Supervisory Management

WILEY SERIES IN MANAGEMENT

Supervisory Management

Second Edition

Robert W. Eckles, *University of Wyoming*
Ronald L. Carmichael, *University of Missouri—Rolla*
Bernard R. Sarchet, *University of Missouri—Rolla*

John Wiley & Sons New York Chichester Brisbane Toronto

Copyright © 1974, 1981, by John Wiley & Sons, Inc.

All rights reserved. Published simultaneously in Canada.

Reproduction or translation of any part of
this work beyond that permitted by Sections
107 and 108 of the 1976 United States Copyright
Act without the permission of the copyright
owner is unlawful. Requests for permission
or further information should be addressed to
the Permissions Department, John Wiley & Sons.

Library of Congress Cataloging in Publication Data:

Eckles, Robert W   1927-
    Supervisory management.

    (Wiley series in management)
    Includes indexes.
    1. Supervision of employees—Problems, exercises,
etc. 2. Personnel management—Problems, exercises,
etc. I. Carmichael, Ronald Lad, joint author.
II. Sarchet, Bernard R., 1917-   joint author.
III. Title.

HF5549.15.E25   1981   658.3'02'076   80-21684
ISBN 0-471-05947-1

Printed in the United States of America

10 9 8 7 6 5 4 3 2 1

To
Sue
Eila
Le

Preface

Job boredom, employee dissatisfaction, lowering productivity, and the need for more effective and well-trained supervision are more pronounced today than ever before. More workers throughout the world enjoy a higher standard of living and consequently expect more respect and efficiency from their supervisors.

Organizations throughout the world have become more sophisticated in the last decade, and the new, emerging supervisors of the 1980s have been accepted by progressive organizations. This has placed a greater burden on the newly appointed supervisors who must have the updated training to insure their success. This edition updates the concepts presented in the first edition in a more logical sequencing of the chapters.

This edition includes two new chapters on productivity and time management, Chapters X and XVI, respectively. Both subjects are interrelated and emphasize the serious need for American public and private sectors to increase productivity to compete effectively with foreign manufacturers. The supervisor is at the heart of this productivity crisis and Chapters X and XVI stress this need and its probable resolution.

All other chapters have been updated, condensed, reorganized, and/or rewritten. Some of the new material includes the emphasis on the work of supervisors at all levels rather than only first-line, including the planning and organization processes. Newer techniques of flextime, and the four-day week are included in the section on job design. We show how the quality-of-life program offsets job boredom. Motivating the worker includes newer theories. Using the computer is covered since it has become such an integral part of supervision. Personal characteristics have been overhauled and reorganized. Transactional analysis has been added to the communications chapter since its use has become a commonplace technique. Training and development has been rewritten to reflect organizational development processes. Labor relations has been updated along with safety and health, which reflects the latest activities of OSHA.

Only four of the first-edition incidents remain the same. The rest are new or greatly revised and updated. The new incidents are more comprehensive and more substantive, permitting students and instructors to receive more "hands on" treatment of the chapter concepts and techniques. As in the previous edition, these incidents are real-world experiences.

The questions for discussion have been added to and completely revised.

We appreciate very much the efforts of many users of the first edition who submitted suggestions to improve the book, many of which suggestions have been incorporated into this edition. Reviewers who have made the most significant contributions for this edition were Professor G. Schneider, Austin Community College, and Professor T. D. Cramer, Fullerton College. We again thank our typists who have performed admirably in the face of adversity so that a clean copy could be submitted to the publisher. We are very grateful to Rita Hughes, Gerry McKay, and Betty Lindsey.

We also thank all who have contributed to this edition. But, in spite of our efforts, all errors that still remain are our sole responsibility.

R. W. Eckles
R. L. Carmichael
B. R. Sarchet

Cheyenne, Wyoming
Rolla, Missouri

January 1981

Contents

Preface

Chapter I   *Supervisory Responsibilities Within the Organization*   1

    Learning Objectives   1
    Introduction   1
    Differences Between Management and Supervision   1
    Universality of Supervisory Management   2
    The Need for Effective and Efficient Supervision   2
    The Challenge of Supervision   4
    The Modern Supervisor   4
    Supervision and the Organization   4
    The Many Faces of a Supervisor   5
    Technical Aspects of the Job— Structure   9
    Aspects of the Job— Activating   9
    Supervisors' Personal Goals Versus Company Objectives   10
    Goals and Responsibilities as Perceived by the Workers   11
    Summary   11
    Key Concepts   12
    Important Terms   13
    Incidents   13
    Questions for Discussion   15

PART I   SUPERVISING WORK   17

Chapter II   *Planning*   19

    Learning Objectives   19
    Introduction   19
    Understanding Corporate Plans   20
    Types of Plans   23
    The Supervisor's Role in Planning   25
    The Planning Process   26
    Some Practical Aids in Supervisory Planning   31
    Planning for Change   35
    Summary   37
    Key Concepts   38
    Important Terms   39
    Incidents   39
    Questions for Discussion   42

Chapter III   *Organizing*   43

    Learning Objectives   43
    Introduction   43
    Corporate Organization   44
    Supervisory Organization   59
    Summary   64
    Key Concepts   65
    Important Terms   66
    Incidents   66
    Questions for Discussion   69

Chapter IV   *Informal Organizations and Groups*   71

    Learning Objectives   71
    Introduction   71
    Nature of Informal Organizations   72
    Types of Informal Organizations   72
    Activities of Informal Groups   76

Relationship of Informal Groups
  with Supervisor's Formal
  Group 80
Supervisory Control and the
  Informal Group 81
Summary 83
Key Concepts 84
Important Terms 84
Incidents 84
Questions for Discussion 86

Chapter V The Human Side of Control 88

Learning Objectives 88
Introduction 88
Control as a Managerial
  Function 88
The Nature of Control 89
The Human Problems of
  Control 97
Making Human Control More
  Effective 102
Summary 105
Key Concepts 105
Important Terms 106
Incidents 106
Questions for Discussion 108

Chapter VI Operating Control and Coordination 109

Learning Objectives 109
Introduction 109
The Organizational Control
  Process 110
Intradepartmental Control and
  Coordination 111
Interdepartmental Control and
  Coordination 122
Summary 125
Key Concepts 126
Important Terms 127
Incidents 127
Questions for Discussion 129

Chapter VII Financial Control 130

Learning Objectives 130
Introduction 130
Accounting System 131
Cash Budgets 135
Production Cost Budgets 140
Use of Budgets for Control 146
Management by Exception 148
Zero-Base Budgeting
  (ZBB) 149
Summary 149
Key Concepts 150
Important Terms 150
Incidents 151
Questions for Discussion 153

Chapter VIII Decision Making and the Supervisory Function 154

Learning Objectives 154
Introduction 154
The Decision-Making
  Process 156
A Supervisory Application of
  the Decision-Making
  Process 162
Summary 166
Key Concepts 167
Important Terms 167
Incidents 168
Questions for Discussion 169

PART II SUPERVISING PEOPLE AT WORK 171

Chapter IX People as Workers 173

Learning Objectives 173
Introduction 173
The Supervisor and People 174
Needs and Wants of
  People 176
Human Behavioral Patterns Are
  Motivated by Both Biological
  and Learned Needs 180

Summary of Factors that Influence a Worker's Behavior 181
Workers as People 182
Summary 185
Key Concepts 186
Important Terms 187
Incidents 187
Questions for Discussion 188

Chapter X The Need to Improve Productivity 190

Learning Objectives 190
Introduction 190
Why Is Being Competitive So Important? 191
What Is Productivity? 192
Productivity Slowdown—Three Points of View 193
A Synthesis of the Productivity Problem 194
Human Approach to Improved Productivity 194
The Supervisor and Productivity 195
Supervision and Training 196
Summary 198
Key Concepts 199
Important Terms 199
Incidents 200
Questions for Discussion 202

Chapter XI Job Design and Job Boredom 203

Learning Objectives 203
Introduction 203
Productivity and the Worker-Supervisor Relationship 204
Flextime—Is It a Panacea? 204
Four-Day Work Weeks 205
Job Design 206
Time Study 214
Job Design and Job Boredom 216
Other Cost Reduction Suggestions 224
Summary 225
Key Concepts 226
Important Terms 227
Incidents 227
Questions for Discussion 229

Chapter XII Communications 230

Learning Objectives 230
Introduction 230
The Elements of Communication 231
The Nature of Communication 234
On-the-Job Communication Processes 238
Types of Communication Within the Organization for Supervisors 240
Good Communicators Are Made, Not Born 243
Communications and Leadership 245
Summary 248
Key Concepts 249
Important Terms 249
Incidents 250
Questions for Discussion 252

Chapter XIII Motivating the Worker 253

Learning Objectives 253
Introduction 253
The Competitive Economy 254
The Individual 255
Motivational Research 256
McGregor's Theories of Motivation 261
Gellerman's Theories of Motivation 262
Argyris' Explanation of the "Why" of Motivation Problems 263

xii   Contents

        Motivation Theory in
          Perspective   266
        Summary   267
        Key Concepts   267
        Important Terms   268
        Incidents   268
        Questions for Discussion   270

Chapter XIV Personal Characteristics of the Supervisor   272

    Learning Objectives   272
    Introduction   272
    Personal Characteristics—
      Conceptual   273
    Personal Characteristics—
      Human   275
    Personal Characteristics—
      Technical   276
    Successful Supervisory Behavioral
      Patterns   278
    Summary   281
    Key Concepts   282
    Important Terms   282
    Incidents   282
    Questions for Discussion   284

Chapter XV   Leadership   285

    Learning Objectives   285
    Introduction   285
    Types of Leadership   286
    Nature of Leadership   289
    Choice of Leadership
      Pattern   292
    Leadership Techniques   293
    Leadership and You   297
    Summary   297
    Key Concepts   298
    Important Terms   298
    Incidents   299
    Questions for Discussion   300

PART III   THE SUPERVISOR'S DAY-TO-DAY ACTIVITIES   301

Chapter XVI   Time Management   303

    Learning Objectives   303
    Introduction   303
    Time Management and
      Productivity   304
    Time Wasters   304
    Time Management and Self-
      Discipline   307
    Time Management
      Techniques   307
    Summary   309
    Key Concepts   311
    Important Terms   311
    Incidents   311
    Questions for Discussion   313

Chapter XVII   The Supervisor and the Selection Process   314

    Learning Objectives   314
    Introduction   314
    Recruitment   314
    Selection   317
    Interviewing   321
    Induction   324
    Summary   328
    Key Concepts   329
    Important Terms   329
    Incidents   330
    Questions for Discussion   332

Chapter XVIII   Training and Development of Workers and Supervisors   333

    Learning Objectives   333
    Introduction   333
    Supervisory Responsibility for
      Training   334
    Learning Theory in
      Training   335
    Employee Training   337
    Employee Development   341

Supervisory Training and
   Development   345
Organization Development   349
Summary   350
Key Concepts   350
Important Terms   351
Incidents   351
Questions for Discussion   353

Chapter XIX Counseling, Giving Orders, Introducing Change, and Conducting Meetings   355

Learning Objectives   355
Introduction   355
Counseling   355
Giving Orders   359
Introducing Change   363
Conducting Meetings   367
Summary   371
Key Concepts   372
Important Terms   373
Incidents   373
Questions for Discussion   374

Chapter XX Performance Appraisals   376

Learning Objectives   376
Introduction   376
Performance Appraisals   376
Summary   389
Key Concepts   389
Important Terms   389
Incidents   390
Questions for Discussion   393

Chapter XXI Maintaining Discipline and Morale   394

Learning Objectives   394
Introduction   394
Effective Discipline   395
The Supervisor's Role in Inspiring
   Discipline   399

Procedures in Disciplinary
   Action   402
Employee Morale   405
Measuring Morale   407
The Morale Improvement
   Program   408
Summary   410
Key Concepts   410
Important Terms   411
Incidents   411
Questions for Discussion   412

Chapter XXII Handling Complaints and Grievances   414

Learning Objectives   414
Introduction   414
The Nature of Complaints and
   Grievances   415
Sources of Complaints and
   Grievances   418
Settling Grievances at the
   Supervisory Level   421
Formal Grievance
   Procedures   424
Grievance Procedures in the
   Nonunion Firm   426
Arbitration of Grievances   428
Summary   431
Key Concepts   432
Important Terms   433
Incidents   433
Questions for Discussion   435

PART IV THE SUPERVISOR AND THE ENVIRONMENT   437

Chapter XXIII Labor Relations and the Supervisor   439

Learning Objectives   439
Introduction   439
The Early Labor
   Movement   440

The Modern Era in Labor
  Relations   443
Summary   453
Key Concepts   454
Important Terms   454
Incidents   455
Questions for Discussion   456

Chapter XXIV   *Safety and Health Responsibilities Under OSHA*   *457*

Learning Objectives   457
Introduction   457
What Is OSHA?   459
The Effect of OSHA   469
Safety and Accidents   471
Summary   481
Key Concepts   482
Important Terms   483
Incidents   484
Questions for Discussion   485

Chapter XXV   *The Organization and Its Environment*   *487*

Learning Objectives   487
Introduction   487
Business Defined   489
Role of the Individual in
  Capitalism   492
Role of Capital in
  Capitalism   493
Role of Marketing   494
Role of Profit   496
The Environment of
  Business   497
Legal Forms of Business   501
Summary   503
Key Concepts   504
Important Terms   505
Incidents   505
Questions for Discussion   506

PART V   A FINAL WORD   509

Chapter XXVI   *Closing Remarks*   *511*

Learning Objectives   511
Introduction   511
Constant Study and Research
  Needed   512
Supervision in Perspective   513
The Supervisor of the
  Future   516
Questions for Discussion   517
Subject Index   519

CHAPTER I

Supervisory Responsibilities Within the Organization

LEARNING OBJECTIVES

- *To see the differences between management and supervision.*
- *To understand the universality of supervisory management.*
- *To see the need for effective supervision.*
- *To appreciate the challenges of supervision.*
- *To know the technical and human aspects of supervision.*
- *To see how the supervisor fits into the organization.*
- *To appreciate supervisory goals and responsibilities.*

Introduction

The terms "management" and "supervisor" are often used interchangeably so it is necessary to clarify the semantical difference right away. *Managers* create and try to maintain an internal environment in an organization so that other people can perform their jobs more efficiently to meet organizational goals. A manager performs managerial functions of planning, organizing, activating, communicating, and control over people, jobs or positions, technology, capital goods, and time. *Supervisors* are managers whose functions emphasize leadership, coordinating, activating, motivating, and controlling people.

DIFFERENCES BETWEEN MANAGEMENT AND SUPERVISION

The major difference between a manager and a supervisory manager, then, is the focus of the effort. Managers may manage all types of organizations including a laboratory, a chemical plant, or a power generation plant where few people may work because of high capital intensity or automation. Supervisors must perform all the functions of a manager in addition to being a leader of people. But whenever the leadership of people becomes the dominant factor, then supervisory management has to be stressed.

Using the people variable as the major differentiating factor between a manager and a supervisor is very significant and warrants the treatment of supervisory management apart from general management. A manager in a library department can order books, borrow books, and discard unwanted books without being overly distracted by people problems. A supervisory manager in a governmental office or the business office of a university whose responsibility is to maintain orderly workflows cannot discard people and their needs if they expect to be productive. Obviously, supervisory management can refer to the management of people at all levels of an organization. However, in many organizations, the supervisor frequently refers to the first- or second-line manager. In this book supervisory management refers to all levels of management that focus primarily on the management of people and their resources. This includes line managers, administrative or staff managers, and central or corporate management levels.

UNIVERSALITY OF SUPERVISORY MANAGEMENT

Every organization regardless of its purposes, objectives, politics, resources, societal importance, or size has need for supervision. This includes hospitals, universities, schools, junior colleges, community colleges, factories, local, state and federal governmental units, retail stores, wholesalers, mines, mills, and agribusiness organizations. Wherever people are involved in a workflow or have goals that need to be achieved, supervisory management is not only necessary, but absolutely mandatory.

THE NEED FOR EFFECTIVE AND EFFICIENT SUPERVISION

The first-line supervisor is in the best position of any manager to know and to understand what is happening in his or her department or work unit. They have the closest contact with the men or women who are actually producing the company's products or services. Therefore supervisors must understand people, so that they can lead and motivate workers on a day-to-day basis in order to meet the needs of both the company and the employees.

Management has spent a great deal of time and money trying to find out what makes people work more effectively, thereby increasing productivity at lower costs. Every few years new theories and methods have been tried. In the 1940s managers tried to relieve the worker of financial worry so that work could be improved. Wage rates increased but production (output per man-hour) increased at a modest 2-3 percent. During the 1950s security became the answer to increased production. Millions of dollars were poured into fringe benefits such as improved retirement programs and hospitalization, but production or output per man-hour increased at a modest 2-4 percent. In the 1960s the slogan was to make the worker part of the overall company team. Bowling leagues and softball teams flourished; house organs carried newsy bits of information and baby pictures. Stock purchase plans were introduced. A 3 percent increase in production was realized.

In the 1970s the blue-collar labor force increased by only 9.8 percent between 1968 and 1977 whereas white-collar workers jumped 27 percent in the same period registering a 1.6 productivity rate. The latter part of the 1970s actually experienced a decline in productivity. However, the emphasis placed on white-collar productivity helped to reduce this trend. Many managers believe that continually refining the productivity of the blue-collar worker while ignoring the white-collar worker is analogous to swatting flies while elephants rampage.

Productivity is not a problem solely for blue- or white-collar workers. Evidence has been uncovered that productivity is directly tied to managers as well. Savin Corporation produces copiers in Japan, California, and Connecticut. They have found that their one plant in Japan and one of their two plants in California, run by Japanese, are more efficient than their other California plant and their Connecticut plant, both run by American managers.[1] Savin offers this as proof that Japanese managers are beating American managers at their own business since the United States has prided itself at being the wellhead of management and marketing expertise. Savin Corporation contends that Americans can produce as good a quality product as the Japanese but the difference is in attention to detail, the respect for quality and productivity, and pride in their workmanship.[2] The difference between Japanese and American managers, according to Savin's president is the discipline that takes place on the part of management, their expectations of top quality, and their insistence that everything be done right the first time. Supervisory managers at all levels are responsible for encouraging and demanding this care and attention to detail and quality. With a tougher competitive battle looming on the horizon supervisors have a much more significant role

---

[1]"Rising One . . . Japan 'Outmanaging' U.S. in Production Game," L. A. Times-Washington Post Service, *Evansville Courier*, March 26, 1980, p. 37.
[2]Ibid.

to play in achieving organizational goals, their own development, and the development of their people. The critical productivity activator many organizations use is the supervisor who manages so that people can produce.

THE CHALLENGE OF SUPERVISION

Good supervision is extremely difficult to practice, and any successful organization requires good to excellent supervision. The graveyards of business and industrial organizations are littered with firms that did not have good supervision. Supervisors are the people who make things happen. They are the ones who manage the employees working to develop and complete products and/or services.

The supervisory skill of *leadership* and its relationship to employee motivation and productivity has not always been fully understood. The confusion stems from the belief that if you are a supervisor, the position and the authority that can be exercised in the position automatically designates the supervisor as the leader. Better-educated employees of today expect and deserve good leadership. The work group wants to follow a leader rather than be driven by a *"boss."* Therefore the successful supervisor aspires to become an excellent leader of men or women. Any supervisor can become a more effective leader if he or she sincerely desires and attempts to develop his or her managerial, technical, and human understanding skills.

THE MODERN SUPERVISOR

The development of the modern supervisor has paralleled the historical changes in society's image of the worker-manager relationship from the humble beginnings of master-slave, to the modern supervisor. The modern supervisor must be well-educated, technically well trained, and be an efficient *leader* of people to meet the competitive market demands of high quality output at the least cost. A high quality management program requires a well-trained supervisor who understands people, supervising people, supervisory skills, organizational behavior, teamwork, developing people to develop themselves, generating support from their superiors, time management, and the technical aspects of the work to be done.

SUPERVISION AND THE ORGANIZATION

The supervisor's position in the overall organization can provoke both misunderstanding and uncertainty. Middle and top management people have their clear allegiance to specific organization. Workers have an allegiance to the union, if applicable. However, first-line supervisors tend to be between the two groups. This places the supervisor in a strange dilemma in that he has part of his allegiance as a manager to the company, and part of his allegiance as an ex-worker to his work group. One of the peculiar responsibilities of the supervisor is that he or she is the only manager who manages nonmanagement people. The one exception to this particular statement would be a manager of professional staff people. In addition to their particular problems, responsibilities of the first-line supervisor are, indeed, very important and very significant to the well-being and efficient operation of the entire organization.

In the remainder of this chapter we explore the problems the supervisor faces within the total organization. This material will include the first-line supervisor's responsibility toward technical efficiency, the human aspects of the job, in addition to his responsibilities to the company, to himself, and to the employees.

THE MANY FACES OF A SUPERVISOR

The first-line supervisor is expected by his superiors to be both a *production specialist* and a *human specialist*. He is expected to produce so that his production meets predetermined quotas. But in the process, the supervisor must be a human specialist and able to work with and through people by understanding, motivating, and satisfying their needs.

Before we investigate the technical and human aspects of the job, we should review the five different concepts concerning how the first-line supervisor's position has been, and is, viewed by some within the organization. These roles are (1) the key person in the organization, (2) the person in the middle, (3) the marginal person, (4) another worker, and (5) a human relations specialist. However, in certain companies, one or a variation of these five roles would be actually practiced. Whether the single or multiple roles are practiced would depend on the chore.

KEY PERSON The "*Key person* in the organization" role tends to make the supervisor someone who is in control of his or her work. Top management people expound about the supervisor as being a person who is in complete control of his or her operation. The supervisor interprets management policy to the worker level but is the key person in getting it done.

PERSON IN THE MIDDLE The second role, *the person in the middle*, emphasizes the serious dilemma of the supervisor. He or she is caught between opposing social forces of both the formal and informal group, between management and the worker and, as expressed earlier, between being affiliated with a specific group and not being affiliated. Since the supervisor can become the victim of circumstances, he may not be able to manage the situation. Therefore this type of person feels very insecure and becomes the scapegoat of both management and the worker.

MARGINAL PERSON The third role is called the *marginal person*. Here the supervisor is pictured as the one who is left out. He has the marginal job. He controls only when *regular* management is not around. For example, the night-shift supervisor can exercise a degree of control when other management people are not around at night. The night shift is out of the mainstream of daytime activities, and seldom do "regular managers" appear at night.

ANOTHER WORKER The fourth perspective of the supervisor is the role as *another worker*. He or she is seen as only a manager in name. This supervisor is an elevated worker who doesn't possess any more qualities of a supervisor than any other worker. Workers tend to view an ex-worker promoted to first-line supervisor from this same perspective. Obviously, this view could be detrimental during stress periods.

HUMAN RELATIONS SPECIALIST The fifth and last role is the *human relations specialist*. Here, the supervisor interacts with staff people, workers, and his or her immediate superior. The specialist becomes a strong component of the entire system. However, this supervisor is seen as a specialist or staff person rather than as a line person responsible for decision making. The supervisor is people oriented and merely carries out orders from above.

THE KEYSTONE OF THE ORGANIZATION None of the above roles explains the supervisor's responsibilities within the organization; however, they do shed some light into the black box, and they do illustrate the images actually followed in many companies.

A down-to-earth but realistic picture of forces that interact with the supervisor (foreperson) within the organization has been diagrammed by F. J. Roethlisberger, as illustrated in Figure 1-1. As can be seen, the supervisor (foreperson) is interacting with a number of people. He or she is in the middle reacting with other supervisors who are requesting cooperation. Technical specialists are interacting with the supervisor as far as standards of performance and evaluation of technological change are concerned. His or her immediate supervisor is interacting with the foreperson concerning the company's policies, rules, regulations, instructions, and orders. The immediate supervisor demands explanations and information of "how come," because that supervisor is interacting with top management people up the line. The shop steward is interacting with

The Many Faces of a Supervisor 7

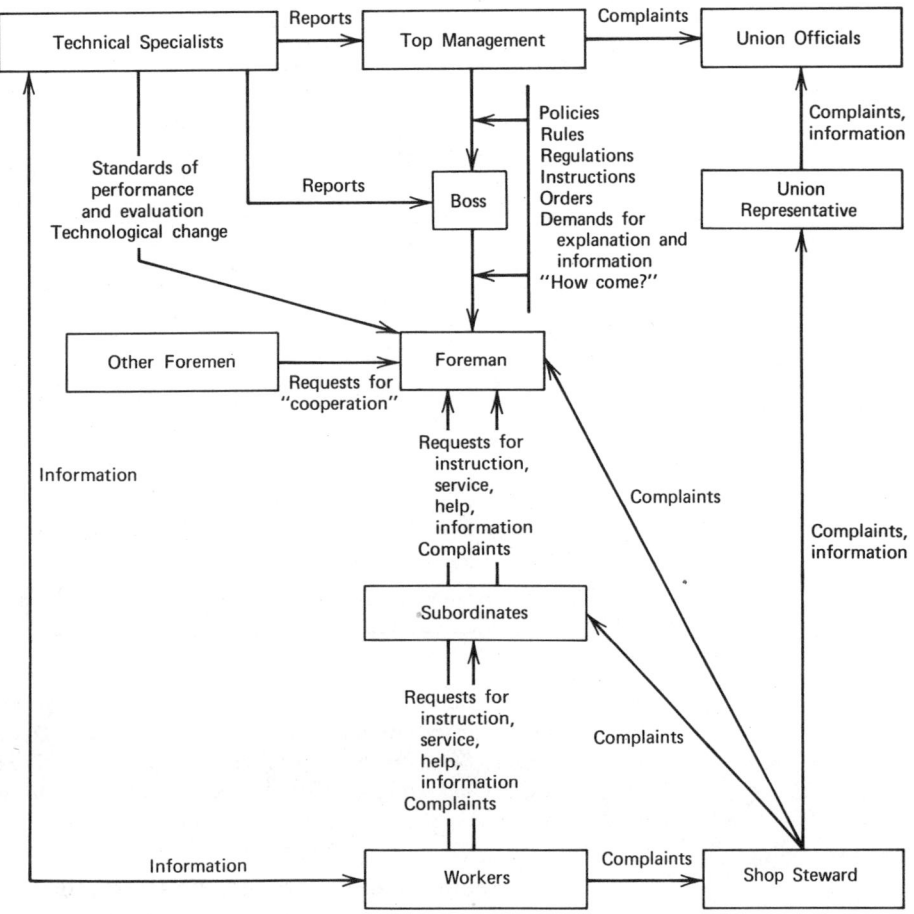

Figure 1-1   Forces impinging on the supervisor. (Source. From F. J. Roethlisberger, "The Foreman: Master and Victim of Double Talk," Man-In-Organization, Essays of F. J. Roethlisberger. Belknap Press of Harvard University Press, *Cambridge, Mass., 1968, p. 40. Reproduced with permission.)*

complaints directly to the foreman, and obviously the workers are interacting with requests for instructions, service, help, information, and complaints.

In addition to the direct forces pressing on the supervisor, many indirect forces prevail that affect the role played by the supervisor within an organization. Technical reports originating from technical specialists that concern the supervisor's job are submitted to the supervisor's boss or to top management people. In either case, technical changes within the reports must be implemented by the supervisor. Complaints from workers that are channeled to the shop steward or union representative find

8   Chapter I   Supervisory Responsibilities Within the Organization

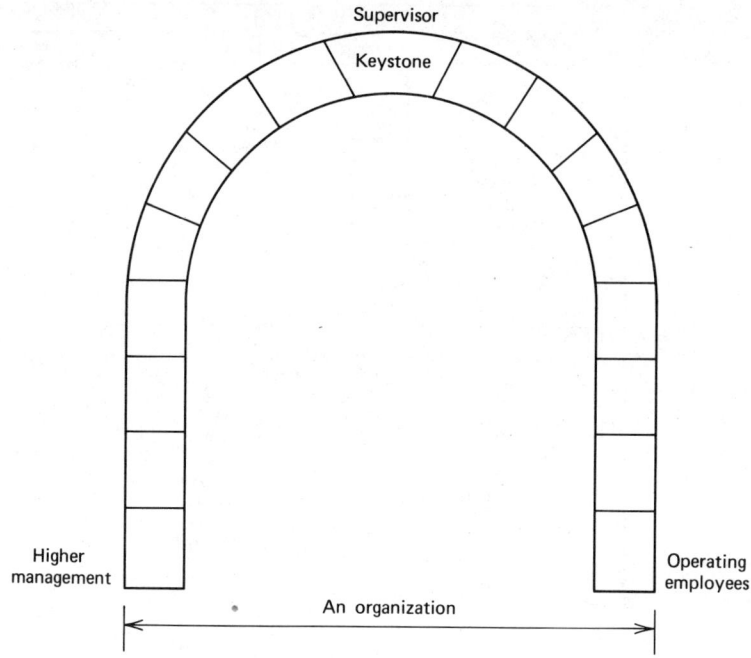

Figure 1-2   Supervisors are the keystone in the organizational arch. (Source. From Human Relations At Work: The Dynamics of Organizational Behavior *by Keith Davis. Copyright 1967, McGraw-Hill Book Co. Used with permission of McGraw-Hill Book Co.)*

their way through the union organization to top management people and can be seen as serious incidents, or flagrant violation of union contracts, or as mistreatment of workers. Once top management has been disturbed by these incidents, pressure from the top is exerted on the supervisor. Between the direct and indirect forces within the organization, these pressures tend to make the supervisor's life a bit hectic. Responsibility to other factions within the organization helps to distract the supervisor from focusing full attention on the management of his own work group. However, this is reality and the organizational environment requires that a supervisor be better educated and trained to cope with the pressures of the position. All managerial positions have pressures being exerted from different sides, at different times. In the supervisor's case, these pressures are many and occur frequently.

The discussion of the five roles, plus the discussion concerning the forces that interact with the supervisor, indicate the significance of the supervisor's position within the organization. However, just what should be the supervisor's role? Which of the five roles, or which combination of roles, best explains the supervisor's responsibilities within the organization? Although all five roles represent explicit parts of the position, none fully explains the supervisory position as it is and should be practiced in progressive firms.

The supervisor is more than a supervisor of workers, which is very significant in and of itself. The position is more than the *key person*; it is the *keystone* of the entire organization. As illustrated in Figure 1-2, the supervisor's position lies at the critical stress area between higher management and workers. The greater stress between the two legs of the arch culminates at the keystone block. If the block were removed, the arch would fall. Similarly, a weak supervisor can seriously affect the strength of the entire organization. The supervisor implements policies, plans, and directives by motivating, activating, and successfully managing himself, other individuals, and groups to attain growth, to develop, and to make decisions that satisfy both company goals and subordinates' needs.

As in all forms of management, a person cannot manage something he doesn't understand. The supervisor must know the technical aspect of the work to be preformed as well as his job. First we shall discuss the technical aspects.

TECHNICAL ASPECTS OF THE JOB—STRUCTURE

The supervisor is responsible for carrying out the assigned technical functions of his job. This means that he has to understand production methods and processes, production control, job design, budgeting, disciplining, decision making, and control. Whether it be the production line or the office, the work has to be done in the most efficient way and the process or system followed in order to get the work done efficiently must be handled through the supervisor.

HUMAN ASPECTS OF THE JOB—ACTIVATING

One of the more important human aspects of the job is trying to cooperate with the individual worker and maintain his or her desire and motivation to work. These are the emotional, behavioral, and psychological aspects of supervision. Maintaining this balance depends on the supervisor's ability to understand and use different leadership models, introduce change, counsel, and effectively interpret and communicate the goals and objectives of the firm to the work crew. Getting along with people, and working with and through people, are complex human relations or activating techniques, but the supervisor's responsibility to the firm is to activate the human resources by support to attain both the company goals and the satisfaction of workers' needs.

SUPERVISORY RESPONSIBILITIES AND COMPANY OBJECTIVES

Essentially the supervisory responsibilities become the implementation of company objectives utilizing the human, material, and machine resources within the supervisor's jurisdiction. The implementation of company objectives is the screening and interpretation of goals, work orders, worker motivation, support, and production control within the work group itself.

The crux of supervisors' production control problem is the fact that they are constantly faced with the dilemma of having to keep their superiors informed as to what is happening at the work level and, second, they must communicate this information in such a way as not to bring unfavorable criticism upon themselves and the workers.[3]

SUPERVISORS' PERSONAL GOALS VERSUS COMPANY OBJECTIVES

The supervisors have to reconcile the conception of an idea and its production. Their personal goals certainly are not met when they feel that they are in the middle. The best thing to do under these circumstances is try to understand and interpret company objectives. Supervisors are responsible for carrying out the goals of the firm. They do have control over their own workers, and they can provide some input into the interpretation of the objectives.

One investigation concerning supportive involvement was conducted on the Chesapeake and Ohio Railroad among section groups and their immediate supervisor. The major findings were as follows. (1) The supervisors of the highest producing sections considered themselves leaders and not supervising workers. (2) The workers perceived the supervisor as having a good planning ability. (3) The supervisors of high-producing groups were more positive toward their people. (4) High-production section supervisors evaluated their sections more highly than the ratings that low producing supervisors gave *their* groups. Supervisors of the productive groups took a personal approach—the employees' needs were considered rather than the job involved. The high-production section supervisor had pride in the work group and in the pride of the individual members in the work group. Togetherness and a feeling of belonging were stimulated under these conditions.

The *people-oriented* supervisor can better understand the differences that exist among the employees. The supervisor's recognition of these differences will enable him or her to make better use of the talent possessed by each employee. Productivity can be enhanced, along with improving

---

[3] F. J. Roethlisberger, "The Foreman: Master and Victim of Double Talk," *Man-In-Organization, Essays of F. J. Roethlisberger*, Belknap Press of Harvard University Press, Cambridge, Mass., 1968, p. 41.

each employee's work attitude and toward the company, if each employee knows that he or she is treated and respected as an individual.

Supervisors have to be the defender of the work group to their immediate supervisors. Supervisors have to be the guardians of the morale of the work group, in spite of the fact that they are getting pressure from staff people and perhaps also from their immediate supervisors. The "defender" atmosphere promotes the satisfaction of the basic safety needs of the supervisors in addition to the satisfaction of worker needs. When a group is under attack, its members tend to be more cohesive. Therefore, with some imagination and slight interpretation, company objectives become the vehicle by which supervisors can satisfy their own basic needs.

GOALS AND RESPONSIBILITIES AS PERCEIVED BY THE WORKERS

A basic conflict between workers' goals and company goals may exist. Workers perform in line with what *they believe* are legitimate objectives for themselves. The worker will judge whether or not these work objectives are attainable, communicable, simple, or acceptable. Since employees have to do the work, they will perform what they think they are capable of performing or what they think should be a part of the job. For example, in a strong unionized shop, the shop steward gladly will support a worker's objections to what is considered to be an inhumane operation or an excessive work load. The labor people are being paid by workers' dues to protect their interests; when workers do not accept company goals, policies, and plans as related by the supervisor, turmoil can develop.

Placating the worker's needs, and matching these needs with company objectives, is indeed a very delicate task. Numerous ideas can be used, such as motivating support, participatory management, fear, dominance, and conditioning the worker. However, if company goals are not achieved, the worker's goals may not be achieved either. Higher benefits force higher costs. This may force the firm out of business. It may be better to take a pay cut than to stand in the unemployment line. The worker's needs, goals, and ambitions have to coincide with the firm's needs and objectives, as both parties desire security and survival.

SUMMARY

Supervisors can be at all levels of an organization's hierarchy but are most frequently at the first-line level. Supervisors, at all levels, are managers who focus their attention on people and their problems and how they interface with the technical aspects of their jobs.

Supervisory management is practiced in any type of organization whether it be governmental, business, industry, retail, institutional, non-profit, or religious. Supervision is necessary, if people are working to achieve common goals.

Productivity is a very serious problem that is close to a practicing supervisors area of authority and concern. The need for better quality products at lower costs are absolutely necessary for an American organization to survive in a competitive market world. The challenge of supervision is the achievement of personal and organizational goals while enhancing the necessary productivity.

The conflicts in authority, role playing, and politics complicates the supervisors position within an organization. Regardless of the power struggles, supervisors have to be productive and enforce their peoples' productivity.

KEY CONCEPTS

Managers. Managers create and maintain an internal environment so that other people can perform efficiently. Managers plan, organize, direct, and control the activities of other people, jobs, markets, events, technology, and capital goods. In other words, managers deal broadly with people, machines, money, and time.

Supervisors. Supervisors are managers whose major functions focus on people and all their attendant problems. Usually the concept of a supervisor is a person in lower management, whose major function emphasizes leadership, motivation, direction, and coordination with others within the business or industrial setting. All levels of management have supervisory functions, but the supervisor's major function is working with and through nonmanagement people to meet the needs of the employees and the objectives of the organization.

Leader versus boss. Historically, the supervisor has been a boss—one whose word cannot be refuted or denied. The concept of today's supervisor is one of a leader in that he or she promotes the climate of trust and respect so that a worker will want to be led, and possibly in some cases lead and direct him- or herself.

Keystone position of supervisor. Among the numerous concepts of the first-line supervisor's position within the organization, the concept of the keystone position perhaps mirrors reality the best. The key person, person in the middle, marginal person, another worker, and human relations specialist—all these images of the supervisor have degrees of truth in various situations, but none fully explains the supervisor's position as it is practiced in an efficient and an effective organization. The supervisor's position lies at the critical stress area between the structural aspects of higher management and the activating needs of the workers.

Technical and human understanding. The supervisor's responsibility embraces both technical and human relations understanding, but conceptually, this means the supervisor must cope with both of these aspects simultaneously and be able to manage and balance both aspects in order to perform on the job and be responsible to the company objectives, self, and the workers. This may be akin to juggling a number of balls at the same time, but it is the supervisor's major responsibility to see that all aspects and functions are working at the same time in a coordinated way.

IMPORTANT TERMS

Another worker	Managers
Assembly lines	Marginal person
Automation	Mass production
"Boss"	Modern supervisor
Human relations specialist	Person in the middle
Industrial revolution	Person orientation
Key person	Production specialist
Keystone position	Supervisors
Lead people	Time and motion study
Leadership	

INCIDENTS

The Rule Maker

Frank McKee had graduated from Purdue University with a major in civil engineering and recently was promoted to an engineering supervisory position in a large defense contracting company in Lima, Ohio, that built the latest model MXI tanks for the U. S. Army. Frank was intelligent, self-confident, considered himself a good leader, and a good "company man" who knew if he were to get ahead he had to impress his superiors with his work. He believed no supervisor should spend any company money needlessly. Part of Frank's views of his new supervisory position were reflected in his desire to be parsimonious or economical with both his personal and company funds. He ran a tight ship at home and at the plant. Some workers went so far as to call him "tight" and an "Old Scrooge" with money. However, Frank's indominable economic motives were unbendable.

McKee's financial hang-up was duly noted by his superiors, used as the butt of many jokes, but inwardly respected by his superiors as it reflected on their own costs control and managerial abilities.

After Frank celebrated his first year in the new supervisory position by treating his wife to an outing at the local McDonald's franchise, much discontent among the engineers in his section began to emerge and reached a disturbing level. Although this discontent originated at many different points with some discontent always prevalent, a rather clear profile of effects emerged.

1. Project completion dates were not being met as before.
2. Absenteeism had increased over the previous year.
3. The number of early retirements had increased over last year.
4. The development of new processes, products, and related areas had dropped significantly.
5. Many of the engineers expressed the attitude of "who cares?"

Analyze the situation and propose probable causes. Also propose possible, workable solutions. Concentrate on what Frank McKee may not have done as well as what he did.

A Leader Versus a Driver

Role play the following two situations by assigning students to act out each situation.

1. Gary Lee is a supervisor in a wooden TV cabinet manufacturing plant. He believes all people are lazy, seek the easiest ways to complete a job, and look forward to their leisure time more than they do to their individual job tasks. Gary's solution to this problem is to drive the worker, put pressure on them to produce, constantly check them for errors or poor workmanship, mistakes and low quality, closely supervise every item, and never give the worker much opportunity to determine his or her own work pace.

Gary is following up a directive he gave earlier to George Lohr concerning policing the work areas by picking up scrap wood and sweeping up sawdust and other debris. After following George on his clean-up route, Gary notices two large pieces of wood scrap overlooked by George. Gary is incensed but picks up the pieces. Start the role play as Gary approaches George to confront him. One person should play Gary and a second person play George.

2. Terry Schmidt wants workers to perform to meet production schedules in the same wooden TV cabinet manufacturing facility but he also praises workers, offers rewards, attempts to make the workers feel successful, and frequently reminds them that quality output is the difference between the company's success or failure.

Terry is following up the same directive about policing the shop area given to George Lohr in the first question.

Have a third person play Terry's part and the same individual who played George in the first situation play George in this situation. Start the role play with Terry picking up two scrap-wood pieces as he approaches George.

Analyze George's impressions between the two situations. Have George determine the good and bad aspects of each supervisory style.

QUESTIONS FOR DISCUSSION

1. Is a supervisor a manager? If not, why not? If yes, what are the differences between the two?
2. Management has spent a great deal of time and money trying to find out what motivates people to work more efficiently and effectively. Why is this objective so difficult to attain?
3. How and why has the image of the supervisor-worker relationship been created over time?
4. Why must the modern supervisor be a leader-motivator and organizational man?
5. Why must a supervisor earn his or her leadership of people?
6. Selected people must be properly trained to fill supervisory positions. Why?
7. Why is the role of the supervisor an uncertain position in an organization?
8. Contrast the five views of the supervisor's position and determine how the relationship between supervisor and top management changes.
9. What is the difference between the key person and the marginal person's views of the supervisors within the organization?
10. What direct forces or factors influence the supervisor and complicate his or her position? Why?
11. If the supervisor's two main responsibilities are technical and human relations, how are they related and how can they be used toward achieving both company goals and the satisfaction of workers' needs?
12. Why is the supervisor in the best position to match or balance company goals and objectives with the satisfaction of workers' needs?

PART I
Supervising Work

Effective supervisory management must master the skills of management. Included in this section are topics on planning, organizing informal organizations and groups, the human side of control, operating control and coordination, financial control, and decision making.

CHAPTER II
Planning

LEARNING OBJECTIVES

- *To understand what planning is and why it is critical.*
- *To recognize the different types of plans and to see how they interrelate.*
- *To understand and appreciate the supervisor's role in planning.*
- *To learn the logical steps in the planning process and to realize that these steps are a systematic way of establishing objectives and determining how to achieve them.*
- *To develop an understanding of some of the techniques helpful in planning.*
- *To know why supervisory plans sometimes must be changed and how to go about this.*

Introduction

Effective planning must answer several questions relevant to future action: What is to be done? Where is it to be done? When will it be done? Who will do it? How will it be done? *Planning* is, essentially, a form of decision making. If there were no more than one way of achieving an objective, planning would be unnecessary in most instances.

A *plan* is a recommended future course of action. It is a guide to achieving previously established objectives in an optimum manner by means of an orderly sequence of steps. Planning is the first of the managerial functions because it is basic in carrying out all other activities. Planning is a pervasive function performed at all levels of management. The kind, duration, and amount of planning done by the company president is quite different from that of the first-line supervisor—but the planning at all levels is equally important.

The supervisor needs to have some knowledge of the corporate planning process in order to understand better how his or her own planning fits into the scheme of things.

UNDERSTANDING CORPORATE PLANS

OBJECTIVES *Corporate plans* developed at the top level of management are based on broad objectives over the long range and are expressed in general terms. For example, *corporate objectives* over the next few years might be to increase the company's share of the total market to 20 percent, to build two new plants, to expand its marketing territory into the west coast area, or to convert from manual to automated operations.

The "broad-brush" corporate objective and plan is, in effect, divided into major functional components and handed to the first echelon of top executives, who develop *subobjectives* and *derivative plans* for their respective functional areas of responsibility. These components are, in turn, divided and redivided into smaller and smaller components as they are assigned downward through the organizational hierarchy. As this happens, the subobjectives and tasks become more specific and the derivative plans more detailed.

To illustrate, let us assume that a new objective for our company is to expand its marketing effort into the West Coast area. Out of this basic objective comes a set of fairly general subobjectives for the top executives. The Vice-President of Finance has the subobjective of determining the best way to finance the new activity. The Vice-President of Production's subobjective is to assure that the company's production facilities will be ready to meet the demands of the new market. And the Vice-President of Marketing will have as his subobjective the development of an overall marketing strategy—the how, when, and where of moving into the new territory. Each of these executives will develop derivative plans to achieve his or her subobjectives.

In so doing, each executive will assign somewhat more specific tasks to his or her subordinate managers, who will have to develop their own derivative plans to meet these lower-level subobjectives. The Vice-President of Marketing, for example, will request the Sales Manager to develop a sales force in the new territory by the target date, ask the Director of Marketing Research to determine the size and nature of the new market, and request the Advertising Manager to determine the most effective mix of the media to be used. These managers will assign even more specific tasks to their subordinates. Eventually the supervisor in charge of field interviewing crews within the Marketing Research Department might wind up planning a door-to-door taste sampling test for selected neighborhoods in Los Angeles. These are but a few examples of the literally hundreds of subobjectives and derivative plans that must be developed at all levels within the company to assure successful accomplishment of the stated primary objective.

Most product manufacturing companies and other types of organizations develop total organization plans covering a 5 year period. The most notable exceptions are the public utilities and extractive industries which, by nature of their purposes, must plan ahead for 15 to 30 years or more.

The usual practice is to maintain a continuous, or running, five-year plan which is updated at uniform intervals, often one year. The five-year objective is very general, but the plan gets more specific as it works back to the present. Obviously, the plan must be quite specific with respect to activities in the six months or one year ahead. The continuous plan concept is illustrated in Figure 2-1.

The upper horizontal bar represents the five-year plan as it is today. The objective to be reached in five years is very general, and its timing is not necessarily precisely fixed. The first year of the present plan will include subobjectives and low-level derivative plans outlined in considerable detail. The derivative plans for the second year will be less detailed, and so on up to five years.

Now, assume that one year has passed and it is a "new today" one year later than the "old today." The first-year portion of the original plan is now history. Its subobjectives may be ahead of or behind schedule, depending on the situational factors that have occurred over the past year. The second year of the old plan is modified accordingly, and it now becomes the first year of the new five-year plan. Each subsequent year of the old plan also is modified, renumbered, and a fifth year is added with a new five-year objective. The new objective will differ from the old to the extent indicated by the present situation and current forecasts of future events. This process is repeated each year.

BASES FOR CHANGE   In a dynamic economy, change is the rule, not the exception. This is the major reason why corporate long-term plans are expressed as objectives and in general terms. The company that develops a detailed five-year

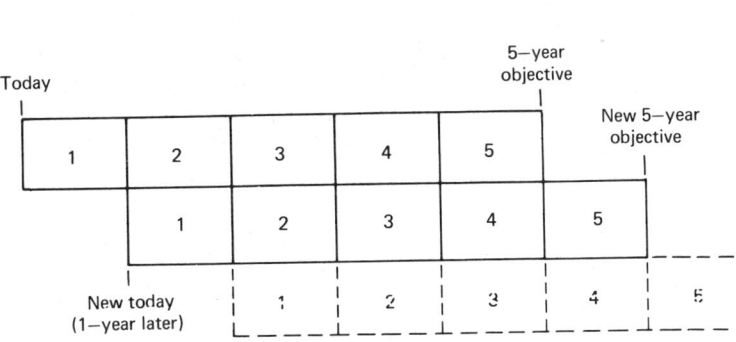

Figure 2-1 The continuous five-year plan.

plan and then tries to adhere to it rigidly will, sooner or later, find itself in very hot water indeed.

A long-term plan must always be subject to change as changing conditions dictate. Plans should have a *built-in flexibility* permitting adjustments with minimum disruption as the organization progresses toward its broader goals. Like a boxer, the successful enterprise must be light on its feet. One way to develop flexibility is to develop and have on hand several alternate plans to meet the more likely contingencies.

What are some of the situations that can necessitate changes in corporate plans? They are numerous, but four of the more common and important ones are changes in market conditions, the financial situation, new product development, and new laws or regulations.

We all know that the demand for a given product or service can change—slowly or rapidly, up or down. Let us assume that the demand for our product has increased more rapidly than forecast by the marketing research department. To meet this demand, we may have to expand our present operations sooner than planned or face the prospect of losing part of our market share to competitors. Derivative plans are affected relating to personnel recruitment, work schedules, material and equipment acquisition, inventories, financing, and many other areas. Conversely, if the market does not grow as rapidly as predicted, planned expansion may have to be delayed.

The general economy as it relates to the financial needs of the company also can cause changes in plans. Suppose that corporate plans call for starting construction of a new facility this year. Suppose also that money is in tight supply and interest rates are at a new high. We may, therefore, decide to change our plan and delay construction until next year in hopes that the money supply will improve and interest rates decline.

New product development, by our own company or by a competitor, is one of the factors most difficult to anticipate but which can have a dramatic effect on plans. The more radical the innovation, the greater may be the effect. Suppose that our R & D department comes up with a revolutionary new product that makes an instantaneous hit in the marketplace. Corporate and derivative plans must accomodate themselves to the new realities. Similarly, if a competitor develops a new product that gives him a competitive edge, our plans must be adjusted to catch up or get ahead. This situational factor may apply to a new manufacturing process or new service concept as well as to a new product.

The development of the radically different Xerox electrostatic copying process is a good example of the tail wagging the corporate dog. When the former Haloid Company (now Xerox Corporation) first acquired the rights to the newly developed Xerox process in the early 1950s it was looked upon as just another copying process that might help reverse a long and gradual downtrend in company fortunes. The results far exceeded all expectations and became the success story of the generation.

Demand for the new process was so great that Haloid had to expand and expand to keep pace. Earnings were plowed back into expansion for a number of years, and stock value increased a hundredfold. During this period Haloid changed its name first to Haloid-Xerox and then to Xerox Corporation. Other manufacturers of copying equipment experienced slim times until they were able to develop competing devices.

Numerous instances illustrate how new laws and regulations, or a change in enforcement policy with respect to an existing law, cause major changes in organization plans. Think for a moment how the federal ban on cigarette advertising on television must have affected the planning of the networks, tobacco companies, and advertising agencies. Similarly, the several civil rights and employment practices acts of recent vintage have had significant planning implications for personnel departments in most kinds of organizations. Many other examples could be mentioned.

The supervisor receives only a small piece of the total organization plan. Supervisors may wonder why superiors give them new objectives, tasks, or instructions and may think that the "top brass" can't make up their minds about what they want to do. The preceding discussion shows, at least in part, why this may be.

TYPES OF PLANS

Many different bases have been suggested by various authorities for classifying different types of plans. Effective supervisors should be familiar with a logical classification system for several reasons. This knowledge assists in defining supervisors' authority and responsibility when administering some types of plans developed by their superiors. It will help supervisors to understand the interdepartmental relationships of many company activities of which they may see only a part. And it will aid supervisors in logical, orderly development of plans in their own area of responsibility.

Plans may be classified initially according to (1) duration, (2) function or use, and (3) breadth or scope. Plans then may be subclassified under each of these three areas. Any given plan may be typed under each of these broad classifications. For example, a plan that is procedural in scope may pertain to the retailing function and be short range in duration.

BASED ON DURATION Any plan may be described in terms of the time span it is designed to cover. *Short-range plans* obviously cover actions to be completed over short time periods, and *long-range plans* over a longer time period. There is no definite dividing line between the two. To a supervisor, a six-month plan might seem long range, but his company president might

| | Period Covered by Plan | | | | |
Organizational Level of Manager	Current (Day to Day)	1 Month Ahead	6 Months Ahead	1 Year Ahead	5 Years Ahead
President	2%	5%	20%	25%	48%
Vice-president	5	15	40	30	10
Middle manager	25	50	15	10	—
Dept. superintendent	50	30	15	5	—
Supervisor	80	15	5	—	—

Figure 2-2 Estimates of planning time of various levels of managers distributed according to period covered by plans. (Source. From George R. Terry, Principles of Management, *5th ed., Richard D. Irwin, Homewood, Ill., 1968, p. 256.)*

view it as short range. Regardless of its length, however, a derivative plan often is considered short range if it is part of a larger plan or program.

Short-range planning takes place chiefly in the lower levels of the organizational structure, as illustrated in Figure 2-2. Involvement in long-range planning increases as we proceed up the managerial hierarchy. Roughly one-half of the company president's planning effort may be devoted to corporate plans extending five years into the future, whereas 80 percent of a supervisor's planning may be of a day-to-day nature.

BASED ON FUNCTION OR USE

Plans may be classified in terms of the function or use to which they are applied. These may include the *primary business functions* of production, marketing, and finance and their subfunctions or supportive functions such as personnel, purchasing, maintenance, research and development, engineering, and so on—the list is almost endless. The supervisor in charge of Personal Demand Deposit Bookkeeping in a bank might develop a special plan for handling those accounts on which no more than ten checks per month were written. This would be a long-term (duration), bookkeeping (function) plan that might be procedural in scope.

Functional grouping of plans assists management in visualizing interdepartmental relationships and in determining if, and how, plans of one department might affect operations in another department. This can be vital in avoiding potential conflicts and problem situations.

BASED ON BREADTH OR SCOPE

Another basis for classification of plans is their breadth and scope. On this basis, a plan could be classed as intradepartmental, interdepartmental, or company-wide in its application.

An *intradepartmental plan* is one that is applicable to part or all of a single department. A supervisor's plan for on-the-job training of new members of his or her work group would exemplify this.

Interdepartmental plans affect more than one department but not necessarily the entire company. The plans for evacuation and damage control of a refinery in the event of fire or other emergency would be applicable to all departments in that plant, but might have no bearing at all on other types of company operations at other locations.

Companywide plans, as the term implies, affect most, or sometimes all, of the operations of the total organization. The total organization budget is a form of companywide plan. The plans for negotiating labor contracts may be companywide in scope if the company's labor relations function is centralized.

In a sense, policies, procedures, and methods are also plans. The terms themselves imply different degrees of breadth and scope. A *policy* is a general statement designed to guide managerial thinking and action during the process of achieving objectives. It establishes broad limits, provides direction, but permits some initiative and discretion on the part of the manager. A corporatewide policy, for example, might state that all new products should be compatible with the existing marketing and distribution system. This still permits leeway in developing new products but does put some bounds on the process.

We tend to think of policy formulation as being restricted to formal, written statements developed at the top level of management and organizationwide in application. This usually is the case. However, policies also may be developed at other levels in the organization and be applicable to smaller organizational units. Policies sometimes are implied rather than formalized in writing, although this normally is poor practice.

Procedures are plans that establish customary ways of handling specific, recurring activities usually involving group effort. The key element is establishing a sequence of steps or operations. Because procedures are more specific than policies, somewhat less discretion is permissible in application. Examples of procedures would include the manner of making up the weekly payroll, or the sequence of steps in firing up a boiler.

Methods are even more specific and detailed than procedures in that they set up the manner and sequence of accomplishing recurring, individual tasks. Virtually no discretion is allowable. The steps in cementing a gasket, attaching a wiring harness, or operating a mimeographing machine are examples of methods.

THE SUPERVISOR'S ROLE IN PLANNING

As stated previously, the individual supervisor sees, and participates in, only a very small slice of the total corporate planning process. This does not mean that the role is correspondingly unimportant. Rather, the reverse is true. Supervisors are responsible for planning the day-to-day activities of the work force. If these activities are not carried out within the scheduled time and with efficient utilization of resources—people, money, equipment, and materials—then the total structure begins to falter. The supervisor's role is vital indeed.

The supervisor's job does not require participation in all of the types of planning previously described, although it is helpful to be familiar with the classification system. The typical supervisor is involved chiefly in short-range planning (see Figure 2-2). Rarely is there a need to plan for activities more than six months into the future.

Large numbers of supervisors in manufacturing industries are concerned with planning for production subfunctions such as specific manufacturing process groups, operations groups, maintenance, inspection, or construction. Supervisory practices and planning are not limited to production functions, important as these are. Supervisors in many other kinds of industries and organizations are in charge of people engaged in retail sales, filing, packaging and mailing, and the processing of various kinds of paper work. Planning in these areas may fall under any type of function.

Supervisors ordinarily are not called upon to determine policy, although they will be responsible for explaining policy to their people and seeing that it is followed. Supervisors are more likely to participate in developing procedures and methods or in providing input for these.

The relationship of supervisory planning in general to overall corporate planning is like that of building blocks. When put together, the derivative plans developed at each level make up the total planning structure. The individual supervisor will develop some plans alone and will administer other plans, or parts of plans, developed by superiors. The supervisor often is called upon to provide input data for planning by higher-level managers.

THE PLANNING PROCESS

Planning all too often is conducted in a hit-or-miss fashion. This should not be. The planning process is amenable to the systematic procedures of the scientific approach to problem solving.

STEPS IN PLANNING Managerial experience shows that the most effective plans result from a rational *planning process*—a logical, orderly sequence of steps. The authors suggest the following sequence.

1. Define the objective.
2. Establish premises and constraints.

3. Analyze the data.
4. Develop alternative plans,
5. Select the best plan.
6. Develop derivative plans.
7. Provide for follow-up.

The dynamic relationships between these steps are presented in pictorial form in Figure 2-3.

Define the Objective Defining the objective, or stating the problem, is the first step. All too often this is fuzzily done because of its apparent obviousness. It is sometimes surprising how a clear definition of the problem may suggest the answer.

". . . In making tennis balls, the first statement of the problem was how to pump air into tennis balls to pressurize them without leaving a sealing plug which unbalances the ball. As restated, the question was asked as to how a ball could be made with higher-than-atmospheric pressure on the inside. With the formulation of the problem the creative solution in this case was relatively easy. Simply make the tennis balls inside a pressurized room without worrying about pumping them up and sealing them off."[1]

In stating the objective, take care not to conflict with higher-level policies or plans. Consider the question of whether a new plan actually is needed or if an existing plan will suffice.

Establish Premises and Constraints Premises and constraints include applicable policies, existing plans, forecasts of future conditions, and factual data. They are the assumptions and facts on which the plan will be based.

In almost every planning situation, one or a few of the premises and constraints may be *limiting factors* (also referred to sometimes as *critical* or *strategic* factors). These are the factors that must be observed and which the planner cannot change or modify. Limiting factors often constitute the basis for choosing between alternative plans. They may be difficult to identify, but is is necessary to search for them because they determine "the size of the ball park and the ground rules of the game." Limiting factors might, for example, be a specific policy, a time deadline, a budget, or a forecast of the work force available at a future date.

Analyze the Data Analysis of the data and of the assumptions developed during the premising step will vary in its complexity, depending on the complexity

[1]Delmar W. Karger and Robert G. Murdick, *Managing Engineering and Research*, 2nd ed., Industrial Press, New York, 1969, p. 89.

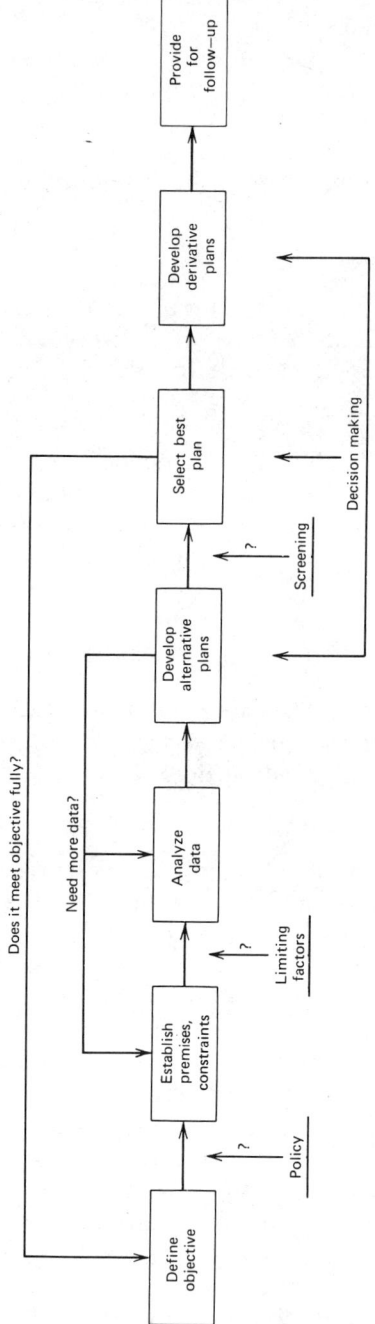

Figure 2-3 The planning process.

of the planning situation. Data should be ordered, classified, and causal relationships sought. Extraneous data are discarded. As analysis continues, gaps in our data may appear, requiring the gathering of additional material.

Develop Alternative Plans
The planner should determine as many different ways as possible of reaching the stated objective. It often happens that the best plan is overlooked because a hasty manager jumped at the first obvious way of doing something.

A surprising number of alternatives usually exists. Suppose, for example, that our objective is to paint small metal castings. A few of the alternative methods of applying paint include brushing, rolling, splashing, dipping, and spraying. This does not exhaust the possibilities. In a class experiment, the students came up with fourteen different methods of applying paint to the article in question. Ingenuity and imagination help.

Select the Best Plan
Selecting the best plan from among the alternatives is the major decision-making point in planning. If the preceding steps have been done effectively, this may be the easiest part of the entire process.

A preliminary screening will eliminate the obviously unsuitable, but several reasonable alternatives probably will remain. A number of factors and possible trade-offs must be weighed carefully in evaluating the alternatives and selecting the best one. Some examples are the following.

1. How well does each alternative satisfy the objective?
2. How does each alternative affect other operations and plans?
3. Is there a difference in complexity between alternatives?
4. What is their relative flexibility?
5. How acceptable is each alternative to the personnel involved?
6. What is the requirement of each alternative in terms of utilization of existing resources versus need for new resources?
7. How do the alternatives compare in risk versus profit? In profit versus investment?

The number and kind of determinants in the evaluation process depend on the type and complexity of planning.

In the painting example previously mentioned, use of a roller to apply paint might be eliminated because of irregular shape. A spray painting booth might be eliminated because of capital investment cost if only a few pieces are to be painted.

Develop Derivative Plans
This may or may not be necessary. If the basic plan is complex, then specific plans will be needed for each task or supportive activity comprising the whole. If the objective is merely to develop, say, a work method, then no derivative plans will be needed and this step may be eliminated.

Provide for Follow-Up

This step to assure that plans are carried out properly and on time is actually part of the control process covered in later chapters. It is mentioned here because provision for follow-up should be incorporated into the basic plan during its development.

THE SUPERVISOR AND THE PLANNING PROCESS

A formalized planning process with its concomitant paper work is a *must* in major organizational planning. Such plans take an appreciable time to develop, have many people working on them, cross many organizational lines, and require coordination. The structure of the planning process becomes less elaborate as we proceed to lower organizational levels. However, a formal process committed to writing still is needed for most intradepartmental plans.

At the supervisor's level, most plans are derived from the plans of higher-level managers. They are shorter in the time span covered and simpler in objective and content. Further derivative plans often are not needed. Even so, many of the supervisor's plans should be developed through a consciously followed sequence of steps and be committed to writing—for example, planning work schedules for his people over the next month, or planning a sticky repair or maintenance job.

On the other hand, much of the supervisor's daily planning does not require either that he or she try consciously to follow a sequence of steps or that the plan be put in writing. To illustrate:

The manager of the men's wear floor at Rendorff's branch store in the Town and County Shopping Center arrives at work one morning and finds that because of an error by Inventory Control the men's shoe department probably will be out of two or three popular styles of shoes by midafternoon. After a few minutes' thought, he telephones the parent store downtown and finds that they have a plentiful supply of the shoes in question. He then telephones the store's delivery department and next the mailroom. After hanging up the phone, he calls one of the floorwalkers over.

"Oh John, Men's Shoes are going to have supply problems by the middle of the afternoon. I hate to ask you to be an errand boy, but we're in a real bind. Would you please take a long lunch break and pick up three cases of shoes at the downtown store? I just checked with Delivery and they're too busy to help us. But the mailroom can lend you a station wagon if you'll drive it. Those cases weigh about a hundred fifty pounds each, so you'd better borrow a two-wheel dolly from the stock room and one of their stock boys to help you."

Within a few minutes, this supervisor subconsciously went through the logical planning sequence. He recognized the problem and established an objective. His experience and knowledge of store operations supplied all the data he needed. After a quick mental review of these data, he was able to consider two or three different ways of getting the shoes when and where he needed them. He selected the best way in view of all the circumstances. He did not consciously go through a step-by-step process; rather his mind subconsciously integrated all factors and quickly arrived at the logical decision. It would have been silly in this instance to sit down with paper and pencil and laboriously work out the steps of such a simple plan.

SOME PRACTICAL AIDS IN SUPERVISOR PLANNING

Several techniques, devices, and methodologies exist that can serve as practical aids to the supervisor in planning. The discussion of these aids proceeds from the simple to the complex.

ADAPTING OLD PLANS Before starting on development of a new plan, the supervisor should ask if it really is necessary. If a similar job has been done in the past, perhaps an existing plan is on file that can be dusted off, updated and modified as necessary, and adapted to the present situation. The foresighted supervisor will keep records of past projects and activities for which plans were developed.

To illustrate, suppose that our supervisor is faced with the job of relining a high-temperature, heat-treating furnace. This is a moderately complex operation requiring a formal written plan. The sequence of job steps includes shutting down the furnace, cooling off (hours to days), dismantling, tearing out old lining, repairing or replacing damaged structural members, relining with refractory brick and mortar (usually several different kinds), reassembly, curing of mortar, and firing up. Along with planning for the operational steps in relining, there are additional tasks: production and other affected operations must be rescheduled, the different classes of skilled labor must be scheduled as required, and arrangements made for the proper amounts and kinds of materials and tools.

With luck, the supervisor can find a plan for a similar relining job from the past. He or she may have to do no more than change the dates, time schedules, and identity of the work crew. However, furnaces vary in make, size, and purpose. Thus the supervisor may also have to change other elements of the plan. Nevertheless, if the supervisor has a framework on which to build the present plan, much time, money, and effort will be saved.

GANTT CHARTS Charts can be a big help in planning. A list of the names of the supervisor's work group is a form of chart and serves as a memory aid. If the job classification is added after each name, the chart is even more useful. Charts can be developed into quite elaborate devices.

The term *Gantt chart* is applied to the many varieties of a type of chart useful in both planning and control of repetitive operations. The common element in all such charts is the use of time as the key ingredient in planning and scheduling production or other activities. The concept originated with Henry L. Gantt, an early pioneer in scientific management. The variety of Gantt charts in use today is limited only by the ingenuity of the users.

A typical Gantt chart used in production planning and scheduling is shown in Figure 2-4. Specific operations and the number of workers customarily assigned to each are listed in the columns to the left. The columns to the right represent the work days and weeks during part of June. As orders are received, they are assigned job numbers and an estimate is made of the number of hours of work required to complete each operation on each order. The time estimates are converted to days and marked off to the right of each operation as a light line with the job number indicated above. The light line is positioned to indicate scheduled starting and completion dates.

If we assume an 8-hour shift and 5 days per week, then one day of work by the stamping group represents 32 hours of work (4 × 8). Job number 27 requires 80 hours of stamping operations, which are scheduled to start on Monday morning, June 12, and be completed by noon on Wednesday, June 14. It then goes to trimming.

The heavy solid line opposite each operation represents the cumulative days of scheduled work for that operation group. It is the sum of the light lines. The heavy dashed line represents previously scheduled work not yet completed. The trimming group is behind schedule by 1½ days. The forming group has the smallest cumulative load. Perhaps some of its people could be transferred temporaily to trimming.

The Gantt chart permits the supervisor to tell at a glance the status of each job order, the total load schedules for each group, and when and where time is available in each operation for new work. To be effective, it must be kept up to date. Gantt charts can be devised for activities other than shop production: individual workers, trucks, routine maintenance operations, paper work processing, and so on.

Sophisticated Gantt-type planning and scheduling boards with magnetic and/or color-coded markers are commercially available from a number of suppliers. These are tailor made for a wide variety of routine office, laboratory, and shop activities.

LINE BALANCING

Line balancing, sometimes called *line of balance*, is vital in planning a production or assembly line. The term refers to the equality of output of each successive operation in the line. If the outputs of each operation are equal (balanced), production flows smoothly. If the outputs are unequal

Some Practical Aids in Supervisor Planning 33

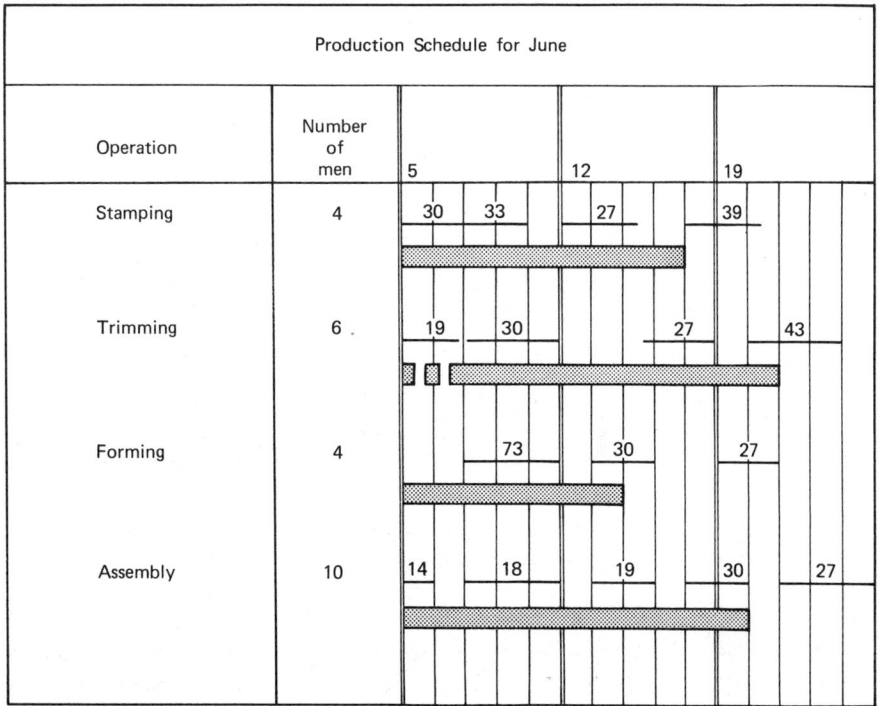

Figure 2-4   A Gantt chart for production scheduling.

(imbalanced), then the slowest operation in the sequence (bottleneck operation) determines the maximum possible output of the entire line. Wasted capacity exists in all operations except the bottleneck operation.

The steps in assembly line balancing are as follows.

1. Establish performance times for the smallest possible whole units of activity, such as positioning a gasket or inserting a bolt.
2. Determine necessary sequences in these tasks or activities, noting flexibility (if any) of sequences. An example of a sequence limitation would be that a washer must go onto a bolt before the nut. In contrast, sequence might be irrelevant in the order in which nuts are put on several bolts.
3. Task times and task sequence restrictions are summarized in a table on the basis of smallest whole activities.
4. Construct a flow diagram, based on the table, illustrating sequence requirements and times.
5. Group the tasks in the diagram into balanced (as nearly as possible) work stations.
   (a) If there are no restrictions on capacity, try the lowest common multiple approach. For example, three operations require 3.5,

1.5, and 4.5 minutes, respectively. If we provide seven workplaces for the first operation, three for the second, and nine for the third, then capacity of the line will balance by producing 120 units per hour at each of the operations.

(b) If line capacity is specified, then the approach is to establish a desired cycle time and task level for grouping into stations. For example, assume that the total for all task times is 38.6 minutes. If a 5-minute cycle is desired (i.e., the line must produce one completed unit each 5 minutes), then a minimum of eight stations would be required. Any solution involving more than eight stations would be wasteful of direct labor.

Although described above in terms of a factory assembly line, the concept of line balancing can be applied to other types of work planning such as multistep paperwork processing in offices, mailroom and packaging operations, and the like. For large-scale, complex line balancing, linear programming, computerized biased sampling techniques, and other sophisticated methods may be used.

ADVANCED SCIENTIFIC APPROACHES

Beginning at the time of World War II, several so-called advanced scientific approaches to decision making in planning have come into use. As might be suspected, they were originated to solve highly complex planning and control problems in which great numbers of interrelated activities must be considered and in which some degree of uncertainty may prevail.

Most of these approaches are based on the use of higher mathematics. It might be said that their development was dependent on the concurrent development of computers. Only the computer could handle the tremendous volume of complex calculations required within any practical time span.

One of the approaches developed for the military during World War II and subsequently applied to business situations is *operations research* (OR), defined by Churchman and coauthors as

"An application of the scientific method to problems arising in the operations of a system which may be represented by means of a mathematical model and the solving of these problems by resolving the equations representing the system."[2]

Some of the mathematical techniques grouped under the general term of operations research include linear programming, game theory, Monte Carlo technique, queuing theory, and probability theory.

---

[2]C. West Churchman, Russell L. Ackoff, and E. Leonard Arnoff, *Introduction to Operations Research*, John Wiley and Sons, New York, 1957, p. 18.

Operations research has been applied with considerable success to managerial problems requiring optimization of factors such as time, cost, or profit. Examples include setting warehouse inventories, location of warehouses, transportation problems, budget allocation, and determining degree of risk.

Another approach is broadly described as time-event-network analysis. Two such techniques—PERT (program evaluation review technique) and CPM (critical path method)—were developed almost simultaneously, but independently, in the late 1950s. PERT is employed chiefly on one-of-a-kind projects where some uncertainty exists and cost is not as important as time. CPM emphasizes cost as well as time and is used on complex projects where both cost and time are important and there is some basis for making reliable estimates of both. PERT in particular has seen many variations since its introduction, including, for example, PERT-COST, in which cost is the critical element rather than time.

The preceding discussions of operations research and time-event-network analysis are barely more than a brief, overly simplified mention that such techniques exist. A more detailed discussion appears in Chapter 6. Also, many excellent books and articles on these subjects are available to the student who wishes to pursue the subjects in depth.

The supervisor is most unlikely to initiate planning on a scale requiring these approaches. However, it is well to be familiar with the terms and to know a little about the concepts. It is always possible that the supervisor may have to supervise a segment of a larger plan developed by these means and will hear references to them.

PLANNING FOR CHANGE

Some of the reasons why corporate plans must be changed were discussed earlier in this chapter. Similarly, there can be many reasons why the supervisor's plans must be changed. He too must be flexible.

The effective supervisor will perform the following steps.

1. Anticipate, when possible, the necessity to change plans.
2. Determine what is to be changed.
3. Determine effect on personnel, equipment, and so on.
4. Alert the work force in advance if possible.
5. Replan.

PERSONNEL CHANGES The make-up of the supervisor's work force can change at times for a variety of reasons: vacations, retirement, rotation for skills, promotion, absenteeism, illness, quitting, and emotional factors.

The first two of these, vacations and retirement, generally are known and scheduled far enough in advance that the supervisor can anticipate and plan for their effect.

Promotions and rotation of members of the work force to acquire new skills may be known in advance. If so, this can be taken into account in planning. But sometimes these events occur on comparatively short notice and cause difficulties in scheduling work assignments.

Absenteeism, illness, and just plain quitting usually are unpredictable and may therefore upset plans. There are some exceptions. For example, if a flu epidemic occurs, the supervisor can reasonably forecast that up to 40 percent of the force may be off. The chronically absent employee also is semipredictable. However, this calls for disciplinary measures rather than accommodation through planning.

Emotional factors in an employee may not change the work force but can cause the supervisor to change plans under some conditions. Suppose, for example, that the operator of a stamping press has a seriously ill child at home. He or she is likely to be thinking about the child and to become careless about work. This job involves the operator's hands being close to fast-moving, sharp, cutting dies. Carelessness can cause severe injury. The effective supervisor will be aware of such problems and should transfer this worker to a safer job until the personal crisis is over.

EQUIPMENT CHANGES   New equipment is rarely isolated. When it is brought into the work place, plans must be made as to where to put it, how to rearrange existing machines, utilities hookup, and training people to operate it. These problems normally are known in advance, and plans can be made ahead of time.

People sometimes forget that no machine ever purchased worked exactly right the first time. "Bugs" have to be ironed out that can take from a few hours to six months. In the meantime, other machines and operations may be affected. The wise supervisor will make allowances for this in planning.

NEW OR MODIFIED PRODUCTS   Introduction of new products often requires changes in equipment, materials, and personnel. The production department normally knows about this sufficiently in advance to plan the necessary changes.

If the new product is made concurrently with the old, and particularly if there is some similarity of component parts, the supervisor must plan for control to prevent intermixture.

Modifications of existing products may have side effects not always anticipated by the engineering or design staff that affect the shop supervisor's planning. The tightening up of dimensional tolerances by no more than a few mils[3] can, for example, slow down the production rate of a machine with consequent disruption of schedules.

---

[3] A "mil" is a unit of measurement equal to 1/1000 inch. The term is widely used in machine shops.

WORK-LOAD CHANGES

Fluctuations in the work load provide headaches for the supervisor in planning work assignments and other activities. The average supervisor probably feels that life is always feast or famine. Some fluctuations can be forecast, but certainly not all of them. A new, big order, or cancellation of an order, may cause a sudden increase or decrease in load.

When the load is heavy, it is vital that the supervisor establish priorities. Which jobs must be done right now? Which ones can be put off? Almost every department or section has some nontime-critical jobs that must be done sometime, but it does not matter when. Certain types of maintenance, shop housecleaning, rearranging equipment, restacking supplies, cleaning out files in an office all fall into this category. It is good planning to save these jobs for slack periods.

COMPANY POLICIES AND RULES

Changes in company policies and rules of a nature to affect supervisors and the work group are another source of difficulty in planning. This is particularly true if the supervisor disagrees with the change or is only lukewarm toward it. The supervisor still has to support the change, enforce it, and explain it to the group.

Not all changes in policies and rules cause changes in supervisory planning, but some do. Company liberalization of the vacation time allowed for hourly employees will cause a major reshuffle of work assignments and schedules. But at least the supervisor does not have to sell this change to his or her group.

Other kinds of policy or rule changes may require hard work by the supervisor to gain acceptance of them by his or her workers; they may also require changes in plans. Some examples might be tighter restrictions on where and when smoking is permitted, elimination of overtime work (and pay), or introduction of new work standards.

The most effective supervisor is the one who is successful in "educating" his or her superior to give advance warning of such changes.

SUMMARY

Planning is the first of the managerial functions. All subsequent activities are based on it. Planning is pervasive in that it is performed by all levels of management. The corporation president engages chiefly in long-range planning to achieve companywide objectives. The supervisor, in contrast, is concerned with more immediate goals such as planning the day-to-day work of the group.

It often is helpful to classify plans according to some rational system. One suggested system is to classify plans initially on the basis of duration, function or use, and breadth or scope; most plans can be described in terms of all three.

Planning is accomplished most effectively by following a logical sequence of steps: define the objective, establish premises and constraints, analyze the data, develop alternative plans, select the best plan, develop derivative plans, and provide for follow-up. The last step actually is part of the control process but should be built into the plan. The planning process normally should be formalized, and the resultant plan should be put into writing. But from the practical standpoint, much day-to-day planning of simple activities is done by the supervisor in his or her head—a process of subconsciously integrating the steps we have discussed.

The supervisor may be able to save time, effort, and money by adapting an old plan to a current situation. Another aid to supervisory planning is the Gantt chart, and its numerous variations, in which time is the common denominator in planning and controlling repetitive operations. Line-balancing techniques also may be helpful in office work as well as in the factory. Advanced scientific techniques such as operations research, PERT, and CPM aid in planning complex multi-activities at higher organizational levels but are unlikely to be used directly in supervisory planning.

Planning at any level is subject to change as the many facets of the business environment change. Among the factors that can cause changes in the supervisor's plans are personnel changes, equipment changes, new or modified products, fluctuations in work load, and changes in company policies and rules. The effective supervisor must anticipate these factors to the best of his ability and be prepared to modify his plans accordingly.

KEY CONCEPTS

Continuous plan. An organization's long-term plans for achieving broad objectives should be developed and maintained on a continuous basis. At periodic intervals (often one year), the plan is updated and extended one more time unit into the future. In so doing, the plan is modified, as necessary, to take into account any deviations from planned performance during the preceding time period and new forecasts of future conditions.

Planning process. This concept maintains that the planning process is rational and is amenable to the scientific approach to problem solving. It may be divided into a logical and orderly series of steps.

Pervasiveness of planning. The planning function is pervasive throughout all parts of any type of organization. It is performed by all levels of management from the first-line supervisor to the top executive and across the full width of the organization in all departments and units at any level.

Flexibility in planning. The probability of change is one of the few certainties in business life. The manager who develops a plan and then adheres to it rigidly is likely to be in trouble. Plans should be developed with built-in flexibility to facilitate adjustment to changing conditions with minimum adverse effects.

IMPORTANT TERMS

Built-in flexibility
Constraint
Companywide plan
Corporate objective
Corporate plan
Critical factor
Derivative plan
Follow-up
Gantt chart
Interdepartmental plan
Intradepartmental plan
Limiting factor
Line balancing

Long-range plan
Methods
Operations research
Plan
Planning
Policy
Premise
Primary business function
Procedures
Short-range plan
Standing plan
Strategic factor
Subobjective

INCIDENTS

Plans, Panic, and Fashions

It was early April and Miss Kelsey, supervisor of sales for women's sportswear at the fashionable Monteith Department Store, was reviewing her plans for the display of summer sportswear in the store's Annual Spring Showing. All departments participated in this popular event, traditionally held on Good Friday, in which summer fashions of all kinds were first introduced to the general public. The date was less than two weeks away, good weather was forecast, and the crowds were expected to be heavier than usual.

Miss Kelsey ticked off items in her mind. The event would tax her sales force to the utmost, but by having the part-time salesgirls who helped out on Saturdays come in on Friday, they could handle it. Space was a bit crowded too. Cosmetics had taken over part of her counter area when they added two new lines last Christmas. Fortunately, she had been able to "borrow" some floor space from Coats and Furs adjacent to her area, since this was their slack season.

Miss Kelsey reviewed her plans complacently. Everything seemed in order. But wait a minute: one more item to consider. The west mezzanine was to be closed off during Easter week for installation of new carpeting. This would change the normal pattern of movement through the store, diverting too many customers away from her area. If she could get Store Security to block off the steps at the north end of the mezzanine on that Friday, this would help the traffic flow. Miss Kelsey relaxed.

At this moment, Mr. Xavier, public relations director, entered her office. "Miss Kelsey, the buyer [department manager] has recommended you for a special job. The Retail Clothiers Association is holding their regional convention in our city during Easter week. As part of the program for wives of Association members, their entertainment committee has asked our store to put on a fashion show of summer sportswear. This will have to be on Good Friday because of other program commitments.

"As you know, Mr. Monteith is an officer of the Association, and he particularly wants this fashion show to be a swank affair and a big success. Incidentally, he has suggested that we serve light refreshments to the ladies. If this show goes well, it could mean something nice in the way of a promotion. But I know that I don't have to emphasize this — you always do a good job."

After the PR director left, Miss Kelsey's head was spinning as she tried to fight down panic. Imagine! Responsibility for a posh fashion show on top of the Annual Spring Showing! Mr. Xavier had mentioned a possible promotion, but she knew very well that it could also mean demotion if the event fell flat.

Miss Kelsey mentally tore up her original plans and began to think afresh. How many women would be attending the fashion show? What would be their age group? This could influence the styles to be shown. Would they want the show to be scheduled over the luncheon hour, in the afternoon, or in the evening? This would determine the availability of models and other help. Better get hold of that committee chairman and get some answers.

And what did Mr. Monteith mean by "light refreshments"? Cocktails or just coffee? Sandwiches, a salad, or what? Should it be catered, or could the store restaurant handle it on top of their routine work? She had better see Mr. Monteith's secretary and the Store Services about this.

Miss Kelsey could see that additional sales help, models, and coordination of timing would be critical problems. Her regular and part-time sales force already were fully committed to the Annual Spring Showing. Maybe she could get some girls from the local junior college for usherettes and models. She had used them before. But wasn't this spring vacation for the colleges? Have to find out. How busy are the local model agencies? Check on this. If the fashion show can be scheduled at just the right time, maybe we can shuttle some of the regular sales force back and forth between the display floor and the fashion show.

Better check with Purchasing and Inventory Control to be certain we will have enough samples on hand for both events. And she would need some extra stock boys, too.

Where to hold the fashion show? The executive dining room probably would be too small. Wait! How about the west mezzanine? If she could just get Store Maintenance to hold off a couple of days on the new carpeting, it would be ideal.

And what about . . . ? Miss Kelsey's head was buzzing with a dozen other questions and thoughts as she reached for the telephone and started to work.

Put yourself in Miss Kelsey's place. Which key concept in planning does this situation illustrate? How would you classify this planning problem in terms of duration? In terms of breadth and scope? Identify the limiting factors that will govern your planning. In the ultimate development of your plan for the two events, could you make use of a Gantt chart? Explain.

The Overly Ambitious Plan

Tim Brewster is supervisor of production machine maintenance at Billiken Tractor Company. Although he is the youngest supervisor with the company, Tim already has attracted the attention of Mr. Connors, the plant manager, because of his innovative ideas and willingness to do more than is expected of him. Consequently, when Billiken decided to automate the machining operations on tractor engines and hydraulic control cylinders, Mr. Connors assigned Tim the job of planning appropriate changes in maintenance procedures for the new system.

Tim was delighted with this evidence of Mr. Connors' confidence in his ability and enthusiastic about the challenge. He spent several evenings and a weekend of his own time working on the assignment. He studied the manuals for the automated machines, scheduled specific maintenance procedures, listed equipment and supplies needed, and rearranged the work assignments of the maintenance crews. It was with considerable pride that he presented the results of this effort to Mr. Connors on the following Monday morning.

Mr. Connors reviewed Tim's report quickly and a slight frown appeared on his face. He went over it again, more slowly and carefully. Finally, he looked up. "Tim," he said, "I can see that you put a lot of work into this but it just won't do. I think you let yourself get carried away by this job. For example, these six pressure-lubricating machines you list here cost $1800 each. That's well over what our maintenance budget allows. Also, you've set up a split shift for the maintenance people on the hydraulic cylinder operation. The union contract won't permit that. And you have located electronic controls maintenance in Bay No. 12. The Assembly Department is using that bay for storage and there's no other accessible area they can use in its place." Mr. Connors paused a moment, and then "I think you had better do some more work on this." Tim left the office in a deflated mood. He shook his head in frustration, wondering how he had gone wrong.

What principles and concepts of the planning process had Tim ignored? What had he forgotten to consider? Does any of the fault rest with Mr. Connors?

QUESTIONS FOR DISCUSSION

1. Why is planning considered to be first in the sequence of managerial functions?
2. It has been said that "planning is essentially decision making." Explain the reasoning behind this statement.
3. What are derivative plans? Under what conditions are these necessary?
4. Why is the typical supervisor involved chiefly with short-range planning?
5. Identify the premises that existed for some plan you developed in the past. Were there any limiting factors?
6. In arriving at a major, complex plan, why is it desirable to develop initially as many alternatives as possible?
7. How do you interpret the return loops in Figure 2-3?
8. What would be advantages, if any, of a supervisor putting low-level policies into writing?
9. For what kinds of activities or purposes are Gantt charts useful?
10. Why must a supervisor be flexible in planning?
11. Develop a role-playing situation in which a supervisor attempts to "sell" the work group on a new company policy with which the supervisor personally disagrees.

CHAPTER III
Organizing

LEARNING OBJECTIVES

- *To distinguish between "organization" as a structure and "organizing" as a process.*
- *To understand the logical sequence of steps in the organizing process.*
- *To identify the various bases for dividing work into logical units (departmentation) and to understand why different patterns of departmentation may be desirable.*
- *To recognize that organization structures and levels are influenced by the span of management and to ascertain how this span is affected by a number of situational variables.*
- *To better understand the nature of authority-responsibility relationships inherent in any formal organization and the nature of specific line, staff, and functional types of authority.*
- *To appreciate the particular characteristics of organizing at supervisory levels and the extent to which this differs from corporatewide organizing.*

Introduction

The term *organization* is often used with either of two meanings: as a structure (entity) or as a process. In the first sense, we say "the organization" with much the same meaning as we say the company, the army, the church, or the club. In this sense of the word, an *organization* is a group of people bound together in a formal intentional structure of roles or positions to achieve certain goals.

In the second sense, the process of organization creates the structure by establishing relationships between people, work, and physical resources. The purpose of organizing is to provide a framework within which people can work together effectively, utilizing resources, to achieve common goals in an optimum manner.

Emphasis should be on people and the relationships between them. Managers do not organize facilities; they organize people and their activities as these relate to the use of all kinds of resources.

CORPORATE ORGANIZATION

Although almost all managerial functions are performed concurrently, they tend to be recognizable as somewhat more distinct and separate activities at the higher levels than at the lower levels in the organization. At the supervisory level, considerable overlap may occur between the functions of planning and organizing. It can be difficult in many instances to say when planning stops and organizing starts.

THE ORGANIZING PROCESS An organization is a dynamic thing—its structure and the relationships between its members undergo continual change. Interrelated internal and external factors are responsible for the need for organizational change. Perhaps the most important factor is the normal growth and expansion (or, sometimes, decline) of the company. Other factors may include changes in business conditions, government regulation, organization interests and objectives, relative importance of various activities, and available resources.

Because of the dynamic nature of organizations, what we call *organizing* often is, in actual fact, the process or *reorganizing* to adapt the existing structure to handle effectively these changing factors. The organizing (or reorganizing) process is essentially the same whether the manager has the task of organizing a simple departmental unit or the entire company. Basically, it is the dividing up and assigning of work to people.

Organizing, like any process, is more effective if the manager breaks it down into a rational sequence of steps. A suggested sequence is the following.

1. Define organizational objective and derivative objectives of departments.
2. Determine the activities or tasks needed to accomplish objectives.
3. Group these activities according to some logical basis.
4. Assign each grouping to an individual and delegate appropriate authority.
5. Provide for coordination.

To make an intelligent beginning, managers must know what they are attempting to achieve. Defining the objectives should emphasize the specific work to be done by the company and/or by any organization unit with which they are concerned. For most enterprises or smaller groups, the nature of the work objectives is fairly stable, providing a reliable base on which to start the organizing process.

The complexity of the second step—determining the activities or tasks needed to accomplish objectives—depends on (1) the scope of the objectives, (2) whether we are reorganizing an existing structure or developing a new organization unit from scratch, and (3) the level at which we start. This breaking down of activities involves division and subdivision, level by level. Depending on the organizational objective, this task may be carried on until we reach the activities of individual hourly employees. To illustrate, higher-level activities might be marketing, production, and finance; lower-level activities could be billing, credit checking, accounting.

Once the objectives have been broken down into component activities, these activities must be reassembled by grouping them into manageable organizational units, or "work packages." Grouping should be done according to a logical system. Several different bases for grouping are in use and are described in the next section of this chapter. Small groups are combined into larger groups, establishing the different levels in the organizational hierarchy. It is at this stage of the organizing process that the structural framework, which may be depicted by an organizational chart, first begins to emerge.

Each grouping of work activities is assigned to a qualified individual who will be the manager or supervisor of that unit. This individual's responsibilities are spelled out, and he or she is granted sufficient authority to accomplish his or her tasks.

With reference to grouping and assigning, particular attention should be given to the strengths and talents of the individuals available. This should influence which, and how many, activities are grouped into a unit under a particular individual. Organizations are continually changing. Management cannot fire everyone and hire all new employees every time it revamps the organization structure. It must make do with the resources available, human and material.

The final step is to provide for coordination of activities of all groups. The necessary types of authority-responsibility relationships (described later) between groups and individuals are established along with information/communication systems. This is the cement that binds the parts of the framework together and turns it into a unified, effective entity.

BASES FOR GROUPING ACTIVITIES

The grouping of activities into *organizational units*, and single units into groups of units, is called *departmentation*. Departmentation can be done according to any of several logical systems or bases that have been developed over the years and that are well known, accepted, and proven in practice.

The reason for having more than one basis for departmentation is that the unit structure should reflect the tasks to be accomplished. It should facilitate the most effective utilization of available resources and simplify coordination and control. For the same reason, different bases often are employed at different levels and/or along different lines of command within the same organization. This is particularly true for medium-to-large enterprises.

Terminology associated with the division of work should be examined before looking at the bases themselves. A number of terms are used to designate organizational units or combinations of units. In the business and industrial world, some examples include division, department, section, group, operation, and plant. In government organization, terms such as department, bureau, agency, office, commission, district, and authority are employed. Religious organizations, the military, and other social institutions have their common terms.

The intention of such designations is to give an indication of *organizational level* and, possibly, of importance or size. However, the usage is not at all precise or consistent in practice. Ordinarily, for example, a division in industry is of higher organization level than a department, and a department is of higher organization than a section, but sufficient exceptions exist that this cannot be stated as a rule. The authors follow a common practice of using the term *department* in referring to any grouping unless indicated otherwise.

Frequently used bases for departmentation are listed as follows:

1. Function.
2. Product.
3. Matrix.
4. Process or equipment.
5. Territory (geography).
6. Customer.
7. Time.
8. Simple numbers.

Function Departmentation by *function* is the grouping of activities on the basis of similarity of skills required or because of a common purpose. In the case of common purpose, diverse activities might be grouped on a functional basis because in combination the result is accomplishment of a larger specific goal.

Function, the most widely used basis for grouping, is applicable at any level. However, it probably occurs most often at the top and the lowest levels. Functional departmentation is depicted in Figure 3-1.

Most industrial/commercial enterprises must perform the fundamental activities of production, marketing, and finance, although the activities are not always called by those names. It is quite common to organize in terms of these three broad functions at the *primary level* (first level below the chief executive). Other functions also may appear at this level if

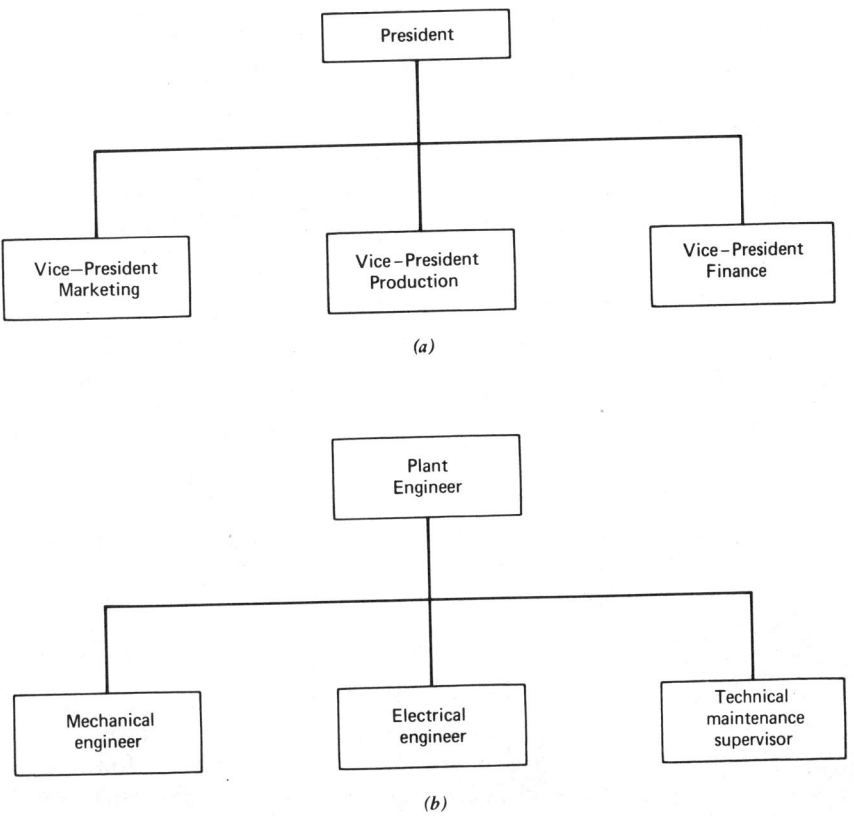

Figure 3-1 Departmentation by function. (a) Grouping by enterprise functions at the primary level. (b) Grouping by derivative functions at lower level.

sufficiently important to company objectives. At lower levels, functional grouping is more on the basis of similarity of specific skills or activities.

Product Organizing on the basis of product is increasing. Large companies with diverse product lines often find that full functional groupings become too complex and unwieldy. Also, multiproduct companies frequently consider it desirable to pinpoint profit responsibility for individual products. Product departmentation may solve either or both problems.

Grouping by product may take place at the primary level, as illustrated in Figure 3-2. It may also take place at intermediate or lower levels with other forms of departmentation above and/or below. For example, the production and/or marketing departments of a steel company could be subdivided into product groups of plate, sheet, bar, tubing, and so on.

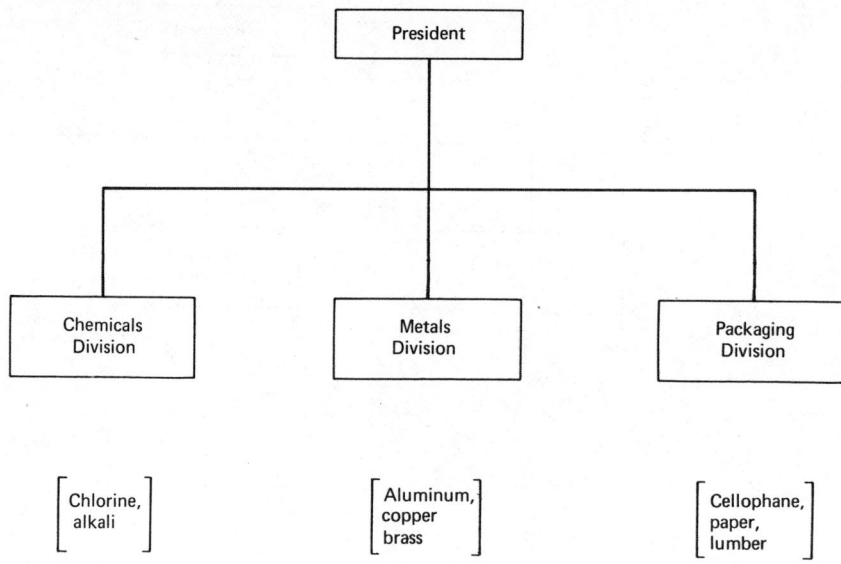

Figure 3-2 Departmentation by product at the primary level.

Matrix Organizing in a matrix form is a compromise between function and product departmentation. It is an outgrowth of project management systems developed by large aerospace firms following World War II. Technical specialists from functional engineering departments were assigned temporarily to project teams for development of new weapon systems. This form of departmentation subsequently has been adopted by many engineering and R & D organizations outside the aerospace industry.

Matrix systems, modified somewhat from aerospace practice, also are finding a place in more conventional areas of business and industry. One such instance is shown in Figure 3-3, a real-life example of recent matrix organization at one major plant of a nationally known chemical company. Under this plant's orginal setup, the functional service departments and the product production departments were organized along conventional lines, with the former providing support services for the latter as needed. A recent reorganization created the matrix system shown in Figure 3-3. Personnel from the service departments are assigned on a permanent basis to teams. Each team, under a supervisor, provides specialized service to a specific product group on a continuing basis.

A major reason for matrix departmentation is to establish responsibility for end results of certain activities. Another is to make better use of specialized skills. A third is that although specialists could be assigned permanently to a product or project group within a conventional organization structure, the matrix system permits them to be allied organizationally to their professional group—a situation that most specialists prefer. It is vital that the respective authorities of functional managers and the product or project managers over members of the teams be delineated carefully and understood by all.

Because matrix organization is a compromise, many variations in practice are found. Some companies actually are practicing matrix management in marketing and other business areas without calling it that, and without depicting it as a grid on the organization chart.

Process or Equipment This form of departmentation is found most commonly in manufacturing operations where the unique nature of the process or equipment makes this grouping logical. This is illustrated in Figure 3-4.

More recently, this form is showing up in offices where electronic data processing and similar activities are being grouped on the basis of process or equipment.

Territory The grouping of activities on the basis of territory or geography is common when the activities are widely dispersed, as in national or international companies. Territorial departmentation is most frequently employed in connection with sales activities. An example of this is shown in Figure 3-5. However, it is not uncommon for manufacturing operations to be so grouped when plants are widely scattered. The reason for territorial grouping usually is based on certain economies of operation. The desirability of local decision making, or a unique local situation may also be a contributing factor.

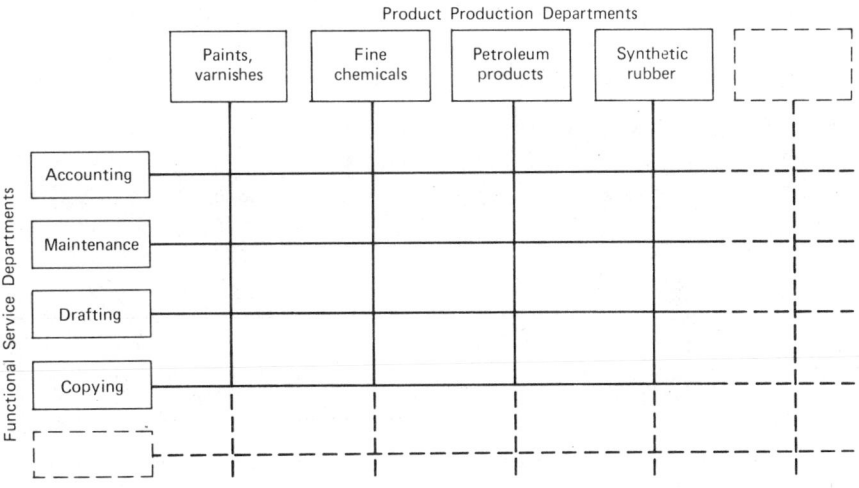

Figure 3-3 Departmentation in matrix form. (Note. At each intersection of authority-responsibility lines is a team of service specialists.)

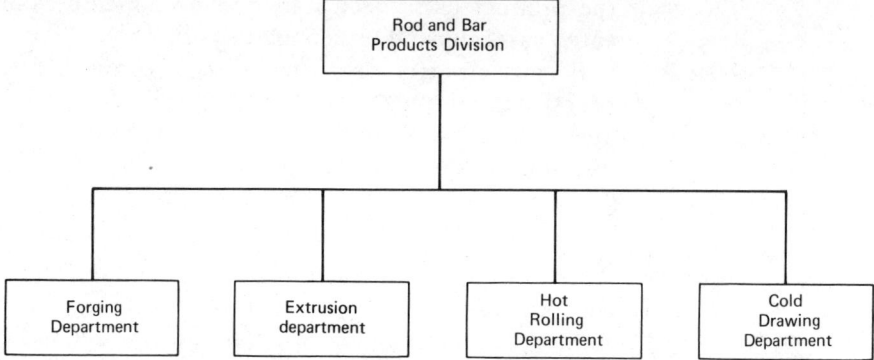

Figure 3-4 *Departmentation by process or equipment.*

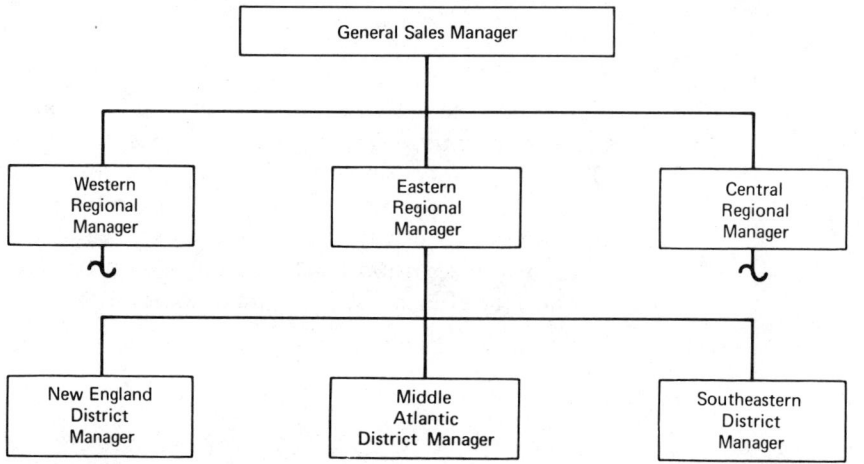

Figure 3-5 *Departmentation by territory.*

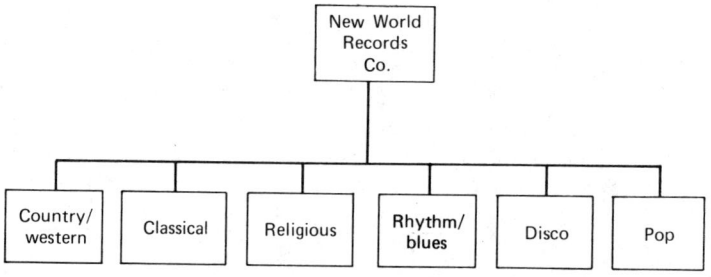

Figure 3-6 *Departmentation on the basis of customer.*

Corporate Organization

Customer Departmentation on the basis of certain categories of customers is logical when service is a major objective. The customer groupings and their particular needs must be clearly definable.

Departments in retail stores catering to specific age groups are examples of customer grouping. Many producers of semimanufactures such as aluminum, steel, lumber, refractories, and other products will establish marketing, engineering, or service groups on a customer basis. At International Nickel Company the Application Engineering Department, which is under Market Development, is subdivided into 13 industry (customer) sections each headed by a manager. The sections include Aerospace, Automotive, Building and Construction, Electronics, and so on. Figure 3-6 illustrates a possible customer basis for departmentation in a stereo record company. The selection of artists to make recordings, distribution, and marketing might be organized on this basis. Because manufacturing of records is essentially the same, regardless of type of recording, this activity would not be organized on the basis of customer.

Time In many types of industries, technical or economic reasons may cause operations to work 16 to 24 hours a day. In such instances two to four shifts will be established. This basis for organizing is shown in Figure 3-7. Departmentation by time normally is practical at the lower levels only.

Simple Numbers Division of work by simple numbers is applicable when manpower is the major criterion and skills or other bases of similarity are relatively unimportant. Grouping by numbers occurs when undifferentiated labor is divided into manageable units; a specific number of workers is assigned to each supervisor.

Common labor crews frequently are organized on the basis of simple numbers. Other examples are certain types of agricultural labor and door-to-door salesmen. In billing departments, essentially the same system is used when the posting of accounts is subdivided according to initials of customers' names, telephone numbers, or credit card numbers.

Organizing on the basis of numbers is disappearing rapidly in industrialized nations. It still is very common in the underdeveloped countries.

SPAN OF MANAGEMENT The problem of grouping individuals into manageable work units and small units into larger organizational units always raises the questions: How many hourly employees can one supervisor manage effectively? How many departments can one higher-level manager handle effectively? This subject is known as the *span of management*.[1]

---

[1] By common usage, this phrase refers to direct subordinates and excludes administrative assistants, personal staff, secretaries, and the like.

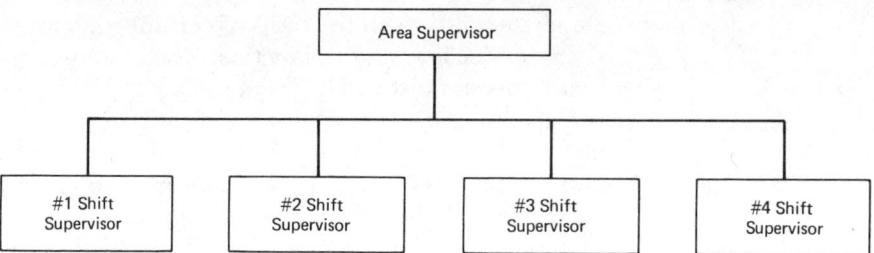

Figure 3-7 Departmentation on the basis of time. (Note. Operating 24 hours a day, seven days a week, requires four shifts.)

It is an important question. Limitations on span definitely influence the total number of departments, their arrangement, and the number of levels in the organization structure. Departmental structure, in turn, influences the length of *lines of communication*. By length, we mean the number of levels through which information items must pass, up or down, along the chain of command.

As a business grows, human limitations force an increase in the number of departments and levels. However, we can generalize and say that, for a given size of enterprise, the wider the span of individual managers, the fewer are the levels and the shorter are the lines of communication. The converse is true — the narrower the span, the more levels there are and the longer the lines of communication will be.

Arguments have developed over the desirability of wide or narrow spans. Proponents of wide spans claim facilitation of communications and individual satisfaction through forced development of highly capable managerial talent. Proponents of narrow spans claim faster, more effective problem resolution and better group performance.

The authors are of the opinion that a manager/supervisor should have as wide a span as is commensurate with *effective* supervision. There can be no question but that levels are costly. Numerous levels and departments complicate planning, control, and communications. The problem of span of management has been with us since Biblical times. However, it was not recognized as a distinct subject worthy of attention and research in its own right until the 1920s and the 1930s. As might be expected, the initial approach was quantitative in nature and consisted largely of efforts to devise a formula or system for determining the ideal number of subordinates.

Later studies recognized that more is involved than just one-to-one contact between a manager and individual subordinates. The number of potential *interactions* between a manager and any combination of all subordinates was calculated. At the same time, it was recognized that not all of the potential interactions actually would occur in real life. This early work came to a generalized conclusion, supported by empirical data, that the best span of control at top levels is 4 to 8 and at lower levels is 10 to 15.

How does practice agree with early theory? We find wide variation in span even among companies generally considered to be equally well managed. In terms of the number of subordinates reporting directly to the president, the median number is 8 or 9 for large companies and 6 or 7 for medium-size companies. The range is about 1 to 24 for large companies and 1 to 17, for medium-size companies. At the lowest-levels the median is assumed to be much higher, although research apparently has not been done in this area.

What specific number of subordinates provides effective span? Generalizations do not appear to provide the answer needed. This is shown by the wide variations in span found between apparently successful companies. According to Koontz and O'Donnell, the current view is "that there is a limit to the number of subordinates a manager can effectively supervise, but the exact number will depend on underlying factors, all of which affect the difficulty and time requirements of managing."[2] These underlying factors include the following.

1. The degree of subordinate training.
2. The degree and quality of delegation.
3. The rate of change of the enterprise.
4. The effectiveness with which communications techniques are used.
5. The amount of personal contact.[3]

Some other students of management include such factors as the size of the enterprise, competition between managers, routine or innovative nature of the work, and the ability of managers themselves.

Instead of considering a span as a fixed number at a given level, the organization planner must balance all pertinent factors in arriving at the most effective span.

AUTHORITY-RESPONSIBILITY RELATIONSHIPS

It was stated at the beginning of this chapter that an organization is a group of people bound together in a formal relationship to achieve organizational goals. This relationship is one of authority and responsibility between superiors and subordinates. Without authority, organizations could not exist—no matter how extensively participative management might be practiced.

Authority is an abstract concept. Several schools of thought exist regarding the ultimate source of authority, its nature, and the manner in which it should be exercised. For our purpose, we take the view that the

---

[2]Harold Koontz and Cyril O'Donnell, *Essentials of Management*, 2nd ed., McGraw-Hill, New York, 1978, pp. 179-180.
[3]Ibid., pp. 180-183.

ultimate source of authority lies in the institution of private property. For the business enterprise, the ultimate source rests with the owners (stockholders in a corporate organization). For convenience in discussing organization structure and departmentation, we often assume that organizational authority starts with the chief executive, although we recognize that, in fact, this authority comes from the stockholders by way of the board of directors.

Authority in the business firm may be defined as the right to decide, to act, and to command others to act (or not to act) in achieving organizational goals. The power to employ rewards and penalties is implied in the exercise of authority, although it may not always be present. The decisions and actions of any manager must, of course, be within the scope of granted authority. Authority rests with a position, and the holder of that position inherits this authority and its corresponding responsibility.

The relationship between superior and subordinate is one of both authority and responsibility. *Responsibility* means the obligation of the subordinate to superior to carry out the assigned duties and functions of the position in a satisfactory manner. In the superior-subordinate relationship, it is necessary for the superior to *delegate* to the subordinate an amount of authority sufficient for the subordinate to be able to make the decisions and take the actions required in performing assigned duties. Otherwise, the subordinate could not meet the responsibility commitment. Without delegation, a formal organization could not exist. The *delegation process* is necessary because the span of any manager is limited. However, managers cannot delegate the entire body of their own authority. To do so would be to give up their jobs to subordinates.

Even though a superior delegates authority to a subordinate, and the subordinate is responsible to the superior, the superior is always answerable to his or her own superior for his or her own actions and for the actions of his or her subordinate. Managers cannot abrogate responsibility because they assigned a task to a subordinate who fell down on the job. Manager must account to their superiors for any failure of work done under their command.

The delegation of authority is not permanent. It can always be retracted by the granter. The recovery and redelegation of authority is almost always involved in the reorganization process.

Formal authority starts with the chief executive and flows downward until it reaches all the lowest levels of employees. This downward flow follows each of the authority-responsibility lines as illustrated in Figure 3-8. The route branches and rebranches as managers delegate portions of authority to subordinates. The line of direct authority relationships from top to bottom throughout the organization is referred to as the *scalar chain,* the *chain of command,* or the *line of command.* It may be seen from Figure 3-8 that a single line of command can be traced from the chief executive to any employee in the organization. Similarly, a sin-

Corporate Organization 55

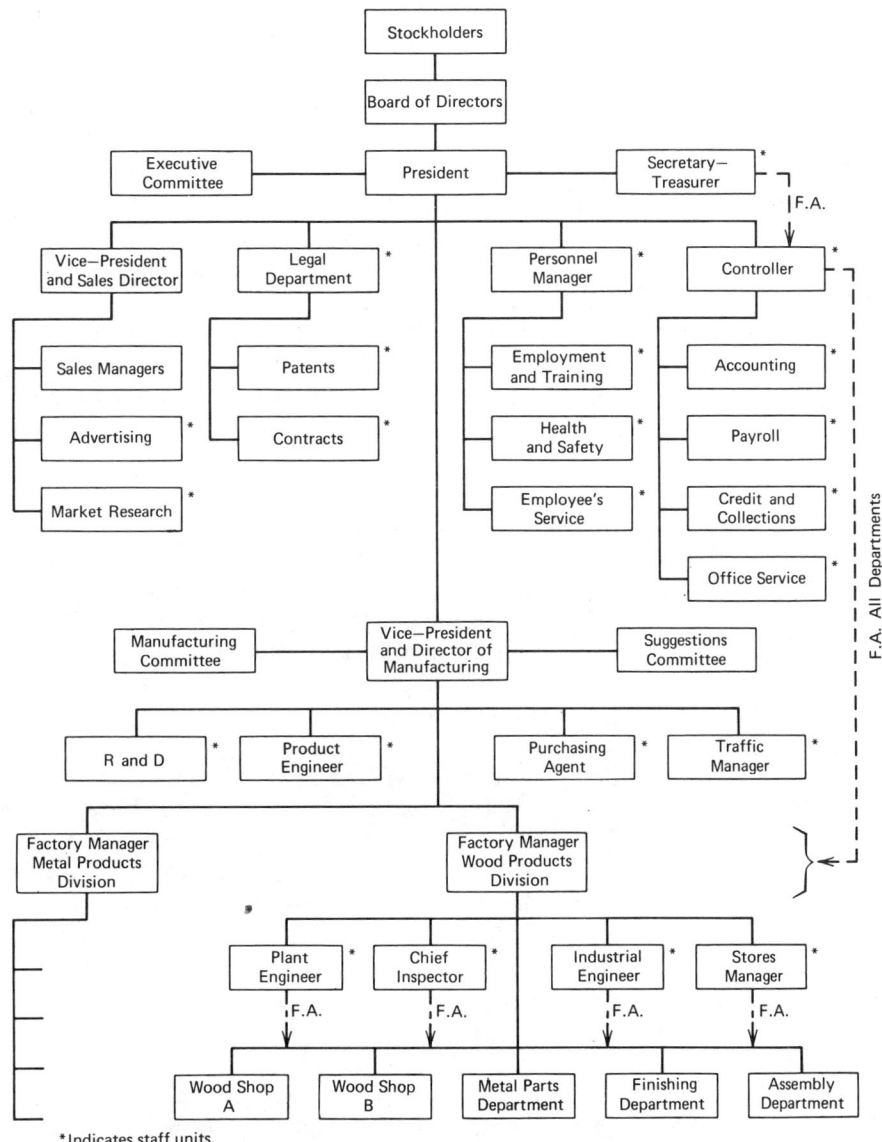

Figure 3-8 Organization chart for typical manufacturing company showing line, staff, and functional authority.

gle line can be traced from any individual manager to any subordinate under him or her in his or her branch of the chain.

Superiors have the right to direct the actions of those subordinates immediately below them in their chain of command. Theoretically, they have authority over those persons directly below their subordinates.

However, good managerial practice dictates that superiors leave it up to their subordinates to issue direct orders to their subordinates.

Ordinarily a manager does not have authority over other managers or their subordinates in other branches of the chain of command. Exceptions do exist. These exceptions, plus certain connotations attached to the term *line of command*, bring us to the subject of the different kinds of authority relationships.

The *organization chart* is a useful device to depict the framework of the structure and its authority-responsibility relationships. In a typical organization chart, as shown in Figure 3-8, the boxes identify specific work activity units and the groupings of units into major components. The lines connecting the boxes show the formal authority-responsibility relationships between superior and subordinate individuals and units, and these lines also indicate the number of organizational levels in the enterprise or in any part of it.

It is important to remember that in many printed organization charts, the limited size of a page may cause crowding and prevent an orderly symmetrical arrangement of boxes. Thus the position of a particular box on the page does not necessarily indicate its level in the hierarchy. However, the *authority-responsibility lines* connecting one box to other units will always determine its proper level and relationship to other groups.

It is common practice for medium-to-large companies to develop a master organization chart depicting the top levels of management down to division or major department managers. Supplemental charts then depict each division or major component in detail. *Organization manuals* often are prepared in conjunction with charts. These give concise written descriptions of each position and department: the functions, activities, authority, responsibilities, and relation to the entire structure.

We should never forget that an organization is a complex, dynamic entity undergoing continual change. The limitation of an organization chart is that it reflects the structure at one point in time. The chart is like a single photograph, whereas the organization is a motion picture.

LINE AND STAFF AUTHORITY

Traditionally, two types of organizational authority have been recognized: *line* and *staff*. Misunderstandings and confusion concerning the nature of line and staff are sometimes a source of friction in organizations. Line managers generally are considered to have more status and power. Staff managers contend that their advice is ignored and their contributions undervalued. Disagreements over respective authority are not uncommon.

The concepts of line and staff may be approached, or defined, from two different points of view: (1) the function or kind of work performed or (2) the nature of the organizational authority relationships.

The traditional view, widely held by many, is that line and staff are defined in terms of the functions performed in the enterprise by the manager and by the degree to which these functions contribute to achievement of enterprise objectives. On this basis, a *line manager* is one who supervises, and has direct responsibility for, activities that contribute *directly* to achievement of enterprise goals. All other managers and officials are staff. In other words, *staff managers* and functions are those contributing *indirectly* to achievement of primary goals.

In the typical manufacturing company whose primary goal is to manufacture and sell products, the production and marketing functions are considered to be line. The finance function is considered line by some authorities and staff by others.

Staff activities then, are those that provide advice, service, and support to line managers or departments. Staff helps the line to do a more effective job. The market research department is a staff group providing information and advice to the vice-president of sales, a line manager. The maintenance supervisor in the shop provides a staff service to the line production departments. Both line and staff groups are shown in Figure 3-8.

Perhaps the greatest drawback to the traditional view in determining what is line and what is staff is in defining *direct* and *indirect* contributions to enterprise goals. In a manufacturing company, purchasing would be considered staff, but in a large mail order firm, buyers are key line officials. Similarly, R & D may be staff in many manufacturing companies but would be considered line in an aerospace company or research institute.

The more current view is that line and staff should be defined in terms of the nature of organizational authority relationships. According to this view, a *line manager* is one who has relatively unrestricted authority over those whom he or she directs or supervises. It is, in essence, a command relationship between superior and subordinate. A *staff manager* is one whose authority over another person or department is advisory or is restricted to matters concerning the functional area of specialty.

From this viewpoint, it is obvious that the manager of what would ordinarily be called a staff department would have a staff relationship to his or her superior (who could be line or staff) but would have a line relationship to subordinates in his or her own department. Similarly, the line manager of a production department might be asked for advice or a recommendation by a superior. In this instance, he or she would have a staff relationship. Thus relationships, not activities, are the determinants.

Many authorities divide staff into either *personal staff* or *specialized staff*, and classify specialized staff activities and authority as advisory, service, control, or functional in nature. Some take a broader view and contend that the nature of staff authority is advisory only, and that service departments are neither line nor staff. According to these persons, *service departments* represent the grouping of activities that could be carried on in other departments but that are brought together in a specialized department for reasons of efficiency, economy, and/

or control. In this sense, service could be considered a basis of departmentation.

FUNCTIONAL AUTHORITY Functional authority is another kind of authority that some writers consider staff and others consider a distinct type in itself. Actually, it partakes a little of the characteristics of both line and staff. *Functional authority* is so named because it is specific or it concerns certain functions only. It should not be confused with functional departmentation.

Functional authority exists when an individual (it can be a department) has delegated to him or her a limited command authority over a specified segment of activities performed in departments other than his or her own. The possessor of functional authority is restricted in its application to the area in which his or her functional specialty interlocks with some phase of activities in the other departments. The restrictions usually confine his or her authority to how, and sometimes when, an activity is to be performed.

To cite some examples, the Quality Control Manager is given authority to tell a Production Supervisor to modify a procedure which is causing too many rejects. The Safety Inspector has the right to order the Plant Manager to slow down a conveyor belt. Without functional authority, these specialists would have to submit recommendations upward to a common line superior who would, in turn, order the respective actions. Functional authority is granted in these instances for convenience and efficiency.

Functional authority may be delegated to line, staff, or service managers (usually the latter two because of some specialty skill) and exercised over other line, staff, or service people. It must, of course, be granted by a line superior who is common to all parties concerned.

The exercise of functional authority is along channels other than the formal superior-subordinate lines of command. In fact, it crosses or breaks the scalar chain. The dotted lines in Figure 3-8 represent functional authority relationships. This form of authority is recognition of the fact that much work in an organization is done horizontally or diagonally across the structure pictured in the charts and, therefore, that horizontal and diagonal relationships must exist along with vertical ones. Incidentally, the joint pooling of authority by two or more different managers and the use of committees are two other techniques for accomplishing work across the structure.

Persons subject to functional authority have multiple responsibility. Although such persons may feel that they have two or more bosses, they still are primarily under the supervision and control of their line superior.

Even so, functional authority violates at least partially a basic principle of management that states that an individual should be accountable to one superior only. This is one reason why functional authority must be carefully restricted and used only where a real need exists. Another reason is that functional authority may interfere with the line manager by taking away some portion of his or her managerial functions.

SUPERVISORY ORGANIZATION

As with all other members of management, one of the supervisor's functions is organizing. Relationships among people, work, and physical resources must be established that will achieve the desired goals. The supervisor's primary goal is to get out the planned production or service as scheduled, within or below cost allocations, and meet or exceed quality parameters.

Of the resources at the supervisor's command, the greatest control normally is over time and people, and the next greatest control over materials and equipment. Probably the least control is over space in that this often is fixed. There are exceptions, of course. Control over money usually is indirect in the sense that the other five items represent costs, and money is controlled through control of the cost items in preparing work force budgets.

Because the supervisor usually has the greatest control over time and people, a majority of the organizing effort may be in dividing and assigning work, and in scheduling time and activities, both for him- or herself and for the work force.

DEPARTMENTATION AT THE SUPERVISORY LEVEL

Organizational units at the supervisory level—shifts, sections, groups, or departments—commonly are set up on one of the following bases for departmentation: function, matrix, process or equipment, time, or simple numbers. (See Figures 3-1*b*, 3-3, 3-4, and 3-7). The relative importance of these bases is difficult to assess. It is likely that function, time, and process or equipment are in much greater use than matrix and simple numbers. Departmentation on the basis of simple numbers is virtually restricted to nonspecialized work at the lowest organization level.

Departmentation on the basis of time is fairly common. However, many work groups organized on this basis will, at the same time, be essentially function, process, or equipment groups. To illustrate, let us assume that the first-level production groups in a chemical plant are organized on a process basis. This distillation process must be operated around the clock. Therefore, we have the no. 1 distillation shift, the no. 2 distillation shift, and the no. 3 distillation shift.

The average person tends to think of *staff* as a high-level position in the military, government, or business. The supervisor is well aware that staff operates at all levels. The transition from nonstaff to staff relationship at the first line is illustrated in Figure 3-9. In Figure 3-9*a* we have a situation in which each foreperson is responsible for quality control in

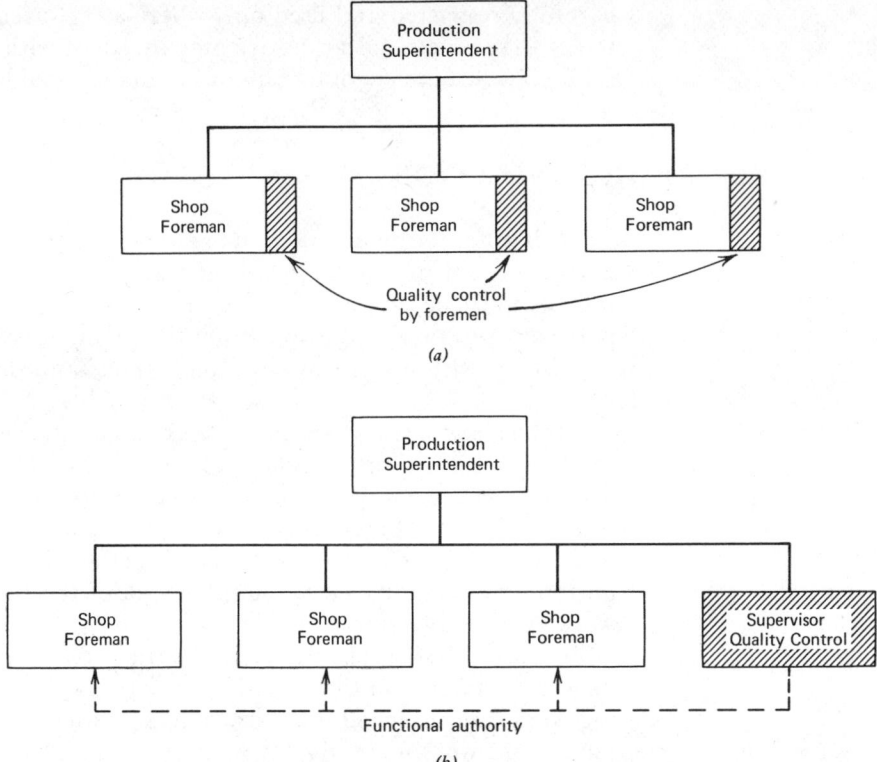

Figure 3-9 Transition to staff relationships at first-line supervisory level. (a) Quality control as part of foreman's responsibilities. No specialized departmentation. (b) Specialized quality control group with functional authority over line production groups.

that particular shop area. If we assume that the amount or complexity of quality control work increases to the extent that efficiencies and economies may be derived from specialization, then we have the situation pictured in Figure 3-9b. In this instance, quality control has been taken out of the hands of the individual forepeople and organized into a staff group. The quality control supervisor now has functional authority over the line forepeople.

Too many line supervisors resent staff and complain of interference with their work. The effective supervisor, regardless of personal feelings, recognizes staff as a fact of organization life and will establish cooperative relations with staff individuals and groups dealing with the unit. The "smart" supervisor usually can figure out some way to use staff to increase group productivity and will improve his or her own knowledge in the process.

TYPICAL DEMANDS ON THE SUPERVISOR

The duties and responsibilities of the average supervisor probably appear to be almost infinite. This emphasizes the need to plan and organize supervisory activities first. If this is not done, the supervisor will spend too much time jumping from crisis to crisis. This is known as "action and reaction management."

What are the duties and responsibilities that must be incorporated in the supervisor's planning and organizing? Dale Beach has developed the following list.

Production
    Requisition materials and supplies
    Expedite the flow of materials and supplies
    Plan utilization of machines and equipment
    Schedule flow of work through department
    Assign employees to operations and jobs
    Check progress of employees
    Help employees clear production problems
    Maintain records of production
    Meet production schedules

Maintenance
    Check equipment for correct operation
    Order repairs to equipment
    Maintain clean and orderly working environment

Methods Improvement
    Devise new and improved work methods
    Cooperate with staff groups such as industrial engineering in developing and installing better methods and procedures

Quality
    Insure that quality standards are met
    Analyze quality reports and take corrective action on defective work
    Inspect incoming materials
    Act on changes in quality standards
    Cooperate and coordinate with quality assurance, engineering, and inspection personnel

Costs
    Control and reduce costs
    Analyze budget
    Determine causes for variances from standard costs and budgeted costs and take corrective action

Personnel Management and Human Relations
    Request additional employees as needed
    Make final employee selection decision
    Orient new employees to their environment, the requirements of the organization, and their rights and privileges
    Train employees

Provide face-to-face leadership
Appraise performance
Coach and correct
Counsel employees
Recommend pay increases, promotions, transfers, layoffs, and discharges
Enforce rules and maintain discipline
Settle complaints and grievances
Interpret and communicate management policies and directives to subordinates
Interpret and communicate employee suggestions and criticisms to higher management
Motivate subordinates; provide rewards for good performance and behavior
Eliminate hazards and insure safe working practices
Develop own skills and abilities through self development activities and participation in company training programs
Cooperate and coordinate with personnel department in administering the company personnel program within own department."[4]

This is an imposing assemblage indeed. Fortunately, not all of these duties will require specific action in any one day, or even in any one week. The broad areas of duties and responsibilities can be narrowed down to more specific activities. Even so, there is much to demand the supervisor's attention.

ORGANIZING THE SUPERVISOR'S JOB

The supervisor's structuring of his or her own job will depend on four factors.

1. The nature and size of the operation supervised.
2. The objectives, plans, and controls of his or her superiors.
3. The nature and scope of authority given.
4. The facilities provided to do the job.

It is obvious from the preceding lists of supervisory duties and responsibilities that supervisors must build flexibility into the structuring of their own job. Supervisors must be able to shift routine duties when needed to make way for emergencies and special jobs. Recognizing *time-critical* and *nontime-critical duties* and allocating priorities to these will help keep supervisors flexible.

Delegation is considered by some people to be a prerogative of upperlevel managers. This is not so; delegation can be a lifesaver to the supervisor. No one person can handle all of the supervisory duties and respon-

---

[4] Dale S. Beach, *Personnel: The Managment of People at Work*, 3rd ed., The Macmillan Co., New York, 1970, pp. 535–536.

sibilities mentioned previously. Therefore the supervisor should consider carefully the possibility of, and need for, delegation. In selecting men or women to whom work is to be delegated, the supervisor should consider the person's attitude, fitness for the particular duties assigned, supervisor potential, and the training given prior to the assignment. The supervisor should be careful not to overdelegate and to remember that he or she still retains responsibility.

Certain essential functions, such as appraising, counseling, and disciplining, should not be delegated. Such activities as record keeping, training, requisitioning materials and supplies, and checking equipment usually are amenable to delegation. Circumstances such as a union contract or company practices will influence which kinds of activities can be delegated and the extent of delegation.

The possibility always exists that supervisors may become ill, be injured, be promoted or transferred, or change jobs. Therefore they have an obligation to their jobs and their superiors to be sure that one or two subordinates are trained to take over. Judicious use of delegation assists in this training.

It is a good idea for supervisors to check on planned versus actual distribution of their own time. An honest record of the actual time spent on activities over one or two weeks can be very surprising.

ORGANIZING THE WORK FORCE

Supervisors are responsible for three categories of work done by the people in their department.

1. Normal, day-to-day work.
2. Special or unusual projects.
3. Emergency work.

The normal day-to-day work relates to the department's primary production or service function. It is the reason for existence of the department and occupies the bulk of its time.

Some but not all, departments occasionally will be faced with special or unusual projects. These, of course, are nonroutine and may or may not have priorities.

Emergencies always occur, even in the best-managed departments. They almost always have priority but do not necessarily affect all other work.

It is the supervisor's duty to keep the crew productively busy, particularly when piecework or incentive pay programs are in effect. To do this, the different kinds of work to be done must be balanced with the people and facilities available.

True supervisors do not engage in direct production work. Ordinarily, the only occasions when they would do so are in emergencies or when instructing an employee by demonstration. Numerous studies bear out the fact that the most productive work groups are under the charge of supervisors who concentrate on their management functions rather than trying to be a superior production worker.

Effective supervisors organize work so that they can tell each man what to do, not how to do it. The principal rule in accomplishing this is to take maximum advantage of the job skills and capabilities of the individuals in assigning work. In other words, a five-dollar-an-hour electrician should not be assigned to sweeping floors. Also, work should be scheduled sufficiently far ahead that the right skills will be in the right place at the right time.

In addition to taking individual skills and capabilities into account, the supervisor in assigning work must also consider the following factors.

1. Physical characteristics required.
2. Effect on other individuals and groups.
3. Training needs and opportunities.
4. Attitudes, particularly dependability and sense of responsibility.
5. Seniority (if specified by union contract or company policy).
6. Safety (when applicable).

Supervisors have several tools or techniques available to them in dividing up and assigning work. They should make full use of such aids, which include job designs, job descriptions, methods, work standards, time and motion studies, and job layouts.

SUMMARY

Organizing creates a structure of relationships among people, work, and resources for the effective achievement of common objectives. An orderly sequence of steps is involved in the process of organizing. Activities and tasks are assembled into logical units, and units are combined into larger groups, according to any of several bases of departmentation: function, product, matrix, process or equipment, territory, customer, time, or simple numbers.

The number of direct subordinates, or departments, that one manager can handle effectively, *span of management*, is limited and influences the total number of departments, the interdepartmental relationships, and the number of levels in the structure.

Organizational relationships are based on the concept of authority and concomitant responsibility. Authority must be delegated, because there is a limit to the span of management. A superior assigns tasks to subordinates and delegates sufficient authority to them to accomplish the tasks. Even though a superior exacts responsibility from subordinates, he or she remains responsible to his or her own superior for his or her own and their actions. The series of authority-responsibility relationships between superiors and subordinates extend from the chief executive down to the lowest level along what is known as the *scalar chain*.

The different types of organizational authority include line, staff, and functional relationships. One view of line and staff contends that these are defined by the kind of work done. By this view, line function and authority relate to activities contributing directly to corporate goals (e.g., production and sales), and staff functions and authority are advisory or supportive to the line. The other view is that line and staff are based on organizational relationships—that line authority is relatively unrestricted command authority and that staff authority is advisory in nature or restricted to a functional area of specialty. In this view, an individual could have a staff relationship to one person and a line relationship to others.

Functional authority has some of the characteristics of both line and staff and exists when an individual is delegated limited command authority over a specific segment of activities performed in departments other than his own. It usually involves highly specialized functions.

Organizational structure at the first-line supervisory level commonly is based on function, process or equipment, time, or simple numbers.

Supervisors have an imposing number of duties and responsibilities. This, plus the fact that their planning is comparatively short range, makes it imperative that they carefully organize their own time and work prior to organizing their work force. Several factors influence the nature and extent of organizing the supervisor's own job. In organizing the activities of the work force, the supervisor considers, first, the kind of work to be performed; second, the skills and capabilities of the members of the group; and third, several supplementary factors. The supervisor then makes the work assignment.

KEY CONCEPTS

Organization. For the purpose of this text, we are most interested in the concept of an organization as a process in which a structure of relationships is created among people, work, and resources. People interact through a system of authority-responsibility relationships to utilize resources in achieving goals.

Basis for departmentation. The division of work and the assignment of tasks to create organizational units (the outward form of the organization structure) can be done in a logical, systematic way that should reflect the nature of the tasks to be accomplished; facilitate the most effective utilization of available resources; and simplify communications, coordination, and control. There are several such bases commonly used in the departmentation process.

Span of management. There is a definite limitation to the number of direct subordinates that any manager can control effectively. The exact number depends on identifiable factors that affect the difficulty and time requirements of managing.

Authority-responsibility. To provide effective leadership and to direct and coordinate the efforts of others in working together to achieve common goals, a manager must have authority. This is the right to decide, to act, and to command others to act or not to act. In the business world, authority stems from the institution of private property. Authority rests with a position and is inherited by the holder of that position. With authority goes responsibility, an obligation to one's superior to use delegated authority judiciously and to carry out assigned duties and functions satisfactorily.

IMPORTANT TERMS

Authority	Organization chart
Authority-responsibility lines	Organization manual
Chain of command	Organizational level
Delegate	Organizational unit
Delegation process	Organizing
Department	Personal staff
Departmentation	Primary level
Function	Reorganizing
Functional authority	Responsibility
Interactions	Scalar chain
Line	Service department
Line manager	Span of management
Line of command	Specialized staff
Lines of communication	Staff
Nontime-critical duties	Staff manager
Organization	Time-critical duties

INCIDENTS

A Problem in Expansion

Clegg Industries, Inc., develops and manufactures a variety of small tools and equipment, manual and powered, for yard and garden work. These include edge trimmers, shears, powered leaf rakers, garden tillers, and others.

The New Product Development Department contains an Engineering Design Section that is responsible for converting ideas for new products and for improvement of existing products into finished designs ready for production. This section also has been responsible for building a few prototype models of each new design for testing by the Testing Section of the same department. Testing procedures result in suggestions for changes in design in about one-third of the instances.

The Design section is made up of four or five graduate engineers and a half a dozen draftspersons. The draftspersons are nonexempt salaried employees. Because of the comparatively small size of this operation, the design engineers and draftspersons have been grouped in one large room—desks in one half and drafting tables in the other. The Section Head would assign a new design project to an engineer. As he or she performed his work, the engineer would give rough sketches and notes to whichever draftsperson was least busy, for conversion to finished drawings. The system worked very well. Everyone knew what everyone else was working on, and there was considerable exchange of ideas.

Prototype construction is done in a small shop at the rear of the Engineering Building in which New Product Development is located. This location makes it easy for the design engineers to check on progress of their projects. The prototype work is performed by a handful of older hourly employees—skilled workers who have been "promoted" from the manufacturing plant. They are under informal supervision of the senior worker, who reports to the Engineering Design Section head. Prototype work is considered a soft job by production workers in the plant.

The leisure-time market is booming, and Clegg Industries has decided to add riding mowers and small garden tractors to its product line. A considerable expansion in the engineering design operation has resulted. The number of engineers doubled, more draftsmen were added, and the prototype shop workers complained of inadequate facilities. It soon became apparent that the old, informal system wasn't working under the increased load.

Management decided to change the setup. All draftspersons are to be incorporated into a new Drafting Section and moved into a room next door to the old one. Engineer's sketches and notes are to be given to the Drafting Section head, who will assign them to his workers. Management also is considering the possibility of moving prototype construction back to the plant and making it a new section under the Manufacturing Department.

In analyzing Clegg Industries' situation, sketch organization charts showing the relationships of all departments, sections, and groups mentioned in the incident under the old organizational structure and under the proposed new one. What advantages will accrue from the new system? What problems will the new system create? How will it affect lateral and diagonal interactions between various categories of employees? What do you think will be the reactions of engineers, draftspersons, and skilled workers to the new system?

A Question of Authority

The Kitchen-Aid Products Company manufactures disposable kitchen utensils out of aluminum foil. Starting out with 10 employees in 1965, the company has grown rapidly to a present size in 1980 of 300 production workers and 110 office, sales, and managerial personnel. George Briscombe, the founder and President, had a background in marketing before organizing the present company.

During the company's first decade, Mr. Briscombe was concerned primarily with establishing a position in the market. Most of his time was spent in developing new sales outlets through contracts with supermarket and discount-store chains. Only recently has Mr. Briscombe appointed a general sales manager and begun to devote more time to other aspects of the business. Now that he is paying more attention to other functions, Mr. Briscombe has become aware that costs have been rising more rapidly than income during the past two or three years. Although department budgets are prepared annually, no real system for control of expenditures was developed during the period of the company's emphasis on sales.

Mr. Briscombe has spoken forcibly about this to his department managers on several occasions recently but without apparent result. After some thought, he has decided to create a staff position for financial control. To this end, he called Ed Driscoll, the assistant accountant, into his office to discuss the matter.

After describing the situation, Mr. Briscombe concluded with "Ed, you're not overloaded in the accounting office so I would like you to take on as an extra duty the responsibility for keeping expenditures under control. You will have the authority to approve or disapprove all expensed items over $25 in amount. Wages and salaries are excluded, of course, and I will continue to approve capital expenditures as in the past. Now go to it and let's see if we can't get costs back in line."

Ed approached his new task with enthusiasm. The first thing he did was to prepare a memorandum to all department heads, over the signature of Mr. Briscombe, advising them that all invoices for operating supplies in excess of $25 must be submitted to him for approval prior to payment. It further stated that salespeople's expense accounts and office telephone bills and copying machine rentals must be initialed by Driscoll. Several department managers grumbled about being "bossed" by an assistant accountant, but generally decided to wait and see how things worked out.

Shortly thereafter, several office personnel complained to the Office Manager that Mr. Driscoll was limiting the number of copies they could run off in any given day. The Office Manager soothed their ruffled feelings, but when Ed disallowed a long-distance phone bill, he hit the ceiling. The Office Manager appealed directly to Mr. Briscombe, pointing out that the total phone bill was under the budgeted amount. Mr. Briscombe overrode Driscoll's action on the bill.

On another occasion, Driscoll refused to approve a $150 item for "entertainment" on a salesman's expense account. The Sales Manager also appealed directly to Mr. Briscombe. "Look, George, you know from your own experience that we've got to play a few rounds of golf with these people and take them out to dinner if we're going to keep their accounts." Mr. Briscombe initialed his approval without question.

Matters came to a head when the purchasing agent went fuming to the Plant Manager with the story that Ed Driscoll was telling him that he should be able to buy heavy-duty aluminum foil more cheaply.

The Plant Manager, Sales Manager, and Office Manager asked for an appointment with Mr. Briscombe. They complained that Ed Driscoll has a "swelled head" and demanded that the financial control position be abolished. After some brief discussion, Mr. Briscombe agreed.

In analyzing this incident, what type of authority was Ed Driscoll given? What errors did he make in exercising this authority? What errors, if any, did Mr. Briscombe make in this organizational change? What factors may have contributed to the complaints made by the department heads to Mr. Briscombe?

QUESTIONS FOR DISCUSSION

1. What are the factors that cause an organization to be dynamic in nature?
2. How does coordination act to bind the parts of an organization together into a unified, effective entity?
3. Define the term *departmentation*. Why do we usually find different types of departmentation within a large company?
4. How is departmentation by function likely to differ within a company at the primary level and the lowest level?
5. Compare matrix and product departmentation on the basis of any similarities that exist between the two.
6. How does the question of wide versus narrow spans of management affect lines of communication?
7. What is the difference between authority and responsibility?

8. What is the ultimate source of authority in a business enterprise from a theoretical viewpoint? From a practical viewpoint?
9. What are two limitations of organization charts in depicting organization structure and relationships?
10. What would be your arguments, pro and con, on the question of considering a service department to be neither line nor staff in function?
11. How does functional authority differ from line authority?
12. What bases for departmentation might you expect to see in use at the first-line supervisor level?
13. What are the factors that influence the style and degree of organizing the supervisor's job?

CHAPTER IV
Informal Organizations and Groups

LEARNING OBJECTIVES

- *To understand the importance of informal groups and their impact on the efficient operation of an organization.*
- *To understand the nature of informal groups.*
- *To know the types of informal groups.*
- *To know the activities of informal groups.*
- *To realize the relationship of the informal group with the supervisor's formal group.*
- *To know how a supervisor's control is related to the informal group.*

Introduction

In addition to understanding the skills of leadership and communication, the supervisor is required to work with both formal and informal groups. Formal groups, as discussed in Chapter III, are established by the organization to fulfill useful functions and goals. The formal organizations that exist within the corporate or company environment are established to perform specific operations; for example, the work group directed by the supervisor is commissioned to produce a given number of products, if possible, at a specific cost or set of standard costs. Formal groups are established for specific purposes and are a structure designed to accomplish the company's goals. Formal groups are usually based on authority that is delegated by a superior to subordinate members within an organization. Although the supervisor is aware of formal groups, this chapter is concerned with the discussion of the less obvious, but very significant, informal groups that play a very important role within the formal organization.

NATURE OF INFORMAL ORGANIZATIONS

Whereas the formal organization has been established by the company to accomplish specific goals and tasks, the informal organization is a social structure primarily designed to meet the social needs of its members. Similar to formal groups, the informal group has to have authority, which is usually based on personal acceptance. Usually informal groups organize spontaneously. This is one of the major distinctions between formal and informal groups. Informal groups can come and go. They can rise when needed, and they can pass from the scene when no longer required. The duration of the informal groups depends on the problems and/or needs that have to be mastered or fulfilled and the degree of uncertainty and fear that exists among the members of a given informal group.

The informal group is limited to individuals who desire to communicate with each other. The informal group will survive so long as its *communication network* operates effectively and efficiently. Whenever people gather for a common purpose, the natural gregariousness of the people usually generates the informal organization.

The specific purposes of the informal organization can be many and varied, but usually the informal groups fulfill four important functions.

1. Satisfaction of social needs.
2. Satisfaction of communication needs.
3. Establishment and maintenance of work, conduct standards, and how to perform on the job.
4. Determination of quality or quantity of work produced.

Often formal organizations are not suited to provide the social satisfactions that an informal group can provide. Therefore, informal groups are held in suspicion by some managers. Unfortunately, suspicion is not the answer, or even an adequate replacement to understanding how and why informal organizations evolve. A brief review of historical data may be helpful for a better understanding.

TYPES OF INFORMAL ORGANIZATIONS

Any classification of informal groups or informal organizations is arbitrary. For the sake of our discussion, we classify and discuss the types of informal groups and organizations under the following categories: (1) work groups, (2) grapevine communication groups, (3) social groups, and (4) cliques.

WORK GROUPS

The supervisor has the closest contact with work groups. The supervisor will be able to observe this group very closely. The informal organization in the *work group* is composed of the straw boss or boss and the other workers. The straw boss may take over or strongly influence the group in the absence of the supervisor. When observing a group of 12 workers, it may not be easy to identify the straw boss, since the most obvious suspect may not be the informal leader. A good way to recognize the straw boss is to observe whom the workers look to for leadership besides the supervisor during a minor crisis or decision-making process. In the work group setting, the informal leader has a great deal to say about the conduct of the work group and the setting of standards of work and work output. For example, if a new member of the group attempted to increase his production higher than what the work group approves, the group would check the new member and notify him that he had violated the work accomplishment rules. The violation of rules of conduct as sanctioned by the informal organization within the work group could be a serious situation. Since the informal group within the work group is cohesive, a threat to the informal group's survival could provoke the group to take action toward policing its standards. To maintain its solidarity, the group will develop its own values, such as work design, amount of work that should be done, and conduct. The informal group will place pressure on its members if they do not bend toward or conform to the group's norms. As the informal leader represents the group's purpose, the person who is best able to communicate the group's purpose to both the group and the supervisor, stands the best chance of achieving the position of straw boss, or informal leader.

GRAPEVINE COMMUNICATION GROUPS

Grapevine communication groups or networks arise from social interaction and are broad in nature and very fickle and dynamic. *Grapevine communication* groups provide social activities and a feeling of importance to the participants. Although it is difficult to determine their exact structure and specific purpose, grapevine communication groups tend to permit the participants to feel important by strengthening their feelings of uniqueness and their feelings of unity against any challenges that may be common to the members. Thus common problems tend to foster grapevine networks. "Birds of a feather flock together." In addition, these groups provide working ties between various organizations, such as work groups in different parts of the plant, store, or office. Also, these groups create traditions and customs, and provide an avenue for discussion of common experiences. Grapevine networks become established informal organizations when they have acquired influential members from formal groups who are credible and appear to be informed about what is going on in the organization. The source of information directly affects the strength and duration of grapevine networks. Moreover, the severity of shock and believability created by the information passed along the grapevine network also influences the effectiveness of this type of informal organization. The greater the shock and believability, the more legitimate the grapevine seems to be.

In almost every formal group there is at least one individual who appears to know what is going on, because of past experience or personality or ability to hear rumors, gossip, and information flowing in and through the grapevine. This individual usually has access to information because of friends or privileged position. The participant achieves a place in the firm as the one with the most information. If this person does have this facility, he or she gains respect, or at least attention, from colleagues. These rewards are usually sufficient for the informer to continue his or her activities, which can stimulate the informal grapevine communication network's existence.

The features of grapevine communication are usually as follows. (1) They have tremendous capacity to channel information. (2) They have a fast pace in that given data, or information, may travel throughout an entire organization in an extremely short period of time. (3) They can be extremely influential. These features can be threatening, but also can provide assistance to the supervisor. It depends on how the supervisor uses the grapevine and how he may be able to cope with it on a day-to-day basis.

The grapevine is usually the product of a situation rather than an individual's personality. Individuals seeking power can initiate rumors, but situations provoke grapevines that will survive. This means that anyone can become active in the grapevine, given the proper situation and motivation. An individual may be viewed as a very steady, conservative member of a formal work group but may participate actively in the grapevine operation if he or she feels threatened by the formal organization or work environment.

The grapevine thrives whenever excitement or insecurity becomes prevalent within an organization. For example, an expected layoff, organizational shutdown, or a major change in the firm's management can generate active grapevines. When individual workers do not fully understand a piece of information going through the grapevine, often they will fill in the missing parts according to their own perception of the particular information. Usually these filled-in parts represent what the workers want to believe. Therefore it is important to management that the right story gets out as soon as possible. The grapevine can thrive and be extremely dangerous in spreading false information.

Grapevines are like other forms of communication; they usually are fast and in constant change. One person can tell another person, who tells two others at the same time, so that now you have a coincidental operation occurring. However, the same information or similar information may be distributed throughout the channel of communication over four, five, or six separate networks simultaneously. During periods of excitement where feelings of insecurity are prevalent, individuals are primed for solutions to situations that would be believable to themselves. Therefore favorable or believable information can easily travel at this time.

SOCIAL GROUPS

The social activities of informal organizations become a very integral part of the formal organization. Whether the social activity is a bowling league, softball operation, or social encounters on the job, it still performs the same basic functions. On-the-job informal social groups usually take the form of small communication networks or small groups that perhaps cluster around the water fountain during coffee breaks, work breaks, or lunch. These groups provide an emotional and social outlet for the individuals, particularly if the workers perceive their jobs as uninteresting. Although boredom can be a state of mind, as it is perceived by the worker, the need to gain recognition and the need to feel satisfied are emotions that can be vented in the small informal social groups. These groups permit the members to unburden themselves or complain about their problems. Reinforcement is received as the listeners agree or restate the situation.

Some small informal social groups are formed in order to have members become better acquainted. This occurs among the younger workers, since they are striving for social contacts. Young married or unmarried workers tend to gravitate toward this type of social group. Their needs to belong and socialize are fulfilled in this way.

CLIQUES

Cliques, as used in this book, refers to social groups whose members have a strong affiliational need for each other, such as friendship support, a sense of power, and/or security. In addition, cliques tend to include a sense of identity and to provide the maintenance of self-esteem for these members. Cliques are a hard-core type of informal social organization that appear on the job as well as off. One of the common denominators of a clique usually is the similarity of psychological and personality features of its members. The members have a bond or unity because of their common interests and traits. As in other forms of informal groups, cliques are established for the need satisfaction of their members. However, the major difference between cliques and social groups is the degree of affinity among the members. A social group may be made up of friends with similar likes and dislikes, but a clique is a social group composed of members who have very strong psychological goals that conform with each other. A member of a clique strongly identifies with his or her cliques and will readily defend the clique at every opportunity.

Cliques appear to emphasize the following factors. (1) They influence aspirational levels of the members of the group, and (2) they influence the kinds of behavior of members. Although both of these influential factors are prevalent in the other groups, the clique tends to have the stronger effects because its members are more closely associated and have more common needs that provoke greater involvement and identity to the group.

ACTIVITIES OF INFORMAL GROUPS

Whether the activities of informal groups are advantages or disadvantages to the supervisor depends on how the supervisor recognizes the activities and how he perceives their value. Few of the informal group activities can be used directly to the advantage of the formal organization. Some activities are disadvantageous unless they are understood and coped with by the first-line supervisor.

Informal groups can affect a supervisor's job in seven different ways.

1. It can start rumors.
2. It can create attitudes.
3. It can shape morale.
4. It can threaten.
5. It can carry true or false information.
6. It can promote conformity.
7. It can develop natural leaders or straw bosses.

RUMORS Informal groups, as stated earlier, can be very powerful organizers. An informal group, whether it be a work group, the grapevine, a social group, or a clique, can be a very formidable function. First, groups can start *rumors*. People will purposely fill in the blank spaces in the chain of communication. People will initiate stories to fill in missing information gaps that provide logic or reason. Informal groups can start rumors that often may be true. Sometimes the rumor is the analysis by some of the workers concerned with the problems that confront the organization. In either case, rumors are usually started as solutions to problems that disturb the affected groups. The grapevine communication system thrives on this type of "inside" information.

ATTITUDES Groups can perpetuate attitudes favorable to the group. Obviously, conformity or tendencies to conform to the group in order to satisfy social needs do help to create attitudes or ways of perceiving activities. This is accomplished because norms are established by the group as a means toward satisfying the needs of the individuals in the group. For example, a work group's informal structure, headed by a straw boss, may believe that its supervisor is unduly oppressive and a new member of the group is quickly indoctrinated to this fact. This mild form of conformity forces the person to bend to the ways of the group, which helps to establish greater solidarity among the group's members.

Attitude formation by informal groups can become extremely important, because these attitudes are constantly reinforced by the informal group. If the attitudes are favorable, the informal group's reinforcement is beneficial. When attitudes are unfavorable to the supervisor and organization, the attitude formation and reinforcement by the informal group can become a disadvantage. Unfavorable attitudes may affect work performance, quality of output, morale, and the formal organization's will to achieve and perform. Moreover, unfavorable attitudes can help to expedite the decline of the formal organization's efficiency over time.

Since the informal group's attitude-formation powers place supervisors in a difficult position, what can they do and what role should they play in this situation? Although this subject is covered in depth later in this chapter, the supervisor must understand the nature, purpose, and direction currently being taken by the informal group's attitude. Once the supervisor can plot the direction, he or she must then determine how to promote it, work with it, or kill it immediately. The supervisor can stop a negative group attitude by disseminating all the pertinent information, changing his or her use of supervisory and managerial techniques, or seeking out assistance from superiors or staff people as soon as possible. If an unfavorable attitude is permitted to survive without corrective activity being taken immediately, it will grow and expand as long as the informal group's needs are being satisfied. The supervisor who can determine that the group's needs are not being satisfied can stymie the growth of an unfavorable attitude and replace it with another, more favorable attitude. For example, if the employees believe that the supervisor is too harsh in his or her treatment of them, the supervisor should convince the employees that it is for their own safety, health, and well being. The attitude of harshness is saying that the supervisor doesn't care about the employee and is motivated by self-gain only. Once the workers are convinced that self-gain is not the culprit, but that the supervisor has the good of the group as the major goal, the employee's attitude toward the supervisor may soften.

Constant attention and awareness on the part of the supervisor are necessary in this volatile area of informal group attitude formation. There are no panaceas. Good, effective, considerate, and intelligent supervision can be of great assistance. This is one of the major supervisory functions that all good supervisors must master.

MORALE Groups can shape morale.[1] *Morale* can be defined in many different ways. It can be defined as the "attitudes of individuals toward their work

---

[1] Morale is covered in greater depth in Chapter 21.

environment and toward voluntary cooperation to the full extent of their ability in the best interests of the organization."[2] Formal groups affect the respective actions taken by the workers toward the organization, the job, the company, and the products it makes. Companies emphasize the drive to produce good work rather than emphasize the worker's contentment. However, the workers with high morale will like their jobs and will have greater drive to work cooperatively with others to achieve common worker/company goals. The exchange of communication among and within the informal groups helps to shape and sustain the level of morale. High morale can be perpetuated by informal group communication systems. High morale is considered by many managers as the hallmark of a well-managed organization. The informal group structure is seen as a subsystem by these managers as well. The informal groups, however, can help managers and supervisors by perpetuating high morale, eagerness, and sensitivity to the tasks at hand. Whether morale improves or declines, informal groups can be instrumental, in part, in the creation of the change in morale and the perpetuation and the momentum of the change.

THREATEN Informal groups can be threatening to the formal chain of command, especially to the supervisor. The amount of respect that the group has for the supervisor will greatly affect the way the informal group structure will respond to the supervisor's leadership or direction. If the informal leader (straw boss) believes that the supervisor is performing properly, he or she will assist in the accomplishment of those tasks. But if the informal group leader believes that the supervisor is not performing, the informal group may drag its feet, rebuke the present leader, or become an obstacle in the path of the supervisor. An incensed informal group could jeopardize a formal group by rebelling against authority or by slowing down production.

TRUE OR FALSE INFORMATION Informal groups can carry information at an unbelievable speed, regardless of its source. There have been examples discussed in the literature in which rumors have spread from one continent to another in one day. The advent of rapid transportation and communication has enhanced the spread of true or false information within a company or organization. The danger lies in the informal group's ability to disseminate false information.

CONFORMITY Informal groups can also promote conformity. *Conformity* is usually a change in an individual's behavior or belief toward a group as a result of

---

[2]Keith Davis, *Human Relations at Work: The Dynamics of Organizational Behavior*, 3rd ed., McGraw-Hill Book Co., New York, 1967, p. 58.

real or imagined group pressure. The formal work group will apply pressure with the leadership of the supervisor in such a way as to bend the group toward the accomplishment of the goals of the organization. Factors such as work load, attitudes, productivity, and beliefs are instrumental elements in a group's survival. The informal group will bend individuals toward meeting the established standards of the group.

Since conformity is such an important activity in informal groups, one might ask why people conform. Three reasons can be listed as to why people conform to groups: (1) need to be liked, (2) maintenance of existing relationships, and (3) need to be correct. We would rather "fit in" than "stand out"; therefore, if the group does meet our needs, we will tend to conform to it. A need to make a living is powerful enough to make a person want to fit into a group. Conformity to informal groups, whether in an office, a production line, or a store, is a very active relationship.

Conformity within an informal group has four stages of development. These four stages enforce or police a group's unity and purpose. When a person objects to the group's will, the members of the group will be threatened and fight for the group's survival or maintenance of the group's correctness. First the group will attempt to seduce the individual (*deviant*) with a pat on the back, a smile, or a joke about the individual's objections to the group's will. If this doesn't work, the second stage starts. The group reasons with the person, trying to point out why the deviant should bend to the group. The second stage usually includes examples of how the individual can benefit from belonging to the group. If the deviant still insists that his or her views are correct, the third stage evolves. Now the iron-fist approach appears. The individual is attacked verbally by the members of the group. Reason is no longer used, and emotion becomes commonplace. If this still doesn't work, the fourth and last stage appears. The individual is completely cut off from the group. He or she no longer exists as a human being to group members. This fourth stage becomes a very delicate situation for the supervisor.

DEVELOP LEADERS

The last factor of informal groups is that they can develop natural leaders. The first-line supervisor will have an informal assistant whether he likes it or not. The informal assistant can be appointed either by the supervisor or by the informal work group. Sometimes the straw boss can be appointed by the formal leader. Informal groups can act as a training ground for future leaders. Although the informal organizations may be a good place for potential formal leaders to develop, it doesn't follow that an informal leader will always make the best formal leader. The informal leader may like to hide behind an informal position and still exercise power within the group. If something goes wrong, the formal leader — not the informal leader — will be held responsible.

RELATIONSHIP OF INFORMAL GROUP WITH SUPERVISOR'S FORMAL GROUP

HARMONY The informal group or organization can be advantageous or it can be detrimental. Whether a supervisor likes or dislikes the informal groups, they will exist. They cannot be ordered about or stamped out by managers or supervisors. Therefore a supervisor's attitude toward informal groups becomes very important. Any effort to eliminate the groups would, in fact, help to make them grow. The supervisor's feelings toward the informal organization have to center on the question of the group's usefulness in achieving the goals of the organization and the goals of the workers.

First-line supervisors have two choices concerning the formal groups' relationship with informal groups. The first choice is to operate with the group in harmony and attempt to further the ends of both groups. The second choice is not to use the informal group, but to attempt to ignore it in hopes that it goes away.

Harmony calls for *understanding* the informal groups, or the grapevine, or clique, or informal work groups. It calls for purposeful action by the first-line supervisor so as to clarify the goals of the organization. The informal group is basically a dormant organization that springs to life when needs are *not* being satisfied. We should know that the informal leader thrives on these needs and rallies the worker into an informal organization so as to perpetuate his own position of power and influence.

In the famous Hawthorne studies of the Western Electric Company, an interesting contrast of informal and formal group relationships existed between two departments within the plant — (A) the relay assembly test room, and (B) the bank wiring observation room.

In the relay assembly test room (A), the operators changed continuously in their rate of output during the test. Yet in a curious fashion, their variations in output were insensitive or were not responsive to most of the significant changes introduced by the experimenters. On the other hand, in the bank wiring observation room (B), the output was being held relatively constant, and there existed a very *strong* sensitivity to change among the workers. In fact, this sensitivity was so strong that it could have been described as an opposition to change. In the case of the relay assembly test room (A), the informal organization was a network of personal relations that had been developed over time by working together. This informal organization in room (A) satisfied its members' needs and maintained harmony between the aims of management and the workers. However, the output of room (B) was held constant because the informal organizations rejected any cooperation with the management people. Collaboration in room (A) was at a much higher level than in room (B).

LACK OF USE In contrast to working with informal groups in harmony, the second alternative is to accept the informal group's existence but to avoid any direct or substantial contact or cooperation with the groups. Here the supervisor does not threaten the organization's existence nor actively cooperate with the informal groups but remains neutral.

The second alternative has some distinct advantages. Working directly with the informal organization could improve the supervisor's general understanding, but it may communicate to the employees that the supervisor is attempting to take over the workers' informal group. This could cause the formation of another informal group that would work underground. In this case, harmonious activity could create a monster.

Probably the worst degree of lack of use would be the complete breakdown in communications between both the formal and the informal groups. Pushing the informal group out of reality could force the group to develop underground and to create a breakdown in any communication between the two groups. Cooperation and use of the informal group would be almost nil. Thus, extreme cooperation or extreme disuse could have the same result—an underground group.

Whether to work in harmony with a group by involvement and participation; or to tolerate its existence, but avoid any substantial contact or cooperation; or completely to avoid the group, would depend on the particular circumstances that prevail. One of the most serious tasks for the supervisor is to make timely decisions that are relevant and pertinent to the given situation. What may work for one supervisor at a given time may not work with another supervisor. The supervisor is paid to make these decisions. It is probably best to understand the group, listen and sympathize, and offer support. This will at least provide an avenue of communication until the supervisor collects enough facts to make a better decision. This is a form of cooperation that just may be sufficient in recognizing that, if any serious problems do arise, then more harmonious organizational contact would be appropriate. But in order to achieve the goals of the formal organization, such as cost cutting or revenue maximization or productivity, overly cooperative ventures with informal organizations would not necessarily be desirable either for the supervisor or for the worker. After all, an informal organization does want to feel that it is unique; when management people invade the group, the workers believe that they may lose this desired position.

SUPERVISORY CONTROL AND THE INFORMAL GROUP

Basic understanding of an organization's behavioral pattern permits the supervisor to predict an informal group's behavior. If the supervisor can predict the group's behavior, he or she then can control the group and guide the group's behavior toward accomplishing the formal organization's goals. The serious control factors that face the supervisor involve (1) the dissemination of information, (2) maintaining a proper power relationship between the formal and informal groups, and (3) instituting changes.

CONTROL OF INFORMATION

Workers tend to use idle gossip and "scuttlebutt" to solve their problem when threatening conditions prevail. Misinformation carried throughout an organization can spread rapidly and create numerous unpleasant situations. Although management cannot stop rumors and falsehood, it can anticipate the informal grapevine's usefulness by publicly announcing complete information before the rumor mill can manufacture misinformation.

In the case of an existing rumor, supervisors should exercise much discretion in order to avoid condoning the rumor. For example, stating, "You have heard the rumor that the office is going to be moved—well, this is not true," is giving the rumor a degree of credence. The supervisor has repeated the rumor, and regardless of what else he or she has said, the workers have heard the rumor from an authoritative source, so therefore it must be true. In this case the supervisor should state, "The office will remain in its present location during the remodeling, which should take two weeks. The remodeling will provide a modern facility for our people." This straightforward newscast stops additional rumors.

POWER RELATIONSHIPS

Care should be taken to insure that the informal organizational or group systems remain secondary to the formal group. If informal systems do not remain secondary, long-term employee objectives may be lost in the labyrinth of small group interests and vested *power structures.* When the formal system appears to be too weak to get the job done, the informal organization grows stronger by rushing in to fill the power void. This kind of arrangement may generate good or passable productivity, as long as the informal system does support the formal organization's objectives. However, informal organizations do not have the same goals or objectives as the formal organization. The informal group can easily drift into a take-it-easy attitude or develop an antisupervisor or antimanagement attitude. Since some management people may not exhibit strong postures, deviant tendencies that persist in some informal work groups may create serious personnel problems. Forecasting these events is probably the best solution. After-the-fact solutions should be secondary choices.

A HELP RATHER THAN A HINDRANCE

Informal organizations provide a number of benefits that help to alleviate some of the problems of the formal group. The informal group can allow the worker to be more satisfied on the job by permitting freedom for the worker. The worker has his or her own identity. Thus the informal group can help to supplement worker needs that are impossible for the formal organization to satisfy.

SUMMARY

Informal groups, such as work groups, grapevine communication groups, social groups, and cliques, are formed for the satisfaction of social needs and/or other human needs. These social needs include the workers' desire to communicate through unique channels and to possess the latest information or gossip. In addition, informal groups enforce and maintain favorable work standards and contribute to how much work will be accomplished.

Formal groups or organizations tend to breed informal groups within them, and the presence of informal groups strongly influences the manner in which supervisors carry out their job. Informal groups can threaten, create attitudes, promote conformity, and create rumors. Of these functions, the most serious can be the power to threaten. If and when such a condition prevails, the first-line supervisor faces a precarious situation. Failure to exercise power may cost this supervisor his or her future ability to lead. Loss of respect may be encouraged. On the other hand, the group can take care of deviants who do not bend to the group's ways be developing different attitudes within the individual or allowing the normal group pressures to run their course until the group's survival is guaranteed. Assuming that the formal and informal group goals coincide, the supervisor may allow the informal group to assist in controlling a troublemaker.

Supervisors can choose to work with informal groups harmoniously, or they can choose to recognize their existence, but avoid direct contact. But an extreme reaction of either kind can be disastrous. Supervisors must decide early if they are going to work with the informal group; they cannot choose merely to avoid the group's existence.

Control of informal groups can be exercised in various areas. The supervisors can disseminate correct information in time to thwart incorrect rumors before they can start. They can institute changes and generate cooperation by the informal group by recognizing, but not fraternizing with the group.

Supervisors should see informal groups as a powerful force that must be considered on a day-to-day basis. The best choice is to use it as a help rather than to consider it as a hindrance. If you can't overcome an obstacle, learn to understand it and work with it. This means supervisors' attitudes toward informal groups must be positive rather than negative. They must be willing to recognize the informal group's existence and be prepared to use its power for the achievement of the organization's objectives as well as the informal group's objectives.

KEY CONCEPTS

Informal groups. Informal work groups, grapevine communication networks, social groups, and cliques will always exist as long as they serve the members' needs. These needs are to belong; to know and to understand the formal organization and how the individual fits in; to obtain security, social interaction, and general information and news. Informal groups satisfy human needs that the formal group cannot or, in some cases, will not satisfy.

Formal organizations usually breed informal organizations. This is an organizational situation or "nature-of-the-beast" concept. The only thing a supervisor can do is recognize this concept's cause and effect.

Informal groups can exercise great power. These groups have great power potential in affecting worker attitudes and morale. Therefore they are formidable obstacles or aids to the supervisor, depending on his attitude toward each of the informal groups.

Supervisor must understand and work with informal groups. This is an essential concept to practice if the supervisor is ever going to control information, retain the formal group's power and authority, and institute changes by successfully using the informal group as an aid.

IMPORTANT TERMS

Attitudes and informal groups
Cliques
Communication networks
Conformity
Deviant
Grapevine communication groups and networks
Group threats

Morale and informal groups
Natural leaders
Power structures
Rumors
Social groups
Straw boss
Work groups

INCIDENTS

The Cohesiveness of the Informal Group

In a small Missouri town with 5000 population an electrical wire plant hired local labor to monitor highly automatic equipment used in its production process. The wire was stranded and then coated with a plastic cover. Both operations were very automatic. The operator of the line initially wound the wire to start the process and then monitored its run. His main function was to be there if trouble developed so that he could turn off the machine and resolve the trouble. The work promoted operator boredom and a psychological feeling of job detachment.

Management was well aware of the operator's predicament and attempted to foster belongingness by instilling a McGregor "participative management" environment. Many plant decisions were made after an appointed worker committee was involved.

Further involvement was fostered after working hours. Much socializing after work was attended by the plant manager, supervisors, and plant engineers. A favorite spot after each shift was a local bar where managers, supervisors, and workers were on a first-name basis and frequently "kidded each other" about the happenings of that day. In spite of the monotonous jobs, the morale of both management and workers was very high.

Three things contributed to the plant's high morale. First, management's involvement with the workers. Second, constant training for management and particularly supervisors, which stressed three points: (1) treat workers as human beings, (2) respect them, and (3) reward them whenever they make a contribution. Third, a strong informal work group structure existed where many of the people were personal friends both on and off the job. For example, many of the supervisors went fishing and hunting with workers. Frequently the workers were the initiators of the fishing or hunting trip and the supervisors were invited.

In spite of this harmonious environment, a problem developed to disturb the plant's peace and harmony. An employee in materials handling, Ron Martinez happened to talk back to his supervisor, Bill Patterson. The disagreement centered over a forklift truck's maintenance schedule and whether or not Ron was spending too much time greasing the truck. Ron claimed that the truck should be lubricated at least once a month but Patterson responded with company policy that lubrication should take place every six months. The supervisor wasn't concerned about the lubrication as much as the time it took to do it and Ron's propensity to soldier on most jobs he undertook. The disagreement spread rapidly throughout the plant. Ray Matthews, a close friend of Ron Martinez in high school, was a chief spokesman for the workers and was determined to get to the bottom of this predicament. Ray had heard that Patterson had punched Ron and knocked him down. This rumor spread rapidly throughout the plant and was the chief topic of conversation at the local bar. The harmonious environment of the Missouri Wire Co. was in jeopardy.

What does this incident illustrate relative to informal groups, informal networks and their impact on a company? What would you do in this situation if you were the supervisor Bill Patterson?

Conformity in an Informal Group

The business education department of Harrison Junior College in Kokomo, Indiana, included six teachers and a full-time vocational counselor. All six members were graduates of the School of Education of Indiana University, which tended to consolidate their educational philosophies and alumni ties to athletic programs with frequent trips to the Bloomington campus to view intercollegiate athletics.

Last year, Steve Holland, a graduate of Ball State University, became the department chairperson. His educational philosophies and educational practices were influenced by his formal education, which differed from the six other department members. Steve wondered why his colleagues seldom socialized with him or refused to offer him the respect he thought he deserved as a department chairperson. All six members of the department ate lunch together and often waited for each other so all six could walk over to the cafeteria together. Steve accompanied the group when he could find the time, but he was never invited. Whenever he did accompany the group he was questioned about a recent decision or ignored by the group, which took its lead from Chris Lemon. Lemon, unlike his namesake, was an intelligent individual but refused to work any harder than necessary. He complained about the school, Holland's leadership, lack of school support, bad students, and his working hours. Although Lemon was the informal leader, he was not considered by Holland as a productive colleague. Nevertheless the other five members took their lead from Lemon as it appeared his word was law. Since Lemon was a bachelor, the other department members, three women and one man, were very conscious of Lemon's welfare and happiness. Holland observed this behavior and wondered what he as a department head could do about regaining control and a semblance of respect. What should Steve Holland do? Be specific in your suggestions.

QUESTIONS FOR DISCUSSION

1. Would informal groups exist *in spite of* formal groups or would informal groups exist *because of* formal groups? Why or why not?
2. What are the major reasons for the existence of informal groups?
3. Does "work design" influence the creation of informal groups? Why or why not?
4. What are the differences between a grapevine communication network and a clique?
5. Why does every informal group seem to have at least one individual who knows more about what's happening in the organization than the other members of the informal group?
6. Discuss why the grapevine communication group thrives on the insecurity of the organization?

7. How and why can an informal group enforce its group norms of behavior?
8. Can the informal group help to improve morale in the formal organization? How?
9. Why can the supervisor's use of the informal group be a dangerous practice when (1) he or she closely cooperates and becomes involved in the informal group and (2) he or she becomes distant and aloof from the informal group?
10. Can the supervisor control the informal group and meet the formal group's goals? How? If not, why?

CHAPTER V
The Human Side of Control

LEARNING OBJECTIVES

- *To realize why control over the activities of people is necessary and how this impinges on all other managerial functions.*
- *To learn the three basic steps inherent in any control process.*
- *To identify the elements necessary to link the basic steps into a control system and how these elements may differ for control systems directed at people as compared to those designed for machines or processes.*
- *To be aware of the several characteristics required if a control system is to be effective.*
- *To understand why people often resent efforts at control, the several types of reactions they may exhibit toward control, and how the supervisor can minimize undesirable attitudes and reactions.*

Introduction

This chapter is concerned primarily with controlling the activities of people. It emphasizes the human aspects of control and how this function can best be implemented by the supervisor. Operating control of the flow of work and materials within and between departments is treated in Chapter 6.

CONTROL AS A MANAGERIAL FUNCTION

Controlling usually is listed last in the sequence of managerial functions of planning, organizing, directing, and controlling. The first two functions—planning and organizing—are essentially preparatory in nature; that is, they are concerned with getting ready to accomplish the work of the enterprise or department. In the directing function, managers initiate the actual work of the organization: they issue orders and directives, and guide and supervise people doing the work. Finally, managers exercise control by seeing if the work has been done properly and done according to plan. The best plans will have means of control built into them. This points up the fact that all managerial functions overlap and may be exercised concurrently.

The *control function* can be defined as those activities necessary to measure and correct employees' performance in order to assure that enterprise and departmental goals are being achieved as planned. It is a function of all levels of management from the president to the first-line supervisor. There are many things at the working level that cannot be controlled directly by anyone other than the supervisor.

The terms *quality control* and *production control* are almost household words, but the control of the human side of the organization is a less familiar concept and raises the question: Why do we have to control people? One reason is that it is people who make the plans and who design and operate the machines. Behind the need for control is the fact that the success of plans and the productive results of machine operations are influenced by people. Even in a highly automated system, people still push buttons, pull levers, and read dials. Differences from desired performance can be corrected only by changing the attitudes and future activities of the individuals (or groups) responsible. Another reason is that the process of delegation requires the supervisor to control his subordinates because he retains responsibility for their actions. Therefore managers should remember that the higher the quality of all levels of managers and the better the training of hourly employees, the fewer will be the differences from desired performance and the less critical will be the need for control.

Supervisors must recognize that *humanistic systems* are more difficult to control than *mechanistic systems*. Errors in dimensional tolerances in an assembly line product ordinarily are detected and corrected relatively quickly and easily. In contrast, a change in some kinds of employee activities may develop more slowly. Six months might pass before the change becomes sufficiently great to be noticeable to the supervisor.

Once a change is detected, determining the cause and correcting the undesired attitude or activity is not always easy; the exercise of *corrective control* on people often tends to breed resistance. The supervisor must be very careful to avoid the appearance that "Big Brother is watching you."

THE NATURE OF CONTROL

The purpose of control is to assure that enterprise activities proceed as planned so that predetermined objectives are achieved. We cannot change the past, although we do use past experience as a data source in the process of controlling future activities. By its very nature, then, control must be concerned with the future.

A *deviation* in performance is said to occur when there is a difference between the actual performance and what was desired and planned. This deviation may involve a physical measurement, an action, an attitude, and so on. A *control system* detects deviations as they occur, finds the amount and cause of deviation, and takes appropriate corrective action. Even if detection is very rapid, correction often is time consuming. In such instances, prevention ordinarily is less expensive than the cure. Ideally, therefore, the control function should forecast possible deviations before they happen and take action now to prevent future occurrences. Even though the ideal is not always possible, the essence of control is forward-looking action.

THE CONTROL PROCESS

The consensus of students of management is that the basic *control process* is made up of three steps.

1. Establishing standards of performance.
2. Measuring actual performance against these standards.
3. Taking action to correct any deviations from standards.

The three basic steps are applicable whether we are considering machine-to-machine, human-to-machine, or human-to-human operating systems. Appropriate control involves the tailoring of the control system to suit the kind of operating system involved, the plan being followed, its place in the organization structure, and the needs of the manager responsible. It is only the type, not the nature, of control that changes with the situation.

Establishing Standards

Standards serve as the criteria against which results can be measured—they specify the level of performance desired. The objectives of enterprise or departmental plans are expressions of standards; as is, for example, the tolerance of plus or minus three mils specified for a motor shaft.

Many kinds of standards are needed in an enterprise. They may be used to set performance levels for a machine, a task, an individual worker, a department, or the enterprise as a whole. In general, standards establish quantity, quality, or time limitations with respect to inputs and outputs of physical objects, money, or activity functions. Obviously, then, standards can be objective or subjective, tangible or intangible, specific or vague. The average manager will prefer objective, tangible, specific standards. Unfortunately, this does not always happen.

Good standards will have certain characteristics. Usually, but not necessarily, performance standards are expressed in terms of specific units: pounds, inches, degrees, dollars, minutes. Specific physical units are not always possible when setting standards for persons or groups. For example, what kind of standards does a manager use to measure morale, leadership, or the results of the company's public relations program? An important characteristic of all standards, tangible or otherwise, is that they be verifiable. In other words, it must be possible to determine in some way whether or not the desired results have been obtained. It sometimes is necessary to restate the objectives of individuals or groups to get these into forms or terms that will make the results verifiable.

Another characteristic of good standards is that they be achievable. In other words, can the performance level specified by the standard be reached without abnormal effort? If not, the standards had better be reconsidered. Standards do not always have to be established to the proverbial six decimal places. For many types of physical products and human activities, performance may range somewhat above or below the standard without harm. The standards should therefore express the allowable degree of variation from the norm before correction becomes mandatory.

With the variety of standards needed, it is evident that no single method of establishing standards will be practical in all cases. One approach, subjective in nature, is to use the judgment of the supervisor in charge of the activity being controlled. His knowledge and experience are often sufficient to determine what constitutes a satisfactory level of performance.

The analysis of historical data is another useful approach in arriving at standards. Internal company records will contain statistical data on past production or on other performance items of interest. External sources of many kinds of statistical data include professional societies, trade associations, and government publications, to indicate but a few. Statistical data are raw material in arriving at various kinds of standards. But when using past experience to set production standards, the manager should remember that past output may not represent a desirable norm today.

The most objective approach to establishing performance standards is based on the application of engineering and/or cost accounting principles. Examples include motion studies, time studies, standard costs and are referred to in greater detail in Chapter 11. These techniques are applicable mostly to the activities of individuals or groups in the hourly employee class of work. The more recent technique of value analysis is applicable to the setting of standards on a somewhat broader base.

Measuring Performance The measurement of performance when standards are objective and tangible is comparatively easy. The standards themselves often indicate the best procedures for measuring.

The types of activity where performance is based on subjective, intangible standards is much more difficult to measure. This frequently is the case with activities of middle- to upper-level managers. Control becomes more complex as we proceed from the base to the apex of the organization structure.

A *feedback loop* is part of a self-correcting system (human or machine) that monitors output against predetermined standards and feeds information about changes back to an element of the system that corrects output. Measurement of actual performance is part of the feedback loop. Therefore the correction step is highly dependent on the measurement data received. The manager must make decisions on the reliability, validity, and necessary frequency of measurements. He must be sure that the measured data are going to the right person.

A variety of automatic sensor and recording devices are available for monitoring the output of machines and processes. In contrast, direct observation by the supervisor followed by appraisal may be the only practical way of measuring the performance of some kinds of activities by individuals or groups. The possibility of misinterpretation and the quality of the supervisor's perception may be problems here. For broader activities, measurement can be done by compiling current statistical records based on data collected from various parts of the operating system. Time lag is the chief problem with this latter method.

Correcting Deviations

Establishing standards and measuring performance are meaningless unless positive *corrective action* is taken. Corrective action is quick, easy, and virtually automatic when we have a mechanistic control system regulating a mechanistic operating system. The thermostat on a household furnace or a flywheel governor on an engine provide excellent examples of this.

As usual, the humanistic control and operating systems pose more of a problem. Corrective action with people involves the decision-making process described elsewhere. The first two steps of the control process have provided the facts. These must be checked and analyzed. Alternative courses of corrective action are considered, and the most appropriate one is selected and implemented. Follow-up to see if performance did get back to the established norm may be provided by the feedback characteristic of the control system or, in special cases, may be an independent action by the supervisor.

Much depends on the personality and managerial style of the supervisor. A certain number of mistakes must be permitted to any individual; this is part of the process of learning the job. The question is how much leeway to give the worker. Only the supervisor can determine this as he or she examines the situation.

Corrective action in controlling the performance and activities of people can take many forms. The deviation may not be the fault of the individual worker. It may be that the objectives and resultant standards are at fault and should be changed. If the individual's sub-standard performance was due to misunderstanding or inadequate skills, then clarifications, remedial training, or reassignment may be the answer. Perhaps the supervisor needs to improve the overall performance of his or her managerial functions.

When repeated substandard performance occurs in spite of the above considerations, the supervisor has no choice but to get tough. Disciplinary action may be needed.

ELEMENTS OF A CONTROL SYSTEM

The three basic steps of the control process, just described, are minimal and are common to control, regardless of what is being controlled or where. Without any one of these steps, control becomes impossible.

When the control process is applied, however, a control subsystem is created that includes a feedback loop. In other words, an operating system exists in balance. As some aspect of the environment changes, the system gets out of balance. The control subsystem then comes into play, and there is a feedback of information that corrects and brings the operating system back into balance.

In application, then, the basic control process is expanded into a control system. The three basic steps still are present, but now they are interlinked into a feedback loop with auxiliary steps in between for comparison, interpretation, analysis, and transfer of information.

The elements in the control system include the basic steps plus such auxiliary steps (or devices) as are needed. The number and nature of the auxiliary steps or devices depend on the kind and complexity of the operating system subject to control.

The elements of a control system oriented toward a mechanistic operating system are illustrated in Figure 5-1. In this figure, Element 1 is a condition or characteristic of an operating system that is being controlled.

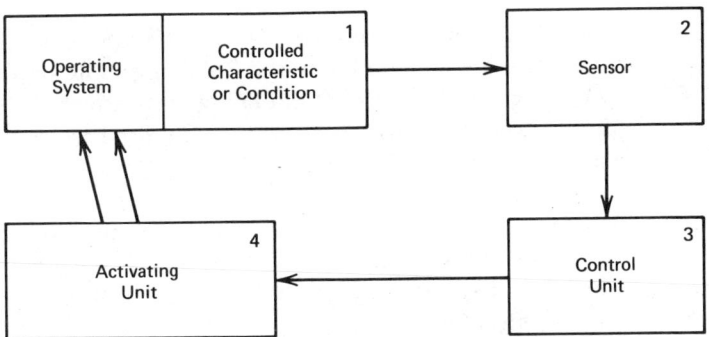

Figure 5-1 Basic elements of a control system for a mechanistic operating system. (Source. From The Theory and Management of Systems, by Richard A. Johnson, Fremont E. Kast, and James E. Rosenzweig. Copyright 1967, McGraw-Hill Book Co. Used with permission of McGraw-Hill Book Co.)

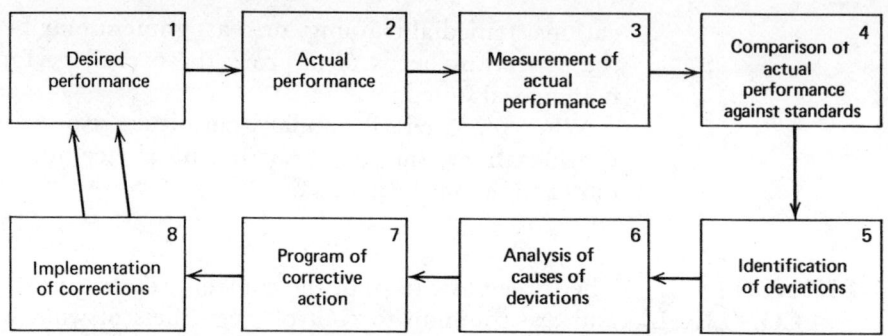

Figure 5-2 Basic elements of a control system for a humanistic operating system. (Source. Adapted from Essentials of Management, 2nd ed., *by Harold Koontz and Cyril O'Donnell. Copyright 1978, McGraw-Hill Book Co. Used with permission of McGraw-Hill Book Co.)*

The item is to be measured against the standard of the operating system. A sensor device, Element 2, measures the controlled item. Element 3 is a control unit that compares the measurement with the standard and, if a deviation exists, sends the information on. The activating unit, Element 4, upon receiving notice of a deviation, brings about the necessary change in the system.

It is interesting to compare this control system with one intended for a humanistic operating system. Such a system is depicted in Figure 5-2. The three basic steps are apparent, but the nature and number of the auxiliary elements have changed to suit the control of individual or group activities.

CHARACTERISTICS OF A CONTROL SYSTEM

The characteristics required of an effective control system for the performance of people include the following: The system must be (1) timely, (2) economical, (3) flexible, (4) appropriate to the operating system, (5) understandable, (6) structured to the organization, (7) strategically located, and it must (8) stress exceptions.

An examination of these characteristics will indicate that they are not limited to control systems. All of these items, except possibly the last two (and excluding even these is debatable), are general requirements for any type of system, for example, a distribution system or a cost accounting system.

They are neither new nor unique. The basic principles of effective control systems have been developed over a long period of time. The characteristics listed here also appear, in one form or another, in many texts and articles on the subject of control. Item 8, for example, is Frederick W. Taylor's *exception principle,* proposed by him in the first decade of this century and still considered applicable today. The only unique feature, if it can be called that, is the fact that these principles are not recognized and practiced as widely as they should be.

The authors wish to stress again that people are more important to results than are systems. A poor system manned by high-caliber people will produce good results even though operating under a handicap. Conversely, the best system possible will result in inferior control if not operated according to sound management principles. This is true of other functions of management in addition to control.

Let us consider the eight characteristics as they relate to control systems.

The control system must be sufficiently *timely* to detect and report deviations before costs become excessive. In general, it is more effective to take continuous (or at least frequent) measurements of performance and make corrections quickly in small increments. Timeliness also involves looking ahead to forecast change (potential deviations) and the rate of change.

An obviously desirable feature of any system is that it be *economical* to maintain and operate. The benefits of control must be commensurate with the costs. It is foolish to install a control system whose costs are greater than those of the deviations it prevents. Cost usually increases with precision of measurement. If approximate measurements are adequate, settle for these. Selection of the best item to be controlled frequently is a trade-off between the item showing highest correlation with objectives and the item most economical to measure.

The need for *flexibility* in control systems arises out of the dynamic nature of business. Objectives, plans, organization structures, and work itself are all subject to change. Effective control systems, therefore, must be sensitive and adaptable to permit desired changes.

To be *appropriate* to the nature and needs of the operating system, both the standards and the controls must be realistic, acceptable, objective and accurate. These features are interrelated. Realistically, the control system should be neither too simple nor too complex, but adequate to do the job needed. This feature influences acceptability of the system to both administrators and hourly employees. In many instances, workers are more likely to correct their own deviations if they have participated in setting the performance standards. Objectivity tends to improve both acceptability and accuracy—it is easiest to achieve with machine-to-machine systems, a little more difficult with human-to-machine systems, and may be quite difficult to achieve in human-to-human systems. Errors in control can occur in all three types of systems; errors result from incorrect information getting into the feedback system. The cause may be mechanical failure, misinterpretation of data, or faulty judgment. Human judgment is the common denominator in all these factors in arriving at the appropriateness of a control system for human performance.

Any control system must be *understandable* to the managers who administer it and to the individuals, groups, and organizational levels subject to its influence. To the extent possible, simplicity is a key factor. Many control systems that looked ideal on paper failed in practice because they were too complex for the level to which they were applied.

The necessity for control systems to be *structured to the organization* stems from the authority-responsibility relationships that make up the framework of the organization. The measurement and flow of control information must follow the pattern of this formal organization structure if it is to be effective. Control of any activity should be exercised at the lowest possible organization level that is consistent with authority-responsibility relationships.

Structuring the control system serves two purposes. First, it pin-points where in the organization the deviations are occurring and who (or what) is causing them. Second, it directs the information on deviations to the manager in charge of the controlled activity. Both purposes must be accomplished before the proper corrective action can be applied.

Strategically located control points extend the range of the manager's control function. Except for the simplest operations, managers can neither watch nor control every single act or item. It is not always necessary that they do so. Ideally, they will be able to identify and establish standards for one or a few items at strategic locations—*critical control points*. If properly selected, the control either of key elements or at critical steps in the operating system will assure successful control of the entire operating system.

The controlled items and their locations are strategic under the following circumstances: (1) if they are limiting with respect to other phases of the operation, (2) if changes in the interrelationships of the measurements of two or more of these items provide the basis for significant decisions, and/or (3) if one or more exhibit direct correlation with objectives of the operating system. Strategic items could include such factors as physical standards, specific types of cost or production data, or specific kinds of individual or group activity. All the other previously mentioned requirements of an effective control system should be observed in selecting strategic control points.

When a control system *stresses exceptions,* information on exceptions only is reported to the manager in charge of the activity. Every minor deviation from a precise numerical standard need not be reported; rather, the manager should be informed when performance strays beyond an acceptable tolerance range. There is a tendency to think of exceptions as comprising only negative deviations from standards. However, exceptionally good performance also should be reported, particularly when human activities are being monitored.

The concept of stressing exceptions is based on the belief that a manager cannot, and need not, handle the large mass of routine information generated in any organization. When the information reported to the manager stresses the exception, he or she can direct most of his or her time and effort at problem areas requiring corrective action. Routine and predictable matters can be left to subordinates.

THE HUMAN PROBLEMS OF CONTROL

Throughout this book, the authors have emphasized the belief that people are more important than systems or physical resources. The attitudes, actions, and reactions of people—from hourly employees up to the chief executive—contribute more to enterprise success or failure than do the mechanistic elements of the operation. Machine-to-machine operating systems normally have a logic that makes them easier to control than humanistic systems. The attitudes and consequent actions or reactions of people may be rational or irrational, and management must take both possibilities into consideration. Unfortunately, the control process often seems to act as a magnifier of the quirks in human nature.

The authors are not suggesting that most people react in an irrational manner most of the time. If a control system for human performance is well designed and administered, following the principles and requirements previously set forth, the reaction in most instances will be as desired: understanding, intelligent compliance. Nevertheless, whenever people are dealing with people, the potential always exists for problems to crop up.

WHY PROBLEMS? Most people instinctively dislike controls even when they understand the necessity for them. When people are asked the reasons for this dislike, the answers usually fall into one or more of the following categories.

1. Standards are incorrect—too tight, improperly selected, erroneous, and so on.
2. Standards are improperly administered.
3. Standards always seem to move up, never down.
4. Measurements are not accurate or do not reflect effort.
5. Corrective action is seen as personal criticism.
6. There is uncertainty or lack of knowledge about controls.

Such answers reflect the "pressure" characteristic of controls, the fact that people tend to associate rewards and penalties with controls, which brings emotional factors into play. It seems to be an inherent trait of human beings to resent and resist pressure. When pushed, we tend to push back. Consciously or subconsciously, we equate control with the violation of our need for freedom, and the desire to be master of our own destiny.

Most people perform best under some pressure, but most people also react adversely (from management's point of view) to too much pressure. When autocratic styles of leadership and management are practiced, managers tend to forget or to ignore this very human trait. The result may be a seemingly unending cycle of pressure and resistance, more pressure and more resistance.

Patterns of leadership flow downward from the top and become pervasive throughout the organization. The supervisor in an autocratic firm truly is the person in the middle and is subject to constant downward pressure from above: "Why can't you get out your production quota?" or "Why can't you keep those fellows in the shop in line?" At the same time, the supervisor is under constant resistive upward pressures from the work force. The average supervisor in this situation is likely to follow the pattern set by his or her superiors, with the result described previously.

Resistance to control is not necessarily limited to autocratic organizations, although it may follow a more predictable path under highly authoritative leadership. Any type of firm contains managers and hourly employees with a diversity of personalities, cultural backgrounds, and job experiences. Unplanned responses to even mild forms of control are bound to happen. The effective supervisor must be aware of the possible forms of subordinate reactions and their causes.

FORMS OF RESPONSE TO CONTROL

Attitudes and reactions toward the pressures of control can take many forms. Too much pressure breeds frustration, and irrational behavior usually is a consequence of frustration. On the other hand, just the right amount of judiciously applied pressure may lead to the performance desired. Thus the response to control can range from aggressive opposition through neutrality to understanding cooperation.

The several possible responses of subordinates to control may be classified as follows.

1. Innovative deviation.
2. Informal group resistance.
3. Formal group resistance.
4. Escape through advancement.
5. Aggressive attack.
6. Line-staff conflict.
7. Neutrality or apathy.
8. Overemphasis on goals.
9. Escape through absenteeism or turnover.
10. Understanding compliance.[1]

---

[1] Adapted, with modifications, from Edwin B. Flippo, *Management: A Behavioral Approach*, 2nd ed., Allyn and Bacon, Boston, 1970, p. 458.

Innovative Deviation Some subordinates will deliberately perform a task in a manner other than ordered, with no intention of actually opposing authority. The reason for such action may lie in boredom with doing things in the same old way, it may be an expression of ego, or it may stem from a sincere desire to improve through innovation the manner of doing work.

Unfortunately, the innovative person is at a disadvantage when he must work under conditions requiring conformity. His experimental approach may represent a genuine contribution to the group effort. However, the organization usually requires orderly activity from its employees for overall efficiency of operations. Letting one individual "get away with" nonconformity, regardless of the level of performance, can hurt supervisory authority in other quarters. The supervisor must be cautious with such people in determining the reason for deliberate deviation, its net effect on operations, and just what to do about it. Too much pressure can stifle creativity.

Informal Group Resistance The informal group provides the employee with a focal point of resistance to counteract the pressure of controls. The strength of the group permits it to do things (or not to do things) that the individual would not attempt alone. Employees may form new groups or cliques for this purpose. Existing groups may become more cohesive and change from their original purpose to one of mutual protection.

Informal group resistance usually is passive. A common practice is to establish *bogeys,* that is, their own standards of output that no worker in the group will exceed. Members of the group will cover for each other against the supervisor. Frequent filing of minor grievances may be used to embarrass or inconvenience management.

An exception to the usual passivity of informal group action is the wildcat strike. Management *may* be able to obtain the help of the union in counteracting this, but had better search for the root of the problem. Wildcat strikes often are instigated for a publicly stated reason that is not the actual cause.

Formal Group Resistance The most common approach to formal group resistance in the commercial or industrial enterprise is unionization. Almost one-fourth of the nation's work force is unionized. Hourly employees look to the union for, among other things, protection from what they may consider pressure tactics by management. The union's strength in this function exceeds that of the individual or of the informal group.

Escape Through Advancement Some individuals, hoping to get out from under the pressure of controls, seek to advance to higher levels in the firm. They believe that managers at higher levels are subject to less control and have more freedom of action and fewer problems. This is analogous to the old saying that "the grass is always greener on the other side of the fence." It is doubtful if the vice-presidents or chief executive of the average business would agree with this belief about their work. The pressures are of a different kind, but they are there.

The hourly employee or the supervisor who has the ability and the drive to climb up the corporate ladder probably will do so regardless of the reason. Escape from pressure may well be just rationalization for ambition.

Aggressive Attack One of the possible reactions to excessive pressure is aggressive attack. This response occurs more frequently when managerial patterns lean toward the authoritative than it does under other leadership styles. Pressures tend to be heavier, which means that the individual's breaking point is more likely to be reached. Also, aggressive response is more likely to be an individual reaction than a group reaction, although exceptions are known. Aggression usually is spontaneous and nonthinking, whereas informal group action necessitates some planning and cooperative effort.

Aggressive attack can follow more than one pattern. The form that we usually think of is outright rebellion. This may involve deliberate substandard performance, sabotage or spoilage, refusal to follow an order, or starting a fight with a fellow worker or the supervisor. Disciplinary action is management's customary response, but this alone does not get to the root of the problem.

Another form of aggressive action is placing the blame for deviations on someone else—co-workers, staff, other departments, or even the supervisor. This reaction is natural when management is more concerned with who is at fault than with solving the problem.

There is another reaction, somewhat similar to the tendency to blame others. A worker under excessive pressure may repress feelings while on the job but later relieve aggressive instincts by striking out at someone who cannot hit back. The worker may vent feelings on an assistant or someone else lower on the job scale. Sometimes the worker will wait until he or she gets home and bawl out his or her family for some minor act.

Line-Staff Conflict Conflicts between line and staff arising out of problems and pressures associated with control might be considered a form of aggressive response. However, such conflict can, and frequently does, occur under even the most liberal styles of management and under comparatively mild pressure.

Much of the difficulty may be because of poor clarification of line, staff, or functional authority and respective responsibilities. However, control activities and pressures certainly contribute to many conflicts. Cooperation is the essence of effective interaction between line and staff.

The need to cooperate while under pressure leads to conflicts between people, particularly if personalities clash.

Neutrality or Apathy In some situations, the response of employees to management's control efforts may be neutral in that there is no obvious or overt resistance, aggressive or passive. Rather the workers and the supervisor arrive at an unwritten, voluntary understanding that supervision will be "reasonable" in return for a "reasonable" output of work. In other words, management is agreeing not to use all the pressures at its command if the employees are reasonably cooperative. This type of arrangement has been called *effort bargaining* or *implicit bargaining*. It assumes that both parties are essentially equal in strength.

An apathetic response is similar to neutrality in that no overt reaction occurs. It is dissimilar to neutrality in that the attitude is one of indifference or apathy to control. Pressures are not so great as to inspire any of the previously described responses. Work is something that is endured because of the need to earn a living, and other need satisfactions are obtained off the job.

Both neutrality and apathy responses offer little opportunity for management to increase production. But in some instances, this is all that can be realistically expected.

Overemphasis on Goals When management stresses production to the extent that standards and controls are oriented toward high performance levels of output, then employees and/or supervisors may respond by overemphasizing production goals. This usually takes the form of neglecting other duties and objectives in order to concentrate on the limited objective of production. The effect is analogous to wearing blinders that narrow the field of vision. The short-range effect may be impressive, but over the long run such policies are harmful.

The production group subjected to this emphasis on output may itself put undue pressure on other line, staff, or service departments to provide it with materials, parts, and services needed to maintain high output. These lateral pressures often lead to interdepartmental conflict and other disruptive consequences. Another effect may be the lowering of work quality in order to keep output high. In extreme cases, falsification of records and reports may be resorted to in an effort to give the appearance of meeting standards.

Escape Through Absenteeism or Turnover To some individuals, the only answer to pressures may appear to be partial or complete physical escape from the job. This is accomplished by chronic absenteeism, requests for transfer to other departments, or resignations. Personnel experts are well aware that absenteeism and quitting can be caused by many other factors in addition to job-related pressure. Thus the supervisor will have difficulty in determining the real cause for this type of action by members of the work force. The termination interviews conducted by some companies cannot be relied on to provide the answer. Many employees give innocuous reasons for quitting because they may want recommendations in the future.

Understanding Compliance The response most desired by management is, of course, understanding and intelligent compliance. This kind of response is obtained when the managerial pattern of the supervisor and the organization, the nature of the job, and the characteristics of the employee match up.

Two types of people can be counted on for the desired response under a moderately wide range of managerial styles and job conditions. One is the person who wants to be work-directed. This person may be intelligent and very capable technically in handling job assignments, but is uncomfortable when left alone. The work-directed person does not need to be told how to do something but does need to be told what to do and possibly when. There are many people of this nature in the world. At managerial levels they make good staff assistants; in the hourly employee ranks, they make good lead people.

The other kind of person who usually exhibits the desired response is equally intelligent and capable but usually is somewhat more willing to accept responsibility. This individual does not feel the need for supervision and may even dislike some aspects of work. However, this person understands the need for control and is intelligent enough to subordinate his or her likes or dislikes to the needs of the organization.

MAKING HUMAN CONTROL MORE EFFECTIVE

Wise supervisors recognize the need for control of human performance and are aware that the response to this control can take many forms other than the one anticipated. They know that "there is a thin line between effective and oppressive control. The major difference between the two is a matter of attitude and relates almost entirely to the manner in which controlling is approached."[2]

We could describe *effective control* as a means of measuring and guiding performance. In contrast, *oppressive control* is a method of goading employees into greater effort. The nature of the job and its environment affect the degree of control possible, the manner in which control logically is applied, and the attitudes and responses of the employees.

Workers have considerable autonomy in those kinds of crafts and skilled trades that cannot be fully mechanized. Nonmechanized work provides

[2]Herbert G. Hicks, *The Management of Organizations: A Systems and Human Resources Approach,* 2nd ed., McGraw-Hill Co., New York, 1972, p. 363.

variety, freedom of movement, status, and opportunity for satisfaction of egoistic needs. A considerable area of overlap may exist between the interests and objectives of management and those of the worker.

The nature of craft and skilled work is such that *close supervision* usually is not feasible. Management cannot apply the same kind of pressures as in more rigidly structured work. The control approach with craft and skilled workers should tend toward the participative—less direct control, more discretion of action, and more emphasis on self-regulation—or what is sometimes called *general supervision.*

Assembly line tasks, semiautomatic machine tending, and similar work are repetitive and rigidly structured. The job cycle is short, the work pace is mechanically regulated, autonomy is limited, and there is less opportunity for satisfaction of egoistic needs on the job. Close supervision is feasible and is practiced by most supervisors of this kind of work.

On many assembly line and other routine jobs, merely adequate performance is all that is needed. The conforming, dependable worker who is not too dissatisfied may well be the best from management's point of view. Even when attitudes are hostile, the effect on productivity is minimal because of the work structure. Participation, job enlargement, more discretion and self-regulation may be meaningless in much work of this kind. Even if theoretically practical, these approaches probably would affect productivity adversely. The traditional approach to control probably is most effective for this type of work. Even so, the supervisor can and should draw the line between effective and oppressive control in establishing standards and taking corrective action.

A third category of work is automation, including continuous-process technology. It is quite different from the conventional assembly line work that some people mistakenly call automation. Examples include modern electric power generating stations, some kinds of petroleum refining or chemical process operations, and basic oxygen furnace steelmaking. Job cycles usually are long, a high level of skill is required, and responsibility is great. Work may require long periods of monitoring activities relieved by infrequent (it is hoped) breakdowns or failures. Job pressure can be intense when breakdowns occur. However, pressures of this kind tend to develop an *esprit de corps* among the group and are not blamed on the supervisor.

The approach to control in this type of work presents some contrasts. Control is continuous and, in fact, is the very essence of automation and continuous-process technology. Standards are set by the technology so that participation of the worker in this respect usually is impractical. On the other hand, control is the responsibility of the worker as well as the supervisor. Corrective action when needed must be definite, specific, and quick; yet oppressive control would be fatal to these operations.

Much of the human problem in control is in trying to satisfy the variety of needs of both the organization and its employees. Regardless of the type of work involved, it rarely is possible to achieve maximum satisfaction of the needs of both the organization and the individual at the same time. Conflicts will continue to exist, and it is unrealistic to expect to eliminate them entirely.

Much can be done to smooth the path for the control function if the supervisor will observe the principles and requirements of the control process set forth earlier in this chapter. Additionally, the following suggestions should lead to more effective control.

1. The manner of administering controls is very important to success. The supervisor must remember that standards often are quantitative and impersonal in nature. They do not take into account the differences between individuals. Administration should be done in a manner that considers the feelings and uniqueness of each person. This will help in integrating persons, standards, and supervision.
2. Controls are a form of downward communication. If we believe in the fundamental principle that communication is a two-way street, then an upward channel must be provided. There should be provision for the employee to express constructive criticism of standards without fear of reprisal.
3. Controls often are designed by staff specialists who are not the direct supervisors of those persons being controlled. Effective supervisors will attempt to study and understand such staff personnel, develop cooperative working relations with them, and, if needed, act as a buffer between staff and their own work group.
4. Supervisors should take a constructive attitude toward nondeliberate deviations and errors. They must remember that everyone is entitled to a reasonable number of mistakes and must try to use mistakes advantageously in training. Frequent errors of the same type by the same person cannot, of course, be tolerated.
5. The fundamental cause of any deviation should be analyzed soon after the supervisor has completed the immediate work involved in correcting the deviation.
6. The supervisor may find it more effective in some situations to employ informal pressure rather than direct action in improving performance. Group interactions, for example, often can be channeled so as to provide motivation for better performance by individuals or groups.
7. People need to relieve tension after emotionally charged or disruptive events. Supervisors should make allowances for this and not overreact to hasty words or actions. Give the situation a chance to cool off and start out fresh.
8. Participative goal setting and job enlargement with consequent greater challenge and more discretion for the worker are suggested by some authorities as means of reducing job pressures and conflicts between management and employees. These techniques are satisfactory under appropriate conditions. However, for many routine jobs (assembly line

tasks, semiautomatic machine tending, and the like), such methods may be either meaningless or exorbitantly costly.

SUMMARY

The control function of the supervisor includes those actions necessary to measure and correct the performance of subordinates in order to achieve goals as planned. The basic control process consists of three steps: (1) establishing standards of performance, (2) measuring actual performance against standards, and (3) taking action to correct any deviations from standards. These steps are applicable regardless of whether it is machines, processes, or people that are being controlled. A control system is made up of the three basic steps interlinked into a feedback loop with such auxiliary steps as are needed for interpretation and transmittal of information. Effective control systems exhibit a number of generally agreed-upon characteristics.

People-to-people and people-to-machine operating systems are more difficult to control than are completely mechanistic systems. Control systems inevitably exert pressure on people. Although most people work better under some pressure, it seems to be an inherent trait of humans to resist what they consider excessive pressure. In autocratic organizations where considerable control pressure may be exerted, we frequently see an apparently unending cycle develop of pressure-resistance-more pressure. Even under more liberal styles of management, the attitudes and response to control can take many different forms other than the desired reaction of understanding, intelligent compliance.

Effective control of people is largely a matter of the manner in which controlling is approached. The nature of the job and its environment influence the approach selected.

KEY CONCEPTS

Control of people. All managers have the need to assure that organizational activities are carried out as planned so that predetermined goals are achieved. Because people establish the objectives, make the plans, and carry them out, the activities of people must be controlled in order to achieve goals.

Control system. Control of any dynamic system may be achieved by following a basic three-step process of establishing performance standards (goals), measuring actual performance against these standards, and acting to correct any differences. In application, a control system is developed by interlinking these steps into a feedback loop with auxiliary steps in between for comparison, interpretation, analysis, and transfer of information. The concept is applicable to any type of dynamic system: machine to machine, human to machine, or human to human.

IMPORTANT TERMS

Bogeys
Close supervision
Control function
Control process
Control system
Corrective action
Corrective control
Critical control point
Deviation
Effective control
Effort bargaining

Exception principle
Feedback loop
General supervision
Humanistic operating system
Implicit bargaining
Measurement
Mechanistic operating system
Oppressive control
Performance standard
Standard

INCIDENTS

The Problem of Group Evaluation

John Coleman is supervisor of Residential Customer Relations for the Concordia Power and Light Company. His work force includes 18 women whose activities fall into two broad categories. One is handling customer complaints, which usually are about bills but which may also involve service interruptions, meter reading, and the like. The women must correct inaccurate bills, initiate paper work for correcting accounts, and refer some matters to appropriate persons in other departments. The second broad area of activity is answering questions and providing information and advice about many kinds of electric appliances and lighting fixtures.

The women vary, of course, in experience and ability, but they are of generally high caliber. Because of this and because of their ability to meet the public and their versatility in all kinds of office operations, women from this department frequently are promoted into responsible jobs or even supervisory positions in other departments.

In order to maintain and improve individual productivity and to provide a basis for recommendations for salary increases and promotions, John Coleman decided to develop a set of criteria for performance. The women would be judged against these, on the basis of their work during the year.

John sat down at his desk and started to list items that were important in the performance of the women's work. He quickly listed "average number of complaints handled per month" followed by "personal grooming" and "ability to get along with people." After a few minutes thought, he added "skill in using office machines," "initiative," "absenteeism," and "accuracy of work." He pondered what else to add.

Consider his scheme and answer or discuss the following.

What sort of difficulties is he likely to encounter in applying this method of control? Is there anything missing in his procedure? How would you classify each of Mr. Coleman's standards? What do you think will be the reaction of the women?

The Unruly Trouble Shooter

Roy Logan, electronic controls technician with Allegheny Specialty Steels Corporation, stormed into Mill Superintendent Alice Gregory's office and blurted out that he was "fed up with things" and was quitting the company. He went out the door with a parting statement that he was going to the cashier's office to pick up his final paycheck.

Gregory reflected on the problem. Logan had been sent, along with Don Gillies, to this mill 300 miles from the corporation's home mill outside Pittsburgh to iron out some "bugs" in the recently installed electronic control system on the high-speed strip mill. This strip mill rolls billets of stainless and other alloy steels into continuous strip of extremely close dimensional tolerances for use by the aircraft industry. Plant production already was behind schedule and normal output could not resume until Logan completed his adjustment of the highly sensitive instrumentation. One problem was that Don Gillies is, in fact, Logan's "boss" and had been sent along to supervise Logan's work and to do the final meshing of the strip mill controls into the overall control system for the other plant equipment. On several occasions during the past two weeks, Logan had told Gregory that Don Gillies was demanding too much of him, making him work overtime and on weekends. Logan had said that Gillies didn't know a transistor from an extrusion press and didn't realize the stress that he (Logan) was working under.

Gregory also thought of her talk with Don Gillies about this matter two days earlier. She had been told by Gillies that Logan was one of those independent workers who had been pampered in their jobs because of their highly specialized skills. Gillies declared that with the deadline to complete the job less than a week away, Logan was going to finish the job on schedule if he had to sleep in the mill and be spoon fed.

Gregory picked up the phone and called the superintendent back at the home mill. "Bill," she asked, "what can you tell me about Roy Logan?" The superintendent at the home mill laughed. "Has Roy been getting after you too? He's been bucking for a supervisor's job for the past year—says if he could be a boss, he wouldn't have to work so hard."

In considering the above incident, does Alice Gregory have more than one kind of control problem? If so, explain. What may be behind Roy Logan's actions? Is Logan exhibiting more than one type of reaction to the pressures of control? If so, identify each type of reaction. Is there a fallacy in any of Logan's attitudes or reactions? What action would you suggest that Alice Gregory take?

QUESTIONS FOR DISCUSSION

1. Discuss the differences between the control function and the functions of planning and organizing.
2. Why is it necessary in a business enterprise to control the attitudes and activities of people?
3. Describe the elements in a control system designed for controlling a human activity.
4. What does a control system do with respect to deviations in performance?
5. Why is it said that no single method of establishing performance standards will be practical in all cases?
6. How would you describe the differences in measuring the performance of a machine and of a person?
7. Why is it easier, in general, to measure the performance of an hourly employee than that of a member of upper management?
8. One of the characteristics of an effective control system is that it should stress exceptions. Describe some types of exceptions that a supervisor might watch for in the performance of the work group members.
9. In very general terms, how do people tend to react to the pressure of controls? Note: In answering this, do not list the 10 specific forms of response itemized in the text.
10. Can you justify an employee's "right to fail"?
11. Overemphasis on goals is described in the text as one possible form of response to controls. What fault on the part of management may cause this type of response in hourly employees?
12. Contrast the probable degrees of freedom from control experienced by workers in (a) a skilled trade, (b) an assembly-line operation, and (c) a continuous chemical process operation.

CHAPTER VI
Operating Control and Coordination

LEARNING OBJECTIVES

- *To know the organizational control process.*
- *To know controlling and coordinating work flow.*
- *To know controlling and coordinating material and supply flows.*
- *To know controlling and coordinating information flows.*
- *To know importance of computers.*
- *To know control and coordination among departments.*

Introduction

In addition to understanding the managerial functions of planning and organizing, it is extremely important that the supervisor fully appreciate the organizational control process. In this chapter we are concerned with the supervisor's relationships with the organizational operating control and coordination of work flows, material flows (product flows as used in retailing), informational flows, and the departments that affect these flows. Also, vertical lines of control and coordination will be included. Supervisors have a major responsibility in controlling their people but understanding of the broader aspects of control are invaluable to their operating efficiency.

Like other managers, the supervisor has a *control function* that can link two levels of an organization. As indicated in Figure 6-1 each level of management plans, organizes, and directs the level below. The planning and organizing become more specific as you go down the levels. At the supervisory level, orders are issued to the workers or operating people. These orders represent the work planned at the top level. After the operating people execute or perform their duties, informational data,

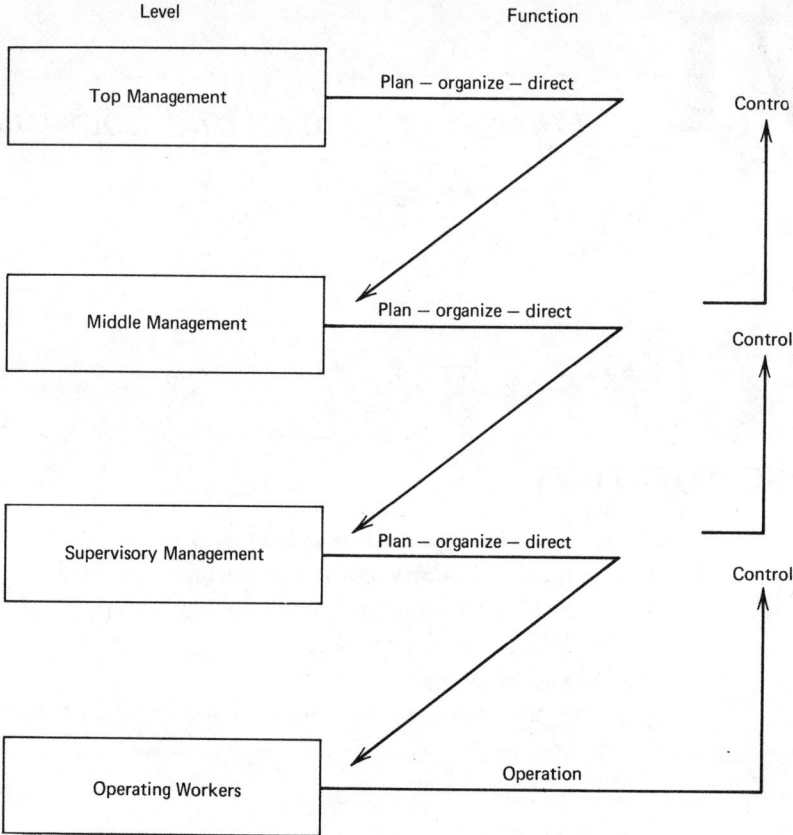

Figure 6-1 Interrelationship of the control function among different levels of management. (Source. Adapted from Edwin B. Flippo, Management: A Behavioral Approach © *1966 by Allyn and Bacon, Inc. Used with permission of the publisher.)*

concerning these results, are initiated and sent up to the supervisor's level. From here the control function flows to middle management people and then on to top management people via reports, both verbal and written. Supervisors are the first level of management to observe these control data. They are in the best position to recognize irregularities of performance and are better able to take corrective action. Thus an understanding of control by the supervisor can take on greater significance.

THE ORGANIZATIONAL CONTROL PROCESS

Organizational control will be treated in three major sections. The first reviews control procedures. The second covers the intradepartmental control processes as they affect the supervisor and his department. This section includes controlling work flows, material and/or product and supply flows, and information flows. The third section covers interdepartmental control processes, which include all the other satellite areas necessary to support the main production-marketing-distribution effort of the organization.

Before we can discuss the control function, a brief analysis should be helpful. Control is the thermostat, or the regulator, of a system that has been planned, organized, and given direction. Information or feedback data are generated as the plan is placed into operation. This information produces the data that can alert the manager to the fact that corrective actions may have to be taken.

INTRADEPARTMENTAL CONTROL AND COORDINATION

The practice of control requires something or someone to control. The supervisor, for example, controls the production of workers, or the activities of sales clerks in a retailing or service operation. We call this *work flows*, since work is passed from one person or section to another until the final product is produced or assembled or the sale is made. Thinking of this as a flow throughout the plant or office or store, we can relate the importance of each department or work group within the organization to each other, and we can relate the significance of each department or work group's contribution to the whole system.

In addition to work flows, raw material, parts, supplies, and subassemblies must flow to the operating units so that the work flow can progress properly. This will be called *material and supply flows*. In distribution and retailing we would be moving products.

Controlling and coordinating these two flows is dependent on the proper information being received at the proper time so that "bottlenecks" and shrinkage, down time, delay, and procrastination do not develop. Thus the two systems must work smoothly. A third system, which we call *information flows*, is necessary for control and coordination.

The next three sections are concerned with the control of work flow, material and supply flow, and information flow and how they affect the supervisor and his or her deparatment from an intradepartmental (within the department) viewpoint.

WORK FLOWS   Production planning and its administration may be the prerogative of the production control department or the marketing-sales forecasting department, but the implementation of work flows affects the supervisor in the form of (1) routing, (2) scheduling, (3) dispatching, and (4) follow-up or expediting. These functions determine the work flows, *what, where, how, when, who,* and a follow-up control to see that all the work has been done properly and on time.

Routing   Fundamentally, routing determines *what* work will be done on what part, product, or process. These concepts are appropriate to offices and distribution organizations as well. In addition, routing also includes *where* and *how* the work will be done.

Routing procedures for a new product or part, or routing customers through a store, may consist of at least seven activities.[1] These activities may be planned by the production control or sales control, or work control department, but before supervisors can understand their role, they must understand the total operation.

1. Determine what to make and what to purchase—make or buy decision.
2. Analyze the product or part to determine what materials are needed—drawings, specifications, standards of quality, and parts list or bills of material. Offices and distribution organizations would be concerned with good inventories, style, sizes, and so on.
3. Determine the manufacturing operations and their sequence—route sheet or operation sheet. Flow of work through an office is similar to flow through a production, warehouse, or service organization.
4. Determine the economic lot size—size of production run relative to least costs. Layout of office, retail store, or warehouse is appropriate to non-manufacturing organizations.
5. Determine scrap factors—shrinkage depends on process-generated scrap. This would be in offices and distribution organizations.
6. Determine cost of product or part—cost accounting department, direct labor, direct materials, indirect cost, and overhead.
7. Determine production control forms—use as few forms as possible.

Routing repeat orders does not include all the steps listed above. Since most of the work has been performed, updated information on cost and the machine use may be necessary. Other than these changes, routing repeat orders becomes a scheduling problem, which is discussed next.

Scheduling   Scheduling is the phase of production control that refers to *when* work will be performed.

Scheduling is usually based on the following factors.

1. Delivery requirements for the finished product or part, including quantities and dates.
2. Production capacity of plant, people, or store.
3. Existing work flow in progress (the availability of open time for new work).

---

[1] For a more detailed discussion of routing procedures, see Lawrence L. Bethel, Franklin S. Atwater, George H. E. Smith, Harvey A. Stackman, Jr., and James L. Riggs, *Industrial Organization and Management*, 5th edition, McGraw-Hill Book Co., New York,, 1971, pp. 221-226.

4. Time required to obtain materials, products, parts, tools, and other setup or display problems.
5. Amount of material or product inventory on hand that is available for new work or display.
6. Time required to perform individual production operations, movements, and inspections.

Scheduling requires the consideration of the resources available and, more importantly, the flow times that are required to control and coordinate all essential work and procurement of materials/products before production or sales can start. Scheduling this lead time along with open periods in a work flow has forced production control people and schedulers, and more recently distributors and retailers, to develop numerous techniques and systems. One popular device, similar to a Gantt chart is called the line-of-balance or LOB flow plan (see Chapter 2). This chart is used to forecast production quantities of required components that will allow the organization to meet its targeted shipping dates. As seen in Figure 6-2, time of processing a part is increased on the X axis (horizontal). The flowchart goes from zero (shipping) time on the right to maximum (ordering) time on the left. Each benchmark or milestone is monitored by various supervisors who report progress on all of these points of different intervals. The LOB flow plan is important because it will enable the manager to pinpoint inconsistencies in processing and opportunities for simultaneous activities. By working backward from the finished product, setup, delay movement, and processing times for all components of a subassembly can be coordinated. For example, it takes 1 hour to machine a hole or 100 hours to machine a 100-piece lot plus setup, delay, and movement time. As shown in the figure, the sleeve actuator (event 5) doesn't have to be started until 15 days after the rod-end extension has started in production.

The advantages of the Gantt chart are the visual, one-shot recognition of work planned and work accomplished as scheduled and performed. The chart will reveal which operations are on schedule and which are not. In addition, the chart will show the sequence of operation over time. Moreover, we can see what operations are necessarily performed in sequence and those operations that can be performed concurrently. Thus the Gantt chart is an excellent device for portraying and controlling time standards of work flows.

A more recent adaptation of the time standard Gantt chart operation is the program evaluation and review technique, commonly called PERT. First developed by the Navy Special Project Office in 1958 and used for national defense projects, PERT has since been employed in highway construction and marketing management (design and development of new products), as well as being widely used in detailed project planning and control. As seen in Figure 6-3, every step or event necessary to finish a project, or achieve a goal, is listed in sequence, with vari-

114   Chapter VI   Operating Control and Coordination

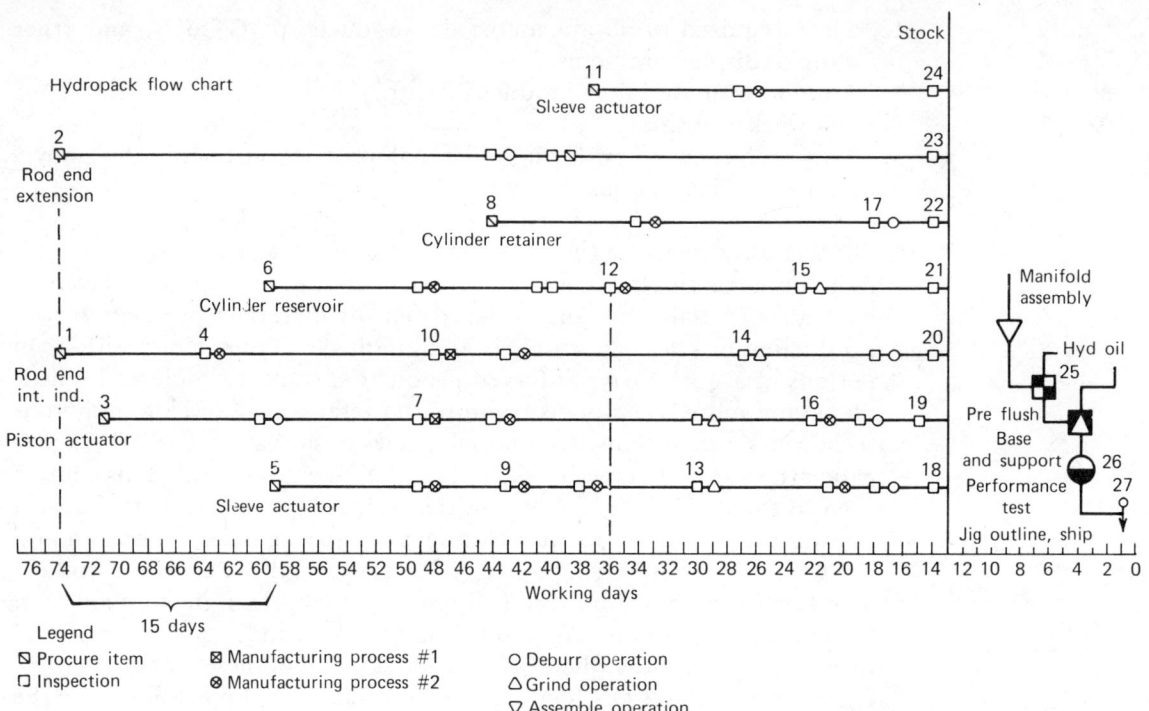

Figure 6-2   Line of balance (LOB) flow plan. (Source. Reproduced with permission from Melvin Silverman Project Management, *Wiley Professional Development Programs, 1976, p. 20.)*

ous dependent prerequisites. In other words, one operation cannot be started until the previous operation is complete. However, concurrent operations can be performed as shown. For example, 1-3-8 is a series, but 1-4-7 can be performed as shown. Moreover, 1-3-8 is a series, but 1-4-7 can be performed concurrently with 1-3-8.

In addition to the time-event-network analysis, PERT's major contribution, compared to Gantt charts, is the technique's ability to show critical paths. The *longest* time for completion of a series of events becomes *the critical path.* All other operations could be completed, but until the longest path is finished, the project or product scheduling will be held up.

Dispatching   Dispatching begins the control side of the production control of workflow process. Whereas routing and scheduling were basically planning, dispatching is concerned with *who* will do the work. Dispatching gives the "go ahead" for work. Its major elements include the following functions.

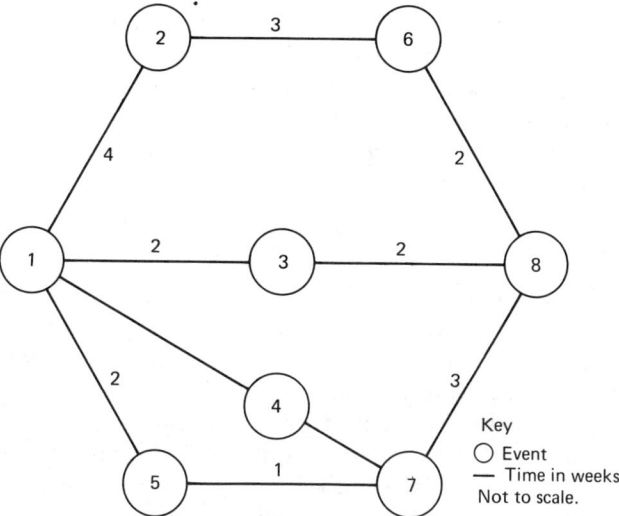

Figure 6-3   Critical path scheduling PERT network.

1. Release of orders, drawing, specifications, and procedural instructions to the production units.
2. The responsibility for controlling the progress of material of each operation.
3. The authority to move work from one operation to another.
4. Service as the liaison function between routing and scheduling offices with performance of the manufacturing divisions.

A shipping dock or production control dispatcher must know at all times the position or progress of all orders, projects, or operations under his or her control. The Gantt chart and LOB control are major visual records of progress. If the dispatcher's judgment is faulty, the efficiency or even the plant capacity is impaired. If the dispatcher's errors are serious, a production bottleneck inevitably results.

Follow-Up or Expediting   Follow-up is also called expediting. This last phase of production control regulates work flow by handling the flow of materials, parts, work in process, and assembly. Dispatchers, or specially assigned expediters, can assist in preventing delays in the accomplishment of the production plan. Dispatchers investigate late deliveries, processing, inspection, and absenteeism errors. They make minor adjustments in scheduling to overcome delays, and recommend corrective measures. The dispatcher literally communicates and makes adjustments to control the work flow. Minor changes are usually communicated to the supervisor for action.

Chapter VI Operating Control and Coordination

MATERIAL AND SUPPLY FLOWS

Material flows include a number of functions, all vital to the smooth operation of a production facility. These operations are usually called production services. *Functions involved in the control of materials are (1) procurement (purchasing), (2) external transportation (shipping, traffic, and receiving), (3) material storage (inventory control), and (4) internal transportation (materials handling).*

Purchasing

The purchasing function deals with outside vendors on all matters pertaining to the procurement of materials, products, parts, supplies, equipment, and tooling. Generally the purchasing agent (or buyer in the case of retailing) is responsible for the four major procurement factors: quality, quantity, time, and price. Quality refers to the kind of goods, as spelled out in the specification. The quantity is determined by production and material requirements set forth in the routing section of production control. Time is important since delivery time is linked with the production schedule. Establishing the purchase price or buyer's cost is the responsibility of the purchasing department or department buyer.

Purchasing procedures include five steps: (1) specifications, (2) purchase requisitions, (3) proposals, (4) purchase orders, and (5) follow-up. Specifications require a meeting of the minds as to the exact features of the materials or products needed. Specifications define form, shape, composition, performance, sizes, style, and specific features desired. Purchase requisitions are forms originated by the user that include how much, when, and where it is requested. The requisition authorizes the purchasing department to proceed with the purchasing function. Next, the purchasing department collects possible vendors' names and gives them information on the material or product specification, quality, quantity, and date when needed. This is a call for a bid by vendors. In the case of distribution, preprinted sales catalogues are available. The vendors submit price proposals in return, based on the bid requests received from the purchasing department. The vendors' proposals or bids are evaluated for price and other factors listed on the bid. A purchase decision is made and a purchase order, "P.O. number," is assigned to a vendor. In the last step, the vendor acknowledges receipt of the purchase order and informs the purchasing department of the delivery date. Follow-up of P.O.'s procedures begin. Expeditors in purchasing are used, as in work flow discussed before.

Shipping, Traffic, and Receiving

Shipping refers to the preparation of goods, both incoming and outgoing. Vitually all outgoing material is packed, marked, and weighed prior to shipment. Breakage or damage of any kind can be serious. Packing containers should be designed to minimize breakage in transit, enhance the packages' handling, and conform to regulations concerning freight packaging.

Traffic is concerned with physical movement and mode of transportation of both incoming and outgoing shipments. The method of movement is dependent on the mode of transportation chosen.

1. Rail.
2. Water (ship & barge).
3. Air.
4. Truck (UPS).
5. Bus.

Railroad freight is probably one of the fastest means of hauling bulky freight. Water transportation, river, lake, and oceangoing vessels, are usually the least expensive modes for bulky commodities. Motor and bus are excellent modes for quick, short hauls, and air freight is quickest for intermediate and long hauls. Although each mode has its strengths, each is used to cover specific needs in transportation.

The receiving department is responsible for checking all material receipts for condition, count, desired location, and then communicate the on-board arrival of the materials or products.

Material Storage Storage is concerned with inventory control. Two values are important in this phase of materials control—first, an adequate supply must be on hand to meet our needs, and second, an excess amount must not be on hand so that our cash is needlessly tied up in stored materials. In addition to location, inventory is the most critical area for wholesaling and retailing organizations.

Five types of general inventories exist in any industrial manufacturing firm. (Distribution organizations are usually concerned only with the last three types.)

1. Raw materials. Materials used directly in the product that have not undergone a major change after receipt by the firm.
2. Materials in process. Those used in the product and whose form has changed as a result of the production process.
3. Finished products. A finished product ready to be packaged and shipped.
4. Supplies. Materials that aid in the production or sales process but do not become part of the product.
5. Equipment items. Jigs, fixtures, fittings, gauges, machine parts, and machines that do not become part of the product, but are used in its manufacture or warehousing.

Inventory control uses sophisticated methods such as operation research, computers, and mathematical techniques. These techniques are necessary to ensure that a sufficient inventory of finished products is on hand to meet customer demand. If a firm has multiple warehouses that store finished goods, the problem is magnified. Sufficient inventory must be available to meet the production scheduling timetable. An out-of-stock condition or the necessary wait for a back order to be filled could cause the loss of a customer or the shutdown of the plant or a severe loss of sales. These consequences are extremely serious.

Materials Handling and Physical Distribution

It has been estimated that 50 percent of each dollar that we, as consumers, spend pays for the cost of transportation both within a plant and throughout the channels of distribution. Much time and effort are expended to get the right *product* at the right *place* at the right *time*. This is the concern of physical distribution. Materials handling is concerned with moving and storage of goods within a plant and between locations at the least cost and shrinkage (damage). Many automatic devices such as hand lift trucks, fork lift trucks, roller conveyers, flat bed conveyers, power conveyers, chain conveyers, tramrail or monorail hoists, and cranes are used in the various transport modes, such as rail, water, air, motor, and bus. Supervisors would be concerned with these specific devices and modes of transportation as they may affect their work group and practices.

Two breakthroughs in materials handling devices and techniques have occurred since 1960 in transportation. Palletization of materials, particularly finished goods, and containerization of finished goods have both reduced the cost of handling goods. In addition, the products have moved faster and with less damage. A banana processor who once shipped the green bananas from the tropics in bunches has since switched to boxing the bananas in the tropics and handling the perishable fruit with modern materials handling equipment all the way to the retailer. Although the boxes increased the product's cost rapidly, the savings in time and shrinkage more than offset the additional cost. Less damaged fruit meant fewer complaints and fewer transportation hangups.

The control of material product flows requires viewing the entire system as raw materials and parts, subassemblies, equipment, and supplies flow into a manufacturing facility and then flow through the channels of distribution. Processing takes place throughout the many assembly or manufacturing activities, as the product is stored, stacked, shaped, and changed in form. After the finished product is packed, a very complex materials flow or distribution system starts moving the product into other uses or eventually through wholesalers and retailers on to the ultimate consumer. In the case of industrial goods, the channels often are shorter — that is, raw material producer to manufacturer or wholesaler.

INFORMATION FLOWS

In both the previous sections, control of work flows and material flows, you have possibly noticed that *informational flows permeate both types of systems*. In the case of control of work flows, information was both disseminated and collected. Material flows, the planning and tracing of the material as it flowed through the system, required control of the information.

In Figures 6-4 and 6-5 we can trace the flow of information of work and materials. Both information flows occur at the same time. However, the material flow becomes the servant of the work flow, in most cases.

Controlling and coordinating a massive amount of information requires numerous reports, as shown in the two figures. The critical element in the entire process is the lead time given to ordering and receiving the materials, so the materials are available when production needs them.

Good planning and control can eliminate idle workers, idle machines, idle materials, idle money, idle delivery promises to customers, and idle product in inventory. Supervisors play an important role within their department in the material/product work and information flows as they affect their work group. Regardless of how carefully planned the production flows are, controlling and initiating corrective action are primarily the responsibilities of the supervisor at the work scene.

COMPUTERS— AN AID TO INFORMATION FLOWS

Supervisors are living in a more complex world where computer technology is a common tool and a basic way of life. Information flows in production could be production reports, inventory reports, cost reports, production schedules, work-in-process reports, and employee payroll reports. For office and business purposes, computers could provide information in the form of payroll statistics, sales analyses, auditing tools, simulation of sales strategy, forecasting, inventory status, and employee's productivity reports.

The computer can assist supervisors in determining problems and seeking possible solutions. The computer contains a data base from which a supervisor may make an inquiry via a CRT (cathode ray tube). In case of goods in progress, inventory on hand, or personnel motivation, the supervisor can index the right product, inventory or an employee's name or code number and receive an immediate display or printout of the desired information. Computers can provide real-time information that makes immediate summaries available. Many wholesalers and retail stores have these systems that automatically reorder a product when supply on hand reaches a minimum size.

Supervisors usually have little input into designing a real-time computer system, however, they are often interviewed, as are other managers, on what information is needed, in what form, and when it is needed. Most computer systems are no better than the software used: hence, if su-

120   Chapter VI   Operating Control and Coordination

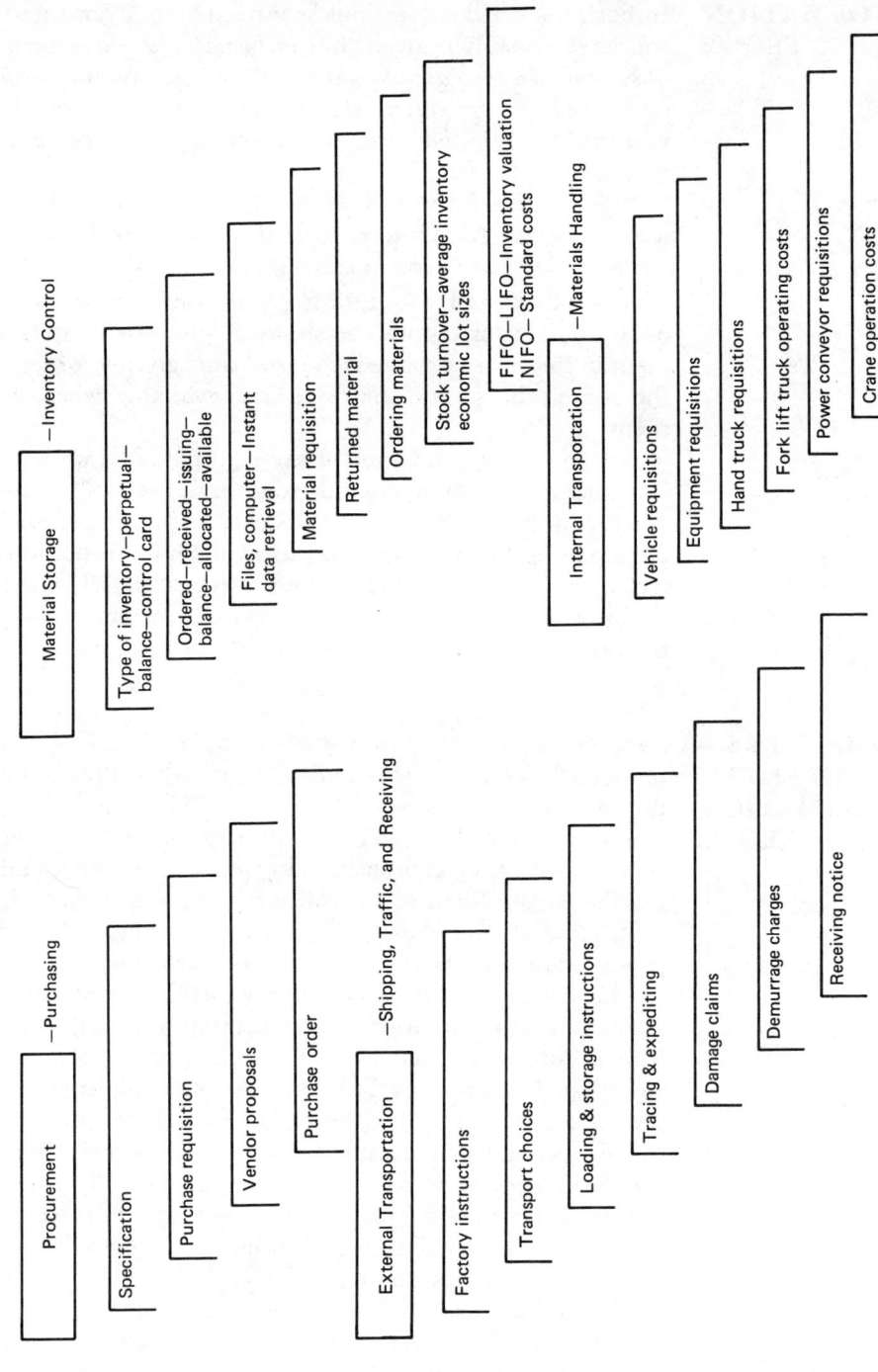

Figure 6-4 *Materials information flow.*

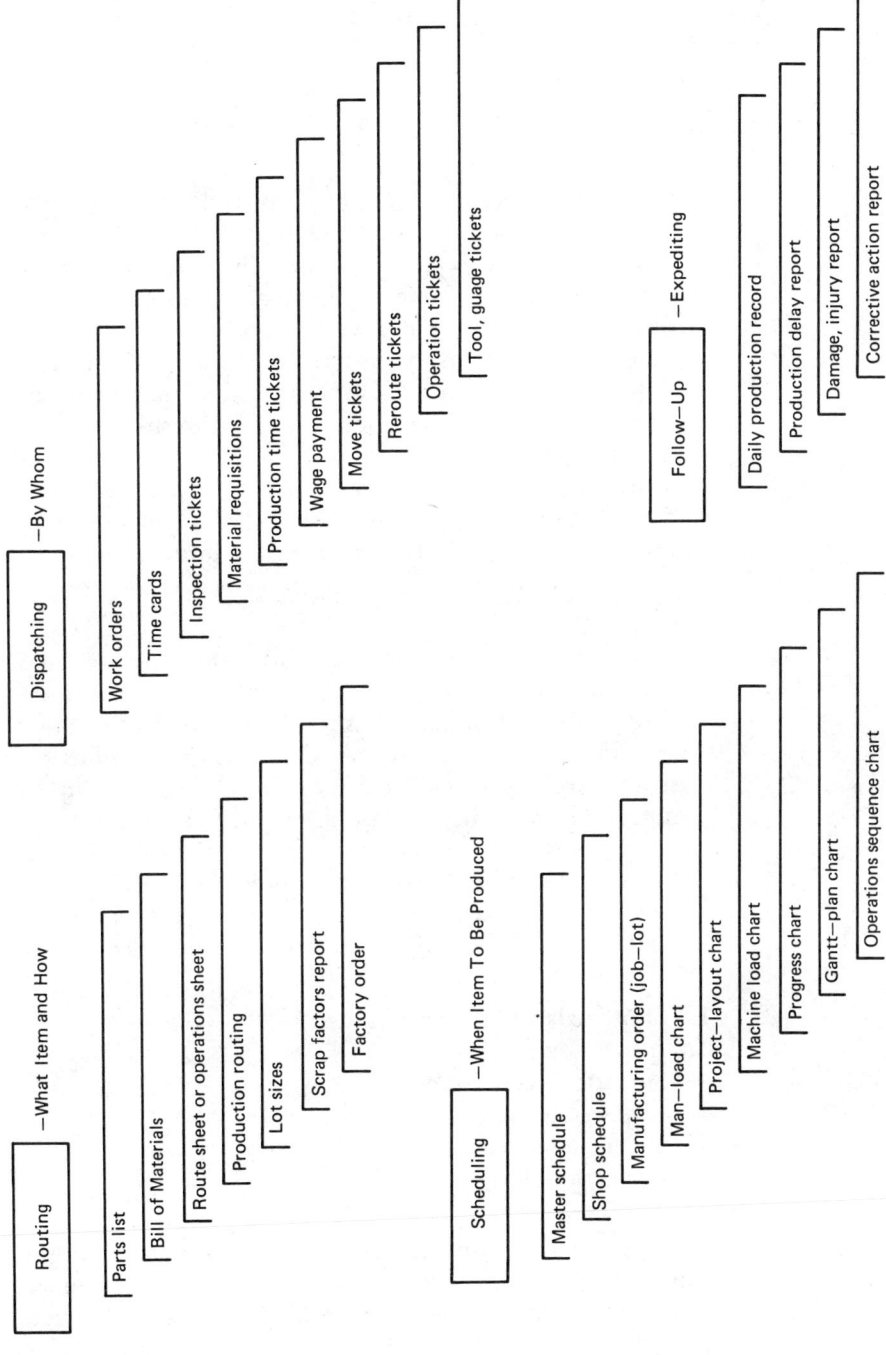

Figure 6-5 Work information flow.

pervisors are overlooked when the system is established, its supervisory use may be limited or impractical.

INTERDEPARTMENTAL CONTROL AND COORDINATION

In addition to contributing to controlling work, material/product and informational flows within the department, supervisors also face control problems as they relate to other departments (interdepartmental), including staff or nonline departments. This section will cover supervisors' relationships with the quality control, procurement, traffic maintenance, company safety, industrial engineering, waste control and pollution, marketing, and research and development departments. Whether or not supervisors like their interrelationship with other departments, they should appreciate their functions in order to better understand their own control operations. Offices and distribution organizations are lucky enough to avoid many of the problems, but interdepartmental control and coordination problems do exist in limited quantity.

QUALITY CONTROL Quality control in its broadest sense refers to a systematic control of relevant variables in the production process that affect the excellence of the end product. Quality control is never absolute—but always relative to certain other considerations. Quality is a nebulous term, since it is abstract. Nothing is really good or bad except by comparison. A product is not good unless its end use and specifications are met as the customer perceives them. Therefore a quality control program has essential elements that can be considered its tools of the trade.

So that the supervisor will not misinterpret the quality controller's methods, the following list contains the tools of quality control.

1. Standards and specifications.
2. Inspection methods.
3. Statistical techniques.
4. Inspection records.
5. Salvage methods.
6. Inspection devices.

The quality control department attempts to follow scientific techniques and methodology in order to perform its mission. At times the quality control people can be policemen and reject the product. This tends to irritate the supervisor, but their "quality" techniques have been devised to save the company embarrassment and, in effect, save the supervisor's job as well as the workers' jobs. Control of quality should not become a serious obstacle for the supervisor. He or she should cooperate as much as possible. Producing quality products that satisfy customer needs, at a profit to the company, is the reason for the firm's existence. Marketing, distribution people, and customers can become very upset if quality does not meet their standards or expectations.

MAINTENANCE DEPARTMENT

Maintenance is the function of keeping the physical plant in effective operating condition and maintaining uninterrupted production. Maintenance responsibility is broad in scope, including care of grounds; painting, roofing, and repair of building; washing windows, sweeping, and other cleaning; oiling, repairing, and moving of equipment; replacement of lamp bulbs; trash removal; and any other housekeeping chores. Further duties of the maintenance department are stocking of repair parts, piping, wiring, reduction of waste programs, and education programs on maintenance.

Some medium-size and large companies have their maintenance section as part of the plant or store engineering department. These departments have mechanical and electrical engineers who inspect designs and install improved or rebuilt systems. Large plant or store engineering departments employ numerous specialists, such as pipe fitters, millwrights, oilers, beltmen, electricians, welders, masons, tool grinders, tool and die makers, machine repair people, machinists, firefighters, guards, carpenters, painters, sanitary engineers, boiler room operators, heating and cooling specialists, and draftspeople.

Rather than wait for deterioration of plant and equipment to run its course, maintenance departments practice what is called preventive maintenance. Inspectors are constantly looking, listening, feeling, and sniffing for predictors or indicators of future failures. Often, maintenance inspectors forget or fail to appreciate that their principal duties are to be of *service* to the rest of the organization rather than vice versa. Maintenance must schedule its work so that it dovetails with the operating department's schedule. Maintenance work is extremely important in terms of preventing breakdowns and costly equipment failure; the preventive maintenance program should give preference to important line production jobs. On the other hand, supervisors sometimes fail to appreciate the technical and scheduling problems of maintenance. Both groups should realize that production scheduling techniques will be used to the advantage of all concerned. Servicing equipment on a regular basis prevents breakdown, but more importantly, the equipment performs more efficiently.

INDUSTRIAL ENGINEERING DEPARTMENT

Industrial engineers cover many fields in industrial production. Most notably, they study factory, office, or store layout, time and motion studies, materials handling, and production operations and control. In addition, the industrial engineer is concerned with inventory control, safety engineering, cost systems and control, merit ratings, supervisory training, and product design.

Each plant, or department, will vary in its utilization of its industrial engineers, but generally speaking, the IE will research, standardize, and control the work habits and work design of the various jobs in the organization. Usually referred to as motion study or methods analysis, the IE establishes standards that reflect the work position's norms.

The supervisor's contacts with the industrial engineer can be many and varied. The most difficult area, of course, will be living with the work standards established by the industrial engineers. This is not to say that the standards are necessarily incorrect, but the motion and time study people tend to use very precise measurements concerning work habits. This tends to overlook individual differences. The supervisor must cope with these differences and learn to live with these differences.

WASTE CONTROL AND POLLUTION

Control of industrial, store, office, or institutional waste is accomplished with a twofold program: (1) waste prevention and (2) salvage. Waste prevention programs endeavor to eliminate and/or control waste at its source. Salvage programs attempt to utilize or dispose of all waste that occurs. These are department-wide and organization-wide programs. Pollution control has been the "in" thing among most ecologists and operating companies. However, much waste control and proper treatment of salvage can start at the first-line supervisory level.

Control of waste is not just the company's or society's problem, it is the problem of every worker and every supervisor. As with company safety, supervisors have to *sell* their workers on good housekeeping, detecting possible sources of waste and pollution, collecting scrap for salvage, and not wasting supplies such as paper towels, rags, power, and fuel.

MARKETING DEPARTMENT

A detailed coverage of the marketing department is beyond the scope of this chapter, but as discussed elsewhere, the supervisor and the marketing department have a very close relationship. Marketing research determines which markets exist and what types of products could satisfy these needs. Pricing, product developments, channels of distribution, consumer behavior, packaging, personal selling, advertising, sales promotion, product service, and product testing are but a few of the functions of the market department. Of all these functions, quality control and production control affect the marketing people the most. The marketing department is very product and service oriented. Marketing personnel have nothing unless they have a fine, durable, valuable product to talk about. Quality, or giving consumers their money's worth, is very dear and close to the hearts of the marketing people. When one unit of a mass-produced product proves to be unusable or does not meet the consumer's or user's specifications or expectations, the marketing agent is very disturbed.

The supervisor's role here is to become cognizant that products are used by customers, who pay money for these products and who expect a product to deliver results for the price paid. Occasionally, poor products will hit the market. Customers complain and these complaints are passed on to the production work crew, making them responsible for the "goof." Then supervisors and their people must correct the situation immediately. Quality control, the supervisor, and the workers are closely allied with the marketing department. In the case of distribution, and particularly retailing, the product is the store, its location, style, friendliness, and selection of products.

RESEARCH AND DEVELOPMENT DEPARTMENT

Research is concerned with the systematic evaluation and analysis of materials and methods that will assist the organization in achieving its basic objectives. Development, on the other hand, is the using of information gained from the research to assist in finding new products and processes, and new uses for existing products and processes.

Research can be classified as (1) basic—conducted for additional data with no specific use in mind—and (2) applied—which utilizes basic research in the development of new products or services.

Product development is closely allied to R & D, except that product development is more concerned with the product's relationship with market potential. Both applied R & D and product development are closely allied with changes in the marketplace that foster changes in product design, production processes, and product control evaluation. Supervisors become involved when changes are made in their work areas or work groups that have been initiated in the R & D department. To remain viable, a firm must continue to invest in R & D. When changes occur, supevisors have to face up to the fact that their world, as well as everyone else's world, is dynamic and constantly changing. Without change and constant improvement, a firm may fall behind its competitors. Change may be disrupting, but managers have to learn to cope with these changes.

SUMMARY

Supervisors have a control function that flows from top managment. Their operation or production provides the data that are analyzed to determine whether plans and activities are being controlled and coordinated.

Control is similar to a thermostat in that changes in output affect input factors going into the operating system. Control procedures are establishing performance standard, measuring performance against these standards, and taking corrective actions. A control system requires a controllable event or condition, sensory devices, a control unit (thermostat), and an activating unit or mechanism that takes corrective action.

The three major systems that must be controlled in an organization are (1) work flows — routing, scheduling, dispatching, and follow-up; (2) material/product flows — equipment, supplies, materials, tools, shipping, traffic, receiving, purchasing, materials storage, materials handling; and (3) information flows — data transmission forms.

Interdepartmental control and coordination force supervisors to work with many staff organizations and many other line organization people. Each of these organizations has some input into their operation. The other operating units that have the most effect, other than their immediate superiors, are quality control, procurement department, traffic department, maintenance department, company safety, industrial engineering, waste and pollution control, the marketing department, and the R & D department.

Working with all these other parts of the organization creates problems for supervisors in the areas of authority, responsibility, and coordination. In the final analysis, as a line person, supervisors bear the responsibility for problems that occur within the confines of their authority.

KEY CONCEPTS

Control. The concept of control is simply the regulation of activities in accordance with a prescribed plan created to achieve an objective. The difficulty that arises in this concept is implementation. Working with other people and departments and contending with inadequate information of the work process itself help to deteriorate the supervisor's ability to establish standards, achieve performance, and take corrective actions.

Flows. The concept of flow is important to the analysis of organizational control procedures and processes. Flow can be visualized as a sequence of various types of processes (transportation, distribution, storage, work, shaping material, typing or changing a service contract, or a change in shape or form). Although flow cannot be described as a fluid flow in manufacturing, retailing, wholesaling, service, institutional, and governmental organizations, it is really a set of discrete items that must fit together in a logical sequence so that time and costs are minimized with a maximization of quantity and quality of product or service output.

Organizational Control. This concept as it relates to the supervisor is a perspective of seeing how the supervisor's position and workers' functions interrelate and fit together.

IMPORTANT TERMS

Control function
Coordinating
Corrective action
Dispatching
Expediting
Gantt charts
Information flows
Interdepartmental control

Intradepartmental control
Inventory
Material flows
PERT charts
Routing
Scheduling
Standards
Work flows

INCIDENTS

Handy House Cleaner

Bret Johnson majored in management while a student at a state university in Pennsylvania. He accepted two corporate personnel positions but each turned sour as Bret had difficulty identifying with specific corporate goals, procedures, and control functions. He investigated the phenomena that over 50 percent of married women were holding down full-time jobs to supplement their spouse's income so their families could maintain their standard of living and combat the prevailing double-digit inflation. Bret believed a market existed for a domestic cleaning company. Upon further investigation he affiliated with Domesticare, Inc., one of a number of franchise domestic cleaning organizations.

Bret was obligated to invest $20,000 in his local franchise to obtain permission to use the franchiser's name and benefit from any promotional campaigns sponsored by Domesticare. Since his financial capital was limited, Bret decided to hire only one assistant, purchase a used Dodge van, and purchase a month's supply of cleaning sprays, disinfectants, rags, and sundry items. Stocked with these items and a young lady who stated she needed a job to help support her family, Bret began his promotional efforts to line up customers. A diligent marketing effort paid off with eight customers, each of whom wanted a full house cleaning, every two weeks.

Bret figured that with his helper they could clean an average three-bedroom home, baths, kitchen, and dining room in one and one-half hours. Given a 10- to 15-minute ride between customers and one hour for lunch, he calculated that about four customers could be serviced every day if he started by 8:20 A.M. and finished up by 4:30 P.M.. Further calculation indicated that if he priced each job at $42.50, his break-even point to cover his expenses, such as labor and travel and materials, would be *three* customers a day.

The first month Bret encountered a number of problems that he believed were responsible for his averaging only two customers a day, well below his break-even point. These problems were (1) locked homes and no keys, (2) van breakdowns, and (3) talkative customers who tied up Bret although he initiated and sustained many of the conversations.

Advise Bret regarding improving his profitability. Is he practicing poor supervisory management? What would you do if you were Bret?

An Irate Office Manager

"Anna, you know I told you to Xerox this report on both sides and not on one side. I'm trying to live within our budget and this is only throwing money away." "I'm sorry Ms. B but I misunderstood." The morning was starting as usual, thought John Garvin, a newly hired office clerk as he overheard Ann Butz (Ms. B) yell at her chief assistant, Anna Place.

John liked working at Winters Manufacturing Co., but the constant bickering, psychological depressions, and domineering behavior of Ms. B, the office manager, was a constraint to the orderly flow of office work as well as being an unstabling influence to the staff.

Every order received by Winters was first checked by John for accuracy in price, extension (quantity $\times$ price), total of the order, application of proper taxes, discounts, credit terms, and customer address. From John, the new order traveled to Anna Place's desk where she checked the availability of the stock and initiated a back order for any items not in stock. The next operation was performed by Ms. B who prepared the forms to be forwarded to the computer section for tabulation, sales analysis, and inventory analysis. Much of these data were used by the computer to determine sales forecasts, cost of sales, and general cost analysis. The last step was performed by the fourth member of the office staff, Glenda Boot, who typed the final invoice and held it for mailing. When the order was filled, a copy of the invoice, called the packing slip, was forwarded to shipping when the office was notified the order was ready. The invoice was mailed at this time.

The system worked well except in those cases where Ms. B was not feeling good enough to work and she hybernated in her office. Ms. B's on-the-job illnesses occurred at least once a week, but she refused to delegate any of her authority or share any of her responsibility.

Correct the invoice flow process and make it more efficient. What is Ms. B doing to her fellow workers? Is she a good supervisor?

Role Play Role play the above incident by using a situation where Anna Place is suggesting an improvement in the invoice system but Ms. B is standing her ground and is objecting to the change.

QUESTIONS FOR DISCUSSION

1. Describe control systems and discuss why it is necessary for the supervisor to understand these systems.
2. What clues can be used to determine the critical points in a situation before corrective actions have to be taken?
3. What are the differences, if any, between the control objectives of work flow versus control objectives of materials flow?
4. What are the differences between the Gantt chart system and PERT?
5. Explain, in detail, the importance of product quality control as perceived by (a) supervisor, (b) marketing people, (c) customers, (d) production people, and (e) cost analysts.
6. Discuss the role that waste and pollution control plays in an organization's operating control system?
7. How best should informational flows be instituted among the R & D, marketing and finance functions?

CHAPTER VII

Financial Control

LEARNING OBJECTIVES

- *To understand how the income statement and balance sheet present useful control information.*
- *To gain insight into the usefulness of the cash budget.*
- *To learn to prepare a production budget.*
- *To learn how to use budgets for control.*

Introduction

Perhaps the most widely used method of exercising comprehensive control over the entire organization, or over a major segment of it, is through financial control. After all, inflows and outflows of money are common to all types of organizations, commercial and noncommercial.

Profit planning is the foundation of financial control. It puts together in an orderly fashion the hopes and expectations of sales and production personnel and their many supporting organizations. No ship, no airplane, and no organization can be steered to an objective without having a course charted. Without such a course, deviations cannot be measured, and hence corrections cannot be made so as to reach the desired objective. The purpose of financial planning and control is to chart this course.

The term *profit planning* is used by many managers as a synonym for budgetary controls. However, there is more to the concept than budgets alone. Although profit planning ordinarily involves the development and use of one or more of the several different kinds of special-purpose budgets, it may also include the use of other financial tools, techniques, and operations.

The student will note the references to both planning and control. The two are closely interrelated. For example, preparation of a budget is an exercise in planning, and the completed budget is a plan expressed in quantitative terms. But use of the budget as a standard against which to measure and correct performance is part of the control function.

Profit planning is a major responsibility of the financial manager. Although supervisors are not directly connected with this responsibility, they do supply much of the data necessary for their superiors to do their jobs properly. It is important, then, that they understand some of the tools, techniques, and operations that are involved in financial control.

ACCOUNTING SYSTEM

The *accounting system* is the primary source of quantitative information used in the operation of a business. Accounting records and reports provide the essential data needed for establishing policies, making decisions, and controlling operations. No business can hope to be a success without having the minimum accounting records necessary to keep abreast of cost, income, assets, and liabilities that arise in the company's operations.

Accounting is the tool by which management secures the information necessary for it to make its decisions. Accounting records have as their source the efficient accumulation of data flowing in from various segments of the organization. The data are put together in an orderly manner, as established by good accounting practice. This orderly manner generally provides two of the most useful tools for corporate decisions.

INCOME STATEMENT The first of these tools is known as the *profit and loss statement* or *income statement*. We have noted that the excess of income over cost is termed profit. On the other hand, the excess of cost over income is known as loss. This idea might be expressed in an equation:

$$I - C = P \text{ or } L$$

in which I represents income, C represents cost, P represents profit, and L represents loss.

There are some minor distinctions not explicit in the formula as written. For instance, we sometimes encounter the terms *gross profit* and *net profit*. Gross profit is sometimes described as the margin of profit resulting from subtracting the cost of the goods sold from the total sales. In this case, the cost of the goods sold only includes the materials used plus direct production costs. This gross profit margin is turned into the net by subtracting selling expenses, administrative expenses, depreciation, and bad debts. A typical income statement is shown in Table 7-1.

Table 7-1 Xzy Company, Income Statement, for the Year 198__

Net sales				$600,000
Manufacturing costs				
Raw material inventory, Jan. 1		$100,000		
Purchases	$200,000			
Freight-in	10,000			
Total purchases		210,000		
Total inventory and purchases		310,000		
Less raw materials inventory, Dec. 31		110,000		
Cost of materials used			$200,000	
Direct labor cost			150,000	
Manufacturing overhead cost				
Indirect labor		25,000		
Heat, light, and power		90,000		
Supplies		22,000		
Insurance and taxes		8,000		
Depreciation		35,000		
Total manufacturing overhead cost			180,000	
Total manufacturing cost			$530,000	
Goods in process inventory, Dec. 31		40,000		
Less goods in process, Jan. 1		20,000		
Net increase in inventory			20,000	
Cost of goods manufactured			$510,000	
Finished goods inventory, Dec. 31		70,000		
Finished goods inventory, Jan. 1		60,000		
Net increase in finished goods			10,000	
Cost of goods sold				500,000
Gross profit				$100,000
Selling and administrative expenses				
Selling expenses			40,000	
Administrative expenses			30,000	70,000
Net operating profit				$ 30,000
Other revenue				10,000
Net income before taxes				$ 40,000
Provision for income tax				10,000
Net income				$ 30,000

BALANCE SHEET The second major form in which the accounting data is accumulated produces the *balance sheet*. This is a statement that outlines the assets and liabilities of a corporation at the end of the period under study. Assets such as cash and inventories of goods may increase or decrease during this period. Liabilities or debts incurred through borrowing or from unpaid bills will do likewise.

As in the case of the income statement, a simple equation can be written representing the balance sheet, which is known as the *balance sheet equation:* Assets = Liabilities plus Net Worth. Table 7-2 illustrates a typical balance sheet.

We note that there are current assets and fixed assets. Current assets are frequently defined as those items that could be converted into cash within a year. Fixed assets generally refer to items such as equipment and buildings that are a fundamental part of the operation.

On the other side of the ledger, we have current liabilities, representing those obligations that must be paid off in a relatively short period of time, and those longer-term debts such as mortgages and long-term loans that are due and payable over a more extended period of time. The difference between the sum of these liabilities and the total assets at that point on the balance sheet represents the net worth of a corporation. This is made up of such items as capital stock and retained earnings. *Capital stock* is the firm's own stock held or purchased from stockholders. *Retained earnings* are net profit held in the form of cash or other assets such as inventory or buildings.

A characteristic of the balance sheet is that the total assets always equal the total liabilities plus net worth. *Double entry accounting* facilitates the equation because for every entry to an asset, the same entry must be made in a liability or net worth account.

ANALYSIS OF BALANCE SHEET

There are certain techniques that the financial manager uses to analyze the balance sheet. These are frequently known as ratios. A commonly used one is the *current ratio.* This is determined by dividing the current assets by the current liabilities. As a rule of thumb, we might say that a ratio ranging between 1.5 to 1 and 2.5 to 1 represents a reasonable current ratio. This ratio varies from one industry or business to another. Many bankers and other financial statement analyzers believe that for a business to qualify as a good credit risk, the total current assets should be approximately twice as large as current liabilities.

Because the merchandise inventory might not be readily convertible into cash to pay debts on short notice, another ratio has been devised known as the *acid test ratio.* In this case, cash and receivables are divided by the current liabilities. A ratio of 1 to 1 is the minimum found to be adequate in many companies.

A third ratio often used is obtained by dividing the net income by the net worth. This ratio is called *return on equity,* or *return on net worth.* It is helpful in determining the use of the owner's equity to generate net income, or net profit. Another ratio, obtained by dividing the net worth by the debt, is called the *debt-equity ratio,* or *leverage effect.* It indicates the proportional or combinational use of both debt and net worth.

Dividing the net income by the total assets gives us still another ratio, which measures how often assets have been turned over (dollars used to

Table 7-2 Xzy Company, Balance Sheet, December 31, 198__

Assets			Liabilities		
Current assets			Current liabilities		
Cash	$ 30,000		Accounts payable	$ 40,000	
Accounts receivable	50,000		Tax liability	10,000	
Inventories	100,000		Accrued expenses payable	5,000	
Prepaid expenses	20,000		Total Current Liabilities		$ 55,000
Total Current Assets		$200,000			
Fixed assets			Other liabilities		
Land, building, and equipment	$300,000		Mortgage		50,000
Less: Accumulated depreciation	100,000	200,000			
Other assets			Stockholders' equity		
Investments	$ 10,000		Common Stock	$200,000	
Goodwill	10,000	20,000	Retained earnings	115,000	315,000
Total Assets		$420,000	Total Liabilities		$420,000

generate X dollars of revenue). Obviously, the more turnovers there are, the better utilized are the firm's assets.

None of these ratios are sufficient in their own right to judge the situation of a company. However, by examining a series of them, and particularly by looking at month-to-month trends, it is possible for the financial manager to make some judgement on the performance of his organization.

CASH BUDGETS

Another useful accounting tool for the manager is the *cash budget*. Capital may be invested in either equipment (fixed capital) or raw materials, finished goods, and cash (working capital). *Working capital* is the difference found by subtracting current liabilities from current assets. This is the cash available for payrolls and day-to-day expenses.

The management of this working capital is one of the major concerns of the financial executive. Although the maximization of profit is a major goal of the business enterprise, the availability of cash is a constant problem in achieving this goal. If a smaller amount of working capital is needed to meet current bills, more money will be available for investment in income-producing assets. Thus we see that the management of working capital involves an optimization of the amount required in the meeting of current needs.

We should distinguish in our minds between working capital in terms of immediately available currency (cash) and working capital tied up in inventory, both raw material and finished product. Cash is liquid, but inventory cannot produce cash until sold.

Regardless of its nature, an enterprise must maintain control over its cash position. Failure to do so will affect its profitability or may even bring on bankruptcy. Balance is affected by many items, and the outcome cannot be left to chance. To assist management in the achievement of this purpose, the cash budget has been developed. If managers can plan ahead and provide a smooth flow of funds, the efficiency of the business operation will be improved. If more cash is needed than will be generated internally, plans must be made to secure these additional funds. If a surplus of cash is going to be present, decisions must be made concerning how to best invest these extra funds.

The cash budget may be used either as a simple forcasting device or as a means for effective planning. When used for forecasting, operating projections are made by the various elements of the company, cash inflows and outflows are matched, and the deficiencies are provided for as needed. When used for planning, it involves estimating different levels of operation and determining what mix of inflows and outflows will provide the greatest contribution to the profitability of the enterprise without entailing too much risk. In this context, management must carefully formulate its goals and establish their time dimension.

The cash budget need not be a complex document. It is merely a formalized structure for estimating cash income and cash expenditures over a given period of time. Some of the typical elements used in determining the cash flows are given in Table 7-3.

When the financial manager inserts estimated dollar outflows and inflows into these various elements and adds them together, the difference will represent either the surplus or the needed cash for the particular month or period in question.

When we look at the list of cash outflows and inflows, we see a number of elements of estimation that must be provided by segments of the enterprise other than the financial department. For example, the people in production will be called upon to estimate their direct labor requirements as well as materials and supplies requirements for the period of time under study. The sales people will be required to provide information on anticipated sales and the outstanding receivables. Personnel people may be asked for information concerning the administrative expenses that may be incurred because of corporate policy or union contracts.

We may now take a more detailed look at some of the major departments of the corporation that provide data for the cash budget and how they approach their task.

SALES

The *sales forecast* is the initial budgeting point and, therefore, one of the most crucial factors in the business forecast. From it follows the estimate of the cost of goods sold and the decisions concerning inventory levels, purchase of raw materials, employment levels, selling expenses, and financial requirements. Decisions based on this forecast will also be made concerning administrative and general expenses.

Table 7-3

Cash Outflows	Cash Inflows
Direct labor	Cash Sales
Materials and supplies	Collection of receivables
Administrative expenses	Interest income
Accounts payable	Dividend income
Repayment of bank loans	Tax refund
Retirement of outstanding loans	Bank loan
Repurchase of preferred stock	Sales of bonds and preferred or common stock
Interest payments	
Dividend payments	Sale of plant and equipment
Purchase of plant and equipment	
Taxes	

The means of securing data for sales forecasts will vary somewhat among those businesses and industries that produce industrial products, and those that distribute products. In the case of industrial products, each salesperson will be requested to analyze the probable requirements of customers over a forthcoming period of perhaps six months and on a month-by-month basis. The salesperson will secure the data by talking to the customers as to their anticipated needs and then deciding what share of each customer's requirements he will receive. The salesperson may augment this forecast with anticipated sales to new customers. The forecast may be further altered by anticipated sales of new products.

In most companies there are district offices for sales, and the district manager will receive this information from various salespeople. The district manager will consolidate it and perhaps adjust the figures on the basis of overall judgment. The district manager will probably be required to furnish information on anticipated sales expenses during the coming months. These consolidated figures will be delivered to the marketing manager of the company.

The marketing manager will analyze the data coming in from the various district offices and may, in turn, impose judgment factors on these figures. He or she may use figures from the marketing research department concerning the probable economic climate during the coming months and may alter the figures on the basis of anticipated competitive situations that appear to be developing. The marketing manager may alter them through one of the available methods of statistical analysis.

In a company dealing with the consumer market, sales forecasting frequently is made on a more general basis. The estimates may be based on anticipated demands related to past experience. One system involves the *moving average*. This simply means taking the most recent observations of sales, say the last three months, and calculating the average. The average is then taken as the forecast of the next month. For each succeeding month, then, the average is taken from a different group of months.

Other systems may involve projections of economic changes and the relationship of sales of certain products to these changes. Economic climate, the mood of the country or market, which styles are fashionable, who can afford them—these are some of the more important factors used in consumer goods forecasting.

By whatever system is used, the marketing manager develops a forecast of probable sales of specific products and probable sales expense, including advertising, personal selling, and sales promotion, which may be incurred in the forthcoming period. These data become the basis for the company sales budget projection.

PRODUCTION *Production budgets* are built on the anticipated sales volume. Once the information is available from the sales organization on anticipated demand, the production department can begin to prepare its plans for the forthcoming period.

The demand as forecast by the marketing people will affect the rate of operation of all production facilities. It will also affect the inventory situation within the production department. For example, in some operations, on the basis of a production demand over a three-month period, a production department might find it more economical to operate at a fast rate for a while and then shut the equipment down for a short time, allowing the sales to come from inventory. In other operations, the production department might find it better to hold the inventory level static and reduce the rate of operation to meet the sales demands. It is incumbent on the production people to make such analyses so that they can schedule manpower and raw material purchases consistent with the most economical form of operation. Too much raw material or semifinished goods in process, or an oversupply of labor, all spell expense with consequent reduction in profit.

In the preparation of the data that will ultimately be used in the enterprise budget, supervision plays an important role. Supervisors may be called on to determine the most efficient operation of their particular production equipment and to estimate the manpower they will require and the inventory levels of raw materials and finished products that seem to be consistent with this measurement. As in sales forecasting, this information will move further up the management hierarchy through general foremen, superintendents, and finally to the plant managers, each level will adjust the figures in the light of its overall analysis of the anticipated environment.

The plant manager, taking into account the study of past performance, union contract provisions, inventories, space physically available, cost of storage, and similar factors, will complete his or her examination and correction of these cost estimates and deliver them to the financial manager.

Doing this allows the plant manager to provide any other useful information to help the financial manager, such as cash demands that may be necessary during the forthcoming period for equipment repair, purchase of unusual quantities of raw materials because of availability at a low price, or similar items that will have a distinct effect on the cash requirements.

INVENTORY CONTROL

The management of *inventories*—which are (1) raw materials, (2) work in process, and (3) finished goods—is an important factor in the short-term liquidity position and longer-term profitability of the enterprise. Inventories represent a major investment of working capital and frequently constitute a major portion of the total assets of the corporation. Therefore their importance cannot be discounted. The firm must have the right amount of inventory on hand at the right time to meet the demand. The inventory must be salable in the short run.

In the adjustment of investment in inventories, the sales/marketing and production groups frequently may have different philosophies. The financial manager may be forced to take a strong position in order to keep from investing too much. The sales manager is primarily oriented toward sales volume and customer satisfaction. Both of these are achieved primarily by having the goods at all times available to meet the customer's needs. If the goods are out of stock, the sales manager's attitude is that he or she has lost a sale. Therefore the tendency of all sales managers is to strive toward high inventories of product.

Production managers normally like long production runs. These runs reduce the number of times production managers must expend money for setup costs in certain types of operations and also allow them to make inventory raw material purchases as economically as possible by buying large quantities. Both of these items—infrequent cash outlay and large-scale purchases—reduce the unit cost, which is what production managers strive for. However, both of these items tend to raise the average level of all kinds of inventories carried by the enterprise.

The holding of inventory is costly. In addition to tying up money that might otherwise be used for capital investment, it requires the payment of interest. The matter of inventory level is such an irritant in many corporations that when economic conditions tighten, the tendency often is to sell off the inventories or allow them to decrease rapidly, thereby freeing cash. Frequently this may be the wrong move, because when situations become serious financially, the loss of inventories may weaken the competitive position of a company. When this happens, the loss of sales will further decrease the profitability and a snowball effect results. Therefore inventories should not be reduced without an adequate study of the overall effect.

Various techniques have been developed for estimating the demand for products and, therefore, the probable level for carrying inventory. The inventory development system is somewhat different in industrial sales from the system in consumer product sales. With respect to industrial sales, much emphasis is placed on the judgment of the sales and production people. In the case of consumer sales, and particularly retail sales, a concept such as probability analysis may be used in order to determine the optimum inventory levels required. What is the probability that a given style will become fashionable? Which color will be popular?

Another system used is that of the *economic order quantity*. This system quantitatively balances benefits against cost and requires an analysis for determining the optimum production run. Buying or producing large quantities reduces the order cost or the setup cost per period, but it raises the average inventory and its carrying costs. Small orders or shorter production runs reduce the carrying costs by reducing the average inventory level, but raise its value for the period because of reordering costs and setup costs.

The financial manager, then, must secure data through the help of both sales and production people to determine, under the estimated sales and production, the most economic inventory levels for the forthcoming period.

PRODUCTION COST BUDGETS

The terms *production* and *manufacturing* are quite often used interchangeably. However, production has a much broader meaning and includes all activities in which something of value is created. On the other hand, manufacturing generally means the production of tangible goods such as chemicals, metals, cars, and foods. We devote our discussion here to the production of goods, or manufacturing, but most of the concepts are the same as those used in distribution and retailing organizations.

ELEMENTS OF PRODUCTION COSTS
We have earlier mentioned the cost of goods sold. Let us now look more closely at one element of this: cost of goods manufactured. The manufacturing costs for a given operating period are the sum of the raw materials used, labor, factory overhead, and capital costs. The last item represents the cost of the equipment required to convert raw materials into finished products.

Let us examine each of these more closely. Raw materials are the chemicals, steel, and partially manufactured goods that are acquired for conversion into an article of value or for upgrading. As we have previously noted, it is necessary to buy some raw materials in excess of current usage so that there will be an inventory against which the production people may work. To determine the raw material used during the month and its cost, we could set up a formula that reads somewhat as follows: Raw material cost = Value of beginning material inventory plus Purchases of additional raw materials, minus Value of ending raw material inventory.

Our main concern in production management is how efficiently we convert the raw materials actually consumed into salable finished products. Therefore this manager is more concerned with the raw materials consumed. However, we have noted that the financial manager is more interested in how many of these raw materials we keep in stock.

Labor costs represent those elements of direct labor involved in the unloading and handling of raw materials, the conversion of raw materials into a finished product, and the handling and loading of the finished product. In some companies the first and third items of labor are included in other factory costs or in overhead costs. Of course, if they are included as part of direct labor cost, then the monthly cost figures will not be wholly accurate since some of the raw materials may have gone into storage and some of the finished products may be in storage at the end of the period. Therefore it is normally preferable to include only direct labor in this item.

Labor costs are provided to the financial manager for inclusion in his or her overall budget through time sheets and the allocation of man-hours of labor to various activities. Even through this mechanism, however, an absolutely clear picture of the amount of labor involved is not necessarily obtainable. At the beginning and end of the month, there will be partially finished materials, which are called *work in process.* By normal accounting procedures, some of this labor will be carried into the work in process item. How much to carry in is frequently a matter of discussion among financial and production executives. Some companies, to be very conservative, value their work in process at only raw material value, putting all of the labor costs against the materials produced during the period of time in question.

Also recognize that all of the labor utilized during that month did not go against the goods that were sold that month. This is because there may have been a change in the volume of finished goods inventoried, and since this carries labor cost, there would be a certain amount of the labor allocated to this product.

Capital cost allocation of the investment is identified as depreciation of the tangible fixed assets. Although these are noncash costs they are vitally important in computing the overall corporate profits. Depreciation rates are established by the financial manager frequently in consultation with an auditing firm or with the Internal Revenue Service. Having identified the rate of depreciation and the capital invested, it becomes a simple matter to determine a depreciation figure to use each month. Depreciation alerts the management to the fact that a cash outlay for replacing equipment and/or improving current equipment will be needed in the coming years. In effect, it represents the accumulation of income from current sales for use at a later date for replacement of current investment.

Other factory costs include several items. Almost all operations require a certain amount of supplies. These may be oil, gasoline, cleaning cloths, paint, and so on. These supplies are normally classified as indirect factory costs.

No operation can proceed without a certain amount of maintenance and repair. The maintenance cost of a given unit is normally determined by an allocation of a portion of the materials and labor employed by the maintenance department.

Most operations require heat, light, and/or power in order to produce goods. Where this item can be determined specifically for a given production operation, it is allocated to it.

Some operations utilize indirect labor that comes from a central pool much in the same way that maintenance and repair labor does. Frequently this labor is allocated as a direct cost, depending on the number of men used. These employees may be used for cleanup work, handling of materials, and similar activities.

There are a number of other costs that cannot be allocated directly against a given production unit. They are normally accumulated for an entire plant and are known as overhead costs. They frequently include salaries for such people as the plant manager, superintendent, personnel manager, secretaries, clerks, accounting department personnel, safety department personnel, procurement department personnel, insurance, and taxes. Since these items are not specifically identifiable to a segment of a plant, the normal practice is to accumulate them for the entire plant and then to allocate them in proportion to the direct labor that each segment of the plant uses. Direct labor is used as the allocating mechanism because it is measurable with reasonable accuracy.

DIRECT MATERIAL COSTS

Let us now look at the source of data on *direct material costs* and the role that the supervisor has in providing this information. In our raw material cost formula, we noted that raw material inventories are required at the beginning and the end of a period in order to figure this cost. The securing of this information is frequently the responsibility of a supervisor. If the supervisor is in a chemical plant, then at perhaps 7 A.M. on the first day of each month, the supervisor will read all the gauges and determine the inventory of raw materials in the plant. If the supervisor is in a plant using solid materials or partly finished materials, this information will probably be secured by a personal inspection of the items involved.

There are occasions, however, when physical inventories are too difficult to perform routinely on a monthly basis. In such cases they may be performed quarterly or even annually. When this occurs, estimates are made of the beginning and ending inventories. These are corrected at the time of an actual, physical inventory.

These data are normally put together by a clerk and forwarded to the accounting department. None of the data that come out in the financial statement are any better than the quality of information provided by the supervisor.

The other item of the equation is raw material purchases. This information is also frequently supplied by the manufacturing unit; it will keep a record of all purchased materials that arrive during a given income statement period. These materials may or may not have been actually paid for, but their costs are recorded as purchases for the sake of the income statement. A freight figure is needed to adjust these to total cost, and this may come either from the producing unit or from the purchasing department.

The supervisor will perform another function here in the determination of the in-process inventories at the beginning and ending of the period. If the supervisor is in a chemical operation, this determination is quite complex; the composition of the materials may be different at the beginning and at the end of the period. Deciding what is the real value of these materials often causes considerable discussion. In the solid-product industry this is an equally difficult problem. For example, a radio chassis partially completed would require considerable work to determine all the elements involved in the product at that particular time. It may be easier to establish a standard value for this in-process material. Since we are dealing with dollars, this works satisfactorily.

In both the liquid-product raw materials and the solid-product raw materials, there will be losses. These may be due to spills in the chemical industry, or due to defective products or pilferage in the solid-material industry. If the total amount of direct materials used is obtained from purchases and inventory changes data exclusively, then any losses will indicate a greater apparent consumption of direct materials than might actually be true.

Although these losses must be paid for in the long run, it is important from an analytical standpoint to know whether part of the raw material use was due to losses. Therefore the supervisor finds it advantageous to report any definitely known losses. This allows the supervisor to report accurately the raw materials used and, therefore, to obtain a better idea of the efficiency of the unit.

DIRECT LABOR COSTS

Direct labor normally indicates labor that can be assigned directly to the manufacturing process. In a typical plant this will be the men who operate the machines and sometimes the supervisor. Since many other costs are apportioned to the direct labor cost, it becomes an important element.

The supervisor may be called upon to allocate certain portions of the time of his or her people to specific operations producing a product. The supervisor bears the responsibility of seeing that these allocations are accurately made. The supervisor may bear the further responsibility of signing time sheets indicating that this does represent the amount of work that was expended. If the supervisor feels the distribution is impossible, then he or she should bring this to the attention of his or her immediate supervisor.

In large, continuous-process chemical factories, once the direct labor allocations have been agreed on, there is frequently little change from week to week or month to month. The same is true in continuous mechanical manufacturing processes.

In job shops or small industries requiring a switch from one product to another in short periods of time, direct labor allocations will vary sometimes from day to day, week to week, and month to month. These areas, in particular, require us to have a clear understanding of what really constitutes direct labor costs.

Since labor is frequently a major portion of production costs in this country, it becomes a target of efficiency studies. This is still another reason why the allocations must be made as carefully as possible. If the information is inaccurate, then any improvements in efficiency become difficult to determine. The supervisor becomes the major link in this information chain.

No operation can run for long without maintenance work being performed. If possible, this maintenance labor is allocated against a unit since it occurs in the improvement of the operation of some specific unit. Because it is allocable, maintenance labor is frequently included along with direct operating labor in determining the direct labor figure.

FACTORY OVERHEAD COSTS

Factory overhead costs represent those items that cannot be assigned directly to a particular product, product line, or specific function. They are normally allocated or prorated on the same basis as direct labor.

Manufacturing overhead costs are frequently broken into variable and fixed costs.

Variable Costs

Indirect labor may vary with the rate of production. This item covers labor involved in handling materials in process, labor involved in handling raw materials and finished products, and labor involved in clean-up. Since all of these costs are somewhat difficult to assign against a specific operation in the multiproduct plant, they are included in overhead costs. Because they may be affected by the production rate, we consider them variable.

Heat, light, and power are also considered *variable costs*. Their consumption in some plants, however, may be a virtually fixed item. Let us consider two examples. In a chemical plant, heat and power are particularly important factors in running the operation. Since power is normally electrical, light is lumped with this item. The amount consumed will vary with rate of production.

However, in a small mechanical-process factory employing a minimum of tools, heat, light, and power may have little to do with production. The heat may vary with the time of year as will the light (depending on when the lights must be turned on). Therefore the supervisor of each particular operation will have to decide into which category these particular items fall.

Supplies are partially fixed and partially variable. Supplies sometimes mean paper, pencils, cleaning cloths, and so forth. On the other hand, they may mean small items utilized in the process that cannot necessarily be called raw materials. In most cases, their use will vary somewhat with the amount of operation.

Fixed Costs

Insurance and taxes are normally levied regardless of the rate of operation. It should be pointed out, however, that they may have a variable element; if a company carried an amount of insurance depending on the raw materials or finished products on hand, this would vary by production output and might be related to production. Likewise, if the area happens to have an inventory tax, the amount paid might well be related to production. But for the most part, they are fixed costs.

The wages and salaries of certain indirect labor such as the plant manager, his foremen, accounting people, personnel people, and other indirect hourly or salaried personnel are essentially *fixed costs*. These people would still be employed regardless of the volume of output.

Depreciation is also considered a fixed cost. This represents a figure outlining the amount of money acceptable to the Internal Revenue Service as representing the accounting reserve of funds required to replace the currently operating equipment. The acceptable rate will vary for buildings and equipment. These figures are normally determined by the finance department and/or auditing firm. Past experience with the Internal Revenue Service normally indicates what will be acceptable.

In practice, the breakdown between variable and fixed cost is not important except for the development of a *break-even chart* as shown in Figure 7-1. Here there is some value in trying to consider the distinction. Normally, however, these overhead costs are summed up at the end of the month and allocated back to the individual parts of the operation on a pro rata basis relative to the direct labor cost in a particular operation. This system is arbitrary, but is helpful in developing a reasonable idea of the total cost of production between corresponding units.

As seen in Figure 7-1, a total fixed costs are shown as a straight line. By definition, total fixed costs would not vary at a given production rate. Total variable costs increase as quantity increases. The total revenue line beginning at the apex in the lower left hand corner shows a direct rela-

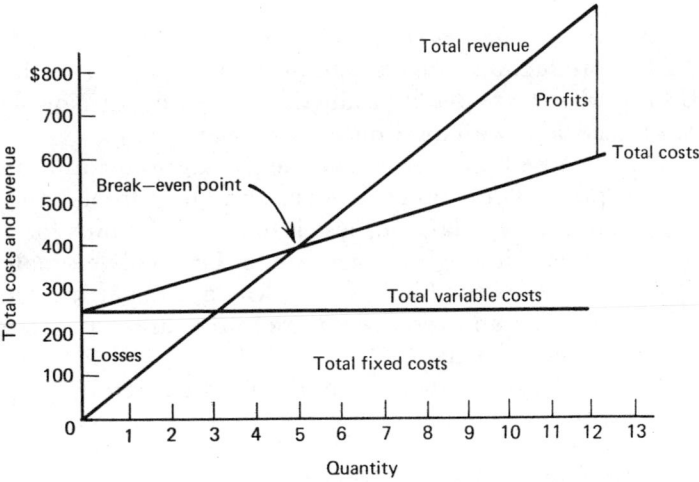

Figure 7-1 Example of a break-even chart.

tionship between quantity (x axis) and cost and revenue (y axis). The intersection of the total revenue line and the total costs line indicates the break-even point. Producing, at that quantity, at these given costs, would be just sufficient to cover all known costs.

DETERMINING FACTORY RATE

With the procedures outlined above, it is then possible for the financial department to accumulate the direct materials used, the labor costs, and the overhead costs allocable to any given product line. The supervisor can then receive a monthly report of the cost of production of each product line under his supervision. This may be broken down into raw materials, direct labor, and factory overhead costs.

It is quite likely that in the larger companies these costs will appear in the form of a computer printout. In smaller companies, these costs may be typewritten numbers incorporated into a form.

The financial department may report these costs to the manager as the factory cost versus a standard that has been developed from the current year's budget and a *variance* or difference from the standard. His or her boss may then ask the supervisor for an explanation each month as to why he or she had deviated from the standard, which is called *management by exception*.[1] The more a supervisor knows about any unusual losses encountered during the month that may have affected raw material cost or any unusual efficiency factors that may have affected labor costs, the more the supervisor can judge why costs have deviated. This will help the supervisor plan for further improvements in future months by knowing what has caused his or her problems in a past month.

USE OF BUDGETS FOR CONTROL

COMPARISON OF BUDGETED AND ACTUAL COSTS

In this chapter we have spoken of profit planning involving sales budgets, production budgets, and inventory budgets. We have examined in somewhat more detail production cost budgets. Now let us consider what can be done with these once they are available.

A well-planned budget helps management in several ways. Perhaps its primary function is to serve as a guide in planning financial operations. But a secondary purpose is to establish limits for departmental expenditures. Although budgets are, at best, only estimates, they are usually accepted as the limits within which a department must operate. If there must be an overexpenditure in one area, an attempt is made to curtail expenses in another area.

Another important purpose of a carefully prepared budget is to encourage administrative officials to make a careful analysis of all existing

---

[1] This concept is discussed later in the chapter and also in Chapter 8 on decision making.

operations. On the basis of their analyses, present practices may be justified and even expanded, eliminated, or restricted. We shall review here a more limited comparison between budgeted and actual cost in a production operation.

Direct Material Costs   Probably monthly, the financial department will provide the production unit with its direct material cost figures. The report may also show the budgeted direct material costs. To be useful, these figures are per unit of product. In the case of chemical operations, there may be a host of incoming raw materials, certain proportions of which are supposed to be used per pound of finished product. In the case of a mechanical or electronic operation, there may be a certain number of parts per unit of finished product.

The supervisor, upon receiving this information, is in a position to study in detail how costs for the month in question differed from those that were budgeted. He or she may find that there have been changes in raw materials cost that affect the dollars per unit even though the pounds or gallons per unit of finished product have not changed. This alerts the supervisor to the fact that he or she may need to look for substitute raw materials in order to keep costs in line. The supervisor has, then, a tool by which he or she can investigate his or her performance in some depth with the objective of improving the operation each month; this is the advantage of practicing management by exception. Such information is highly useful in pointing up efficiency changes due to poor operating equipment. This may mean that the equipment should be replaced with a new unit, or it may mean that more adequate maintenance is required. But in any event, it is a tool that draws the supervisor's attention to the problem.

Direct Labor Costs   As previously mentioned, this is a very important figure because certain overhead costs are allocated against it. Again, when supervisors receive their figures for the month, they can look at the direct labor costs involved in the various product lines under consideration. As in the case of raw materials, they may find that they are deviating from the standard because of a wage decrease that was not planned at the time of budgeting. On the other hand, they may find that their units of labor are higher than budgeted. With this tool they can investigate what has happened to bring about this change. They can then determine whether it is a correctable item or not. If they find that it is not correctable, then it is important for them to see whether there is any need for modification through use of new equipment or new processes that will improve the situation.

Again, a budget is only a tool. It serves no useful purpose in its own right other than to alert the supervisor to cost changes.

Overhead Costs On the information sheet furnished supervisors, will be found an allocation of overhead costs to their product line. They may find that the allocation is higher than they had budgeted. They must then go back to study the independent elements of the overhead costs. They will look to see whether their variable overhead costs are out of line compared to the production rate, or they will examine to see if the fixed costs have been raised for some reason unknown to them. Although supervisors cannot directly control these overhead costs, they are in a position to point out to plant management the effect that these costs are having on their operation. This becomes a powerful tool for alerting the plant management to the effects of overhead on costs.

VARIANCE We have said that we are looking at a comparison between the actual data for a given month and the preestablished standard data. For the sake of comparison here, we have used the standard data as those data developed for the budget. In some operations, however, standard data are developed through standard costing or other methods.

In cost accounting, the difference between actual and standard data is called a *variance*. The words *variance* and *difference* may be used interchangeably.

As we have shown previously, the use of variances from budgeted or standard data allows us to decompose a total difference in cost into its elements. The study of these elements helps us to plan effective action. Detailed descriptions of the use of variance factors may be found in many books on management accounting and financial mangement.

MANAGEMENT BY EXCEPTION

A management control system operated on the exception system is one in which management's attention is focused on the relatively small number of items in which actual performance is significantly different from the standard, or budgeted, amount. In such cases, little or no attention is given to the relatively large number of situations where performance is satisfactory as indicated by the financial records.

Unfortunately, no financial control system can make a perfect distinction between the situation that attracts management's attention and situations that do not. The exception system may point out certain items that significantly exceed the budgeted amount but that, according to investigation, were entirely warranted. On the other hand, an item that happens to match the budgeted amount may, upon closer investigation, prove to represent an unsatisfactory situation. For example, the cost of a raw material might have significantly decreased, but poor performance may have caused the monthly figure to just equal the budget figure. Therefore the principle of management by exception must be handled with some care. Nevertheless, management by exception has become a useful tool that signals the need for a follow-up investigation, and many books and articles have been written dealing with its practice.

ZERO-BASE BUDGETING (ZBB)

Zero-base budgeting is a new technique for controlling discretionary costs more effectively.[2] It was developed in 1970 by Texas Instruments, Inc., and spread rapidly to other companies and many governments. ZBB requires that each expenditure must be rejustified every time the budget is made. Previous budgeting techniques had simply carried items forward at "last years" level regardless of productivity or environmental changes. It integrates the planning and budgeting process, and causes managers at every level to put expenditures in some priority order, rather than continually adding appropriations and never cutting any. Supervisors may well be required to make such hard decisions if their company adopts ZBB.

SUMMARY

Three of the major tools in financial control are the income statement, the balance sheet, and the cash flow statement. The income statement or profit and loss statement records how a firm's financial progress is accumulating over a period of time. The balance sheet is a picture of the firm at a given time. The cash flow is used to determine cash income and cash expenditures, or where the cash is coming from and how it is spent.

We have noted the importance of the marketing people in preparing a sales budget as a guideline for the preparation of production inventory budgets. These budgets represent the best estimates that can be made by the various operating units within the economic and environmental situation predicted.

When the sales budget is available, it becomes possible to set production rates and to produce estimates on various elemental costs of production. These costs include direct material, direct labor, and a host of allocable items incorporated in factory overhead.

Once these budgeted figures have been obtained, a useful control can be built around comparison of actual figures with budget figures. These are only tools to help management and the supervisor pinpoint areas of difficulty. It must be remembered that the numbers are not absolute and that they should be considered as useful tools.

[2]P. A. Pyhrr, "Zero-Base Budgeting," *Harvard Business Review*, Vol. 48, No. 6, pp. 111-121, November-December 1970.

KEY CONCEPTS

Profit planning and the supervisor. Profit planning combines sales, production, and all the support functions necessary to produce a product or to provide a service at a profit. Supervisors are involved in the cost side of this planning process. What they do can help either to increase or to decrease the costs in their department. Without a profit, the firm may not survive.

Accounting records and the supervisor. Accounting records are tools to be used to control an activity. Accounting records are generally historical facts that can be used to predict the future. Budgets, on the other hand, are estimates of future costs and require planning input by the supervisor. These records are used for the financial control of a supervisor's operation and to make future decisions.

Financial control. Conceptually, this type of control is based on quantifiable measures. Usually a dollars-and-cents measure is the common expression. Thus financial control cannot be used directly or effectively when certain activities—that is, morale, people investment, and job satisfaction—are important to the supervisor. However, financial control data do provide a specific tool that the supervisor may use as a standard measure within his department.

Budgets. As estimates of the future, all budgets are based on the sales forecast. If the sales forecast is inaccurate, necessary changes in the production budget or the allocation of funds to specific production operations may change. Conceptually, supervisors should realize that this eventuality may take place and should prepare to remain flexible in planning budgetary items.

Management by exception. This is the managerial technique of having established policy or, as discussed in this chapter, cost standard by which a supervisor can determine if some activity is not up to par. Subordinates do not have to check with the supervisor if policy and standards are established. When an exception occurs, then supervisors can give special attention to this exception.

Zero-base budgeting. This is a new technique for controlling discretionary costs more effectively. It integrates the planning and budgeting process, and causes managers at every level to put expenditures in some priority order.

IMPORTANT TERMS

Accounting system	Balance sheet equation
Acid test ratio	Break-even chart
Balance sheet	Capital stock

Cash budget
Current ratio
Debt-equity ratio (leverage effect)
Direct labor costs
Direct raw material costs
Double entry accounting
Economic order quantity
Fixed costs
Inventories
Inventory control
Leverage effect
Management by exception
Overhead—factory and/
   or manufacturing
Production cost budget
Profit-and-loss statement
   (income statement)
Profit planning
Retained earnings
Return on equity
   (return on net worth)
Sales forecast
Variable costs
Variance
Working capital
Zero-base budgeting

INCIDENTS

What Price Intermediates?

John Dancy is plant manager of a plant producing alkylated phenols, a raw material for liquid detergents. The process is new and is the main product line of the plant. The plant is suffering losses of $150,000 per month and John is continually looking for ways to improve his situation.

In production of alkylated phenols he is dealing with two major raw materials and one finished product. In the production of the finished product, however, the process goes through several intermediate steps. These so-called "intermediates" must be valued in some manner so that the cost of production can be determined by the end of the month.

A lot of judgment is required in determining what price to place on these intermediates. If the price is too low then the cost of production of the finished product will be higher and the loss at the plant will be greater. If high values are placed on the intermediates, then a lower cost of finished product will be shown and the loss will be reduced.

Mr. Dancy, in the course of operation of a year or so, has been tempted to place ever-higher values on the intermediates in order to alleviate these losses. The intermediates contain certain by-products and he continually hopes that something of value might turn up from them.

But now the day of reckoning has arrived since auditors have just completed a review of his plant and made a report to the home office. They have reported that the intermediates are overstated in value and should have their value reduced immediately.

Mr. Dancy has been called to the vice-president's office to explain how he managed to get into such a situation and more importantly how he is going to get out of it. To reduce the value of the intermediates will cause what are known as "write-offs," meaning significantly higher losses for the plant.

How would you react in John Dancy's position? What would you tell the vice-president? Has the accounting system served as a valuable tool in uncovering this potential difficulty? Are there ethical matters involved?

Hoffman Manufacturing Company's New Department Cost System

Hoffman Manufacturing Company was in the business of producing plumbing and pipe-fitting equipment. Gary Hoffman, the owner's son, believed it was necessary to increase the control of costs. He believed a new method for cost control was required.

Young Hoffman decided to start in the valve department because it produced 40 percent of the firm's sales revenue. The valve department had three sections that included various types of machines such as drilling, grinding, welding equipment, and lathes. An assembly space was provided. Clark found that all the factory costing in the valve department (excluding material costs) was done on a departmentwide, direct, labor-hour basis. That is, each lot of products going through the department was costed at a certain rate for each direct labor hour spent on the lot.

Hoffman believed this type of costing was too loose and did not provide the necessary control to run the department more effectively. He proposed that costs be apportioned to jobs according to the amount of time spent in each section of the department.

When young Hoffman's proposal was explained to the heads of the operating department, it met with immediate and strong opposition. The strongest voices were heard from the supervisors of other departments who had work done by the valve department each month. They thought it unfair to change a sizable part of their departments' costs particularly since they had no control over the costs in the valve department.

Mr. Hovelman, supervisor of the pipe-fixture department, adamantly stated, "The valve department does my machinery work or all overload work my department can't handle. If you raise the costs on this work, I won't be able to stay within my budget. The valve department is already overcharging me more than what it costs me to do the work. If I had the capacity, I'd do it myself."

Lenore Jones, the supervisor of the valve department, voiced opposition to the plan. She said, "I'm too busy with getting out the production to fool around with more paper work. The department is carrying all its costs now. Why put in more work for my section leadman? They're too busy already."

What benefits does young Hoffman hope to derive from the new system? Are the supervisors right in their contention that the present system is fine? What would you say, under the circumstances illustrated in the incident? Do you believe it should be necessary for supervisors to have to defend their department from staff people?

QUESTIONS FOR DISCUSSION

1. Why is profit planning important in the operation of business? Why is an accounting system important in the operation of a business? What does it consist of?
2. Describe how the balance sheet can be used to provide information on the health of a business.
3. What constitutes the cash budget? Of what value is it to the decision-making process?
4. In developing a profit plan where does one start? Why is this the necessary and important starting point?
5. Do inventory levels play an important role in the operation of the business? If so, why?
6. As a supervisor in a plant, discuss what contribution you can make to the preparation of the budget.
7. Is direct labor an important element in budget preparation? Discuss why it may or may not be.
8. Discuss the role that material cost plays in budget preparation.
9. Explain the construction of a break-even chart. What is its value?
10. Zero-base budgeting has become a buzzword in recent years. What is its most important characteristic?

CHAPTER VIII
Decision Making and the Supervisory Function

LEARNING OBJECTIVES

- *To understand the decision-making process.*
- *To know the critical steps in the process.*
- *To understand a supervisory application of the decision-making process.*

Introduction

The managerial functions of planning, organizing and controlling are important concepts for the supervisory level of management to use and to understand. Much of the planning and organization, however, is performed at higher levels of management, and what remains for supervisors may not occupy the majority of their time. Understanding the immediate environment for purposes of control and coordination provides the constraints that keep supervisors and their department from doing whatever they care to do. Thus far, these are the tools for performing the managerial functions entrusted to the supervisor. As important as these functions may be, decision making is used more often by the supervisor than any other managerial functions described so far. The decision-making process and the supervisory use of it are the subjects of this chapter.

Supervisors are constantly called on to make decisions. Someone must recognize that problems do exist that may affect the department; someone must choose a solution, "live" with the action, and appraise the result. Many of the problems faced by the supervisor may be routine or may occur frequently. These situations can be *routinized* or *systema-*

tized, or a policy can be established that would provide a ready solution. In these repetitive situations the decision-making process is used at the beginning and then the solution is repeated over time. Exceptions to these established routines or policies become the difficult decisions that have to be made by the supervisor. This is called *management by exception* (also discussed in Chapter 7). These are individualized or nonroutine decisions or courses of action that someone in management must determine. Since these exceptions pop up everyday, this chapter will concentrate on solving the exceptional problems (which require management by exception) as well as new problems that constantly bombard a supervisor. This may sound overpowering. If these decisions could be made by a computer or by policy, would we even need a supervisor? Obviously the answer is no. The fact remains that some supervisors tend to shy away from making decisions and relegate themselves to playing traffic cops. By policing established policy, this type of supervisor merely interprets rules and regulations. We must have rules, but rules are not the managers/supervisors' only concern. They must manage the department, work crew, or section. Their job requires a strong working knowledge of how to make decisions that they can live with and achieve the planned objectives.

All supervisors make decisions since this is a vital function of being a manager. But making a decision can have many far-reaching results. A supervisory decision may affect the technical performance of a specific job, office, or plant. A decision may influence society such as the deletion of a new product or the addition of a product that fails, costing the firm and eventually society a sacrifice. Supervisory decision making is very pertinent to the firm's future success as well as influential to society's well-being.

Decision making is a skill that can be learned. Natural skill and intelligence are very helpful, but a person can become proficient in this skill with practice, effort, and understanding. The essentials of the managerial decision-making function performed by the supervisor involve making day-to-day decisions that affect the workers in the department, the allocation of effort, the materials to be used on the job, and how to do what, where, and when.

The supervisor's skill in decision making can also influence the employee's ability to use the same skill. Most employees learn and develop by observing their immediate superior. Good decision making by supervisors can foster and encourage good decision making by subordinates. This proficiency can pay substantial dividends because workers may not be able to call or contact the supervisor in every situation so that the supervisor can make all the decisions on the job. Workers may be forced to become involved in the decision process whether they like it or not. Practical training for the workers in decision making can be beneficial for the department's operating efficiency.

THE DECISION-MAKING PROCESS

Making a decision is relatively simple, but determining *how* to make a decision is complex. A decision can be a simple yes or no. A decision can be the choice of an alternative. The difficulty lies in what analysis precedes making the decision of yes or no or the choice of a specific alternative.

The nine steps in the decision process, as shown in Figure 8-1, are (1) determining that a problem exists, (2) recognizing and analyzing the problem, (3) determining workable solutions, (4) identifying key uncertainties, (5) gathering data, (6) estimating the value of each alternative or workable solution, (7) choosing a solution (8) taking action, and (9) following up the action.

DETERMINING THAT A PROBLEM EXISTS

Before we get into decision making, a few definitions have to be made to clarify the subject matter. The literature differs in its use of decision making and problem solving. We will use these terms, defined as follows. *Decision making is the process of making a choice between workable alternatives to solve a specific problem or situation.* Hence decision making is a part of problem solving. However, we have to determine if a problem exists before we can apply the tools of decision making. Here is where problem analysis comes into play. *A problem exists when the supervisor's desired state is below his or her actual state and the super-*

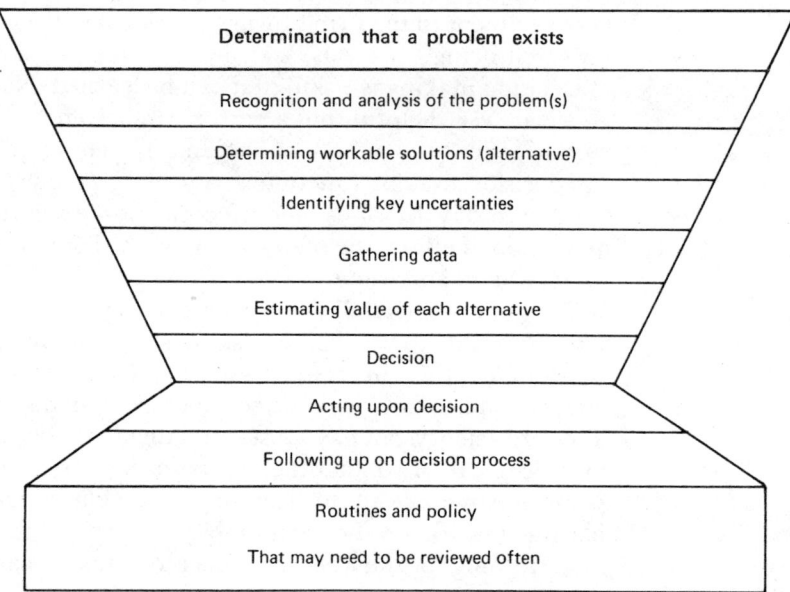

Figure 8-1   The decision-making process.

visor does not know what is causing this discrepancy. If a supervisor knows what *is* causing the discrepancy between the desired and actual states, then a problem doesn't exist, but a situation exists that requires a subsequent decision-making analysis to remove the discrepancy. Therefore, problem solving is the process for determining the cause of a problem and its subsequent decision-making process. This is illustrated in Figure 8-2.

RECOGNIZING AND ANALYZING THE PROBLEM

The first prerequisite of problem solving is to correctly *define the problem*. This might seem obvious. Some people say that problem recognition is easy; the hard part is the solution. This is—wrong. Supervisors and managers are too easily swayed by a solution orientation that forces them to belittle this first and most important step in the decision-making process. If a supervisor or employee doesn't solve the right problem, then all the activity up to this point has been wasted. The danger in decision making is that so many solutions are proposed or acted upon for problems that don't even exist. A flurry of activity, but no real solutions are achieved. We must be able to state the problem and determine what is causing it. This means recognition of the right problem.

The first step is to *define* the factors that are causing the trouble. We as individuals can recognize trouble, but most often we see the symptoms rather than the causal factors. If the symptoms are defined as the problem, all subsequent activity will only create more trouble and confusion. It can be rather frustrating to think we have solved a problem and then to see it reappear. For example, if two employees are constantly at each other's throat, each one complaining about the intrusion of the other on his or her work schedule, the symptoms may appear as a difference in personality or a personality clash. Or the supervisor could pass off the squabble as a political one. However, the real problem, or causal factor, could be more profound; the problem could be the supervisor's failure to delineate job duties between the two employees. If the problem of a personality clash were recognized, the solution could be to ignore, tolerate, or attempt to pacify the situation. This could be a painful experience for the supervisor and the two workers involved. If the real causal factors,

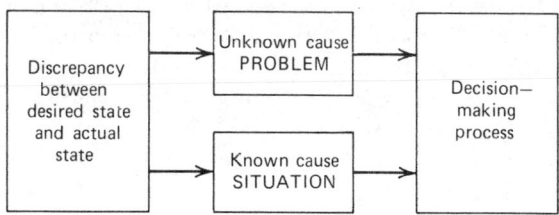

Figure 8-2 Problem solving analysis and decision making.

rather than the symptoms, were recognized as the problem, a different approach to solving the problem would be discovered. This problem definition means recognizing the causal factors by not confusing the symptoms of the problem with the problem itself. Like a medical doctor, the supervisor/decision maker must diagnose the problem correctly before prescribing the proper solution.

After problem definition, the problem has to be analyzed. *Analysis* in this instance means identifying the important facts relevant to the problem as defined. These facts can be tangible as well as intangible. Intangible elements would include morale, motivation, personal feelings, concepts, and impressions. The tangible factors could be activities such as the assignment of work, the work schedule, a conversation, or an order given by the supervisor.

DETERMINING WORKABLE SOLUTIONS

Now that the decision maker can identify the specific problem to be solved and can isolate the facts pertinent to the problem, the next step must be to search for and state workable alternative solutions. The term *workable* has been used here to preclude possible alternative solutions that are too expensive, are too time consuming, or require a truckload of fantasy to work out.

The best approach in determining *workable solutions* is to state all possible solutions and then eliminate the ones that are *not* workable. The remaining alternative solutions provide the basis for subsequent decision-making steps. Investigating all the possible routes helps to prevent eliminating the "most appropriate" one. A decision is as good as the best alternative solution evaluated.

Most problems faced by the supervisor will provide more than one or two workable solutions. By referring to the problem of the squabbling employees mentioned in the previous section, we can perhaps determine workable alternatives. Since the problem was defined as the supervisor's failure to identify the job duties of each employee, what possible activities are available to correct this situation? The supervisor could (1) call in the time and motion study people to do a study of both jobs; (2) perform a job analysis, by himself, with the assistance of the personnel office; (3) ask each employee to describe his or her own job, then analyze overlapping and duplicate duties; (4) ignore the problem and let it work itself out; (5) step in and get both workers together to thrash out the problems; or (6) transfer or replace the one employee who appears to be causing the most trouble. As you can see, this one problem has many workable alternatives. Undoubtedly the list has not exhausted *all* the workable alternatives for this problem. Can you think of more?

The important thing to remember in this step is to state or "brainstorm" all the workable alternative solutions without trying to analyze their value. A list of the alternatives should be made so it can be evaluated in a later step. Otherwise, the cart can get before the horse and a possible breakdown in the decision process could occur. Each step is a unique and discrete operation. The decision maker must concentrate on one thing at a time. This way his efficiency and effectiveness can be maximized.

IDENTIFYING KEY UNCERTAINTIES   Key uncertainties refer to unknowns that are the result of pure chance. Regardless of the solution chosen, the chance variables or key uncertainties would play an important role. These variables could prove to be pluses or minuses. To illustrate, let us see what key uncertainties could exist in the case of the disgruntled employees. If the supervisor investigated the two jobs, what would the other employees think or demand? They could force and identification of all the jobs in the section. Another chance variable could be the reaction of both or either one of the employees involved. What would happen to their productivity when they were investigated? Which way would these variables fall, relative to each of the workable solutions? Thinking out or reasoning by *a priori* means is an important step. This can be very helpful in making the final determination of the decision-making process.

GATHERING DATA   Often this step is included with the first or second, but for the supervisor's purposes and for better decision making, it has been separated. In order to improve the process, formal research of the gathering of facts should be postponed until the supervisor has thought out all aspects of the problem. This includes identification, statement, and analysis of the problem; a listing of all the workable solutions; and the identification of the key uncertainties of the problem. *Now the decision maker knows where he or she is going. How to get there becomes the function of the data-gathering step or the actual investigation of the problem.*

In the course of gathering data, it is quite possible that new insights will develop and lead the supervisor to return to earlier steps that might lead to a redefinition of the problem. Let's assume that, by talking with the two disgruntled workers, the supervisor learns that the problem is not laxity on the supervisor's part but the fact that supply of the material used by the two employees is erratic and undependable. Both workers were blaming each other for the delays and overlapping duties. This event could force the supervisor to set up new workable alternatives and identify new key uncertainties. But for the sake of simplicity, let's assume that the original problem prevails.

ESTIMATING THE VALUE OF EACH ALTERNATIVE   After reviewing the data gathered in the previous step, the supervisor must now analyze each alternative. He or she has to mentally test each alternative by judging the good and bad events that could occur if each alternative were put into effect. He or she has to simulate in his or her mind what would happen with each alternative and its effect on the system under investigation.

Certain probability factors must be considered in the evaluation of each alternative. The questions of the state of risk, the state of uncertainty, the state of ignorance have to be considered. Strictly speaking, there is no single best criterion for decision making where perfect knowledge of all the facts is present. Therefore a set of criteria must be used as determined by the supervisor for the problem at hand. *Risk* is a state of imperfect knowledge where the decision maker judges the different possible outcomes of each alternative and can determine the probabilities of success for each. In a state of *uncertainty*, the decision maker judges the possible outcomes of each alternative, but lacks any feelings for their probabilities of success. Here a supervisor wouldn't know, with any certainty, which alternatives would be the best. Often this situation exists when the supervisor is faced with a production problem, or where a choice between alternatives is present. *Ignorance* is a state in which the decision maker can't even judge the different possible outcomes, let alone their probabilities. This situation may be incurred when a supervisor is faced with a complex personnel problem involving personalities, minority status, ethnic backgrounds, educational backgrounds, or work expertise. Although these states tend to be theoretical, an analysis of this type can indicate to the supervisor the level of imperfect knowledge he is in and can show the possibility of achieving a successful outcome. If the third state, ignorance, prevails, the supervisor hasn't done his homework.

Another facet in evaluating each alternative is the aspect of timing. The probable outcome, its advantages versus its disadvantages, are affected by *when* the alternative solution may be implemented. The "most appropriate" alternative may be the one that is most appropriate at a given time. Following the disgruntled worker example, each alternative would be evaluated in depth as if it were the one being chosen at that time.

CHOICE OF SOLUTION

As the "moment of truth" arrives, the decision maker/supervisor has to make a choice. He/she alone must decide and stand responsible for the subsequent steps — implementing and following up the decision.

The supervisor must make a choice among the alternatives or compromise by choosing a combination of the various alternatives. The decision or choice can be assisted by the supervisor's experience, past judgment, advice from others, or even hunch (but with high probability of success); but the fact remains, he/she must "live with" the outcome. Study, analysis, and contemplation are necessary ingredients. Self-confidence is the best element for the supervisor to possess at this stage. The supervisor must be confident that he/she has the right problem, the most important workable solutions, the key uncertainties, proper data, and a proper evaluation of each alternative. If all these previous steps have not been fulfilled, then the choice can be painful. Often the supervisor does not have the time to back up or procrastinate a decision. They can't hide or shift the responsibility to someone else. The heat is on, but as former President Harry S Truman was credited with saying, "If you can't stand the heat, get out of the kitchen." So it is with the supervisor. She must make the decision. She must practice all the decisions steps effectively. Obviously, she is paid to make decisions. All of her decisions will not be perfect or even be right. We learn from our mistakes, but a poor practice of the decision-making art is one mistake that should *not* occur. Poor judgment is a human failing, but poor management cannot be tolerated very often in a profit-making organization or any organization that seeks to be efficiently run. In the case of the disgruntled worker, we should choose to do an informal job analysis in order to discover the overlapping job activities; this might seem the most appropriate of the various workable alternatives.

ACTION There is a long road between making a decision (determining a plan of *action*) and the action itself. The supervisor has to plan, organize, and control the actions so that the entire effort exerted on the preceding steps is not wasted by poor practice of the managerial functions. As a manager, the supervisor has to work with and through others, and this task may require communication, motivation, and leadership skills.

In the example of the disgruntled worker, the supervisor could initiate an informal job design by arranging an interview with each of the two workers. From the data and their analysis, a proper job design for each position could be drawn.

FOLLOW-UP After the action is taken to implement the decision, a *follow-up* and appraisal of the solution is necessary. This last step can take many forms, depending on the type of decision, the environment, working conditions, desires of superiors, the workers involved, and technical production problems.

Often reports are necessary for a supervisor's superior to learn of the decision's outcome. A very scholarly investigation and reporting of the results may be necessary.

Usually follow-up will only require a supervisory visit to the work station, desk, or section of the change or activity initiated by the decision. The main function of the follow-up is to determine that the problem has been resolved. If not, the supervisor may have to repeat the entire decision process if a new problem has been generated by the solution. It is better to discover this failure during the follow-up period rather than be unaware of a new problem provoked by the solution implemented. Unsuccessful follow-up can be very frustrating, but the other situation—the generation of a new problem—could mean the supervisor's terminal notice if it occurs too often.

A SUPERVISORY APPLICATION OF THE DECISION-MAKING PROCESS

The list of steps in the decision-making process may require a concrete illustration in order to be fully understood. The decision process is not a series of academic steps, but rather a proven process that can be applied in different degrees to numerous situations. Its worth can be measured by its timeliness in increasing the efficiency of the first-line supervisor in today's dynamic and ever-changing society.

We shall assume that a given situation exists that involves many of the contemporary problems faced by the modern supervisor. Then this situation will be analyzed and a solution will be recommended, as an illustration of applying the decision-making process described in this chapter.

SITUATION Tom Angus is an office manager of a small manufacturing firm in a large Midwestern city. The firm, Mason Manufacturing Company, acquired an electrical power generation unit that had been developed by two ex-soldiers while on overseas duty. The revolutionary aspect of the power generator was its portability. Competing instruments were fixed to the floor, but Mason's unit, the Benson Power Source, could be used to run power tools by garages, service stations, and repair crews when on emergency calls. Moreover, the portable power source could be used on farm calls or calls to remote areas. With a few attachments the unit could be connected to an automobile engine. Sales were rising very fast. During the rapid increase in sales, numerous problems began to appear.

Six months ago, the office employed two workers who kept books, did accounts receivable (A/R), prepared invoices, handled accounts payable (A/P), and wrote the payroll for the firm's 22 employees. Today 8 employees perform the same functions. Obviously the increase has been due to a rapid sales volume increase and a rapid increase in production facilities. The firm has been adding to its present manufacturing facilities by building corrugrated steel additions. The growth has been so rapid that the concrete hardly dries before the production line has moved onto the floor. This is an improvement over the previous method of expansion, when the production line was extended onto the dirt floor that held up the pouring of the concrete floor.

The office staff of eight are crowded into an office that measures 25 by 30 feet or 750 square feet. Tom Angus foresees further increases in sales, and he contemplates that he will have to hire additional personnel to handle the increased accounts receivable. credit checks, and payroll. Tom has to make a decision concerning what he should do before the office is inundated with paper work and employees.

IS THERE A ROBLEM? A problem does exist since Tom doesn't know what is really causing the discrepancy he experiences between an efficiently run office and the overcrowded predicament he is in. Tom may feel that he doesn't have a problem since he has pinpointed that the increased sales volume is the cause. If he feels he doesn't have a problem, then the analysis could stop here and Tom would continue to "muddle along." But Tom needs help. However, let's not get ahead of ourselves.

PROBLEM A first impression would indicate that the problem faced by Tom Angus is overcrowded conditions owing to the rapid growth of the Mason Manufacturing Company. On second thought, this problem could be a symptom. The overcrowded conditions are symptomatic of poor planning, poor leadership, and lack of a systematization of the office procedures. Sales orders, production facilities, and office personnel have grown in a linear relationship. As new orders come in, additional people are hired to type, work the bound ledger books, and post in the pegboard accounting systems.

The recognition of the problem and the casual factors creating the symptoms are the first step. The problem has to be defined. Remember, this is the most crucial step and probably the hardest. In this case it is necessary to design some sort of system that will practice economies of scale in the office production. We must find something that will break the lockstep in which Angus appears trapped. Therefore the statement of the problem is to search for and find a reasonable production system for the office so that increased business can be handled without increasing personnel.

After the definition of the problem, it becomes necessary to analyze and identify the important facts relevant to the problem. The production system will be simple compared with the intangible aspects of the present personnel. Without going into detail concerning the personalities of each of the eight workers in the office, suffice it to say that morale, motivation, fear of a new system, fear of the unknown will be very relevant variables.

ANALYSIS Once the problem and the important variables have been identified, next we have to determine the relevant, workable solutions. In this case we can "brainstorm" by spelling out all the possible, workable alternatives. They can be as follows.

1. Specialize the work of each worker.
2. Divide the workers into teams of two or three each, to work on specialized accounting routines, such as A/R, A/P, or payroll.
3. Install a wide-carriage calculator.
4. Install a computer.
5. Do nothing but expand supervisory control in hope that the workers expand their capacities to get out the work.

6. Place the workers on an incentive program with extra pay and/or a bonus tied to each unit of output.

Assuming that we have exhausted the workable alternative solutions, it now becomes necessary to identify key uncertainties. These appear to be the morale and motivational aspects of the present eight employees. Regardless of the alternative chosen, Tom Angus would still have to make it work. The present employees present a formidable obstacle that could short-circuit a successful change.

Next we have to gather data to solve the problem by choosing the best workable alternative. Here the question becomes: How can we get the best data? The mechanization of the office alternative could be to call in a factory representative from three firms who specialize in these applications. Second, an informal investigation with key people could be conducted. The investigation would seek to discover unrest that might exist among the workers, involve them in making a change, and present the needed change as a problem that they could help solve. Another method for gathering data would be to call in the firm's accountants for their advice and counsel. At this point we may not be sure that all the necessary data have been collected.

Other data that may be needed would involve the type of production improvements needed. A rearrangement of the desks, the available "canned accounting" systems, available support items to assist a billing clerk, and many other pieces of data may be required.

After the data are collected, we must evaluate each alternative listed above. Since there is no single best criterion, we must establish a set of criteria so that we can evaluate each of the alternatives. The states of risk, uncertainty, and ignorance should be included among these criteria. Timing of the alternatives' implementation is also essential. Each of the workable alternatives can now be evaluated. Notice that we evaluate each one by itself in the light of how it will affect the production system in the office.

1. Specialize the work of each worker. This presumes that Tom knows how to systematize the office routines. Immediately this alternative becomes spotty. The risk involved in using Tom as the systems man is far too great. Remember, risk is calculable in that we can judge the possible outcomes. This alternative is very unfavorable. Anyone who would get into a mess like this certainly can't get us out.
2. Specialize the operations of the workers by function in teams of two or three. Sounds good. The risk appears to be tolerable. Notice that ignorance is not involved. However, one important facet, the reaction of the girls and their abilities, remains an uncertainty. It is difficult to judge the probability of success as far as the workers are concerned. Therefore, because of the uncertainty, scratch this alternative.
3. Install a wide-carriage calculator. Sounds great, but who will install it? How much will it cost? How competent is the installer? How will the

workers react? Is the equipment suitable for the jobs that have to be done? A flurry of questions is provoked here, but Angus will not install the new system. This will be turned over to the experts at this sort of thing. Cost-benefit analysis may still require more analysis. Risk exists but can be calculated.
4. Install a computer. The same questions can be asked as before, but the major question is, How much better is a computer system relative to cost than a calculator? Risk still exists but can be calculated.
5. Do nothing. Absolutely not! Doing nothing has helped to create the problem that we are in. This alternative is out. Since a high degree of risk is known, increased supervision appears to be out as well. You can't squeeze blood out of a turnip.
6. Use an incentive program to get out the work. The major question is, Will it work? The problem and its variables tend to isolate an important element: the workers do not have the proper tools to increase their productivity. It appears that this alternative of using an incentive program has a high degree of uncertainty in that we cannot even judge any probability of success. Scratch this alternative.

The two best alternatives, numbers 3 and 4, appear to have survived the evaluation. More data must be collected to narrow the degrees of risk to a tolerable state. An important aspect in this subsequent analysis is to determine the timing of the implementation of either of the two systems.

For the sake of simplicity, we can say that we have contacted three companies that provided us with the data concerning analysis, support, cost, performance, and timing of the operation. This information is further evaluated against the decision maker's feelings of compatibility with each company's representative and the cost, performance, and delivery of each supplier's equipment. These data are as follows.

SOLUTION The moment of truth has arrived. After viewing each of the three systems as advocated by each of the three companies, the single choice is up to us. The data are laid out by each company. We have rated the performance of each, the cost of each, and how long it will be before starting on the new system. With this data, how would you make the choice and live with it? Will it be company A, B, or C? Our choice is company B. We need to get into operation as soon as possible. Company B gives a very satisfac-

Company	Type of Equipment	Cost ($)	Performance	Timing (Mo.)
A	Minicomputer	16,500	Very satisfactory	3
B	Minicomputer	7,600	Satisfactory	2
C	Calculator	1,300	Unsatisfactory	2

tory performance versus an outright purchase. Company C can be eliminated immediately. Company A requires three months, but its initial cost is much higher than Company B's. Timing has played a very important part in our analysis, in addition to initial costs.

Once the decision has been made, we must proceed to preparation of the workers, the office training, and completion of all the new systems. Action must be instituted immediately. If the workers see delay, they will build up more fear of the uncertainties involved. Thus Tom Angus should bring in the employees as soon as possible. Watching a demonstration of the chosen system would be an excellent means of involving the key workers. They can be enlisted to help with the change.

The last step in the solution phase would be the follow-up or "debugging" process once the new equipment has been installed. Most new systems take four to six months of close follow-up so that all the shortcomings can be overcome and all the unforeseen events can be corrected. Small problems may develop during this stage that require more decision making.

It is hoped that this example of a supervisory decision-making process has shown that a decision process does belong within the managerial tools of an effective supervisor. Decisions may not always be as complex as the one illustrated, but the process is the same. After defining the problem and establishing workable alternatives, the choice is made after each alternative is mentally carried out to completion. Then follow-up and appraisal must be made to determine that the problem has been solved.

SUMMARY

Decision making is one of the chief responsibilities of a supervisor. He/she is trained and paid to make decisions, such as planning, organizing, controlling, motivating, and leading. Many of the supervisor's problems can be solved by routinized or systematized procedures. Others will be a matter of policy or a set way of taking care of recurring problems. The important aspects of decision making for the supervisor will be managing the exceptions to policy and routine decisions. Here he/she needs to know how to make decisions.

Decision making is a skill that can be learned, and the good practice of it can influence the worker's ability to make better decisions.

The decision-making process has nine steps. First, you must (1) Determine that a problem exists. (2) The problem then has to be recognized and analyzed. This requires defining the specific problem and its causal factors, and the facts relevant to the problem. (3) A set of workable solutions has to be stated. (4) Key uncertainties have to be identified. These help to influence the outcome of any of the solutions. (5) Data have to be gathered that are relevant to the problem and its solution. (6) Each alternative solution has to be evaluated, using the data collected in the previous step. The evaluation takes each solution and attempts to simulate what would happen if it were chosen. The states of risk, uncertainty, and ignorance will help the decision maker to determine the probabilities of success for each alternative. Moreover, the timing of each solution's implementation is evaluated. (7) A choice of a solution is made with which the supervisor must "live." (8) Action must be taken to implement the solution. This may require more planning, organizing, and controlling to accomplish the task. (9) Finally, the decision must be followed up to see that it has worked out correctly.

The steps of the decision-making process are real and extremely useful for the supervisor. It is advisable that he learn and practice these steps so as to enhance his operating efficiency.

KEY CONCEPTS

Supervisory decision making. This concept is not an academic treatise, but a very real and practical aspect of the supervisor's job. Decision making requires intelligence, thought, and analysis. Knowing the logical steps can assist the supervisor's natural talents. Determining how to make a decision is a difficult task. The supervisor has to live with the course of action chosen.

The decision-making process. The eight steps are the elements of the process, but conceptually these steps build on the logical analysis involved in decision making. The logic becomes: Do we know what is causing the trouble? What is the trouble? Why is it causing trouble? What can be done in all possibilities? What are the probabilities of success of each of the actions or solutions? What is the proper choice? When can it be implemented? What is the best way to implement the solution? Has the activity to achieve the solution solved the original problem? If not, let's start over again. Also, the decision process is not a building-block approach, but can be a "push through and then pull back" to evaluate approach. Where data show the wrong problem has been identified, it may require that we discard all the work up to this time and take a fresh start.

IMPORTANT TERMS

Action follow-up
Action on solution
Key uncertainties
Ignorance
Management by exception

Problem definition
Routinized decisions
Risk
Uncertainty
Workable solutions

INCIDENTS

Fiddle, Faddle, or Frugality

Big Three Industries was formed in Cincinnati, Ohio, by three young men who desired to go into business for themselves. The initial business venture was the manufacturing and marketing of the Clarkson Tire Changer.

The tire changer was invented by John Clarkson and Tom Moore while they were stationed on a lonely South Pacific Island during World War II. The product had a stand on which the tire was placed so the operator could work at table height. This eliminated the drudgery of the prevalent method where the operator had to wrestle the tire on the floor. In addition, the Clarkson Tire Changer had all the tools that fit on the stand for breaking the tire rim from the wheel, depressing air from the tire, and reinflating the new tire. The time saved by the new tire changer over the old method was at least 60 percent. The readily demonstrable advantages of the Clarkson Tire Changer, the first of its kind on the market, enhanced its sale to garages, service stations, and automobile dealers.

Fred Jonkoff, the company's sales manager, realized the product's desired advantages and quickly exploited the market opportunity. He purchased an air-conditioned step van and had a Clarkson Tire Changer installed complete with wet bar, lounge chairs, and music. Fred or one of his two salespeople would drive the van up to a garage and invite the owner to see a demonstration of this new marvel. Fred's orders were quick and lasting as the product filled a long-felt need in the market. He closed approximately 70 percent of the demonstrations with solid orders. Since "success breeds success," Jonkoff's enthusiasm grew with each order.

Big Three Industries was not capable of filling all the orders generated by the sales department. Back orders, delayed shipments, shoddy workmanship, higher costs, and lower quality-control problems set in. The company built extensions to its present manufacturing facility and frequently went into production before the concrete floor of the new addition was laid. The high enthusiasm on the plant floor (dirt in some cases) wavered as the production problems mounted and conflicts developed. The plant supervisors encountered numerous problems related to hasty manufacturing, packaging, storage, and shipping. Big Three's once-lucrative profit potential began to shrink perceptibly. The three owners realized they had serious problems, and an emergency meeting was called to resolve the issues.

If you were called to attend this meeting, what would you suggest as the correct decision processes to follow? Be specific and detailed in your answer.

What could the plant supervisors do? What should Fred Jonkoff do?

Decision to Accept a New Job

Barbara Miller is considering accepting her first job after graduating from a small college in southwestern Arizona. She is faced with the problem of finding a position that is challenging, but one that can also use her psychology background. Since Barbara trusts and respects you, she asks your opinion.

Miller is intelligent, attractive, and gets along well with people. She doesn't want to work in psychology but wants to meet her goals in another field.

What would you suggest Barbara do to solve her problem? Is she aware that a problem exists? Why or why not?

QUESTIONS FOR DISCUSSION

1. Comment on this statement: "Decision making is the *most* important managerial function of the supervisor."
2. What kind of situation may exist that requires a decision but doesn't involve a problem?
3. Why may some supervisors shy away from making decisions?
4. Of the nine steps in the decision process, which steps are the most critical? Why?
5. Why can the problem definition step become troublesome?
6. Why is it helpful to state all the workable alternatives in the decision process before attacking subsequent decision steps?
7. When estimating the value of each alternative, why is setting up probabilities of success so important?
8. Why is the action step in the decision process so difficult to implement?
9. What are the possible outcomes of the follow-up and appraisal of a solution?

PART II
Supervising People at Work

This section focuses on the supervisor's interface with the most important variable in supervisory management—the person. Supervisory management tools are only effective as long as the person or employee produces quality output and meets the needs and goals of both the organization and the individuals. The important topics in this section are people as workers, productivity, job design and job boredom, communications, motivating the worker, personal characteristics of the supervisor, and leadership.

CHAPTER IX

People as Workers

LEARNING OBJECTIVES

- *To realize that employees are people.*
- *To know that people have wants and needs.*
- *To know that some needs are learned.*
- *To see that people are individuals.*
- *To know that supervisory success is largely based on how others are treated.*
- *To realize that productivity can be enhanced if supervisors understand that they are working with people rather than machines.*

Introduction

Supervising people at work involves management of time, machines, and paperwork as support duties, but the major task is leading the workers in the day-to-day tasks faced by the work crew, office unit, store, or field party. Since leadership and the personal characteristics of the supervisor have been discussed, it is now time to cover the topic of *who* is being led. Employees are people. A supervisor must understand people for who they are and what they want to be. All of us are subjected to individual needs, wants, desires, social groups, personal experience, education, cultural values, and the impact of our total psychological, sociological, economic, political and physical environment. Indeed, people are complex entities.

Supervisors must be able to work with and through people before they can effectively master their own position. If one thing characterizes the uniqueness of a supervisor's position, it would be the need to manage and lead people. This is a tall task. This chapter attempts to unravel some of the more difficult aspects of people as workers. We shall discuss the needs and wants of people, group and societal influences, and learned needs and how they affect and influence a worker's behavior. This is followed by a discussion of how a supervisor can use these factors in supervising employees as people. Being people centered in his or her thinking, recognizing opportunities for participation and recognition for the employees, developing teamwork, listening, developing positive worker attitudes, and understanding how attitudes are formed are factors that can affect the supervisor's efficiency and effectiveness significantly.

THE SUPERVISOR AND PEOPLE

The supervisor must probe into questions, such as: Why do people work? What motivates people to increase their productivity and quality of output? Employees work to satisfy their own needs. If company needs are satisfied in the process—well and good. If the reverse were true—that is, if people worked primarily to satisfy company needs—then the supervisor would not have to contend with many of the problems generated by subordinates.

Understanding people as workers involves to a high degree the ability to accept people as they are. Each person is an individual and is unique. He or she has wants, needs, ambitions, desires, and goals that he or she tries to satisfy. Previous management attempts to motivate workers as part of a group have failed because an individual's unique personality often was downgraded. For instance, companies have spent much money on fringe benefits to make workers feel more secure and provide the workers with economic security, but other basic needs were left unsatisfied. Provision of financial security by management in earlier decades was based on the assumption that people wanted to satisfy needs of hunger, thirst, and shelter. This idea has prevailed for many decades in the worker-supervisor relationship. But we now know that what workers wanted then, and they want now, are what human beings have always wanted—to satisfy their basic needs as human beings. Workers want to be accepted as individuals, and not be treated as spokes in a gigantic wheel.

Supervisors must involve themselves and become more sensitive to differences among individuals. The wants and desires of one worker may not be identical to the wants and desires of another. Just as we have many different sizes and weights and colors of people, we have many different desires and needs among individuals. The supervisor should realize that people are humans and that they desire to be treated as human beings rather than as inanimate objects or as parts of a production line. It might be said that we are unique enough to be "one in a million." This saying, popular a generation ago, can be substantiated in research findings.

This uniqueness of the individual must be recognized by the supervisor. This does not mean that the supervisor must use introspection, depth interviewing and analysis, but should be constantly aware of individual difference by being people-oriented as opposed to being only production oriented. Greater understanding of each individual employee allows the supervisor to allocate work assignments more efficiently. When people are recognized as individuals, they tend to respond favorably to group goals by encouraging favorable interpersonal relationships among themselves.

Further understanding of people requires the supervisor to increase his/her ability to respond, understand, and communicate with his/her workers. Communicating with workers requires, first, the understanding of the logical content of verbal communication and, second, comprehension of the implied feelings and sentiment also contained in the communication. The supervisor must be able to read between the lines when conversing with the worker. He/she must ask: What did Charlie really mean when he said he wouldn't take the new job? Did Charlie mean that he was fearful of the new job, or that he was incapable of performing on the new job, or that he was completely satisfied with the job he was now performing and didn't want to change? Evaluating the content of messages becomes a difficult judgmental problem for the supervisor. However, he/she is in the best position to understand the communication, since he knows more about the worker than anyone else in the entire organization. This knowledge places the supervisor in the very important position that higher levels of management have just recently recognized.

Supervisors must become involved in the awareness of themselves in how they are perceived, or seen, by the workers. Managers must understand their own feelings, desires, wants, and needs and how all of these factors fit into their job as a manager of people. Attempting to understand other people is difficult in itself, but understanding oneself becomes more difficult because our prejudices and our biases tend to screen out our objective view of ourselves. We view ourselves as the *center of our universe* (self-centeredness), protected from some day-to-day problems by our previous experience and knowledge. Self-centeredness tends to develop a *cocoon effect* that becomes stronger as we grow older. This effect is represented by the heavy black circle at the center of Figure 9-1. In effect, we say to new experience, "Don't confuse me with facts; my mind is already made up." Workers operate in much the same manner. They see themselves as the center of their universe, and they filter out communication and observation of the supervisor's behavior to justify their previously held notions about their superiors. Thus the workers may see the supervisor differently from the way the supervisor sees himself.

Referring to Figure 9-1, you can observe that the self is surrounded by concentric circles that include face-to-face groups, work task groups, supervisors, workers, economic conditions, working conditions, and company policies. With this brief introduction we can explore the nature of a worker in greater depth.

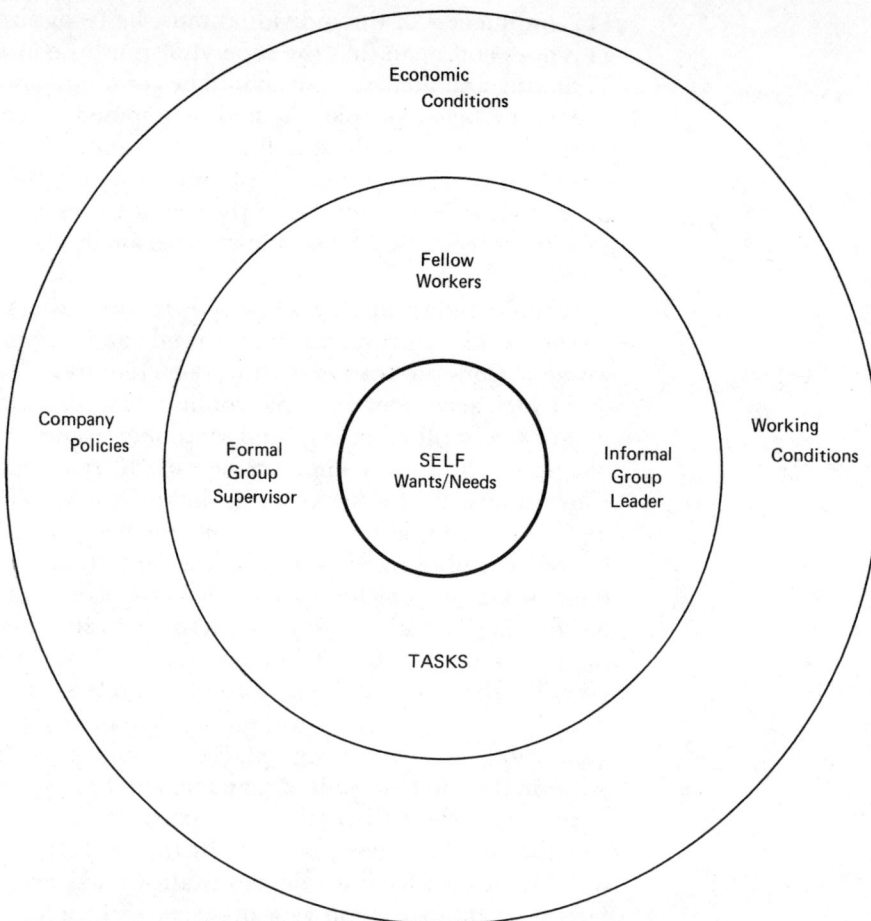

Figure 9-1 Self-centered view by an individual of his immediate work environment.

NEEDS AND WANTS OF PEOPLE

BASIC BIOLOGICAL AND PSYCHOLOGICAL NEEDS

Although each person must be treated as an individual and dealt with as such, we as individuals have much in common. Understanding common features among human beings can provide the foundation on which supervisors can base their treatment of each individual. Lists of needs common to all human beings are many and are varied in their content.

Although this discussion offers a representative sample of human needs, they are presented as useful background material for a leader's use on the job in order to manage and motivate people. One of the most widely accepted and practical sets that lists man's basic needs is Maslow's *need priority* model.[1] Humans are viewed as complex beings (which they are) who attempt to satisfy their needs in an orderly manner similar to climbing stairsteps. Where humans' primary needs have been partially or completely satisfied, they try to achieve partial or complete satisfaction of higher-level needs. People can only partially satisfy a need before they feel the push for the next level of needs. Insufficient satisfaction of a need causes frustration, which could result in the overcompensation of the next need.

As shown in Figure 9-2, the first step common to humans includes the *physiological needs* of hunger and thirst and protection of oneself from the environment. Need number 1 is the basic survival need. Once this need has been fully or partially satisfied at a given time, then humans, who are never really satisfied, desire to achieve the second-level needs, which are safety needs. These needs involve physical protection, housing, protection from the elements, desirable working conditions, and other physical environmental factors that would satisfy this need.

Once these two basic, or primary, needs (1 and 2) are partially or completely satisfied, humans then feel the push to move on to the three higher-level needs, which are principally psychological needs. These higher-level needs have become more predominant in the last ten years, because humans in our economic environment have been able to satisfy the first two primary needs, physiological survival and safety.

The three higher-level needs are more difficult to identify and do not present as limited a picture as the primary needs. These higher-level or *psychological needs* create many problems that have to be solved, or satisfied, by activities of the first-line supervisors. They represent social and self needs.

The third-level needs are the belonging and love needs. Humans are social animals who desire or need to belong to groups of like kinds. The

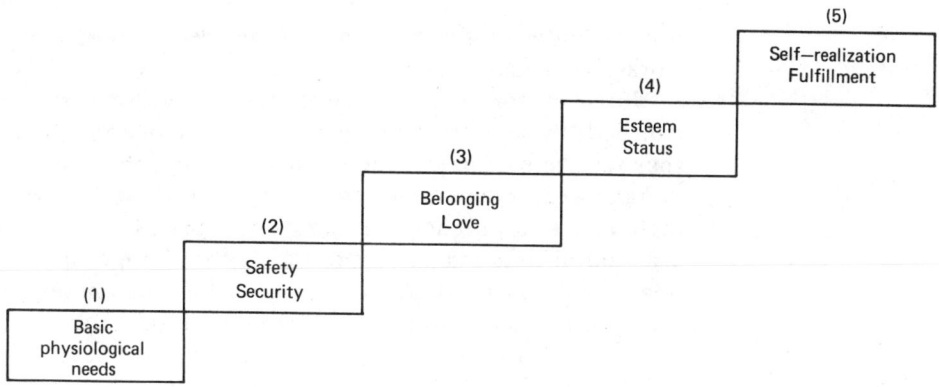

Figure 9-2 Order of priority of human needs.

[1]A. H. Maslow, *Motivation and Personality,* Harper & Row, New York, 1954.

old adage "Birds of a feather flock together" typifies this point of view. In addition to belonging to a group, to an institution, to a family, or to a work group, humans also need to love and to be loved. Love in this context is much broader than romantic love as the word is used in our culture. Affection for a friend, a father, a mother, a son, a daughter, a good boss, a good worker, or a good company are examples of fulfilling this need.

Once the third-level needs are partially or completely satisfied, humans then desire to move on to the fourth-level needs, which are called self-esteem and status needs. These needs are represented by humans' feelings toward themselves, such as pride in themselves and their accomplishments, high self-evaluation, and the feeling that they can live with themselves as worthwhile, productive human beings. Humans must feel that what they are doing is justifiable, worthwhile, and productive rather than being irrelevant, unproductive, and oppressively detailed work.

When self-esteem and status have been partially or completely satisfied, humans then move on to the highest-level need, that of self-realization or self-fulfillment. This last need, which is the most difficult one to achieve, is humans knowledge that they can become everything that they feel capable of becoming. This need is less apparent than others, because many persons have not unleashed it. They are still busy with needs 3 and 4. Although self-realization dominates few people, it influences nearly everyone. In fulfillment of this need workers may believe that they can become the best drill-press operator in the plant or the fastest typist in the office. Then they will pursue this goal until it is attained. In the attainment of this goal the worker has achieved self-realization or an inner feeling of accomplishment. To the degree that the fifth-level need can be satisfied, people will find their work a challenge.

The five-step classification of needs is somewhat artificial, because all needs are interacting together within the whole person. Maslow's need priority model, however, does provide the supervisor with a convenient way of understanding which type of need is most likely to dominate a worker's drives in a given situation.

Moreover, the need priority model does not suggest that workers' needs can be fully satisfied by giving them some of each of the five needs. As they receive partial satisfaction of one need, the need itself can increase or take a different direction. A mountain climber who has climbed a high peak sees a higher one. Someone satisfied by eating hamburger over a period of time may aspire to satisfy that hunger need by eating sirloin steak. Workers' needs are never static. They can never be satisfied. Need satisfaction is a continuous problem for all time.

The need priority model essentially tells us that satisfied needs do not help to motivate. Workers are motivated by what they are seeking. Supervisors have to recognize what need workers are trying to satisfy in order to motivate them.

GROUP NEEDS AND THE INDIVIDUAL

Humans have contact with others that affects or influences behavior. Humans are social animals; they join groups. Individual personalities can be altered, or modified, when they become members of certain groups. Basically, humans join the group in which they feel the most comfortable. But as members of a group they learn new ways called *group needs*. They learn to behave differently. They learn to accept different ideas. They learn to want different things to satisfy their basic needs. The satisfactions of many individual wants (those needs one is aware of) are geared partially to the desires of the group. On the job workers learn they can achieve some goals by bending or conforming to the wishes of the work group. The individuals in the group may act differently when in the group than when they are alone.

The group on the job also becomes a powerful force in that the sum total of the talents of individuals in the group may be less than the total talents of the group when together. Phrased another way, a group of workers is capable of more output than if those same workers were to operate alone with the same materials and production facilities. Thus teamwork does mean something. But to individuals it can mean belonging to a group in which they can derive satisfaction, a chief basic need.

Group behavior can also have disadvantages in an organization. If a plant, office, or store were to have poor morale because of inadequately trained supervisors, poor working conditions, low pay, or lack of understanding from management, the workers in a group may band together for solace and generate pleasurable feelings among themselves by complaining about the company, their immediate supervisor, or general company policies. Productivity could be high or low in this situation, but the employees' morale is improved when the workers complain within their group. This gives them something in common that satisfies group and belonging needs. However, company needs may or may not be met in such a situation. The supervisor is very concerned with this situation when it begins to affect company needs.

INFLUENCES OF SOCIETY

As humans grow and mature both physically and mentally, their value system, or what they believe is important, is influenced by society. Society's norms of behavior may become their own. Their mannerisms, factors they consider important, ethics, and moralities are dictated or learned from society and are included in their behavior. These *cultural values,* both national and subcultural of various sections of the country, become very involved and deep-seated. Many of the things we believe to be the truth can be traced to these social or societal values. These value systems strongly affect what we are, as managers or workers, and what we believe to be right or wrong. Prejudices, biases, the way we look at things, are influenced by cultural values. Workers of a different national origin from ours may have different values from ours. We may look down our noses at these individuals because of the difference between these value systems. However, it is important for the supervisor to understand the importance of values held by persons from different cultural backgrounds. It is important to realize that these values cannot be changed quickly, but may take months or years to change, or they may never change.

HUMAN BEHAVIORAL PATTERNS ARE MOTIVATED BY BOTH BIOLOGICAL NEEDS AND LEARNED NEEDS

Although human behavior is influenced by people's own personalities, their group, and society in general, how they act in a given situation will also depend on their experience. Everyday living behavior is usually motivated by *learned needs*. Needs have been used in Maslow's need priority model as biological and psychological needs common to all. For example, the need to belong to and be identified with a group of our liking is the psychological need. This explains the "why" of our behavior. How we implement the satisfaction of this need is within our discretion and becomes a learned need. We *learn* to satisfy a biological or psychological need; we do not always follow natural ways. Belonging to a particular work group may be reinforced by the same worker's participating in a company-sponsored sport. Workers' needs to belong are implemented by certain groups that they choose. Belonging to a team in the company bowling league becomes a learned reaction to satisfy a biological-psychological need. Therefore we learn to want things so that our inherent, biological and psychological needs can be satisfied. However, what we learn to want is the result of our experiences. A third-grade-educated rural farm worker's learned needs can be very simple compared with the needs of a high school graduate from a large suburban neighborhood. Although television and better transportation have reduced the differences between these two types of people, learned needs still vary according to one's experiences or exposure to the means of satisfying biological needs.

Learned needs can take many different forms. We learn to want a new car, to want a new house, to want a new job. We learn to want to belong to certain organizations or activities, on or off the job. We don't need a new Cadillac, but we need transportation to fulfill our basic psychological, social, and physiological needs common to all human beings. Because we do have learned needs, a supervisor can help to play a role by exposing workers to different experiences.

Learned needs, as the phrase is used here, really are wants. Wants, then, become a realization of needs—we become aware that we need something as part of the learning process. We, as individuals, may not always recognize our wants, but as these wants grow in intensity within us, they trigger us into activity to achieve the goals established by the wants. "That new car I pass every morning on the way to work strikes my fancy. Someday I'm going to have one just like it." This person wouldn't desire the new car unless she were exposed to it frequently. This desire grows more intense as her exposure to the car increases. Frequency of exposure wouldn't affect this person if she did not perceive the car as a stepping-stone toward achieving a basic or psychological need, such as self-esteem. This stair-stepping process of goal recognition is called *levels of aspiration.* We aspire to bigger and better things or bigger and better goals. Levels of aspiration become a very important tool. They can be used by managers to motivate workers. If workers believe that they can live better lives by joining a particular group, they may aspire to join that particular group. Workers' behaviors may be influenced by these aspirations, and their manners will reflect these aspirations accordingly.

SUMMARY OF FACTORS THAT INFLUENCE A WORKER'S BEHAVIOR

Numerous factors influence a worker's behavior, and supervisors should understand these factors so that they can cope with the complexities of understanding workers.

1. Each worker is an individual, one in a million. Each one wants to be accepted as an individual. Our personalities are unique, and we as individuals should be treated as if we were unique.
2. Each worker attempts to satisfy his/her basic needs, with organizational needs being treated secondarily.
3. These basic needs are partially or completely satisfied on a priority basis — one step at a time at a given moment in time. However, it is possible to fall back as more pressing needs reappear.
4. Primary needs for physiological satisfaction (hunger and thirst) and for safety (shelter, clothing, and working conditions) represent first-level needs. First-level needs hold priority over higher-level needs such as belonging and love needs (group interrelations, fondness for another individual), self-esteem and status (self-respect, need to be able to live with ourselves), and self-realization (becoming everything we feel capable of becoming).
5. Group belonging influences an individual's behavior so that he/she changes or tends to conform to the behavioral norms of the face-to-face group to which he wants to belong.
6. Cultural values of society affect a worker's behavior as expressed in his/her mannerisms, communication, attitudes, and how he/she perceives his/her surroundings. Cultural values are extremely difficult to change.
7. Basic needs are biological and psychological, but from experience individual workers learn to want and desire objects that help to satisfy these basic needs.

8. Workers learn to establish obtainable goals to satisfy basic needs. The level of the goal is called the level of aspiration.
9. Workers' levels of aspiration can be influenced by the supervisor through exposure and reinforcement.

WORKERS AS PEOPLE

Now that we have discussed factors that influence a worker's behavior, we should determine how to use this knowledge on the job. Since we have suggested that workers are people and that they do have basic needs that are recognized as wants and desires, managers can use these needs to motivate people and to increase the workers' job satisfaction. Although it is dangerous to try to manipulate workers by using human relations techniques, the supervisor can use these concepts to increase his understanding of worker behavior. The major points discussed below can provide a framework that a supervisor can put into practical use.

PEOPLE ARE INDIVIDUALS Often a manager who wants to be fair to all of the people believes that being fair is treating everyone equally. If supervisors treat workers all alike, they are really being unfair to the workers, because the workers are not all alike. A rapport or understanding can be and should be developed between the worker and the supervisor. A supervisor who is interested in each worker as an individual is showing recognition of the worker as an individual, in addition to satisfying the worker's basic need for self-esteem. Although this approach is more difficult for the supervisor to accomplish because of its more time-consuming features, it bears more fruit in terms of a happier work environment, greater productivity, and higher quality of productivity. Humans are not equal in their talents, but they should be given an equal opportunity to succeed or to fail. It is hoped that failure doesn't occur very often, or the supervisor may be replaced for incompetency.

PEOPLE-CENTERED SUPERVISION Supervisors should tend to be people-centered rather than work-centered. It is very easy to cope with numbers or production reports because they are tangible, quantifiable factors. It is difficult to cope with the complexities involved in psychological man because these factors are inherently difficult to measure accurately. The operation of an organization or a business unit may be expressed in production output, sales quotas, costs, efficiency, and other suitable means of quantifying activities of workers within the organization. Because the supervisor sees reports that display statistical information, he or she may have a tendency to become work centered or production oriented to the extent of meeting their production schedules. By emphasizing the means to the end (being people centered), the end result of production will be accomplished more easily. This does not mean that supervisors are not bosses or that they shouldn't make production; it means saying "Hey, Fred, come here," rather than "Hey, you, come here." We as individuals have names that we carry throughout our lives. We prefer hearing our name rather than a number. People want to be treated as people in their employment.

OPPORTUNITY, PARTICIPATION, AND RECOGNITION
Workers must be provided the opportunity for participation and recognition. Although workers may never try to achieve promotion within the organization, this does not necessarily mean that they do not want to be recognized as achievers. Even if they refuse the promotion, once it's offered to them, they still want to recognize their own ability, or capabilities, of doing a job better. Workers in dead-end jobs believe they will never go any higher in the organization. They may recognize their situation, but once their immediate supervisor has shut the door on any change, the worker may lose much initiative. A serious morale problem could develop. A reasonably good worker could be abandoned, thus coloring an otherwise favorable image of the supervisor by the other workers.

TEAMWORK
People desire to belong to groups, and they tend to work best in groups. The word *teamwork* has been used widely in industry and, at times, over used. Workers feel more secure as members of a team and of a larger organization. They like to work in teams and sometimes compete as one team against another. People work better in teams to accomplish specific tasks because the feeling of belonging and the spirit of cooperation are involved. One worker who might be slightly deficient in a particular task is helped by the stronger worker if they're on the same team. A group effort may be more productive if it is on a competitive basis, but it is also more psychologically rewarding to an individual, since basic needs may be satisfied by working and achieving in the group.

A word of caution about group competition is warranted here, since research has shown that competition between teams or competition between individuals can produce side effects harmful to the organization's productivity if improperly handled. Some sociologists and psychologists are adamantly opposed to competition in any form because conflict and unsatisfactory inner group consequences could develop. However, experience indicates that competition handled adroitly is a very helpful and rewarding experience for both the worker and the company. The handling of competition should be very subtle; the supervisor can point out one worker's production record to another worker who is not performing as well. Publication of performance or production records for the purpose of creating competition among groups can be favorable. However, competition is not advisable unless economic gains or tangible rewards are offered. Most of this type of motivation and competition is appropriate in marketing, distribution, and retail sales organizations, but the concepts of competition can be useful for consideration in plants and offices as well.

Motivation by competition between individuals or among groups or teams should follow a few simple guidelines. First, the competition should be among those approximately equal in ability so that a wholesome rivalry can result in higher achievement, not only in production but in the workers' feelings of achievement. Second, competition is best when it fosters or develops team spirit and good morale. Third, the groups involved should be balanced in the number of equivalent tasks to be performed and should receive equal treatment in working conditions, time, and assistance.

The team spirit will decline, however, unless the employees are informed frequently about their progress or score. If they are not kept informed, interest and motivation can dissipate rapidly. The supervisor should encourage and support team improvement and offer praise immediately after the completion of each step.

A SUPERVISOR LEARNS BY LISTENING

A democratic climate must be maintained between the worker and the supervisor. This does not mean that the supervisor should permit the worker to vote on making decisions in the work group. Rather, it refers to freedom on the part of workers, as well as the supervisor, to express their opinions concerning the tasks to be accomplished. This is usually called an open-door policy, but what is meant is that there is a two-way communication between the supervisor and the worker. A common practice of many supervisors is that they do not listen to the worker's ideas, complaints, or other forms of communication. The worker may have a better solution to the supervisor's problems than the supervisor has. Recognition of the worker's suggestions are important, regardless of how rushed the supervisor may be. Listening provides workers with recognition. If the supervisor listens, obviously workers believe their ideas or suggestions are important. The fact that the supervisor has taken a few minutes to listen is recognition in and of itself.

POSITIVE WORKER ATTITUDES

Positive attitudes must be developed in the workers toward management, toward their immediate supervisor, toward their work task, toward their fellow employees, and toward the public. It is important that these positive work attitudes be developed, because this mirrors how employees see themselves in regard to their own situation, to their own worth, to society, and to the company. An attitude is a state of mind. A job may appear boring to the supervisor, but it may not be boring to the worker. Boredom is a state of mind and is not always a functional aspect of a particular job or task. It is how we, as individuals, perceive the situation that is important. Therefore the supervisor should not set up a negative attitude in the worker by telling the worker that a particular task is boring. Another approach the supervisor could use would be simply to ask the worker her opinion of the job or situation.

How workers see themselves and how they fit within their company's environment helps to determine whether they are happy or not. If they are happy, they tend to be better co-workers and will often achieve more. Happy workers will listen to new ideas; they will be more prone to raise their level of aspiration; they will be more receptive to changes if and when they are presented to them so that they can understand changes and how the changes will benefit. *Therefore the first step in developing positive attitudes in workers is for the supervisor to be worker oriented.* This is the first step the supervisor should take when achieving the goals of the company.

ATTITUDE FORMATION

Many factors influence a worker's behavior, but attitudes are predispositions to act in a certain way. Behavioral factors influence attitudes, but the attitudes themselves strongly affect the worker's day-to-day behavior. Worker attitudes are built on the facts of both past and present experiences. Workers' experiences with their supervisors, their formal organizational groups, and their informal groups strengthen or weaken their attitudes. If worker's attitude toward his/her pay is unfavorable, any mention of this sensitive subject could trigger an immediate response, such as "This is a lousy company to work for." The worker will complain because she sees the work environment through her negative pay attitude. However, the same worker may have many positive attitudes toward family, friends, immediate supervisor, or working conditions. Attitude formation is a complex subject and will be treated in greater depth in subsequent chapters.

SUMMARY

Managers must get work done through people. Work tasks are achieved by working with and through people. People-oriented supervisors tend to perform better and achieve better results than supervisors who tend to be only work-centered. The work-centered supervisor overlooks many opportunities to motivate his people. The worker-centered supervisor is constantly observing many opportunities for greater production by satisfying worker's needs that also coincide with the organizational needs.

People must be understood and treated as individuals. We are all unique. We have common needs, but we have unique wants that are learned through our asssociations, our own observations, and our cultural norms in society. We want to be recognized as individuals and to be treated as human beings.

All human relations are based on contact with others on the work scene. The relationship between the supervisor and the worker is one of the most critical relationships in any company. All the policies and plans and organizational structure established by top and middle management people are useless until someone has developed the product, produced it, shipped it, sold it, and collected the money. So the accomplishment of the tasks laid out by the top managers lies in the hands of the supervisor-worker relationship. This contact is generally a verbal, face-to-face contact on the work scene and becomes the most critical link in the total communication and organizational chain in a company.

KEY CONCEPTS

Individual uniqueness. The need to understand human behavior on the job cannot be overemphasized. Each individual is unique unto himself and must be treated as such by the supervisor. This one concept is justification enough for hiring first-line supervisors rather than using computers to cope with individuals in order to achieve company goals.

Basic biological and psychological needs. Although unique, each individual does have broad, common biological and psychological needs that can be satisfied in many different ways.

Needs versus wants. The concept of *need* is used differently in different contexts, but a need is basic to all human beings. Human beings are born with needs. On the other hand, a want is a learning experience in that an individual's desire to achieve something is a result of experience or a recognition of a basic need.

Humans and groups. Humans are social animals and desire to belong to groups that can help to satisfy basic needs and learned wants, and to achieve personal goals.

Humans and culture. Society and culture influence the worker's behavior in that ethnic background, race, national origin, place of birth, and early childhood can strongly influence a worker's behavior.

People-centered supervision. It is easy for a supervisor to think in terms of production figures (i.e., number of parts, reports, pages typed) as a measure of success, but work is accomplished by people, and only by working through people can the supervisor advance personal and company goals. Worker recognition, participation, and opportunity to grow are integral parts of this concept.

Positive worker attitudes. Attitudes are predispositions, or how we as individuals see something and react. Since human beings develop attitudes through learning, experience, and exposure to our environment, it is necessary that the supervisor help to develop positive worker attitudes toward the supervisor, company, product or service, society, and customers.

IMPORTANT TERMS

Aspiration level
Attitude formation
Cultural values
Group needs
Individual differences
Learned needs
People-centered supervision
Physiological needs
Positive worker attitudes
Priority of needs
Psychological needs
Self-centeredness (cocoon effect)

INCIDENTS

The Preoccupied Supervisor

Ada McDonald was proud of her accomplishments as a creative copywriter for a large New York City advertising agency. Although her position seemed secure having been with the agency for over four years, Ada was troubled. Her colleagues said she was one of the "best" in the business.

Last month's recognition banquet for outstanding copywriting work didn't list her name as one of the honorees. She had been a faithful worker for over four years. The two previous years Ada's name had been on the honoree list at the annual recognition banquet. She wondered what had happened that her name had not appeared on the list for last month's recognition banquet?

For about a month, since the banquet, Ada's quality of work seemed to be less than her previous output. Her aspiration to succeed had eroded and she became more listless. She developed a "don't care" attitude toward her work and toward the agency.

Jo Arnold, her supervisor, recognized Ada's listlessness and new attitude and called Ada into her office for a consultation. Since Jo had been promoted two months ago to supervisor from a copywriter position, she didn't believe in "hovering over" people nor did she believe in kissing them on the forehead every time they accomplished something. Jo thought a copywriter's reward was knowing they did a good job. They are professionals and she treated them as professionals by giving respect to their opinions, giving directions, and allowing the copywriters the professional courtesy to manage their time so they would meet the deadlines established by the account executive. Jo believed her job was to hold the department together and make sure that people were producing.

Ada asked Jo why her name was not on the honorees list at the banquet. After searching for the list Jo discovered mistakenly she had not included Ada's name because she was so busy learning her new job.

If you were in Jo's position what would you do and say? What activities would you intend to follow to prevent such a situation from occurring again?

The Thunderheaded "Bull of the Woods" Supervisor

Jack was a 62-year-old, experienced, respected, product inspector for a decorative plastics manufacturer. He was well respected by his co-workers and by the plant's management. Jack's supervisor had received a promotion and was transferred to another plant. His new supervisor was a brash, forceful young ex-worker who had worked in the paint department before his promotion to Jack's department. The third day on the job, the new supervisor had an exchange with Jack:

Supervisor: "Hey old man, how long have you been inspecting parts?"
Jack: "For eighteen years, why?"
Supervisor: "Your rejection rate is too high and that makes me look bad. I don't like to look bad, understand?"
Jack: "My job is to see that quality is maintained and . . ."
Supervisor: "I'll tell you what your job is and how to perform it. So don't give me any trouble and you won't get into any trouble."

What needs are being fulfilled by the new supervisor? Which of Jack's needs are not being fulfilled as illustrated by this exchange? If you were Jack's supervisor, what gratification would you receive in this exchange? Should a successful supervisor attempt to satisfy his needs or the worker's needs? Why?

Incident Problems

1. Role play the first incident by assigning one individual the part of the disappointed copywriter and another individual the role of the preoccupied supervisor. Start the scene in Jo's office.
2. Incident 2 can be role played by starting the scene where the incident stops. Have the person playing Jack respond to the supervisor's last remark, ". . . So don't give me any trouble and you won't get into any trouble."

QUESTIONS FOR DISCUSSION

1. Discuss the reasons why a supervisor is in the best position of any manager to know and understand what is going on in his or her department.
2. Why do people usually see themselves as the center of their work environment? How can the supervisor best cope with this situation?

3. What are the five steps in Maslow's need priority model? Of what benefit is this model to a practicing supervisor?
4. Humans join groups where they feel the most comfortable. Why?
5. Humans learn to like things. How can a supervisor use this aspect of human behavior to enhance quality output?
6. Even if an employee will not take a promotion or a job change, why shouldn't he or she be given the opportunity by being offered the change? What results may occur if the employee, who desires the consideration of a change is not given the opportunity?
7. Attitude formation is a double-edged sword that can cut both ways. How can the supervisor help to develop employee's attitudes favorable toward the supervisor, the company, and the company's products?
8. What is so significant about fostering an atmosphere of teamwork among workers? Can it have disadvantages as well? When?

CHAPTER X
The Need To Improve Productivity

LEARNING OBJECTIVES

- *To understand the importance of productivity.*
- *To know what productivity is.*
- *To understand the relationship between productivity and an organization's viability.*
- *To realize why a productivity crisis exists in the United States.*
- *To see the supervisor's impact upon and responsibility for improving productivity.*

Introduction

The United States still has the highest absolute rate of productivity among all the industrial nations in the world, but over the last decade this leadership has been quickly eroded by our chief competitors. Our rate of growth or productivity has been well below that of our key competitors: Japan, West Germany, France, The Netherlands, and Italy. As seen in Figure 10-1, the United States has bested only the United Kingdom in percentage of increase. Obviously the slower U.S. rate of growth foretells the eventual loss of this nation's prestige and dominance in world markets and a rapidly deteriorating position in the domestic market, as well. This may come as a shock, since America has given superb instruction in the art of industrial excellence to many of the nations who now comprise the bulk of our competitors. Unhappily, the teacher has lost sight of some of its own lessons.

Products once poured out of American factories that set worldwide standards in quality for automobiles, steel, light and heavy machinery, and stereos. Now products flow into America from other countries

PRODUCTIVITY INCREASE IN MANUFACTURING 1968–1978

Country	%
United States	23.6%
Japan	89.1%
The Netherlands	93.7%
France	61.8%
Germany	63.8%
Italy	60.1%
United Kingdom	21.6%

Figure 10-1 Productivity increase in manufacturing, 1968-1978. (Source. Bureau of Labor Statistics, U.S. Dept. of Labor, December, 1979.)

usurping market share or completely controlling markets in automobiles, steel, and stereos. This is helping to create economic stagflation with its heavy trade deficits. Soaring energy costs, our aging manufacturing facilities and our precariously inadequate capital investment have helped to fuel inflation as well. It could get worse throughout the 1980s since other countries have hit their industrial stride and are likely to pull ahead even further in their growth percentage.

WHY IS BEING COMPETITIVE SO IMPORTANT?

If we as a nation are so intense about productivity and being number one in the world, why won't we settle for number two or even number three? This is a good question. In a competitive marketing world where different producers try to grow and to capture market share with improved products, new products, or with least cost manufacturing, an organization or country that doesn't grow at the same economic rate as the rest is declining relative to the others. If the United States isn't growing in productivity at the same rate as others then eventually the faster growing countries will catch up with America and the United States will lose economic power in the world.

Aside from national defense and the ability to arm ourselves in event of war, economic growth, maintaining our productivity, and remaining competitive, can be justified from two other perspectives. First, economic growth encouraged by offering competitive products provides employment, and the standard of living to which we have become accustomed. Lower productivity and increased costs per unit is inflationary and curtails competitiveness. Hence, lower productivity increases the cost of living and reduces the standard of living. If we are willing to accept a lower standard of living, then we might settle for a number two or even three position. The fewer goods we sell, the less money we will have to buy goods from other countries.

Second, when a country suffers an economic decline or sluggish growth, as in the case of the United Kingdom, the country loses power, prestige, and respect. Foreign capital and investments are reluctant to come into the country. Because of the economic uncertainty, lower capital investments, and lower productivity, many conflicts between labor, management and government occur. Whether we like it or not, productivity is a vital issue for all parties involved. The only differences lie in the biases and prejudices of the concerned parties.

WHAT IS PRODUCTIVITY?

Productivity is an input/output analysis, compiled by the Bureau of Labor Statistics (BLS) of the Department of Labor. It is a measure of output per man-hour worked and becomes a measure of efficiency. It is determined by dividing the goods produced by the number of hours worked. It is not much different than figuring a baseball batter's average (hits ÷ turns at bat). The BLS publishes productivity measures quarterly and yearly. The BLS also publishes separate productivity data for manufacturing, farms, nonfinancial corporations, and for 75 selected industries. The total measure of productivity does not include government because government workers primarily provide services and the output of services is most difficult to measure.

of data may partially cloud the issue. For example, the BLS, in measuring output for the construction industry, uses input price indexes to correct for inflation. These indexes measure the cost of labor and materials but do not include any cost savings incurred at the production site. Therefore, these indexes understate the total value of an output and do not reflect a true productivity measurement. The output of finance, insurance, and real estate and services like health, legal, and repair services is also difficult to measure. Productivity for these sectors is based on gross dollar receipts for each sector that does not count physical output increases, if output goes up faster than prices. Hence productivity would be overstated in a high or double-digit inflationary period, since the hours worked would be divided into a larger gross receipt without an actual productivity increase.

This may be more than the reader cares about, but it's important to understand that productivity figures may be inaccurate in some jobs, but is fairly accurate where an end product can be identified and deflated to a base period. Nevertheless, the productivity problem appears to be a never-ending malaise that will not go away, as long as we continue to slip in growth, relative to competitors. Regardless of all the smoke that can smother the productivity issue, the real villain is our loss of markets and control to other countries that becomes the *central issue* in the productivity crisis.

PRODUCTIVITY SLOWDOWN—THREE POINTS OF VIEW

The three interested parties in the productivity debate are (1) business, (2) labor, and (3) government. All three groups are claiming our overall decline in productivity is caused by the other two.

Business makes claims that government should reduce paper work and that workers should return to the work ethic, reduce absenteeism, be more quality conscious, and put in a day's work for a day's pay.[1]

Labor says that productivity in the manufacturing sector has not declined and overall decline is the result of poor measurements in the nonmanufacturing sectors that reflect unfavorably on the union member. They believe productivity will increase when better ways are found to produce and distribute goods and services enabling each worker to produce more in each hour worked. They concede that a better-trained work force, better machinery, and better scheduling of work flow will improve productivity.[2]

Government believes that since they aren't the producers, but only the facilitators, they have generated sufficient incentives for business to increase the flow of money for investment and R & D, the two areas that should improve our product quality and their production processes. Some government officials believe that management's preoccupation with immediate payouts, ROI's (return on investment, expressed as a percentage of investment), and profit forces them to invest in sure things and not practice a more liberal entrepreneur's art by investing in long-term projects, as well.[3]

Three legitimate points of view help to illustrate the complexity of defining the productivity crisis or determining if it really is a crisis. We could ignore the productivity problem, but common sense would tell us that we, as a nation, can't continue to lose markets, both foreign and domestic, without realizing the seriousness of the consequences (i.e., inflation, unemployment, stagnation, and a lower standard of living). Instead of pointing accusations at each other, the three parties should attempt to shoulder some responsibility for the problem.

Since all three parties do agree that productivity is a serious problem that has to be met, although using different remedies, it is our purpose to synthesize the problem and analyze where major improvements can be made. Unfortunately, past conferences with all three parties have deteriorated into a name-calling, buck-passing affair. What starts as a conference on productivity ends up in a mess.[4]

---

[1]Joseph V. Barks and Keith W. Bennett, "Why America Can't Afford to Overlook the Human Side of Productivity," *Iron Age*, October 1, 1979, pp. 28+.
[2]Bill Cunningham, "Bringing Productivity Into Focus," *AFL-CIO American Federationist*, May, 1979, pp. 1-8.
[3]Frank A. Weil, "Managements' Drag on Productivity," *Business Week*, December 3, 1979, p. 14.
[4]"Why America Can't Afford to Overlook the Human Side of Productivity," p. 31.

A SYNTHESIS OF THE PRODUCTIVITY PROBLEM

All three parties are guilty of contributing to the productivity crisis. Some people say that government has *too* much control with excessive regulations, high taxes, and the forced allocation of company resources to nonproduct or nonproduction process areas. This shift has the effect of eliminating engineering on improved products of higher quality and lowering the costs of production. Government controls the situation because it can allocate company efforts to nonproductive ventures in its quest for greater quality of life (i.e., less air pollution, water pollution, and so on).

Labor controls when it's not on the job because of chronic absenteeism or work stoppages that could negate any improved equipment-related addition. Labor is in control when it leaves and jumps from one job to another and disturbs the configuration of the work force. Labor is in final control because it's the closest thing to the last word by virtue of its being where the action is. Labor can forget to lubricate a new machine, or not care about quality work, or, simply, put time in to make a living. These accusations have been widely expressed but it doesn't mean they are correct.

Management is in control of the money and has much to say about the whats and whens of the investment that could improve productivity. Technological change and productivity increases are absolutely necessary to increase the standard of living. Many business people have emphasized the financial side of investment, immediate return, payoff, ROI, and break even rather than the marketing side, long-term growth, future returns, and product and company viability.

Regardless of the circumstances, labor cannot be blamed entirely, nor will government cease to be an important factor, so the only factor that can be charged to improve productivity is the management side. Management has to reemphasize the human side of their workers. Much of labor's problems tend to be cultivated by management's ignorance. Until managers, or—more specifically—supervisors, realize that workers are more than blue-collar machines and are people who have wants that need to be satisfied, productivity improvement and competition could be stymied. "If there is anything to comparisons which show America losing ground to other countries, it's probably management's fault."[5]

HUMAN APPROACH TO IMPROVED PRODUCTIVITY

Supervisors work with and through others at all levels of management. Successful supervisors must have effective face-to-face relations with their people. This appears to be one of the major keys in improving productiv-

[5]Ibid., p. 37.

ity on the plant floor, in the office, in the board meeting, on the hospital floor, in the insurance office, in the retail store, in the government office, and in the mines, forests, and the farmlands of the nation. The most workable set of solutions for improved productivity appears to be all too simple, but many knowledgeable people haven't discovered these solutions. "Obviously, good management can cause people to work a lot more enthusiastically than bad management,"[6] stated the president of the National Association of Manufacturers (NAM). *People will respond if the boss treats them like they would like to be treated.* Sounds too simple, doesn't it?

While one school advocates the key to productivity improvement lies in investment in new equipment and technology, the human-element people counter with the following argument. Any investment designed to increase productivity will be hard pressed to pay off to the fullest—if at all—if the people involved fail to realize that *they* play more than a bit part in the show. If investment were the answer, why didn't the United States improve its productivity when real fixed investment, as a percentage of real GNP, was actually higher in the late 1960s and early 1970s—periods followed by alarming slowings in productivity increases—than it was in the 1950s and early 1960s when productivity growth was at a generally acceptable level. Clearly, the human factor is one of those interlocking aspects which can't be assigned second string status if the U.S. expects to lick its productivity problems.

THE SUPERVISOR AND PRODUCTIVITY

If productivity is so important for an organization's survival, and if the human element is the driving force behind improved productivity, given proper tools, technology and financial assistance, why can't more organizations capitalize on what's happening? Although productivity increases are not an end in themselves, productivity is a means to achieve a variety of social as well as economic goals. As covered in the previous chapter, people have needs that must be fulfilled. A supervisor can fulfill people's needs on a day-to-day basis better than anyone else. How a person is treated, how the person is involved in change, and how a person is encouraged to "do the job right the first time" are human keys to improved productivity. As in the case of the Savin copier machines, *high expectations* and required *quality of output*, was backed by management's desire to spend more money up front to enhance quality the *first time.* Eliminating rework and customer complaints improved morale and improved the people's "pride" in being part of a *class* organization. Some scholars may call these results by many names, but, simply put, these activities encourage a person to want to come to work, stay overtime, and believe what they are doing is of value to society, and to themselves.

---

[6]Ibid., p. 28.

It's easy for workers with a poor attitude toward their supervisor to forget to maintain or lubricate a moving part—thus contributing to a worn-out bearing, or the earlier replacement of a company vehicle when the person doesn't care about the job or the company. These attitudes can be directly attributed to poor management and poor supervision. Treating people as a part of the machine is dehumanizing. The work ethic in the United States isn't dead, according to C. Jackson Grayson, founder of the American Productivity Center. Motivation of better-educated people requires better supervisors with better training. This sounds simple but perhaps this simple solution may foster a more productive, quality-conscious individual who does the job right the first time.

Motivation to produce higher quality products requires a better-skilled supervisor in all the facets of the supervisor's job: technical, human, managerial, and communicative skills. With better-educated people, greater mobility, and a greater desire to be involved in decisions and procedures that affect their worklife and future, people have to be recognized as people. Managers have to recognize that employees will contribute when involved and when asked by their supervisors. So it appears that participative management with its involvement, people awareness, and willingness of the supervisor to delegate some authority, is the way we have to go to increase productivity.

People are more self-assertive now in their relationships with supervisors and managers. They know productivity is declining and expect supervisors and managers to be responsible for turning the whole situation around. Workers are less likely to say, "Well, that's what the boss says, that's the way it goes." Today, there is a greater sense of dignity and self-respect among workers, which means they are less likely to take unreasonable orders in comparison with workers a decade or two ago. Workers are more prone to challenge authority or at least ask for reasons or explanations. They have greater concern for doing their own thing. Thus supervisors, in particular, must bear the brunt of change and be able to cope, motivate, and produce quality products in the right quantity. *The key to improved productivity is good supervision and better supervision means better training.*[7]

SUPERVISION AND TRAINING

Making a person feel like coming to work and reducing absenteeism and then producing when they arrive is largely a function of how well that person feels they belong or "fit in" with the organizational workplace. Picking a good supervisor and then not training them in communications, management principles, job instruction and human relations, is expecting too much from the individual supervisor.

[7]Ibid., p. 44.

A successful supervisor must understand the people he or she is managing. To achieve that understanding, the supervisor must listen to his or her employees, must behave so that the employees will trust and respect them, and speak more frankly to them. The supervisors must be alert to observe things around them and between themselves and the employees and the working relationships which develop. In short, the supervisor must be trained as a researcher, aware of problems, be able to diagnose these problems, prescribe a solution, and be able to carry it out.

People productivity must be a philosophy, a way of life, a business ethic. Being able to find out what can be done to get more out of what is put into each operation personifies participative management. This attitude has to be taught so that improved productivity in all sectors of the U.S. economy and political life can cut waste, duplication, boredom, and lack of pride in doing a job right. Obviously, this is a tall order as the United States competes with rapidly growing economies such as Japan and West Germany, who tend to practice these managerial-supervisory perspectives. Remember, productivity is a supervisor who helps subordinates grow.

Although many American firms, particularly assembly operations, have suffered from employee neglect, many plants personify the will and ability to produce high quality products with enthusiastic workers. General Motors' 55-year-old assembly plant at Tarrytown, N.Y. produced Chevrolet Citations and earned the reputation of being perhaps the giant automaker's most efficient assembly plant.[8] Strangely this same plant in the early 1970s was infamous for having one of the worst labor-relations and poorest quality records at GM. What happened?

The turnaround at Tarrytown grew out of the realization by local managers *and* union representatives that inefficiencies and industrial strife threatened the plant's future viability and very existence. GM, as in the case of other automobile manufacturers, closed inefficient, higher-cost plants if sluggish auto sales warranted such action. Tarrytown lost a truck production facility in 1971 for these reasons. The bosses and workers were fearful for their jobs and decided to get together to find better ways to build cars.

At first with hesitancy but later with enthusiasm, they embarked on an experiment to improve work and tap shop floor expertise for running the factory. Absenteeism was running at 7 percent of the work force and a total of 2000 grievances against management prevailed at the offset of the experiment. Confrontation and conflict resulted in sloppy work, rapidly rising dealer complaints and an unprecedented number of disciplinary and dismissal notices.

The first payoff in the experiment and the new mood at the plant came at model changeover time in 1972 and then the following year. GM management showed workers the proposed changes in the assembly line

---

[8]"Stunning Turnaround At Tarrytown," *Time Magazine*, May 5, 1980, p. 87.

and invited their comments. Many good ideas came forth concerning problems that management hadn't realized existed. Missed items were picked up and managers had time to implement corrective action. The cost savings produced by these suggestions spurred the plant executives to move further. In 1972 the plant's supervisors began holding regular meetings with workers, on company time, to discuss worker complaints and ideas for boosting efficiency. Both sides agreed to bring in an outside consultant to organize worker participation projects.

The first breakthrough in the trial project came with Tarrytown's 30 windshield installers. Half of these workers had been disciplined during the previous six months for poor work. During discussion it was revealed that each worker selected a different point around the windshield to begin applying the sealant. One worker started at the spot where the radio antenna wires emerged from the windshield because you get a little extra adhesive in the form of a puddle and that stops leaks. That little trick was new to the rest of the crew, the supervisor, and the plant engineers. This method was quickly adopted and resulted in a rapid reduction in the number of dealer complaints.

A similar breakthrough resulted in the plant's body shop. Within months the percentage of bad welds dropped from 35 to 1.5 percent.

As a result of these programs of worker participation, the plant's atmosphere changed radically. No longer were workers ready to "knock heads" with supervisors but felt ready to inform supervisors when they were ready to discuss problems. If management had a problem, they sat and discussed it. Giving labor a greater voice in the job participation experiment improved productivity by bringing declines in grievances, absenteeism and waste. Since 1976 the Tarrytown plant has turned out high quality products, lowered absenteeism to 2.5 percent and drastically reduced disciplinary orders, firings, worker turnover, and breakage. "Tarrytown represents in microcosm the beginnings of what may become commonplace in the future—*a new collaborative approach on the part of management, unions, and workers to improve the quality of life at work in its broadest sense.*"[9]

SUMMARY

One of the major keys to an organization's success or a country's success is to maintain a market competitive edge and remain profitable. Productivity or the output of products given the input of resources, such as men, materials, money, organizational assets, appears to be *the* major reason for an organization either winning or losing its market competitiveness. Whether an organization competes on a domestic or international mar-

[9]Ibid., p. 87.

ket basis, lower output and higher costs can be the harbinger of an organization's demise.

The manager closest to the actual output or where the work is actually done, regardless of level of management is the supervisor. The addition of new or improved plant equipment and technology can boost output and significantly increase overall production at lower cost per unit of output, but the major ingredient in substantial output appears to be people and their attitudes toward their quantity and quality of work. An effective, well-trained supervisor can instill pride, trust, and willingness to work or he/she can provoke distrust, suspicion, and an unwillingness to work.

KEY CONCEPTS

Employee productivity. This concept has changed in recent years from methods design and time standard incentive programs to involvement, concern, quality of work life, job satisfaction, and self-fulfillment. Productive workers must want to work and be motivated to work to produce *quality* output.

Participative management. Supervisors have to elicit employee input in making changes, job improvement, and generally be willing to listen to others with concern to develop trust and feeling that their subordinates are doing something worthwhile. People should be treated as you would want yourself to be treated.

Market competitiveness. An organization must produce up-to-date products that sell at a low enough price but also make a profit. Favorable revenue, volume, and cost relationships culminate in quantity and quality of output or productivity. High productivity is essential for a firm to be able to compete effectively in domestic and world markets.

Well-trained supervisors and productivity. Good supervision will and can insure high quality productivity by working with and through people. A willing worker can be a productive worker with proper training and tools. An unwilling worker can be nonproductive, regardless of the environment, tools, pay, or other variables. Losing the race in productivity means the decline or even demise of the organization.

IMPORTANT TERMS

Competitiveness	Productivity
Involvement	Quality of work life
Participative management	

INCIDENTS

The Supervisor's Dilemma

Howard Lilly is the supervisor of the cultural scribing department in a large map-making government agency. His department's responsibility is to scribe the cultural aspects (houses, schools, barns, and so on) on the maps that already have contour lines for elevations, woodlands, water, and stream characteristics. Howard and his workers are very conscientious in their placement, identification, and representation of these cultural aspects. The scribing jobs, however, are tedious and boring after a few hours. A scriber has to sit on a high stool or stand over a 2½ foot by 3½ foot line map master and position himself or herself so that his or her perspective is perpendicular to the plane of the map. This is very necessary to present an accurate representation. Inaccurate representations of any of the map's characteristics, such as distances could provoke serious errors by engineers who use these maps for construction and excavation projects.

Since the tedium of the job is so high, Howard is very lenient on the workers and how they spend their time on the job. This leniency, however, appears to be carried too far in some instances since outside visitors believed that the entire department was taking a continuous coffee break. A complete lack of urgency appears to exist. When questioned by his immediate superior, Beth Goldman, the assistant branch chief, about production delays, Howard insists that precision and accuracy are more important than speed and meeting a self-imposed production schedule. Goldman can't counter with much ammunition since the agency's average time to complete one sheet or line map is four years from flyover to finished line map, ready for sale to users. Goldman couldn't help but think about some private and state map agencies who could do the same product in an average of a year. She worried about these competitors taking away business but quickly dismissed this fact as she justified the agency's existence since it was established by Congress in 1879.

The branch chief, an engineer named Greg McCamment, doesn't see the situation as do most of his colleagues. McCamment worries about production delays and loss of business to private and state organizations. He knows that many bottlenecks exist in the agency's productivity and wants to correct as many as possible.

Maps can become obsolete over time as new roads, buildings, dams, and excavations change contour, cultural, and water characteristics. Scribing is one of the most noticeable bottlenecks and McCamment decides to put pressure on Howard Lilly's department to increase productivity. With many new mapping techniques developed during the space program of the 1960s and 1970s, new mapping technologies are available but are not being used by McCamment's agency.

Next week, McCamment will hold a staff meeting with all the department supervisors and assistant branch chiefs. In the meeting he will forceably point out that productivity *must* be increased or else. Both Goldman and Lilly, who will be in attendance, will get the message and begin to worry about possible solutions.

What clear areas of supervisory responsibilities can be identified? If you were Howard Lilly, the supervisor of the cultural scribing department, what would you do? How can McCamment's orders be carried out effectively?

Role Play the Supervisor's Dilemma Apply the preceding situation to a conversation between Howard Lilly, the supervisor, and one of his scribers, Bill Bissel. Lilly is trying to implement his supervisor's wishes and increase his department's productivity. Bill Bissel is the department's informal leader and can help Howard establish the new work patterns and quantity of work for the department since Bissel was instrumental in establishing the present work standards. Obviously, Bissel wants to protect his position of power.

Start the role play with Lilly approaching Bissel's worktable.

The Power Struggle

Young Karen Yoho, a recent community college graduate, was appointed a supervisor in the major appliance stockroom of a large Milwaukee department store. She had seven men working for her. The department filled orders from stock to be shipped to customer's homes throughout Wisconsin and northern Illinois. Orders from the downtown store and from the three suburban stores were filled in Karen's department.

The major task of the department was to maintain accuracy and speed in locating the specific appliance, shipping it safely and expeditiously, and choosing the proper transportation method. Most customers were impatient when their appliances were not shipped as soon as possible after inspecting the store's floor samples. Shipment also required installation of the washing machines, dryers, microwave ovens, trash mashers, refrigerators, ranges, and freezers.

Karen understood the technical, structural aspects and the objectives of her department's productivity but she failed to understand that her six workers were not as enthusiastic about working for the company as she was. This situation created a few tense encounters with her employees, including some insubordination and angry words. No incident was serious but the frequency of these minor irritants caught the attention of both the union steward, Pete Wilson and the store's personnel director, Merle Olsen.

Both the union steward and the director of personnel who also handled labor relations saw Karen's predicament as the ideal test case for the next bargaining session where supervisory training and worker educational benefits were two primary issues. The union used Karen Yoho's case as a prime example of the company's poor hiring practices and inadequate training system. The store saw Karen's situation as an example of the union's insistence that workers and supervisors should be trained on company time rather than their own time. The store insisted that all worker training should *not* interfere with their obligated 40 hours per week but be on the worker and supervisor's time. All other management training was not on store time so why should any other training be on store time?

As the union and personnel director bickered and bargained, poor Karen was caught in the middle and rudely became aware of the ensuing power struggle. She complained that she couldn't get her job done with all this interference. She attributed the incidents with her people to have been instigated by the union-store power struggle. The increased recognition of her workers also helped to increase the seriousness of each small encounter she had with her men. Being inexperienced, Karen Yoho was uncertain as to what was her best solution.

What would you do if you were Karen Yoho? What avenues are open to the supervisor in this power struggle? What responsibilities does Karen have to the store, to the workers, and to herself? How can she correct and coordinate these growing problems?

QUESTIONS FOR DISCUSSION

1. If you were in a conversation with a friend of yours and he or she stated "American cars are not as well built as Japanese or German cars," how would you respond?
2. If the United States is still the most productive nation in the world, why do we hear so much about productivity?
3. Why won't number two or even number three or four suffice for the U.S. standing in the economic foot race?
4. What is productivity and how is it measured?
5. Is productivity higher in white-collar or office jobs than it is in blue-collar or manufacturing jobs?
6. Why can't labor, management, and government agree on workable solutions to the productivity problem?
7. Explain why the human approach to improved productivity may be the best approach.
8. What may provoke a worker into carelessness?
9. Why are people more self-assertive now than ever before?
10. Explain how and why well-trained supervisors may be the major key to improved productivity.

CHAPTER XI
Job Design and Job Boredom

LEARNING OBJECTIVES

- To become acquainted with the latest productivity improvement techniques.
- To understand job design.
- To understand what work methods and time studies are and how they can be used.
- To know what techniques, procedures, and communication processes are available to increase productivity.

Introduction

Given the seriousness of the productivity crisis and the supervisor's significant contribution toward its improvement, we now turn our attention to the task of how to implement improved productivity.

A movement called "Quality of Worklife" exemplifies the major direction being taken to improve productivity. Quality of worklife concepts are difficult to identify and even more difficult to evaluate, but generally they include groups of both management and labor formed to improve working conditions, supervisory effectiveness, employee benefits, worker involvement, and worker control. Workers respond best to programs they help to create and that benefit them. Many supervisors are terrified that it will mean giving up control to the workers. Obviously this is not correct. It forces the managers, including supervisors, to deal honestly and directly with workers, which appears to be the supervisory *modus operandi* of the 1980s and 1990s.

PRODUCTIVITY AND THE WORKER–SUPERVISOR RELATIONSHIP

The preceding discussion illustrates a growing need for greater productivity in our business, industrial, service, institutional, and governmental organizations. Lack of motivation, insufficient desire to work or produce a quality product, outdated work rules, slowdowns, inefficient supervisory and management methods, and just plain boredom on the job have helped to stymie the necessary increase in productivity. Supervisors can't sit on the sidelines in this complex set of problems. They are in the middle and have been, and will continue to be, held responsible by top management and society for an increase in productivity. (Up to this time, at least one-half of the recent increase in national worker productivity has been the result of improved machinery, technology, product design, and capital investment in new plants and equipment, rather than from the improved efforts of employees.) The potential increase in productivity from a new generation of technology—such as computer-assisted or directed machine (numerical control), automated factories, and breakthroughs in production techniques—will greatly assist in this productivity problem. However, nonproduction employees now make up approximately 62 percent of the work force in business, industry, and the service industry. These nonproduction, or white-collar employees have difficulty in establishing predetermined rate of productivity.

All types of organizations are faced with the need for greater productivity per worker. No longer can most organizations afford to keep a well-paid worker who collects eight hours pay for only two hours work. World competition will deter featherbedding on the part of employees as well as featherbedding practices by management.

In this chapter, both current and historical concepts are discussed so that a supervisor may see clearly the problems that exist in the set of economic complexities involved in supervising people at work. The chapter will cover the more recent work schedules such as flextime and the four-day week, in addition to work methods and their facets and job design.

FLEXTIME—IS IT A PANACEA?

Flextime is one of the major developments in employment policies of the 1970s. First introduced in Germany in 1967, it was first used in this country in the early 1970s and spread rapidly. Under flexible work hours (flextime for short) employees choose their arrival and departure times, within limits, to and from work. The organization established core hours when everyone must be at work with a flexible band at both ends of the working day. Flextime is sufficiently versatile to permit some people to borrow time off from one work week and make up for the lost time. This enhances long weekends, visits to distant relatives, and extended leisure excursions.

Flextime is a highly regarded employee benefit and morale builder. It appears to be an innovative way to increase employee self-esteem, dignity, involvement, and satisfaction. More importantly it may yield a hard dollars-and-cents productivity gain to a firm. It also gives hope toward resolving serious nationwide problems of lagging productivity.

A research study that surveyed over 445 organizations and more than 10,000 employees in drug companies, banks, insurance companies, electronics companies, transportation companies, utilities, and governmental agencies provided the following trends and patterns concerning the effectiveness of flextime.[1]

1. Reductions in paid absences, idle time on the job, fewer employees leaving or arriving at once, and more actual labor from the same number of hours.
2. Greater productivity because of better organization of work.
3. People have different biological clocks, being "morning people" or "night people."
4. Better employee morale and job satisfaction usually produces an increased productivity.
5. Flextime may bring about better supervisory and management practices such as a change from a negative controlling style to a more positive, facilitating style.
6. May induce better labor-management relations with greater worker involvement, quality of worklife, more training and new organizational development programs.

Flextime may sound as if it were a panacea or cureall, but it must be judged within its sources of information and constraints. Few flextime failures are reported and successful programs may be exaggerated. Supervisors report that flextime is less successful than as reported by the employees—success being measured by quality increases and productivity gains.

The key to productivity gains using flextime may be *how* it is managed. Flextime says to employees, "we are paying you to get the job done, not to put in your time." Faced with this proposition and positive challenge, employees tend to respond. However, supervisors are often skeptical since some of their control is dissipated with greater employee involvement in their own work schedules. Control Data Corporation found that managers and supervisors are more effective under flextime because they have to *plan* in order to make flextime work. So improved supervision may be the significant part of the productivity gains reported.

FOUR-DAY WORK WEEKS

Another system for improving employee morale and productivity is the four-day instead of the five-day work week. Forty hours a week are stand-

[1] Standley D. Nollen, "Does Flextime Improve Productivity?", *Harvard Business Review*, September-October, 1979, pp. 12+.

ard in both plans but the four-day work schedule contains a 10-hour day rather than an 8-hour day as in the five-day week.

Most evidence shows a reduction in absenteeism and tardiness, but an increase in quality, safety, and productivity are insignificant, washing out the expectation of significant gains in both quality and productivity. Labor unions claim that four-day weeks will be standard as was the five-day, 40-hour week when it became standard in 1938 with the passage of the Fair Labor Standards Act.

The major controversy over the four-day work week is the union's contention that a four-day week should be an 8-hour or 9-hour day rather than a 10-hour day. This would compute to a 32- or 36-hour week. Management believes unions are really trying to create more jobs. If the issue is more money for less work, then the firm could be placed in jeopardy, thus mitigating the possible productivity offerings of the four-day week.

THE SUPERVISOR AND JOB DESIGN

A supervisor's responsibility to the organization is the motivating, directing, and controlling of the efforts of the workers in production while at the same time satisfying the worker's social and emotional needs. With the changed worker and the change in leadership styles required today, a worker-centered rather than a production-centered attitude can get out more work. However, being worker-centered does not excuse the supervisor from being proficient in the technical methods of production. Workers like to have their supervisor interested in them as individuals, but they also desire his technical support and direction so that they can do their jobs more efficiently. If their jobs are not rewarding, it behooves the supervisor to take steps that will correct the situation, such as a transfer, a change in the job, elimination of waste motion, or establishment of new standards and procedures for the job. *Job design* is concerned with the job content, the methods, and time study of the job. It is necessary that the supervisor understand these concepts so that she can call in professionals and be able to interpret these needs to both the worker and the specialist.

JOB DESIGN

Among the many problems of efficient productivity, job design is one of the major topics of concern. A supervisor's knowledge of this important technical aspect of the job can be quite rewarding because the supervisor will be required to work closely with methods engineers, time and motion people, personnel people, wage and salary administrators, and job design people. *Job design*, in its current sense, is the specification of *job content* (what the job requires), *work methods* (the best way to do it), and the relationships between the two in order to satisfy technological and organizational requirements as well as social and personal requirements of the job holder. The traditional or historical approach to job design has concentrated on technological requirements of cost cutting and production standardization.

Starting in the 1930s, social scientists became interested in job performance, work analysis, and man's relationship. Elton Mayo and F. J. Roethlisberger found in their Hawthorne experiments that social and egotistic needs affected workers' performance as much as the economic considerations.

Following World War II early studies performed by the Tavistock Institute on job design were called "sociotechnical" systems studies of the relationship between social needs of the worker and the task performed. The new job design people, with their social science perspectives of Herzberg, Maslow, McGregor, and McClelland believed that current sophisticated practices of motion and time study viewed man as an integral part of the mechanical operations of the job. Despite the often repeated statement, starting with Taylor, that work methods "fit the job to the person," Louis E. Davis[2] and his colleagues insisted that firms rarely tried to do this in spite of the sizable amount of scientific research on individual "capability for creativity" toward work.

The gap between job design research and existing methods of structuring jobs can be explained partly in terms of management's willingness to live with the traditional concepts of division of labor, paced work, engineered standards, repetitive operation orientation, and the fact that these perspectives had been tested and proved. The new social sciences techniques, discussed later in this chapter, have not had a sufficient number of tests to prove their validity.

Despite incentive programs, profit sharing, improved equipment, better working conditions, and a proliferation of fringe benefits greater worker performance is still a problem. Historically, job design has been a meeting place for industrial engineering techniques, and social science perspectives and research findings.

WORK METHODS

Work methods, sometimes called methods analysis, motion study, work simplification, or work improvement, are concerned with cutting costs by making products at minimum costs. Moreover, work methods attempt to determine how to make products or perform a task with less human effort, how to reduce the cost of material or supplies, and how to simplify the work methods involved in a job. It is a constant struggle to shave unnecessary movements, inappropriate procedures, and poor work arrangement as these are practiced by a number of workers and tolerated by their supervisors. Improving the efficiency of doing a job starts with questioning whether the job is necessary or not. Methods study tries to reduce human effort by directing people to work smarter, not harder.

Curiously, many people dislike the thought of increasing efficiency in their work methods. The "efficiency analyst" image generates thoughts

---

[2]Louis E. Davis, "The Design of Jobs," *Industrial Relations*, October 1966.

of a threat to job survival, mechanistic movements, spying, and interference. Work methods study attempts to reduce tasks to their simplest elements and to view these elements so that an economy of motion can be achieved and costs can be reduced. In redesigning a job, certain parts may be eliminated; as a result, a person may do the remaining parts of the job more often, thus increasing the number of units produced. Or in another case, the person may take an additional task with the time savings. In a third case, the job may be reduced to something a machine can do better, and the person can be transferred to another, more creative position. Making a job more repetitive disturbs some people, but most methods people believe it is easy to exaggerate this matter. According to the methods point of view, some people object to being transferred from a repetitive job because the job offers security without any upsetting problems. A repetitive job permits the worker to daydream or talk to his or her neighbors, and it has a pleasant lulling effect, according to the defenders of traditional methods study techniques.

Objectives of Methods Study

The methods person attempts to find the best way to do a job in the time-honored Gilbreth tradition. In reality, he or she is attempting to find a better way. The difference is important. Once perfection is achieved, the job content may be changed or a new operator, clerk, or typist can introduce other variables that destroy the perfection. A work methods engineer must be satisfied with a better way at reasonable costs.

The analyst, whether an industrial engineer or a supervisor, has three objectives that should be achieved.

1. Eliminate as many wasteful human movements as possible.
2. Shorten the movements that can't be eliminated.
3. Make the necessary movements less tiring.

Techniques for Work Methods Study

The first tool a methods analyst should possess is a research orientation coupled with an inquisitive nature. This person must ask all the pertinent questions of any good researcher—who, what, where, when, how, and above all *why*. Status-quo or "we have always done it that way" attitudes have to be considered but tolerated in the analysis. The methods analyst assumes that the job is not being performed correctly and that he or she is there to improve it. Obviously, a critical analysis can be harmful and upsetting, as already stated. Once the worker understands the objectives of the study—and if the methods analyst treats the worker with respect and courtesy—a better working relationship can exist.

The methods analyst has five major working tools to use in the analysis. Of the five, the first two are used frequently and the other three are used in special cases where the higher costs of analysis can be justified.

Job Design   209

1. Process charts.
2. Motion study principles.
3. Suggestive questions.
4. Micromotion study.
5. Therblig analysis.

Process Charts There are a number of different charts that can be used, depending on the function or relationship that we wish to chart. A chart is a method to record movements so that the analyst can see the possible waste in movements. Therefore, when charting, the analyst must record what is happening rather than what is supposed to happen. Once these data are in the chart as observed, then the chart becomes a useful tool for analysis.

Process charts of all kinds show the details of activities. Performance, or what is done, is described in words. In addition, all charts show a symbol for each detail, as shown in Figure 11-1.

Motion Study Principles The second kind of job improvement technique views human motion from the standpoint of *principles of motion economy*. Over the years, the industrial engineers have developed a set of general statements, called principles of motion economy, which concern work arrangements, use of

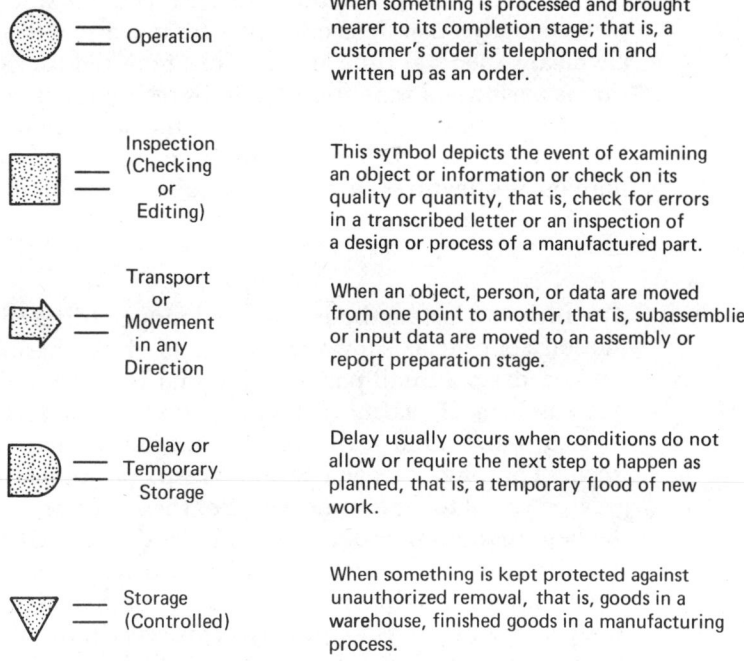

Figure 11-1 Five charting symbols for manufacturing analysis and their definitions.

human hands and body, and the design and use of tools. These principles are described in an abbreviated form in Figure 11-2. Figure 11-3 shows the basic motion elements. The twenty-two rules or principles of motion economy can be profitably applied to shop, office, store, or household tasks. Although not all the principles are applicable to all work situations, they do form a basis for improving efficiency, in addition to reducing fatigue in manual work. Figure 11-4 illustrates work areas for most efficient operations. This type of illustration can be included in an operator's process chart, as discussed above, but is included here to illustrate some of the parameters or values of motion economy.

Suggestive Questions The third tool used in work improvement or methods analysis uses a series of very detailed questions. These questions are much like the principles of motion economy but are more detailed in their analysis. Such a list, as applicable to a marketing organization, appears in Figure 11-5. These questions contain the six research W's of who, what, where, when, why, and how (how ends with a W). The great amount of time required for this approach prohibits the wide use of this technique.

Micromotion Study A fourth way of analyzing work methods is through the use of motion pictures, running them slowly through a projector and analyzing each motion and the time it takes to perform. By studying the pictures, a trained analyst can determine how to improve even short-cycle jobs. (Cycle means the total time and motions required to complete an operation that is performed repetitiously.) This technique is very precise but costly in time expended; however, unions and workers dislike it because they believe the worker is placed under a microscope, and they reject the dehumanizing features of the technique. Short, highly repetitive jobs are best for this technique.

Therblig Analysis The fifth and last methods study technique utilizes the Gilbreths' therblig motion concept as shown in Figure 11-4. A therblig (Gilbreth spelled backwards) is a small part of a job that is much too short to time with a stopwatch, such as move hand, get ready to pick up wrench, grasp wrench, move hand with wrench, position wrench, turn wrench, and so forth. Therbligs of each move, grasp, position are analyzed in their greatest detail to determine which of these motions can be combined into the best methods in order to expedite and economize on human motions. A trained analyst can spot a series of these movements and determine whether a worker has reached too far or too high. However, therblig analysis is not used as frequently as process charts and motion study principles because of its high cost. The technique is usually limited to fast, highly repetitive operations in which an extremely small movement, if changed, can improve the operation appreciably.

I. Use of the Human Body
1. The two hands should start and finish their motion at the same time.
2. The two hands should not be idle at once — except during rest.
3. Arm motions should be opposite and symmetrical directions simultaneously.
4. Hand motions should be at a minimum for job performance.
5. Momentum should be used to assist the worker but be reduced to a minimum if muscular effort is needed to overcome it.
6. Smooth, continuous motions of hand are correct rather than zigzag motions.
7. Ballistic movements are faster, easier, and more accurate than restricted or controlled movements.
8. Rhythm is essential to smooth, automatic performance that requires proper work arrangement to expedite and enhance the rhythm.

II. Arrangement of the Work Place
9. Tools and materials should have a definite and fixed place.
10. Tools, materials, and controls should be located directly in front of the operator.
11. Gravity feed and containers should deliver material close to point of use.
12. Drop deliveries should be used whenever possible.
13. Materials and tools should be located so that the best sequence of motions can be sustained.
14. Good illumination is the first requirement for satisfactory visual perception.
15. Height of work place and chair should be located so that alternate sitting and standing at work are possible.
16. Good posture chairs should be provided for each worker.

III. Design of Tools and Equipment
17. The hands should be relieved of all work that a jig, fixture, office equipment, or foot-operated device can do better.
18. Two or more tasks should be combined whenever possible.
19. Tools and materials should be prepositioned.
20. Where each finger performs a specific movement, that is, typing, the load should be distributed in accordance with the capacities of each finger.
21. Handles of tools should be designed so that a maximum hand contact surface can be maintained.
22. Lever bars and hand wheels should be located so that operation can manipulate them with the least change in body position and with the greatest mechanical advantage.

Figure 11-2 Principles of motion economy. A checklist for motion economy and fatigue reduction. (Source. Adapted from Elwood S. Buffa, Basic Production Management, John Wiley and Sons, New York, 1971, p. 338. Originally appeared in R. M. Barnes, Motion and Time Study: Design and Measurement of Work, 6th ed., John Wiley and Sons, New York, 1968).

Group 1	Group 2	Group 3
Useful elements that usually accomplish work—but not necessarily in the most effective way	Elements that retard work usually by slowing down Group 1 elements	Nonaccomplishment elements that add nothing to completed task
Reach Apply pressure	Change direction	Hold
Move Turn	Preposition	Unavoidable delay
Grasp Sino motion	Search	Avoidable delay
Position Body, leg, foot	Select	Rest to overcome fatigue
Disengage Eye travel	Balancing delay	
Release Eye focus	Plan	
Examine		
Do		

Figure 11-3   Three groups of basic motion elements grouped according to the action comprising the element (therbligs).

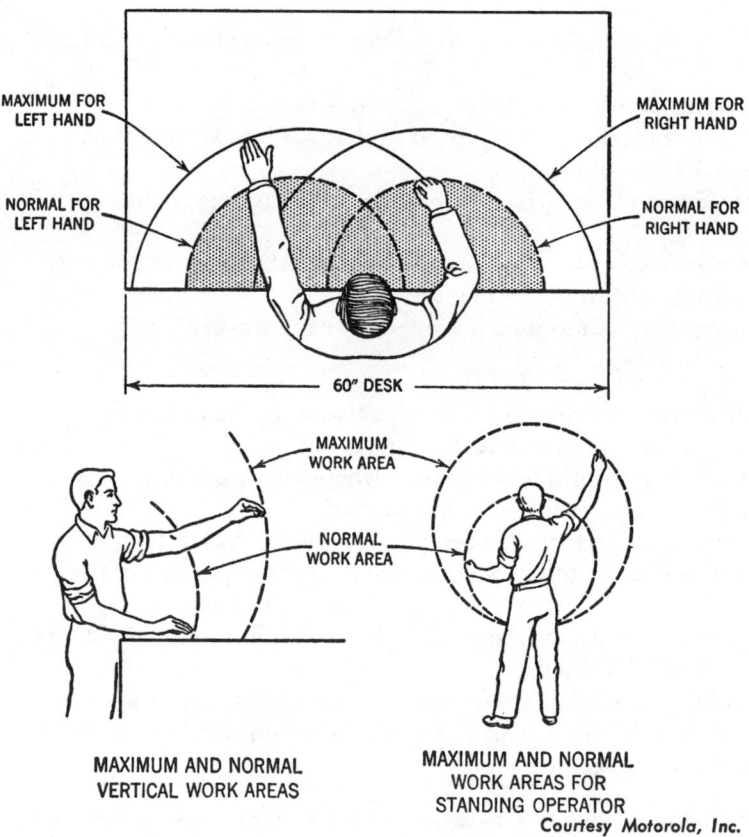

Figure 11-4   Work areas for most efficient operations. (Source. From William R. Spriegel and Edward Schultz, Elements of Supervision, 2nd ed., John Wiley and Sons, New York, 1957.)

1. Is the scope and purpose of the investigation clear?
2. How far is the organization and work done affected or likely to be affected by recent events or developments?
3. Have fringe activities been investigated or reported on recently?
4. Is an organization chart available? Is it up to date? Is the total staff strength included?
5. How much of the work is routine, how much is specialized, and how much is technical?
6. What are the main conditions under which the work is done? Is there a dependence on another section or department? Must the work be completed within a specific time cycle? Is this cycle logical or traditional?
7. Are other people's interests involved in the work situation?
8. Are there work standards, timetables, or programs? Are these being achieved or followed?
9. What time is taken on the main phases of the work? How much time is taken up in waiting for work, clerical activities, selling?
10. Where are documents kept and how are they stored? How are the papers arranged and what is the degree of accessibility to them?
11. What are the relationships with other sections or departments and between individual jobs within the section or department?
12. How is the staff deployed? What have been the fluctuations, if any, in the numbers employed on specific activities?
13. What is the current and historic volume of work at the various stages?
14. Are there any arrears of work? Is there a pattern? Are there any particular trouble spots?
15. What are the activity costs in terms of staff, accommodation, equipment, and materials?
16. What facilities are provided for the user or customer? Are there records of their complaints?
17. Have there been any complaints about the ways in which the section or department has operated?
18. Is there a measure of the cost or effectiveness of the service provided to the customer?
19. Are there any comments or problems which the staff could contribute to the study?
20. What are the effects of layout, accommodation, and environment on job performance?
21. How is work supervised? Is there visual contact or is it physically remote? Are there checks during the job or at the end of it? How effective are the checking procedures?
22. What is the ratio of supervision to employees? Does supervision restrict its activities to just supervising or does it undertake other activities? If it does, what are they?
23. Is supervision given adequate guidance and backing by management?

Figure 11-5 Checklist of questions for work study. (Source. From Ronald Dow, Marketing and Work Study, Pergamon Press, Oxford, England, 1969, p. 23.

TIME STUDY

Time study can be defined as a procedure for determining the amount of time required, under certain standard conditions of measurement, for tasks involving some human activity. The result of such a measurement is called a *standard time*. A standard time indicates how long a given rate of work input must be maintained to produce a unit of output. Time study, sometimes called work measurement, is used to determine what is a "fair day's work." A production standard established through work measurement provides the methodology and rationale for determining a fair day's work for different jobs. Incentive pay systems use these standards in setting a piece rate. However, piece rate or other production incentive pay systems are not the only reason to use time study. Time study standards can help to determine an operation's cost, how long a job takes, and how much a machine can produce. Moreover, time study can help estimate new jobs never performed before; set quotas; divide up work along an assembly line, store, or office so that the workers performing the work will have equal work assignments; compare costs of doing a job in different ways; help in figuring how many workers and machines will be needed for future production in a shop, office, laboratory, or institution.

Taking an Observed Time Study

The detailed techniques of taking a time study are beyond the scope of this chapter, and it is suggested that the supervisor study the technical aspects of time study in one of the many excellent books available. However, it is necessary for the supervisor to understand the different methods employed in time study and to understand the use and benefits of time study.

Three major steps taken by the time study analyst are as follows.

1. Observe time of a job from a decimal minute, or hour, stopwatch.
2. Calculate normal time for a job.

Normal time = Observed time × Rating factor (recorded in a manual)

3. Calculate standard time.

$$\text{Standard time} = \text{Normal time} + \text{allowance}$$
      (a) Personal.
      (b) Delay.
      (c) Fatigue.

These three steps illustrate the most common time study analysis. However, no matter how precise are the data that a time study analyst presents, there are certain disadvantages inherent in the system.

The first step, observing time with a decimal stopwatch, can be done by almost anyone who stays alert to starting the watch at the beginning of an element in a task, stopping the watch when the element is finished, and then recording the correct reading. This appears easier than it really is; observing the correct movements requires experience and judgment.

The second step, calculating *normal time*, becomes a little trickier as the analyst's judgment, experience, and training begin to show themselves. Observed time is multiplied by a *rating factor*, sometimes called a leveling factor. This rating factor represents the major area of controversy in present day time study. Unions object to the so-called subjective nature or judgment involved.

The third step, *standard time* calculation, again, has some judgment in estimating *allowances* for personal time, delay, and fatigue. As an example of delay, the worker may not have correctly inserted the paper into the typewriter, and thus a delay for paper adjustment can occur, or the operator may have to wait for an automatic machine to complete its cycle before starting operations. Fatigue is a catch-all term but generally refers to resting time allowed on heavy jobs. Personal time refers to time for clearing up, visiting the restroom, and other necessary human activities.

Limitations of Time Study

Time study does have its limitations of which a supervisor should be aware. The following points illustrate these limitations.

1. You can time only what you see.
2. A job to be timed must be a specific job with starting and stopping points.
3. Jobs have to be repetitive before time study is very useful.
4. The worker has to control the work before time study is beneficial. If a worker is paced by the machine, time study loses its significance.
5. If quality is difficult to define, standards may cause quality to fall off.
6. Time study must be properly introduced to the employees. This makes psychological demands on the engineer for which she may be unprepared.
7. Union opposition may stop the use of time study. Here the supervisor may assist in the educational process.

After all has been said, motion and time study can be an extremely valuable tool for the supervisor to understand and work with the experts in these fields. However, ignorance, mistrust, and fear can destroy the usefulness of these techniques. The reason for these studies is to assist the worker in becoming more productive so that he can share in the fruits of his labor. The unions and sometimes the workers have not agreed with this philosophy. In other quarters, some scientists believe that methods and time study have helped to dehumanize the worker. They point to the worker's lack of motivation, lower productivity, and apathy on the job. These are real problems in mass production, mass distribution, and general assembly or report preparation duties. Routinized, perfunctory jobs have apparently hurt some organizations' worker involvement. In addition, management-worker attitudes, societal changes toward the worker's role, and the greater sophistication of the worker of today have exaggerated the situation. The next section treats this subject in greater depth.

JOB DESIGN AND JOB BOREDOM

TRADITIONAL VIEWS
Methods design and time study have been techniques to increase the efficiency of the worker by applying scientific analysis to his already designed job. A job could be analyzed and condensed to its common elements. Productivity, if measured by output per worker, could be used in incentive programs, such as piece rate systems. The worker's productivity or output could be rewarded once standards of a normal output were measured. This philosophy of rewarding worker productivity has much merit and has been successful in many places over the last 100 years. However, a gradual change in workers and their attitudes has been occurring since World War II. Repetitive jobs are causing job boredom, which precipitates lower-quality work, lower productivity, and low morale. Today organizations are designing new jobs and redesigning old ones with some new values and techniques in operation.

Today's work force appears to be a new breed in which people are less easily controlled, less dependent, less submissive and passive, less willing to work "harder and smarter," in spite of better economic rewards, improved working conditions, better training, and enlightened supervision. People at work don't appear to be motivated by the "carrot and stick" formula used so often in the past. Part of this lack of motivation has been due to the character or job content of work itself, according to a number of behavioral scientists. For the mature individual, work may be a means of personal growth in that it may satisfy needs for achievement, creativity, and self-fulfillment. As discussed earlier, work has become more than a means for economic survival. In our age of affluence, people won't work long or well at a job that offers no challenge or meaning. This newer development may be the result of our economic affluence, better education, better transportation, better communication, and higher levels of aspiration among workers. Newer attitudes generated by these developments have affected worker productivity as measured by traditional methods and time study in assembly and mass production jobs.

In a household survey 1515 workers, representative of all major demographic and occupational groups, were asked a series of questions about

	Percent responding to "Very True"	
	1973	1977
1. Good hours, pleasant surroundings, and job free of conflicting demands.	38.4	30.2
2. Interesting work, opportunity to develop abilities, freedom to decide how to do the job.	51.3	41.5
3. Good pay, fringe benefits, and job security.	45.7	33.8
4. Sufficient information and authority to get the job done.	63.3	52.3

Data 1973 and 1977 "Quality of Employment Survey," University of Michigan Survey Research Center, Work In America Institute, Inc.

Figure 11-6   Four Year Decline In Job Satisfaction

employment. The results are shown in Figure 11-6.[3] Various polls of the same subject matter indicated that job satisfaction had shown little change but the 1977 survey shown in Figure 11-6 is a significant change because it's the first confirmed decline in the national level of job satisfaction. Jobs may not be getting worse but people are getting better educated. If this trend were to continue, it may not result in strikes and other overt forms of protest but it would probably mean increasing friction between supervisors steeped in authoritarian production attitudes and workers who want more challenge and more voice in decisions affecting their jobs.

According to the same survey over half of the respondents complained about having no control over job assignments, 76 percent believed that workers should have complete say or a lot to say on decisions affecting worker safety, and 77 percent mentioned the lack of control over the days that they work as a problem. The growing concern about working days and hours points to a sizable group of workers who would favor *flextime* where workers could determine their own work schedules.

METHODS FOR JOB DESIGN

There are a number of different approaches to job design and the increased interest in job content. The use of any one method depends on the product or service requirements of the organization, the managerial style practiced, and the motivational level of the work force. The most common approaches used in job design to enhance job content for motivation include the following seven policies.[4]

[3]"A Warning: The Worker Discontent is Rising," *Business Week*, June 4, 1979, p. 152.
[4]Harold M. F. Rush, *Job Design for Motivation, Experiments in Job Enlargement and Job Enrichment*, The Conference Board, New York, 1971, pp. 12-14.
"Hot UAW 'Quality of Work Life'" Business Week (September 17, 1979), pp. 120-122.

Job Rotation Employees move from one task to a related task within their "home" work unit. Advocates of this method believe that the motivational factors are the stimulation from learning new skills, increased employee interest, and knowledge of the job.

Job Enlargement The employee assumes several related tasks instead of a single task previously performed. The scope of the work is enlarged, and the job is designed to include several tasks. The proponents of this approach believe that boredom will be decreased and the increased challenge will act as a motivator.

Job Enrichment The difficulty of the task is increased to demand more of the employee's capabilities. The employee accepts more responsibility and accountability for "managing" the job. Advocates of this method insist that job enrichment, and not job enlargement, is the best means for building real motivation since it includes an enriched job content and self-actualizing opportunities. Enriched jobs usually include responsibility, achievement, recognition, advancement, and growth.

A number of companies have instituted "enrichment" programs to give workers a sense of satisfaction on the job and to send them home with a feeling of having accomplished something. General Foods' Gaines Pet Food plant in Topeka, Kansas, has started a work team approach, numbering from 6 to 17 per group, in which the workers hire, discipline, fire, set work standards, work schedules, and settle problems as a group. The supervisor takes a passive role and sits in the group to guide and direct the group whenever needed. The supervisor actually works as a lead man on the production floor. General Foods claims that the Topeka plant gets a 20 to 30 percent higher production rate than the Kankakee plant, which follows the traditional supervisory style for dog food production.

General Motors' GMC Truck and Coach Division that assembles its motor homes was experimenting with assembly techniques previously used by the Swedish firms Saab and Volvo. Basically, General Motors used the concept of group assembly, in which a team of workers perform a variety of operations on the production line, instead of one worker performing a single operation repeatedly. The team approach was designed to create more variety and interest in the job and, it is hoped, to assure a better product. GM officials believed the design would work well in the motor home plant, since it is a low-volume operation. They believed that the technique might not be appropriate in passenger car assembly, which is a high-volume operation. For example, in the Saab and Volvo plants, their group production volumes are, at most, one-fourth the volumes currently reached by most American passenger automobile plants. At the time of this writing, GM has closed down the group approach because it failed to meet the desired motor home production quota.

The Travelers Insurance Company headquarters in Hartford, Connecticut, was suffering from high absenteeism and low morale and productivity. A three-year-old "enrichment" program was instituted by transferring some supervisory functions to the card punch operator and broadening the operator's jobs. Originally, a worker would handle receipts or collections or any other single punch card function. Work was rearranged so that one employee became responsible for the entire punch card operation for a particular corporate or individual customer. This established a strong operator-customer relationship. In the first year of the pilot project, productivity increased by 26 percent and absenteeism decreased by 24 percent.

Common statements have been made by employees involved in the case studies described above. Generally, these comments show more concern by them, a feeling that less badgering by their superiors occurs, that more decision making by the workers was practiced, and, above all, that they had more involvement in planning and control. Workers tend to have a better opportunity to identify with the organization. They feel that they have input into the system. They can have a say about their jobs, their output, and how it is to be performed.

Plan—Do—Control This system carries job enrichment a step further by including the managerial functions of planning and controlling the actual job. This usually involves a team activity or a group of workers as described in the dog food plant example.

Work Modules This approach seeks to fit the job to the individual and assumes that the individual is best qualified to create that fit.[5] The work module is simply a time-task unit. If a basic unit were 2 hours, then a worker on a 40-hour week would have 4 modules a day or 20 modules a week. Workers could choose which 4 jobs they would work in a given 8-hour day. This could provide the freedom they desire so that intrinsic job satisfaction could develop. Their greater involvement could improve their productivity.

Organization Development This approach holds that organizational change can be made simply by improving the way people work together. In essence, this means allowing employees a larger voice in how they do their jobs and assuring that management does not treat employees as impersonal and interchangeable spokes in a wheel. This requires that attitudes be changed by both super-

---

[5]Robert L. Kahn "The Work-Module—A Tonic for Lunchpail Lassitude," *Psychology Today*, February 1973, p. 351.

visors and subordinates. It requires a delicate balance to maintain the supervisor's authority without stifling the employee's incentives. The workers must be treated as human beings.

Quality of Worklife

The need for more worker input and control over his or her work environment, work procedures and work control has been called the quality of worklife movement (QWL). Leading companies in this movement have been General Motors, Proctor & Gamble, Exxon, General Foods, TRW, Cummins Engine, and Polaroid. Many firms are engaged in these projects but few are willing to talk about them, citing propriety and other reasons.

General Motors and the United Auto Workers (UAW) have jointly set up QWL programs in 18 to 24 plants. They had great success with work teams and other QWL programs since they improved human satisfaction and performance. At the GM Oklahoma City plant, the 2300 workers were divided into teams of 10 to 15 people with elected leaders who made work assignments and represented the workers in dealings with supervisors. The team had the right to vote on matters normally governed by provisions in union contracts, such as overtime scheduling, and promotions. The unions became disillusioned with the system and the workers voted 2-1 for UAW representation to replace the system, citing the work teams as the major reason for discontent. However, the GM Tarrytown, N.Y. plant had high praise for its QWL program. The QWL program set the stage for better overall labor-management relations. More freedom of expression and more trust had developed. It appears that a firm must embrace some form of work improvement or face an alienated work force if it doesn't.[6]

Swedish firms have long touted QWL systems. Volvo has only one assembly plant at Kalmar that was built *without* a conventional assembly line.[7] This new line eliminates noise, monotony, and pressure which the auto workers find repugnant. Although the plant costs 10 percent more than a conventional plant, worker morale has improved, there is less costly personnel turnover, and less absenteeism occurs than at other Volvo plants.

Volvo's largest assembly line plant at Gothenburg uses optional work schedules to improve quality of worklife. Workers have the option of organizing into groups of six or more and working as teams. For example, one group of women inspects a sealing compound in all seams and installs sound-dampening insulation. They rotate the group's 15 functions so that no one gets a sore back from having to reach for long periods into remote crevices or grows too bored performing the same job. Since the

[6]"Hot UAW Issue: 'Quality of Work Life,' " *Business Week*, September 17, 1979, pp. 120-122.
[7]"Taking the Monotony Out of the Production Line," *Fortune*, February 12, 1979, p. 112.

line creeps at an almost imperceptible pace, the teams can finish their assigned work before the next batch of cars reaches them. During the waiting time, the workers are free to go for coffee or read a book. This appears to work in Sweden, but similar experiments in U.S. auto plants have not had the same results. Cultural differences may be important, mismanagement by supervisors may be another causal factor, or even labor's unwillingness to cooperate, may be a third reason.

ASSUMPTIONS OF APPROACHES

All of the above approaches to job design attempt to decrease job boredom by including different perspectives that are useful to the supervisor. But many assumptions have to be made before these concepts can be used successfully. These assumptions or theories are common threads that run through the contemporary job-design-for-motivation movement.

1. Most jobs can be improved. Too little attention has been paid to the human element, other than how man adjusts to technology.
2. Job design is aimed at economic development—increased productivity through more efficient use of human resources, materials, machines, and money, in addition to the social, emotional, and involvement aspects for the employees.
3. Job content is related to job satisfaction. An uninteresting job does not enhance job satisfaction.
4. Motivation is a function of job satisfaction and personal freedom. Humans seek responsibility and more commitment to a course of action that they help to plan and control.
5. Job design can be a means for individual as well as organizational growth. Challenged workers can be an effective vehicle for learning, and if channeled toward organizational goals, they can be an asset.
6. Motivation and productivity are inextricably intertwined. In spite of improved technological advances, without worker motivation a large segment of the sought-for productivity is missing. Human resources can be underutilized.
7. Humans seek and need meaningful work. Psychological health depends on people involving themselves in creative and rewarding work. Every effort should be a form of self-expression. If work cannot provide the opportunity for creative expression, apathy and boredom may result and the creative drive may be directed elsewhere.

Understandably, the advocates of the newer approaches to job design have an enthusiastic approach to the problems of job boredom, absenteeism, low morale, and low productivity. However, it is up to supervisors to know and to understand their people so that they can properly place each individual in the most opportune spot so that these newer techniques, attitudes, and practices can work. This could benefit the individual and enhance the achievement of the organization's objectives. This is only good supervision of the resources at hand as practiced on a day-to-day basis.

BARRIERS TO JOB DESIGN

Numerous obstacles may exist that could impede us from approaching a job design from the Theory Y perspective. This means that the supervisor should assist in the implementation of these newer techniques by understanding certain barriers, either (1) organizational or (2) attitudinal.

Organizational barriers include many elements. Some say that economic structures that emphasize or need mass production, such as high-volume passenger car output, cannot return to a "whole" job. Moreover, it is often claimed that skill levels among the workers may limit the expanded and broadened use of job enrichment or plan—do—control. A few workers may not be able to plan and control their jobs. They lack managerial talent. The supervisor should be careful in allocating workers to sensitive jobs. Some theorists say that certain jobs cannot be changed if the company's profit picture is to remain favorable. Redesigning jobs closely related to highly automated processes might incur exorbitant costs that a company could not recoup. Thus short-term profit concerns may hold up a switch over to more job enrichment. Physical conditions may prevent changing job content. Lack of money and lack of administrative practices may prevent a company from incorporating newer job design concepts. These reasons could be short-run defenses. Union-management relations may be such that any change in jobs may threaten the union's survival. This may be partly attitudinal as well, but unions could resist changes because of jurisdictional lines, particularly in the craft unions. Presently unions are sitting on the sidelines waiting to see who is right in the issue of boredom and quality of worklife versus greater productivity.

Attitudinal barriers include aspects that prevent changes. These barriers tend to be the most formidable. The work force may see job design changes as a tool to get more work out of them without considering the workers' needs. Although the opposite is true, everything depends on the supervisor's attitude. Lack of training of the supervisor in these new perspectives has created tremendous barriers in some companies that have experimented with the contemporary job design concepts. Challenging the assumptions of supervisors about the people who perform the jobs was the biggest attitudinal obstacle in an electronics firm with considerable experience in job design for motivation.[8] *The real problem wasn't so much to enrich the lower-level jobs, but rather to change supervisory attitudes that assumed that people who do menial tasks have different needs and values from people in more highly skilled jobs.* This situation provoked development training for the supervisors. Finally, some people have said that a lack of professional guidance, low priority, inertia, and a

---

[8]Harold M. F. Rush, op. cit., p. 25.

"programmed" approach to job design may have limited its use in some organizations.

In summation, barriers to job design tend to be social, attitudinal, interpersonal, and environmental. The climate of the organization, as created by top management or as created by union-management relations, can influence the success of the job design techniques. It behooves supervisors to become acquainted with the needs of today's workers, rather than continue to hold on to all of their precious authority.

SUPERVISORS HAVE TO BE BETTER MANAGERS

Leaving job design up to the supervisors or assuming that it will be carried out routinely may be a barrier. The supervisor may place higher priority on production output or on other aspects of his job. Lack of knowledge or skill in designing work, and the unfavorable climate of the organization, may help the supervisor to be a "bottleneck" in implementing the new concepts of job design. There are a variety of reasons given for the lack of implementation of job design on the part of the supervisor, but it is not uncommon for organizations to report that the supervisor's reluctance to *trust* people with greater responsibility is the major barrier. People are crying out for more meaningful work, but many supervisors appear to be reluctant to delegate, to give up doing the job themselves and making corrections for their people. "If we could somehow get the foremen to be real managers and leave the production to the workers, we'd have more success."[9] Job design requires an all-out effort in changing job content according to the behavioral sciences. Behavioral scientists warn that superficial changes in job content can be more damaging than leaving the job alone.

The messages here are quite clear. Supervisors must be better managers, they must delegate authority and assign responsibilities. Moreover, the challenge to the modern supervisor is mirrored in his training; he must be trained in human relations, understanding of organizations and human needs, and practicing the managerial functions of planning, organizing, controlling, communicating, motivating, and the latest—involving the workers in all these functions.

JOB DESIGN FOR MOTIVATION AND EMPLOYEE SATISFACTION

Since we have covered a number of techniques in cost cutting, methods analysis, and time study analysis, it is appropriate that we include some guidelines for job design as advocated by the contemporary behavioral scientists. Limited experience does not allow these practitioners to develop a manual of "how to do it" as in the case of methods analysis, but job design stresses the general guidelines listed as follows.[10]

[9]Ibid., p. 27.
[10]Ibid., p. 29.

1. Analyze all possibilities. If a job can't be made more challenging and fulfilling, automate it out and train employees for other more meaningful jobs.
2. Work on a problem. Select jobs in which a lack of productivity, efficiency, or good morale exists. Thus a better opportunity exists to measure success or failure and to determine cause-and-effect relationships between redesign of the jobs and resulting motivation and productivity.
3. Begin with a pilot study. Experiment with a small unit of the work force that makes observation, measurement, and evaluation easier.
4. Assess employee motivation. Determine needs and motivations of employees.
5. Communicate. Let employees know the real intent of the changes and how they personally are affected.
6. Develop assessment mechanisms. Measure in a systematic way.
7. Gain supervisors' support.
8. Train supervisors to delegate more, and to be more willing to give up some of the "managing" aspects of the supervisory job.
9. Train job incumbents.
10. Gain union support.
11. Build feedback mechanisms into the job.
12. Set expectations high. Demand a good performance. *Increased responsibility carries with it increased accountability for performance and satisfaction.*

Actually, job design for motivation as seen by many is a change in management philosophy. Some companies don't include such terms as *job enlargement* and *job enrichment* in their vocabulary. Some other firms have been practicing these techniques without giving them names. Inertia on the part of companies as well as supervisors are the biggest obstacles in using these newer techniques to increase worker moitivation. It is imperative that the modern supervisor understand these approaches so that he or she can work with and through his or her people effectively.

OTHER COST REDUCTION SUGGESTIONS

Job analysis and job design are not just ways of recording, improving jobs, making jobs more efficient, and providing data for incentive programs. They represent valid techniques for cost reduction and job satisfaction. However, other methods exist that the supervisor should be aware of and understand.

Cost reduction programs tend to pop up whenever sales decline or an economic downturn is foreseen. Actually, cost reduction programs should be constantly followed by the operating supervisor on a day-to-day basis so that high morale and productivity are realized.

Cost reduction is really a state of mind or an attitude as much as it is an activity. Unfortunately, a person will not concentrate on this phase of production when worried about getting out production, working with and through people, and keeping everyone informed about the activities in the department. In the heat of battle, a supervisor may become careless and overlook vital cost reduction techniques.

Supervisors do not have a great deal of latitude in reducing basic costs in the organization because of lack of control, but a supervisor is in an excellent position to influence some actual costs that may occur. Directly related to productivity per worker are things such as idle time, detailed assignments of jobs, giving orders properly, efficiently using time, working with the employees, supervising the speed and efficiency of work done, reducing the amount of scrap produced, and properly utilizing the raw materials used in the jobs. Of these controllable variables, the proper use of motivation, involvement, and satisfaction of worker needs is the most important. People can cut costs if the climate encourages them to develop this attitude.

COST REDUCTION TECHNIQUES

The most useful cost reduction tool available to the supervisor is a questioning attitude toward the job. The progressive supervisor doesn't go through a daily routine questioning everything and everybody but is constantly on the lookout for ways of doing a job better (job design or redesign, methods and work measurement).

The following questions can be helpful to the supervisor in cost reduction analysis:

1. What is being done, and what purpose does this operation fulfill?
2. Who is doing the work, and is that person the right person? Does the worker believe she or he is in the right slot?
3. Can modifications be made so that another person with less skill can do the job? Can the high-skill, high paid people be moved to critical jobs that require their skills?
4. Where does the work need to be done, or is this the best place?
5. Are the materials and tools needed to perform the job readily available to the worker? How can supervisors support their people?
6. Can operations be performed while material is in transit?
7. Is the work place properly ventilated, heated, and illuminated? Do the employees think so?
8. What can I as the supervisor do to further support the workers and increase their productivity and reduce costs?

SUMMARY

Managers are involved in social changes and behavioral changes, such as attitudes and values. The young workers are questioning their superiors' traditional way of doing things, their goals, their institutions, and their way of life. Greater attention is being paid to the decline in motivation and worker productivity and an increase in job boredom. International firms are invading traditional American markets and are forcing American companies to achieve a painful jump in worker productivity. This situation is aggravated by supervisors who insist on living in the past; but supervisors are involved in this problem whether they like it or not.

One available tool is job design, with its methods analysis, time study, and its contemporary views of job content called job design for motivation. Work methods attempt to find the better way to perform jobs so that greater efficiency and productivity can develop. Time study tries to determine standard times for use in established repetitive jobs, incentives, work allocation, and work assignments. Recent developments in job design have resulted from worker boredom and from dehumanizing effects related to mass production, division of labor, and changes in worker's attitudes and expectations.

Of the numerous new approaches, job enlargement, job enrichment, and plan—do—control have received the most attention using the term quality of worklife. All three methods appear to have barriers in practice. The supervisor's lack of knowledge, comprehension, and willingness to delegate some of his authority to the workers appears to be the biggest barrier. The future will certainly demand a better-educated supervisor, and his knowledge of job design techniques will be an extremely valuable tool in maintaining leadership to attain high productivity, at least costs, and worker satisfaction.

KEY CONCEPTS

Worker productivity. This concept has changed in recent years from thinking in terms of methods design and time standard incentive programs to enlargement of the job so that involvement, job satisfaction, and self-fulfillment are included. Productive workers must want to work and must be motivated to work as a function of their environment.

Job design. For worker satisfaction, job design must embrace job content (what the job requires) as well as job methods (the best way to do it). More recently, a broader point of view, currently used today, would place emphasis on the design of the entire system of jobs within the present sociotechnical systems. The design of new jobs and the redesign of older ones would focus on a man's capabilities.

Human capabilities relative to machines. It is significant to understand that humans have some advantages over machines and vice versa. Although economics enter the picture, it is important to note that substitutions are warranted to improve efficiency and job satisfaction for the workers to meet organizational objectives.

A standard. This concept is basic to time study or work measurement and to the problem in general. Standards are established by people exercising judgment and analyzing observed data. A normalized time is constructed, minus allowances for all tasks of a job.

Optimum job specialization. A job can be too fractionalized for economic division of labor until productivity falls, with a resultant decrease in economic gain. Job enlargement and job enrichment are different ways of attacking this problem. Where the proper balance lies depends upon the job.

Participation. Worker involvement and participation seems to be growing and increasingly accepted. In job design, the principle of participation appears to run counter to the traditional work methods and work measurement techniques used by the methods engineer who can determine the best way; ignoring the human element may not be the best way.

Job responsibility/accountability. More managerial responsibilities are pushed down to the worker level. This change forces greater accountability on the workers part. This is a management concept that the workers will have to accept as they gain greater control of their jobs. Worker satisfaction can be increased as capable workers are given more say concerning their position and tasks.

IMPORTANT TERMS

Allowance
Job content
Job design
Job design for motivation
Job enlargement
Job enrichment
Job evaluation
Job methods
Job responsibility/accountability
Motion study principles (principles of motion economy)
Normal time
Organizational development
Plan—do—control
Process charts
Quality of worklife
Rating factor (leveling factor)
Standard time
Therbligs
Time study (work measurement)
Work methods
Work modules

INCIDENTS

The Updated Job Design

George Kim was a supervisor in the chassis assembly department of a medium-sized electronics manufacturer. This plant specialized in the assembly of small microprocessors for use in industrial control systems.

The company, located in the San Francisco Bay Area, had received an order for 250 microprocessors from a company in the Midwest who wanted to use the box-sized unit for monitoring closed-circuit grain storage systems. Stored grain had to contain a minimum amount of moisture to keep the dust down but too much moisture would cause the grain to rot. Therefore, the microprocessor was a preprogrammed control unit of both a drying machine as well as a moisture adding machine. Both slave machines were activated when the microprocessor's monitoring units signaled the moisture content was either above or below the desired moisture standards.

This order was critical to the company because it represented the initial phase of a new product rollout that could result in many subsequent orders as the product gained market acceptance. Delivery, quality control, initial costs of materials, and direct labor costs were very critical to the success of the venture.

George Kim was worried as the plant manager related the importance of this order and the significant part that George's chassis assembly department would play.

The assembly department's job was to prepare the printed circuit board to receive the capacitors, resistors, and microcircuits that implement the software logic of the system. This requires workers, usually women, handling small parts and soldering their connectors to the printed circuits on the chassis base plates. Women have greater dexterity and can pick up small objects better than men. Of the 15 women in the department, George figured that the most critical quality control point would be the soldering operation performed by five of the women workers.

As in most assembly operations, George's department was faced with absenteeism, fatigue, and job boredom due to the work's repetition and the tedium of high quality control.

The plant manager asked George to design the job so that both product quality and quality of worklife were both enhanced.

If you were an advisor, what would you tell George Kim to do in his job design venture? What are George's major problem areas? How can you design the job and work environment so that quality of worker life can be improved and sustained?

The Unproductive Office

Assume that you were a supervisor of the buildings and grounds crew of a state university in Arkansas. Your people were complaining about the tardiness of their paychecks. Although you didn't believe that one or two hours would cause so much irritation, you were perturbed at the overall inefficiency of the university's accounting department and particularly at the ineptness in getting out the semimonthly payroll checks.

Everytime you visited the accounting office in the administration building, you were faced with cluttered desks piled high with paper and people seated at their desks who were obviously working feverishly to reduce their backlog of work. However, you were not irritated by the inaccuracies of your department's accounting records as kept by the administration's accounting department. It seemed that almost every other month you were forced to visit with the university accountant to evaluate each charge made against your department and determine how much money you had left in your budget. You were convinved that incompetency in the accounting department was the major reason for the inadequate records.

What questions would you ask if you took the time to help alleviate the accounting department's inaccuracies and slowness? Where would you begin?

QUESTIONS FOR DISCUSSION

1. How may the productivity gap affect the supervisor in day-to-day activities?
2. What is meant by quality of worklife and how does this concept affect supervisors?
3. What is job design and its relationship with productivity?
4. "Work methods are techniques used by management to increase the workload of workers." Comment on this statement and determine why it has or why it does not have significance.
5. Is it necessary for a method and time study engineer to understand human behavior? Why?
6. Can motion study be applied to an office or a retail store? If so, name those positions that could be analyzed using methods analysis.
7. Discuss the major problems that confront a supervisor when approached by a worker who questions the rating factor used to derive normal time in time study analysis.
8. What relationship exists between job enlargement, job enrichment, and quality of worklife?
9. Can quality of worklife programs help to reduce job boredom? If so, where and why?
10. What advantages can accompany job enrichment and work module programs?

CHAPTER XII

Communications

LEARNING OBJECTIVES

- *To understand the elements and nature of communications.*
- *To appreciate on-the-job communication processes.*
- *To understand types of communications the supervisor will face in an organization.*
- *To cover the basic steps that make good communications in speaking, writing, and listening.*
- *To appreciate the significant relationship between communications and leadership.*
- *To understand how transactional analysis is a significant communication aid.*

Introduction

As we have seen in the previous chapters, the two basic elements of supervision are (1) being able to lead by working with and through people, and (2) utilizing the basic management skills necessary to meet the goals of *both* the individual and the company. Perhaps one of the most significant managerial tools or skills that can be used by the supervisor is communication. *Communication* is more than talking with or writing to people—*it is the exchange and understanding of meanings*. The common ingredients of management planning, organizing, and controlling require skillful use of proper communication techniques.

The supervisor's major contribution in working with the employees and his or her immediate superior rests on his or her ability to communicate meanings between these two positions. The supervisor represents the link that conveys how plans, policies, and directions coming from above have to be interpreted into meaningful goals and directions for employees. Also, the supervisor has to utilize these communication skills by properly interpreting meanings generated by the workers and passing these meanings upward to their immediate supervisor. Therefore the supervisor controls a two-way communication flow that is extremely vital to the growth of the firm.

Communication with employees has been of increasing concern to management recently. Some firms believe that if the employees are to be active participants in the management process, organized ways must be provided for them to express their ideas to supervisors and other levels of management. Furthermore, they must be confident that management is listening. The missing link in this communication process is the supervisor.

This chapter will cover the elements of the communication process, the nature of the communication process flow as a step-by-step procedure, the dimensions of communication (such as one-way, two-way), the human barriers of communication, and a discussion of how the communication process is used on the job. This latter area includes gathering data, reporting to superiors, listening, and understanding how transactional analysis can be used. The last part of the chapter covers the basic ingredients in becoming a good communicator as a speaker and as a listener. Finally, communication is related to the supervisor's leadership ability to plan, organize, and control the work group.

THE ELEMENTS OF COMMUNICATION

The major elements of the communication process are listed below.

1. *Gestures.* Physical actions, facial expressions, and nonverbal signs.
2. *Spoken words.* Syntax (word arrangement), vocal symbols, and voice inflection.
3. *Written words.* Syntax, word symbols, penmanship, and time element.
4. *The emotional or conscious state of sender and receiver or listener.* During the exchange, readiness of listener or reader to receive a message, trust, respect, and psychological climate.

Gestures, the first major element, are commonly called actions and facial expressions. They have become subtle ways of communicating meanings from one individual to another. Obviously people communicate with each other by words, written and oral, but the facial expressions, gestures, and actions, have a great deal of meaning in a face-to-face situation. For example, a supervisor complimenting one of his workers for a job well done scowls in the process. The worker receives an uncertain meaning. If the worker isn't accustomed to the personality traits of the supervisor, a disastrous communication process could evolve. A new worker, in this situation, probably would not trust the meaning of the supervisor's message.

In everyday life a large part of the social interaction is not verbalized. Visual observation is essential for the full comprehension of communicative behavior. Raised eyebrows, a smile on the face, a wink of the eye, a shrug of the shoulders, a pounding of a fist on the desk, a far-off look in one's eye, the joy expressed on one's face—these are a few of the many types of facial expressions and actions that can convey meanings. The use of these gestures and facial expressions combined with words makes up the total message. Every time you meet anyone, particularly on the job, you not only hear their words but also observe and react to nonverbal cues, such as noting their facial expression, body posture, and muscular tension. You also may look for cues to the feelings as well as the statements made by the individual. We look for these nonverbal cues to sense the sender's underlying motivation. These gestures and facial expressions may be more revealing to the listener than the words used in the communication process.

The second major element in the communication process is the spoken word. Words are the symbols of meanings. How words are placed in sequence within a sentence, called syntax, can influence the meaning conveyed. If words are jumbled, the meanings are garbled, and confusion may be the message that is transmitted. In other cases, poor English used by an individual can communicate much about that individual concerning his education, willingness to learn, self-improvement, and many other factors.

In addition to the arrangement of words, the words themselves can make pictures in a person's mind. A word such as *fall* has a different connotation from the word *cascade*, although each is synonymous with the other. These two words provoke different word pictures in our mind; thus the word symbols used become very important elements.

The spoken word adds a new dimension since inflection and tone of voice help to convey meanings. A supervisor with a deep, resonant voice may convey a different impression to workers than a supervisor with a high, squeaky voice. Both supervisors could say the same thing, but the spoken word could vary in meaning depending on which individual does the speaking.

The third element in the communication process is the written word. Here we have similar problems to the spoken word in that the arrangement of words and the meaning of words are important. The written word, however, can be studied over time and is not as transitory as the spoken word. Supervisors can't deny the written word as they can the spoken word. Much greater care must be exercised with the written word. Care should always be exercised when communicating in any form, but the written word has greater significance since the reader can read between the lines and possibly change the message to fit the reader's fancy.

Supervisors can use the handwritten word to convey messages when they can't be on the job. The style of the writer's penmanship can be an important element in the communication of meaning. For example, the handwritten note may be scrawled in an illegible form that could provoke the reader to either misinterpret or discard the note.

The supervisor may have to prepare warning or instructional signs occasionally; such signs illustrate some of the problems associated with the written word. By shuffling a few phrases and rephrasing a few words, a safety worker in a railroad reduced accidents in half. A little personalization assisted the communication process.[1]

"Remove your gloves when operating this machine" was switched to "Save your fingers and your income by removing your gloves."

"Danger. High voltage." The safety supervisor changed this to "Even 240 volts can kill—there are 660 volts here."

"Wear goggles at this grinder" was revised to say, "Eyes aren't replaceable—goggles are. Please use both at this machine."

Or the typical sign seen in most plants—"No smoking" was expanded to "Lighted cigarettes cause fire, damage, and death. Please don't light up."

"Pick up those tools" was changed to the less bossy and more informal phrase "Scattered tools cause accidents. Pick up your tools and save your conscience."

Although the signs changed by the safety director did convey different meanings to the reader, eventually the signs became fixed in the minds of the reader and lost their meanings. This illustrates another communication problem associated with the written word. This is the fate of all signs, no matter how startling their message. Frequent change in position, design, and phrasing is a good method for keeping signs effective. Humans become conditioned to the environment, and the intended message will not be conveyed after the reader fails to see the sign.

The fourth element involved in the communication process is the emotional and conscious state of the sender and/or the receiver during the exchange of meanings. People's ideas are the basis of their actions, and people's beliefs have a way of proving themselves to their possessors. Humans believe what they want to believe. This affects the communication process, because a breakdown can occur if both the sender and the receiver are not on the same wavelength. Emotional stress in some form can force a supervisor to communicate messages to a worker than can af-

---

[1]Harry W. Hepner and Frederick B. Pettengill, *Perceptive Management and Supervision—Social Responsibilities and Challenges*, 2nd ed., Prentice-Hall, Englewood Cliffs, N.J., 1971, p. 133.

fect a work group performance. At any level of management, a supervisor should not display unfavorable emotion during the communication process. A supervisor's wrath and emotional instability can easily be conveyed during a heated encounter with either her or his superior or a worker. The supervisor's (sender's) problems may be solved, but new problems, such as ill will, may destroy a capable worker or communicate to the worker that the supervisor may not be the easiest person with whom to work.

Trust and respect between and among listeners and speakers can have a great effect on the substance of the message conveyed. Listeners will be more attentive to the words of a person they trust, in contrast to the words used by a person whom they mistrust. In the process, the listener is hearing the symbols—the words, actions, and gestures—and is filtering the symbols to determine the meanings involved. Thus constant trust and respect become very important aspects in the managerial communication process. Even though the communication process may appear to be very complex, we must consider that all management processes pass through this important bottleneck. The only way management can achieve its goals is by the skilled use of all of the communication elements.

THE NATURE OF COMMUNICATION

As we have seen, it becomes obvious that the communication process is far from a simple operation. Although preconceptions held by many people suggest that certain myths do exist concerning the communication process, we should attempt to quell these misconceptions with a discussion of the nature of the communication process.

THE COMMUNICATION PROCESS

The *communication process* usually involves a series of six steps. The first step, as seen in Figure 12-1, concerns the sender or source of the message to be sent; this is commonly called the ideation step. This involves the content of the message, which is an idea or fact at this stage. The old saying, "Don't start talking until you start thinking," becomes a truism in the communication process. Be sure your brain is engaged before putting your mouth in gear. Step 1, therefore, is simply "Know what you want to communicate."

The second step is usually called the encoding step. This is the operation that transfers the message or idea into a series of symbols such as words, gestures, phrases.

The third step is that of transmission of the message from the sender to the receiver. During this step of transmission, the supervisor has to overcome certain barriers such as outside noise and interference.

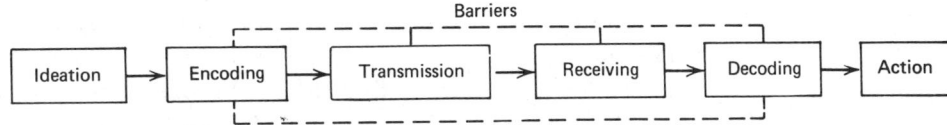

Figure 12-1 The communication process.

The fourth step is where the receiver is tuned to the transmitter. The message being transmitted is picked up in this stage. The human senses of seeing and hearing are activated.

The fifth step is concerned with the decoding of the message; this is the attempt to derive meaning from the symbols picked up by the receiver.

The sixth and last step is the action or behavioral change that comes as a result of the message.

As can be observed from the six-step process, numerous problems can enter into the process of communication. Step 1, the creation of an idea by the sender, can be a stumbling block. There appears to be no substitutes for clear thinking. If the sender doesn't know what to say (idea), the message could be garbled at the source, or a meaningless message could be transmitted.

The second step, the translation of the meaning into a series of symbols, can also be an obstacle. In this step the sender attempts to put his message into a clear-cut form (words, gestures, symbols) that can be conveyed. How good or how successful this step is depends on the sender's ability to symbolize the message correctly. In most instances, the supervisor will use verbal communication in this step. If the message is not well conceived and assembled, supervisors may create hard feelings among their own workers by communicating their lack of leadership and lack of trust to their workers.

In the third step, the transmission of the message, a supervisor may run into a number of difficulties. Barriers are created in the transmission channel, that is, voice, writing, gesture. The sender's voice may not be heard over the noise of the shop or office. The noise may prohibit the actual receiving of the message by the hearer. The sender may have a cold, or the sender may try to overcome external noises by screaming. When the transmission is in writing, the barrier is usually illegible handwriting or unintelligible usage of words strung out in long sentences. In many instances, written transmission problems usually are initiated by poor ideation or poor preparation in both Steps 1 and 2.

The fourth step, receiving, is a barrier as well. The worker may not be listening, or her thoughts may be focused on another activity. Listening, a most difficult procedure, is generally the greatest barrier in the communication process. If the receiver is not properly functioning, the message can be lost. In a verbal message it could be lost forever. Thus listening becomes a major obstacle in this step.

The fifth step, decoding the message by the receiver, is a very critical step also. Here the receiver has picked up the symbols as transmitted by the sender and is attempting to decode what these symbols really mean. A verbal message requires that the decoding operation take place during the transmission, whereas a written transmission provides time for decoding. The written message may be decoded many times. If the receiver doesn't really decipher the meaning during the decoding step, the message is lost. Even if all the previous steps were practiced with a high degree of expertise, the decoding by the receiver is still the *most critical step* in the entire process. *The communication process becomes dependent on the receiver's understanding the message.*

Step 6 becomes the final step in which the action or behavioral change takes place. If the message was understood as it came through, it should precipitate action. However, the receiver may decode and understand the message but may conclude that you don't mean it. Feedback becomes important, since the supervisor or sender should know if his message has been received.

The intricacies of the communication process, as shown, illustrate the tremendous task that supervisors have in conducting their managerial position. Communication as a management activity is an extremely important skill to be mastered by the supervisor. In order to provide the information and human understanding necessary for group effort and to provide the attitudes appropriate for proper motivation and job satisfaction, better communication is an absolutely necessary.

ONE-WAY VERSUS TWO-WAY COMMUNICATION

Another way of looking at the nature of communication is to determine its channel of direction. In a *one-way communication* process the sender develops a message and transmits it to the receiver with no participation other than listening on the part of the receiver. A two-way communication process involves the receiver actively participating in the process by verbally asking questions or making statements to determine his understanding of the message being transmitted.

One-way communication is usually considered faster than two-way communication. One-way communication is good (1) if the appearance of efficiency and speed is important, (2) if the sender doesn't want his or her mistakes to be recognized, and (3) if the sender wants to protect his or her power. The typical "boss" will tend to use the one-way communication process. In order not to have his or her authority thwarted, the "boss" will simply dictate his messages to the listener. If the message is complex, the authoritative "boss" can be in trouble. Perceiving this situation, the authoritative "boss" usually barks simple and direct orders.

In the *two-way communication* process, accuracy is much greater than speed. Here the listener or the receiver becomes an active participant. If the listener doesn't understand the message, he or she has the opportunity to clarify the meaning by asking questions. This may take longer, but accuracy will be enhanced. Under the two-way process, the receiver or listener is more sure of himself or herself. This enables the listener to make more correct judgments in carrying out the directive. However, the sender can find himself or herself under attack in the two-way communication process because of his or her mistakes and oversights, which are mirrored as the listener communicates them back. Two-way communication can be very advantageous in the long run, because the noise of the shop, office, or store conditions tends to garble verbal transmission. What may be sacrificed in speed can be made up in accuracy when complex messages are involved.

Participative management techniques tend to utilize the two-way communication process as much as possible. This requires the supervisor to have a better command of communication skills in order to perform the important managerial functions.

HUMAN BARRIERS IN COMMUNICATION

Barriers in communication become the natural phenomena of human behavior. Barriers in communication between people or between supervisors and workers usually do not screen out all communication; but barriers do filter communication and prevent some messages from going through the channel, while allowing other messages to pass. However, since the purpose of communication is to develop the information and understanding that are necessary for group effort, it becomes extremely important that supervisors have a full understanding of why these barriers exist and how they can overcome them. Companies rely on supervisors to be the active communicators of management's policies and objectives. This section will describe and analyze these barriers in sufficient depth so that a supervisor will have a better understanding of them.

Believability

It has been said that people see and hear what they want to see and hear. This statement has a great deal of truth. If people define situations as real, the situations are real in their own mind. We see only what we want to see that is pleasurable to us, and hear only what we want to hear that is pleasurable to us. Pleasure is one motive, but in many other cases we try to shut out communication that would be detrimental to what we see of ourselves. If we do not believe a situation exists, we will ignore the facts because we cannot believe a different image of ourselves may even exist. Hearing and seeing what we really want to believe helps to make the decoding, or fifth step, the most critical step in the six-step communication process.

Attitudes

An attitude is a feeling or emotion toward a fact or state of affairs. Attitude formation is one of the principal barriers in communication, since attitudes screen or filter much of the communication for the listener. Attitude development and attitude measurement are very complicated processes. Attitude development is susceptible to change; this fact may shed some light on understanding the problem of attitude development. The behavior or action of a human being is strongly influenced by his attitudes. Attitude development can be the result of previous experiences in the work place. The lack of experience may create attitudes also.

Reasoning Process   Another barrier to communication is the reasoning processes possessed by the sender or receiver. The extent to which a message is perceived by a listener or a reader is a function of both educational attainment and general level of intelligence. A person with a higher degree of intelligence *may be* more aware of the environment than a person of a lower degree of intelligence. However, the person with higher intelligence could be thinking far ahead of the transmission, thus losing some of the message. That person was not listening. A person without a substantial education may not have had the opportunities to expand his reasoning processes or be exposed to word meanings, although his or her native intelligence may be quite high. In this case, when supervisors are communicating complex messages, they should use words that are very understandable.

ON-THE-JOB COMMUNICATION PROCESSES

Understanding the nature and problems of the communicative process is merely the working environment for supervisors. They must know how to cope with this environment in order to survive and still do his job. The following section provides a discussion concerning the important aspects of applied communication.

Using proper *communicative skills* on the job involves the following considerations by the first-line supervisor.

1. Know how to gather data or facts to define problems.
2. Know how to report these data to superiors.
3. Know how to listen.

One of the biggest problems faced by the supervisor is the area of requesting information in order to correct a situation or provide informational input to management. Since one of the chief tasks of the supervisor is being a communications center, it becomes imperative that in gathering information the supervisor qualify the information before writing the report or before passing the information on to his or her superiors. Definition of the problem and choice of the proper solution may rest on the supervisor's communicative skills. For example, determining why an employee's absentee rate is very high may be a very difficult problem to analyze. The situation requires that a manager exercise a degree of research when culling out the information. The opinions of the absentee's colleague and side remarks that the supervisor may overhear, could be sources of information. Observing the absentee employee's attitude and behavioral patterns may help the supervisor to isolate the problem or problems that beset the absentee employee. A supervisor would not necessarily ask an employee a leading question, such as "John's absentee rate is high because he is drinking too much, isn't that right?" This is not a question. It becomes a statement in which you are coercing the employee to agree with you. On the other hand, a broader question asks, "Why is John's absentee rate so high?" We elicit an opinion from the employee. The employee's opinion may be biased and may be influenced by the tone of voice or facial expression or gestures used by the supervisor in the process of asking the question; but the supervisor must search for the actual reasons for the worker's absenteeism. Care must be exercised.

Another difficult communication area for supervisors is the reporting of data to the supervisor's superior. In addition to the normal reports that a supervisor has to fill out concerning the production reports, absentee reports, and so on, special reports may be required from time to time as deemed necessary by the superintendent or the plant manager. Style of writing and English used will greatly enhance or deter the communication process. Correct usage of words may convey different meanings to the reader, as was previously discussed. The written report usually is thought out by the writer during the reporting process. Time is available for thinking. The oral report has its own peculiar problems. A verbal report may communicate incorrect data that could seriously impair an employee's future. Many biases and prejudices of a supervisor can be passed on to his immediate superior. These biases may shade the perception of the truth by the supervisor. The employee may be erroneously accused of situations that were not of his or her making. When reporting orally, the same format should be followed as when reporting in writing. Be sure that what you say is well thought out and that you are reporting fact as seen, rather than an opinion or conclusions based on hearsay or faulty analysis. In many companies it is becoming a common practice to talk over the report first with your superior, and then write it down, in order to avoid errors in both written and verbal communication. In this way, the facts may be spotlighted more clearly and the communication process can be improved immensely. Under these circumstances, the reader or listener will pick up the symbols of communication and the meanings much faster. A short, distinct message is preferred in contrast to a long, wordy message. The wordy message tends to cloud the real meanings involved.

The last major on-the-job communication problem for supervisors is listening. Listening becomes very difficult, not only for the supervisor, but for all human beings. We tend to want to place our own ego ahead of other factors. Many people find it much easier to be in the limelight than to be humble. Considering the two skills involved in the talking-listening process, most people seem to have the greatest difficulty listening. For example, an egotistical movie actress at a cocktail party was talking about her previous films. After approximately 30 minutes of this conversation, the listeners became a little bored and began to leave. The movie actress perceived the situation and stopped the conversation by saying, "I've been talking about myself for some time. Let's talk about you. What did *you* think of my last film?"

TYPES OF COMMUNICATION WITHIN THE ORGANIZATION FOR SUPERVISORS

Managers of all types spend the major part of their work day communicating in one form or another. A study of research concerning communication among managers reported that first-line supervisors spend 74 percent of their time communicating, in contrast to second-level supervisors who spend 81 percent and third-level supervisors who spend 87 percent.[2]

Internal organizational communication is usually pictured as having three directions: downward, upward, and horizontal. These classifications tend to show what the formal communication flows are, but in reality many informal communication flows exist within any organization. This is a fourth direction, which is called multidirectional. As management authority and responsibility are pushed farther down the line of an organization, more informal communication networks appear. Managers are talking out problems, trying to find better solutions. There appears to be a less rigorous downward, upward, and horizontal communication network in informal groups than in formal organizations.

A fifth direction, external communications, exists. It includes all forms of marketing research and intelligence between an organization and its market, society, and environment.

DOWNWARD COMMUNICATION SYSTEMS

This is the traditional line of communication coming from the top and sifting down through each of the management levels to the ultimate worker. Policies, plans, objectives, and philosophies of a firm are implemented in the products manufactured and the services offered as these products are produced to satisfy the needs of the society. The manage-

---

[2] Keith Davis, *Human Relations at Work: The Dynamics of Organizational Behavior*, 3rd ed., McGraw-Hill Book Co., New York, 1967, p. 326.

ment responsibility of the first-line supervisor includes short-run planning, directing, and working with the organization in controlling the organization within a small work group. Supervisors must correctly interpret the messages coming from the top and communicate them correctly to workers. This informational flow requires a great deal of control on the part of the supervisor, since much of the information is purified at each level as it filters down the organization, as illustrated in Figure 12-2. Purification takes place as each level of management interprets the message, as they believe it should be transmitted.

The trend in today's modern firm is toward reducing the number of levels and broadening the lower base in order to shorten the communication channel. Studies have shown that the loss in understanding the original message, which starts at the top and is passed down through many layers of management, may be as much as 75 percent.[3]

UPWARD COMMUNICATION SYSTEMS

Newer management techniques emphasize job enrichment, greater personal involvement, and delegation of more authority throughout all the levels of management. A greater need for accurate upward communication has been created. This need has increased largely because modern management has become convinced that listening to what comes from the worker level and then utilizing these data can help management to create and to improve its own planning and control processes. Upward communication becomes a very important source to monitor the implementation of a plan, such as the production process. Moreover, top and middle management can ascertain the attitudes and the morale of the workers by listening to upward communication. Top management or upper levels of management have known for years that the upward flow of data tends to be distilled by each level of management (see Figure 12-2). This natural filtering process is followed because supervisors are not going to "air dirty linen" in reporting all the facts. They will tend to report and embellish those facts that will place their department or work group

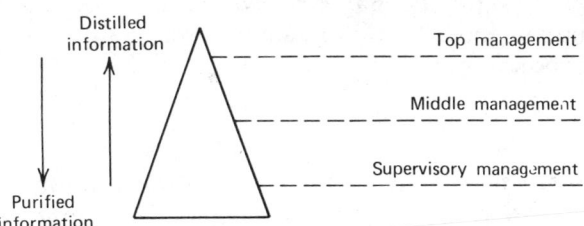

Figure 12-2 Distillation and purification of organizational communicational flows.

[3]Earl P. Strong, *The Management of Business,* Harper & Row, New York, 1965, p. 106.

in a favorable light. As this process goes on, these data reaching the top manager's office could be highly refined. Therefore management desires more accuracy, more involvement, and more participation from the supervisor.

Upward communication from the worker to the supervisor is an important tool that may provide the supervisor with information to improve the work group's operation. A worker may have a better solution to a problem on the production line that the supervisor may have. Upper levels of management tend to listen more, because the supervisor knows more about the events occurring within the work group than anyone else. Accurate data collected from upward communication have always been an important aspect of management. Today the supervisor becomes a more important rung in this communication process.

HORIZONTAL COMMUNICATION SYSTEMS

Horizontal communication usually involves messages being conveyed between departments of the line organization and between staff and line departments. Certain problems do exist in this type of communication, since staff people with a technical background may find it difficult to communicate with nontechnical people. For example, a graduate engineer may not be able to convey his or her technical expertise to the supervisor, and a communication barrier may exist.

Since the supervisor is a line manager, he or she must have contact with other staff experts such as personnel management people, industrial engineers, time and motion study people, and systems people. Although this important area is covered in more detail in later chapters, it does concern horizontal communication. Staff people do not have to accept a line person responsibility since the staff person's job is to advise and assist. The supervisor has to learn to understand the staff person's jargon, understand the staff person's presence, and attempt to placate the workers when staff people are involved on the work scene. A time and motion study person may not the most beloved person in an organization. Bridging the gap between the time and motion man and the work group is, indeed, an intricate part of the supervisor's horizontal communication responsibility.

MULTIDIRECTIONAL COMMUNICATION FLOWS

A discussion of the traditional downward, upward, and horizontal communication systems may not show all the complexities of communication within an organization; however, multidirectional communication flows, as shown in Figure 12-3, are quite common. All directions may be used at the same time. A union official may be communicating with top management while a colleague is communicating with workers and while another colleague converses with the supervisor. This could trigger rapid flows between the top and middle management people and the supervi-

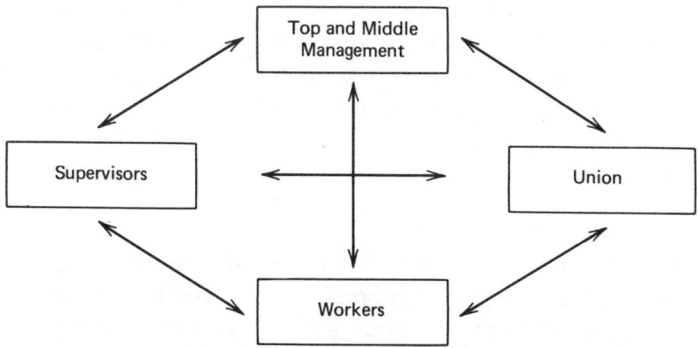

Figure 12-3   Multidirectional communication flows.

sor, who then communicates with the worker. In another instance, the general manager or the office supervisor may stroll the floor, talking directly with the workers, hoping to receive the worker's views and perhaps to communicate his or her own views directly to the workers. The multidirectional communication flow can become an awesome situation; it can further complicate the already difficult process of human communication.

EXTERNAL COMMUNICATION SYSTEMS   External communication usually includes public relations, advertising, marketing research, sales, and customer relations. Supervisors and their workers are involved in external communication, but not in the same way as judged by many people. Workers and supervisors do have external communication functions, even if they are not in sales or marketing. For example, during a social activity after work, the company's image can be affected by the attitudes and opinions expressed by the supervisor and/or by workers to people outside of the plant, office, or store. An unhappy worker may discuss the disadvantages of a given company; the message may be a damning image of the whole company and its products. This could result in a loss of sales, or the loss of stockholders, or the loss of prospective employees. On the other hand, a happy and well-adjusted employee will tend to speak of the good things about a company, which will enhance the sale of its products, the status of its stock, and the recruitment of its employees. The supervisor does have responsibility for external communication. Without sales and profits, the need for in-plant or in-office supervisors could evaporate.

GOOD COMMUNICATORS ARE MADE, NOT BORN

Now that we have discussed the communication process and its barriers, and seen why communication is a very important tool in the management and supervisory process, we can turn our attention toward what makes a good communicator. These principles of good communication can be learned and practiced. Many public speakers who are well known for their oratory started out as timid young men or women, but through practice of principles of public speaking became outstanding people in their field.

GOOD COMMUNICATIONS— SPEAKING

A speaker's major problem in the communication process begins with lack of planning remarks and meaning. Bad communications can not be condoned in the management and supervisory process. Many lists are available concerning the "do's" and "don'ts" of speakers for the enhancement of the communications process. The following eight points illustrate the process most accurately.

1. Plan remarks. Have a purpose for your message that should be related in terms of your listener's reaction.
2. Organize your remarks. Be certain that your main thoughts are clearly symbolized for the listener.
3. Keep a specific purpose in mind so that you do not ramble over many things but remain precise and concise at all times.
4. Be listener centered, not self-centered. Rather than try primarily to provide the listener with a better image of yourself, be intent on communicating with the listener.
5. Be enthusiastic and attempt to project the message so as to elicit a good reception.
6. Provide sufficient evidence to back up statements so that your listener will not question the validity or the reliability of your message but may concentrate on the understanding of the message.
7. Consider the background of the listener, such as natural origin, education, and possible prejudices, attitudes, and biases.
8. Use language the listener understands.

These points for a speaker certainly are all steeped in the basic understanding of both the listener and the speaker or supervisor's knowledge of the message that has to be conveyed.

Remember, if the listener doesn't understand the message, you, as the sender, haven't communicated. Coordinate the spoken work with gestures, silence, facial expressions, and actions. Actions speak louder than words.

GOOD COMMUNICATIONS —WRITING

Frequently a supervisor must write reports and it's helpful to review some of the major points to be followed in effective writing.

1. Determine the purpose of the communication such as (a) circumstances, (b) ideas, and (c) purpose, which is to inform, stimulate

thought, persuade, change attitudes, seek feedback or a combination of purposes listed here.
2. Identify the audience or person and write to that audience or person.
3. Design the message so that it is (a) appropriate for the audience or individual, (b) can be understood, (c) can be acceptable, (d) consistent with purpose, (e) clear, and (f) can command attention.
4. Select an appropriate medium, such as handwritten memo, formal letter, or formal report.
5. Anticipate distortions and opportunities for the reader to distill the report's information.

Remember that written communications can be reread many times with the reader trying to justify his or her position or to protect their stand. So be very careful that a written report can't be distorted to meet an individual's needs. Be truthful, factual, analytical and communicate these facts as well as possible.

GOOD COMMUNICATIONS —LISTENING As a listener or a receiver, the following seven points can be used as guides to enhance the communication process.

1. Anticipate the situation by anticipating the message that the speaker will have.
2. Look for main points. The speaker's voice and the symbols used are much slower than what the listener's brain is capable of comprehending, and a loss of the message may result unless the main points are sought.
3. Analyze the speaker's purpose and try to determine why this message has to be delivered.
4. Weigh the speaker's evidence and try to determine also the message's validity.
5. Be open-minded. Watch your biases and prejudices. Try to find out why the new ideas are espoused and to think before making replies.
6. Analyze the speaker's language in terms of what the speaker means, since the speaker may have a handicap and use incorrect words.
7. Do not concentrate on what you will say in return, but *listen* to the speaker and analyze his or her message before you question the statements or question the message.

COMMUNICATION AND LEADERSHIP

LEADERSHIP Face-to-face relations for the supervisor necessitate the use of proper communication. However, good communication is also an expression or projection of trust in leadership, as perceived by your own subordinates as well as your superiors. Among the many messages communicated may be trust, hope, support, and involvement. These are subtle but extremely necessary aspects of leadership.

Leadership is a complex subject, but we do know that from experimentation and pragmatic experience, leadership is related to whether or not a person is a good communicator. We are using communication in a broad sense including the written word, the spoken word, and gestures. A good leader is one who is a "take-charge type," but in addition one who supports subordinates in time of need. Communicating this willingness to support your people and practice participative management requires an outstanding man. Self-confidence and knowledge of the job are required. Good leaders communicate respect and confidence among their own workers. Good leaders lead a group of people because the workers permit them to lead. The communicative skills of the supervisor are largely responsible for the degree of leadership practiced by the supervisor.

Much communication can be a subjective type of communication, such as that concerning mutual trust. A mutual trust must exist between supervisors and workers in order for the worker even to attempt to involve some thoughts, cooperation, and activity in the work group. When mutual trust does not prevail, the communication process has no rapport. Frequently, the believability of a message is a function of the sender's reputation, and the mutual trust and respect the sender enjoys with the listener or reader.

TRANSACTIONAL ANALYSIS

Much of the trust and respect so necessary for a supervisor's success is in the way the supervisor interrelates with his or her people. This interrelationship is a very complex system, but communications can be improved if the supervisor understands the major concepts of transactional analysis. TA was popularized by Eric Berne, a clinical psychologist and later promoted by a book by Thomas Harris called *I'm O.K.—You're O.K.*

TA is built around various ego states that are defined in terms of experiences, memory, and feelings stored in three basic areas of personality.

1. The Parent—viewed as the source of both critical or supportive behavior, reward, and punishment.
2. The Adult—rational, mature side of personality, problem solving, decision making, questioning, analytical.
3. The Child—emotion, feeling, creative, curiosity.

Figure 12-4 shows these three states of supervisory personality that may influence the communication process.

Generally, the most appropriate transaction would be adult to adult for supervisory-worker relations and communications. A parent-to-child relationship may work *if* the worker accepts the obedient subordinate

	Parent State	
	Critical	**Supportive**
Does:	Frowns when pacing work. Points finger when giving direction. Folds arms before making an important point.	Gives an approving smile. Sends flowers to sick employee. Pats employee on shoulder. Sends a birthday card to employee's spouse.
Says:	My three-year-old kid could do a better job than that. You're absolutely impossible.	Keep up the good work. Excellent, you're doing a good job. You're the best employee I have. I think of you as my son (or daughter).

	Adult State	
Does:	Gathers facts and information. Determines priorities. Seeks opinion of others.	Avoids displays of anger. Promotes a participative, trustful atmosphere. Asks numerous questions.
Says:	What are the facts? What is your opinion? The facts demonstrate that . . .	When did it happen? How did it happen? It's our only logical choice.

	Child State	
Does:	Plays practical jokes. Plots and schemes to get back at someone. Has temper tantrums.	Occasionally tips a few at lunch. Refuses to work with fellow workers. Is a constant complainer.
Says:	Wow! Come look at my new office! Fantastic! We've got the best operation here. Dammit. It's just not worth it.	Wow! We blew it that time. Nothing ever goes right for me. I'm never going to speak to you again.

Figure 12-4   Supervisory Ego States in TA.

role. But this relationship or transaction is not recommended. For example, the worker may respond to a parentlike supervisor and follow with a rebellious, childlike behavior.

Although other TA concepts exist, the three personality states can greatly assist the supervisor in a communication situation. A supervisor should realize what role he or she is playing at the time and what role the listener is playing at the time and then attempt to fit the most compatible and workable states together to enhance the communication process.

SUMMARY

The elements of the communication process include (1) gestures, (2) spoken words, (3) written words, and (4) the emotional or conscious state of the sender and receiver or listener. Two types of barriers—physical and human—tend to complicate the entire process. Physical barriers, such as noise of the plant or office or interference by others, curtails the sender's ability to transmit and the receiver's ability to listen or receive. However, the human barrier, the failure to listen, is the greatest and most significant problem.

Listener hears what they want to hear. They hear or see those things that help to support their mood, expectations, predispositions, past experiences, or aspirations.

The communication process has six steps: (1) ideation, which is an idea or fact; (2) encoding, which transfers the idea into words; (3) transmission, which is the voice, gesture, or written word; (4) receiving, which involves the listener or reader who is tuned into the channel; (5) decoding, in which words are transferred back to idea; and (6) action, which is storage and use of the transmitted message.

Improper communication usage can create numerous problems for the supervisor. It can create misinformation, convey incorrect impressions or images, downgrade the sender's ability to manage, and create morale problems within the department or work crew. Listening, which will help to mitigate these problems, is very difficult for both the supervisor and his workers.

Various types of communication systems exist within an organization. The typical or most obvious type is the downward flow of information from top management to the worker. Upward communication is simply a reversal of the downward flow. Upward communication is important in that policies and plans are often based on some upward flow. Horizontal flow occurs between workers or between supervisors. Multidirectional flow proceeds in different directions at the same time. External communication includes public relations, marketing research, promotion, sales, customer relations, and what workers and supervisors say off the job.

Good communicators have to plan remarks, organize their remarks, keep a specific purpose in mind, be listener centered, and be enthusiastic. Good listeners have to anticipate the speaker's message, look for main points, and analyze the speaker's message.

Leadership ability is directly tied into the supervisor's proper use of communication skills. The "take-charge" person's ability to produce is linked with the ability to communicate.

Transactional analysis with its three personality states of parent, adult, and child can help the supervisor adjust his or her role to enhance the communications process.

KEY CONCEPTS

The communication process. Although the communication process contains discrete elements, it is the flow or combination of these elements and their use which is the most important part of this concept. The various uses of the elements fit into six distinct steps, of which the receiver stage is the most difficult.

Human barriers in communication. The sender's garbled message doesn't help the communication process, but the receiver is the most critical barrier. He believes what he wants to, and hears and sees what he wants. To overcome these barriers the supervisor must understand the listener and cope with the complexities that make up the individual.

Good communication is practice and understanding. By understanding the communication process and its barriers, along with practice and common sense, a person can become a good communicator. The difficulty lies in being able to practice all the rules of communication. As in playing golf, a person must concentrate and be a scholar of the subject.

Good leadership and supervision rest on good communications. Lasting leadership is directly tied up with a person's ability to communicate. Better communication skills, together with substantive message content, are indispensable tools for a successful supervisor.

Personality state of communicators. Colors the sender's and receiver's psychological readiness to communicate. The supervisor must recognize the listener's psychological state so that he or she can assume the proper role in communicating with that individual. Determine "where the listener is" and then determine where you "should be coming from."

IMPORTANT TERMS

Communication	One-way communication
Communication process	Spoken words
Communication skills	State of sender or receiver
Downward communication	Symbols of communication
External communication	Two-way communication
Gestures	Upward communication
Horizontal communication	Written words
Multidirectional communication	Transactional analysis

INCIDENTS

Mismatched Personality States

Sue Smith gritted her teeth to avoid saying anything and tried to retain her composure as her customer, Tony Valleti, continued his tirade that occurred everytime Sue made a call on Tony's bank. Six months previously, Sue had sold 20 calculators to Tony's First State Bank. Two of the 20 calculators experienced some difficulty. After Tony had complained loudly, Sue agreed to replace the 2 defective calculators with 2 new ones. However, a waiting period of two months would elapse before delivery. Again Tony went through a tirade. Sue loaned Tony's bank 2 machines to replace the defective ones, thus alleviating any of the shortcomings. This had all transpired six months earlier and now Tony had all 20 calculators in working order but went through the entire tirade on every call Sue made.

Sue thought, after meeting all of Tony's calculator needs: Why does he persist on discussing all the details in an abusive manner everytime I call?

What do you think was the matter? Do you believe that transactional analysis might help to explain this behavior? Was Sue's behavior correct by not saying anything during the tirades?

Role play the situation by assigning members to play both Sue's and Tony's parts.

The Cookie Salesperson

Anne Leflore is a successful 28-year-old salesperson for a cookie manufacturer. She works a New England territory but her company's main plant is located in Richmond, Virginia. Her job is to sell to grocery chain buyers in Boston and then distribute and stock the cookies in each of the chain's stores. The job requires keeping accurate inventory records, sales records, and maintaining fully stocked shelves for each store. Until the product moves out of the store, Anne will not be able to get more orders in Boston. She likes her job, its pay, and her customer contact. Her sales record is near the top in the zone.

Anne's zone sales supervisor, Mike Finn, started in the same type of job and was promoted to his present position four years ago. He believed that women shouldn't have sales positions since he felt that men were better performers, however, he never communicated this fact to Anne, the only woman in his zone.

Finn would visit Leflore every quarter and travel with her for either a whole day or part of a day. Anne dreaded these visits as Mike was constantly telling her, "Don't chew gum," "You should visit the store manager before taking shelf inventory," "Be sure the front row of every cookie is stocked to the top," "Write down your mileage before you forget it," and so on.

Anne could cope with these "helpful" suggestions but the one comment that really angered her was, "Anne, you need all the help you can get."

What has Finn been communicating to Anne? What's the message that Finn thinks he is communicating? If you were the supervisor, Finn, how would you have handled this situation?

Incident Problems

1. Ask a good friend of yours to describe a spiral staircase while he sits on his hands.
2. Take two tables approximately six feet long and place them together forming a "T." Have one person sit at the bottom of the "T" and two people sit at the top or cross bar as far from the first person as possible. Place a tinker toy set on the table next to the two men at the top, and give the plans and instructions to the person at the bottom of the "T." The man with the plans must communicate to the others. Please observe leadership qualities, different forms of communication, inflections of the voice, language used, gestures, symbols, signs.
3. A young office worker in her early twenties has just entered her supervisor's office with a large smile on her face that spreads from ear to ear. She had just become engaged the night before and wanted to show off her new ring. Obviously, the worker is in ecstasy and quite delighted to inform her supervisor of the previous night's event.

   The supervisor, an unmarried woman of 40, has had a rough morning at home, and few things at the office have gone well. The supervisor had just left her superior's office after being informed that her department's production was too low. The supervisor is not in a good mood.

   Play out the two roles and observe the communication process, hidden meaning or feelings, breakdowns in the communication process, and perhaps turned-off receivers.

Communication Goofs

1. An oppressive supervisor who locks up all the paper and pencils so that they are not lost or stolen makes the following comment: "If it weren't for me this place would close down tomorrow."

   What did this supervisor communicate? Did he follow proper communication procedures? What did he do wrong?
2. A sympathetic supervisor's comment to one of her most productive workers in a large insurance office: "You can take the promotion if you want but if I were you, I would consider my own inabilities to cope with the rough and tumble of the business world."

   What message has been communicated by the supervisor? What message has been picked up by the employee? What would you do to clarify this situation?

QUESTIONS FOR DISCUSSION

1. Why is communication an important tool for supervisory management?
2. What are the four elements of the communication process? Which one is the most critical? Why?
3. How can conflicting use of communication elements distort the communicated message?
4. How can voice inflection change a message being communicated?
5. Can handwriting or penmanship create barriers in the communication process?
6. What other human barriers exist in the communication process?
7. "If listeners don't understand the message, then the sender hasn't communicated." Comment on this statement.
8. Can a written report be distorted? If so, how and why?
9. What are the steps that a good speaker or communicator follows?
10. Explain why the most desirable transactional state between a supervisor and employee is adult to adult. What's wrong or right with other possible combinations, such as parent-child, child-child, and adult-child?

CHAPTER XIII

Motivating the Worker

LEARNING OBJECTIVES

- *To learn the role of machinery, technology, and people in our competitive economy.*
- *To gain insight into a number of early motivation studies including the Hawthorne experiments, Herzberg studies, and Texas Instrument studies.*
- *To learn the changing ideas in motivation starting with Taylor's scientific management, through McGregor and Gellerman to Porter and Lawler's model.*
- *To understand how these motivation theories can help you as a supervisor.*

Introduction

As a background for examining the importance of motivating the worker, we need to examine a few elements of our industrial society.

Ours is a competitive economy based on the *capitalistic system.* Profit is the motive power for investment by shareholders. But productivity of the workers affects the return on the investment that is necessary to secure sufficient capital for the business. And at this point we encounter motivation, which affects productivity.

Years of research and study have brought forth certain principles that show promise of influencing productivity in today's society.

THE COMPETITIVE ECONOMY

CONTRIBUTION OF MACHINERY AND TECHNOLOGY

Ours is a so-called free-market capitalistic economy. It is based on the principle of the investment of capital, that is, money and materials, into production systems. It requires the assistance of people to create a new or improved product to capture a segment of a lucrative market. This product must be in demand by these same workers or other elements of society, who are willing to receive it in exchange for money. We are a free market because no one tells us what we must buy. Usually we can make a choice from a number of products.

There must be a difference between the cost of production and the sales price of the product. This difference is known as profit. A portion of this profit is paid to those who provided the money to buy the original machinery and materials. Another portion is returned to the system to repair and replace or provide new machinery for improved processes.

In this simple model, then, we see a number of factors. First, there is normally a mechanical device involved, known as a machine. There may be a collection of pieces of equipment that are capable of working together to perform a function. The more efficiently this machinery works, the greater is the profit generated for the same sales price; that is, the opportunity to provide a lower sale price increases. Likewise, if new and improved machinery provide new or improved products for which there is a demand, there is more likelihood of increasing the amount of profit. If the profit is increased, more income can go to the *investors* (those that provided the capital) or be available to provide new and improved machinery. Thus we see that more efficient machinery and improved technology allow for greater profit margins or reductions in prices. Or they may provide greater volume of sales and therefore more dollars of profit even though the margin may be constant. This means that worker motivation is directly tied into the need for more efficient plant operations, fewer wasteful practices, fewer absentees, and greater productivity.

CONTRIBUTION OF PRODUCTIVITY

Today we frequently encounter the word *productivity* in union contracts. We hear it related to the matter of *inflation*. We hear that if the productivity increases 3 percent, then we can increase the wages 3 percent without causing inflation. Without entering upon a discussion in depth, it does seem apparent that if for the same dollar of labor expense we can produce a greater value of product for sale, then relative to labor cost we shall have increased the productivity. This may be accomplished by more physical output per man-hour of labor. Greater productivity, however, normally occurs by placing more efficient machines on the line that require fewer man-hours of labor per unit of product output. Since labor costs are usually higher than machine or material costs, more efficient utilization of machines can increase productivity, given the same number of workers. It is this factor—more efficient use of machines—that has accounted for the significant increase in productivity over recent years.

IMPORTANCE OF MOTIVATION

Another factor intimately related to this situation is *motivation*. Even if we place improved machinery in the hands of employees, productivity may still lag if the machinery is not utilized efficiently. By lack of interest in learning how to utilize the machinery; by planned misuse of machinery; or by other means, productivity may fail to increase despite increasing capital investment. Furthermore, many industries and segments of some industries still require considerable man-hours of labor input in order to produce the product. In these industries, the efficiency of the worker has a significant effect on productivity. Motivation of this worker becomes of significant importance to the management of the firm.

Since motivation affects employee performance at all levels of the corporation, it is important that we study this matter in some detail.

THE INDIVIDUAL

WHAT DO WE KNOW ABOUT PEOPLE?

We might first ask ourselves what we know about people. If we cannot answer this question, then we can do very little toward motivating them. Psychologists, in general, agree that a number of the following items represent common behavior patterns.

1. *All behavior is directed toward the satisfaction of needs.*[1] People aim at some goal that represents a relief from some discomfort, as discussed in Chapter IX. For example, when you are hungry, you eat in order to relieve this discomfort of hunger. When you are cold, you put on additional clothing or enter a warm place in order to relieve this discomfort. Therefore we can say that our behavior tends to satisfy some need that we are experiencing.
2. *People generally take the easiest way of satisfying their need.* We might call this the principle of least effort. Learning, as practiced in our growing up, may really represent the process of finding an easier means to the satisfaction of needs. For example, the person who goes on through a college education to become an engineer may do this as a means of providing what he or she considers an easier way of satisfying his or her financial needs.
3. *When people encounter obstacles in the satisfaction of some need, they may become aggressive.* For example, a person might commit some underhanded acts in order to achieve a promotion that he feels he needs for his own satisfaction. Or a person may strike out against her com-

---

[1] A. H. Maslow, *Motivation and Personality,* Harper & Row, New York, 1954.

pany in some manner because she does not have sufficient information to satisfy her needs of importance or belonging.

4. *We frequently forget that what counts most to people is what they see from their point of view.* They are not necessarily concerned with the truth, but what they feel to be true. This means that if we are to change someone's behavior, we must change his or her attitude toward things as *he or she sees them.*

WHAT DO PEOPLE WANT FROM THEIR JOBS?

Normally, a supervisor will feel that the employee is interested in such things as higher wages and job security. However, when a series of questions are addressed to the person—the one being supervised—the responses often are quite different. Frequently such things as appreciation for work done, feeling of belonging, help with personal problems will rank at the top of the list, whereas high wages and job security rank farther down.

SUPERVISOR'S RESPONSE TO PEOPLE'S WANTS

This points up a very important matter. If the supervisor thinks that things are important that employees do not think are important, the supervisor obviously is going to have difficulty in motivating them. If the supervisor satisfies needs that the employees do not think they have motivation will not result. On the other hand, if the supervisor fails to satisfy needs employees feel they have, once more motivation will not result.

It is apparent that if supervisors try to provide what *they think* the employee needs, then job performance will be less than satisfactory. Therefore it is very important that supervisors understand employees' needs *from their point of view.*

MOTIVATIONAL RESEARCH

HAWTHORNE STUDIES

The first significant study of the relationship between motivation and productivity took place in 1927 at the Hawthorne works of the Western Electric Company.[2]

The investigators were trying to discover the effects of fatigue on the output of females assembling relays. They worked with a group of five women who were segregated from the other assemblers and "protected" from supervision by the researchers. The investigators explained the purpose of their research to the women and then began a series of experimental changes in their rest periods and working hours, as follows.

---

[2]F. J. Roethlisberger and W. J. Dickson, *Management and the Worker,* Harvard University Press, Cambridge, Mass., 1939.

Women were on a 48-hour week, no rest periods.

First they introduced two 5-minute rest periods; production went up.

They added four more rest periods; production went up.

Then they gave them a 15-minute midmorning lunch, plus a 10-minute afternoon rest period; production went up again.

Then they cut their working day by 1/2 hour; production went up.

Then they cut their working day by another 1/2 hour; production went up again.

They eliminated Saturday work; production went up.

Finally, they took away all changes. Girls returned to a 48-hour work week with no rest periods; *production skyrocketed!*

This completely confused the investigators, so they interviewed the women to find out why production had continued to go up. They learned that the fact that they were a select group, helping the company to solve a problem, made the women feel important since their work now had a new purpose. The investigators concluded that working conditions themselves had less effect on output than worker attitudes. They discovered that, in setting up the experiment, they had done several things that were different from the way the women normally were treated by their bosses.

They asked for their cooperation.

They consulted them about changes before they were made.

They held conferences with the girls and listened to their reactions.

They allowed the girls to talk at work.

They paid a great deal of attention to their results and showed them their output charts.

The Hawthorne studies stimulated a major shift in emphasis from scientific management, where the objective was to break down as many jobs as possible into simple, repetitive operations, to a concern for relations and the attitudes of the people doing the work.

HERZBERG STUDIES In 1959 a group of psychologists at the Psychological Service in Pittsburgh achieved another major breakthrough in our understanding of what it is that people want from their jobs.

Herzberg and his colleagues interviewed 200 engineers and accountants in the Pittsburgh area. Each was asked the following.[3]

---

[3] F. Herzberg, B. Mausner, and B. B. Snyderman, *The Motivation To Work*, John Wiley and Sons, New York, 1959.

1. Think of a recent experience that made you feel particularly good about your job.
2. Think of a recent experience that made you feel particularly bad about your job.
3. What effects did these incidents have on your attitudes and performance?
4. How long did these effects last?

Herzberg found that when people felt good about their jobs, it was because something had happened that showed that they were doing their jobs particularly well or that they were becoming more expert in their field. Typical responses were of this nature: "Six months ago I was given an assignment which meant more responsibility and an opportunity to learn something new." Bad feelings, on the other hand, were usually due to feelings about unfair treatment — low wages, poor working conditions, or some other factor *not* specifically related to the job itself.

These findings led Herzberg to conclude that there are two sets of factors that affect performance: (1) job content factors, and (2) *hygiene or maintenance factors.*

1. The true motivators, for the most part, were the job content factors of achievement, growth, recognition, responsibility, advancement. The job content factors were the real motivators because they had the potential of yielding a sense of satisfaction to the worker.
2. The other factors, which Herzberg labeled "hygiene" factors, were made up essentially of pay, benefits, working conditions, and so on. He called these hygiene factors because they did not produce any *improvements* in worker attitudes or performance; they merely prevented dissatisfaction and poor morale. They were not related to the work, but to the work environment. He also concluded that lower-order needs were pretty well satisfied today.

Inadequate attention to these hygiene factors had a significant negative effect on attitudes, but they had no important *positive* effect when properly administered. Also, hygiene factors, once given, were taken for granted from then on.

TEXAS INSTRUMENTS STUDIES About two years after Herzberg published his findings, a group of research psychologists at Texas Instruments decided to test Herzberg's theories on their own people.[4] They followed the same interview pattern used by Herzberg, but expanded the groups interviewed to include scientists, engineers, manufacturing supervisors, hourly male technicians, and hourly female assemblers. Their study supported Herzberg's conclu-

[4] M. Scott Myers, "Who Are Your Motivated Workers?," *Harvard Business Review*, Vol. 42, No. 1, (January-February) 1964, 73–79.

sion that motivation stems from the challenge of the job through such factors as achievement, growth, responsibility, work itself, and earned recognition. These motivational needs are shown in the inner circle of Figure 13-1. Satisfaction of these needs, according to Scott Myers, who led the research at Texas Instruments, can be accomplished by the mechanisms and factors listed in the inner circle. The inner circle contains needs that are job related.

Characteristics of motivation factors are as follows.

1. Task or job centered—derived from the job itself.
2. Individually as opposed to group administered.
3. Double edged—can become dissatisfiers if taken away.
4. Low cost.
5. Not satisfied in industry today—in fact, little attention is given to these needs.

The hygiene factors, or what Dr. Myers calls "maintenance needs," which appear in the outer ring, are classified as economic, security, orientation, status, social, and physical.

Characteristics of maintenance factors are as follows.

1. Not directly related to the job, but surround it.
2. Group administered.
3. Potential dissatisfiers, little motivational value.
4. Expensive.
5. Generally satisfied in industry today.

In considering the many groups tested in the Texas Instruments experiments, it is interesting to note which factors motivated which group the most. To the scientist, work itself and company policy and administration were the most important. Among engineers, advancement, responsibility, work itself were considered the most important. The manufacturing supervisors recorded a resounding preference for advancement, with responsibility running a close second. Hourly male technicians chose responsibility by a vast majority over advancement. Hourly female assemblers believed competence of supervision and friendliness of supervision were the most important, with achievement running a close third. All five groups believed achievement was necessary since this one factor, in all cases, had the highest frequency of mention.

SUMMARY OF MOTIVATION STUDIES

1. People at work are more productive if they are motivated.
2. People at work are constantly seeking to satisfy personal needs (see Chapter IX).

260 Chapter XIII Motivating the Worker

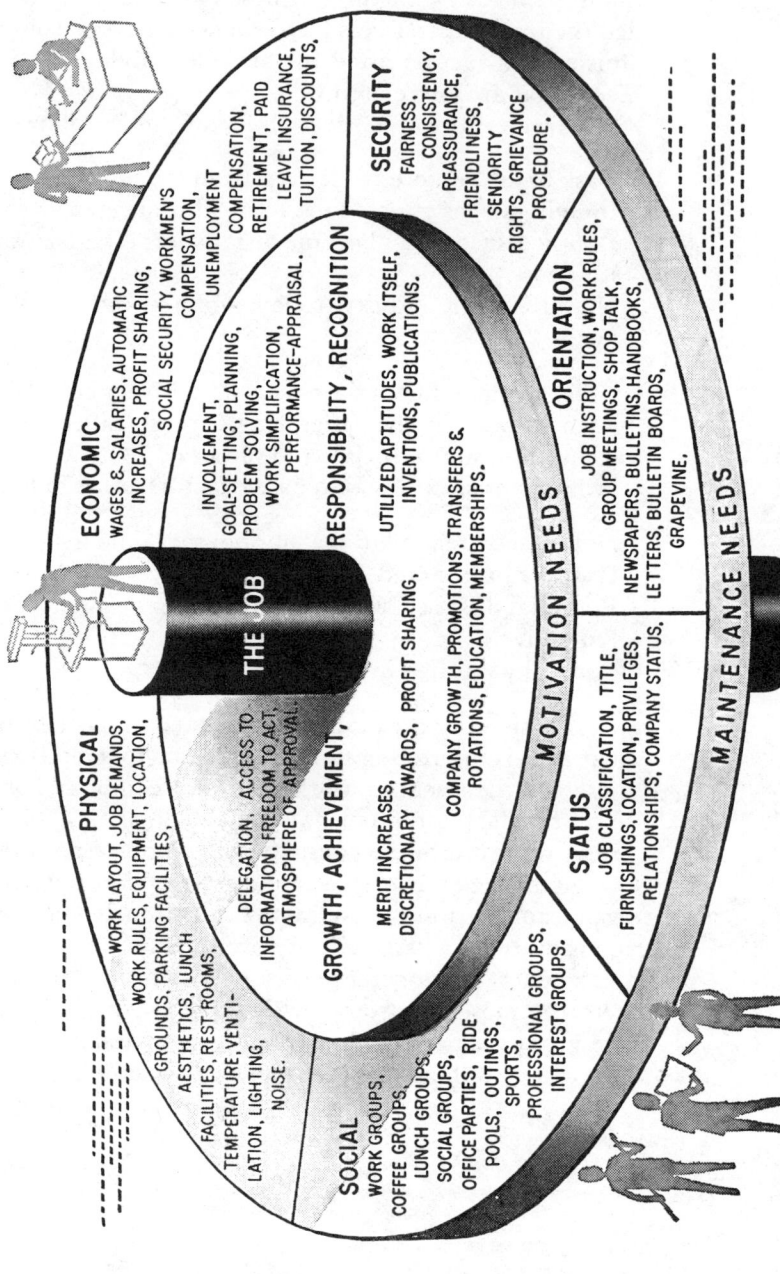

Figure 13–1 Employee needs—maintenance and motivation. (Source. M Scott Myers, "Who Are Your Motivated Workers?", Harvard Business Review. 42, No. 1 (January–February 1964), p. 86.

3. Industry has provided most people the means to satisfy lower-order needs.
4. Providing the means to satisfy higher-order needs has the greatest motivational value.
5. Lower-order needs must be *kept* satisfied or low morale and productivity will result; however, once they are satisfied, they lose their ability to motivate.
6. Professional satisfaction and prestige are becoming relatively more important in industry.

SCIENTIFIC MANAGEMENT

Frederick Taylor and his associates developed the concept of *scientific management*.[5] It was their idea that the way to improve productivity was to break the job into its movements and scientifically determine the best way to make each movement. The use of this approach did result in a marked increase in productivity for each worker.

However, this management style is based on the assumption that employees are motivated by monetary incentives—that pay is the most potent motivator. Its application tended to increase production and pay to the point where it was self-defeating, because higher needs were awakened as the lower needs were satisfied.

This system is still practiced to some degree today. We see it in the industrial engineer's activity in setting job standards for production facilities. However, it is normally a part of some other management style.

McGREGOR'S THEORIES OF MOTIVATION

To fully appreciate the changes that have taken place in management philosophies, it is important to examine a few additional theories. The first one will be *Theory X and Theory Y* of Douglas McGregor.[6] According to McGregor, the traditional mangement assumptions about human behavior are incorrect. He classified traditional theories of management (Theory X) and new developments (Theory Y).

Traditional philosophy called Theory X is as follows.

1. The average human being has an inherent dislike of work and will avoid it if he or she can.
2. Because of this, most people must be coerced, controlled, directed, and threatened with punishment to get them to put out "a day's work for a day's pay."

[5]F. W. Taylor, *The Principles of Scientific Management,* Harper and Brothers, New York, 1911.
[6]Douglas McGregor, *The Human Side of Enterprise,* McGraw-Hill Book Co., New York, 1960.

3. The average human being *prefers* to be directed, because he or she doesn't like responsibility, has relatively little ambition, and wants security above all.

New developmental assumptions of Theory Y are the following.

1. People enjoy work as naturally as they enjoy play.
2. Most people are capable of exercising self-control and self-direction if they are motivated to achieve a goal.
3. The average worker will not only accept, but will actively seek, responsibility.
4. The capacity of the average worker is only partially utilized.

In any organization you will find managers at both ends of the spectrum. Most of us fall somewhere in the middle, between Theory X and Theory Y.

Most people who work for a manager who believes in Theory X will become "maintenence seekers"; under managers who believe in Theory Y, they will become "motivation seekers." The assumptions you make about people will determine, to a great extent, whether they are maintenance seekers or motivation seekers.

GELLERMAN'S THEORIES OF MOTIVATION

Gellerman has presented some other insights into the matter of management.[7] He speaks of two major styles of management: (1) the method involving coercion, threat of dismissal, and (2) the method involving compensation, reward.

Both of these methods are based on the assumption that people must be subjected to external controls to be productive. Management's problem is often "how best to play on human fears and appetites to regulate behavior." The traditional view is that people must be managed by manipulation. Coercion and manipulation are always with us, but they are no longer to be considered potent motivators.

Gellerman said that the manager must know why people believe and act as they do. One must get to the root of behavior, rather than react to behavior. This new approach to human relations is an analytical approach to understanding people, rather than a set of techniques for handling them.

Gellerman defines morale as the attitude a worker has toward accomplishing work, rather than emotions displayed during work. Therefore the happiest person is not necessarily the best motivated or the most productive worker. This helps to explain the failure of the human relations type of management as practiced in the earlier part of this century.

[7]Saul W. Gellerman, *Motivation and Productivity*, American Management Association, New York, 1963.

Motivation needs and the rise of the labor unions are related. The union has developed as the result of needs that employees felt were not being satisfied. They felt they needed an organization to protect their interests and offset the power of the company. Union organizers have capitalized on this belief of the employees, and many companies by their actions have reinforced this belief.

ARGYRIS' EXPLANATION OF THE "WHY" OF MOTIVATION PROBLEMS

Argyris has addressed himself to the question of meaningful work.[8] He has said that "we must make work worthwhile." He then proceeds to tell us how we have destroyed the worthwhileness of work.

1. We have simplified and specialized jobs to the point where little skill is needed.
2. Monkeys do some assembly jobs better than people.
3. If the job doesn't satisfy the worker's needs, he becomes preoccupied with wages and working conditions, and exhibits hostility and resentment toward management.

To overcome the problems we must change the nature of work in the following ways.

1. The job must be made more interesting and challenging in order to provide means to satisfy needs.
2. We must take more advantage of our people's talents. Workers are capable of doing more than their jobs allow them to.
3. To provide meaningful work, we must include planning, doing, and controlling in a manner consistent with Theory Y.
4. Most managers have meaningful work to do, but few hourly people do. Therefore, by allowing them to plan, we provide an opportunity for growth and recognition through goal setting and problem solving. By allowing them to control, we provide opportunity for feedback, a sense of achievement, and self-actualization.

Now that motivation research and contemporary theories have been covered, it appears that these "emerging concepts" can be contrasted with the traditional views. This is shown in Figure 13-2.

SKINNER'S OPERANT CONDITIONING B. F. Skinner, a Harvard psychologist, has a theory known as *operant conditioning*, referring to his standard practice of making a subject operate in a certain way to receive a certain reward.[9] His idea is that people

---

[8]C. Argyris, *Integrating the Individual and the Organization,* John Wiley and Sons, New York, 1964.
[9]B. F. Skinner, *Science and Human Behavior*, The Macmillan Company, New York, 1953.

Traditional Views	Emerging Concepts
1. Set goals for subordinates; define standards and results expected.	1. Participate with people in problem solving and goal setting.
2. Train subordinates how to do the job.	2. Create the situation for learning to occur naturally.
3. Check subordinates' performance to make sure they are doing things right.	3. Enable people to check own performance.
4. Discipline to keep people in line and set examples.	4. Mediate conflicts and help people see the need for rules and the consequences of violations.
5. Stimulate subordinates by forceful leadership and emotional appeals.	5. Allow people to set challenging goals.
6. Develop and install new methods.	6. Provide opportunity for methods improvement by job incumbents.
7. Develop and free subordinates for promotion.	7. Provide opportunity for people to pursue and move into growth opportunities.
8. Recognize achievements and point out failures.	8. Recognize achievements and help people learn from failures.

Figure 13-2 Motivational research—traditional versus emerging concepts.

are what they are because of their environment, not because of any internal drives, needs, or other unexplainable influences.

Skinner developed certain terminology. An operant response is the desired behavior probability followed by a pleasant experience. Since we prefer pleasure to pain, the subject repeats that which brings pleasure.

Stephen Jablonsky and David DeVries[10] have suggested several rules for gaining maximum motivation through operant conditioning. A few of them are as follows:

1. Avoid relying on punishment as a primary means of motivation.
2. Positively reinforce desired behavior and if possible, ignore undesired behavior.
3. Minimize time lag between operant response and reinforcement.
4. Determine the response level of each individual.
5. Determine the environmental factors that are considered positive and negative by the individual.

[10]S. Jablonsky, and D. DeVries, Operant Conditioning Principles Extrapolated to the Theory of Management," *Organizational Behavior and Human Performance*, April 1972, pp. 340-358.

VROOM'S PREFERENCE EXPECTATIONS

Victor H. Vroom in 1964 describes how two variables (preference and expectation) work on each other to determine motivation.[11]

Preference refers to the multiple possible outcomes that workers might have for any activity. They have preference for certain rewards related to their performance.

On the other hand, workers have a certain *expectation* that the desired outcome will happen. Their enthusiasm to receive a reward is tempered by their expectation.

For example, a union worker would like a raise for working harder, but he knows the union contract does not provide a raise for this extra effort. Therefore, he will not be moved to act. On the other hand, a factory where employees are paid on a piece work basis would provide the incentive to work harder.

PORTER AND LAWLER'S MODEL

Porter and Lawler expanded Vroom's theory by the concept that continued performance depends on worker satisfaction, and that satisfaction is determined by how closely the actual rewards given compare to what the worker feels he or she deserves.[12,13] If the reward for performance equals or exceeds what the worker perceives to be his or her due, he or she will be motivated to repeat the action. If it falls short of expectations, the worker's dissatisfaction will prevent motivation to continue the effort. While this helps to explain some motivation phenomena it is difficult to apply in practice.

FRUSTRATION AND UNSATISFIED NEEDS

Frustration is the feeling of insecurity and dissatisfaction arising from unresolved problems or unsatisfied wants.[14] The mind generally attempts to cause behavior designed to aid the frustrated person to adjust to an unresolved situation, a type of behavior termed adjustive reaction. Some adjustive reactions are positively directed; other reactions are negative.

An understanding of psychological concepts, such as this, will enable you to be sensitive to your own complex mental problems or those of others. Persons with chronic and severe problems should seek professional assistance. An awareness of major adjustive reaction may enable you to deal more effectively with the relatively normal stresses of everyday living. Kossen discusses related areas of compensation, negativism, resignation, repression, rationalization, obsessive thinking, displacement, flight, and conversion.

---

[11] V. H. Vroom, *Work and Motivation,* John Wiley & Sons, New York, 1964.
[12] E. Lawler, and L. Porter, "The Effects of Performance on Job Satisfaction," *Industrial Relations,* October 1967, p. 23.
[13] L. Porter, and E. Lawler, *Mangerial Attitudes and Performance,* Richard D. Irwin, Inc. Homewood, Ill., 1968.
[14] S. Kossen, *The Human Side of Organization,* Harper & Row, New York, 1978, pp. 117-126.

MOTIVATION THEORY IN PERSPECTIVE

What do all these theories mean to the supervisor?

First, he or she must recognize that knowledge of human nature is a changing thing. As more research is done, more theories will develop or the present ones will be reinforced. The amount of research done in human relations is so insignificant compared to that done in technical fields that we can expect many changes in the coming years.

Second, at the present time in America the weight of opinion says that maintenance needs are pretty well taken care of and that we must concentrate on the job content factors, a subject covered from a different perspective in Chapter XVII. The maintenance factors are generally beyond the supervisor's control, but the job content or motivation factors are not. Therefore the supervisor can improve the operation of his or her group if he or she takes note of the motivation factors of Herzberg and Myers. The supervisor should operate in such a manner that subordinates feel they are intimately associated with the decision making. The supervisor must keep them informed so that they can evaluate the quality of their decision. Thus they will do better the next time. The supervisor must cultivate their aspirations for advancement, even at his or her own sacrifice. The supervisor must search for ego-satisfying criteria for each person in the group.

To the authors, the various motivation theories appear to provide reasonable bases for improving the supervisor's performance. He or she must recognize that they are not exact mathematical laws, but rather clues to behavior. The Theory X or Theory Y person does not exist *per se*—each person is some blend. However, the fact that we know the dimensions of the blend is helpful.

The Hawthorne studies were important because they gave the first clue to the fact that managers had the wrong idea about their employees' needs. Herzberg reconfirmed and validated this first work. He brought it into focus, analyzed it, and classified it.

Myers at Texas Instruments tended to build on Herzberg's work and demonstrated how this theory could be applied in an industrial enterprise. He contributed the thought that unsatisfied maintenance needs can be "dissatisfiers."

McGregor provided parameters to human behavior with his Theory X and Theory Y. Directly, their practical application is limited. However, knowledge of their existence helps us to better study ourselves and our colleagues. It is important to note that whichever way we lean in our management theory, we tend to pull those we supervise into operating in a similar manner.

Gellerman urges us to study our men and get at the root of their behavior. This is a good suggestion, and as we build along participative management lines we can see the importance of this analysis.

Argyris helps us to consider the value of meaningful work. If the work can be made meaningful, the excitement of operation under participative mangement will help us to develop the team we want.

Skinner has told us that people are what they are because of environment, not because of any internal drives, needs, or other unexplainable influences.

Jablonsky and DeVries have given us some rules to obtain maximum motivation through operant conditioning.

Vroom describes how preference and exceptation work on each other to determine motivation.

Porter and Lawler provided the concept that continued performance depends on worker satisfaction as determined by how closely the actual rewards given compare to what workers feels they deserve.

The theories are, then, not individually important or necessarily directly useful. However, woven together they form a fabric that helps us to become better supervisors.

SUMMARY

We can now summarize the role of the supervisor as it has been in the traditional format of management, and as it will be in the emerging format of management. We live and operate in a competitive capitalistic economy where productivity is important. Productivity depends to a considerable degree on the motivation of the individual. Supervisors cannot motivate individuals unless they understand them. Supervisors must know what their people want from their jobs.

Motivation research has demonstrated that people are no longer interested in the so-called maintenance needs of money and fringe benefits, but rather are interested in job satisfaction and self-realization. These latter factors have become the true motivators.

Over the years various management styles have evolved. They normally came to the fore because of the circumstances of the time. All are still used in various forms today. However, the most accepted style today is primarily participative mangement. It utilizes the elements of McGregor's Theory Y. A major change is necessary in corporate operations so that the supervisor can fully use the theories that have developed.

KEY CONCEPTS

People motivation. Conceptually, most human beings are very complex and difficult to understand. A supervisor's biggest problem with workers or subordinates will be motivation, or getting people to do a high-quality job when it is needed. Motivation comes from within an in-

Chapter XIII   Motivating the Worker

dividual. He or she must want to do something. It becomes the supervisor's job to activate this desire within the individual.

Supervisory use of motivational theories. The theories included in this chapter help to shed light on the complex nature of human motivation. These theories can be useful for broadening the supervisor's understanding so that he can practice them to get the job done. It is important to understand that human motivation is a culmination of these theories and how they fit the individual supervisory style used with the employees. Flexibility is the key, because no panacea or absolute answer can fit all situations the supervisor will face.

IMPORTANT TERMS

Argyris' studies
Capitalistic system
Frustration and unsatisfied needs
Gellerman's studies
Hawthorne studies
Herzberg's studies
Hygiene or maintenance factors
Inflation
Investors
Motivation

Motivational factors
Motivational research
Operant conditioning
Preference expectation
Porter and Lawler's model
Scientific management
Texas Instruments studies
Theory X and Theory Y
   (McGregor)

INCIDENTS

The Motivated Worker

As Pete Smith, the supervisor, was walking down the production line, one of the workers, Joe Walker, called to him. The supervisor walked over "What's the matter, Walker?"

"Nothing," replied Walker, "but I've been thinking that if we get rid of those wooden boxes that move down the production line we could—" "Look, Walker, I don't want you to get upset, but you're paid to work, not think. Just stack the boxes as I showed you, and forget about telling us how to do it."

Walker shrugged his shoulders and went back to stacking the wooden boxes as they came off the end of the production line. He began to think more about his idea of a machine that could replace the tedious and monotonous job he had. Boy, he thought, if I had gone to college, maybe I could have become a supervisor and tried out some of my ideas.

At that moment one of the wooden boxes jammed on the line. A nail sticking out of the box had become engaged with one of the joints in the steel guides along side the belt. The box twisted sideways, and the following boxes piled up behind. The weight and force that built up finally caused the jammed box to literally explode from the pressure. Wood splinters flew in all directions, some of them landing in the belt rollers jamming the belt. The circuit breakers popped open, shutting down the whole line. The belt stopped, and the 125 workers across the plant had to stop work. The supervisors hurried up and down the line looking for the problem. Finally two maintenance men spotted the jam near Joe Walker's work station. Pete Smith ran up to Joe and said, "Walker, why didn't you do something about this?"

"I am," replied Joe. "I'm stacking the boxes."

Disgruntled, Smith thought of the union rules that stated workers had to be paid for down time of less than three hours.

One of the maintenance men said, "This is some jam. We'll be down for better than an hour."

Smith groaned as he turned to face Joe Walker. "Walker, why didn't you see that jam coming?"

Walker replied, "I'm stacking the boxes as you told me to do. My back was toward the belt, and I didn't see the jam. I was only following orders, Mr. Smith." Smith walked off in a huff muttering something under his breath.

What type of motivational factors were present here? Which motivational factors were allowed to operate? Which were not permitted? What would you have done if you were Smith when Joe first called you over? What would you have done after the jam?

Unusual Motivation at the Warren Company

Sam Brown was plant manager of the Warren Company located in southwestern Ohio. Most of the workers in the plant lived close at hand and were accustomed to a rather paternal treatment by the management of the company. They were accustomed to certain privileges and felt as long as they did their job management should leave them alone. They were hostile toward management when disciplined but obedient when they had their own way. Among their privileges were lateral job shifting achieved by bidding on vacancies and a right to use company materials for home repair.

One day Brown got a call from the home office indicating that $5 million worth of new equipment had been approved by the board. He was also told a new production manager was being sent to him. The new production manager was known for his strong autocratic leadership characteristics.

The new production manager, Henry Rose, soon moved to deny the workers access to company equipment. He also eliminated the policy of job shifting. The workers were obviously irritated by both of these moves but since his policy was to only pay attention to employee grievances when they reached a critical stage, he made no immediate moves.

While Rose made a number of technical changes that speeded up production and reduced labor cost during his first several months, tensions continued to build among the employees. They began to focus their attention on the new equipment that was being installed. They felt that if the company could spend $5 million on machinery they ought to be able to increase their wages. At the end of his first year Rose was sent off to a three-month managerial seminar in Boston. Brown decided to leave Rose's job vacant during his absence and instructed the shift foreperson that they would be responsible for their particular shift with no further supervision. He also told them that they should feel free to handle minor grievances.

A number of things began to happen. The women requested some improvements in their restroom. The plant manager responded by instructing the maintenance crew to take care of the job. Some workers requested a change in their six-day week. Brown made a deal with them that if production reached 40,000 pounds a day (about a 20 percent increase) he would institute a four-hour work schedule for Saturday. Within a few days, production reached the indicated level.

Other changes in attitude were noted. A worker suggested that a public address system, rather than a whistle, be used to announce beginning and end of shift and rest periods. This was adopted and shortly employees were even returning to work before the announcement was made.

During the first month of the absence of the production manager the daily output increased from 50,000 to 70,000 pounds. Brown, the plant manager, was puzzled. He could not understand why production was up 30 percent when the production manager was absent.

Discuss the motivating factors that were present in this set of circumstances. Do they represent situations that could be used on the long term? What should Brown do when Rose returns from his managerial education?

QUESTIONS FOR DISCUSSION

1. Discuss why the profit of the corporation is not an adequate motivating force for the employee.
2. Why is it important to know something about the characteristics of people before we can decide how to motivate them? What early research can help us to understand some important characteristics of people? What did it teach us?
3. Summarize some of the characteristics of people that the various motivation studies have shown.

4. Is scientific management a viable motivation tool today? Why or why not?
5. How would you, as a first line supervisor in a unionized organization,, effectively use some of these motivational theories?
6. Explain operant conditioning. As a supervisor, how could this help you in motivating your employees?
7. Define frustration. What causes it?
8. List six things that you have learned about people. How would you use this knowledge to motivate your group?

CHAPTER XIV
Personal Characteristics of the Supervisor

LEARNING OBJECTIVES

- *To realize the importance of time management and personal characteristics.*
- *To realize the importance of time management and personal characteristics.*
- *To be concerned with successful supervisory behavioral patterns toward other levels of management.*

Introduction

We will review leadership styles in the next chapter. Now we will examine in somewhat more detail the supervisor's inherent and acquired personal characteristics that are helpful for the development of successful relationships with associates and for the leadership of people.

Many attempts have been made to isolate those characteristics of a person that will assure his or her success as a supervisor. The net result of this work has been to conclude that the presence or absence of a long list of characteristics does not insure that the person will or will not be successful. The actions of a person who has leadership responsibilities are all too complex for easy cataloguing.

It is useful to review some of the characteristics that will help a supervisor to become successful. Some of these characteristics may be inherent while others may be acquired or learned. Regardless, the successful supervisor has both native talent and learned skills.

Authority and responsibility will be part of the discussion and should be defined. *Authority* is the right delegated to a position that allows the incumbent to manage a group of individuals in such a way that enterprise or department goals are set and achieved. The authority of any manager can be traced up through the organization, to the board of directors, and thence to the stockholders, who hold their authority by virtue of the institution of private property.

Responsibility is the obligation of a subordinate to perform assigned and implied duties. Responsibility cannot be delegated. It is a person's obligation to perform as owed to his or her superior.

A successful supervisor, regardless of managerial level, must possess basic skills in at least three areas: (1) conceptual, (2) human, and (3) technical.

Conceptual ability—able to think in the abstract concerning decision making, managerial and technical systems, importance of the organization relationship with the total economy and societal impact.

Human ability—able to show empathy, concern, leadership, and the willingness to listen and be concerned with others.

Technical ability—able to perform the technical aspects of leadership, motivation, and knowledge of the job.

PERSONAL CHARACTERISTICS—CONCEPTUAL

INITIATIVE AND DRIVE A characteristic of a well-managed organization is that each member will carry forward the execution of his or her responsibilities expeditiously within their delegated authority. This implies that each manager or supervisor possesses the characteristics of *initiative and drive*. The characteristics are usually fostered by our American cultural values. We accept the need for initiative and drive, but not everyone has these characteristics or the ability to grasp the initiative and to drive toward a goal.

Many people are born with these abilities. Given other necessary talents, they may rise to high positions in their particular fields. If one is endowed with these characteristics, his or her future as a manager can be enhanced. On the other hand, there are people who are not so richly blessed. These people must acquire the traits through training or through certain motivational influences provided by management.

Although it is possible for a person to be a relatively good supervisor without these qualities their progress will be considerably enhanced if they possess them. Therefore it should be a matter of concern to the supervisor and the superior that these characteristics be developed.

DECISION-MAKING ABILITY Decision-making ability is related to the preceding characteristic. If one enjoys carrying responsibility, it is likely that he or she will be a better decision maker than one who shuns such responsibility.

A good decision maker must be able to identify the problem, request the data required for a solution, make the decision, and be willing to live with the result. It is in this last step that the one who enjoys carrying responsibility excels. Many people have destroyed their lives by worrying about their past decisions. The old quotation, "Its better to have tried and failed than never have tried at all," is most appropriate to supervisory decision making. Supervisors have to give it their best shot and then live and learn from their successes and failures. This is an important aspect of personal development.

Decision making, however, requires another personal characteristic: an analytical mind. Once a supervisor has identified the problem, it is important that he or she be able to identify the data necessary to make a decision. They must be able to analyze the problem in order to arrive at the proper decision.

An example might clarify the situation. Suppose that you are a supervisor in charge of a chemical operation and that you are on the midnight shift. At four o'clock in the morning the packing gland on one of the pumps develops a serious leak, emitting combustible liquids and vapors. To shut the plant down in order to fix this particular pump means the loss of considerable production and the producing of low-quality materials for a number of hours. Should you stop the leak as best you can, keep the plant running, or leave the problem for the day shift to worry about?

Any choice you make will have certain consequences. The real decision maker is the one who will make the decision to the best of his or her ability, and live with those consequences. Obviously the boss will have an opinion about what you should have done. To choose the wrong course of action opens the door to his or her wrath. The more able you are to analyze the data presented to you and to make the proper decision, the more likely you are to receive roses rather than ashes.

INTELLECTUAL CAPACITY   Leaders must have an intellectual capacity that will allow them to do many things. They must be creative in order to find ways to organize and inspire the group toward greater achievement. One of the main factors that should be coupled with the intellectual capacity is common sense and judgment. Without these the leader's intellectual capacity becomes quite ineffective.

INTEGRITY AND COURAGE   Finally, perhaps two of the most important characteristics of all are integrity and courage. This must include both moral and intellectual integrity. Only if their followers clearly see their stature in these areas will they achieve the maximum success. As they exhibit this moral and intellectual fiber, their followers will have faith in their decision-making ability and their ability to lead them to the goals that they see. In the final analysis, it is the common purpose of these goals that will ultimately unite the followers in their pursuit of the leader.

PERSONAL CHARACTERISTICS—HUMAN

ENJOYMENT OF RESPON-SIBILITY A leader must *enjoy carrying responsibility*. This is another characteristic that is partly inherited and partly acquired. However, it is sometimes the dividing line between the person who will make a successful supervisor and the one who will not. Many individuals possess a host of excellent characteristics but have deficiency in this area. For some supervisors, carrying responsibility means loss of sleep and appetite. When these two items are affected, a supervisor must consider whether the positive values associated with being a supervisor are worth the penalty.

For those who are born with these characteristics, sharing of other people's problems is like bread and meat. For those that must acquire them a real psychological change must take place. One good rule for the person trying to acquire such a capability is not to carry the problems of yesterday, today, and tomorrow at the same time. The decisions of yesterday and their consequences must be put behind. The problems of tomorrow must not be assumed until that day has arrived. With this kind of an attitude it becomes possible for the supervisor to find joy in problem solving while devoting his/her efforts to the day's activities.

This is a trait worthy of serious study and consideration by anyone desiring to rise through the various management levels of an organization. The higher they rise the greater the problems. If there is not joy in carrying responsibility, then the price may be too great.

EMOTIONAL STABILITY Supervisors must have as much interest in the problems of others as they have in their own. Human beings tend to have problems and to interrelate with one another in such a manner as to cause additional problems. The supervisor is always the focal point of such conflicts. If he or she is going to lead these people toward a definable objective, they must be able to handle these conflicts without their conflicts affecting them emotionally.

In addition, it is difficult to follow a leader who is unstable emotionally. Such a leader finds it difficult to establish a course of action and stick to it. The follower finds himself or herself trying to follow a moving target. Such action tends to damage the image of the supervisor as a leader in the eyes of the led.

MOTIVATION *Motivation* is somewhat similar to initiative and drive. However, we can look at it in a slightly different light. We can consider how susceptible a person is to being motivated. Do factors such as achievement, recognition, responsibility, growth, and advancement inspire leaders to do a better job? On the other hand, how susceptible are they to disappointments that may make them dissatisfied with their job? Disappointments might involve such matters as pay, supplemental benefits, company policy in administration, and working conditions.

Perhaps a good supervisor is one who is susceptible to the motivation factors, and not overly affected by the dissatisfaction factors. This characteristic is probably inherent in the particular nature of a person, but it can be cultivated in someone who is not so richly blessed.

VITALITY AND ENDURANCE

The leader must have *vitality and endurance.* General Brehon Somervell said many years ago that the leader must be up in the morning before those being led and must be in bed at night after those being led. Such leadership requires an endurance surpassing that of the followers. In addition, because of the decision making involved, the leader is under considerably more stress than the followers, and they have to respond to this stress either with quietness and calmness or eagerness, initiative and a positive disposition, depending upon the circumstances. For example, an emotional circumstance should elicit calmness and a depressing circumstance should elicit eagerness.

PERSONAL CHARACTERISTICS—TECHNICAL

COMPETENCE TO PERFORM THE JOB TECHNICALLY

The supervisor must have a *working knowledge of the job* being performed by the people supervised. They look to the supervisor to help them over rough spots in their operations. If he or she is unable to assist them, credibility as a supervisor is weakened. The supervisor who has risen from the ranks should find it easy to meet this requirement.

On occasion a new college graduate without practical experience may find himself or herself in a first-line supervisor's job. Sometimes management has placed the graduate on the line working with the hourly people prior to making him or her supervisor. To develop respect from people under such circumstances requires considerable finesse on the new supervisor's part. Normally he or she can succeed by showing respect for the worker's specific knowledge and by showing how his or her own technical knowledge can be used to improve the operation for the benefit of the worker and employer.

As a person progresses further up the organizational ladder, the need for technical knowledge of subordinates' activities tends to decrease. For example, the president of a company may be a lawyer or an accountant who knows nothing about the technical details of the operations he manages. As seen in Figure 14-1, the relationship between technical, human, and conceptual skills and personal understanding changes as a manager advances in the organization.

PERSUASIVENESS

Leaders must be persuasive because they must communicate the plans and goals of the group. They must communicate any changes in these plans and goals. They must communicate to the group the orders that must be followed in the achievement of these goals. Communication re-

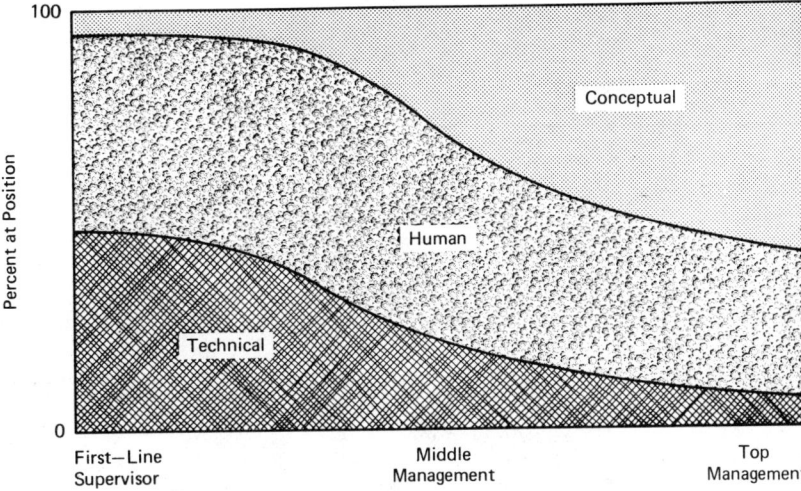

Figure 14-1   Differences in the nature of skills and personal understanding required of different levels of management.

quires an ability to express views clearly. Leaders must have the perception that will allow them to understand the receptivity of these views by the followers. They must be sensitive to their followers' needs and must satisfy these needs in such a manner that they will not interfere with the achievements of the goals. All of this must be done in a manner that is inspiring to those being led.

USE OF TIME   A supervisor is a leader to the degree that he or she has a voluntary following and where the supervisor demonstrates to the people the best method of getting what they want, by doing it in the most effective way. Many supervisors believe that no matter how hard they apply themselves and reallocate their time, they can't escape a nagging feeling that they have more work to do and more people to see than they can satisfactorily handle.

Time is a finite factor that is directly related with a supervisor's productivity and quality of output. How supervisors use their time is a major determinant to their efficiency. Managing one's time rather than being managed by time is often a characteristic successful supervisors find indispensable. Some people have a talent to be orderly and on top of everything, but practicing time management can lead to more productive output and more satisfied supervisors. Time management is not a mystical operation but one that can be learned. For example, successful supervisors utilize their time better by giving priority to events and things that have to be done that day. Daily activities may follow (1) things that must be done, (2) things that should be done, and (3) things that would be nice to get done, as shown in Figure 14-2.

THINGS TO DO TODAY

As of: _____

I. Must be done:

    _____

    _____

    _____

II. Should be done:

    _____

    _____

    _____

III. Nice to be done:

    _____

    _____

    _____

Figure 14-2 Time Planning by Prioritizing the Things to be Done Daily.

SUCCESSFUL SUPERVISORY BEHAVIORAL PATTERNS

Supervisors should have personal behavioral patterns that can assist them to cope with their environment on the job. These behavioral patterns include relationships with subordinates, higher management, other departments, unions, technology, and performance standards.

TOWARD GROUP MEMBERS We see our surroundings from a personal perspective, so we might say that "beauty is in the eye of the beholder." This statement might also be applied to leadership. We might say that the leadership ability of the supervisor is in the eyes of the followers. No matter how good a leader a person thinks he or she is, unless this impression of leadership ability is conveyed to the employees, workers will not be led. The supervisor's personal characteristics and performance, must convey to the subordinates that he is, in fact, the leader of the group.

One of the most effective ways for a supervisor to convey this leadership is to define clearly the objectives for the group. For example, the supervisor should make certain that the employees clearly understand that their obligation is to operate effectively within the organization and to produce the desired quantity of product at the desired quality.

Supervisors can make themselves look better by enhancing the performance of those who work for them. This factor becomes even more important when the supervisor moves to a higher management level. Frequently supervisors have made the mistake of not grooming subordinates to take their places. Some supervisors have felt threatened by too good a performance on the part of employees. Therefore they have depreciated the importance of subordinates' jobs and failed to assist them in preparing for future promotions. These supervisors have paid the penalty of this action by failing to be promoted themselves, since there was no one to step into their shoes.

Another way to convey the idea of the group member's importance is through the utilization of the participative leadership style. Through this type of management the worker feels that they are an important part of the problem-solving process. Participative management provides a forum in which attitudes are developed that lead the subordinate toward greater accomplishments.

The successful supervisor matches the appropriate leadership style with the treatment of workers, as people. Although people want to be led and given direction by a competent supervisor, nevertheless they are not always willing to be led. Convincing the workers that they want to be led, the supervisor must relate his personal characteristics to their best advantage. Therefore a successful supervisor has to create his/her opportunity to lead and manage; he/she cannot expect this opportunity to already exist. It's most critical to make the proper match between leadership style and the situation in which workers are involved.

TOWARD HIGHER MANAGEMENT

The supervisor shows the employees his/her attitude toward them by the way he/she defends their interests with higher management. If he/she has proved that he/she supports their request to the fullest, then they will rest their case with him/her. On the other hand, he/she should demonstrate to them that he/she can act as a buffer between higher management and the employee. If an error is made, the supervisor takes the responsibility and does not try to find a scapegoat.

There is one other point that is frequently neglected. When higher management sets a policy with which supervisors may not wholeheartedly agree, it is their responsibility to convey this policy to the department as though it were their own. He/she is not to blame the management for establishing policies unpopular to his/her people. Rather, he/she is to defend the position of top management. The good supervisor will spend time in helping the employees to understand what is behind such a policy. This can be done much better by the supervisor than by a document coming from on high.

TOWARD OTHER DEPARTMENTS

Two or more departments frequently must work together to meet corporate goals. Supervisors should be willing to cooperate, and they should be capable of helping their employees to understand the importance of such cooperation. While his/her men are a team with them, they as supervisors are part of the supervisory team that must work toward common objectives.

TOWARD UNIONS

The supervisor must recognize that the union has a viable place in an industrial society. Although they may not like some union methods or motives, the supervisor must recognize that they do perform a service such as providing management with a somewhat united group with which to deal.

The supervisor must know the union contract and its provisions. They should recognize that this is an operating agreement between management and its employees. It is a contract to be honored like any other contract. Their obligation then is to become familiar with every provision of the contract. If they have questions, they should have them answered by the personnel department.

Frequently a union contract spans two or three years during which time mutual agreements are made between union and management. These mutually agreed-upon changes in the initial union contract have to be understood by supervisors so they can cope with the variety of problems workers face every day.

Here again, supervisors have the opportunity of establishing credibility. If they administer the contract fairly and if they cooperate with the union leaders fully within the spirit and letter of the contract then supervisors can expect that the union leaders will trust them. This trust may become very important at some later date; supervisors will be able to assure the union leaders that they will operate in a particular manner in a given situation because they operated the same way in an earlier situation.

TOWARD TECHNOLOGY AND PLANNING

The good supervisor should always be interested in the efficient operation of the crew. He or she should be a leader in making requests to management for equipment changes that will contribute to the efficiency of operation. The employees will understand that this will bring more benefits to their unit and to them.

The supervisor should call on his people to come forward with suggestions that will lead to more efficient operation. There is no better way to build the morale of a crew than to have them alert and searching for improved operating procedures. Once good suggestions are found, it is the supervisor's responsibility to see that action is taken to implement the improvements.

The ability to plan is an integral part of the supervisor's personal characteristics. The supervisor must encourage worker confidence in the supervisor's ability to do the job. Planning in advance and making provisions and contingencies to cover future events can be a big help in demonstrating a supervisor's managerial abilities. For example, if a potential equipment failure were diagnosed early enough and its replacement were on order, an expensive shutdown could be averted. Thus an ability to see the future, planning for it, and acting to resolve these problems before they occur, is an important supervisory characteristic.

TOWARD PERFORMANCE STANDARDS

The setting of performance standards is always a very delicate matter, particularly where unions are involved. The immediate reaction of the employee is "The company is trying to get more work out of me for the same amount of money." The appearance of the industrial engineer with clipboard and stopwatch has frequently been as explosive as a red flag in front of a bull.

On the other hand, it is important to establish fair and high performance standards for the employees. If this is not done in certain types of operations, some employees will receive more money than they should, and others will get less. Ample time must be spent with the employees, explaining the need for standards as they are developed. The employees should clearly see and understand the importance of this work. They must see that the company will be able to appraise their performance more fairly against such measurable standards.

It is here that the supervisor's leadership abilities are tested to the fullest. If he/she has developed the image of a fair-minded, responsible supervisor, then it will be much easier to organize to accomplish the task. The employees will be willing to ride with their judgment that "the boss" will look after them. The supervisor must try to avoid anything that will alter such an image in the employees' eyes.

SUMMARY

A successful supervisor has a number of personal characteristics that include competence, initiative, drive, enjoyment of responsibility, decision making, problem-solving ability, emotional stability, motivation, vitality, endurance, persuasiveness, intellectual capacity, integrity, and courage. As a leader, the supervisor demonstrates these talents and capabilities to workers, peers, and superiors through leadership, management of time, planning, directing, and controlling the departmental people's activities. A team effort is used to help set goals.

The supervisor uses new technology to improve the department's efficiency along with fair performance standards to encourage quality of output.

The supervisor stands between employees and higher management and must have the ability to absorb problems from both directions and attempt to resolve these problems in order to attain greater efficiency. Finally, the supervisor must recognize the union's importance and attempt to work fairly with the union contract to properly administer the supervisory position.

KEY CONCEPTS

Personal characteristics. Successful supervisors may not possess all the characteristics listed in this chapter, but conceptually, they do have intelligence, leadership ability, vitality and, above all, the ability to work with and through people. This ability is observable in their relations with people inside or outside their department.

Enjoyment of position. A successful supervisor likes what he or she is doing. They accept the position for its intrinsic advantages rather than accepting the position as a job and accept the supervisory position for the power and opportunity it gives to try out their own ideas.

IMPORTANT TERMS

Authority
Decision-making ability
Emotional stability
Initiative and drive

Motivation
Responsibility
Time management
Vitality and endurance

INCIDENTS

Promotion Based on Supervisory Characteristics

Assume that you are a sales supervisor and have been asked by your supervisor to recommend one promising salesperson in your zone for promotion to a sales supervisory position in another sales zone. You looked at the seven people in your zone and eliminated all but three from the promotion list, for different reasons, such as inexperience, poor sales record, or have already refused a promotion. The remaining three people had backgrounds as follows:

1. Roger Dodge has been a territory manager for four years. He has exceeded his sales quota for the last three years. He is friendly, outgoing, loves to tell stories, and is easy to get along with and to understand. Roger's major disadvantage is his self-centeredness when under stress. Customers and sales colleagues have complained about

Roger's aggressiveness and his inability to deliver on all of his promises.

2. Ray Arnold has been a territory manager for two years. He has been very productive, personable, outgoing, and the "life of the party" when with his peers. However, when discussing business with you, he tends to become quiet and reserved. You wonder if you are doing something wrong or if Ray really wants to contribute, but suffers from some imaginary hang-up. His sales record is outstanding and his peers believe he is a valuable member of the organization.

3. Barbara Hume has been a territory manager for three years, the last two have been outstanding sales years having won the company's highest sales award, the Legion of Merit. Barbara, in contrast to Roger and Ray, is not outgoing or the life of the party but appears to be a steady, quiet producer. She is a team person as she is most willing to be included in conversation but feels uncomfortable when the discussion turns to her, as an individual.

Which person would you choose for promotion to a sales supervisor position? What characteristics (either stated or inferred from the description) helped make your decision?

The Analytical Dentist

Dr. Clyde Harker, a prominent dentist in Denver, Colorado, was known in the profession for his exceptional abilities to run his practice profitably. Word came down to a young, struggling dentist named Dr. Greg Altman about the prominent Dr. Harker. Dr. Altman figured he had everything to gain and nothing to lose, so he called Dr. Harker for an appointment to talk about his problems and his practice. Typically, Dr. Harker was most hospitable to the young dentist and gladly set a date for the meeting.

Upon entering Dr. Harker's offices he was struck by the expensive furnishings, spacious room, and inviting living room setting of the waiting room. He noticed a TV monitor in the corner being watched by young patients who could change video tapes whenever they tired of the current children's show.

Dr. Harker showed Dr. Altman the business office and introduced him to each of the three secretary-receptionists who managed the office. The office workers appeared to be intelligent, happy, knowledgeable, and productive as they explained their duties to Dr. Altman. Dr. Altman noticed their desks were not cluttered with unfinished work, but demonstrated efficiency of movement and care for detail.

Upon entering Dr. Harker's four patient rooms, Dr. Altman chatted with each dental assistant and dental hygienist. Each appeared efficient, knowledgeable, and productive.

The walls, decor, dental equipment, and the personal grooming and appearance of all Dr. Harker's employees were modernistic and colorful but still communicated the latest in dental technology and efficiency.

Impressed with what he had seen, Dr. Altman asked Dr. Harker what was his secret. Quietly, but distinctly, Dr. Harker stated, "Greg, I built up my practice by using the latest techniques and equipment, but above all, I made sure my people were involved in making the practice a success by giving them the opportunity to grow with the practice. I pay my people well, but they know that I expect their best effort without my hovering over them."

What favorable personal characteristics do you believe Dr. Harker possesses? What unfavorable characteristics may Dr. Harker possess? Would these characteristics be common to only dentists or would they be common to other supervisory positions?

QUESTIONS FOR DISCUSSION

1. Why is technical competence so important in a supervisor?
2. How may a supervisor's initiative and drive be a favorable influence on workers and when may these characteristics have an unfavorable influence?
3. What are some of the most important characteristics of effective supervisory decision-making ability?
4. Outline which characteristics are most important for a supervisor when faced with the following situations:
   (a) Reprimanding an employee.
   (b) Planning the day's work.
   (c) Giving praise to outstanding work by an employee.
5. Discuss why emotional maturity is a very important supervisory characteristic.
6. Why is planning so important to the supervisor?
7. Assume that top management has sent you a procedure to enforce with your people but the procedure is in conflict with your own morals and ideals. What is your attitude toward management in such a case and what will you do to implement this procedure?
8. Is it important for the supervisor to be interested in the operations of other departments with whom he or she has to work?

CHAPTER XV

Leadership

LEARNING OBJECTIVES

- *To learn the characteristics of autocratic, democratic and laissez-faire leadership styles.*
- *To gain insight into the nature of leadership.*
- *To understand the importance of varying leadership style.*
- *To learn how to secure cooperation, use power, lead, maintain discipline, and develop morale.*

Introduction

Leadership is the ability of a manager to bring people to work together efficiently in a common cause. Its methods of operation have varied somewhat over the years, but the styles of autocratic, democratic, and laissez-faire are still identifiable. The most useful style will depend on the leader and the led.

Although some characteristics of a leader are inborn, others may be acquired. It is important that the supervisor augment inherent abilities with acquired abilities.

You can improve your chances for success when you get an opportunity to lead by cultivating certain behavior. You should be *aware* of the factors that make for leadership effectiveness and you must practice them. You must have *empathy* for your subordinates. You must see things from their point of view. You must walk in their mocassins. You should try to look for the causes of events *objectively*, even though the problem may be brought to you by an emotional subordinate. You must evaluate it from a distance. It is important that you *know yourself*. You must know and understand your attitudes, words, and actions. You must know the effect your attitudes have on others. And to complicate matters, people do not all respond the same way.

TYPES OF LEADERSHIP

Leadership may be defined as the ability of a manager to accomplish group objectives by working with and through people. The need for leadership is present at all levels of an organization from the supervisor to the president or chairman of the board.

Years ago leadership was identified as the ability of one person to tell another what to do. However, with the advent of unions, the manager, or leader, was no longer able to tell workers what to do in quite the same manner as before. This forced consideration of other means by which to secure sufficient productivity from the work force. When scientific management arrived on the scene, the idea of leadership changed.

Under *scientific management* the role of the leader was determined as a result of certain assumptions concerning human behavior. Scientific management offered a means of correcting the normally slothful habits of people and thereby strengthening the organization. This correction was made in two ways: (1) by improving the structure and definition of the organization, and (2) by improving the methods used in the operation of the organization.

The improvements in the structure were directed toward the management. Under this system the manager must respect the organization at all times. The reward was economic security and continued employment. The manager might advance along well-defined paths of promotion.

The improvements in the methods of operation by procedures and standard practices were directed toward overcoming the human frailties of the worker. Improvements in methodology were primarily directed toward changing the job to meet the capabilities of the worker. For example, if problems in quality control appeared, the answer lay in engineering of the products or operation so that the errors of production were reduced to a minimum—not in training the worker to perform at his greatest level of skill.

This approach to organizational control was next modified by the *human relations approach*, which emphasized the contribution and strength of each member of the organization, rather than the organizational structure methodology. Instead of changing the organization, management tended to try to motivate the members to reach their full potential. People were viewed as individuals with certain basic psychological needs that not only must be satisfied, but could be satisfied within the framework of the industrial organization.

For a number of years this motivation approach tended to concentrate on keeping people happy. This was in full flower during the 1940s and 1950s, and the results of it were exemplified in increasingly large pay raises and fringe benefits.

Today emphasis has gone away from merely wages, fringe benefits, and treating people nicely as a means of securing adequate productivity. As was covered in Chapter IX, it has been found that people will produce better under certain motivating conditions affecting his group participation, his sense of belonging, and a number of similar nonmonetary items. Therefore today we speak in terms of group goals and democratic (participative) management.

Three broad styles of leadership are normally recognized: (1) autocratic (boss), (2) democratic (participative), and (3) laissez-faire (free rein).

AUTOCRATIC (BOSS) With this leader the decisions are his or hers alone. An *autocratic* or authoritarian manager centralizes power and decision making in himself or herself (see Figure 15-1). He or she is "boss." The workers do what they are told to do. The autocratic leader assumes full authority and responsibility. When the authority of the autocratic leader becomes oppressive, negative results may occur among the workers, such as being uninformed, insecure, and afraid of the leader's authority.

The autocratic leader can become a *benevolent autocrat*. This is a high-status, powerful individual who makes the decisions but who is accessible to group members and genuinely concerned for their welfare. He or she can develop effective human relations and deal with the workers effectively. Some workers would derive a sense of security and satisfaction working under this style of leadership. In turn, this type of leadership provides strong motivation and psychological rewards to the leader. This leader feels that "he or she is running the show." There has been some attempt to break the benevolent autocrat down into three types.

1. Tends to give orders, and the subordinate tends to take them.
2. Uses ample praise and a pat on the back. Demands loyalty in the acceptance of his or her decision.
3. Makes subordinates feel that they are actually participating in decisions even though they do what he or she wants.

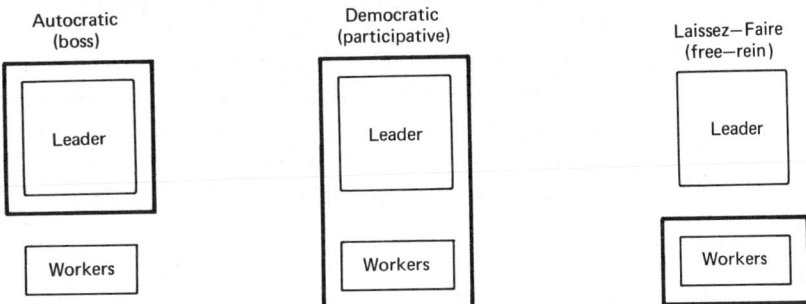

Figure 15-1 Three styles of leadership. (Note. The heavy line indicates the location of power and decision making.)

The industrialist of the late 1800s or the small company operator of today tend to follow this order of leadership. The give the orders and they expect them to be obeyed.

This type of leadership often runs the danger of building resentment among the employees if carried to extremes or if attempted among strong workers who also desire to exercise power.

DEMOCRATIC (PARTICIPATIVE)

The democratic leader wants to share some of the decision-making responsibility with followers, as shown in Figure 15-1. She or he consults the group on questions that interest them and to which they can make a contribution. There are obviously some decisions for which she or he cannot do this. This leader attempts to develop a certain sense of responsibility in the group for their accomplishments. This leader may use both praise and criticism. Although the decision making is shared, the ultimate responsibility still rests with the leader.

In this type of management the leader appeals to people's higher needs, as pointed out in Chapter IX—his needs for belonging, for self-esteem, for status, and for fulfillment. This management recognizes that people's higher needs are most important in today's situation and therefore caters to them. It provides a work environment that allows the worker to satisfy these higher-level needs.

In practice this management allows the people to participate in problem solving and goal setting. This is done in several ways: by creating situations in which people can learn naturally; by enabling people to check out their own performance; by allowing people to set challenging goals; by providing opportunities for method improvement by the job incumbents; by providing opportunity for people to pursue and move into growth opportunity; and finally by recognizing achievements and helping people to learn from their failures.

Many of the organizations to which we belong illustrate this kind of leadership. We as participants develop a plan of action under the guidance of a chairperson. He/she then develops a plan of implementation.

This type of leadership is today considered to have the greatest promise. It will be noted that the term *participative* has been used parenthetically with *democratic*. The term *democratic* has been used for many years; however, recently some writers have introduced the word *participative* feeling perhaps that it better defines the action. Under this title many corporations are today bringing subordinates into the decision-making process.

LAISSEZ-FAIRE (FREE REIN)

The laissez-faire or free-rein leader avoids power by effectively delegating the power to subordinates, as shown in Figure 15-1. This leader depends on the group to establish its own goals and solve its own problems. The group tends to be leaderless except when the leader deals with outside persons to bring the group necessary information, materials, and resources. This leader gives little or no direction and allows supporters a great deal of freedom. This style is not generally useful, but it is effective in highly motivated, professional groups.

This system is sometimes used in research work—in order not to inhibit independent thinking. We often see it in civic organizations, where the leader is weak and the leaderless group tries to act in unison.

This is a difficult method of leadership, demanding much understanding and perseverance by the leader. It is very useful under some circumstances, however, and in these cases has no equally effective substitute.

ANALYSIS OF LEADERSHIP STYLES

In actual practice no one uses any of these three styles exclusively. The ideal managerial style is the one that utilizes all leadership types to the best advantage. We may use autocratic management when necessary. We may use free-rein style to serve a particular purpose. We may use democratic (participative) management to best develop the talents of our employees. We use the democratic style because it is the only system that recognizes and takes advantage of individual differences and capabilities. An example might help to clarify how the manager uses all three types under different situations.

Suppose that John Doe is a successful plant manager. He may direct his secretary to make up a report on all overtime work on a specific order till the order is completed. In doing this he has employed the autocratic approach. He may consult with his five department heads on the best way to push this special order through their department with a minimum of disruption of regular production. In doing this he has used the democratic approach, or participative method, in that he has allowed the five department heads to participate in the decision.

He may suggest to the assistants that it would be a good idea to figure out ways in which they could handle special orders a little more smoothly in the future. In doing this he is using the free-rein, or laissez-faire, style of leadership.

The skill of leadership, then, lies largely in knowing when to use which method. Your problem as a supervisor is to vary the technique to fit the changing positions under which your people are working.

NATURE OF LEADERSHIP

The supervisor, or leader, has been compared with the bus driver whose passengers will leave unless she takes them in the direction in which they want to go. The *employee-oriented leader* will be sensitive enough to the feelings of her subordinates and use enough restraint so that she will be unlikely to lose her passengers. Ordway Tead has stated: "And that leader will be most successful in retaining his right to lead who can help a group to get what it wants with the least friction and the most sense of unity and self-realization."[1]

Seen in this light the leader, in effect, becomes the agent of the led. The leader's approach is "Let's go," whereas the old-time boss says "Go." Instead of having power over people, the leader earns power and authority by his or her day-to-day behavior, decisions, and actions with people. They confer on the leader the privilege of leadership, and they expect the leader to exercise authority when the situation calls for it. The formal authority the leader exercises is inherent in his or her position and allows him or her to utilize discretion in such a way that enterprise or department objectives are set and achieved. The leader's informal authority comes from the acceptance by subordinates of his/her right to manage. True leadership that brings forth teamwork in a common cause depends on this kind of support from below.

The leader's first responsibility is in defining the goals of the group. What purpose do they have in being? Toward what objectives are they working? How do they relate with the objectives of the enterprise? Once these points are clearly defined and understood by the group, it becomes the leader's responsibility to bring the individual and group goals into effective working harmony with the purpose of the department and the overall organization. Beyond this, the leader's unique contribution is to vitalize and energize subordinates into meaningful, cooperative efforts by providing inspiration. The leader is a symbol to subordinates. The leader becomes the personal embodiment of the cause or objective he/she is serving—the company. If the leader is convinced and purposeful about his/her goals and sensitive to employee needs, the employees will tend to follow the leader's example. When a leader gathers prestige and articulates ideas, programs, and aspirations that appeal to people, the response to his/her leadership will be improved teamwork and unity. In extreme circumstances, inspirational leadership helps the followers to become identified with him in a cause beyond themselves.

Much study has been given to the correlation of characteristics that identify the leader. At one time it was thought that leaders were born, not made. However, over the years it has been discovered that there are no real stereotypes and that there is no absolute way of relating human characteristics to leadership success. Rather, leadership is related to the leader, those whom he/she leads, and the situation under which he/she leads them. Let us look at each of these aspects of leadership.

THE LEADER

Certain leadership characteristics will always be important. Among them may be intelligence, self-confidence, sociability, sense of reality, and human relations attitude. Gordon Lippitt reports that in 106 studies of

---

[1] Ordway Tead, *The Art of Leadership,* McGraw-Hill Book Co., New York, 1935, p. 29.

leadership traits, only 5 percent appeared in 4 or more studies.[2] A few of the most important characteristics are a strong will, inner drive, understanding of others, a sense of mission, stability, integrity, and communication skill.

These traits, however, will not explain the success, or lack of it, of all leaders in all situations.

THE LED A leader is without a job if there are no followers. A leader is also without a job if he/she is unable to relate to the people and to cause them to follow. A leader might be able to relate to certain types of individuals and not to others. For example, one leader might be able to command the respect of manual laborers but be totally unsuccessful in inspiring research chemists. The reverse, of course, could also be true.

The success of the leader is dependent to a large extent on those whom he leads. He/she must be a part of the group that he leads but still be apart from it. The group must see the goals in the same manner that the leader does, but it is the leader's duty to coordinate and direct each person toward these common goals.

McGregor speaks of three major aspects of superior-subordinate relationships, at any level of an organization, that influence the subordinate's feelings of genuine security:

"The most important of these is what we may term the 'atmosphere' created by the superior. This atmosphere is revealed not by what the superior does, but by the manner in which he does it, and by his underlying attitude toward the subordinates. It is relatively independent of the strictness of the superior's discipline, or the standards of performance which he demands . . . . Security for subordinates is possible then only when they know they have the genuine approval of their superior. If the atmosphere is equivocal, or one of disapproval, they can have no assurance that their needs will be satisfied, regardless of what they do. In the absence of a genuine attitude of approval subordinates are threatened, fearful, insecure. Even neutral and innocuous actions of the superior are regarded with suspicion. Effective discipline is impossible, high standards of performance cannot be maintained, 'sabotage' of the superior's efforts is almost inevitable. Resistance, antagonism, and ultimately open rebellion are the consequences."[3]

THE SITUATION Regardless of leadership style with a group, a leader may be unsuccessful in certain situations. Although a leadership style may be very effective with one group, the same style may be a disaster with a totally different

---

[2]Gordon Lippitt, "What Do We Know About Leadership?", *Leadership in Action,* National Training Laboratories, National Education Assn., Washington, D.C., 1961, p. 7.
[3]Douglas McGregor, "Getting Effective Leadership in the Industrial Organization," *Journal of Consulting Psychology,* 1944, pp. 149-150, reprinted in *Advanced Management,* October-December 1944.

group. For example, a person who was a successful leader of labor unions or management in the early part of the twentieth century might be ineffective today.

The brash, dominant, autocratic "boss" leadership style practiced by many firms in the early part of this century would be frowned on today by the better educated and informed worker. Improved transportation and communication allows today's worker to move to other jobs. Moreover, the number of different company leadership styles has grown rapidly. Thus there is a wider choice of leadership styles allowable to the worker. If the worker does not like one superior, he/she can request a change to another department. Union shop stewards can assist the worker under these circumstances. However, today's leader may not be able to cope with the situation as it existed then. The founding and growth of many organizations required strong, autocratic leadership that provided specific direction and goal orientation. A young, growing company needs strong, dynamic leadership for its survival. The more mature firms can expand their leadership styles over a broader spectrum.

The same is true at different levels of management. One who is a successful leader at the first level of management may be unsuccessful at the top management level.

It seems apparent then that we cannot precisely define the nature of leadership, because it cannot be isolated and applied only to the leader apart from consideration of the led and the situation.

CHOICE OF LEADERSHIP PATTERN

A person may well be a leader in one group and a follower in another. In the case of a supervisor, he/she is a leader of the people reporting to him/her. But likewise he/she reports to a general foreman or someone farther up the line. An in this situation he/she becomes a follower. Therefore each individual will at times be in one role or the other. Let us look a moment at the situation as it concerns each party at any given time.

In order for subordinates to be effective members of a group to be led, they must recognize their position. They must help those in their group to see a common goal. They must see that it is to their benefit that this goal be achieved. They must further understand that in the achieving of this goal someone must coordinate the activities of the group for maximum efficiency. Finally, they must see that to achieve, they must be willing to submit their will to that of the supervisor who is doing the coordinating.

Supervisors, on the other hand, must also see this goal clearly. They must be assured that this group fully understands the goal and that the individual members are willing to work toward it. In the achievement of this, they must be sensitive to the characteristics of each of the individuals in their group. They must be willing to work harder than any member of the group. They must be willing to bear the responsibility for achieving the goals that have been set. They must be willing to suppress their own personal biases for the good of those whom they supervise.

When these relationships are attained, it is then possible for the leader to work effectively and for the group to attain its goal.

The group that is led may vary in size. According to many theories, there should be a supervisor for every 6 to 10 people. However, this varies greatly from one organization to another and from one situation to another. It is easier for a supervisor to effectively control a large group of people doing essentially identical things than it is to supervise a small group in which each individual may be doing something different. Therefore it is necessary to adjust the number of leaders, as well as the type of leadership, to the group and to the activities in which the group is engaged.

We see that in order to choose the proper leadership pattern and to choose the proper ratio of supervisors to subordinates, we must consider many factors. We must consider the size of the group and the activities in which it is engaged. We must consider the characteristics of the available supervisor. We must consider the situation in which the supervisor will be operating. With a careful analysis of these things it then becomes possible within an organization to utilize the proper supervisor, and it becomes possible for this supervisor to employ the proper leadership pattern.

LEADERSHIP TECHNIQUES

SECURING COOPERATION To be successful a leader must secure the cooperation of those who are to be led. This can be achieved more satisfactorily if the employees are properly oriented. This means that they must understand where they are being led and why they are being led. They must also understand their relationships to one another and how they as a team are going to achieve their goal.

The story is told of the sergeant who had a squad of eight men assigned to move a building weighing 1200 pounds. Each man could lift 150 pounds. He advised each man of the objective and that each must lift his own 150 pounds if the building was to move. If any one of them failed to cooperate, they would not achieve their objective—that is, the moving of the building to a new location.

It is important that some performance criteria be developed so that the men can understand their success in moving toward this goal; otherwise they have a feeling of moving in a wilderness without a definite course of action. The leader must then follow up with them and communicate to them the performance that they are giving. This follow-up tends to give confidence and prompts the person to do better because he knows his performance is being watched. Therefore, if a leader will establish the goals of the group and communicate them to the group, establish criteria for measurement of performance, and communicate this performance to the group, he/she will greatly strengthen his/her position.

In the operation of the group there is bound to be some friction and some difficulty. Some members of the group will undoubtedly have complaints or grievances. Their willingness to continue to cooperate will be a function of how fairly these grievances are handled. Therefore the leader will do well to be considerate of the welfare of the others and to promptly and expeditiously handle their problems as though they were his/her own. He/she should clear the lines of communication so that these grievances can come to his/her attention quickly and so that he/she can effectively move to eliminate them.

In the course of operation the plans and goals may change from time to time. It is important that leaders communicate to the followers these changes and that particularly they explain the "why" of the changes. They must try to see the "why" from the employees' point of view. Their followers will be much more willing to follow and will spend less time in complaining about their leadership if they clearly explain the "why" of the change.

Leaders' orders should be clear and nonconflicting—and they should be compatible with the achievement of the goals.

From time to time there will be the opportunity to promote people to other segments of the organization. The fairness with which leaders appraise the ability of their people and make recommendation for their promotion will greatly enhance their effectiveness as a leader.

From time to time financial considerations will alter the way in which the group can operate. Once more it is important that he communicate the "why" to the workers so that as it becomes necessary to tighten the belt they understand the reason for it.

USE OF AUTHORITY AND POWER

The leader has a certain *authority* evident to the followers and identified with his/her position on the organization chart. However, this organization chart authority becomes useless unless the leader is an effective leader and exercises power to fulfill the position's authority.

To maintain the effectiveness of *power* the leader must exhibit fairness in dealing with the employees and must be considered reasonable in handling of their grievances. The leader must always clarify for them the purpose of their work. As long as the leader does these things, the authority inherent in the position will assist the leader in using power to motivate the personnel.

Supervisors cannot hope to maintain effectiveness if they discipline an employee for sloppy workmanship on a part for which no standards have been set. On the other hand, if they have clearly set the standards and pointed out the necessity of following these standards, then other members of the group will support them if they find it necessary to correct one of their members who has been slipshod.

LEADING Leaders must exhibit a unity of command. If the situation is such that they must have help from time to time, their followers must know precisely the amount of authority that they have delegated to their helper. Leaders must clearly identify whether or not anyone outside of the group has the power to direct their activities. The most effective leader will be the one who in the eyes of the followers represents the single unit of command.

Personal contact with those supervised is an important characteristic and an important leadership technique. It is impossible to discover the feeling of the employees toward yourself without talking with them. Likewise, it is impossible for them to understand what you mean if their sole contact is by means of memorandum, or word, passed from others. Therefore the effective leader will spend time with subordinates.

The effective leader, then, depending on the situation and on the people to be led, will from time to time use the autocratic, the democratic, or the free-rein type of leadership. The leader's effectiveness will depend on choice of the proper style at the proper time.

Second only to the unity of command is the clarity of command, or communication. Communication is two-way. A room may be filled with radio waves, but they mean nothing to us until we tune in a receiver to receive these waves and convert them into audible sound. Messages of importance could be transmitted into the room, but they would mean nothing to us until they were received, converted into audible sound, and understood. Therefore an order means nothing unless it is received by another individual and understood.

The command must be possible to execute and must be acceptable to the one being commanded; otherwise nothing of importance will happen. To be successful a leader must be reasonable.

The leader must also be a good listener. Most of us listen poorly, however. Think for a moment of a typical return home at the end of a long workday.

Manager: "Evening, dear. Is the paper here?"
Wife: "Yes, but first let me tell you what Johnny did today. That little tyke almost got hit by a car. He was playing on his new skates — the ones mother sent him — and he started down the driveway, and etc., etc., you are really going to have to do something about him, Sam."
Manager: "Hmm, yes, I suppose so . . . now where did you say the paper was?"

The manager did not really want to talk to his wife. He wanted to settle down with the evening paper and let some of the cares of the day ebb away. His wife, however, had been waiting all afternoon to tell him about Johnny, and she was really worried and anxious for her husband to do something.

This is illustrative of the listening situations we often find with supervisors. The subordinate has a problem and wants the supervisor's help. The supervisor may be engrossed in another problem, one of his own with his boss, he may be on his way to lunch, or he may have a hundred and one things on his mind. However, he invites the subordinate to speak. He turns his ears in the subordinate's direction, nods periodically, smiles sympathetically. But he is not listening!

If, on the other hand, he is that rare breed of manager who really concentrates on listening, it will pay dividends in a better understanding of both the subordinate and his problem. And the better a manager knows and understands his subordinates and their problems, the more effectively can he motivate them.

MAINTAINING DISCIPLINE

Discipline can only be maintained effectively if the rules have been clearly communicated and understood. The rules will be better obeyed if the reason for them is clear in the mind of the employee. Therefore it is important that leaders go out of their way to make certain that their rules make sense and are understood.

If the rules are broken, then the discipline meted out must be consistent and reasonable. Supervisors are frequently helped in their consistency and restrained in their actions by a union contract under which they may be operating. These contracts define very clearly the limits of management's authority and the right of redress of employees if they feel they have been unjustly treated. Moreover, the courses of action to be followed by an aggrieved employee are clearly defined.

The supervisor should generally look at discipline as a means of bringing about corrective action—not as a means of punishment. On the other hand, there are occasions when employees will specifically flaunt well-recognized rules, and in such cases the supervisor's response must be firm, consistent, and clear.[4]

The wearing of safety glasses in some areas or on some jobs is a good example of this problem. The rule itself will generally not cause the person to wear the glasses. They are hot and heavy and they are uncomfortable. However, if through education the person can see the importance of safety to future livelihood, then reasonable cooperation can usually be achieved. However, in this particular instance it is difficult, and frequent deviations will be found.

[4]Discipline will be covered in greater detail in Chapter XXI, "Maintaining Discipline and Morale."

DEVELOPING GROUP MORALE	High group morale can only be obtained if the group understands its goal and if some proper measure for performance is used. Depending on the type of subordinate and the situation, the proper style of leadership can be chosen.

Group morale is an individual matter. Individual members must be inspired to achieve the goal. They must thoroughly understand that this achievement can only be obtained through teamwork on the part of the group members. Each member understands his/her own situation most clearly, and therefore it is well for the leader to think of the members of the group as individuals and not as a mass. This means looking at each one's individual goal, then helping the person to see his/her performance in relationship to that of the group. The person begins to develop the feeling of teamwork. |

LEADERSHIP AND YOU

Supervisors may have varying degrees of education, industrial experience, and supervisory training. Despite this you are forced to cause 5, 10, 15, or 20 men to follow you in achievement of a common goal.

As we have seen, you may have certain innate characteristics that will assist you in bringing these people along behind you. However, you may have to develop other characteristics in order for you to successfully become a leader of men. However, it is well accepted today that if you possess certain inherent characteristics of leadership, then many others may be developed, through practice, to the point where you may successfully become a supervisor and fit yourself for progression up the line.

There is real satisfaction in leadership. As a single individual you are stimulated by those goals that you can achieve personally. These are limited for one individual, but someone who leads 5 or 20 people has the opportunity of participating in the success of all of these people. As a result, greater satisfaction comes to the leader than to the individual worker. It is for this reason that the leader should be willing to exert greater effort to cause these workers to become ideal followers and to be loyal and faithful to the end.

SUMMARY

It is normally recognized that there are three styles of leadership, that is, autocratic, democratic (participative), and laissez-faire (free rein). The successful leader will use all three styles under varying conditions.

Successful leadership is dependent on the leader, those being led, and the situation under which the leader leads them. A leader must define clearly the objectives and goals of the group. The one being led must relate to other individuals in the group and assist in the work toward a common goal. The situation may affect both the leader and the led. A person who is successful at a lower level of supervision may be unsuccessful at a higher level of supervision.

There are many leadership techniques, including securing cooperation, use of power, directing, maintaining discipline, and developing high group morale.

If these techniques are practiced successfully, a supervisor may have the real satisfaction of leadership.

KEY CONCEPTS

Leadership. By definition, leadership is the ability of a supervisor to accomplish group goals by working with and through people. Conceptually, leadership includes the inherent authority of the supervisor's position that allows him to lead. This is enhanced by the subordinate's respect and trust in the supervisor, which also permit the supervisor to lead. Therefore leadership is a position of authority, power, ability, and respect and trust from those being led. Within an organization this includes a unity of command, discipline, and favorable group morale.

Leadership's persuasiveness. A person may be a leader in one group and a follower in another because of the hierarchical nature of an organization, because of the position occupied relative to others, because of the possession of a specific type of leadership quality that is exercised in times of danger, or because of special knowledge or experience. All people have a degree of leadership ability if it is ever tapped. The supervisors can use this hidden resource to help achieve the organization's objectives by tapping leadership qualities in the men and women they supervise.

Leadership styles. The three leadership styles—autocratic, democratic, and laissez-faire—appear to be separate and distinct, but in practice they are not. Supervisors may utilize each separate style in certain given instances, or they may use combinations of two or all three. Conceptually and in practice the leader/supervisor must know which leadership style is appropriate to lead people at a given time, or with different individuals. Since each person is unique, leaders must tailor their leadership style to fit each individual. Leading the group would, of course, require a degree of consistency; otherwise frustration could easily develop among the subordinates.

IMPORTANT TERMS

Authority
Autocratic (boss) leadership
Benevolent autocrat

Democratic (participative) leadership
Employee-oriented leader

Laissez-faire (free rein) leadership
Leadership
Power
Scientific management

INCIDENTS

Poor Planning in a Chemical Plant

Joe McIntosh was plant manager of a large chemical plant outside Philadelphia, Pennsylvania. He had reached his plant managership by way of the maintenance department and was an expert at organizing the 300-worker maintenance group to tackle emergency situations. However, since he was so capable in emergencies he ran from one crisis to another, always on the defensive. As a result it was difficult to meet the delivery dates of orders placed upon the plant by the sales department. This inability to supply the customer brought about a loss of orders and in due course produced an effect upon the profitability of the plant.

The vice-president of the division tried repeatedly to get Joe to mend his ways, without avail. In desperation he decided to give the plant managership to a former general foreman in this large plant who had in the interim period been plant manager of a smaller plant. He felt that this man, Jim Jones, had the characteristics of leadership and planning that were necessary to stabilize the plant operation. When Jim took over he found, as would be expected, a certain amount of resentment among the three assistant plant managers who were 10 to 15 years older than he. Furthermore, he found discipline in the plant in shambles. The workers began to line up to leave work a half hour ahead of quitting time, the 5-minute rest periods in the morning and afternoon were extended to 30 minutes and the workers generally ignored rules dealing with safety glasses and smoking. Superimposed upon these problems were the matters related to plant operation.

Discuss ways in which Jim Jones should move to reestablish some discipline within the plant. How should he eliminate the crisis situations that were so detrimental to the plant's ability to perform? Should he use one leadership style or would several be needed? If several would be needed, name some specific situations in which he would use a certain leadership style.

The Accounting Office Manager

Daniel O'Brien is the accounting office manager for the New Market Coal Company. He was the company's chief accountant for 12 years prior to acquiring his present position, and as chief accountant he performed extremely well. He acquired his present position when the office manager retired.

Daniel had nine employees reporting to him, but since taking over as the office manager two years ago, four of the original nine have quit the company. As a result, the work in Daniel's office is often late, the office has become messy, and morale appears to be extremely low.

Daniel O'Brien is a rigid and formal man who lacks a sense of humor. The office employees joke behind his back about his face cracking if he were ever to smile. O'Brien insists on being called "Mr." or "Sir" by the office help. His word is law and shall not be challenged by his people. O'Brien has little patience with subordinates who do not understand his orders or who do not perform to perfection as he, O'Brien, defines it. He often loses his temper and reprimands a subordinate in front of his colleagues.

Mr. O'Brien appears to have an insatiable desire to have everything conform to his direction and leadership. He refuses to praise anyone, but demands that his work have the highest priority even when the office employees are fighting a deadline to close the books for a given accounting period.

What are the major problems in this incident? What action would you recommend if hired as a management consultant to investigate the office's low morale and productivity?

QUESTIONS FOR DISCUSSION

1. Define leadership. Discuss its evolution into the three accepted styles of leadership.
2. It has been said that leaders are born, not made. Do you agree or disagree with this? Why?
3. Is it important for a supervisor to use different styles of leadership under different circumstances? If so, how does the supervisor decide which style to use?
4. What is a leader's first responsibility to the group? Why is this important?
5. Due to the hierarchy of command in any organization a person may be a leader in one group and a follower in another. Because of this relationship the person may be called upon to administer company policies in the group that are not entirely to his/her liking. Discuss how a good leader should function in such a situation.
6. A leader cannot be successful without the cooperation of those being led. Discuss how she can secure the cooperation of the members of her group so that it can perform most effectively.
7. What role does authority play in successful leadership?
8. Discuss the importance of communication.
9. How can discipline be used to weld a group into an effective unit?

PART III
The Supervisor's Day-to-Day Activities

The immediacy and intimacy a supervisor has with his/her people and the need for quality production requires excellent management of day-to-day activities. This section contains seven chapters: time management; the supervisor and the selection process; training and development of workers and supervisors; counseling, giving orders, introducing change, conducting meetings; performance appraisals; maintaining discipline and morale; and handling complaints and grievances.

CHAPTER XVI
Time Management

LEARNING OBJECTIVES

- *To see the relationship between time management and productivity.*
- *To understand what constitutes a time waster and what are some more prevalent time wasters.*
- *To see how time management and self-discipline are necessary correlates.*
- *To show what time management techniques are available, including guidelines, delegation, control of interruptions, improved reading skills, and a time management system.*

Introduction

The effectiveness of a supervisor is governed by the way he or she practices the managerial skills on a *day-to-day* basis to achieve the planned output. However, the incorrect use of time, a very limited resource, can reduce the supervisor's effectiveness. How often has a supervisor said, "No matter how hard I apply myself and reallocate my time, I can't escape a nagging feeling that I have more work to do than I can satisfactorily handle. On the average, I put in more time on the job than any worker. What's frustrating is the fact that I spend so much of my time on day-to-day operating problems." This supervisor has a time management problem since he/she cannot meet his/her production goals within the time allowed. This chapter investigates what a supervisor can do about correcting this common problem.

TIME MANAGEMENT AND PRODUCTIVITY

Many statements exist about time, its use, and its relationship with productivity. Among these many statements are the following. Time is a limited resource that should be treated as a precious commodity. Time on the job should not be wasted or "filled in" as a requirement of the job. Time shouldn't manage a supervisor, but the supervisor should manage time. Time management is really self-management. Supervisors who have trouble managing their own time find it most difficult to manage, lead, direct, and control the work of others. Good time management is the best example a supervisor can show his or her people. If time and its management is so significant, just what is time management and why is it so very important?

A supervisor is charged with authorities and given responsibilities to carry out. Among these many responsibilities is a major one called productivity. Whether the supervisor is in the plant, office, or institution or whether the supervisor manages factory workers, office workers, nurses, sales people or retail clerks, production is the major objective. How much output is achieved, given the number of manhours input, is the most widely accepted measure of productivity. The supervisor's job is to generate quality productivity in the most effective way. Hence much of what the supervisor does is measured on the productivity of his or her department, branch, zone, or section. Given the slower rate of productivity in the United States, it's even more important that efficient use of time and quality output be maintained and even increased. No longer can we afford to waste our resources by frittering away our work hours, by just putting in time, by acting as if we are working, and by trying to get jobs that force us to do the least amount of work. In a competitive world of markets, an organization can't survive in the long run, following these practices. Attitudes that encourage low work outputs, loitering on the job, and deceptive work practices frequently can cause an individual physical and psychological problems. When people are not actually involved in a worthwhile project, both their physical and mental capabilities can suffer. A productive, involved worker and supervisor appears to be one of the best answers to job satisfaction and happiness.

TIME WASTERS

Successful supervisors have to manage time and use it to their best advantage. In running this gamut, many time-wasting obstacles have to be dealt with. It is so easy for a supervisor to hide behind a time waster and use it as an excuse to cover up or justify not doing everything planned for that day. When supervisors fail to manage these time wasters, then other people will manage their time for them. Time wasters include (1) inefficiency, (2) tension, (3) heavy workload, (4) indecision, (5) overcommunication, (6) meetings and conferences, (7) lack of planning and priorities, (8) visitors and socializing, and (9) routine work. As you can see, some time wasters are external and some are internal or peculiar to the supervisor.

INEFFICIENCY —POOR INFORMATION A job done poorly, whether in haste or carelessness, that has to be done over, is a waster of time. Frequently a poor job may be the result of improper information or inaccurate specifications. Due to time restraints the job went "on stream" before adequate information was available. Inefficiency in any form or for any reason is intolerable because the costs of repeating a job can be measured in both financial terms and in sheer grief for the supervisor and the department. Although it isn't always possible to attain, adequate information should be in the supervisor's control if he/she is expected to manage a project.

TENSION— INDISPENS- ABLE Tension is anxiety often caused by pressures from superiors, subordinates, or feelings of inadequacies, and/or a lack of understanding of what the job entails. One of the major causes of supervisory tension appears to be the supervisor's inability to manage and control his/her job. The supervisor who can't plan and control his/her job but merely reacts to all the changes encountered is doomed to a constant flow of frustration and irritation that manifests itself into poorer performance. Staying on top of a job can ease tension, but more importantly it can help to build a supervisor's self-confidence and her people's trust and respect in her.

Tension can also develop when a supervisor believes he or she is indispensable or irreplaceable. When the workload increases to dismal heights, the indispensable supervisor may develop tension if she/he believes that no one can do the job better. Under heavy loads, delegation of authority to others can alleviate much of the tension. This has to be accompanied by discarding the feeling that one is indispensable and replaced with a feeling that a supervisor must manage events and not be managed by these events. The net effect of both tension and lack of delegation is poorer performance and lower productivity. It is better to do a few jobs well than do many jobs poorly that have to be done over.

HEAVY WORKLOAD AND POOR MANAGEMENT A supervisor has the choice of steering the departmental ship or stoking the department ship's boilers. If the captain of a ship, or the supervisor in this case, vacillates between the bridge and the boiler room, a higher head of steam can't compensate for steering the ship in circles. Harder work can waste time if the department is going in the wrong direction. Work smarter—not harder. Clarify objectives and steer a clear path toward those objectives. To do otherwise is wasting time, motion, and money.

INDECISION—PROCRASTINATION

Change, uncertainty of the future, and lack of information can encourage indecision or the willingness to delay a decision or action. Indecisiveness can waste time for subordinates as they wait on the supervisor's action. Making decisions has been taken for granted as one of the major skills a manager/supervisor must have, but many supervisors tend to delay making a decision because they may not want to accept the responsibility but prefer to push the responsibility on to others. Indecision can waste the supervisor's time and the time of those employees directly affected by the supervisory procrastination.

OVERCOMMUNICATION—PAPERWORK AND TELEPHONE

Most managers are inundated with paperwork that passes over their desks. Much time is spent reading each piece of paper to determine if they should be reading it. Guilt may force the supervisor to read everything in detail for fear that he/she will miss an important message or report. Hence a forced reading of all messages, including junk mail, takes up much valuable supervisory time.

The telephone can be disruptive, disconcerting, and waste more time. A long-winded customer, boss, fellow supervisor, or staff person can literally rob a supervisor of precious time. Individual phone calls have to be treated as such but the frequency of telephone interruptions is another force the supervisor has to guard against in the fight to avoid time wasters.

MEETINGS

Meetings can provide a forum for certain individuals to voice their emotions and frustrations, but such displays can waste the time of the other people in attendance. Meetings play an important role in a supervisor's life, but attending numerous unproductive meetings is another time-robbing force.

LACK OF PLANNING AND SETTING PRIORITIES

If the supervisor doesn't know what should be done or which tasks are more important than others, low productivity and poor management can result. A supervisor must be a good manager. To be anything else can be a waste of valuable time.

VISITORS AND SOCIALIZING

Plant or office visitors or unexpected visits by customers can be a waste of time since the supervisor hasn't planned to cover these activities. Unexpected visitation by superiors or anyone else can't be helped and the supervisor should try to turn the visits into an advantage, such as asking the visitor for information, cultivating the visitor as a legitimate sales prospect, or impressing the visitor with the efficient operation of the department.

Socializing or the individual who wants to stand and talk can be controlled or mismanaged by the supervisor. Since time is a finite commodity, much of it can be wasted with idle gossip or unproductive gathering around the favorite watering hole, or listening to long-winded peers complain about or brag about their groups. A terribly overworked person may take 45 minutes at least twice a week to discuss their problems and stress overbearing workload rather than getting the job done. Not only do these people waste their own time, but they waste the time of others, as well. It seems that the most productive people don't have to constantly discuss their problems, progress, and their successes with others, since they are too busy. Socializing needs vary with individuals but if overdone, socializing becomes nonproductive.

ROUTINE WORK Routine work by the supervisor can be both boring and time consuming. If the supervisor's time is valuable, routine work can be done by subordinates while the supervisor uses this time for more productive purposes. Supervisors who have trouble managing their own time often hide behind routine work and use it as an excuse for not doing the more important tasks. Their story usually is they are overworked because of operational, day-to-day routines that preclude doing the more important supervisory tasks of planning, organizing, implementing, and controlling.

TIME MANAGEMENT AND SELF-DISCIPLINE

Supervisors have to manage their own time and selves before they can effectively manage others. Being productive means to "work smarter" and not harder. That means the time a supervisor spends with a given task must be creative and each task encountered must be worth the supervisor's time to spend on it.

These requirements necessitate self-discipline when supervisors must constantly remind themselves of the need to plan, organize, implement and control activities, and be as effective as possible. Self-discipline takes concentration, practice, and some helpful techniques, which follows in the next section.

TIME MANAGEMENT TECHNIQUES

The secret of practicing good time management lies in two widely known management skills: (1) establishing goals and (2) putting these goals on a priority basis. Proper implementation of these two secret words can slash wasted time at work.

TIME MANAGEMENT GUIDELINES

Productivity can be increased not by time and motion studies but by allocating priorities to various tasks. The circulation manager of *The New York Times* suggested 12 ways to get control of your time and consequently get control of your life.[1]

1. List goals and put them into A, B, C priority, A being the most important.
2. Set priorities to goals that will endure. Do a job better rather than doing more jobs. This is quality versus quantity.
3. Work smarter—not harder.
4. Each day do all the A priority jobs first.
5. Don't procrastinate. Do goal jobs *now* even if there is a long lead time available and you have the time.
6. Make a daily "to do" list.
7. Schedule time for best advantage.
8. Don't confuse efficiency with effectiveness. Do the job right, so you don't have to do it over.
9. Ask what is the best use of your time, *right now*.
10. Handle each piece of paper only once. Skim read it to see if it is necessary to read in detail.
11. Find ways to delegate tasks both to your boss and subordinates.
12. Keep on top of your reading and paperwork on the job by doing it in nonproductive times such as waiting for an appointment or commuting.

DELEGATION

Its inexcusable for supervisors to labor under heavy workloads because they refuse to delegate some of the workload to others. The refusal to delegate is a sign of the supervisor's distrust of subordinates or the feeling that only she/he can do the job.

Following principles of good time management, supervisors should do the top priority jobs that are the most critical and for which they may be the best qualified and delegate the other top priority jobs to subordinates who are the best qualified. Quality productivity can be more easily achieved.

CONTROL OF INTERRUPTIONS

A supervisor's work or concentration can be broken by outside interferences such as a socializer or the ubiquitous telephone. Control of the socializer is easy if the supervisor remembers to never sit down with the socializer or ever invite the socializer to sit down. Never shut the door with the socializer inside. Never act as if you are very interested in what the socializer has to say if the impending conversation appears to be a

---

[1]"Set Goals and Priorities to Slash Wasted Time At Work," *Marketing News,* September 7, 1979, p. 12.

long one. Politely ask the socializer to come back at a later date since you have to finish a job or meet a deadline.

Control of the telephone is more difficult. If the supervisor has a secretary who can screen the calls, then no problem exists. Without a secretary, the supervisor can explain the need to meet a deadline and ask the caller if he/she can't return the call at a later date when the supervisor has more time to spend with the caller. If the caller is long winded, the supervisor can say he/she is very busy and unfortunately cannot spend much time on the phone.

IMPROVE READING SKILLS

Learn to skim read paper that flows across the desk. The easiest procedure may be as follows:

1. See how many pages are in the message.
2. Read the headings or topic sentences in each paragraph. Forget about details at this time.
3. Determine if you should read any further. If not, learn to quit as soon as possible. Knowing when to stop will save much time.
4. Read details at this time if the judgement made in step 3 is positive.
5. File the message and make notes on your day planner to take specific actions.

A TIME MANAGEMENT SYSTEM

The prerequisites to good time management are an alert mind, good health, a desire to get accurate data, a preparation to expect the unexpected, and a desire to store your energy for use when it is absolutely necessary. This entails eliminating self-criticism or brooding over past events and replacing them with a look toward the future.

Carry a pocket planner with you that lists each day's date and time during the workday as illustrated in Figure 16-1. List results to be accomplished and place a priority number in the "NO" column before each workday. List any appointments and their times. Work the task around the appointments. Record the accomplishments of that day. Compare performance with the tasks planned and the priority number. If discrepancies exist, correct your control over your time whenever possible.

SUMMARY

What supervisors do with their time is a direct function of their department's productivity. Being able to manage their own time is a prerequisite to being able to manage their people's time by assigning jobs, controlling work, meeting quality and production schedules.

NO PRIORITY RATING	TASKS TODAY	APPOINTMENTS	TIME OF APPT.	ACCOMPLISH TIME
		June 3, 198		Thursday
			8	
			9	
			10	
			11	
			12	
			1	
			2	
			3	
			4	
			5	

Figure 16–1   A daily planner book.

Time wasters are numerous and present formidable obstacles in the supervisor's quest for quality production. Included in the time waster category are (1) operating inefficiency, (2) personal tension, (3) overwork, (4) indecision and procrastination, (5) overcommunication and the telephone, (6) meetings, (7) lack of planning and setting priorities, (8) visitors and socializing, (9) routine work that's boring to the supervisor and workers.

Proper time management is directly related to an individual's self-discipline or ability to time plan and follow up on the time plan.

Time management techniques generally revolve around two basic concepts. First, each day must be planned with stated goals and results. Second, these goals and results have to be assigned a priority rating. The daily schedule should be followed as much as possible with top priority jobs done before lower priority jobs.

Overworked supervisors can delegate as many jobs to others as there are qualified people to perform the tasks. Controlling interruptions and doing paperwork are two tasks the supervisor must master. Effective time management is always asking: "How best can I spend the time to the advantage of the organization and myself?"

KEY CONCEPTS

Time management and productivity. How a supervisor spends his own time and how he directs his people to spend their time is a direct function of the department's productivity. Time is a precious commodity and if wasted, cannot be regained.

Time wasters. Time wasters are interruptions, personal hangups, or environmental forces that force a supervisor to waste valuable time. Frequently, these time wasters can be used by supervisors as an excuse to justify their own lack of productivity.

Time management techniques. The most useful major concepts are planning each day's events and results expected, their priorities from highest to lowest, and controlling these plans.

IMPORTANT TERMS

Delegation	Procrastination
Indecision	Self-discipline
Meetings	Socializing
Overcommunication	Tension
Planning	Time wasters
Setting priorities	Time management
Productivity	Time management systems

INCIDENTS

Plans, Football, and Basketball

As a sales supervisor (zone sales manager), Tom Scott was well-liked by his salespeople. He was intelligent, gregarious, a good leader, and easy to work with. Generally the people in his zone respected his leadership and knowledge in computer sales. However, one personality trait was annoying to his people and to his superiors. He had trouble developing and carrying out plans because he was easily interrupted.

Tom would attempt to plan his week's work on a Sunday afternoon while watching football, baseball, or other sports events on TV. Frequently the plans were rough sketches of what should be accomplished rather than detailed plans on a day-to-day basis.

One fixture in Tom's plans was the weekly sales meeting at 7:30 every Monday morning. Contests, pricing, planned demonstrations for the week, sales expectations, and problems, both competitive and personal that should be discussed, were the major topics of most of the meetings. Tom conducted a tight meeting and avoided lengthy gatherings, unless relevant information was to be presented.

Tom enjoyed his job talking with customers, helping his salespeople over the numerous hurdles encountered by a salesperson in the computer field. All of these activities required planning, which Tom earnestly endeavored to perform, but with difficulty. While making plans Tom was often distracted by conversation coming from the sales room, distracting conversations about college or professional football, baseball or basketball, depending on the season. He was a staunch fan of his son's Big Eight school. Whenever the university's name was mentioned, Tom couldn't resist dropping everything and entering the conversation, leaving whoever was in his office to wait. He would voice his well-thought-out predictions of success and failure of the various athletic teams being discussed. Never was he without an answer to a sports question.

Tom's people admired his sports knowledge, which he frequently used in conversations with customers. The time of a sales call with Tom was automatically doubled if a customer was a sports buff. The customers liked it in most cases, as Tom could match wits with the most knowledgeable customer. His people were a bit frustrated, however, and time was believed to be wasted.

What do you believe is good and bad about a supervisor who has the propensity to be easily interrupted? Is this really wasting time? Justify your answer, relative to Tom's effectiveness with both customers and his people. What would you suggest to Tom, if given a chance?

Plans, Plans, Plans

Dr. Howard Berman was a management department chairman in a small school of business in the mountain states. His claim to fame was his ability to research, write, and consult in addition to his regular duties as department chairperson. His secret was to plan each day's activities and live up to his plan. When an outside source tended to disrupt these plans, he would usually become angry and take his frustrations out on the nearest person, be it a professor, secretary, or student.

Dr. Berman prided himself on the effective use of his time that enabled him to produce a quality output as he defined quality. He would cut meetings short and angrily walk out of meetings he considered a waste of time. Students and professors were afraid of his temper and would try to avoid him rather than waste his valuable time. He soon became known as a hermit, unfriendly and unsociable. People refused to stop in his office and socialize with him. Soon Dr. Berman resigned himself to the fate that high productivity was achieved at the expense of cultivating a social life.

Analyze Dr. Berman's statement on productivity and friends. Do you agree? What's wrong with Dr. Berman's behavior? What's good about his behavior? If you were commissioned to improve communications in the department, what practices or points would you suggest? Be specific.

QUESTIONS FOR DISCUSSION

1. What does a supervisor mean when she/he says, "I don't have enough time to do all the things I have to do"?
2. Why is productivity a function of the supervisor's use of good time management concepts?
3. What are time wasters? Would they apply to any supervisor regardless of industry or product class?
4. Explain how inefficiency can waste time for a supervisor of retail clerks in a large Eastern department store.
5. How can supervisory tension be a time waster? Give examples.
6. Why should a supervisor learn the skills of reading fast? Where could such a skill save time?
7. Doesn't socializing cement employee relations and provide a climate of trust and respect? Aren't these factors favorable to greater productivity?
8. What are the major concepts in time management techniques?
9. Why is it better to do a job *now* when sufficient lead time exists rather than to put it off until later?
10. Could delegation of authority to others waste time? When and how if you answer yes.
11. How can time management be viewed as a system?

CHAPTER XVII
The Supervisor and the Selection Process

LEARNING OBJECTIVES

- *To understand the concept of recruiting.*
- *To appreciate the philosophies and practices in the selection process.*
- *To understand the importance and techniques of interviewing in the selection process.*
- *To understand the importance of the induction stage of the selection process.*

Introduction

The acquisition of qualified people in any organization is a very critical step for the establishment and growth of the organization. A supervisor's position involves him in this process. The selection process, sometimes called the *staffing* process, has numerous steps. This chapter is concerned with four of these steps—recruiting, interviewing, selecting, and inducting. Chapter XVIII covers two additional steps in the staffing process—training and developing.

Although the first step, the recruitment of new workers, usually is performed by the personnel department, it directly affects the supervisor. It is essential that the supervisor understand this phase of selection since it greatly affects the later steps of the selection process, the steps in which the supervisor plays a major role.

RECRUITMENT

THE LABOR MARKET   Employees are recruited from the existing labor pool, and the characteristics of this pool must be understood so that the personnel department and the supervisor can determine what sort of potential employees are available. Four areas of concern are involved in this determination.

First, the *labor market boundaries* are established, as set by geographical limits, to estimate the available supply of qualified employees. The actual boundaries of the market, that is, the supply (people looking for work) and the demand (employers looking for people to hire), depends on the type and number of job candidates being sought. For example, the labor market for unusual types of skills may embrace a section of the United States or even a continent, and the market for clerical workers may be housewives or students unwilling to travel more than a few miles from home.

Second, *economic conditions* in the labor market can affect recruitment. Upturns and downturns in economic activity can affect the number of people in the labor force (those looking for work). In times of recessions, many secondary workers—wives, older men, students, teenagers, retirees—may not enter the labor force because of cutbacks. In times of prosperity, many will enter the labor force because of the brighter prospects and greater expectations of earning more money. Consequently the total labor force tends to rise in prosperity and shrink in times of recessions.

The third area of concern is *available skills*. An organization will hire specific skills rather than hire labor. The actual location of plants, offices, and institutions is often influenced by the available supply of specific types of skills. An organization that may require a large number of people with specific skills has a much different recruitment problem than a firm that hires many different types of skills. An insurance company must hire hundreds of stenographers every year. This influences the location of the office and the firm's recruitment procedures.

The fourth area in the labor market is the *attractiveness of the organization*. The progressiveness, profitability, and growth of an organization help to determine the image of a company to the unemployed worker. The image may include wage rates, steady employment, rapid promotions, and a fringe benefit program.

SOURCES OF MANPOWER

Workers that are included in the available work force, or who are potential members, can be categorized into three broad groups: (1) the new employee taking the first job, (2) the already employed but dissatisfied worker, and (3) the unemployed worker. This classification may help the supervisor's judgement in subsequent selection steps and in the final judgment.

An inexperienced worker taking his/her first job has a limited idea about job possibilities. He or she is likely to take several jobs during the first five or six years of employment before settling down. Growing family responsibilities, maturity, and experience in different types of jobs help to mature the worker. The supervisor may also help to influence the worker. When this person seeks his/her first job, he/she will be strongly influenced by numerous factors, including peers' opinions, parents' occupations, his/her own level of education, geographical preference, and personal achievement level.

The already employed, but dissatisfied employee, represents a different type of recruitment situation that can present problems for the supervisor. Every job has its disadvantages, and firms that require special job skills may often recruit employed workers who are looking for a better job with better benefits, working conditions, and opportunities. If a worker believes his/her talents and abilities are not being utilized or are not being utilized properly, he/she places himself/herself in the job market again.

The dissatisfied employee may not be actively seeking a new job, but the dissatisfaction may make him/her more receptive to tips, rumors, and actual job offers that may come. If the job dissatisfaction grows in intensity, this type of worker may eventually quit his/her job.

The unemployed worker has been laid off because of slack times or may have been released because of an infraction or altercation with his/her previous employer. If the unemployed worker has been laid off, many organizations will hesitate to hire him/her for fear of his/her returning to the old job when better times arrive. Seniority rights, pension rights, and vested interests with a worker's previous employer may influence this worker's return. The unemployed worker released by an employer for infractions of rules can cause a great deal of harm. A worker who has a history of "getting into trouble" can become a two-time loser. The turnover, or the number of jobs this type of person has held, may also indicate problems. In the case of a young worker, he/she may have learned a lesson and can become a valuable employee. The chronic job hopper is another case. A small percentage of the labor force cannot tolerate the restrictions imposed by life in an organization. These people either move on their own accord or are dismissed for nonperformance of their job. These people are difficult to contend with in delicate situations.

RECRUITMENT METHODS

Once the labor force factor has been isolated and the sources of manpower determined, the next activity involves the promotion or active *recruitment* of the worker. An organization may have in their personnel files many applicants, but if a needed skill is not readily available, aggessive action is required.

The different modes of active recruitment include word of mouth, government employment agencies, private employment agencies, school recruiting, advertisements, and working with the union. Recommendations from satisfied friends and relatives are among the best sources of recruitment that an organization can have. Many organizations, and particularly supervisors, actually conduct regular programs to encourage their workers to seek additional people through friends and acquaintances.

Word-of-mouth recruiting has two major disadvantages of which the supervisor should be aware. Friends and relatives of the present workers foster *nepotism* (hiring relatives) and violate the equal opportunity employment regulations of the federal government. Hiring minority group members requires active promotion if a firm is to stay in line with public policy. Present employees who are nonminority group members usually will not have many friends or relatives among minority groups, so other means must be used.

Government and private employment agencies offer very broad services and usually have access to a network of job opportunities throughout the nation. Some disadvantages appear here. A few applicants who are registered with the government agencies may be more interested in the unemployment benefits than in the jobs being offered A private agency where fees are paid usually will not handle this type of individual.

Advertisements in local papers or over local radio stations are effective ways of communicating job opportunities. This mode can generate a flood of applications but may include less qualified job applicants.

The union's role in recruitment can be significant when building trades or the maritime industry are involved. Union's stock in trade becomes its ability to maintain a full complement of skilled employees readily available. In these industries the traditional union hiring hall becomes a combination employment and recruiting office. The disadvantage is that the union maintains complete control over an organizations recruitment process and can control the entire selection process. The organization, and the supervisors involved can be at the mercy of the union's hiring hall. The control by the union is exercised by requiring each applicant to be a union card holder and to be sanctioned by the union.

SELECTION

Attracting qualified job applicants is only the first step in the process of acquiring new employees. The next step is the screening of qualified people from the list of applicants. Since hiring and training costs are rather high and represent a sizable investment, the selection process becomes critical at this point. With the advent of union standards, seniority, community pressure, and minority hiring practices, it often is difficult for an employer to fire an individual. Once a worker has been selected, an organization may have to tolerate him. Several hundreds of dollars may be expended to place an unskilled worker on the payroll. To compensate for any failures in the selection process, a probationary period is used as a check. The newly hired employee does not become a regular employee until he has successfully completed a one- to three-month or even a one-year trial period. Although numerous instruments and techniques are available to help measure the success of an individual, the desire to work after being hired is one major factor that the selection process cannot measure with any degree of accuracy.

SUPERVISOR'S ROLE IN SELECTION

Many of today's selection process steps have been taken over by the employment or personnel department, but the supervisor must understand-and/or contribute to each step. Most firms still require the superviosr to be involved and to make the final judgment. The personnel department and its specialists go through an extensive screening process, saving the supervisor much time and energy. Applicants who have passed all the interviews and tests before arriving at the supervisor's interview should have previously determined qualifications listed in the job specification as worked out between the supervisor and the personnel department.

The personnel or employment department can provide a real service to the supervisor. They are in a better position to recruit, apply scientific testing procedures, conduct preinterviews, and they can refer only qualified applicants to the supervisor for his final interview.

The fact that the supervisor has the final say in the employment of a worker has a number of advantages. First, the supervisor can control his/her departmental personnel since he/she is recognized by the workers as a man of authority and an integral part of management's hiring practices. In situations involving unions, the supervisor may not have the final say. Requisitions are processed through personnel in many cases and a supervisor's new employees may come as a new hire, layoff bid, and/or a bump from another job. Personnel departments can assist and cooperate with the supervisor in the selection process so that each party can perform the duties that each is best suited to perform and meet the contractual agreement, if any.

Another advantage to having the supervisor conduct the final selection interview is that it gives the supervisor the opportunity to be more accountable for the production of his/her department. Since top management holds the supervisor responsible for the results in the department, it is only right that the supervisor have the biggest say about who shall work with him/her. Supervisors can take a greater interest in, and feel more responsible for, people they helped to select. Otherwise a supervisor may feel that he/she has lost control of the department,

SELECTION PHILOSOPHIES

Organizations try to develop and follow hiring methods that are consistent with their overall organizational philosophy of selection, and it behooves the supervisor to understand them so he can function effectively. These methods differ significantly in actual practice from company to company. Whereas recruitment is a positive program, selection becomes a negative process. Selection is really a screening or filtering process, since all the applicants enter the screening process at the top and the undesirable applicants are rejected at each immediate step of the screening process.

Selection offers opportunities for mistakes, often serious ones. Errors in decisions at this point can be costly, whether they involve the failure to hire a promising prospect or the hiring of someone who subsequently fails to achieve the organization's expectations. The right choice can be a fine investment. Investment in good people can produce a very high rate of return.

Three philosophies are usually followed by firms when implementing their selection process. First, they can attempt to screen out applicants who do not fit the company's image. Those prospects who "don't belong" are rejected. This point of view can be the result of an informal system, and it may be practiced whether management likes it or not. The second philosophy followed is fitting the job to the person. Job method analysis, split shifts, innovations for handicapped people are all examples of this philosophy. The third and most widely used philosophy attempts to fit the people to jobs. To match jobs and people becomes the philosophy's objective. The major assumption made here is that a job, as well as a worker, is unique and explicit; this assumption allows a firm to make an intelligent match between the two. Finding the best person for the job is a positive selection process, rather than trying to screen out the worst, or change the job to fit the person.

SELECTION PROCESS

As illustrated in Figure 17-1, the selection process is a screening or filtering of job applicants until employment and the end of the probationary period. After applicants are recruited, an initial job interview is conducted by the personnel department to gather preliminary data for *screening* at lower levels. Most of this interview tends to be *directive*—asking direct questions. A minor part of the initial employment interview in the selection process tends to be *nondirective* in that it encourages the applicant to discuss whatever subjects he regards as relevant and interesting. This latter approach provides the initial interviewer an opportunity to "size up" the interviewee.

If an applicant has passed the initial interview, most large organizations have specialists conduct a follow-up interview after the applicant has filled out his application blank. Once an applicant has succeeded in passing this obstacle, he or she is given a battery of tests that can range from graphology (the study of a person's personality by studying her/his handwriting) to interest, aptitude, and psychological testing.

After the testing procedures are complete, the applicant is usually required to take a physical examination. In addition, the personnel people make an examination of the applicant's work history, if previously employed, and a check of the applicant's references.

Examination of the data may suggest slotting the applicant into a specific work environment or job. From here the applicant is interviewed by

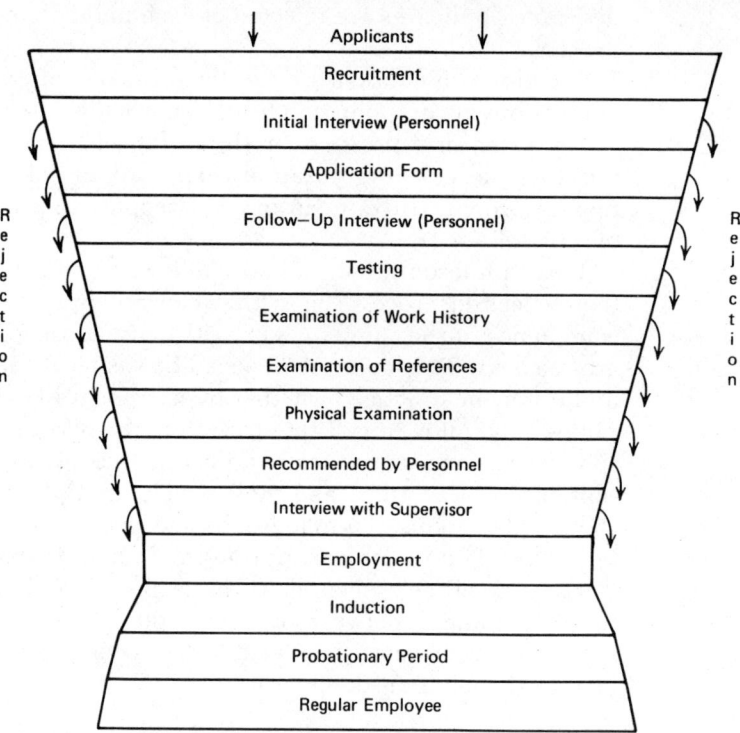

Figure 17-1 Selection as a filtration process.

the supervisor of the work unit or department (interviews are covered later in the chapter) before employment is offered Following employment the new worker enters the induction phase and then goes on to the probationary status.

The applicant who passes all of the steps in the filtering process is presumably hired, but often the step-by-step process is short-circuited to save time and money or to cope with the immediate pressures of the organization's needs. Since new employees have high turnover at the beginning of their employment, it is necessary to gain the favorable reaction of fellow workers so that the new recruit can be accepted and welcomed to the group.

TESTING IN SELECTION Formal testing procedures are carried out by the personnel department or professional counselors or psychologists. It is important that the supervisor understand their value and their limitations so that the supervisor can work with them effectively. Tests are generally given to determine potential job proficiency, for example, in clerical tasks, a firm would want to measure ability and intelligence. Testing in the selection process is based on the assumption that human behavior can be forecast by sampling it, and then measuring the individual's test results against past data or "norms" to predict success or failure of the applicant. Tests create situations to which the applicant responds. These responses or reactions can provide clues to the applicant's likely behavior in the work for which the applicant is applying. The fact that tests establish a simulated situation can be a limiting factor in their use, because the situation may not mirror the exact situation of the job. For example, clerical work and administrative tasks require native talent and intelligence. Work that involves dealing with people, such as supervision, instruction, and sales, require stable temperament, and social and emotional maturity. Jobs that require manual dexterity or physical strength, rhythm of movements or speed (motor skills), require muscular or motor, physical and sensory skills. All jobs require a certain degree of intelligence, sociability, and muscular power, but it is sometimes difficult to establish specific tests to precisely measure the human traits or talents peculiar to each job. Therefore a general set of tests can be used to measure traits believed to be appropriate to the job.

Another disadvantage that has to be recognized concerning testing is the public policy of equal employment opportunity. Tests must be culture free in that the test selection must not be significantly influenced by cultural factors that are not clearly related to job requirements. Many tests have been devised by middle-class white psychologists using words and idioms familiar to the value system of this group. Minority groups and even nonminorities in today's world may not have the same cultural values and may not understand words or idioms used in the test. For example, if a test asks, "When riding a streetcar, would you rather be the motorman or the conductor?", how many people today know or have ever ridden or seen a streetcar, let alone attempt to understand and cope with what a streetcar motorman and conductor do.

INTERVIEWING

Every time a supervisor talks with a worker, a prospective worker, a group, or superior, she/he is interviewing. Interviewing is one of the most widely used methods for communicating, whether it involves getting ideas across to others or obtaining information from them.

In almost every situation that involves a conversation, the interviewing process is being used in one form or another. This includes employment interviews, inducting a new employee into the job, explaining company policy or procedures, giving instructions, giving directions and orders, talking with worker committees, handling complaints and grievances, exit interviewing, and day-to-day office, field, store, or shop activities. Other activities, such as settling a low morale situation, taking care of some resistance to change, merit rating and evaluation, settling disputes, and informing a worker about work methods and time study analysis results, are different forms of interviewing. You can see that the applications of interviewing techniques can be an endless list. Interviewing is more an art than a science. No set procedure can be exposed that could even come close to meeting the needs of all people in all situations. No two people will interview exactly alike. Interviewing is widely practiced at all levels of management. Although interviewing has certain disadvantages since it is an art form, there are few substitutes for it in most situations. Supervisors must be well trained in interview techniques.

Before discussing the elements and "do's" and "don'ts" of interviewing, it may be wise to differentiate between employment interviewing and counseling. For our purposes, interviewing is related to giving and receiving information, solving problems, getting acquainted, and motivation. Counseling, on the other hand, is problem solving that is surrounded by and involved in an emotional state of affairs. Interview techniques are very useful in counseling, but because of this basic difference, counseling will be covered later.

PURPOSE OF SUPERVISORY EMPLOYMENT INTERVIEWING

Before an interview, supervisors should have definite points in mind that they expect to cover. These points or objectives can be made by allowing the worker to respond to direct questions. Supervisory employment interviews usually have three general purposes.

1. To secure information—items needed for the record, opinions, feelings, and beliefs, to determine if applicant has requisite ability.
2. To give information—answers to questions, explanation of policies and procedures so as to acquaint applicant with the details of the position.
3. To determine if worker matches the requirements of the position and to make the new employee a friend of the organization.

WHAT MAKES A GOOD INTERVIEWER

A perfect interviewer does not exist, and even if she/he did we would be unable to agree about what makes her/him perfect. However, some helpful hints are very useful in assisting a supervisor during the interviewing process. The supervisor-interviewer should keep the following in mind.

1. Show an attitude of interest and sympathetic curiosity.
2. Ask the applicant about previous positions at the start to break the ice.
3. Be free from personal bias and hide prejudices from the interview.
4. Participate to the extent of guiding the applicant along desired lines.
5. Establish rapport (put people at ease).
6. Be innovative and adaptable in hearing and conducting the interview.
7. Be knowledgeable about worker, job, management policies, and working conditions.
8. Communicate with the worker in language he/she can understand.

9. Keep records and remember names, faces, and facts about the interview.
10. Be alert to any additional bits of evidence not already on the interviewer's list of factors.
11. Try to improve your interviewing technique after each one.

INTERVIEW TECHNIQUES

Interviewing is learned better from practice than by reading about it in a book, especially if the interviewer understands the workers and knows how to communicate with them. Each supervisor should develop his/her own technique and try to be himself/herself. In addition to helpful hints, some "do's" can be enumerated, which are followed by "don'ts" in the next section.

Get the Interviewee to Talk

The supervisor should not try to monopolize the employment interview for any length of time except to extract more information through questions, to explain something about the company, or generally to place a person at ease. He/she should listen as much as possible.

Listening is not easy. It is so much easier to talk about what we already know than to really listen so that we may learn something. Abe Lincoln was quoted as saying that whenever he talked, he only expressed information he already knew, but when he listened, he could learn many things. Remember, a good interview is a two-way street, so let the other fellow talk freely and *listen intently*.

Probe for Facts

The supervisor should try tactfully to find the interviewee's underlying feelings. Before acting on employment, the supervisor must get as many pertinent facts as possible.

Rarely does an interviewer know the "right" questions to ask. If he/she did, he/she would probably already know the answers. The complexities of interviewing cannot be unraveled by a series of questions.

If possible, the interviewer should avoid questions that elicit a flat "yes" or "no" answer and avoid questions that provoke meaningless answers or small talk. In order to probe for data, the interviewer should ask questions that stimulate the interviewee to talk so that proper information may be disclosed for analysis by both parties. This is a difficult task, and only a trained, experienced interviewer can come close to perfection in this area. One simple rule a supervisor can follow is not to ask leading or meaningless questions unless they might help to stimulate thinking or fact finding.

Give Information and Communicate

The worker or applicant may not understand a given situation, company policy, or production technique, which provides the supervisor the opportunity to inform him/her. But the biggest problem in any interview may be the lack of communication. Fresh ideas, clearly thought through, well-defined problems, and well-conceived solutions are all very necessary elements in a well-communicated two-way interview.

COMMON ERRORS TO AVOID

Excessive Warm-Up — A new applicant can be nervous, and rapport must be established. The common error however, is to waste *too* much time. A short warm-up of perhaps 20 seconds may be sufficient

Judging from Appearance and Halo Effect — In the employment interview or when first meeting another person, we tend to size up or judge the individual by his/her clothes, manner of speaking, length of nose, and length of hair. We attempt to judge the book by its cover. Often it is difficult to determine a person's character from first appearances. There may be little relationship between personality and physical appearance. Clothes do help to project the individual's personality, because he/she chooses the items that make him/her feel the most comfortable.

The judging from appearance or prejudging an indivdual during an interview is using the halo effect. Originally, the term was applied to people who were thought by their superior to be "little angels" incapable of any wrongdoing. A more current use of the term refers to the bias held by an interviewer for the interviewee. Obviously, both approaches do not enhance getting the facts for a successful interview.

Premature Judgment — The interviewer should avoid giving any clue or hint to the applicant that what he/she says displeases or pleases him/her. The supervisor should refrain from passing judgment during the interview or before all the facts are in. This restraint is very important, because interviewees may be very sensitive to any verbal or facial clues that will tip them off to what the supervisor wants them to say or not to say.

INDUCTION

Induction — or introducing a new employee to his job, the company, fellow workers, and company policies — is an important final step in the selection process. When a new employee reports for work the first day, the way he is handled by the supervisor may be critical to his future job satisfaction and performance. First impressions by the new employee concerning his new position are always the most lasting, regardless of how valid they may be.

THE SUPERVISOR'S RESPONSIBILITY

When a new employee enters her first job or a present employee enters a new job, she may be anxious and frightened. The new uncertainties, strangeness, and unexpected situations of the new place, new people, and new supervisor can create anxiety and shake a person's self-confidence. As human beings we resist change, not because we fear change as such, but because we fear the uncertainties of change. What will happen to me in the new job? Will the new supervisor like me or dislike me? These are a few of the common apprehensions that we as human beings experience on a new job. Therefore it is absolutely necessary for the supervisor to ease this strain and bridge the uncertainty gap. Until the unknowns become familiar and the mystery is gone, a new employee cannot gain self-confidence and the reassurance that she can perform in the new job. Self-confidence is directly related to job performance. The supervisor plays a major role in the induction or introduction phase of the selection process. A supervisor who fails to take the time to properly introduce a new employee only creates more problems for both in the long run.

ROLE OF SUPERVISOR IN INDUCTION

Although the personnel department handles all the duties of the selection process, including partial introduction to the organization, company policies, and employee benefits, the responsibility of intoducing the employee to the job rests entirely on the supervisor's shoulders. The supervisor will find it a safe practice to review with each new employee the wage rate, increases, pay period, payday, shift, hours, holidays, company absentee policy, and sick pay benefits. In many cases progressive companies issue a booklet to each new employee that contains all of this information. Such a booklet's table of contents and the plant manager's letter of welcome are illustrated in Figure 17-2. An organization that does not provide published information of this nature is missing a golden opportunity to promote a friendly relationship for the new employee.

The induction role of the supervisor also includes the giving of needed information that can ease the transition period for the new employee. Communicating the rules that restrict the new person, as well as communicating just exactly what is expected of the new person, can save much time and grief later. Once the employee knows what is expected, a large amount of his uncertainty vanishes. The dissemination of rules also can provide security and reduce some of the uncertainty in the new employee's mind. The new employee will get the feeling that someone is looking after him, and, at least, someone has been considerate enough to assist him in his new job. The opposite of this feeling would be the introduction of a new office worker who did not have a chair, desk, or a place to hang his coat. His job was vague and no goals or rules were exposed. If

Chapter XVII The Supervisor and the Selection Process

TABLE OF CONTENTS			
Section I	Welcome	1	
	Olin Pledge	2	
	History of the Company	3	
Section II	The New Employee	6	
	Employment	6	
	Equal Employment Opportunity	6	
	Facilities	9	
	Housekeeping and Quality	10	
	Personal Counseling	8	
	Personal Interest	9	
	Personnel Records	7	
	Probationary Period	6	
	Protective Clothing	8	
	Safety	8	
Section III	Employment Benefits	11	
	Annual Military Training	20	
	Death Benefit Payment	18	
	Educational Assistance	22	
	Group Insurance	13	
	Accident and Sickness	15	
	Hospital/Surgical	14	
	Life	14	
	Accidental Death and Dismemberment	15	
	Term	14	
	Paid-Up	15	
	Long Term Disability	16	
	Major Medical	15	
	Travel Accident	18	
	Holidays	11	
	Jury Duty	19	
	Absences	19	
	Civic, Community and Governmental Activities	19	
	Maternity Leave	21	
	Military Leave	20	

Section III	Employment Benefits *(continued)*		
	Non-Occupational Sickness and Disability	19	
	Medical Services	18	
	Personal Absence	19	
	Personal Leave of Absence	20	
	Retirement Plan	16	
	Service Awards	23	
	Social Security	17	
	Thrift Plan	22	
	Vacation	11	
	Vacation Termination Pay	13	
	Workmen's Compensation	18	
Section IV	Pay Plan	24	
	Lines of Progression	27	
	Emergency Call-In Pay	30	
	Emergency Shut Down	31	
	Job Posting	28	
	Reduction and Recall	31	
	Overtime and Premium Pay	26	
	Pay Schedule	28	
	Payroll Deductions	25	
	Severance Compensation	33	
	Service Credit for Reinstated Employees	32	
	Shift Premium	27	
	Temporary Reclassifications	28	
Section V	Hours of Work	35	
	Gate Control	35	
	Timekeeping System	35	
	Work Day and Work Week	35	
Section VI	Internal Communications	37	
	Complaint Procedure	37	
	Employee Supervisor Communication	37	

WELCOME

I

Fellow Employee:

We are delighted to welcome you to the Olin Conductor Sedalia Team. We believe our plant is a pleasant place to work and that the work will be interesting.

As a new employee, you will find this handbook particularly useful in helping you to become acquainted with Olin Conductors, as well as a helpful source of information about the Olin Conductor Sedalia Plant. You will find it useful in answering questions that might arise from time to time.

Although you may be new on the job, we hope you have already sensed a certain spirit among your co-workers—people who work well together and enjoy working together. This spirit might best be described as a strong desire to produce the best electrical conductor and wire possible—products that are shipped on time and cannot be surpassed in quality and reliability.

Our employment plan is very selective and you have been chosen because we feel you can contribute to attaining these goals.

In the long run, the only real measure of our success is how well we satisfy our real boss—the customer. It's up to all of us to do our part in helping to build electrical conductor and wire that will create the kind of customer satisfaction that means more jobs and better job security at the Olin Conductor Sedalia Plant.

R. H. HARDWICK, Plant Manager
October 1, 1971

Figure 17-2 Employee handbook contents. (Courtesy Olin Conductor, Sedalia Plant.)

you were in this situation, don't you think you might wonder if the organization wanted you or even needed you? The supervisor's role in achieving an easy transition is extremely important.

GOOD INDUCTION PROCEDURES

The steps of induction are not complex, but significant. Six steps are common to the induction of most workers.

1. Conducting an initial "get acquainted" interview.
2. Giving the employee essential information about the company, products, policies.
3. Giving the employee information about the work.
4. Introducing him to other supervisors and fellow workers.
5. Checking up on progress, with frequent visits to make sure the new employee is comfortable and fits in.
6. Listening to the employee and finding his/her needs and feelings.

The introduction of a new employee does not have to be a long, drawn-out process. A minimum of one hour over two days may be necessary. The supervisor is interested in getting reacquainted or becoming acquainted with the employee if the supervisor hasn't already met the employee. In addition, the supervisor is interested in giving the new employee essential information about the department and the work, which can help to start the process of gaining the new employee's confidence.

After the interview, a supervisor can turn the new person over to a trusted employee who is capable of completing the introduction process. This is a common practice, but one that can generate problems. The more sophisticated worker of today desires that the supervisor complete the introductions, rather than be turned over to fellow employees. Using a trusted employee tends to lessen the importance and the prestige of the induction process. It is best that the supervisor make the introductions to other supervisors and fellow workers. The new employee wants the respect, approval, and friendship of the supervisor. Supervisors can be a steadying influence if they guide the new employee through this adjustment period in a friendly, sympathetic manner.

Some organizations give the new worker a complete guided tour of the entire plant or office to show what products or services the organization handles and to explain why the functions being performed are so important. This is becoming a more common factor in the induction process because it provides a more meaningful experience to the new person.

Once the new employee has been oriented to her/his new surroundings and begins to feel comfortable, it is important that the final step in the induction process be followed. Check up on the progress of the new worker with frequent visits. This should be instituted by the supervisor. It is to the advantage of the organization and the supervisor's department that the new person be recognized by the supervisor who stops by to say hello. Just to support the new employee by seeing him after a week or two on the job can help the new person's self-confidence and feeling of belonging. In addition, these follow-up visits provide the supervisor an opportunity to answer questions that might be bothering the new employee.

When the supervisor follows up new people, he/she can also invite them to his/her office rather than see them at their work place. Frequently the work place is more convenient, but a visit to the supervisor's is more effective. Talking to the new person in the supervisor's office can add more prestige to the meeting and can give the new employee a feeling that the supervisor really cares about his/her progress. The follow-up interview in the office helps the supervisor to give the new person undivided attention. The doubts or fears that the new employee may have can be discussed and possibly solved in the privacy of the supervisor's office. The plant floor or the chatter and clatter of an office or store doesn't help the communication process.

Proper induction procedures can turn a new person into a well-balanced, satisfied, and productive worker, as soon as possible. Improper induction procedures can provoke problems that could last for months or years.

SUMMARY

The selection process is a very critical step in the employment of new people or the transfer of employees from one position to another. The steps in the selection process—recruitment, selecting, interviewing, and induction—are integral parts of acquiring the right people to do the right jobs. The human element in an organization is the most significant element.

Starting with reviewing the labor marketplace for available skills, evaluating the economic conditions, and determining the sources of manpower, the active involvement of the organization in attracting and recruiting qualified people becomes a basic management responsibility. A flow of qualified people is necessary for the survival of the department or of the entire organization.

The actual selection process begins with the initial interview and becomes a filtering process as an applicant successfully passes through each stage of the process. The supervisor's major role in the selection process is met at the final interview before the decision to employ or not to employ is made. It is important that supervisors have this control in the selection process so that they maintain the status and control of the people in the department. Supervisors are responsible for leading, motivating, and controlling employees so they should have the final say about who is acceptable or not acceptable to work in the work group.

The selection process involves testing, interviewing, physicals, and evaluations at each step, but interviewing becomes an important part of the role played by the supervisor. Among the many objectives of interviewing are securing information, giving information, training, motivating, changing behavior of the worker, and creating a friendly relationship between the supervisor and worker.

Common errors of interviewing include excessive warm-up periods of chitchat, judging from appearance or halo effect, premature judgment, putting the interviewee on the spot, and arguing. Committing some of these errors can lessen the supervisor's effectiveness.

Induction is the last step and probably the one that involves the supervisor the most. Introducing the unfamiliar worker to new surroundings, new colleagues, new superiors can be a frightening experience for almost everyone. The successful introduction of a new person by the supervisor is a major ingredient in producing a happy, satisfied, well-balanced, and productive employee. An unhappy experience during the induction stage can haunt the supervisor for many months. The supervisor must bridge the gap with follow-up visits.

KEY CONCEPTS

The selection process. This concept involves getting the right people placed in the right job. It is important to be critical and analytical during the selection process. Under present constraints of public policy, unions, and public opinion, it is difficult to release a person once she/he has passed his probationary period. Therefore the importance of the selection process has grown enormously in recent years.

Induction process. A person's first impression of his new job, supervisor, company, and fellow employees can either precipitate future trouble, job disssatisfaction, and low productivity, or be the beginning of high job satisfaction, amiable working relationships, and high productivity. The decision between these two alternatives is generally in the hands of the supervisor. The new employee wants to belong and wants to be accepted in the new environment but may feel strange, frightened, and uncertain. The supervisor must support, inform, and help the employee to bridge this critical gap in work life.

Manpower system flow. This concept embodies recruitment, selection, and induction processes as steps in the total view of all manpower management. The selection and induction processes maintain the needed levels or flows of manpower to fill the right jobs, cope with expansion or contraction of the organization, and provide replacements for the normal turnover caused by promotions, resignations, retirements, and illnesses.

IMPORTANT TERMS

Achievement tests
Applicant
Aptitude tests

Economic conditions in labor market
Halo effect

Induction
Interest tests
Labor market boundaries
Nepotism
Personality tests

Recruitment
Screening
Selection
Staffing

INCIDENTS

The Unexpected Job Applicant

The personnel office has just called you on the plant intercom. As the supervisor of the materials handling department, they have asked you to interview an applicant for your department. The materials handling department in an amusement company, such as yours, includes the normal storage and movement of materials for your company, such as pool tables, basketball hoops, backboards, and dart equipment from receiving the materials to the finished products. Your department is also responsible for all movement of products to and between the assembly lines and storage of semifinished and finished goods.

You recall the applicant's name is Bob Stubbs from the application he had filed last week. He is a 21-year-old high school graduate who has worked for three other local manufacturers for short periods of time. His references appear to be good and personnel's recommendation for employment is quite high. Stubb's application specifies a truck driver's position. You hurry to your office to meet Stubbs for the 2 P.M. appointment.

On your way one of your workers stops to ask about a relief person for tomorrow since his wife is scheduled for surgery. You assure him the relief person has been lined up and he can have tomorrow afternoon off, with pay, if he takes sick leave. This conversation takes five minutes, making you a little late for your interview appointment.

As you hurry through the shop to your small 5 foot by 6 foot office you notice a person already seated by your desk. "Dammit," you mutter under your breath, "I'm already late, what an impression I'll make."

Entering your small office you are startled by a huge, bearded individual seated by your desk. He is approximately 5 feet 9 inches tall and must weigh at least 300 pounds. Stubbs appears grossly overweight as he sits sideways in the chair to accommodate his bulk. You introduce yourself and Stubbs reciprocates. Numerous thoughts race through your head. This Stubbs is as broad as a truck. Can he adequately move around to maintain his vehicle? What will be the other driver's impression of Stubbs if he is hired? Why has he not been able to hold any previous job for more than a year?

Given this situation, how would you interview Mr. Stubbs? What types of questions would you ask to determine the information you need?

Set up a role play beginning with the exchange of greetings between the supervisor and Mr. Stubbs.

The "Eager" New Salesperson

David Moore was a successful zone sales manager (first-line supervisor) for a large computer peripheral manufacturer. His zone included seven territory managers (salespeople) who produced an annual sales volume of $1,500,000. This volume was partially attainable because David's zone covered the western side of Dallas, Texas, plus three counties north and west of Dallas. The growth of the city and surrounding territory helped to make this a lucrative zone.

David had always prided himself on hard work, perceptive analysis of customer needs, being truthful, and hiring people who mirrored these values.

Part of David's many supervisory duties was interviewing, making recommendations, and introducing new sales people to the job. His recommendation for hiring an individual was one of many but his superior, the branch manager, could overrule any of David's recommendations.

Two months previously, a young lady named Rita Cruz was interviewed and recommended for hire over David's objections. The company checked out her qualifications and found them to meet all the company's prerequisites. David's objection was based on the fact that she was a female. He believed the computer peripheral business has no place for an attractive young woman such as Rita. He believed she would find it difficult to cope with the hard work, male environment, and occasional irate customer. Although David's objections still stood, he was obligated to induct Rita into his zone the next Monday morning.

Monday rolled around and David arrived at the office at his usual 8 A.M. to find Rita waiting for him. He quickly accumulated two books and two brochures so Rita could spend the day reading them. The books were success stories on positive thinking by Dr. Dennis Whately and Earl Nightingale. The brochures described the company's history, products, organization, and business philosophy. David instructed Rita to read as much of the material that day as possible since he was not going to be able to spend any more time with her because of other obligations. However, his burning desire to let Rita know she was hired over his objections couldn't be satisfied. He blurted out his thoughts by first reiterating his belief that this was no job for a female. With that he led Rita to her new desk. For the remainder of the day, Rita sat behind her desk in a room that contained approximately 12 other desks. No one else was in the office except the secretaries and their clattering typewriters and occasional business conversations. For the remainder of the day, Rita sat and read and wondered what kind of a supervisor David Moore was. When 4 P.M. rolled around, Rita looked at her watch, picked up her reading material, and went home.

What do you think of this induction of a new salesperson? What changes do you believe should be made to improve Rita's introduction to her new job? If you were David would you have voiced your opinion concerning females on this job or not?

QUESTIONS FOR DISCUSSION

1. If labor market economic conditions created a short supply of a skill, such as computer programmers, what possible steps could be followed to correct or lessen the effect of such a situation?
2. Discuss why or why not the supervisor should be an integral part of the selection process.
3. If the recruitment stage is a positive, active operation, why are the selection and screening stages of an applicant generally negative operations?
4. What is the contributory role of employment testing?
5. What is the difference between interviewing and counseling?
6. Why can the "halo effect" be dangerous? In what ways?
7. A good interviewer must show an attitude of interest and sympathetic curiosity. In interviewing a young 17-year-old for her first job as a stock clerk in a grocery store, how could this statement be practiced?
8. When probing for facts during an interview, does this mean (1) psychoanalyzing the interviewee or (2) getting the interviewee's opinions?
9. When a person enters a new job, why is the induction process the most critical part of the selection system?
10. Should a supervisor turn a new employee's induction over to another employee? Why or why not?

CHAPTER XVIII

Training and Development of Workers and Supervisors

LEARNING OBJECTIVES

- *To see why the supervisor must exercise input into the training of workers to improve productivity.*
- *To understand the types of training and development processes available.*
- *To understand supervisory training and development processes.*

Introduction

The preceding chapter covered the selection process, with a breakdown of recruiting, selecting, interviewing, and induction. This chapter will cover the subsequent activities of training and development, which are areas of great concern to the supervisor. Induction begins the training of the new worker, but the supervisor has the responsibility for assuming that all members of the working organization have an opportunity to learn and to develop their talents and skills in order to maintain their potential and contribution to the organization in the long run. Increased employee capability can offer a greater contribution to the organization and the achievement of its goals than can be effected by taking a disinterested view of development. The supervisor and the management of the organization have a stake in training and development for both the workers and the supervisors.

Often we think that training involves workers but the group that receives the most frequent training is supervisors. A survey was made by Prentice-Hall and the Society for Personnel Administration of 1006 employers on what kinds of training programs they offered and who got them.[1] Nearly 86 percent said they gave training to first-line supervisors compared with only one-half who provided training to prospective supervisors. Training for managers included only 73 percent of the respondents. The same survey showed that 17 percent of the respondents have separate training departments, 42 percent assign the matter to the personnel department, and 33 percent decentralize the function by department. Personnel departments are assuming the training role more often, but still a third of all training is in the hands of the supervisor.

Since personnel departments are staff functions, allowing their takeover of the training function could be a mistake. In the busy workday of a first-line or middle management supervisor, it's easy to permit personnel to usurp the entire training and development functions. But supervisors are in the best position to determine what subjects need to be emphasized and which topics shouldn't be included at all. Frequently, personnel people do not understand production functions, unless recently educated. Frequently, production managers refuse to permit their supervisory people to participate in training sessions unless they have had the opportunity to participate in the planning of these training sessions. If realism and pragmatism is a prerequisite for training, perhaps personnel people should take temporary jobs in the organization's production, marketing and finance sections so they can use their training expertise to design more realistic training programs.

SUPERVISORY RESPONSIBILITY FOR TRAINING

PRODUC-TIVITY Supervisors manage the people in their department. In so doing, they direct their efforts in order to achieve the organization's objectives as well as to meet the workers' goals. The supervisor is responsible for instructing and training subordinates. A supervisor can scarcely expect top performance from workers if their knowledge or skills are less than the job demands. The better workers are trained, the more productive they can be as individuals and as members of the work group.

IMPORTANCE OF PEOPLE INVESTMENT Supervisors work with and through people. Their attainment of success is highly correlated with the degree of success, need satisfaction, and self-development of the people in their department. Progressive organizations realize that proper *investments in people* can pay lucrative dividends by means of higher and more efficient productivity. The most important capital that any economy can possess is the skills of human potential. These skills or potential talents can be typing, taking dictation,

---

[1] "Supervisors Get Job-Training Programs More Often Than Other Employees," *Wall Street Journal*, September 11, 1979, p. 1.

tending a machine, doing assembly work, solving problems, leading others, developing improved methods of doing a job, and developing enthusiasm, to name only a few. Every opportunity should be made to allow the employees to become better trained and to develop their potential talents and skills.

LEARNING THEORY IN TRAINING

Learning is generally considered by psychologists to be any change in an individual's response or behavior resulting from practice or experience. This tends to be rather a stiff definition, but as you can see, learning takes place all the time. Learning causes changes in response. We as human beings learn many things during formal training or any other experience, but the majority of our learning is difficult to observe. Only the result of the learning process, or what has been learned, is observable. We don't understand the inner workings of the mind in learning, but that limitation really shouldn't stop us from analyzing the input and output factors involved. For example, we know much about the behavior of atoms, but we have yet to see one or fully understand their existence. Learning is measured by its effect—just as temperature is measured by the effect on a column of mercury. Learning's effect can be demonstrated in performance self-development and employee need satisfaction. The supervisor is interested in performance and should understand how learning theory can help him achieve his training objectives.

Whatever training problems a supervisor may face, some attention to the principles of learning is very worthwhile. The human elements of learning include (1) motivation, (2) conceptualization—image, (3) practice—involvement, (4) reinforcement, and (5) feedback. A flow of these learning elements is illustrated in Figure 18-1. Although this picture may not be totally correct in the interworkings of a person's mind, it does represent a flow or input-output system that can be readily observed by the supervisor during and after a series of training exposures.

As seen in the figure, the learning process starts with personal motivation to learn and to improve oneself. As the numerous sets of cues, such as teaching, gossip, reading, observation, bombard the personally moti-

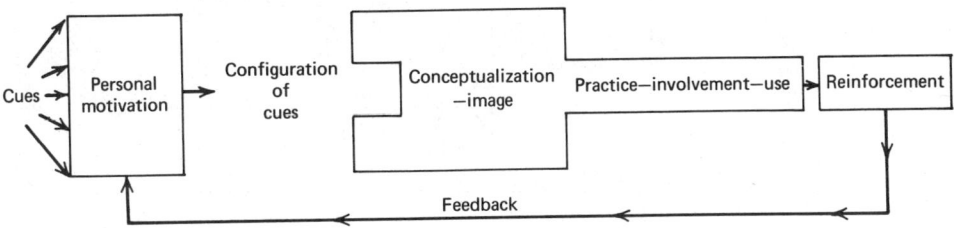

Figure 18-1 The learning system.

vated learner, one establishes a configuration of these cues by setting them in proper perspective, or eliminating, modifying, or somehow treating them so that they are meaningful. Setting up a meaningful representation of these data is then translated into a conceptualization or overall image of the process. This conceptualization includes the meanings of a word and the qualification of an image's virtue concerning its goodness or badness. Somehow the learner assembles these facts and works them out in his/her mind so that he/she can understand. Now this indicates that all people will not learn the same thing or learn it equally fast. Some people can see the significance much more quickly than others. Therefore the trainer must realize this difference and must gear her/his teaching to each person's ability to perceive these images.

After the perception of the image, the learning process is carried farther by the learner's practicing, using, and becoming involved in the thing he or she is to learn. At this point the learner wants some reinforcement to see that he/she is performing correctly. As the learner gains confidence in trial and error, this provides feedback and becomes another cue in the learning process. Thus the learner can go on to the next stage in his/her learning process.

It is helpful for the supervisor to see how a typical learning curve is shaped, as shown in Figure 18-2. Learning does not follow a nice, neat pattern of growth. Rather, learning grows by fits and starts. In the first stage, the trainee tends to be frustrated as all new information is bounced

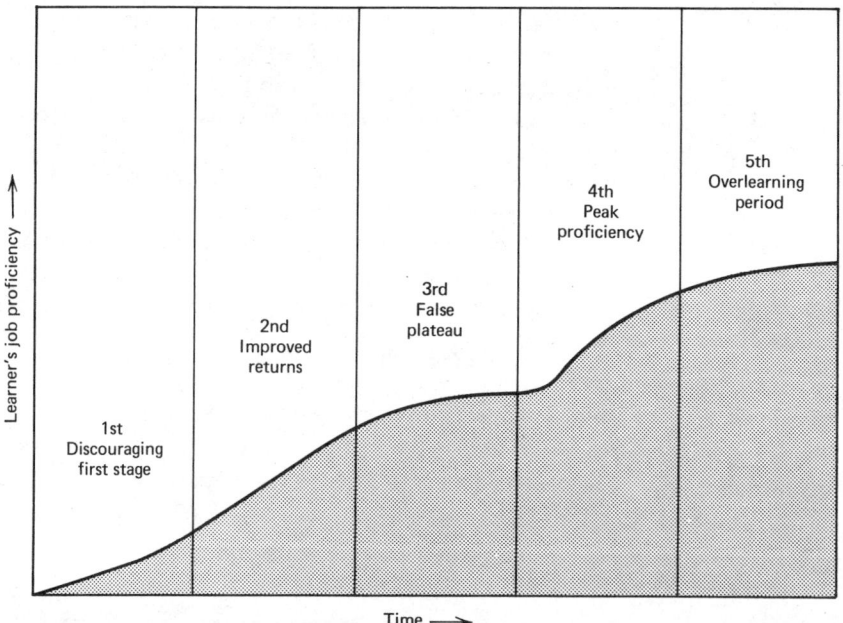

Figure 18–2 The learning curve.

off him/her. This is a very discouraging and frightening period for one who prides himself/herself on ability or agility. What happens in this stage is a test of the trainee's self-confidence and requires a great deal of patience, understanding, and support from the supervisor.

The second stage is a very rapid growth stage as the information gets sorted out by the trainee, who then develops concrete images. Increasing returns are the first indications that the learner is finally catching on. Practice in small amounts generally accounts for these first increases, but they encourage the employee to build up self-confidence, and as a result, satisfaction rises.

The third stage is a plateau in which additional training does not result in a very significant increase. Both the supervisor and the trainee may be deceived into thinking that the optimum proficiency has been attained. Two reasons generally account for the plateau: (1) The trainee loses motivation as early successes fade and further progress becomes extremely difficult, and (2) the trainee needs a substantial block of time to practice and use the additional bits of information received.

After a settling process takes place and the trainee grows more self-confident of his/her skill and understanding, the trainee enters the fourth stage—peak proficiency. Training should not stop at this stage, but should continue until the trainee enters the next stage.

The fifth stage is the overlearning period, achieved by continued repetition, reinforcement, and feedback. Overlearning diminishes the likelihood that the learner will forget if transferred to another job temporarily and then returned.

The learning curve is a representation of a typical learning sequence and should not be misconstrued as being applicable to every trainee. Each training opportunity is affected by several major variables, such as individual differences, talents, communication problems where transfer is impeded, levels of motivation, and the supervisor's skill in instructing. The learning curve does show that learning grows by leaps and bounds, rather than as a smooth progression.

EMPLOYEE TRAINING

As important as employee training is to the success of an organization, many additional types of training exist. The different types of training for employees will be discussed, followed by a coverage of job instruction methods and job instruction training (JIT), and then a section will be presented on how to instruct.

TYPES OF TRAINING How do we decide which types of employee training are best suited to a specific organization? The answer depends on a number of factors such as job skills required, candidate's qualifications, and the kinds of production, distribution, or marketing problems confronted by the organization. It is important that the training program be developed to meet the specific needs of both the employee and the organization. Thus one type of training may work well in a certain training situation but may fail in another. It is the responsibility of the training director and/or the supervisor to determine the best type for each job. In addition to types, the length of each session of training should be determined so as to optimize the learning curve.

The various types of employee training and their relative advantages may be outlined by the approach taken and by the methods and place of training, as follows.

Classroom Training   This may be arranged by contacting the local vocational-technical school, correspondence courses, professional societies, or training institutes. These off-the-job classroom training periods can be used to supplement another type of training, such as on-the-job training. Such skills as welding, steam fitting, typing, and shorthand can benefit from this type of training.

On-the-Job Training   *OJT*, as this type is commonly called, is the most frequently used type of training. The supervisor is very involved and is expected to devote extra time and attention to the trainee. Occasionally, an experienced employee may be assigned to help break in a new worker, but it is necessary that a competent instructor be used. This type of training can be very effective for rapid training of large numbers of unskilled and semiskilled workers. The contribution of a competent OJT program can be an important asset to any supervisor and to the entire organization. The pressures of limited time on the supervisors, and sometimes their lack of preparation for extended training activities, precipitated the training format called job instruction training (JIT) that was developed during World War II. (JIT is discussed in another section.)

Vestibule Training   This is a combination of on-the-job and off-the-job training. Often this type is used as an introduction to the on-the-job sequence, but frequently many job skills cannot be learned in slow motion or on the floor but require a simulated situation in a plant classroom away from the noise of the operating floor or the clatter of an office.

Programmed Learning   Many company training programs have changed as newer technical aids have appeared on the market. Computers, projectors, tape recorders, TV, professional films are often utilized as part of employee training. In addition, there is programmed textbook material available that offers the advantages of feedback, involvement, and repetition. These devices are self-teaching techniques that can help to free a supervisor's time. However, use of some of these newer tools should supplement and not replace the actual instruction by the supervisor or training specialist. Automated teaching techniques are impersonal and cannot be used effectively in every case, unless personal aspects of training are included.

Role Playing This technique has become very popular as trainees are asked to play roles, included at the end of many chapters in this book. The advantages of role playing are twofold: (1) the role playing involves the participants and creates a live situation from which the other participants can evaluate, and (2) role playing provides a totally different diversion to training as it can add variety, enjoyment, and satisfaction to the participants.

Case Method Cases are enlarged role plays where the participants are involved as analyzers rather than as characters, as in role playing. The major contribution of this technique is the participant's opportunity to evaluate, in detail, the incident being studied. Cases allow the trainees to learn from each other. The instructor/supervisor can then evaluate the trainee's educational process.

JOB TRAINING METHODS Training means changing behavioral patterns, and this is always a difficult task. An individual's way of doing things, skills, energy, and the thought process used, all reflect the person's own personality structure. Instructing a worker is a major responsibility of the supervisor, and it is important that the supervisor be completely familiar with all aspects of a given job as well as the essentials of adequate preparation for training. In getting ready to instruct on a specific skill, four basic procedures should be followed.

1. Plan a training schedule. The supervisor should plan the complete program and establish goals that the trainee can be expected to achieve. By committing himself in advance, the supervisor will force himself and the trainee to use their time to best advantage. Then the supervisor should lay out the schedule in a proper sequence, with the date and amount of time required to attain each goal.
2. Do a written breakdown of the job. Knowledgeable people often take things for granted, but to the novice or trainee, a new job may encompass many unknowns and uncertainties. Therefore it is important to write a job description, for training purposes, to remind the instructor so that he covers all the important steps and key points.
3. Have the right equipment and materials available. Substituting or simulating materials or work situations is less than adequate. It is im-

portant to have the proper equipment and materials available so that the instructor and trainee can concentrate on learning the job at hand.
4. The work place must be arranged properly. In addition to the right materials and equipment, the place of work should be arranged as the trainee can expect to find it on the job. Simulating or telling him how it should be arranged is not as effective as actually showing him (involvement).

JOB INSTRUCTION TRAINING (JIT)

Job instruction training (JIT), has been widely used by supervisors and has been an important contribution to the training of workers. How to instruct, as listed below, provides all the steps from preparation to follow-up. Since these are tested techniques, it is important for a supervisor to refer to them whenever needed.

HOW TO INSTRUCT

Practical methods to guide the supervisor in instructing a new employee on a job, or a present worker on a new job or a new skill, can be illustrated as follows.[2]

FIRST, here's what you *must do to get ready* to teach a job.
1. Decide what the learner must be taught in order to do the job efficiently, safely, economically and intelligently.
2. Have the right tools, equipment, supplies and material ready.
3. Have the work place properly arranged, just as the worker will be expected to keep it.

THEN, you should *instruct* the learner by the following four basic steps:

STEP I — PREPARATION (of the learner).
1. Put the learner at ease.
2. Find out what the person already knows about the job.
3. Get the person interested and desirous of learning the job.

STEP II — PRESENTATION (of the operations and knowledge).
1. *Tell, show, illustrate and question in order to put over the new knowledge and operations.*
2. Instruct slowly, clearly, completely, and patiently, one point at a time.
3. Check, question, and repeat.
4. Make sure the learner really learns.

STEP III — PERFORMANCE TRYOUT
1. Test learner by having learner perform the job.
2. Ask questions beginning with *why, how, when*, or *where*.

---

[2]*War Manpower Commission, The Training Within Industry Report*, Washington, D.C., Bureau of Training, Training Within Industry Service, War Manpower Commission, 1945, p. 195. This is the original source from which many more recent adaptations have been made.

3. Observe performance, correct errors, and repeat instructions if necessary.
4. Continue until you *know learner knows.*

STEP IV — FOLLOW-UP
1. Put him "on his own."
2. Check frequently to be sure learner follows instructions.
3. Taper off extra supervision and close follow-up until learner is qualified to work with normal supervision.

REMEMBER — If the learner hasn't learned, the teacher hasn't taught.

A very simple example, such as starting a lawn mower, can further illustrate how to instruct under the JIT method. Assume that you were to teach your brother or sister how to start a manual pull lawn mower. Following the steps enumerated above, you would decide what has to be taught, the proper setting, and available tools. Then the first step, preparation of the learner, would be to mention the ease of starting the mower, and how much time could be saved if it's performed properly. Once the learner is prepared, then the actual presentation can begin. Tell the learner to set the carburetor to the choke setting, then do so. Show and tell the learner how to place his left foot between the left front wheel and the mower casing so that the mower doesn't move. Show and tell the learner how to grasp the starting cord and pull. Go through the operation again. Ask for any questions. Then step 3, performance and tryout: have the learner perform. Correct any errors you observe. Then follow up and make any necessary corrections later on.

EMPLOYEE DEVELOPMENT

Besides training an employee in a specific job, the supervisor should endeavor to help develop qualified subordinates for supervisory and administrative skills. Moreover, the supervisor should help promote the growth of each individual so that individual can develop beyond his/her present job and progress as far in the organization as his/her abilities can carry him. The supervisor can provide the climate — such as support, conditions, tools — and some of the means for employee development.

If the workers know that the supervisor legitimately wants to help them to improve and succeed in their development, they usually repay the supervisor by performing better at their present jobs. The hope that improved performance and development can lead to a better job and more pay can motivate most people. However, the abilities of each individual are limited, and it is impossible for any individual to develop beyond his/her talents. The only problem is that most of us do not know our talents. We are constantly learning about our talents every day. Basic needs of individuals dictate that they grow, mature, and advance in their own estimation. Therefore development means growth in the eyes of the developer.

From another point of view, employee development can be advantageous to the supervisor. The more capable and self-confident a subordinate becomes, the greater will be his/her productivity. This can reflect on the supervisor's ability because he/she provided the opportunity for the development of good workers. Rarely can a supervisor move into a more responsible job with greater authority unless he/she has developed people to take his/her place or has shown the ability to develop subordinates. This supervisory development is closely linked with employee development.

Employee development will be covered by first considering the principles of employee development, then on-the-job development, and finally off-the-job development.

PRINCIPLES OF EMPLOYEE DEVELOPMENT

From studies conducted at General Electric by managers, psychologists, and professors concerning the growth and development of people, five principles have emerged. These principles are very broad, but they do provide a basis from which supervisors can help to establish an understanding, proper climate, and active support program for the workers in their department.

1. *Development is a personal matter and should be tailored to the individual.*

    Individual differences among people cannot be ignored. Group training methods are very effective for common group needs. An organization should provide the opportunity for each employee to develop his/her own talents pertinent to his/her growth and advancement within the organization.
2. *Self-development is the basis for all development.*

    A motivated person must exist before any training or development process becomes meaningful. Any effort or responsibility for development is taken on by the individual because he/she wants to do it. A supervisor can help to establish the climate for the employee to want to develop by support, suggestions, providing opportunity, information, and direction.
3. *The day-to-day experiences are the most important part of a person's development.*

    The most stimulating aspects of a person's individual development are the contacts made every day. Formal education and training are important, but the daily contacts the worker has with her/his supervisor have the most profound results. The work climate appears to be one of the most significant factors in a person's development.
4. *Development opportunity must be available for everyone.*

    Although the most able workers may be recognized first for development, it is important that all workers have an opportunity to develop.

"Diamonds in the rough" still exist. Predicting the success of an individual is very risky. By broadening the self-development opportunities, the supervisor can help to improve morale for one and all.

5. *The supervisor is directly responsible for the development of people who work under his/her direction.*

    The supervisor cannot delegate the development responsibility to someone else. Others may assist, but the responsibility rests on the supervisor's shoulders. Only the supervisor can best motivate the people toward self-development. The supervisor can provide the immediate climate and the immediate example for the rest of the department to follow. Leadership in self-development is a critical aspect of supervisory management.

ON-THE-JOB METHODS On-the-job techniques for development can be very effective if used properly by the supervisor. Four techniques are available: (1) delegation, (2) coaching or understudy, (3) special assignments, and (4) job rotation.

Delegation When workers show promise, a supervisor can delegate as much authority and commensurate responsibility as possible to the individual. Exercising authority helps the individual to grow and develop. By trying their wings and correctly accomplishing the tasks assigned them, workers can receive reinforcement and feedback for learning and development progress. This type of on-the-job technique develops an employee's self-confidence.

Coaching Coaching means giving individuals an assignment and then personally assisting them. It is a one-on-one relationship where the superior adds suggestions and tips to the subordinate, without telling the subordinate what to do. If the supervisor performs the job in an impatient way, the pupil who is being coached will not necessarily learn. Good coaching allows the employee to learn by mistakes but encourages the employee to seek advice from the supervisor as often as needed. Coaching is a delicate art and must be practiced with a keen sense of understanding for the employee. The example set by the supervisor is critical. Specific goals must be established. Each member must know what to expect. Coaching respects results, since they are more important than methods. Praise is extremely important. A good coach reviews the employee's progress and provides constructive criticism when needed, and praise when desired.

Special Assignments By assigning special projects once in a while, a supervisor can encourage growth by increasing the employee's self-confidence. Sensitive situations that the supervisor does not have time to unravel can be assigned. Presenting a plan to a group or the department, correcting office or production problems, helping to develop new product ideas—these can be types of special projects assigned. The challenges of the new assignment can be sufficient stimuli to assist the employee's personal development.

Job Rotation Job rotation can also be used for broadening an individual. Moving a man or woman from one responsible job to another can expose the individual to different problems, variables, decision processes, and solutions. Moves made too often can be dangerous, however. Once a person has reached overtraining in a specific job, then job rotation can be implemented. Moving people too soon can create frustration, destroy self-confidence, and create low morale. Instead of development (building up), these tactics would help to destroy (tear down).

OFF-THE-JOB METHODS Productivity can be increased by opportunities for development offered off the job as well as on the job. These opportunities are as follows: (1) formal education, (2) company-sponsored programs, and (3) short courses.

Formal Education Almost anywhere in the United States, formal educational opportunities exist. A listing of these facilities usually is available in the personnel office. The most readily available formal, credit-type educational programs are night classes at the local high schools or vocational-technical schools. Courses ranging from sewing to logic can help an individual to become a better person.

Universities and colleges may offer night credit courses appropriate for employees that could help to broaden and improve their development. Both credit or noncredit offerings are usually available in urban areas.

Company-Sponsored Programs Larger organizations may offer a wide variety of educational programs taught either by company officials or by visiting college professors, high school teachers, or outside consultants.

Additional programs can be self-teaching or programmed learning courses. Similar to formal teaching, but graded for the individual's speed and comprehension, programmed learning courses are becoming more popular.

Short Courses Special two- to three-day courses are available that are taught by professionals or outside consultants on the company premises. These short courses do not carry college credit, but are tailored for the advancement of groups. Courses for workers could include workday planning, tool crib operation, or mail room operations.

SUPERVISORY TRAINING AND DEVELOPMENT

An important part of any training and development program is the supervisory training and development. The critical position that the supervisor holds requires that an organization have adequate programs to train and develop supervisory personnel. In the case of the first-line supervisor, it is doubly important that he or she have special training since many are promoted from the workers' ranks. The need for special training is obvious as supervisory jobs become more complex as a result of higher educational levels of workers, unions, more sophisticated labor markets, equal employment opportunity laws and campaigns, public policy, and the normal day-to-day problems that confront any manager who has to motivate, lead, control, and appraise the workers in his department.

TRAINING OBJECTIVES Supervisory training programs have two major objectives: (1) improve the supervisor's performance in her/his present job and (2) prepare her/him for promotion to the ranks of second- and third-line supervisor or middle management position.

TRAINING CONTENT Among the many supervisory courses available, the most popular areas covered appear to be people management, that is, human relations, leadership, communications, and motivation. The curricula are constantly changing, but generally the content mirrors the management's perception of supervisory problems. In addition to the people management, production problems and general management such as planning, organizing, decision making, and control techniques are widely recognized. An inclusive program covering all of these areas appears in Figure 18–3.

PEOPLE-CENTERED SUPERVISORY TRAINING PROGRAMS In study after study, it becomes clear that if supervisors showed some concern or consideration for employees as human beings, and if they were worker centered, then subordinates would be more productive. Thus people management or people-oriented supervisory training programs have been the most important. However, in the experience of the authors, teaching a people-oriented supervisory course is most difficult. The difficulty lies in the area of properly communicating to the supervisors the highly complex variables of human nature and how they relate to the organizational goals, to the interpersonal relationships in groups or in informal organizations, and to the total formal organization. What may appear as a people-oriented or a people-centered supervisory training program may be a technique-oriented or general management supervisory program.

	Introduction **Purpose and Objectives**
Course 1	Leadership
	You as a department supervisor Personal characteristics of a supervisor Leadership styles The use of authority Case study
Course 2	People
	What motivates people? What is motivation? Maslow's hierarchy of needs Herzberg's theory of job enrichment for motivation Theory X and theory Y Case study—role plays
Course 3	Planning, organizing, and control
	Planning function for each job Organizing for the job Organizing work Job description
Course 4	Communications
	Effective communications to management The communication process Written communications Oral communications Case study and role playing
Course 5	Performance appraisals and discipline
	Performance standards Management by objectives Discipline, morale, and grievances Reinforcement theory Case study and role play

Figure 18-3   A Supervisory Training Program.

Such technique-oriented training programs attempt to provide an opportunity to learn the necessary skills of supervision that are considered essential for an effective performance. For example, some courses seek to help the supervisor become an effective communicator, which includes how to listen and how to develop a consultative approach. Other courses might include training in public speaking and writing to increase a supervisor's communication skills. Still other programs may include consultative supervision in which supervisors cultivate suggestions from members of the crew. Finally, to improve a supervisor's leadership skills, they can be exposed to human relations training in which they can learn about group influence, behavior norms, and the complexities of interpersonal relations. Identifying the problem(s) and determining a solution are the immediate goals of the training; this fact is of paramount importance to all of the programs. People management is extremely difficult and requires extensive training; exposure and practice are necessary before a person can even cope with the problems.

SUPERVISORY TRAINING METHODS

The training and development of supervisors have produced a number of effective methods over time; they include the following four methods.

Lectures

This is one of the oldest means of teaching. The limitations of lectures are known, but for disseminating concepts and details for the first time, this method is effective if followed up by some of the other methods that follow.

Conferences

The supervisor shares mutual problems with others, and the group members attempt to pool their ideas and experience. The conference method may include *buzz sessions* that divide conferences into small groups of four or five for intensive discussion. Conference groups may take projects in which they try to improve conference leadership, communications, or disciplinary actions. For example, *cases* or games may be used in a conference that focus on an illustrative example that can help the participants to develop principles from each incident.[3] Human relations case studies, as used in this book, are very common teaching devices.

Job Rotation

This technique is a form of job enrichment, but for training purposes a supervisor is shifted from one group to another. In this way the supervisor can gain broad experience and can meet a variety of problems. This technique is more common in management training techniques.

Simulation and Role Playing

These are favorite supervisory training methods. Role playing is widely used because it allows the student supervisor to become actively involved in a game of supervision without serious repercussions. Usually a case, such as the ones appearing at the end of each chapter, is outlined and the principal roles are described briefly. Then the actors are chosen and the

---

[3]The authors have found that Tinker Toys are very useful in games for teaching leadership, communication, planning of work, and a host of other functions and skills.

scene is enacted in front of the group. Simulating specific problem areas and role playing provide a workshop experience with which the participants can easily identify.

A SUGGESTED SELF-DEVELOPMENT PROGRAM

It is impossible to measure out a precise self-development program that could, or even would, be suitable for everyone, but the following list of ideas have been proven successful by many people. In a nutshell, self-development for supervisors and managers means improving four things.

1. Ability to think.
2. Understanding of yourself and your environment.
3. Effective speaking.
4. Effective writing.

All four of these things are interrelated. Now it becomes necessary to determine how we achieve these four objectives. The following list will help to supply the means. Notice that reading is the key.

1. Discipline yourself into reading as frequently as possible. Set up a systematic reading schedule. A chapter a day, perhaps.
2. Read for information and adventure, as if you were looking for treasure and had to find it in the shortest period of time and in the most direct fashion.
3. Learn to read under pressure, because it is difficult to read only when you are completely relaxed. Besides, you will probably fall asleep. Reading should be an active, aggressive search for answers.
4. Make a habit of casing a book or article before you actually read it. Who wrote it? When? What are his qualifications? What is he trying to say? Then you can determine if reading it is worthwhile or not.
5. Be impatient in your reading habits. Get the meaning as fast as possible. Don't wait for lengthy paragraphs to bog you down.
6. Organize what you have read by detecting the control theme of the book or article.
7. Set up a habit of writing down all the words that you don't understand. Look them up in a dictionary, and if they are useful, absorb them into your vocabulary.
8. Observe effective speakers' and writers' logic and their methods of communicating.
9. Observe effective decision makers, and try to incorporate their methods and logic as your own with practice.
10. Avail yourself of all the training and development programs offered by your organization or community that meet your personal goals of development. This presumes that you have already set these goals.
11. Speak a great deal to peers, superiors, and subordinates concerning mutual problems and possible solutions or conjectures.

12. Write about these identified problems, alternative solutions, analysis of each of the alternatives, and the best workable solution. Then determine why it is best and write up a concise defense of your solution.
13. Take notes as ideas come to you.
14. Take aptitude and interests tests to try to determine who you are. Analyze yourself and try to be honest about your strengths and weaknesses.
15. Set immediate and long-range goals for personal development that can coincide with your promotional or self-confidence goals.

ORGANIZATION DEVELOPMENT

The work climate must support behavior for development. Many management consultants believe work-related problems are caused by deficient work environments that affect productivity. Efforts to turn this situation around have been called quality of work life projects. However, a host of strategies, that interrelate with quality of work life programs, are grouped under the title of organizational development or OD. Figure 18-4 shows a summary of popular OD interventions.

Team building
  The objectives are to build cohesive and cooperative work teams such as (1) analysis of supervisor and work groups, (2) analysis of groups organizational problems, and (3) group goal setting.

Job enrichment
  This entails restructuring jobs so individuals can experience more satisfaction from their work.

Feedback and reinforcement systems
  Individuals perform at higher levels when they receive information concerning their previous performance.

Conflict resolution
  This includes methods of identifying the conflict, discussing it, and developing action plans to reduce it.

Goal setting
  Explicitly stating organizational goals via management by objective process (MBO). Workers define their major organizational and individual goals as periodic reviews are made.

Transactional analysis
  This includes lectures and exercises that help to identify transactions which create communication problems. Informal agreements are made to decrease destructive communications.

Figure 18-4   Summary of Popular OD Interventions.

SUMMARY

The difference between training and development tends to be a thin line, but it has been said that you train dogs and develop people. Training and development programs cover a number of areas, from induction training to training for development.

Learning theory tells us that learning is a change in our behavior and that we learn in "fits and starts." To be effective, learning must be preceded by motivation, conceptualization of the cues of data, practice, reinforcement, and finally feedback to bolster our images and motivation to learn.

Types of employee training include classroom training, on-the-job training (OJT), vestibule training, and programmed learning, role playing, and case analysis. Job training methods start with (1) planning a training schedule, (2) making a written breakdown of the job, (3) having the right equipment and materials available, and (4) arranging the work place properly. JIT (job instruction training) advocates that you first get yourself and the trainee ready to learn. Then four steps follow—first, preparation of the learner; second, presentation by telling, showing, illustrating, and questions; third, performance try-out; and fourth, follow-up.

On-the-job methods for employee development include delegation, coaching, special assignments, and job rotation, but these methods should attempt to use development tailored to the needs of the individual since self-development is the basis for all development. The day-to-day experiences are the most important learning devices, and the supervisor is the most important person in employee development. Off-the-job development programs are formal education programs, company-sponsored programs, and short courses from local schools and universities.

Supervisory training and development attempt to achieve two objectives: (1) improve the supervisor's job performance and (2) prepare him for promotion. Training content can vary, but generally people-centered supervisory training programs are the most popular and are the most needed.

Methods used in supervisory training include lectures, conferences, simulation and role playing.

A suggested self-development program would attempt to achieve the following goals: (1) increase a person's ability to think, reason, and solve problems, (2) promote better understanding of self and environment, (3) make a person an effective speaker, and (4) develop a person into an effective writer.

KEY CONCEPTS

Training and productivity. This concept is rather obvious, in that a better-trained individual can also be a better producer. However, a better-trained individual can also promote employee satisfaction and more happiness and prosperity for himself as well as for the organization.

People investment. Organizations have to make investments in their people in formal and informal off-the-job training and development programs as well as programs on the job. People can have ideas, can think, can solve problems, can create new products, can improve jobs, and can increase the firm's profitability and the organization's effectiveness. Therefore investment in people can pay handsome dividends.

Development influenced by supervisor. Day-to-day contact can be the most important variable in a person's development if a favorable learning environment is provided. This concept is vital in making the supervisor aware that training and development of an individual occurs every day and not necessarily in formal training situations.

Self-development. As people we have to grow, develop, learn, and mature in order to fulfill our needs of being human beings. Self-development starts with wanting to improve, and it is implemented by a plan and much practice.

IMPORTANT TERMS

Case analysis	People investment
Coaching	People management
Conditioning—operant	Practice—involvement—use
Conferences	Reinforcement
Conflict resolution	Remedial training
Development	Self-development
Job instruction training (JIT)	Simulation and role playing
Job rotation	Trainer—trainee
Learning curve	Training
Learning theory	Transactional analysis
On-the-job training	Vestibule training
Organizational development	

INCIDENTS

From TVs to Bathroom Fixtures

It was Lou's second year as an inspector in a decorative plastics company that made parts for TV sets, auto dashboards, calculators, computers, and photocopy equipment. The precise design and manufacture was an important facet of Lou's job. He worked on the production line inspecting parts as they came off the line. Lou had spent both years at various lines that made large cases for TV sets. He liked his supervisor, the company, and the people he worked with.

One day the plant superintendents asked Lou if he would work as an inspector on the new bathroom fixture line. This line made a decorative plastic figurine that became part of the bathroom fixture handle. This line required much more attention to detail and precision than the TV line.

Lou had heard that the fixture lines supervisor, Chuck Conrad, required hard work, loyalty, and little backtalk from his people. Most of the fixture line employed women, which pleased him since he believed women were more precise and accurate than men on such a line. This feature would make his job as an inspector easier.

The next morning Lou met with his new supervisor for training in the inspection of the decorative plastic fixture handle. Conrad, the supervisor, took Lou to one of the inspection points and described the critical points to watch for. Conrad told Lou to observe as he inspected so Lou could ask questions as Chuck thought out loud as he inspected. The training session took 15 minutes and then Chuck turned the line over to Lou. Conrad left telling Lou to call him if he had any questions, any trouble, or needed any assistance.

1. If you were Lou, how would you feel about this training session, given Conrad's reputation for quality?
2. What learning steps did Conrad overlook? Which steps did he use successfully?
3. If you were Conrad, would you have done anything different?

Self-Development Plans Compared

As the supervisor of the transit department of a large commercial bank in Des Moines, Iowa, you are asked to seek ways to help develop the office personnel. You believe it's best to develop an inventory of your present personnel: two administrative assistants, six proof machine operators, and three microfilm operators. You start with the two administrative assistants as the basis of your development program.

Both administrative assistants, Karen Parker and Kathy Hillenbrand, are earnest and hard working. You decide to quiz the women to get some feedback concerning their feelings, impressions, and goals as they see their self-development in their present jobs. The following statements are collected from both:

Karen Parker (Rules for Self-Development)

1. Do what the supervisor tells me to do.
2. Watch TV and stay abreast of current events.

3. Read the local newspaper.
4. Do what my friends and business peers do.
5. Be careful with my work.
6. Attend any training sessions my supervisor wants me to attend.

Kathy Hillenbrand (Rules for Self-Development)

1. Have a good attitude toward supervisor and the co-workers but keep in mind that my job is the most important function.
2. Be cheerful, don't begrudge work or extra jobs since the more I can alleviate my supervisor's workload makes me more important to my supervisor and further assures my opportunities for advancement.
3. Concentrate on transmitting happiness, enjoyment, and satisfaction into the lives of others. Don't be a grouch!
4. Be aware of everything happening around me, be willing to listen and learn from others. The other person may be flattered by my attention but I may learn something useful in the process.
5. Always do each task as well as I can by pushing for speed, accuracy, and efficiency.
6. Take courses related to my field of business interests. Try to realize my potential and try to develop it. The only restraints on what I can learn are the ones I impose on myself.

What are your impressions of each secretary? What steps can you take, as their supervisor, to improve their self-development plans? What changes, modifications, deletions, or additions would you suggest for Karen Parker's or for Kathy Hillenbrand's plans?

QUESTIONS FOR DISCUSSION

1. What are the differences between training and development?
2. Why is motivation an important prerequisite for learning? Why can't a supervisor force learning on an employee?
3. Discuss why each of the following training methods would be effective for an insurance claim clerk. Which could be the most effective? Why?
   (a) Classroom training.
   (b) On-the-job training.
   (c) Vestibule training.
   (d) Video cassette.
   (e) Films.
4. What are the advantages of programmed learning over other types of training techniques?
5. Why can role playing and case method techniques be more effective than other techniques?

6. "If the learner hasn't learned, the teacher hasn't taught." Comment on the relevance of this statement for the following positions:
   (a) Ice worker installer on a refrigerator line.
   (b) File clerk for a large insurance company.
   (c) Accounts payable clerk in the accounting office of a large manufacturer.
7. In what ways does supervisory training differ from worker training?
8. If reading is one of the most important variables in self-development, why should the reader be self-disciplined to emphasize discovery rather than pleasure?
9. How can the ability to think be enhanced?
10. How can day-to-day contact with a supervisor or immediate superior have a greater effect on an individual's development than formal courses or outside educational exposure?

CHAPTER XIX

Counseling, Giving Orders, Introducing Change, and Conducting Meetings

LEARNING OBJECTIVES

- *To appreciate the significance of counseling employees and the various practices available.*
- *To understand the order-giving process and how consultative supervision may accompany this process.*
- *To appreciate the importance of introducing change and the role the supervisor plays.*
- *To see how resistance to change can be overcome with increased two-way communication and employee involvement.*
- *To understand how to conduct meetings effectively.*

Introduction

In addition to the previous day-to-day activities of the selection process, interviewing, training, and developing functions, the supervisor is confronted with the duties of counseling, giving orders, introducing change, and conducting meetings of all sorts. This chapter will discuss these latter activities in detail.

COUNSELING

Today's supervisors frequently find themselves in a personal counseling situation with their workers. The essence of counseling is to determine the possible solutions and courses of action to be taken after the employee has a full understanding of his/her problem. Basically, the first thing to do is to follow a nondirective type of approach (explained later) by encouraging and questioning the worker to talk so that the worker can identify the problem. Second, the supervisor should see the problem from the standpoint of the worker rather than from the supervisory point of view. Third, the supervisor should involve the worker and help him to sketch out solutions and courses of action that would best fit the worker's needs.

When a supervisor tries to counsel a worker, there must be a proper atmosphere that provides communicative rapport. First, the proper place should exclude noise and interference that will cause static in the communication process. A place of quiet, away from the work scene, over a cup of coffee in the cafeteria or after work, can be most appropriate. Counseling and communication are really an educational process that includes problem solving. Until the communication process has been structured to optimize the transmission of the messages, little will be achieved.

Counseling, as the term will be used here, is defined as discussions with an employee who has a problem with emotional overtones. The objective of counseling is to decrease the emotion and/or to help the employee solve the problem. Counseling involves communication, by voice usually, so that emotional problems can be shared. The supervisor/counselor must learn to understand, and help to decrease, an employee's emotional state.

THE ROLE OF COUNSELING AND THE SUPERVISOR

Now that counseling has been defined, it is necessary to see how the supervisor's role fits into the counseling situation. Whether or not a psychiatrist or clinical psychologist is on the organizational staff, a worker may not always contact the professional first. Often workers will seek out their supervisor. Normally, persons who have problems that generate emotions suffer from temporary problems that stem from the stress and strain and complexities of work and social life. Temporary problems that appear gigantic—such as marital problems, a broken love affair, in-law difficulties, trouble with others, problems with retirement, a new job, a transfer, or a promotion—are the most common counseling situations. Supervisors become involved with these situations because the workers' emotional states prohibit them from maximizing their job efficiency. Moreover, unhappy workers can influence fellow workers and elicit their pity or anger or both. Gloom can hang over the work crew if the supervisor doesn't try to help or to counsel the unhappy employee.

The supervisor's role as a manager requires that she/he help to solve the on-the-job problems or else refer the employee to competent professionals for further help. The supervisor should not practice psychiatry.

Advantages of Counseling

The major objective of counseling is to reduce the workers' emotional tensions. This is best achieved over the long run by offering support to the workers, by listening and assisting the employee in working out their problems alone. A neutral, supportive role should be assumed. Put yourself in the worker's shoes.

The supervisor's supportive role often can have various positive results, but the predominant goals are to help the worker to be reassured, to release emotional tension, to clarify thinking, and to reorient himself/herself.

A supervisor can *reassure* emotionally upset workers by giving them the courage and confidence to identify a problem, face it and then try to solve it. Sometimes a formal counseling session, in which the worker and the supervisor sit down in an office, may be needed, but a little encouragement and support by the supervisor can be of great assistance. It can be helpful simply to have the supervisor say, "Jane, everything will turn out all right," or "You're doing fine, Joe," or "Time heals everything." In the case of mental illness, attempts at reassurance could be dangerous. The supervisor should seek out professional help immediately. Any delay here would be more harmful than helpful. The supervisor is only trying to counsel employees who are temporarily upset. *This does not include sick employees.*

Releasing *emotional tension* is an advantage in counseling, because the supervisor listens or becomes a sounding block for the upset worker. The worker has the opportunity to unburden his or her troubles on a sympathetic, listening superior. The workers' tensions or anxieties subside as they become more relaxed. Being a sympathetic listener, without trying to practice psychiatry, can help to dispel the worker's problems by releasing the worker's tensions. This could be the solution in many cases.

Allowing workers to *clarify their thinking* and especially their feelings is another major advantage of counseling. The counseling supervisor should attempt to help them identify the problem or problems by themselves, and then should assist them in clarifying their thinking by skillfully questioning them so that the questions do not intimidate or belittle.

Finally, *reorientation* is an advantage in that the supervisor can help the workers revise their level of aspiration so that it more closely fits their level of attainment. The supervisor's job is to recognize those in need of reorientation before their need becomes serious or before the worker really disrupts the productivity of the work crew. If individuals refuse to accept their lack of abilities in the achievement of a specific goal, frustration can easily set in. In this case, the supervisor can help to redirect the worker's efforts toward pursuits more appropriate to the employee's talents.

Danger Signals Since all human beings are endowed with emotions, it can become difficult to maintain an emotional balance. When a person's automatic balancing mechanisms get out of order, there are usually one or more symptoms that make it apparent. It is necessary for the supervisor to spot these symptoms. The supervisor should be aware of problems that stem from more profound causes and refer the individual to professional help by notifying his superior immediately.

The most common danger signal is *anxiety*. This is not the normal worrying, but rather a restless, sleepless, insecure, fearful, unhappy feeling that keeps a person from concentrating. Anxiety is the body's method of triggering our defense mechanisms to fight off danger. Fear signals are dry mouth, sweaty palms, and a rise in blood pressure. But continued or constant fear becomes anxiety.

Another danger signal is *depression* or lengthy periods of discouragement and "feeling blue." This feeling is experienced by all of us at times, but a lengthy period can be a significant signal of an emotional problem. Another signal can be the occurrence of depression without any significant reasons. The supervisor may not be able to diagnose depression, but he may be able to see the results of depression, which are dullness, apathy, severe self-criticism, and even crying.

On the other end of the depression spectrum, *continuous excitement* is also a danger signal. Excitement in a worker when there is no cause for such excitement can be dangerous. This is similar to running a car at 120 miles an hour: sooner or later the mechanism falls apart.

When workers *consistently avoid* other people and social groups, they are giving another danger signal. A radical change in behavior is indicative of emotional problems. If a normally sociable person becomes withdrawn and doesn't want to talk or be in the company of others, then some emotional problem with deeper meanings may be present.

Doing something that a worker doesn't ordinarily do is still another signal of emotional trouble. If a person who is normally quiet and considerate suddenly assumes a rude and noisy manner, this is an indication that something in his/her personality is not functioning properly.

The important thing for the supervisor to remember and understand is not to try to change the individual, but to recognize these symptoms as danger signals that trigger the need for professional help. *The supervisor should assist only in spotting the symptoms, not correcting them.*

DIRECTIVE VERSUS NON-DIRECTIVE COUNSELING

Two different approaches can be taken during a counseling interview. Like other types of interviews, the counseling interview can be either directive or nondirective.

Directive counseling is a process of hearing a person's emotional or rational problem, deciding with the person what he/she should do, and then advising and motivating the person to do it. Directive counseling is the same as giving advice, except that it also includes assurance, emotional release, and perhaps some clarification of the client's thinking. Generally, giving advice in an emotional counseling situation is not as effective as giving advice in a rational type of interview. The emotional stress in the former counseling situation may preclude any giving of advice.

The nondirective counseling technique is usually the one used by counselors. This approach is client-centered in that the supervisor listens and encourages employees to explain their problem and tries to have them understand the problem. Then the counselor has the employee determine the proper course of action. Emotional release can take place faster with this approach than with directive counseling. Usually clearer thinking follows, as well.

EFFECTIVE COUNSELING SITUATIONS Before effective counseling can take place, six conditions and assumptions must be met. First, the supervisor must assume that the workers are responsible for themselves, and must continue to assume that the workers are responsible enough to carry out their responsibilities. Second, the supervisor assumes that any change in the workers' emotional problems must originate within the workers. Third, the supervisor must provide an atmosphere where the workers feel free to express themselves. Fourth, the supervisor should establish a permissive attitude or a research attitude to determine facts as uncovered by the workers. Fifth, the supervisor should show a reflective nature by rephrasing the statements made by the workers so that they can understand and help the workers to understand. Sixth, supervisors should keep quiet; rather than probe or blame or give advice, they should offer suggestions or offer reassurance during the stage when the workers vent their emotions.

GIVING ORDERS

As the supervisor manages the work crew by planning, organizing, directing, controlling, communicating, motivating, understanding, and coordinating, the giving of orders becomes a part of the total process. Directing means the issuance of instructions, assignments, directives, and orders. Giving orders is a very major part of the supervisor's managerial directing prerogatives and communication skills; it occurs every day.

CHARACTERISTICS OF GOOD ORDER GIVING Although supervisors may learn to issue orders from their own experience and common sense, research has indicated that common characteristics do exist that will assist the supervisor to be more effective in this area. The experienced supervisor knows that poorly given orders can unsettle the best laid plans, regardless of how effective the preliminary planning, organizing, and thought processes have been.

Giving orders is simply good communication; the order must be reasonable, understandable, and use proper verbal or written symbols. In addition to good communication, order giving also incorporates two other elements—orders must be compatible with the needs of both the organization and the employees, and orders must specify a definite time limit. These two additional points will be discussed here.

A supervisor should avoid giving orders that may countermand the direction or policy of the organization or violate the needs of the employees. For example, the supervisor may tell the workers to stop work on a given project that originally had been given top priority by the organization. Employee confusion could reign. The supervisor's reasons for changing direction may be initiated by a shortage in materials or parts or supplies, but to the workers on the project, this represents a conflicting directive. The supervisor must explain why such an action is necessary.

Good order giving includes the specification of how much time is allowed. The amount of time will vary for each employee and each job combination; however, it is important to specify the exact time so that proper control and motivation can be exercised by the supervisor. Knowing when the order has to be carried out gives the employees a time frame that can be used to organize their resources properly.

ORDER-GIVING PROCESS

Giving an order is but one step in an entire process. The first step, as seen in Figure 19-1, is planning. Supervisors must consider what action is necessary to meet desired results. Moreover, they must plan who, what, where, and when such activity will take place. Next supervisors should plan what kind of order (the message) should be given. They must decide how the order can be reasonable and understandable, without provoking employee confusion or conflict with previous orders.

The second step is to prepare the worker. This means that supervisors must understand how to communicate properly with the worker. Before issuing the order, the worker has to be prepared to listen and be prepared to understand the order. You might say it is necessary to get the worker's mental machines ready to receive by explaining the objective to be achieved and what needs of the worker can be achieved. This is the "why" of order giving that involves the worker in the process.

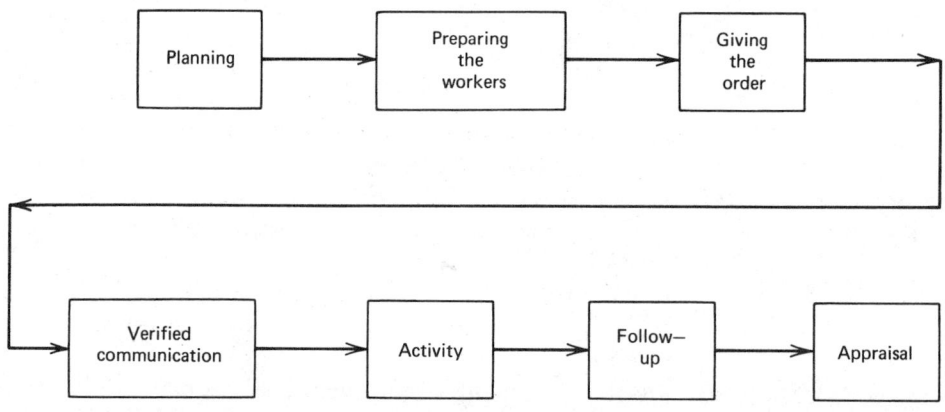

Figure 19-1 The order-giving process.

The next step is the actual issuance of the order. Words, tone of voice, gestures, facial expression, and surroundings that are conducive to good communication become the tools in this step.

The verification step is next. Here the supervisor tries to see if the order is completely understood. Often workers will hear only the first part of the message and may neglect to hear the rest. This could become a touchy situation. The supervisor shouldn't ask the workers to repeat what he/she said, because this might insult their intelligence and destroy the entire process. It is better if the supervisor tests the workers and involves them by appealing to the satisfaction of their needs and by asking their judgment concerning some of the details. For example, if the supervisor were to give an order to a warehouse fork lift truck driver to stack pallets in a certain section, he/she could consult with the worker as to the height of each stack relative to the floor strength in the warehouse. However, if the supervisor refused this approach and stated, "Stack them three high," the worker could have heard "four high." If the worker knows four high is ridiculous, he/she may perform the work anyway with the thought: I only work here and if the darn things falls, I'm only following orders.

The action step follows next. Here the worker carries out the orders.

Follow-up of the order takes place. Even though the worker has heard the order and attempts to follow it correctly, unforeseen events may occur, such as a failure to receive the proper material or support to perform the task. Tact should be used in follow-up because if the follow-up is too close to the order giving, the worker will feel badgered. It is best to have the worker feel involved.

The last step is appraisal. The supervisor checks to see how effective he/she has been and what he/she can do to improve his/her communication, planning, use of organizational skills, motivation, satisfaction of worker's needs, and control.

CONSULTATIVE SUPERVISION AND ORDER GIVING

Giving orders can be a means of accomplishing many things, such as worker involvement and motivation, spreading positive attitudes, praise, correcting workers, and generally creating a better climate for better leadership. *Consultative supervision* means exercising a participative leadership style. Although many supervisors are quite capable of making their own decisions, they use the consultative approval to bring the workers into the issuance of orders. Workers can appreciate being consulted *before* the decision or order is given. Some appreciate having a "say so" about the problem.

Consultative attitudes in order giving are very beneficial as the supervisor asks the worker's opinions or bounces his ideas off an experienced worker for his response. If the technique is properly handled, the supervisor shouldn't lose any prestige or weaken his formal authority, because the right to decide and the right to give an order are still reserved. A supervisor who is willing to share, gains respect and trust. The following example illustrates an order-giving process in which the supervisor sincerely requests a worker's input.

Supervisor: "Charlie, the visual inspection of the packaged beer bottles creates a great deal of monotony for an inspector."

Inspector (Charlie): "Gus, you're right. I fight that job every time I get it."

Supervisor: "What do you think should be done to improve that situation?"

Charlie: "If the inspector could be moved to a few other jobs during an eight-hour shift, the bottle inspection could be a little easier."

Supervisor: "I agree, but what do you think the other jobs should be?"

Charlie: "Bottle cleaning and bottle sterilization with Hank and Joe."

Supervisor: "I've given this a great deal of thought, and I agree with you completely. Tell Hank and Joe to meet with us at the break."

Charlie: "Okay."

(At the break.)

Supervisor: "After talking with Charlie, I've come to the conclusion that we have to beef up the packaged bottle inspector's job to alleviate boredom by rotating you three among bottle cleaning, bottle sterilization, and packaged bottle inspection. I could suggest that each of you pull a two-hour watch on each of the three jobs. I've written out the assignments and the flow of the changes starting with the day shift. We'll start tomorrow and check it out. Any questions?"

Hank: "Sounds good, except why can't I start the sterilization first rather than the cleaning?"

Supervisor: "Hank, you're the most experienced in that job, and I want a strong start on each shift."

Consultative order giving does not appear to the employee as an order, but it becomes the direction and application of a solution that involved the workers. Employee morale is bound to improve when their ideas are valued and used. Of greatest importance, however, is the fact that the workers and supervisor are closer in communication and trust and respect for each other. A better order-giving climate can be achieved under these circumstances.

COMMON ERRORS IN GIVING ORDERS

If a supervisor practices good communications and gives the reasons for the orders, the supervisor usually gains the workers' cooperation. In spite of these circumstances, three common errors might crop up to which some attention should be given. The first of these errors is giving too many orders at once. This can confuse or add heat rather than light to the subject. In this situation, the supervisor should increase two-way communication so that he/she knows for sure that the worker understands each facet of the order. Better still, it is more effective to write the order down so that the worker can remember.

A second error involves too much or too little detail. Highly detailed orders may insult the worker's intelligence or suggest that the supervisor is a child, whereas too little detail leaves the worker out on a limb. Whether too much or too little detail is involved depends on the worker's intelligence, motivation, experience, and job knowledge. A supervisor must communicate with the individual receiving the order.

Third, orders given as commands may also cause problems. Wherever possible, an order should be a suggestion rather than the "you will do this or else" type of attitude. An order in the form of suggestion comes out as "We have to get that report out by five, Alice; do you want Jane and Suzy to help?" or "How's your work schedule? Can you fit this illustration in before quitting time?" An order phrased as a question does not show weakness, but strength. Commands show weakness in that a poor leader has to resort to them to drive rather than lead. Real leaders have seen that the less authority they show outwardly, the more they actually have. A good, strong leader shows a great deal of concern for working with and through people rather than against them.

Consultative order giving can break down in situations where a firm leadership stand has to be taken by the supervisor. When the supervisor's authority is openly questioned by workers or when confusion has developed over previous orders, the supervisor should exercise direct orders at these times with no doubt as to who is running the show. This style should be held in reserve since most people would rather be led than driven.

INTRODUCING CHANGE

Initiating and controlling changes can be among the supervisor's very significant roles in day-to-day activities. Mishandled changes can provoke the ill will of the work group. This, in turn, may develop into a full-scale morale problem that might affect productivity and quality of output. Building mountains out of molehills can be illustrated in the following case of a plant engineering operation in a medium-size manufacturing plant. In this room 14 employees sat behind drawing desks. These employees had been with the company for many years. The vice-president of engineering wanted to expedite the flow of work in the office and decided to tear down a half-wall that had separated the 14 desks into two groups of 7. Without consultation with the group, carpenters entered the design area and began to tear down the wall. This so unnerved the informal organization of the long-term employees that they generated rumors to satisfy their need for information. Eventually, as the whole thing snowballed, the firm was forced to hire a human relations expert at a considerable expense to straighten out the entire matter. This case shows how important it is to use the informal organization and satisfy the employee's needs when instituting changes. The work group should have been told, in this case by the vice-president of engineering, that the wall was going to be torn down and why it was going to be torn down.

The lesson to be learned in this particular situation is never to make changes without first preparing the people for a change. People do not fear change as much as they fear the many uncertainties created by change. If an unknown event exists, the uncertainty of the event is feared. Once people are set for change in that they can see advantages for themselves, and are informed of the changes, the informal group can assist in making the change and possibly even pass along some valuable information that would improve the change.

TYPES OF RESISTANCE TO CHANGE

Perhaps the most commonly recognized resistance concerns technological change. Improved machinery, new processes, or automation and the new social relationships are feared by employees the most. A worker may be required to learn new skills, learn a new approach to work, become a helper rather than run the new equipment, or face the prospects of changing jobs with all the new social relationships provoked by the change.

The second type of resistance, as depicted in the previous example, involves change in organizational structure or social relationship. A change in communication lines, new responsibility, a new superior, a new location, or new co-workers are all examples of what organizational changes can mean to employees.

WHY RESISTANCE EXISTS

Resistance to change may not occur in all change situations. If the worker can see that an improvement or advantage for himself is being added, little resistance will exist. If this is the case, the worker may insist on the change. For example, if one of the typists has been promised a new typewriter after she has requested it, no resistance will exist. However, if the new machine does not fulfill her expectations, she may complain after receiving it. Thus you can see that change is really not resisted; the resistance is caused by the meaning of the change to the individual. Uncertainties, the unexpected, and the unknowns are the factors that affect the individual and enhance fear of change.

Introducing Change

Economics Workers will resist automation when they fear losing their jobs. Arguments to sway their fears are pointless when workers foresee losing "bread on the table" for themselves and their families. If a skilled worker lost his/her economic hold in a given job because of automation, and if the worker's particular skills were reduced in importance as the result of a technological change, the worker would strongly resist change for economic reasons only.

Inconvenience Learning new ways to do things forces a worker to forget what has become habit, and the expenditure of energy to learn new ways creates the resistance. "The extra effort isn't worth it" can become the worker's attitude. This is a form of laziness, but it also indicates a lack of self-development, as well as boredom and lower employee morale. In general, a worker learns the "tricks of the trade," whereas a new situation forces the worker to master new "tricks."

Uncertainty Strange unknowns are always threatening to most people because of ignorance and a failure to understand the change or the need for change. The familiar status quo gives security. A change disrupts this security and the status quo. The lack of factual information is the primary reason for this fear. This type of resistance can be corrected by providing answers to questions and by communicating support.

Another form of fear from uncertainty is generated internally rather than by external factors. People's fears of how *they will react* to the new, changed situation creates more uncertainty. Fear of inadequacy or fear that they may break up under the strain can create a great deal of resistance to change. This is always noticeable when a group of people who are unacquainted sit down to take a short course in supervision. Their uneasiness comes from the new social relationships, their inability to know what will be involved, and their fear that they may not be able to learn. Breaking the ice is always a very standard feature in this type of program. Friendliness and a casual atmosphere help. Once the participants realize that the instructors and fellow students are human and don't know all the answers, they tend to lose some of their fear of the course and its unknowns.

Threats to Interpersonal Relations Workers develop social relationships on the job that can be deep rooted. These social relations help to set standards as well as providing security and communication, and generally satisfying the worker's need to belong. A change in the organizational structure can disrupt these informal groups and pose a threat to the worker. A new supervisor is an unknown to the worker, and the worker may be anxious about the new supervisor's attitude toward informal group relationships. An exception to this statement would occur if the old supervisor were so bad that everyone wanted a change. In this case anyone would be an improvement, but some fearful souls might say, even under these circumstances, "Yes, but we know the present son of a gun and we don't know the new person."

Resentment of New Orders and Increased Control Change necessitates many new orders, directives, and control. Managers exercise control so that the change can be made successfully. The increased attention, which puts workers in the spotlight, and the intensified communications can be interpreted by many workers as an increase in control or an invasion of their privacy. Both perceptions by the workers will help to develop resistance or foot dragging.

REDUCING RESISTANCE TO CHANGE

Resistance, as has been discussed, is basically the individual's lethargy in learning a new job that disturbs the status quo (mostly social relations) and thus creates a fear of the uncertainties of the change. Obviously, to reduce this resistance to change the supervisor must placate or pacify these fears and/or involve the affected workers in the change through participative leadership techniques.

Economic Incentives Economic motivation is still very important in our life. We never have enough money. As ably put by C. Northcote Parkinson, our expenditures rise to the level of our income. We spend everything we make, or so it seems. However, a supervisor can overcome economic resistance to change by offering guarantees to workers that their jobs will not be eliminated or reduced in importance by the change.

Two-Way Communication Change is uncomfortable, and the changer seldom thinks about the changee's objectives and motives. Workers must accept change themselves, because a supervisor cannot do it for them. As in training and self-development you can lead a horse to water, but you can't make him drink—unless he wants to.

In two-way communication the supervisor convinces the worker that the change is for the best and that the worker will be disappointed and feel left out if the change is not made. A supervisor makes the worker's present position seem undesirable by encouraging the worker to spring forward and anticipate the change.

Involvement People have a strong desire to participate in decisions that affect them directly. Involving individuals in the decision process is another way of reducing resistance to change. Involvement in the change itself and in the planning of the change gives workers a sense of control over their present and future environment.

Involvement actually means consulting with the workers so that they have a say about how the change will be implemented. The supervisor then becomes the leader of an active, involved group of workers. Resistance to change will tend to dissipate as each worker understands and helps to provide input into the change process, providing that the workers are convinced that the reasons for the change are correct or are favorable to them.

CONDUCTING MEETINGS

MEETINGS AND THE SUPERVISOR

Conducting meetings may not appear to be within the realm of a supervisor's day-to-day duties, but with the increased use of committees and conferences, it is wise for a supervisor to understand their advantages. Meetings can be very useful for the supervisor (1) in decision making, (2) as a participative instrument, (3) for giving information or developing a cooperative climate, and (4) for training. Each of these functions is performed every day by the typical supervisor.

All supervisors should familiarize themselves with the various techniques of leading group discussion, because they will be called on to lead when the departmental business is discussed among subordinates. The ability to lead this type of interpersonal communicative group or group dynamics is, indeed, an important supervisory talent needed for future growth.

TYPES OF MEETINGS

Before we discuss meetings in detail, it might be best to define what we are talking about. The term *meetings* usually refers to the following types of interpersonal relationships in a group—committees, conferences, and possible other groups that meet face to face to discuss work problems, convey information, give advice, make decisions, or develop creative thinking.

A committee is a specific type of meeting in which the members have delegated their authority to the group concerning the problem at hand. This authority is one vote for each member. This means that when a supervisor serves on a committee with some of the workers, the supervisor's role has to be changed for the time being.

A conference is very similar to a committee except that its intention is different. Whereas a committee is usually formed to solve problems or identify a problem, a conference is established for training communication and is led by a designated conference leader. It is the conference-type meeting that the supervisor will conduct most frequently.

BENEFITS AND LIMITATIONS OF MEETINGS

The benefits of meetings can be varied, depending on the supervisor's ability to conduct a meeting. The major advantage of a meeting is the face-to-face contact between the supervisor and the workers. This permits the supervisor to show concern and human relations abilities as the supervisor asks for and receives the workers' ideas.

In addition to participation and feedback, another benefit of meetings is the development of creative thinking. An individual working alone finds it difficult to generate new thought process unless they are triggered by others. We are forced to think and to question our own predispositions when another person questions their validity. Transforming another person's creative thoughts for use in solving our own problems becomes possible in a meeting if an attitude of free exchange prevails.

Meetings encourage support for decisions, because the climate is favorable for the dissemination of information. The participants gain a feeling for the problem and the possible workable alternative solutions to the problem as related in the meeting. Meetings are probably one of the best means available to commit persons to a course of action.

Finally, the development of teamwork is an important by-product of meetings. When people are performing tasks together in quest of a common goal, the activity helps to precipitate feelings of belonging and teamwork. The essentials of teamwork are a small group, a leader, a common goal, regular interactions, contributions by each member, a team spirit, and a conscious coordination.

Limitations of meetings are numerous, but the possible overexposure of the supervisor is a major disadvantage. If the supervisor exhibits a lack of concern for the workers and their ideas during meetings, the meeting will magnify the problem. A supervisor would be better off to have as few meetings as possible if his/her personality does not fit the proper image of concern and trust. Perhaps he should be transferred if this situation continues.

Meetings can become habit forming and can be used to avoid accountability. If the entire crew decides to take a given action, it can take the supervisor off the hook. A group or committee can decide something that no one individual really wants to do. If the first response to any problem is always to have a meeting, a habit-forming, behavioral pattern is present.

Meetings can be a waste of time, expensive, and slow. Attitudes and predispositions brought to a meeting can become an obstacle to getting anything accomplished. A meeting offers a forum for certain individuals to show their intelligence, power, spite, or just plain cantankerousness in front of the supervisor or anyone else involved in the group. A noisy, irritating member in a meeting may be trying to satisfy personal needs, rather than trying to contribute to the problem or discussion at hand. However, a very quiet group with little or no noise or response indicates that the communication lines may be plugged or that everyone is bored. In any case, it is better to promote rather than limit communication.

Time may be wasted, but a worker may have satisfied needs by blowing off steam. The supervisor must exercise discretion when handling this situation.

Finally, a meeting may provoke compromise or even conformity. People may feel a compulsion to agree to a statement made by the leader or an influential member in the group. Some people may compromise something about which they feel very strongly. Group pressure serves to temper unreasonable ideas and possibly curb the responses of the dissonant member of the group.

HOW TO CONDUCT A MEETING Conducting a meeting takes patience, understanding and, above all, plain listening. Although a supervisor's mind may be already made up, a meeting may be necessary to involve the workers or to permit them to express their views and offer their suggestions. Participation by the members is the most welcome part of meetings. Ideas, solutions, or additional information can make a supervisor more effective and can compensate for the many limitations of meetings.

In developing an understanding of meeting or conference leadership, the following suggestions may be helpful.

1. Hold meeting at a regular time each week, or month, but watch for habit-forming, boring sessions. Cancel meeting if no business is to be transacted.
2. Develop and distribute an agenda so that the group has a right to participate.
3. Hold the meeting where distractions, noise, and the interference of day-to-day chores are minimized.
4. Plan your questions carefully so as to generate input from members so that you don't run the show.
5. If asked a question, use the question as a stimulus for group discussion.
6. Be honest if you reserve the right to make the decision; relate this fact to the group.
7. Encourage as much participation as possible in line with the subject discussed, but watch for long-winded discussions that waste time.
8. Do not offer your opinion at the beginning of the discussion unless you want to railroad a topic through or curtail an easy flow of communication.
9. Take notes of pertinent statements and ideas so that they will not be forgotten.

The Sales Meeting This type of meeting, doesn't enjoy as much acceptance by sales managers as a major vehicle for supervising their people. Many meetings are treated as necessary evils by managers and salespeople. The predispositions of both parties may also be slightly negative concerning any type of meeting which may carry over into the sales meeting setting.

However, as important as written and face-to-face communication can be, the sales meeting is a very significant vehicle in building respect, trust, and willingness to work cooperatively. It can also be a vehicle of poor morale, a waste of time, or the lowering of the salespeople's trust and respect for their sales manager. The sales meeting therefore presents a formal setting for the sales manager to be at his/her best or at his/her worst. Input by the manager into the meeting may be reinforced numerous times as the salespeople meet informally in small groups. Improper input or poorly conducted meetings reflect upon the sales manager and can be used by dissidents to magnify problems.[1]

In spite of the importance of every sales meeting, regardless of size or objectives, some sales managers attempt to "wing it" without proper analysis and organization beforehand. Some people may be capable of conducting a very successful sales meeting, given these circumstances; but the majority of sales supervisors have to be well-prepared before the meeting. Figure 19-2 lists possible topics.

Informative and Educational	Sales Techniques	Personal
1. New product description	1. Prospecting	1. Individual quotas
2. New product sales strategies	2. Sales approaches	2. Recognition
3. Product promotion	3. Demonstrations	3. Awards
4. Present product	4. Answering sales objections	4. Motivation
5. Company policies	5. Sales presentations	5. Inspiration
6. Corporate benefits	6. Effective closes	6. Reprimand
7. Buyer behavior analysis	7. Customer relations	7. Entertain
8. Product sales remuneration policies	8. Qualifying prospects	8. Gripe session
9. Territory assignments	9. Establishing an itinerary	9. Solution of personal problems and feedback
10. Paperwork, reports, and individual responsibility	10. Reading customers	10. Planning involvement
11. Competitive product	11. Competitive understanding	

Figure 19-2 Objectives and Purposes of Sales Meetings.

[1]Robert W. Eckles and Susan A. Eckles, "How to Conduct a Successful Sales Meeting," *Louisiana Business Review,* April 1979, pp. 10–12.

The oversight of the importance of all sales meetings may be due to a lack of understanding of the ways a meeting should be conducted, the different types of sales meetings, the salespeoples' roles in a specific meeting, or the reluctance of the manager to conduct a sales meeting other than as a forum to demonstrate who is in control.

After the agenda, time, and place of the meeting have been determined to accomplish the meeting's objectives, the next task becomes its conduct and control. There is no singular way to conduct a meeting, but the objectives will lead the sales manager into how the meeting should be conducted. There are common components.

First, the announcement of the meeting should be in writing, giving date, time, place and purpose. Frequent meetings, for example every Monday at 7:30 A.M., needn't be announced each time, but it is important to have an agenda prepared.

Second, the leader must know the sales force participants—if not personally, at least in background, experience, and probable problems.

Third, supplementary equipment, such as a slide or overhead projector and screen, should be set up and ready to go.

Fourth, the meeting should start promptly and follow the time frame as closely as possible. Elongated sessions are both boring and wasteful.

Fifth, the meeting should be conducted by stating the purpose of the meeting and then allowing as much input from participants as necessary without allowing any one participant to monopolize the proceedings. Participation must be recognized, but a good sales meeting leader soon learns to minimize extraneous individual activity.

SUMMARY

Counseling, giving orders, introducing change, and conducting meetings are four day-to-day activities of a supervisor that have two things in common. First, these four activities require face-to-face interrelationship between the supervisor and the workers. Second, each activity requires a strong ability to communicate meanings, understanding, support, and the supervisor's authority.

Counseling takes place in many situations, but it is different from interviewing because the worker is upset. The supervisor becomes a counselor whether he or she likes it or not. The supervisor has to solve problems that affect a person's efficiency. Counseling provides a supervisor the opportunity to gain trust and respect from the workers by reassurance, releasing emotional tension, and helping the worker to clarify thinking, relate feelings, reorient thinking, and change aspiration level. In addition, a supervisor should understand the psychological danger signals that precede a serious emotional problem so that he/she can become aware of the need for professional psychiatric help. Extended periods of anxiety, depression, continuous excitement; a radical change in behavior; and isolation from others are the important danger signals. The supervisor must not try to treat these symptoms; if the individual is sick, he/she needs professional help.

Counseling can follow either a directive or a nondirective approach. In the directive method the supervisor leads the session, whereas the nondirective approach is worker centered. The nondirective approach places the supervisor in the worker's shoes. A modified approach that is a combination of both the directive and nondirective is best for the supervisor to use.

Giving orders is part of directing and requires the use of all the rules of good communication. The order-giving process follows a seven-step process: (1) planning, (2) preparing the workers, (3) giving the order, (4) verifying the communication, (5) carrying out the activity, (6) follow-up, and (7) appraisal. Giving orders is a vehicle that can be used to involve and consult with workers. Common errors in giving orders are giving too many or too few at once, and commanding results rather than communicating requests.

Introducing change is one of the most difficult day-to-day chores faced by the supervisor. People resist change for a number of reasons, such as economics, inconvenience, uncertainty, threats to interpersonal relations, resentment of new orders, and increased control. Resistance to change can be reduced by removing the reasons for the resistance with economic incentives, two-way communication, involvement, and the presentation of the change to the subordinates by involving them in a problem-solving venture.

Conducting meetings also becomes an important facet of the supervisor's day-to-day operation. Meetings—both committees and conferences—can be beneficial in providing face-to-face contact, participation, feedback, and the development of a team spirit. Limitations, however, include avoiding accountability, wasting time, and provocation of compromise and conformity. Conducting a meeting takes patience, understanding, and the desire to listen and learn on the part of the supervisor. It is a valuable tool for disseminating trust and respect between the employees and the supervisor.

KEY CONCEPTS

Nondirective counseling. A supervisor manages people, and success is measured by the success of the department and its productivity. The concept of nondirective counseling is to become aware of the employee's feelings by allowing the employee to talk in order to establish facts. The significance of this concept is to solve problems by researching with the employee rather than "playing boss" and dictating. This basic counseling and interviewing technique is applicable to almost any face-to-face relationship of the supervisor and the employee. The magic word is *listen*.

Consultative supervision. This concept has wide usage, but it means to involve, motivate, develop positive attitudes by bringing workers into the process of giving orders and announcing decisions. Allow the workers to participate by asking them rather than commanding.

Preparation for change. This concept embodies one of the more difficult tasks faced by a supervisor. Change is always present, and when a supervisor must implement change, he must prepare the workers for the change. Resistance to change is a result of disturbing one's interpersonal equilibrium. Therefore, to reduce resistance to change, the supervisor must reduce those factors that magnify a change. Involve the affected people in some way in order to prepare them for the change. Support, communication, direction, and effective use of authority are necessary ingredients to facilitate effective change preparation.

Effective conference leadership. Leadership of conferences starts with the fact that the leader doesn't know it all. Leadership means leading, directing—not domineering, or closing off the participation of others. It also means managing the conference so that a productive output can be realized and the meeting will not be a total waste of time.

IMPORTANT TERMS

Anxiety	Depression
Clarify thinking	Directive counseling
Committees	Emotional tension
Conferences	Inconvenience of change
Consultative supervision	Involvement
Continuous excitement	Nondirective counseling
Counselee	Reassurance
Counseling	Reorientation
Counselor	Resistance to change

INCIDENTS

The Insecure Worker

Rick Tabor enjoyed his supervisory position at Outland Container Corp. in Troy, New York. His responsibility included overseeing the box board scoring operation for containers used for air conditioning units. The job wasn't difficult except for an infrequent accident where a worker caught a finger in the scorer. Rick was very conscientious and attempted to tell each worker to be aware of hanging a finger on the scorer. He would insist that each worker be adequately informed almost everytime he passed an operator on the plant floor.

Brad Lewis, a new employee, was starting his second week on the scorer when Rick noticed Brad's productivity hadn't increased sufficiently from the day he had started. When approached on the subject, Brad responded with his fear of getting hurt as previously related by Rick. Although Rick thought common sense would prevail, he couldn't figure out why Brad was afraid of the scorer.

Rick decided to tell Brad to "get on the stick" and increase his productivity if he wished to remain at Outland Container. Brad responded with lower output. This began to hurt finished goods shipments and consequently customer relations. The problem had taken on significant porportions.

Does Rick have a counseling problem, a giving-orders problem, or both? How would you manage Brad out of his predicament if you were his supervisor?

The Unhappy Growth Problem

David Cohen, a supervisor in a men's suit-sport clothes department in a large suburban Seattle department store had received word that his department was being enlarged due to the greater demand and the growing size of the community. The projected growth would double the department's present floor size and increase the number of employees in the department from 12 to 22. At present Cohen had two assistants, Mike Leone, in charge of men's suits and Dan Oates, in charge of men's sport clothes. The store contemplated adding two new lines of sport clothes: ski outfits and summer vacation outfits for those patrons who enjoyed the mountains and desert sun.

Cohen's superior insisted on a change in the organizational structure. He insisted that the two new lines must be set up and headed by a third department assistant. Proper attention could not be given to these new lines unless such an organizational change were made. David knew these demands would tax the emotions of his two current assistants as they would see a dilution of their importance by having a third peer in addition to the loss of control over the two new lines that could enlarge their own power and prestige.

Cohen's major consideration wasn't with the reorganization itself, but with how it would be received by his people. Also he was concerned with how to best communicate this change to both Leone and Oates.

Assume you were David Cohen—how would you make the change and encourage and support your assistants toward accepting the reorganization? Be specific in your recommendations by spelling them out in a chronological sequence.

QUESTIONS FOR DISCUSSION

1. Determine the differences between interviewing and counseling. List the most likely situations where you would use each process.

2. If a worker were suffering from an emotional imbalance as evidenced by erratic, unnatural behavior such as restlessness, feelings of fear, and depression, what would you do if you were supervisor?
3. If nondirective counseling requires workers to work out their own problems, how can the supervisor best maintain the nondirective counseling approach?
4. Why is good order giving also good communications?
5. How and why are order giving and consultative supervision related? Is this good or bad supervision?
6. Discuss why resistance to change is so much a part of human nature.
7. Under what circumstances does a change fail to cultivate resistance in the person involved in the change?
8. What are the forces that promote work output and the forces that limit work output? How can a supervisor cope with these forces?
9. What does teamwork in a meeting mean and why is it such an important ingredient for a successful meeing?
10. Why are patience, understanding, and being a good listener among the many tools of a successful meeting leader? What other tools must he or she have?
11. What may differentiate sales meetings from production floor meetings?

CHAPTER XX

Performance Appraisals

LEARNING OBJECTIVES

- *To understand employee and supervisory roles in the appraisal system.*
- *To be able to differentiate performance appraisal from day-to-day interpersonal contact.*
- *To understand the appraisal system and the types of appraisal systems available.*
- *To understand the limitations of appraisal systems.*

Introduction

Employees are in a constant development process, beginning with their selection and continuing through their induction, training, and counseling. An important aspect of this development process is their performance appraisal to determine their merit or value of service to the organization. Related to appraisal of an individual's performance are promotion possibilities and compensation plans.

This chapter covers the most important aspects of employee appraisals, such as their purposes, employee reactions, the supervisor's role, the various types of appraisal systems, their limitations, the supervisory appraisal review, and use of the results of an appraisal system.

PERFORMANCE APPRAISALS

A performance appraisal means a formal rating of how well individuals have handled their job during a given period of time and what goals should be established in the future to correct or improve these individuals' performance. The purpose of performance appraisals is the enhancement of an employee's development and career planning. Performance appraisal is a positive, helpful, constructive review of an employee's record and future, usually performed on an annual or semiannual basis.

EMPLOYEE REACTIONS TO APPRAISALS

Although few data are available to fully determine how employees really see appraisals, the available data indicate the following reactions. First, some employees are skeptical of being judged and at times distrust the supervisor/appraiser's ability. They question even the fairest of systems. They believe that some of the data can be used against them. Second, other employees believe the system provides them with sufficient feedback from the supervisor to judge their own growth and development in the organization. They believe that they know where they stand with the supervisor. A few individuals look forward to the appraisal interview. Third, another group of employees tend to be indifferent to the whole system. They could live with it or without it. The percentage of employees distributed among these three reactions would be dependent on the supervisor, the workers, the company policies, the type of work, and the leadership qualities of the supervisor.

SUPERVISOR'S ROLE IN APPRAISALS

Supervisors see performance appraisal from many different perspectives. As human beings, many supervisors dread the thought of evaluating and appraising employees. It's easy for some supervisors to be embarrassed when forced to rate an individual, whereas some other supervisors may fear that an employee's antagonism may be provoked by a low rating. Still other supervisors see the performance appraisal system as an opportunity to reprimand a given individual or as a system that provides them a power base from which to control their people better. Some supervisors are afraid a formal performance appraisal will only disturb their day-to-day operations and hope their operation will not take six months to recover from the formal performance appraisals system.

These perspectives frequently occur since performance appraisals should be used as a positive, constructive tool to enhance productivity through employee development and career planning.

The first aspect of the supervisor's role in appraisal is to develop a positive attitude toward the system. Supervisors should use the appraisal process as an opportunity to help, support, and improve production in their department and to enhance their respect and trust as leaders.

A benefit of the appraisal system is to have the employee ratings discussed with the worker. This provides a means of praising outstanding performance and of helping to improve performance. The supervisor's role is to use the system as a means toward an end, rather than thinking of appraisal as an end in itself. If they tell the workers that the performance appraisal is a grading system where a worker can pass or fail, supervisors would not be doing their job. Any person who is "flunking" in performance is not being supervised properly.

THE PERFORMANCE APPRAISAL PROCESS

The actual steps taken in the appraisal process may vary in different companies, but a common set of steps can be described. The process usually starts with the company establishing a policy that performance appraisal *will be* made every six months or every year. As illustrated in Figure 20-1, in the first step of the actual appraisal process the supervisor works either alone or with each employee to determine the goals and objectives of each job.

The second step is to establish an appropriate means to measure an individual performance in a particular job. This is discussed in greater depth in the next section.

The third step is the end-of-the-period appraisal evaluation by the supervisor. An evaluation of each worker's performance is made by the supervisor, who judges the worker's attainment of the goals and objectives established in Step 1, using the means of measurement established in Step 2.

The fourth and last step, appraisal review, is conducted with the employee by reviewing and discussing the supervisor's ratings with the worker. This is a trying but most beneficial step since the supervisor can use the appraisal system to praise, recognize, constructively criticize, and offer suggestions and support for employee improvement.

As can be seen by this process, the appraisal system provides the supervisor with an opportunity to set a leisurely, unrushed pace by conducting appraisals throughout the year rather than creating a peak load in one or two months. Additionally, the process's formal nature permits the supervisor to control the process and make sure the reviews are scheduled and performed in the best manner for both the individual's and the organization's future.

TYPES OF APPRAISAL SYSTEMS

Two broad types of appraisal systems exist. The first type is the rating scale, which is the oldest. The second and newer technique, management by objectives, tends to be oriented more toward managerial positions but has gained increasing acceptance as a tool for use by the supervisor.

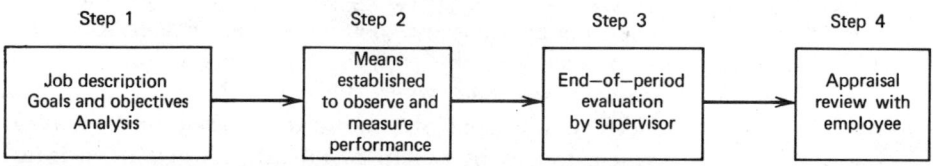

Figure 20-1   The performance appraisal process.

Rating Scales A typical appraisal *rating form* appears in Figure 20-2. The two most widely used kinds of measurement or rating are (1) the graphic rating scale, and (2) the frequency rating scale.

Typical of the *graphic rating scale* is the rater's opportunity to judge an individual's existing or potential talent in a particular trait. For example, the rating of employee loyalty may be as follows.

Employee's Loyalty to the Company

Extremely Low	Low	Medium	High	Extremely High

The rater simply places a check in the category that he or she believes is most applicable to the individual. It is important to stress that the rater's *idea* of the individual, rather than the rating of his *performance*, often is expressed. Obviously, biases and prejudices can easily creep into this type of rating analysis.

The *frequency rating scale* differs from the above in form only. Instead of a descriptive choice, a quantitative choice is provided. For example, in appraising an employee's loyalty, a frequency rating scale would appear as follows.

Employee's Loyalty to the Company

Bottom	10%	20%	40%	20%	10%	Top

The employee's loyalty will be evaluated against that of others by categorizing the trait on a percentage basis.

The two traditional rating scales have been severely criticized for their excessive emphasis on personality traits as opposed to a more objective measurement of performance. Actual performance has been considered secondary, since the appraisal system traditionally has emphasized an employee's potential for future development. To overcome some of these criticisms of objectivity in rating, other rating methods were developed. These are forced distribution, forced choice, ranking, and weighted checklist.

Forced distribution, sometimes called "grading on the curve," ranks subordinates by class. Certain people are ranked high and others ranked low, but the majority are ranked in the middle. The system assumes that a normal bell-shaped curve (statistical curve) is present. This system assumes that a given work crew is representative of the total society, meaning that so many people must be rated high and so many rated low. Obviously this is a serious drawback of this approach.

Forced choice is a technique to reduce bias in evaluation by forcing the rater to choose the most appropriate descriptive word or phrase from a choice of usually four. The most likely words, as well as the least likely words, are chosen. This technique was first developed for use in rating army officers. For example, to reduce bias, the technique would present four statements as follows.

380   Chapter XX   Performance Appraisals

Name: __John Doe__   Job Number: __4798-M__
Date Hired: __March 197–__   Starting Date
    of Present Job: __November 197–__

	Unsat.	Fair	Good	Very Good	Exceptional	
1. Job knowledge: use of practical knowledge and know-how related to present job	1	2	3	4	5	3
2. Judgment: ability to use facts and apply sound judgment	1	2	3	4	5	4
3. Attitude: enthusiasm shown for job; loyalty to company and superiors; ability to accept criticism and changes in company policy	1	2	3	4	5	3
4. Dependability: reliability in carrying out orders with efficiency	1	2	3	4	5	4
5. Creativity: ability to show imagination in job and offer suggestions for improvement	1	2	3	4	5	2
6. Association with fellow workers: ability to get along with others	1	2	3	4	5	2
7. Quality of work produced	1	2	3	4	5	4
8. Attentiveness: willingness to learn new skills or new methods.	1	2	3	4	5	4
9. Honesty and integrity	1	2	3	4	5	3
10. Leadership: ability to work through others and motivate fellow workers	1	2	3	4	5	1
11. Self-confidence and self-motivation	1	2	3	4	5	2
12. Analytical ability: ability to analyze problems	1	2	3	4	5	1
13. Emotional maturity: emotional stability	1	2	3	4	5	3
14. Use of safety practices	1	2	3	4	5	5
					TOTAL POINTS	41

Evaluated By: _____

Figure 20–2   Typical appraisal rating form.

	Most	Least
1. Doesn't try to pull rank	____	____
2. Knows their people's capabilities and limitations	____	____
3. Low efficiency	____	____
4. Speaks in a steady monotone	____	____

The rater would choose the most likely and the least likely characteristic. Two of the characteristics appear favorable (1 and 2), and two appear unfavorable (3 and 4). However, when the appraisal is graded, only one of the favorable items (item 2) gives a plus credit and only one of the unfavorable items (item 3) gives a negative credit. The other two items (1 and 4 in this case) have shown that they have less correlation or relationship with efficiency than items 2 and 3. The rater doesn't know which items count as he gives an objective appraisal by checking the appropriate blanks.

Ranking is a very common practice that requires the supervisor to rank, in descending order, each member in the work group as compared to each other member of the group. This ranking of individuals can be on certain aspects of the worker's job, or it can be on overall performance. A typical ranking process may be as follows.

Names of People	
_____	
	_____ Highest
_____	
	_____ Next Highest
_____	
	_____ Next Highest
_____	
	_____ Next Highest
_____	
	_____ Next Lowest
_____	
	_____ Next Lowest
_____	
	_____ Lowest

All the workers are listed on the left, alphabetically. Then the names are ranked on the right. All the names are listed so that the supervisor will not accidentally leave out a name. First the highest and next highest are entered; then the people are ranked from lowest and next lowest. The rest are ranked in the middle. This method is aimed at improving the appraisal by making it more objective.

The *weighted checklist* is similar to the rating scales, with the exception that a summation of the total points is the result of each item multiplied by a weighting factor. For example:

Knowledge: Familiarity with all aspects and details of the job (0.0 to 1.0 scale)	A Rating	B Weight	A&B
Expert knowledge of all aspects		40%	
Generally well versed		25	
Knows most of the details		20	
Unfamiliar with some important details		10	
Lacks basic knowledge of job		5	
Total		100%	

The ratee would then have all of his scores added for each trait or performance area, and the summation or total would be the appraisal score.

Most rating scales described so far have emphasized personality traits rather than measurable performance. The rating secured from traits is of little help to a worker for appraising job performance.

Management by Objectives   This technique also known as MBO, has been adopted by a number of companies because it is based on quantitative, measurable performance goals that are usually set by both the supervisor and subordinate. Rather than rate the employee, as before, each subordinate is requested to establish, for himself, short-term performance goals. As see in Figure 20-3 a simplified MBO form, both the supervisor and employee fill out the work sheet and then meet in review to develop and agree to a plan or goals for improvement in the subsequent period.

These goals may be a 5 percent increase in production output, or a 10 percent reduction in scrap, or a new job to be mastered by a given date, or a completion of a project as of a given date. The worker, in cooperation with the supervisor, would plan the activities or "game plan" to be followed so these goals could be achieved by the worker within the specified time frame.

When the planned period is over, workers evaluate themselves against standards that they have set at the same time that the supervisor rated them. In the process, the workers' relationships with the supervisor are also evaluated. During the appraisal review interview, in which supervisors and workers sit down to discuss the performance, a good climate and balance can exist between them because the workers have a stake in the final outcome.

Performance Appraisals

```
┌─────────────────────────────────────────────────────────┐
│               U.S. ENVELOPE COMPANY                      │
│                                              Cody/Plant  │
│   Name_____                   │
│   Department_____                   │
│ ═══════════════════════════════════════════════════════ │
│   Performance rating:  Excellent☐   Very good☐  Good☐   Fair☐ │
│                        Unsatisfactory☐    Very unsatisfactory☐ │
│ ═══════════════════════════════════════════════════════ │
│   Job description                                        │
│                                                          │
│   Achievements since last review                         │
│                                                          │
│   Goals                                                  │
│                                                          │
│   Career interest/development plans                      │
│                                                          │
│   Employee strengths/weaknesses                          │
│                                                          │
│   Replacements/position target                           │
│                                                          │
│   Supervisory signature                                  │
│                                                          │
│   Employee signature                                     │
└─────────────────────────────────────────────────────────┘
```

Figure 20–3 Simplified MBO form.

The advantages of MBO over traditional rating systems are many. MBO creates a standard of evaluation for each person based on the special needs and characteristics of a particular job. Workers know the rules of the game, and they know the standards on which they will be judged. Workers have a say about their futures and about the organization's future. The MBO approach sets future goals as opposed to rating scales, which tend to evaluate the past. The future can be changed, but the past is history. Another interesting perspective of MBO is that it requires the supervisor to change his/her role. Relative to the worker, the supervisor is no longer a judge in the appraisal system but is a coach, supporting the worker to achieve the established goals. Greater motivation on the worker's part, in conjunction with better supervisory planning and utilization of the worker, are the two major advantages of MBO.

Certain limitations are contained in the MBO approach. The worker may not be capable of, or want to be involved in, setting goals in cooperation with the supervisor. The two may give lip service to MBO, but the supervisor may really set the goals. MBO is beneficial in that it allows greater involvement on the part of the employee.

An illustration of a modified MBO system appears in Figure 20-4, a faculty effort report. The performance of each professional member is allocated to specific tasks on the basis of a percentage of time. These goals (time allotments to specific tasks) are planned by the professor and his supervisor, the department chairman or dean. After the semester or quarter is over, the appraisal review is conducted to determine the faculty member's rated performance. In this way one of the limitations of a straight MBO system can be overcome, since the performance can be used to determine future potential. Figure 20-4 also permits changes in a member's time allocation, if necessary, so that at the rating time he or she is judged on actual performance. This system permits supervisors to cope with any changes beyond their control that may occur. Obviously this system was established for the professorial ranks but could be applied to numerous positions involving professional people, such as engineers, chemists, hospital personnel, and government agency personnel.

In general, the MBO appraisal and evaluation system can be very effective if a supervisor practices a participative management style. Involvement of a worker on a periodic basis is not effective because many side effects can develop. Mistrust, irresponsible contributions, and difficulty in measurable performance are among the numerous side effects. For supervisors who feel more comfortable with an authoritarian style of leadership, the MBO approach may not be suitable, because the supervisor might feel uncomfortable if he/she didn't set the goals.

LIMITATIONS IN APPRAISALS —HUMAN ERRORS

Some of the limitations stated for the MBO approach are shortcomings of all appraisal approaches. The most common error practiced by raters still remains the rater's inability to judge another individual since bias, prejudice and subjectiveness can't be overruled in some cases. Indeed, this is a very difficult task for any of us, but a knowledge of these common errors can help supervisors improve their appraisal performance. Some of the same errors as discussed in interviewing and counseling also appear in appraisal and evaluation systems.

Human errors in appraisals include inconsistencies, insufficient data, leniency, strictness, halo effect, and biases affected by current events.

Inconsistencies by supervisors as they rate different workers can distort the results and perhaps influence the whole rating system by inspiring a

Performance Appraisals 385

Figure 20–4 Faculty effort report evaluation.

lack of confidence in the entire system. In order to compare apples with apples, rather than apples with oranges, a common definition of what is good, excellent, satisfactory, fair, and poor must be determined. Supervisors can fluctuate in their definition of each term by allowing their impression of the person, the job, and other factors to influence their judgment.

A supervisor may only get a limited view or distorted data to use in the appraisal. Workers' abilities to get along with their supervisor may have greater impact on their ratings than their performance as workers. Judging productivity is very difficult.

Since we dislike rating others, it is common for us to be lenient and rate everyone high. A low rating has to be defended in the appraisal review or be modified under duress. A low rating may conflict with the superior's rating of the same individual, so the supervisor can rate high or rate as his superior would rate the man. The U.S. Army has constantly faced the problem of leniency in rating. To get a next-to-highest rating could mean absolute incompetence on the job. Only the highest rating would be satisfactory.

The opposite of leniency is strictness. A supervisor can build a reputation within an organization by being known as a strict rater, or "hard nose." Other terms could be applied to this type of individual, but it is necessary for strict raters to prove that no one in their work crew or department could possibly be as good as they. Obviously, this is the extreme case, but undue strictness is disadvantageous.

The halo effect in appraisals means the tendency to rate a person consistently according to the supervisor/rater's general feelings and impressions of the worker. If supervisors believe that the worker/ratee is a good person, most of the individual ratings will be high. If they believe that the ratee is poor, they will find it difficult to find any good points in favor of the ratee.

When rating an individual, it is easy to see only the last part of a worker's performance record. We tend to see how the worker performs his/her latest duties and to forget early performance. This attitude by the rater/supervisor could be fostered by recent or current events in the supervisor-worker relationship. A worker who just won a companywide award for the best cost savings suggestion could influence the supervisor's judgment. The worker in question could have been one of the worst producers in the department because he/she spent a great deal of time evaluating cost savings techniques.

SUPERVISORY PERFORMANCE APPRAISAL REVIEW

Many organizations require supervisors to conduct an appraisal review or interview with each worker they have rated. The purpose of the interview is to provide *useful* feedback to the worker of his/her strengths and weaknesses. In the case of MBO (management by objectives), the performance appraisal interview is a mutual meeting of the minds, since the worker has rated his/her performance on a self-evaluation basis and now compares his/her rating against the supervisor's rating.

Interview Preparations

As in other forms of interviewing, certain preparations must be made for a successful review session. A supervisor must carefully prepare for the performance appraisal interview. The review should be scheduled, the employee informed of the time and the place so both can be prepared for the occasion. First, both the worker and the supervisor should understand what results should be expected. Both should be aware of conditions, and of facts and figures that indicate that a satisfactory performance has been obtained.

Appraisal Interview

Once the interview takes place, all the rules of interviewing should be followed. First, establish rapport and allow the worker to talk freely. Beware of an excessively long warm-up, and get down to business after the worker's tensions, if any, have subsided.

When covering the ratings, supervisors should encourage questions while keeping the performance appraisal as the central topic of discussion. Questions can trigger areas for development, improved methods, or plans for improved performance in the next period.

Supervisors should be cautious in making promises or statements that could be construed to mean something that they would regret later. They should keep previous promises, but they should refrain from discussing promotions and pay increases during the performance interview.

At the end of the discussion, it may be advisable to summarize weak points and what the subordinate can do to rectify these situations. Supervisors, at this stage, should accept defense or aggression as shown by the worker, without a fight. The subordinate may feel obliged to save face, so discretion may be the better part of valor. Keeping quiet and not exposing the worker's alibis could be the best alternative. After supervisors have given the ratings that they care to disclose to the worker, and a mutual plan has been worked out for improvement, it is no longer necessary to stretch the interview. Any further delay could encourage the worker to bring up something disagreeable. Workers should leave with a feeling that they contributed to a plan for improvement, and that their supervisors were straight in comment, helpful, supportive and, above all, honest. Any other activity can only do more harm than good. The performance appraisal interview is a form of coaching so that improved performance can materialize with the supervisor's help. Figure 20-5 is a checklist supervisors can use to improve their performance in appraisal review interviews.

	Yes	No

1. Was your performance formally appraised and discussed with you? ____ ____
2. Before your appraisal was discussed with you, did your immediate superior give you advance notice of the discussion he planned to have with you? ____ ____
3. In advising you of the discussion, did he ask you to be prepared to appraise your own performance? ____ ____
4. Was it clear from his preliminary discussion with you that the purpose of the discussion was to help you improve your performance on the job? ____ ____
5. In the discussion of your performance, do you feel that you had sufficient opportunity to raise questions and make comments? ____ ____
6. Do you believe your performance was objectively appraised?
7. Was your "personality" being appraised rather than your performance on the job? ____ ____
8. During the discussion, were you asked to appraise your performance in any areas of your responsibilities? ____ ____
9. Did the discussion clarify what your immediate superior expects of you? ____ ____
10. Did the discussion clarify your responsibilities and authorities? ____ ____
11. Do you understand your immediate superior's job better as a result of the discussion? ____ ____
12. Do you believe your supervisor understands you better as a result of the discussion? ____ ____
13. From the discussion, do you think he knows what you do well and in which areas you need improvement? ____ ____
14. Was he hesitant about telling you that you needed improvement in certain areas? ____ ____
15. Did he have any helpful suggestions as to how you could improve? ____ ____
16. Did you contribute to the discussion as to how you could improve? ____ ____
17. Were specific plans made to help you do a better job? ____ ____
18. If plans were made, who was to follow through to see that they were carried out? _____

	Yes	No

19. Were the plans carried out? ____ ____
20. Did you leave the discussion with a clear idea of what would happen next regarding improving your performance? ____ ____
21. Give any suggestions that you think would make the appraisal and development program more helpful to you. _____

Figure 20–5 Performance appraisal questionnaire useful to the supervisor.

SUMMARY

Supervisors should understand the process of performance appraisals and why they are a necessary part of supervision. Appraisals are a formal rating of the job performance of an individual to determine a change in compensation, a need for additional training or counseling, and promotion possibilities. Just as important, however, appraisals permit supervisors to know the workers better and to inform the workers about their progress in the organization. Although employees generally do not like to be appraised any more than the supervisors like to appraise, this is, nevertheless, a necessary part of supervision.

The appraisal system includes the steps of a job description, a measurable means to determine performance, the establishment of a time period, and the appraisal review interview. Types of appraisal systems can be many; the most common types are rating scales and management by objectives (MBO). Both methods are subject to human errors, but MBO tends to be most suitable in jobs with more responsibility.

Appraisal interviews offer the supervisor a tremendous opportunity to assist the workers in improvement of their performance, growth, and development.

KEY CONCEPTS

Performance appraisal systems. These are complex systems, but conceptually they are instituted because a supervisor may not be properly informing or being informed of each worker's performance, progress and need for counseling, training and support. Therefore, a system is superimposed to aid the supervisor in the performance of his duties in addition to standardizing data for organizational use.

Objective ratings. This may appear to be set, but many abilities and qualities possessed by individuals may not be quantifiable. Therefore objectivity means that these difficult-to-measure qualities should be an intricate part of the appraisal system. Otherwise, politics, favors, and cronies could become beneficiaries of highly subjective types of rating systems.

Management by objectives. This concept can be very useful. It forces the involvement of the worker in performance, planning, control, and appraisal. The major aspect of this concept is communication between the supervisor and the worker.

IMPORTANT TERMS

Career paths   Forced choice rating

Forced distribution rating
Management by objectives
Performance appraisal interview

Ranking as an appraisal
Rating scales
Weighted checklist rating

INCIDENTS

The Perfect Appraisal Interview

"I'm really looking forward to the semiannual performance appraisal interview tomorrow," said Pat Murphy, the supervisor of the packaging department at the Goodall Chemical Company in Jacksonville, Florida. "This will give me the opportunity to really 'come down hard' on Rob Massingale." Pat reflected on this statement's meaning as he related it to his fellow department head, Helmut Wagner. Helmut questioned Pat by saying, "Pat, do you really mean that? Look at the consequences if you use the system to your advantage." Pat thought about Helmut's warnings but he just had to do something drastic to get Rob Massingale back into line. Massingale had been goofing off long enough so that his disinterest had seriously affected the productivity of the entire department. Pat thought he couldn't allow Massingale to further deter the otherwise fine output of the department.

Massingale was the first interviewee scheduled for 9:30 A.M. the following day. Pat looked at his stack of personnel folders piled high on his desk and proceeded to study Massingale's folder that lay on top. Massingale's folder included his own appraisal of Massingale's record, as shown in the exhibit. He began to visualize the impending meeting and his appointment with Massingale.

The door to Pat's office opened and Ron Abercrombie, a supervisor of the bottling department entered.

"What are you mumbling about, Pat?" Ron asked.

"You know the guy that's giving me fits in packaging? I've decided to really lower the boom on him during his performance review tomorrow," Pat replied.

"Look at Massingale's production quality," said Pat as he pointed to the department's annual production statistics spread out on his desk. Ron bent over to inspect the record. Pat told Ron about Massingale's production record and his penchant to slack off. He told about how he was going to use the performance interview as a device to teach Massingale a lesson as he showed Ron his performance appraisal for Massingale.

What do you surmise are the problem(s) indicated in this incident? What would you do in this situation? Do you think Murphy is correct or incorrect in his behavior toward Massingale? Why has Pat told two other supervisors about his intention toward Massingale? Is this good supervision?

Goodall Chemical Company
Jacksonville, Florida

Personal Appraisal Form

Name: __Rob Massingale__   Date: __January 1, 198-__

Job Title: __Packer__   Length of Co. Service: __3 yrs__

Performance Rating

	Low	Medium	High
Quality of production			X
Quantity of production	X		
Intelligence	X		
Willingness to work	X		
Willingness to take orders			X
Overall contribution to dept.	X		
Ability to work with others		X	

Recommended Disposition:

Promote	Pay Raise	Transfer	Layoff
		X	

Department: __Packaging__   Authorized by:

Patrick Murphy
Supervisor

Incident Problem: The Perfect Appraisal Interview—Role Play Role play the above incident during the 9:30 appointment between Massingale with his supervisor, Murphy.

Pat Murphy visited a bar on his way home from work last night and is suffering from the morning-after effects of the night-before overindulgence. Proceed with the role play with one person playing Rob Massingale entering Pat Murphy's office, played by another individual.

Putting Numbers on People[1]

Assume that you are a supervisor working in an engineering organization. You supervise six people that you have to rank from highest to lowest as part of their performance appraisal review. The rating scale ranges from the most outstanding to the most unsatisfactory.

The six people are Simmons, Kelly, Nussmier, Rossi, Lynch, and Snyder.

Simmons can be rated the highest as his record is outstanding in these areas:

Quality of work

Quantity of work

Knowledge of work

Attitudes toward supervisor, company, products, and job

Relations with others

Initiative and responsibility

Dependability

Kelly can be ranked the lowest as his record is the most dismal when using the above criteria.

The remaining four people have to be ranked within these two boundaries. The following information is known about these four individuals:

Nussmier. His wife believes money is going out of style and she is determined not to be caught with any of it. He has an allergy toward work that seems to strike when sufficient sick time leave has been accrued. When working, Nussmier is very productive and he exhibits a high knowledge of the job.

Rossi. He has recently been granted a divorce from his wife who now has custody of their child. They both are living in another city, 200 miles away. He received a promotion about two years ago to a position that you feel is one step above his level of competence (the Peter principle). The quality of his work produced is far less than desirable.

Lynch. He is well motivated, shows excellent drive, but lacks the necessary formal education to meet minimum requirements for promotion.

Snyder. She is well motivated, extremely fast, accurate, and does considerably more than her share of the workload. However, she has made it very clear that she doesn't want any more responsibility or a promotion that would force her to spend less time with her family.

---

[1] The authors are indebted to Mr. Billie R. Taylor for his contribution to this incident.

Where do these people belong on the rating scale? Do you qualify their performances against the criteria and then write down the numbers? Anyone who has experienced this type of rating form is well aware of the difficulty involved in assigning a number that can be justified.

As the supervisor, you must submit the report to your boss. Rate the other four people—Nussmier, Rossi, Lynch, and Snyder—on the following rating scale.

AJAX ENGINEERING COMPANY
Rating Scale

Number	1	Simmons
	2	
	3	
	4	
	5	
	6	Kelly

QUESTIONS FOR DISCUSSION

1. Discuss the importance of a supervisor letting people know their progress within the organization.
2. Can performance appraisals hurt an individual's job satisfaction? If so, how and why?
3. Why do supervisors often dread the performance appraisal system, particularly the interview?
4. Determine what type of appraisal system you would use for the following jobs in a bank:
   (a) Teller.
   (b) Posting clerk.
   (c) Loan officer.
   (d) Cashier.
   (e) Information clerk.
   (f) Bank security guard.
5. If the major limitations of the appraisal system are human error, what are they and why do they constitute limitations to the system's effectiveness?
6. What's wrong with this appraisal interview approach? "Sit down, Matt —I want to inform you that your performance is *not* up to standards."
7. What is the difference between a graphic rating scale and a frequency rating scale?
8. What are the merits of an MBO system over the traditional rating systems?
9. Why must participative supervision be an integral part of an MBO system?

CHAPTER XXI
Maintaining Discipline and Morale

LEARNING OBJECTIVES

- *To understand the meaning of discipline, both as a condition and as an action, and the pros and cons of the two broad approaches to discipline available to the supervisor.*
- *To develop an awareness of the several basic principles and considerations that must be followed to achieve a condition of good discipline and/or to make disciplinary action effective.*
- *To recognize that the supervisor plays the major role in creating a work environment conducive to good discipline, and to identify the supervisory characteristics and actions helpful in this process.*
- *To understand the procedural steps that should be followed in taking disciplinary action if it is to be effective and to protect both the employee and the supervisor.*
- *To recognize that morale is a complex quality, the development of which depends on the employee and on internal and external factors.*
- *To identify the several recognized techniques for measuring and improving the morale of the work force.*

Introduction

Discipline and morale are closely interrelated. Both are major factors influencing the frequency and severity of grievances and related problems. The supervisors, being at the interface between management and the hourly employee, play a vital role in developing and maintaining conditions of good discipline and high morale.

EFFECTIVE DISCIPLINE

THE MEANING OF DISCIPLINE A number of misconceptions exist concerning just what is meant by discipline. Perhaps the most unfortunate misunderstanding is the belief held by many persons that discipline always means punishment. In actual fact, punishment should be the last resort of the effective supervisor in achieving discipline. It should be tried only after all other methods have failed. Punishment alone rarely motivates the worker; it is more likely to result in the minimum response necessary to prevent further punishment.

Discipline involves aspects of both a condition and an action. We will use the term *discipline* to connote the aspect of condition, and the terms *disciplinary action,* and *to discipline* for the aspect of action. The supervisor must approach both terms in relation to the industrial or commercial environment within which he works.

Business and industrial organizations must have a framework of policies, rules, and procedures that enable members of management and hourly employees to work together in an orderly, systematic manner to achieve company goals and at the same time to satisfy personal needs. Without order and system, operations become chaotic and inefficient, and both the company's existence and the jobs it provides are threatened.

The term *discipline* essentially encompasses three interrelated factors:

1. The framework of policies, rules, and procedures established by the organization.
2. The employee's and supervisor's attitude toward, and degree of compliance with, this framework.
3. The leadership process—example, instruction, training, and so on—exercised by the supervisor that largely determines the employee's attitude and compliance.

In other words, *discipline* might be described as orderly conduct based on definite standards catalyzed by effective leadership.

When *good discipline* prevails within an organization, employees follow the applicable policies, rules, and procedures and willingly obey their superior's orders. Employees recognize that they are working for the good of the group, as well as for their own benefit, and avoid actions that would interfere with the rights and privileges of others in the group. They are aware of the standards of conduct and performance expected of them, and of the reactions if these are not met. Above all, they accept the framework as just and logical because they realize that it works to their advantage over the long run.

Conversely, when *poor discipline* exists, the employee is not following the rules of the organization or the orders of superiors. This will show up in conduct and work performance in varying degrees, from a general dragging of the feet to, in extreme cases, outright disobedience. The fault usually is considered to rest on some trait or characteristic of the worker. However, conditions contributing to poor discipline can be caused by weaknesses within the organizational structure or by external factors. The wise supervisor will recognize this possibility and examine all factors for causes before resorting to disciplinary action against the individual.

Disciplinary action consists of the steps taken to correct a condition of poor discipline. It implies some type of penalty backed up by the authority of the organization. The penalty may range from a simple warning through layoffs of varying length to, in the most serious cases, discharge of the offending worker. The term also should include corrective training and instruction, which may be the applicable action in some instances.

Some authorities broaden the scope of the term *disciplinary action* to include steps taken to correct poor discipline when the company or external factors are at fault. Such action might include periodic review of policies, rules, and procedures to see if these are still pertinent; removing the cause; and demonstrating to the employees that the company is trying to be fair. However, these actions might be considered to fall more logically within the area of morale rather than disciplinary action.

It may be seen from the preceding discussion that discipline is, in a sense, a means of motivation. Most people work better under a set of rules. They want to have a definite goal, to know what is expected of them, where they stand, and what will happen if they don't measure up, as the following example illustrates.

The supervisor, Miss Smith, was very sensitive to the opinion of others—she wanted to be liked by everyone. As a result, she did not enforce office rules very stringently. As Alice Newell put it: "Under Miss Smith you could get away with little things. Some of the girls took advantage of this and tried to get away with bigger things like taking an extra half-hour at lunch to go shopping or taking sick leave when they weren't sick. Then, when the office manager would get fed up and complain, Miss Smith would suddenly have to crack down.

"Mrs. Roberts, our new supervisor, is tougher, but at least we know where we stand with her, what we can do, and what we can't do."

APPROACHES TO DISCIPLINE

General agreement exists that two broad approaches to discipline may be followed: negative and positive.[1] In their "pure" form, if such can be found, these approaches represent two extremes. Although some companies may lean predominantly toward one or the other approach, a combination of the two usually works best in actual practice. The negative approach is mentioned first because it is the older, traditional approach.

---

[1]Chapter XV discusses the leadership styles associated with these two approaches to discipline. See also the discussion of Theory X and Theory Y in Chapter XIII.

Negative Discipline   The negative approach to discipline also is referred to as the punitive, judicial, or autocratic approach by some specialists in the field. This approach to discipline is based on the assumptions, proposed by some persons, that work is inherently distasteful—that most people have little ambition, wish to avoid responsibility, and need to be directed.

The supervisor taking this approach tends to abide rigidly by the rule book in determining if an infraction has occurred and in applying the penalty. There is little concern with getting at the root cause in order to improve future performance.

This approach to discipline within an organization is based on the recognized right, or authority, of a superior to give commands to a subordinate. Compliance with the framework of policies, rules, and procedures is attained chiefly through fear of penalties. Disciplinary action is considered as part deterrent and part retribution.

The strongest feature of negative discipline rests on the certainty and uniformity of application. The major drawbacks are that workers may perform just sufficiently to get by without penalties, and that truly corrective or rehabilitative action probably does not take place.

Positive Discipline   The positive approach to discipline also is referred to variously as the corrective, constructive, or human relations approach. It is based on a set of assumptions about people different from the assumptions mentioned in discussing negative discipline.

The positive approach assumes that work is a normal part of human life. It assumes that the average person can learn to accept and even seek responsibility, that he/she has the capability of exercising ingenuity in solving problems, and that he/she can develop self-control and self-direction in reaching a desired goal.

Positive discipline is discipline willingly imposed by the employee on himself as the result of effective leadership by the supervisor. The supervisor has been able to convince the employee that the greatest advantage to the individual and to the group comes from working cooperatively within the established framework. Furthermore, the skillful supervisor, through knowledge of the strengths and weaknesses of each employee, helps each to develop fuller utilization of individual capabilities. Emphasis in this approach is directed at action to improve employees' conduct and their capability for self-direction. It is corrective rather than punitive.

Interdependency of Approaches   No two people are exactly alike. Even under the most modern, progressive mangement practices, an organization will have some "Theory X people" in its employ. Similarly, the most autocratic of organizations will have some "Theory Y people." Extremes in disciplinary approaches, therefore, should be avoided. Most organizations will find it advantageous over the long run to develop a balanced approach, leaning toward the positive, corrective philosophy as far as possible, but making constructive use of the traditional approach when the need for this is indicated.

In actual fact, few companies are completely negative or completely positive in their approach. Most do strike a middle ground. The problem is to determine for a particular organization the location of the appropriate middle ground within the spectrum of possibilities.

SOME BASIC PRINCIPLES AND CONSIDERATIONS

Effective discipline teaches through experience. The analogy of the hot stove illustrates this. At the same time, it points out four basic principles of discipline—the disciplinary process should provide *advance warning* of the consequences of misconduct, and the event of misconduct disciplinary action should be *immediate, consistent,* and *impersonal.* Let us look at what happens when you touch a hot stove.

1. Advance warning. The feel of heat or the color of the stove warned you that the stove was hot.
2. Immediate. You are burned right now as an immediate result of touching the stove.
3. Consistent. You are burned every time you touch the stove.
4. Impersonal. The stove has no feelings toward you individually; everyone who touches the stove is burned.

In other words, discipline is directed against the act, not the person. Following these principles makes the committed act and the discipline incurred seem almost one.

It also is a principle of discipline that supervisors must set the example and follow the same rules, where pertinent, as the hourly employees.

At a small stove factory, a press brake designed for safe operation by one man was used to form sheet metal parts. The general foreman had developed the practice during rush periods of removing the safety fence from the machine. He would then feed material into the machine, a second man would operate the controls, and a third man would remove the finished pieces. This was a hazardous practice and clearly violated safety rules. This practice was not stopped until one day when an inspector from the insurance company walked in on a surprise visit and caught the foreman red-handed. Not only was this a very poor example for the foreman to set, but his prestige was not helped by the tongue-lashing the inspector gave him in front of the employees.

Another principle is that the framework of policies, rules, and procedures must be clear and their requirements must be fair. It is good practice to review these periodically for ambiguous expressions and continued applicability. Poorly phrased statements should be rephrased, and those no longer applicable should be eliminated. In many instances, this will require joint action by the supervisor and his superiors.

Adequate records should be kept for each employee with respect to all infractions, the circumstances surrounding the occurrence, and the penalties imposed or other action taken.

The basic principles of discipline and disciplinary action may be itemized as follows.

1. Policy, procedures, and rules must be established.
2. Rules and standards must be reasonable and reviewed periodically for adequacy, relevancy, and so on.
3. Rules and standards must be communicated to employees.
4. Disciplinary action must be consistent.
5. Disciplinary action must be applied impersonally.
6. Disciplinary action should be applied immediately (within reason).
7. Supervisors and managers must observe the same policies and rules.
8. Extenuating circumstances of individual cases must be considered.
9. The burden of proof rests with management.
10. Progressive penalties are desirable.
11. Adequate records must be kept.
12. Employees must be given the right of appeal.

More will be said later concerning application of all of these principles.

THE SUPERVISOR'S ROLE IN INSPIRING DISCIPLINE

Good discipline is dependent on management's motivating efforts. The major role is played by the supervisor who transmits policies, rules, and procedures to the hourly employees; gives them orders in connection with their work; is the first person to be involved in handling infractions; and, in general, establishes the climate under which discipline either develops or regresses.

The criticality of this role is emphasized by the fact that the most common single source of grievances is a claim by the worker that some disciplinary action was either unwarranted or, at best, too severe or not in line with terms of the labor contract. Disciplinary cases comprise one of the five most common types of grievances carried all the way to arbitration. This subject is treated in detail in Chapter XXII.

THE WORKING ENVIRONMENT   The supervisor is the most important factor in developing the climate, practices, and attitudes leading to good discipline at the lower levels. The supervisor must provide basic orientation to new employees and continue with information, instruction, and training so that all workers will be familiar with what is expected of them.

Within reason, and where emotions are not inflamed, explanation is a useful tool in getting the job done. It usually succeeds better than the "Do it because I say so" approach. Along this same line, the supervisor can help establish a favorable environment by being willing to listen to suggestions from workers. Experience will tell him when it is time to "cut out the gab," whether he is explaining something to a worker or listening to a suggestion.

The personnel department normally is responsible for initial placement of workers in job areas. However, the supervisor usually has considerable leeway in assigning workers to tasks within his work group. Proper assignment of workers is conducive to good discipline. An employee assigned to a job for which he has no aptitude, or which is below his capabilities, is a potential disciplinary problem as well as representing an inefficient use of human resources.

Employees with physiological limitations, or who are emotionally unstable, require careful consideration by the supervisor in matters of discipline. Employees with such problems should be caught during the medical checkup and interview that is customary in most hiring practices. However, some disorders sneak through these check points, and some develop after the worker is on the job.

Finally, the supervisor must remember that people bring their personal problems to work with them. Such problems cannot be turned off and on as the employee enters and leaves the gates. Domestic, social, or financial problems can affect even the best worker on the job, causing him to react adversely. Supervisors who have taken the trouble to know their people and who are alert to changes in behavior patterns will recognize this type of problem more easily.

Counseling ability and skills in nondirective interviewing techniques will help in identifying the exact nature of the problem. In other words, it is highly desirable to take prompt investigative action before trouble starts.

A discussion of the working environment is not complete without emphasizing that inept supervisors can be a cause of poor discipline. For example, they may lack self-discipline, be too lenient or too strict, play favorites, hold grudges, reflect poor attitudes toward company policies and rules, fail to draw clear lines between what can and cannot be done, or fail to take corrective actions when needed. Any of these characteristics in a supervisor can contribute to an environment in which good discipline has difficulty surviving.

CONSISTENCY IN DISCIPLINE Consistency has been mentioned previously as one of the basic principles of discipline. It is quite natural that employees want to know what the supervisor's reaction will be to any given situation. This, of course, points up the need for adequate communication to the employees of appropriate information on rules, penalties, and so on.

Dissimilar treatment of employees under identical conditions weakens leadership and creates morale problems. Occasionally, disciplinary situations may arise that appear identical at first glance, but the supervisor recognizes some slight difference in circumstances that causes him to handle the problems differently. Such situations must be treated very carefully. In particular, all participants must be made to understand the reasons for different treatment.

The changing of rules, or of customary practices, may bring about problems in consistency. Take, for example, a situation in which a "No Smoking" sign has been posted in a hazardous area for a long time. Let us assume, as frequently happens, that enforcement of this rule has gradually declined until workers have become accustomed to ignoring this sign without penalty. Then for some reason, perhaps a fire in a nearby plant, upper mangement suddenly decides that this particular rule must be enforced rigidly. It would be bad for discipline for the supervisor to crack down suddenly with a penalty on the next employee seen smoking in the area even though the sign is in clear sight. The inevitable reaction from the employee would be "Why pick on me? Why didn't you jump on Joe when he was smoking here yesterday?"

The proper approach would be for the supervisor to institute a short transition or learning period of two or three days, for example. It should be announced to the work force that effective on such and such date, the "No Smoking" rule will be enforced rigidly according to the rules and procedures in the manual. The supervisor should be certain that all persons concerned understand fully and clearly why this action is being taken and that the company means business in this matter. Habit is a strong force, as any smoker knows. During the transition period, the supervisor should keep an eye on the area and be ready with a cautionary warning when needed, which, of course, would *not* go on the employee's record.

Consistency, however, does not necessarily mean inflexibility. Most employees want their supervisor to be predictable but not inflexible. The labor relations climate tends to influence the mix of consistency and flexibility that will be practical. When labor relations are good and the supervisors competent, then flexibility is quite feasible. But when labor relations are strained, then emphasis on consistency probably is the wisest course.

LEAVING THE DOOR OPEN FOR CORRECTION

Because the purpose of discipline is corrective, not punitive, the supervisor will provide incentives for improvement in conduct. Nothing should be said or done to discourage or prevent a violator of some rule from voluntarily trying to improve. Effective supervisors know that their goal is to prevent future violations, not just to exercise authority for authority's sake.

DISCIPLINARY ACTION AS A LAST RESORT

Disciplinary action should be applied by the supervisor only as a last resort after other efforts to secure orderly conduct have failed. When the supervisor decides that action must be taken, it should be applied quickly and firmly. Hesitancy or an excessive time lag cause the action to lose much of its effectiveness. Playing "cat and mouse" with the employee, that is, letting the employee worry a little before you pounce, does more harm in terms of future relations than it does good at the present time.

In applying disciplinary action, supervisors must take care not to become emotionally involved. If they have any strong feelings of anger or disgust, they must hide these at the actual time of implementing a penalty. All employees must believe that disciplinary action follows a fair, judicial approach—that it is not vindictive—and that it is their behavior at the moment that is being criticized, not themselves personally.

KEEPING RECORDS

The personnel department normally keeps a record in each employee's file concerning disciplinary warnings, penalties, and other actions plus information concerning the attendant circumstances. It is a good idea for the supervisor to keep similar records on the work crew, at least in abbreviated form since the personnel files always can be checked for details. Records also are helpful when attempting to justify a supervisor's position in an arbitration or Equal Employment Opportunity Commission (EEOC) case hearing.

Records of past violations provide a guide when considering the severity of penalty for a current violation. However, there should be a time limit with respect to consideration of past violations as they affect the current situation. Progressive personnel policies provide for "wiping the slate clean" after a certain length of time has passed. The time limit may vary with the severity of the violation. Three years is a common figure for minor violations.

PROCEDURES IN DISCIPLINARY ACTION

Disciplinary action is a management tool, and like all tools it can turn upon the user if not handled properly. Experience has shown that the greatest effectiveness results when certain steps are followed in the disciplinary process. These steps are as follows.

1. State and accurately describe the problem.
2. Collect all facts concerning the problem.
3. Decide on the appropriate penalty.
4. Apply the penalty.
5. Follow up the situation.

Depending on the nature of the labor contract and union-management relations in general, consultation with the appropriate union officials may constitute an additional step. Unions almost always have an interest in disciplinary matters.

STATING THE PROBLEM

The supervisor's first reaction to an apparent violation of the rules is not necessarily correct. A cardinal rule in applying discipline is "Don't shoot from the hip." This does not violate the principle of immediate action. Employees have the right to expect the supervisor to spend the time necessary to give their case a thorough investigation. It does follow, though, that supervisors should start their investigation as soon as possible. Apparent offenders should be given the chance early in the process to describe their version of the situation.

In stating and accurately describing the problem, the supervisor must determine if a violation actually did occur. Extenuating circumstances can modify the severity of a penalty, or even excuse a violation in some instances. If a violation did occur, which particular rule was broken? It is well to remember that action, or lack of it, by one person can cause another person to violate a rule. Thus it must be stated which person or persons were involved, directly or indirectly.

Time, place, and other circumstances also must be described and recorded. A violation occurring in the middle of a shift may have entirely different causes (and consequences) from the same violation occurring a few minutes before the whistle blows. The "no smoking" rule may prevail in two different plant areas, but a violation of this rule in one area could be much more hazardous than in the other.

COLLECTING FACTS

Some basic facts will have been assembled in the first step of stating and describing the problem. However, if the problem is of sufficient importance to warrant further investigation, additional facts must be sought. Disciplinary records should be checked for the past history, if any, of previous violations by the offender.

It may be desirable to interview participants and witnesses. The supervisor should be careful when interviewing to distinguish between opinion and fact. In all investigations, the appearance of spying should be avoided.

Finally, the supervisor's assemblage of facts must be such that he is confident of their accuracy and completeness and is willing to stand behind them if questioned.

DECIDING ON THE PENALTY

Before the supervisor can decide on the appropriate penalty, it is necessary to know which penalties can be applied to a particular situation. Every company should prepare a chart listing various types of violations and the applicable penalties for the first and subsequent occurrences of each. The more progressive personnel policies use such charts as guides, rather than applying them rigidly, and give the supervisor some latitude in judging circumstances of individual cases and selecting an appropriate penalty.

New employees should be made thoroughly familiar with these charts and their application during the orientation period (the advance warning principle). There is some disagreement, however, among authorities on the value of posting disciplinary charts in such public places as bulletin boards or near drinking fountains. Orientation material, including a list of work rules and penalties for violations, often is printed in a manual distributed to all new employees.

The concept of a sequence of increasingly severe penalties for repeated violations of a rule is commonly referred to as *progressive discipline*. It is a result of the growing belief that disciplinary action should be a learning experience—that its purpose is correction, not punishment.

Penalties become more severe with repeated violations of the same rule, although there are some violations for which a second chance should not be given. A typical chart, for example, might indicate immediate discharge as the penalty for the first occurrence of such serious offenses as theft or deliberate destruction of company property. Offenses of medium seriousness, such as fighting or entering restricted areas without permission, might indicate a one-day layoff for the first occurrence, a one-week layoff for the second, and discharge for the third. Mild violations might start with a reprimand for the first offense and progress through layoffs of increasing length for repeated incidents to discharge for the fifth occurrence of the same offense.

In deciding on the penalty, supervisors must weigh all facts and be careful not to underpenalize or overpenalize. Remember that the action taken may set a precedent.

APPLYING THE PENALTY

It is always unpleasant to be forced to punish someone. Nevertheless, it is necessary on occasion. A positive attitude free of either apology or emotional bias is required. Reprimands or simple warnings should be given calmly and quickly. There is no need to overemphasize such incidents. On the other hand, more serious penalties require some formality that helps to impress the worker with a realization of the seriousness of the situation.

It is imperative that the supervisor recognize the differences in individual personalities and the relation of these to disciplinary action. There is one type of worker for whom a public reprimand or warning causes such embarrassment, and consequently resentment, that the intended effect is lost. More harm is done than good. A warning in the privacy of the supervisor's office may be much more effective with this type of individual. With another type of personality, private warnings seem to go in one ear and out the other. Public action often is more effective in improving the conduct of such people.

Unfortunately, there is an increasing tendency in our society for people to go to court at the slightest excuse. Many supervisors are beginning to feel that no aspect of disciplinary action, from simple warnings on up, should be taken except in the presence of witnesses in order to protect themselves against possible claims of mistreatment. This is a matter of personal judgment and reinforces our often repeated advice to know your people.

The final rule in applying a penalty, once it has been decided on, is not to delay. The greater is the time lag between violation and disciplinary action, the less effective is the action.

FOLLOW-UP

Because disciplining often is unpleasant, some supervisors want to forget it as soon as the penalty is applied. However, the purpose of disciplinary action is to improve future conduct. Therefore it is necessary to follow up a disciplinary case to determine if attitude and performance are improved.

This requires careful handling. The follow-up of mild cases should be unobtrusive. On the other hand, it does not hurt to let offenders in a severe violation case know that they are being checked on. This helps impress upon them the seriousness of the situation.

ROLE OF THE UNION

Most companies would prefer that disciplinary action be an uncontested right of management. If the company is not unionized, then this usually is the case. However, most labor contracts have written into them provisions concerning some aspects of disciplinary action as it relates to the hourly worker. The number and nature of these provisions vary appreciably from contract to contract. Where these exist, the supervisor must, of course, know and follow them.

The supervisor should not automatically assume that the union is a roadblock in the exercise of supervisory functions. It is often possible to enlist the help of the union in disciplinary situations both in the setting up of basic rules and procedures and in the enforcement process.

The supervisor must remember, however, that if the unionized employee feels that the disciplinary action was unjust in any way, then he has the right to file a grievance. The employee has the right to do this himself or to ask the union steward to do it for him. This reinforces the need for the supervisor to be confident of the accuracy of the facts and the correctness of the action. The supervisor will not be right all of the time, but hopefully will be so most of the time.

EMPLOYEE MORALE

THE MEANING OF MORALE

If discipline is described as orderly conduct based on definite standards, then morale might be described as the spirit and confidence with which the worker performs his job. Both are catalyzed by effective leadership.

The preceding explanation is an oversimplification. Morale is a complex, psychological quality impossible to force on someone, difficult to measure, and easily destroyed. It is an elusive subject—there are more different definitions of morale than of discipline.

Conditions of *poor morale* usually are the result of poor management practices by the company, or the result of employees' misinterpretation of management actions. Thus effective leadership and motivational practices by management, and continuous two-way communications between management and hourly employees are vital.

DEVELOPMENT OF MORALE

The level of morale is a result of the degree to which the overall needs of the individual are fulfilled. The needs of individuals, and of workers on the job, are discussed in Chapter IX. For *good morale* to exist in a group, each member of the group must be made to realize that satisfaction of personal needs is mutually dependent on satisfaction of the other workers' needs.

Although many factors influence morale development, it is common to group these into three broad classifications:

1. Employee factors.
2. Internal (company) factors.
3. External (outside the company) factors.

Employee Factors

The characteristics and traits of the individual have a bearing on efforts to develop a high level of morale. These characteristics may include intelligence level, education, introverted or extroverted personality, ethnic background (in some instances), and status in the group. Morale hinges in part on the fulfillment of needs for belonging, esteem, and self-realization that arise out of these factors.

There is little that the supervisor can do to alter or manipulate all of these factors. However, he can recognize their existence and take them into account in tailoring his own actions to fit the situation.

Internal Factors

Management practices in general, and the first-line supervisor's actions in particular, have a major influence on morale. In fact, internal factors are the most important with respect to morale, because it is in this area that the supervisor has the most control.

Internal factors influencing morale include policies or procedures with respect to wages, promotion methods, employee services and benefits, working conditions, handling grievances, disciplinary actions, and many others.

Communication is yet another factor under company control. The degree to which information is free to flow in both directions between management and the hourly employee, and the nature of the channels provided by management for this flow, can have a decisive impact.

External Factors No employee can leave all thoughts of home and social life behind when he goes to work. Consequently, these factors influence thinking and attitudes while on the job.

Included are the employee's relations with, and the well-being of, family; relations with friends and neighbors; community environment (housing, educational and recreational facilities, and so on); union membership; and numerous others.

The company may have a degree of control over a few of these factors—some aspects of the community environment, for example—but certainly not over all of them.

MEASURING MORALE

The elusive nature of morale makes it very difficult, if not impossible, to measure this quality directly. Yet in order to improve morale, we must know its present level. Several methods of measurement are in use, but all are indirect and none are perfect.

PERSONAL OBSERVATIONS Personal observation of the work force by the supervisor can be very useful, but it seldom is employed as effectively as it can be. The supervisor must practice this consciously, continuously, and systematically. A change in employees' work habits is an obvious red flag. However, if the change is gradual, the supervisor may be slow in recognizing it. More subtle measures of attitude, of the kind that only experience can detect, include the expression in a worker's voice, mannerisms in gestures, and even how a person walks.

The principal drawback of this method of measurement is that a significant time lag usually exists between initiation of the cause and observance of the effect.

INFORMAL INTERVIEWS To be effective, interviews should be initiated by management rather than by employees, even though it is wise to maintain an open-door policy. Effective interviewing also must be carefully planned; the questions and path of discussion must be carefully structured. At the same time, the atmosphere must be kept informal. These apparently contradictory requirements can be reconciled by proper training in interview techniques. Effective interviewing is an art and a science—it must be learned. Too many interviews are conducted in a casual, sloppy manner and thereby lose their usefulness.

SURVEYS AND QUESTION-NAIRES

Surveying the work force for attitudes and opinions by means of questionnaires is fairly widely practiced, particularly among larger companies.

As with interviews, the questionnaire should be carefully structured. Questions may be *specific* or *open ended.* In the first instance, a list of answers follows the question and the employee marks the answer that best fits. Specific-type questionnaires are easy for the employee to answer, but are somewhat restrictive. In the case of open-ended questions, employees are asked to express an answer in their own words. This overcomes the restrictive nature of the other type but, by the same token, answers are difficult to tabulate under comparable headings.

Questionnaires may be repeated periodically to determine trends. Some companies summarize the completed questionnaires and then display the results on posters, often with cartoon illustrations pointing up any problems uncovered and promising corrective action.

STATISTICAL METHOD

The *statistical approach* to measurement is somewhat analogous to personal observation. Use of this method involves periodic analysis of data from various records to check for significant deviations from the norm. This type of analysis might cover such data as production, quality, costs, absenteeism, tardiness, frequency of disciplinary actions, or other pertinent indicators.

Trends can be spotted quickly with this approach. However, causes of deviations can stem from factors other than morale, and morale causes are not as readily apparent as with other approaches.

THE MORALE IMPROVEMENT PROGRAM

If periodic measurement of morale indicates a condition of poor morale, or a downtrend in a previously high level of morale, then a corrective program is needed. The major difficulty with all of the methods of measurement previously discussed is in determining the causes behind an indication of poor morale. This is to some extent the fault of the indirect methods of measurement necessarily used.

The steps in planning a morale development program can be laid out in broad-brush form only. Details cannot be filled in until specific causes of poor morale are identified. The suggested steps are as follows.

1. Measure the quality level of present morale.
2. Identify the cause or causes of poor morale. This may require considerable effort and analysis.
3. Locate the areas of poor morale—department and/or individual.
4. Develop plans for counteracting negative factors and strengthening positive factors. This step is highly dependent in detail on identity of the causes.

5. Assign responsibilities for implementing corrective action.
6. Follow up the program after a suitable interval by reappraising morale.

A program of this scope probably will require cooperative action between supervisors and other levels of management. In fact, it is likely to be initiated at an upper level. However, there is no reason why a supervisor could not modify the suggested steps to handle an isolated morale problem within the work group.

MOTIVATIONAL PROGRAMS

Motivational programs often are introduced for purposes other than morale, but they also can contribute significantly to developing or improving morale. A typical program consists of a fairly sizable employee-management committee comprised of various subcommittees responding to the needs and demands of the work force.

A noteworthy example is the PRIDE program (Personal Responsibility In Daily Effort) of Rockwell International's Electronic Systems Group. This program committee includes over 40 persons grouped into subcommittees for such purposes as Innovations, Membership, Communications, Awards, and Special Activities. The PRIDE program has proven very successful and the company frequently is requested to assist other organizations in initiating similar programs.

The so-called Quality Control Circles, implemented at a number of companies, is another example of this general type of program.

EMPLOYEE-ORIENTED SUPERVISION

At a level of effort less formal than motivational programs is the supervisor becoming involved with subordinates in employee-oriented activities. Key factors that also are positive approaches to morale building are recognition, group identification, and goal setting. Actions that supervisors could take might include the celebration of birthdays and hiring dates, taking photographs (instant type) at all occasions and then displaying them, being receptive to "kaffeeklatsch's," and getting a name for the work group and building team spirit around this.

The supervisor might display group goals in the vicinity of the work group area, along with an 8- by 10-inch photo of the group. No individual or group wants to look bad. Opportunities to identify or recognize groups by task should be emphasized. People in general identify with the Boston Red Sox closer than with the American League, and employees with the Claims Processing Section more than with Prudential Insurance. In the Hawthorne studies, described in Chapter XIII, the relay-assembly workers not only increased their production when working conditions improved, but increased production again when conditions were returned to the original state. Recognition as being part of a special test group was a factor here.

SUMMARY

Discipline has been described as orderly conduct based on definite standards catalyzed by effective leadership. *Disciplinary action* consists of those steps taken to correct a condition of poor discipline. A combination of negative and positive approaches (with emphasis on the latter) is most successful in developing and maintaining good discipline.

The supervisor plays the major role in developing the climate, practices, and attitudes conducive to good discipline. The framework of policies, rules, and procedures must be clear and their requirements must be fair. Above all, consistency in the handling and enforcement of disciplinary situations is vital.

The wise supervisor applies disciplinary action only as a last resort after other efforts have failed. Effective procedures for disciplinary action follow a sequence of steps: state and describe the problem, collect all facts, decide on the appropriate penalty, apply the penalty, and follow up to see if improvements occur. Cardinal rules are not to delay or drag out the process, and to keep adequate records.

Morale is closely related to discipline. It is a complex psychological quality difficult to define or measure and easily destroyed. To over-simplify, it might be described as the spirit and confidence with which the worker performs his job.

The development of morale is dependent on the interrelationships of factors in three broad areas: employee characteristics and needs, internal (company), and external (outside the company). The level of morale may be measured by personal observation, informal interviews, surveys and questionnaires, and/or statistical procedures.

KEY CONCEPTS

Discipline. Employees must exhibit orderly conduct within a framework of policies, rules, and procedures if the organization is to be effective in achieving its goals and satisfying the personal needs of its employees. Such a condition is called discipline. Obviously, discipline may be "good" or "poor."

Disciplinary action. The traditional view holds that disciplinary action is a penalty imposed as punishment for misconduct and acts as a deterrent to others. The more modern view is that disciplinary action is a corrective process that may involve penalties on occasion but also includes corrective training and instruction.

Progressive discipline. There is a growing belief that one of the best ways to put the concept of corrective disciplinary action into practice is through progressive discipline. This concept accomplishes the learning or corrective process by providing for a sequence of increasingly severe penalties for repeated infractions of a rule, rather than by always imposing a harsh penalty on first infractions. It recognizes, however, that there are a few types of offenses for which a severe penalty must be imposed for a first occurrence.

Morale. We generally recognize that when any group of people are mutually engaged in some form of organized activity, a complex psychological quality comes into being. This quality is intangible, and its outward form is expressed in the spirit and confidence with which individuals perform their jobs. This spirit, called morale, is impossible to force, difficult to measure, and easily destroyed. As with discipline, morale can be "good" or "poor" from the viewpoint of the organization.

IMPORTANT TERMS

Constructive discipline	Morale
Corrective discipline	Motivational programs
Disciplinary action	Negative discipline
Discipline	Open-ended questionnaire
Employee factors	Poor discipline
Employee-oriented supervision	Poor morale
External factors	Positive discipline
Good discipline	Progressive discipline
Good morale	Punitive discipline
Human relations discipline	Specific questionnaire
Internal factors	Statistical approach
Judicial discipline	Traditional discipline

INCIDENTS

The Practical Joker

Carl Meade has a reputation around the shop as quite a practical joker. He has pulled all the timeworn gags, such as filling a glove with cup grease or sending the new apprentice after a left-handed monkey wrench, plus many more. About three-fourths of the men in the shop think Carl's antics are funny, that he livens things up on dull days. The rest of the men think he is a "pain in the neck" and that someone should crack down on him.

   The supervisor has tended to be neutral, although he has been seen to smile at some of Carl's funnier tricks. However, he did have occasion a couple of weeks ago to caution Carl to "take it easy or someone might get hurt" when one of his practical jokes almost backfired.

Carl did take it easy for a while, but today he greased the seat of the bench stool at Chuck Davis' work place. When Chuck sat down, he slipped off the seat and, in trying to break his fall, wrenched his left elbow and smashed his wrist watch.

The supervisor suspended Carl for three days under Work Rule No. 23 — "General horseplay or other behavior or actions tending to disrupt or interfere with plant operations." Penalties for violation of this rule are a warning for the first offense, three days off for a second offense, and discharge for a third offense. The supervisor considered his cautionary remark made two weeks earlier to Carl to be a warning for a first offense, even though it did not go into the written record.

Chuck Davis, who has been on the receiving end of Carl's jokes before, is furious. He argues bitterly that Carl should be discharged under the last phrase in Work Rule No. 17 — "Willful misuse, destruction, or damage of any company property or property of any employee." The penalty is discharge for a first offense.

In considering this incident, which rule do you think should be applied to Carl's offense? Why? In what way, if any, have the supervisor's past attitude and actions contributed to the present situation? Do you think that either rule should be rewritten in any way?

Incident Problem

Set up and conduct role-playing situations involving different aspects of morale. Divide the class into teams of two or more persons, as appropriate. Let each team first structure a morale situation — developing basic assumptions as to "facts" concerning the type of company and/or departmental unit, company policies and practices, makeup of the work force, the character and personalities of the role participants, the nature of the morale problem or situation, and so on. Teams should vary the locales of their problems between office, shop, warehouse, factory, department store, and the like. Each team then should role play its situation, letting conversations and actions progress naturally, but consistent with the assumed basic "facts."

Some examples of situations that might be developed for role playing are the supervisor attempting to identify the cause of low morale, a personnel specialist interviewing employees in an attempt to measure morale, a motivational program committee trying to decide on the elements of a program, a situation in which an ethnic group within the work force has significantly lower morale than the rest of the work force, and so on. Morale being an elusive subject, considerable imagination and creative effort will be required in developing and setting up realistic situations.

QUESTIONS FOR DISCUSSION

1. Why is a system of rules needed by an organization?

2. Can you visualize a work situation in which "negative discipline" as described in the text might be the best approach for the supervisor to take? If so, described the situation and justify your argument.
3. Develop a set of reasons why most companies strike a middle ground in their approach to discipline.
4. Select any 2 of the 12 basic principles of discipline and disciplinary action itemized in the text and develop arguments to support the principles.
5. What is the purpose in having different levels of penalties that may be imposed for a given infraction?
6. You find two employees engaged in a fist fight. Assuming that disciplinary action will result, what information would you want before handling the situation?
7. Assume that your company distributes a manual containing a list of work rules and penalties for violations to all new employees. In this situation, what would be some arguments for and against the posting of disciplinary charts in public areas of the work place?
8. When will a union steward typically be involved in a disciplinary action case?
9. Three broad categories of factors (employee, internal, and external) are said to influence morale development. From your personal experience, would you consider any one of these to be more important than the others? Why?
10. Does a work environment designed to develop and maintain good discipline necessarily contribute equally to the development of high morale? Why?
11. Compare the advantages and disadvantages of open-ended versus specific questionnaires in appraising morale.
12. Could the statistical approach to measurement of the level of morale identify external factors contributing to poor morale? Explain.
13. Summarize the differences between the "motivational programs" and the "employee-oriented supervision" approaches to development or improvement of morale.

CHAPTER XXII

Handling Complaints and Grievances

LEARNING OBJECTIVES

- *To understand the nature of complaints and grievances, that these may be expressed or unexpressed, and the role that emotional factors and hidden causes may play.*
- *To recognize how complaints and grievances may be caused by factors related to the union contract, to other on-the-job problems, or to off-the-job personal problems.*
- *To become aware of the importance of attempting to settle grievances at the supervisory level, to learn of some factors that contribute to this, and the procedural steps the supervisor should follow.*
- *To understand the characteristics of the typical, formal multistep grievance procedure common in most unionized firms.*
- *To identify the several different procedures for handling grievances that develop in nonunionized firms.*
- *To become familiar with the nature of the arbitration process and its features as the unique and final step in most formal grievance procedures.*

Introduction

In the ideal organization, effective managerial policies and practices should prevent employee dissatisfactions. In real life the ideal is rarely, if ever, attained. Complaints and gripes occur within even the best-managed companies; and it is an unfortunate fact of business life that not all companies are well managed. A keypunch operator gripes to a friend,

"The company should have paid for my dinner when I had to stay late the other night to finish a rush job." A pool typist complains to her supervisor that she gets the difficult reports to type while the typist at the next desk gets the easy form letters. A shop maintenance crew tells the union steward that call-out pay rules were not followed last Thursday. The supervisor contends to the steward that by his interpretation of the union contract, the rules were observed. A formal grievance then is filed by the steward.

What causes these problems? Underlying reasons—to name but a few—may include lack of communications, poor managerial practices, differing interpretations of rules or agreements, personality clashes, and external problems brought onto the job. The direct and indirect costs can be appreciable to both the individual and to the company. In addition to dollar costs, these problems involve considerations of justice and may adversely affect morale and the smooth functioning of operations. It is highly desirable, therefore, to have a systematized procedure, whether formal or informal, to handle such situations as quickly and satisfactorily as possible.

THE NATURE OF COMPLAINTS AND GRIEVANCES

The term *grievance* is defined by some authorities in a narrow legalistic sense as being restricted to those dissatisfactions arising out of alleged or actual violations of provisions in the labor contract. The origin of this restrictive definition probably stems from the customary wording of the articles in the labor contract that cover grievances. A quotation from a typical contract illustrates this usage of the term.

"The term Employee Grievance shall mean any grievance of an employee arising out of the interpretation or application of any of the terms of this Agreement or any alleged breach or violation of the terms of this Agreement. Such an Employee Grievance shall be filed within five (5) working days from the date it was found to exist by an employee or be considered not to exist. The word 'filed' shall mean the first discussion with the supervisor."[1]

When the term *grievance* is used in this narrow sense, then the term *complaint* often is defined as any expressed dissatisfaction over matters other than those covered in the labor contract.

The legalistic approach to grievances is too restrictive to meet the purpose of this book. After all, supervisors are faced with many forms of dissatisfaction, and it is their responsibility to handle them.

[1] Article IX, Section 1, of *Articles of Agreement Between District Lodge No. 837 International Association of Machinists and Aerospace Workers and McDonnell Douglas Corporation,* Effective 17 February 1969.

In this chapter we shall take the broad view and consider the handling of all forms of worker dissatisfaction regardless of cause, expressed or unexpressed, real or imaginary. Many authorities employ the term *grievance* in the broad sense, and we shall do the same.

UNEXPRESSED DISSATISFACTION

Dissatisfactions are not necessarily expressed in verbal or written form. The *unexpressed dissatisfaction* is just as important and worthy of attention as one that is vocalized. It, too, affects employee attitudes, performance, and morale—but with the added disadvantage that, since the dissatisfaction is unexpressed, appreciable time may pass before the supervisor first realizes that something is wrong, can pinpoint the cause, and is able to take corrective action.

The effective supervisor will be alert for the symptoms of unexpressed dissatisfactions. Symptoms may take various forms such as a decline in the quality or quantity of work, sulkiness, overly aggressive actions, indifference, absenteeism, and others. The supervisor should remember that such actions or attitudes are not necessarily, or not always, indicators of dissatisfaction. For example, an undiscovered health problem might be responsible for a decline in work performance or for absenteeism. This possibility emphasizes the need for careful, thorough investigation of possible causes.

There are many reasons why employees may not express their complaints verbally. They may be hesitant because of embarrassment over inability to frame complaints in clear terms. The lack of verbal skills is particularly common among members of some minority groups, although it is found in all categories of workers. Other reasons include the feeling that uttering a complaint may do no good, fear of some kind of retaliation, or the hope that the problem may go away if left alone.

It is here that the skills of the supervisor come to the fore. Supervisory practices play a vital role in establishing the work climate. The supervisor must have gained the confidence of the work group so that they feel free to approach. They must know from past experience that they will receive a fair and understanding hearing, without fear of punitive action. Empathy, ability to analyze human factors, and interviewing skill will enable the supervisor to help those employees who cannot express themselves clearly.

Equally important in handling both expressed and unexpressed complaints is the leadership style of top management. The supervisor's superiors must give him the authority to decide and to act in appropriate situations. Consider the following example.

Stan and Bill are loading castings into crates to be hoisted by a rope sling. The rope is slightly frayed.
Stan: "Hey, Bill, I don't like the looks of that rope. Let's ask the foreman for a new one."

Bill: "Aw, what's the use? Mac's a good guy, but you know darn well that he's got to fill out six forms and ask the plant manager before he can get a drink of water."

THE EMOTIONALITY FACTOR

A characteristic of many expressed complaints or grievances, and one that should not be minimized, is the emotionality factor. Most complaints and grievances involve a combination of facts and emotions. All too often, facts, or alleged facts, are presented to the supervisor in highly emotional terms: anger, bitterness, fear, jealousy. A worker often lets some dissatisfaction build up over a period of time. The more he thinks about it, the more it becomes magnified out of proportion to its true significance. Some minor and perhaps unrelated incident then triggers an emotional outburst. The startled supervisor wonders: "What brought that on?"

The danger here is that the supervisor may not recognize the situation for what it is and may overreact to what he/she thinks is a case of insubordination. The supervisor must remain cool while assessing the situation. An equally aggressive reaction may serve to crystallize the worker's dissatisfaction into a real (to the worker) grievance that he/she will pursue. Emotional outbursts often serve as a safety valve. Once a person has "blown off steam" or "gets a gripe off his/her chest," the matter may go no farther. In many instances, a simple action or a few words of explanation by the supervisor will be all that is needed to arrive at a solution once the air is cleared.

Much depends on the degree of emotionality exhibited by the worker. An abusive harangue, or a belligerent ultimatum, expressed in front of other employees puts the supervisor on the spot. Skillful handling is required to calm down the aggrieved worker without appearing to give in and without suffering a loss of prestige. The work force will respect the supervisor who is fair but firm, decisive but not precipitant in handling such cases.

HIDDEN CAUSES

Another characteristic of some, although certainly not all, complaints is the *hidden cause*. This means that the complaint expressed to the supervisor may not be the real reason for dissatisfaction. The worker is engaging in *rationalization*, one of the most common of several forms of defense mechanisms. Consciously or subconsciously, he is substituting a socially acceptable reason for what he or others might consider an unacceptable reason for dissatisfaction. Broadly speaking, the use of *defense mechanisms* is one method of adjusting to otherwise unsatisfactory situations such as frustrations from blocked goals, the loss of some satisfier, or a threat to one's self-respect. Defensive behavior of this type is used by people in all walks of life and at all levels in the organization. It is considered normal if not carried to extremes.

Money is the most frequently used whipping boy in cases of rationalization. Complaints about company policy, work rules, job classifications, and bias or discrimination also are "acceptable." However, many other "substitute" reasons may be expressed.

Bill's friend and co-worker receives a promotion. Soon thereafter, Bill complains that his wage rate is too low. It is socially unacceptable for him to express feelings of jealousy over a friend's promotion.

Mary Jane requests a change in classification from Typist-II to Typist-I and is turned down. She complains that "Miss Robinson, the supervisor, has a grudge against me." Mary Jane cannot face up to the fact that her own skills are inadequate.

Unless the circumstances surrounding the complaint are clear-cut, the supervisor should consider the possibility of a hidden cause—particularly when the complaint involves wages or other forms of compensation. In the supervisor's subsequent investigation of the complaint, he should be alert for hints and clues as to possible real causes. The supervisor who knows the work force as people and as individuals, not merely as names on a pay schedule, has an advantage in these situations.

SOURCES OF COMPLAINTS AND GRIEVANCES

The causes of complaints and grievances may be classified according to source: (1) those causes related to the labor contract, (2) those causes related to on-the-job problems, and (3) those causes related to off-the-job personal problems.

CONTRACT-RELATED CAUSES

Most contract-related grievances concern violations or alleged violations of terms of the labor agreement. Deliberate violations probably are quite rare. In the great majority of instances, grievances of this kind occur because of differences in interpretation or lack of understanding of some article or section of the labor agreement. It is difficult at best for one individual to prepare a lengthy contract in which the language of all parts is clear and unambiguous. It is not surprising, therefore, that differences of opinion as to meaning occur when we realize that the wording of the average contract is hammered out by two negotiating teams with divergent views and that subsequently it must be followed in practice by persons who had no hand in its writing.

Another type of contract-related cause for grievance may arise from omissions, that is, when no article in the contract covers the problem. Omissions occur most frequently in the area of work rules. It is not always possible to foresee all of the various kinds of problems that can develop. This type of grievance can pose some troublesome questions for the supervisor. Should the supervisor try to handle the matter alone, or should the supervisor "pass the buck" to higher management? If he decides to handle it alone, which of several possible decisions should the supervisor make?

In the long run, the supervisor's decision and action are likely to hinge on the managerial practices of the firm. If the organization practices autocratic leadership, the supervisor almost always will refer the problem to his/her immediate superior. If, on the other hand, the leadership pattern is participative or democratic, the supervisor may decide to handle the matter alone. In any event, the supervisor should proceed carefully; his/her decision or action may set a precedent.

Obviously, it is vital that supervisors be thoroughly conversant with all of the articles and sections of the labor agreement. Supervisors should have a copy of the agreement handy at all times while on the job. Labor agreements usually are printed in booklet form of a size easily carried in a shirt or jacket pocket and are available to both the work force and supervisory personnel. If in doubt about any item in the contract, the supervisor should discuss the matter with his/her superior or the labor relations department.

JOB-RELATED CAUSES

Employee dissatisfactions arising out of factors related to the job but not involving terms of the contract may result in complaints to the union steward or to the supervisor. In such instances, employees frequently feel that they have a legitimate grievance in the legalistic sense of the word. It may take the combined efforts of the union steward and the supervisor to convince the employee that a grievance under the terms of the contract does not exist. Even so, it is the supervisor's responsibility to make every effort to settle the matter to the satisfaction of all concerned.

Job-related causes of dissatisfaction may originate because of (1) job conditions, (2) attitudes or actions of co-workers, or (3) the relationship of the worker to his job.

Complaints about job conditions generally pertain to such things as condition of tools and equipment, supply or quality of work materials, physical comfort, safety, housekeeping, or similar matters. The validity or nonvalidity of such complaints usually is easily determined and the problem is readily solved. Sometimes, however, real ingenuity is required to arrive at a solution. In one of the incidents ("The Problem of the Diesel Trucks") at the end of this chapter, a supervisor developed, in the nick of time, a most ingenious way of solving this real-life problem.

Many complaints are directed at the attitudes, actions, or lack of actions of fellow workers on the job, rather than against management or the company. The validity of such complaints can be difficult to determine. Much depends on the personal characteristics of the supervisor in handling this type of complaint. Supervisors must be tactful, completely fair, and impartial. Above all, they must know the work force—their individual personalities, needs, and backgrounds.

The relationship of the worker to the job may be infinite in its variations. Workers who are inadequate in meeting the requirements of the job are subject to anxieties and fears. They will worry about job security—the possibility of being downgraded or even fired. They may fear losing the esteem of fellow workers because of inability to measure up to group standards. And above all there may be the loss of self-esteem, the fear of failure.

At the opposite end of the scale, we have the situation of the job failing to satisfy the needs of the worker. Individuals bring many different qualities to the job and expect many different things from the job. Some like routine and comfort, whereas others want continual challenge. Others put job security first, and still others are ambitious beyond the limits of the job. The personal needs and the demands placed on the job take many forms. Unsatisfied needs of the competent worker are just as frustrating as the inadequacies of the less competent worker.

Regardless of where the worker is located in the spectrum of possible job relationships, if goals are blocked or if there are conflicting goals, the results are anxieties, fears, and frustrations. In seeking a way out of this dilemma, he may turn to rationalization or to some other form of defensive behavior such as aggression, negativism, or the projection of blame on others. Complaints of the "hidden cause" type often result.

It is far better, and usually easier, to prevent this kind of problem than it is to cure it after it has developed. Prevention is dependent on proper selection and placement of employees, good orientation procedures, and adequate training. Communications play an important role in explaining company policies, work rules, and options open to the employee with respect to assignments, transfers, and channels for advancement.

OFF-THE-JOB PROBLEMS

It has been said that "no man is an island." In the same vein, we can say that no person can isolate fully the off-the-job and the on-the-job portions of his or her life. When an individual walks through the office door or the factory gate in the morning, she or he does not automatically forget the family squabble of the night before, the sick child, or those troublesome mortgage payments. The employee brings personal problems to work and will think about them and worry about them during the work day.

Worry about personal problems while on the job can lead to lowered productivity, carelessness in safety matters, and similar adverse behavior. If personal problems become sufficiently serious, frustrations develop that, in turn, may cause the employee to express dissatisfactions about some aspect of the job.

Most people are reluctant to discuss personal problems with "the boss," feeling that it is none of his business or fearing that the problems may affect his evaluation of them. The supervisor must avoid the appearance of spying or of being "nosy" in trying to determine if personal problems are at the root of complaints. However, if supervisors are familiar with the backgrounds and personalities of each member of the work group, they will spot abnormal behavior quickly and may suspect the real cause. We have emphasized before, and will continue to do so, the importance of supervisors' knowing their people.

There is much that an effective supervisor can do, utilizing the facilities of the organization, to help subordinates with personal problems. For example, most large organizations and many medium-size ones have credit unions, medical services, and even psychiatric and counseling services available to employees and their families. If not, they often have outside specialists or consultants on retainer who are available as needed.

SETTLING GRIEVANCES AT THE SUPERVISORY LEVEL

A basic principle of grievance handling is that the first step in the procedure normally should be an effort to settle the matter in discussion between the employee (and/or the union steward) and the immediate supervisor. There is logic in this. All parties concerned are more likely to be satisfied if the complaint or grievance is handled where and when it occurs, while the facts are still fresh, and by the people immediately involved.

IMPORTANCE OF EARLY SETTLEMENT

Grievance procedures always are costly. In addition to the cost of lost production, the time expended by the supervisor, and by higher management if the grievance is carried upward through channels, is by no means an insignificant cost. Grievance procedures may be costly also in terms of the effect on morale and on labor relations—other employees will be watching to see "just how management fields this one."

The effect of these tangible and intangible costs increases significantly with the number of hierarchical steps through which a grievance is carried before being settled. Conversely, the settling of complaints and grievances at the supervisory level provides many benefits. Loss of production and of managerial time is minimized. Mutual trust and confidence between employees and supervisors is reinforced. The example of satisfactory settlement encourages other workers to bring their problems to the supervisor. The work climate and grass-roots labor relations are improved. As a result, the supervisor's authority and position of leadership are enhanced.

The preceding is not intended in any way to minimize the need for multistep channels for handling grievances. Problems that exceed the authority or ability of the supervisor are bound to arise occasionally. Also, honest differences of opinion will occur between employee and supervisor. Finally, the right of appeal is fundamental in our society's concept of justice. The mere existence of grievance-handling steps beyond the supervisor is reassuring to the average worker, whether the worker uses them or not.

In actual fact, it is probable that, for industry as a whole, about 75 percent of all complaints and grievances brought to the supervisor are settled at the supervisory level. The percentage of complaints and grievances resolved at that level is a good index of how effectively the organization's grievance-handling procedure is functioning.

SOME PERTINENT FACTORS

Top management's basic philosophy—its approach to such matters as managerial style, communications, and labor policy—is an important factor in the likelihood of complaints and grievances being settled at the supervisory level. We have emphasized previously that leadership styles and attitudes tend to flow downward from the top. If higher management takes a "hard-nosed" attitude toward the union, if it is jealous of its managerial prerogatives, and if it is legalistic in its interpretation of the labor contract, then the supervisor will tend to reflect these attitudes. In fact, if this type of pattern has been established, it is doubtful if the supervisor will have the authority necessary to resolve most grievances and it is likely that the grievant will go through the union steward rather than bring the problem directly to the supervisor. The authority of the supervisor must be clearly defined if she/he is to be given the opportunity to make an initial settlement.

The supervisor's attitudes, characteristics, and skills are just as important as higher management's philosophy. They are significant factors in reducing the number of grievances as well as in handling those that are presented. The supervisor must demonstrate a genuine willingness to listen to, and discuss grievance matters with, both the employee and the union steward. The supervisor must remember and accept the fact that under Section 9(a) of the Taft-Hartley Act an employee (or group of employees) can present grievances to management: (1) individually (or as a group), (2) jointly with the union steward, or (3) by having the union steward present it alone. If the individual presents the grievance, then under the same act the settlement must not be inconsistent with the terms of the labor contract, and the bargaining representative (usually the steward) has the right to be present when the settlement is made. In general, the union prefers to be involved from the very beginning.

The supervisor also must accept without prejudice the employee's "right of appeal"—the concept that if employees disagree with the supervisor's solution, they should be able to take their grievance to the next higher step, or steps, in the procedure without fear of vindictive action.

Supervisory training is yet another factor in handling complaints and grievances at the first level. To be effective in this area, the supervisor should be trained in the terms of the labor contract, in the firm's labor policies, and in human relations, interviewing, and counseling skills. A poorly trained supervisor seems to be a magnet for attracting grievances.

Between 15 and 20 percent of labor contracts specify that grievances be put in writing at this first step. Most authorities, however, believe that grievances are handled more readily if not put in writing initially. Workers tend to dislike the task of writing out a grievance for several possible reasons: inability to express themselves clearly, fear that something in writing can be held against them, fear of making a "federal case" out of it, and just plain bother. If the working environment is "right," the informality of oral discussion can get at the root of matters more quickly and easily than a written document.

SUPERVISORY PROCEDURES

Once a grievance has been presented to the first-line supervisor, there is a logical sequence of steps he should follow in handling it. These steps are similar in broad principle to the planning steps described in Chapter II and even more similar to the procedural steps for handling a disciplinary action case, as described in Chapter XXI. There is a reason for this similarity. All three instances represent problem-solving logic modified to meet the particular situation.

The sequence of action to be followed by the supervisor may seem too obvious to put in writing, but it is surprising how many supervisors tend to overlook a critical step.

First is to obtain from the employee a clear and complete oral description of the alleged grievance. Supervisory skills in interviewing will help in drawing out the other person if he has difficulty in expressing himself. Remember, no matter how trivial the problem may seem, it is real and important to the employee and should be treated seriously. The supervisor may wish to rephrase the grievance and see if the employee agrees with this statement of the problem. Also, the supervisor should not forget the possibility of a hidden cause being at work—the possibility that the stated grievance is not the real cause of dissatisfaction.

Once a clear and complete description of the alleged grievance has been obtained, the supervisor may or may not be able to determine immediately whether or not a valid grievance exists. Even if it appears at this point that a valid grievance does not exist, the employee obviously is unhappy about something. The supervisor should go on with the process to straighten out the matter.

The second step is to gather all of the facts concerning the grievance. When, how, and where did the cause happen? What were the circumstances? Was anyone else involved? The nature of the grievance will to a large extent tell the supervisor what kind of facts he needs and where and how to get them. It may be necessary to visit and inspect the scene, interview other persons, check various records, and so on.

In the third step, supervisors should review and study the facts obtained and how they relate to the employee's description of the grievance.

They now should be able to determine, if they have not done so before, whether or not a true grievance exists. If they are unsure of the interpretation of the labor contract as it applies to the subject in question, they should not hesitate to consult their superior or the labor relations department. In some instances the terms of the contract may not permit alternatives, but in other cases they will have a choice as to how the problem can be handled. They should consider these and select the best alternative. Personal experience and records concerning the handling of past grievances will prove helpful.

If the complaint is of such a nature that it does not constitute a grievance as defined by the labor contract, then several alternatives are likely to exist. Here again, precedent in past handling of similar complaints will be helpful.

Fourth, the supervisor should inform the employee of the decision and the action to be taken. This should be done as quickly as possible and in clear terms. Do not forget that even if the aggrieved employee has chosen to carry matters up to this point without the help of the union steward, the steward has the right to be present when the settlement is made.

The final step is to follow up the situation after a reasonable time to see if the employee's dissatisfaction has, in fact, been settled.

FORMAL GRIEVANCE PROCEDURES

The collective bargaining agreement for most unionized organizations will include provisions for handling grievances. Specific sections will define grievances and describe with appropriate detail the procedures for handling them. These sections in the agreement describe a *formalized* grievance procedure that must be followed by both parties.

The presence of grievance procedures in the contract is recognition by both labor and management that disagreements are bound to occur in industrial life. Even though a contract exists, errors in application or compliance and differences in interpretation will happen. The presence of the grievance procedures also is recognition (in most instances, at least) that it is to the advantage of both parties to iron out these disputes in an objective, orderly manner.

PROCEDURAL STEPS The procedures for handling grievances, as found in most labor contracts, have become fairly standardized, although specific details vary from firm to firm. The basic concept is that if disputes cannot be settled at the first-line supervisory level, they will move through successively higher levels of authority until finally settled. Thus the first step typically involves the grievant's immediate supervisor on the part of the company, and his steward on the part of the union. The terminal step, as specified in over 90 percent of labor agreements, is arbitration by an impartial third party. The path commonly followed by a grievance through successive levels and participants in the procedure is indicated in Figure 22-1.

There are usually between three and five steps (authority levels) in the grievance process, from supervisor/steward to arbitration, inclusive. The actual number depends chiefly on the size of the company and its organizational structure. The titles of both union and management participants at these different levels can vary appreciably. The identity of the participants is a function of the organizational setup of the company and the union. In the case of the company, it also depends on policy with respect to direct involvement of line management versus industrial rela-

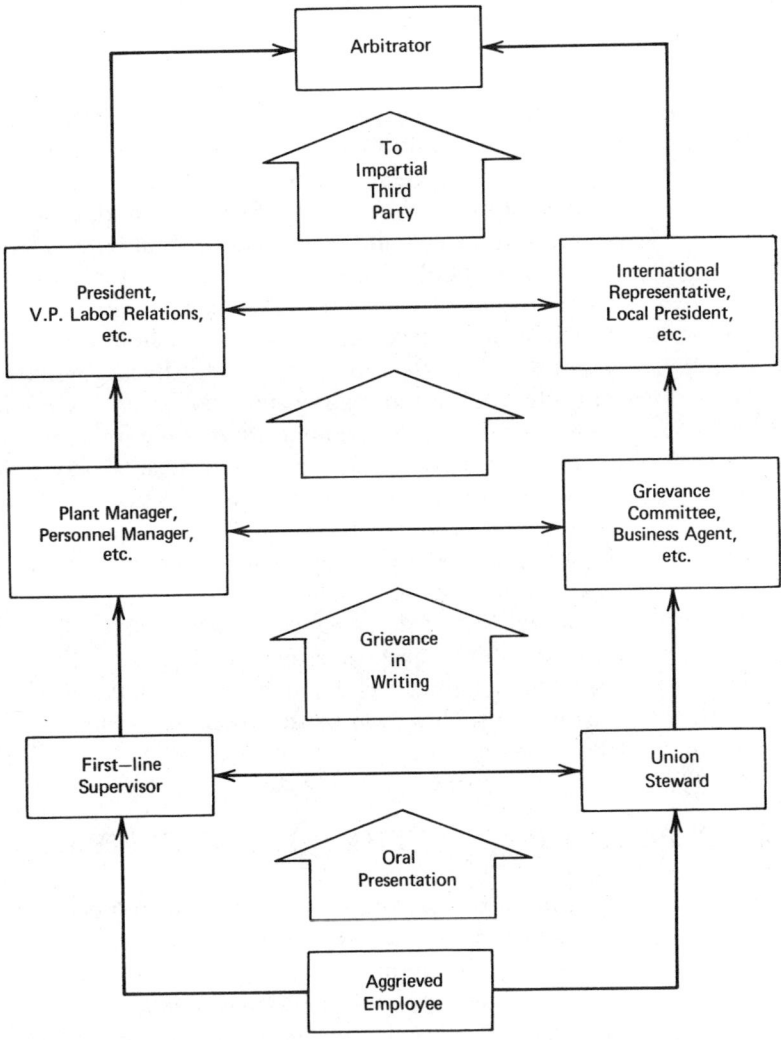

Figure 22-1 A typical formal grievance procedure.

tions staff. At the higher steps, it probably is advisable to involve the labor relations specialists in direct contact with the union representatives. Specialized knowledge is necessary because of the need for consistency in companywide policy and because of legal aspects. Those grievance cases that go all the way to the top often set precedents.

Because of the particular importance of the initial and terminal steps, the handling of grievances at the supervisory level has been discussed in detail in the preceding section of this chapter, and arbitration is covered in detail in a later section. It has been noted earlier that the supervisor has little direct involvement in a grievance case once it has moved upward from his level. However, the supervisor may be called upon to provide background information, or as a witness, at all steps up to and including arbitration.

DESIRABLE FEATURES

In order for a grievance procedure to be effective in accomplishing its purpose, it should include certain features. The structure of the procedure, its language and attendant details, should be comparatively simple and clear-cut so that it is readily understood by all employees.

From the viewpoint of both management and labor, the processing of grievances should not be long, drawn-out affairs. The procedure should include time limits for initial presentation of grievances and for appeals to each higher level. Likewise, there should be time limits for management to give its decision at each step. Because unavoidable delays can occur, the time limits at any step should be extendable by mutual agreement. Most labor agreements do provide for time limits and extensions.

The grievance procedure should be sufficiently flexible to provide for alternate courses of action in special situations. For example, some disputes may involve technical matters about which the average supervisor is not qualified to judge. Disagreements over aspects of time studies, performance standards, wage incentives, job evaluations, and the like, could fall into this category. In such instances, it may be desirable to send the initial grievance directly to a specialist in the personnel or the industrial engineering departments. Supervisors should, of course, be informed of such action so that they are aware of what is going on with their work group.

GRIEVANCE PROCEDURES IN THE NONUNION FIRM

Nonunionized organizations having formal or informal grievance procedures are in the minority. Probably no more than about 25 percent of firms with nonunion hourly workers have some kind of grievance procedure for these people. The corresponding figure for firms employing nonexempt salaried employees probably is no more than 10 percent. Of those firms with some kind of grievance procedure, the majority utilize informal measures. If there is no union contract requiring grievance procedures, then it is only human nature, unfortunately, that many managers will try to avoid the issue.

The need is great for systematic grievance procedures for nonunion employees. The imbalance of power between the nonunion employees and the employer is great. The lack of such procedures is one of the driving forces in unionization efforts.

Some approaches to handling grievances of nonunion employees include:

1. Personnel counseling.
2. Open-door policy.
3. Ombudsman.
4. Multistep grievance procedure.

Under the *personnel counseling* approach, a counselor attached to the personnel department assists employees with all kinds of problems. Although not designed specifically for complaints and grievances, it can be helpful. Even if supervisors were trained to counsel, the question would remain—what to do when the supervisor and employee could not reach agreement.

The *open-door policy* currently is the most commonly used procedure in handling complaints and grievances of nonunion employees. Under this approach, the employee is supposed to be free to see an appropriate top executive (president, division head, and so on) who in theory will hear and investigate all complaints. The method seldom is completely satisfactory. The top executive just does not have sufficient time to handle this responsibility. Also, many employees are hesitant to approach the "top brass," and the danger always exists of undermining the supervisor's position.

The *ombudsman* concept is borrowed from Sweden and Finland, where it was successfully instituted in the early 1800s. In those countries, the ombudsman is a politically neutral official who hears the complaints of citizens against the government and has strong investigative powers. The concept has aroused interest recently as possibly offering some promise in private business.

The *multistep grievance procedures,* as practiced by nonunionized firms, are quite similar to the procedures outlined in union contracts. The chief difference is that arbitration seldom is included—the terminal step is at the top management level.

Of the four approaches described above, only the multistep procedure is a formalized grievance procedure with the right to appeal. The principal criticism is its lack of an arbitration step.

A difficulty with arbitration in nonunion situations would be the expense to an employee and lack of skill in preparing and presenting the case. Various proposals, such as neutral boards of review, have been suggested to overcome this drawback. However, not much has actually been done in this direction to date.

THE ARBITRATION OF GRIEVANCES

Arbitration is a process of resolving disputes by submitting them to an impartial third party for a final and binding decision. It usually is the terminal step in grievance procedures. Provisions for arbitration are found in most labor agreements today, and they commonly specify what subjects may be arbitrated, how the arbitrators will be selected, and other details. The arbitration process is not restricted to unionized firms; it is used to some extent in situations where no labor agreement exists.

Supervisors are rarely direct participants in the arbitration process. However, they should have some understanding of the process. It is likely that they will be asked to provide input to the management strategists planning the company's presentation, and they may be called as witnesses at the arbitration hearing.

THE NATURE OF ARBITRATION   Arbitration may be voluntary or compulsory in nature. Under *voluntary arbitration,* both parties have agreed in advance (by an arbitration clause in the labor contract) to submit differences to arbitration if they fail to arrive at a settlement between themselves. This is by far the most common form of arbitration in the United States.

Compulsory arbitration takes place when the two parties are required by law to submit certain types of differences to arbitration. It is not common in this country, although practiced in some foreign countries. The general feeling in our society seems to be that a forced settlement rarely is satisfactory to both parties and rarely solves a problem permanently. However, there is a school of thought that holds that compulsory arbitration might be desirable in public sector disputes.

Of the many different issues carried to arbitration in recent years, the following five subjects were the most frequent:

1. Disciplinary actions.
2. Job classification and work assignment.
3. Management rights.
4. Seniority—in promotion, demotions, and layoffs.
5. Overtime and hours.

The ranking in comparative importance of these issues varies slightly from year to year.

Labor relations experts generally agree that the increasing acceptance of arbitration in the years since World War II has contributed to labor peace. In some instances, at least, both labor and management consider arbitration to be a preferable substitute for some form of economic pressure—strikes, slowdowns, lockouts, and the like. Letting an arbitrator settle an issue is, in some instances, a convenient face-saving way for union or management officials to avoid making a decision that, for many possible reasons, they may dislike.

As the terminal step in the grievance procedure, arbitration should be resorted to only when all else fails. Every effort should be made to reach an amicable solution by other means. It is unfortunately true, however, that labor or management may let a weak grievance case go to arbitration for unworthy reasons:

1. To avoid unpleasant decision making.
2. To avoid the appearance of being pushed around.
3. Because of pressures from others.
4. Because of poor union-management relations.

SOURCES OF ARBITRATORS

Most *arbitrators* are professional people for whom arbitration is a part-time avocation. They are people who have an interest in labor relations, appropriate knowledge, and a reputation for integrity. Arbitrators are employed most commonly on an *ad hoc basis;* that is, an arbitrator is selected anew each time a case comes up. A few large corporations and industry trade associations engage *permanent arbitrators* for the duration of a labor contract.

Somewhat over one-half of labor contracts specify that the case shall be heard by a single arbitrator. Most of the remainder specify a *tripartite panel* in which one member is selected by each party and the third member by joint agreement.

In seeking arbitrators, the company and union may go to an impartial agency that maintains and provides lists of qualified arbitrators. The most widely known of such agencies are the Federal Mediation and Conciliation Service and the American Arbitration Association. Additionally, several states have similar mediation services. The agencies will provide a list of qualified arbitrators from which union and management will select an arbitrator. If union and management cannot agree on an arbitrator, the agency will, on request, appoint an arbitrator from the list. It is customary for the union and the company to share the arbitrator's fees and other expenses.

Although records are not available on privately selected arbitrators, it is probable that a majority of arbitrators are chosen locally by union and management without going through one of the public agencies.

Acting as an arbitrator has been largely a male prerogative. It is interesting to note that in 1979, 23 women were graduated from the first national program for women labor arbitrators. This 18-month program is jointly sponsored by the two mediation agencies mentioned above and Cornell University.

THE ARBITRATION HEARING

The issue to be settled by the hearing, and the authority of the arbitrator usually are spelled out in advance in what is known as the *submission agreement* or the *stipulation to arbitrate.* In general, both parties have agreed in advance to accept the arbitrator's decision as final and binding. The advance agreement usually provides that the arbitrator cannot add to, subtract from, or modify the labor contract but can interpret, apply, or rule on compliance with provisions of the contract.

Arbitration hearings are quasi-judicial in nature. They may range from very informal to quite formal in conduct, but even a formal hearing is less so than what we would find in a court of law. Much is left up to the arbitrator in conducting the hearing. The arbitrator may question witnesses and representatives of either party, ask for additional information on some point, request documents and records, and so on. This provides for great flexibility, an important and major feature in arbitration.

Arbitrators are not bound by the same rules of evidence as are courts of law. Neither are they bound by precedent, although in actual practice they may take precedent into account. Most arbitrators, however, attach considerable importance to consistency or lack of it in past actions and relationships between the two parties at the hearing in question. The arbitrator is attempting to establish facts and arrive at an impartial decision and is not forced into rigid channels in doing so.

THE ARBITRATION AWARD

After the hearing is concluded, the arbitrator has 30 days in which to study the facts of the matter and arrive at a decision. The decision, referred to as the *award,* is prepared in written form along with a separate review or opinion supporting the decision. The *review statement* summarizes the pros and cons of the presentations made by the two parties and outlines the reasoning followed by the arbitrator in his award.

If the arbitrator has been obtained through one of the previously mentioned agencies, the award and review statement often will be printed and distributed. These are widely read and studied by union officials, management specialists, and other arbitrators.

SOME LEGAL ASPECTS OF ARBITRATION[2]

It has been mentioned that most labor contracts provide that arbitration shall be final and binding. In effect, both parties have agreed in advance not to appeal the decision. The courts have upheld this. The courts can, however, set aside an award for certain reasons:

1. If a fair hearing was not provided, that is, if fraud, corruption, misconduct, or the like can be demonstrated.

---

[2]The authors are not attorneys. This discussion of legal aspects is necessarily cursory and presents only a few of the more important highlights in condensed form. The reader is cautioned that this is a highly complex subject with many ramifications. What to the nonspecialist might appear to be a minor point could make a major difference in any specific case.

2. If the arbitrator has gone beyond the parameters of the labor contract or the submission agreement.
3. If the award goes against public policy.
4. If it is impossible to implement the award.

We note that it is most unusual for an award to be set aside.

The courts can enforce the arbitrator's award in the event that either party fails to abide by that decision. To be enforceable, the arbitrator must have been governed by the terms of the submission agreement and by his interpretation of the labor contract.

The courts also can determine which issues are arbitrable under the labor contract. State laws have varied on this subject. In some states in the past, if either party refused to arbitrate, there was nothing the other party could do about it. A Supreme Court ruling in 1957 (the Lincoln Mills case) held that agreements to arbitrate are enforceable under the Taft-Hartley Act, regardless of state law, when the labor contract contains a no-strike provision.

Other Supreme Court decisions have amplified this general subject. Under an absolute no-strike clause in the agreement, all disputes of any nature are arbitrable unless there is a *very specific* clause excluding certain management actions from arbitration. Moreover, it has been held that the courts cannot weigh the merits of the grievance itself.

SUMMARY

It is inevitable that dissatisfactions expressed as complaints or grievances will arise in any organization. The causes are many: alleged violations of the union contract (the legalistic definition of grievance), job-related factors, untrained supervision, and personal problems. To be effective in handling these, the supervisor must keep his or her eyes open for symptoms of unexpressed dissatisfactions, for possible underlying real reasons for the complaints, and must cope in a mature way with the emotional content present in many complaints and grievances.

We cannot overemphasize the importance of the work environment and the status of union-management relations in minimizing the number of complaints and grievances and in facilitating early and satisfactory solutions to those that do occur. The philosophy of top management and the characteristics, attitudes, and skills of the supervisor are vital factors.

Formalized procedures for handling grievances have become fairly standardized and are spelled out in nearly all labor contracts. These provide safety valves for the employees, contribute to a climate of justice, and are critical to day-to-day administration of the labor contract. The procedures provide for appeal through successive levels of management until a settlement is reached, with discussions between management and union representatives at each level.

The supervisor has the most important role in this process because the initial step is a joint effort at settlement between the supervisor and the worker (and/or the union steward). Approximately 75 percent of grievances are resolved amicably at this level.

The terminal step in the great majority of grievance procedures is voluntary arbitration by an impartial third party, the results of which are final and binding. The arbitration process and its application are being affected by court decisions.

There is a pressing need for more and better grievance procedures for nonunion employees who do not have a union representative to look after their interests. Comparatively few firms have developed grievance procedures for such employees. The informal, open-door approach to handling complaints and grievances predominates. Arbitration rarely is included in the few instances of formal multistep procedures available to nonunion workers.

KEY CONCEPTS

Right of appeal. If an individual receives an adverse decision that he considers unfair, he has the right to appeal the decision to higher authority. It is basic to the broader concepts of justice in general, and of formal grievance procedures in particular.

Early settlement. The direct and indirect costs of lengthy grievance procedures are high. Additionally, an employee who believes that he has received unfair treatment has the right to expect an answer within a reasonable period of time. Consequently, a basic principle of grievance handling is to attempt to reach a fair and satisfactory settlement as quickly as possible. The entire grievance procedure should be geared to encouraging and facilitating settlement of a majority of grievances at the initial step.

Formal grievance procedure. Because disagreements are inevitable in any organization, a system must be established to handle them. The system should serve the interests of justice and facilitate the day-to-day administration of the collective bargaining agreement. The most effective form for such a system developed to date is a multistep (three to five steps) procedure starting at the first-line supervisory level and terminating with arbitration. The aggrieved employee has the right to appeal decisions to successively higher steps.

Arbitration. This is the settlement of a dispute between two parties by an impartial third party. It should be used only as a last resort after all other procedures and efforts have been exhausted. It is being accepted more and more as a preferable alternate to some form of economic pressure such as strikes and lockouts.

IMPORTANT TERMS

Ad hoc arbitration	Labor contract
Arbitration	Ombudsman
Arbitrator	Open-door policy
Award	Permanent arbitration
Complaint	Personnel counseling
Compulsory arbitration	Rationalization
Defense mechanism	Review statement
Dissatisfaction	Steward
Emotionality factor	Stipulation to arbitrate
Expressed complaint	Submission agreement
Grievance	Tripartite panel
Hearing	Unexpressed dissatisfaction
Hidden cause	Voluntary arbitration
Labor agreement	

INCIDENTS

The Problem of the Diesel Trucks

The underground lead-zinc mines of southwestern Missouri are cavernous chambers extending in some areas for miles. Massive pillars of rock or ore are left in place at irregular intervals to support the overlying roof strata ("back" in mining parlance), which may be as high as 50 feet or more above the mine floor. Ventilation never has been a major problem in these mines because of their large size. Huge quantities of air move through the mine chambers constantly, but because of the large cross-sectional areas, the velocity of this air is so slow that a person is not consciously aware of its movement.

Several years ago, diesel-powered trucks were introduced into these mines for ore haulage, replacing old rope-drawn scrapers. Prior to introduction, the mining company fitted the truck exhaust systems with chemical-type fume-control devices. Advance calculations showed that the mine ventilation system was more than adequate (by a factor of several times) to handle the slight amount of fumes that might escape into the mine atmosphere. The company also conducted an educational and training program about the new equipment and its safety features.

Nevertheless, the mine workers were concerned that the diesel trucks might create a hazard. Soon after the trucks were put into service, complaints were heard about stuffiness of the air. A few miners reported headaches and dizziness to their shift supervisor. In consequence, the company engaged an outside firm of consulting engineers to conduct tests of the atmosphere in various locations throughout the mine. The tests proved that the quality of the mine atmosphere was well above normal standards. The fume control devices on the trucks were examined and found to be working efficiently.

In spite of this, the miners were unconvinced. Complaints about the air and reports of headaches and dizziness actually increased. There were mutterings among the men about a possible strike. The mine management was at a complete loss as to what to do.

Assume that you are part of management at this mine. Exercise your ingenuity to see if you can come up with a solution to this problem. Do you believe that the miners had a valid complaint? Do you believe that emotional or psychological factors were at work? Explain your answer.

The Borrowed Calculator

Jo Ellen Kirk is an accountant at the Delroi Paper Box Company. In February, March, and April of each year she does a little legitimate "moonlighting" at home helping neighborhood businesses prepare their income tax forms. This March she was particularly busy with such jobs. Before leaving the office on a Friday, she stopped by the company's office supply room and asked the attendant if she could check out a programmable calculator in order to do some tax work at home over the weekend. The attendant gave her the calculator with a joking comment about "The company making her burn the midnight oil." Jo Ellen returned the calculator at 8:00 A.M. the following Monday, but was observed by her supervisor who immediately discharged her.

Company Work Rule No. 6 provides for immediate discharge for "theft, or removal from company premises without proper authorization, of any company property." In the company's labor contract, Article XI, Section 4, in reference to theft or unauthorized removal of company property, states that "violators are subject to immediate disciplinary action up to and including discharge." Jo Ellen is a member of the Amalgamated Office and Clerical Workers, Local No. 23.

Solve this incident with a role-playing approach. Assume that Jo Ellen has complained to the union steward, who has requested a meeting with the supervisor. Jo Ellen and the office supply room attendant also are present. The steward is considering filing a formal grievance but wants more information before deciding on this. Members of the class will be assigned to each of the four roles. In acting your part in role play, accept the facts as given and assume an attitude consistent with your particular role. Develop reasons for doing what you did and supportive arguments. As the situation progresses, make up additional "facts" or events, as needed, consistent with how it might be in real life.

QUESTIONS FOR DISCUSSION

1. The text states that the supervisor should be alert for the symptoms of unexpressed dissatisfactions. Can you justify this statement?
2. Why should every supervisor be thoroughly conversant with the terms of the labor contract?
3. Do you believe that there are personal factors that may cause some employees to submit more complaints or grievances than will others? Identify and explain.
4. Why is it often difficult to determine the validity of complaints about the attitudes, actions, or lack of actions of fellow workers on the job?
5. How would a manager who believes in Theory X be likely to view grievances in contrast to a manager who believes in Theory Y? (See Chapter XIII.)
6. What are the implications of an employee asking the union steward to take a grievance to the supervisor?
7. Under what conditions might a supervisor not have either the authority or the ability to settle a grievance?
8. Discuss the pros and cons of putting a grievance into writing at the first step.
9. Why is it desirable for every organization to have formal grievance procedures?
10. The "open-door policy" currently is the most commonly used procedure in handling complaints and grievances of nonunion employees. Can you think of some problems with, or drawbacks to, this approach in addition to those mentioned in the text?
11. In your opinion, what importance should an arbitrator attach to precedent?
12. Can you visualize a situation in which it would be impossible for an arbitrator to award a *just* decision?
13. Identify those features of arbitration that make it unique in comparison with all preceding steps in the multistep grievance procedure.

PART IV

The Supervisor and the Environment

Since supervisors must operate within an environment beyond their control, their knowledge of this environment is imperative. This section covers three chapters: labor relations and supervision, safety and health responsibilities under OSHA, and the organization and its environment.

CHAPTER XXIII

Labor Relations and the Supervisor

LEARNING OBJECTIVES

- *To discover how the Industrial Revolution created the factory system and thereby permanently changed the nature of the relationship between owner (manager) and worker.*
- *To understand how laws, customs, and society's attitudes in the 1800s and early 1900s strongly favored management and to realize that labor-management conflicts (often violent) during those years still affect many of the attitudes of organized labor today.*
- *To see how the balance of power in labor relations first swung over to the side of labor with passage of the Wagner Act in 1935, sparked by the Great Depression of the 1930s.*
- *To identify the numerous federal laws affecting labor relations that have been enacted since the 1930s, to understand the reasons why each of these were passed, and to learn the major provisions of the more important pieces of labor legislation.*
- *To understand the mechanics of the unionization process and the nature and importance of the restraints placed on the supervisor's words and actions during the organizing campaign.*
- *To learn something of the nature and characteristics of union organizations.*

Introduction

This chapter provides the supervisor with a general background knowledge of the major pieces of legislation currently affecting labor relations.

Most of this legislation has been enacted within the past four decades, that is, since the early 1930s. For a better understanding of the root causes leading to this legislation, it is desirable to review briefly labor's situation and key events in the labor movement prior to the 1930s.

Two major results of labor legislation—unionization and collective bargaining—have had a profound impact in settling the pattern for labor relations. Civil rights legislation also has affected labor relations, although less directly. It is appropriate, therefore, that the supervisors have some familiarity with these laws and processes.

Labor legislation, unionization, and collective bargaining—important as they are—represent only a part of the many facets to labor relations. Additional aspects—discipline and morale, and handling complaints and grievances—are presented in specific chapters of their own.

THE EARLY LABOR MOVEMENT

In the colonial days of the 1600s and 1700s, the great majority of people lived on the farm. Work was a joint family affair. Most manufacturing was done by the cottage system or in small shops often attached to the home of the owner. A young boy would be legally bound to his master, the shop owner, as an *apprentice* to learn a trade. The boy lived in the home of his master and was given room and board. In five or six years he became a *journeyman* and went out on his own to work for wages. Although abuses existed, the relationship between master and apprentice or master and journeyman usually was close.

EFFECT OF THE INDUSTRIAL REVOLUTION
The *industrial revolution* of the seventeenth and eighteenth centuries was a gradual transition from an agriculture-based society to an industrial-based society initiated by the need for increased production due to population growth. It was made possible by the concomitant development of artificial sources of power (steam) and machinery, the linkage of which gave rise to factories. Factories greatly increased man's productive capacity but permanently changed the previously close relationship of master and worker. The tremendous technological changes during the nineteenth century continually widened the gap.

The early factory system necessitated large numbers of people working together in one place with an interdependency of tasks and place not previously experienced. With this came the need for regimentation. Everyone had to start and stop work at the same time. Strict work rules were needed. Supervision was a completely different problem under these conditions, as contrasted to the former master-journeyman system. Various levels of supervision—foreman, superintendent, works manager, general manager—grew up between worker and owner. All of this widened the social and economic gap between worker and owner.

Both the common law and the statutes of the day emphasized the rights of ownership of property. Labor was viewed as a commodity that could be bought and sold. Labor had few rights, and employers' responsibilities were negligible.

In the early 1800s most workers could not vote. As late as 1835, workers could send their children to public schools only if they swore a pauper's oath. The work week was six days, and working hours were sunup to sundown, usually 75 hours in the winter and 82 in the summer. Women and children worked similar hours in the factories and mines. In 1829 boys as young as seven years worked in Philadelphia factories from dawn until 8:00 P.M.

LABOR RELATIONS IN THE 1800s

The century following the industrial revolution saw an ever-increasing, and gradually successful, effort by workers to organize. Labor legislation and the interpretation of law slowly liberalized, although still favoring the employer up to the 1930s. Occasional setbacks in forward movement occurred, of course, and the period from the Civil War to World War I was marked by considerable labor violence.

In 1792 the cordwainers (shoemakers) of Philadelphia formed the first craft union for collective bargaining. In 1806 the Philadelphia cordwainers were indicted and charged with criminal conspiracy for attempting to raise wages. The *conspiracy doctrine* applied by the judiciary of the period held that any combination of labor to bring economic pressure to bear upon an employer was an illegal act of conspiracy. A number of court decisions upheld the conspiracy doctrine until 1842, when the Massachusetts Supreme Court (the Hunt Case) reversed this doctrine. The court ruled that labor combinations were not illegal as such, that they could have desirable objectives. To be illegal, such combinations must have a criminal or an unlawful aspect.

After 1842 most states allowed unions to organize, but many union purposes, including raising wages, were frequently held to be unlawful. Where purposes were accepted, the means for achieving them—strikes, boycotts, picketing—often were illegal.

There were many attempts through the nineteenth century to form national federations of unions. Several came into existence but were relatively short lived. Business panics and recessions hurt such efforts. Employers also had many means of applying pressure: firing union members, blacklists, refusal to deal with union representatives, and the *yellow dog contract*. This last item consisted of requiring new employees to sign an agreement that they would never join a union while working for that employer.

Immigration also had its effect on the labor movement. By 1850 immigration had reached 500,000 per year. The waves of immigrants swelled to a flood between 1880 and 1920, bringing many millions of new people into the country. Most spoke no English, were desperately poor, and needed work. They often were used as strikebreakers, and the general effect was to depress wages.

The Civil War accelerated the industrialization process in this country. Labor's struggle increased in intensity, and violence became more prevalent. The Molly Maguires, a secret society of Irish miners in the anthracite coal fields, conducted terrorist campaigns in the 1860s in an effort to control relations with mine owners. Ten leaders of the Molly Maguires were exected in 1875. The Haymarket Riot, which occurred in Chicago in 1886, resulted in the deaths of several striking workers and police. Clashes between federal troops and strikers in Baltimore and Pittsburgh during 1877 resulted in killing more than 100 persons. The Ludlow Massacre occurred in Colorado in 1914 when company employees and hired guards sworn in as state militia opened fire on strikers and their families living in tents, and then set fire to the tents.

Although progress was slow, it did occur. In 1840 a ten-hour day without reduction in pay was established for federal employees on public works. And in 1868 a federal law was enacted providing for an eight-hour day for laborers, workmen, and mechanics employed on behalf of the United States government. Several states passed laws putting at least a few restrictions on child labor. The first permanent national federation of unions—the American Federal of Labor (AFL)—was founded by Samuel Gompers in 1886.

A setback to labor took place in 1890 with enactment of the Sherman Anti-Trust Act. This act was not intended as labor legislation. However, employers utilized its provisions to obtain injunctions against strikes and some other union activities, such as a nationwide boycott, on the grounds that unions were "combinations in restraint of trade." Nevertheless, the period from the 1880s to World War I saw a dramatic increase in the formation of labor organizations, creation of state and federal agencies concerned with labor, and individual pieces of favorable legislation.

THE TRANSITION PERIOD

Although wars have tremendously devastating effects, history does show that often they represent turning points in the cultural, social, and economic affairs of mankind. World War 1 was such a turning point in the labor movement of this country.

A war-derived shortage of labor plus patriotic fervor combined to improve the climate for labor relations. The AFl gave President Wilson a no-strike pledge. Various boards and commissions were set up to mediate labor disputes, study working conditions in war industries, and encourage labor-management cooperation. A National War Labor Board was set up as a kind of supreme arbitrator in labor disputes.

Some, but not all, of these advances were abandoned after World War 1. However, the stage had been set. The period between World War 1 and the early 1930s was a transition period between the nineteenth century and entry into the modern era of labor legislation and labor-management relations. Legislation still favored the employer. The right to strike and the right to bargain collectively still remained to be affirmed and guaranteed by law for the majority of workers, but the pendulum was swinging.

Important legislation of this period included the Clayton Act of 1914, which exempted unions from the provisions of the Sherman Anti-Trust Act. It limited the use of injunctions and made picketing legal. It did not protect unions from civil damage suits by employers.

The Norris-La Guardia Act of 1932 overcame some of the deficiencies in the Clayton Act. It drastically limited the conditions under which the federal courts could issue labor injunctions. It also outlawed the *yellow dog contract*, that is, requiring new employees to sign an agreement that they would never join a union while working for that employer.

The Railway Labor Act, passed in 1926, established collective bargaining for railway employees as well as providing for grievance and arbitration procedures, cooling-off periods, and mediation. This was the first time collective bargaining was guaranteed by law. Some labor leaders consider this the beginning of the "modern era," but most labor historians favor the more all-inclusive Wagner Act of 1935 as the start of the new era.

THE MODERN ERA IN LABOR RELATIONS

It is unfortunate that it took the Great Depression of the 1930s to provide the final impetus for the labor legislation that lifted the balance of power from employers.

The foundation of labor relations is based on the *collective bargaining* process. In its ideal form, this is rule by mutual agreement between two parties. The collective labor force bargains with collective ownership (stockholders) to establish the rules of the ball game. This is done through their respective representatives—the union on the part of labor, and professional managers on the part of the stockholders. The resulting *collective bargaining agreement*—also called the *labor agreement* or *labor contract*—is developed through negotiation and compromise and sets forth the rights and obligations of labor and management. It is a critical factor in establishing the labor relations climate.

Bargaining implies negotiating from positions of strength. Much of the history of labor legislation is a history of the shifts in the balance of power. The past and present situation is analogous to the swing of a pendulum, as illustrated in Figure 23-1. The balance of power (or perhaps imbalance would be more descriptive) was almost completely on the side of the employer at the beginning of the nineteenth century. The pendulum gradually swung in the direction of the employee, but it was not until 1935, with the passage of the Wagner Act, that it could be said that the pendulum had passed the midpoint and was on the side of the labor.

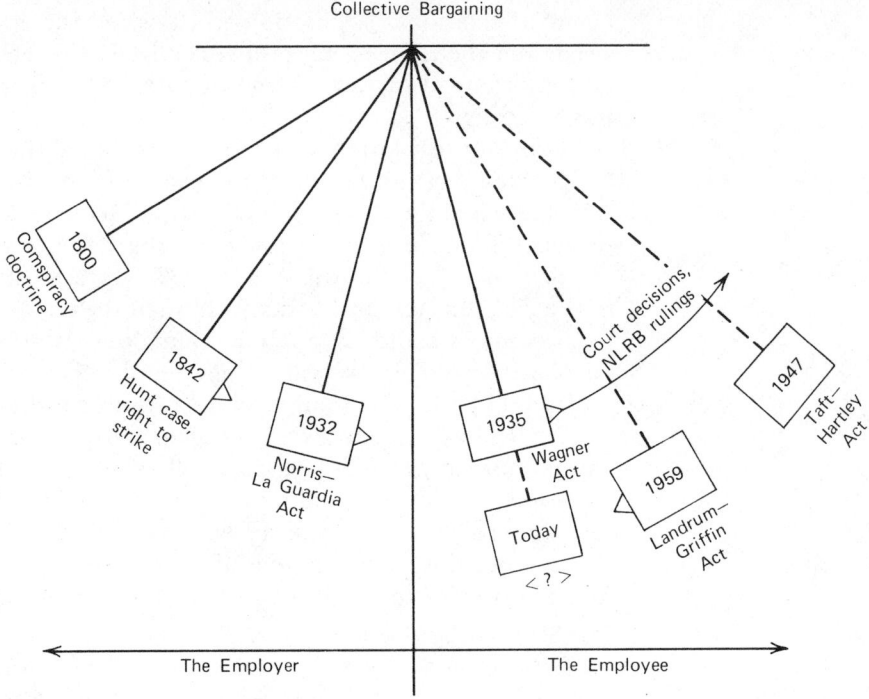

Figure 23-1 The pendulum concept of the balance of power in collective bargaining.

Subsequent interpretations, rulings, and court decisions under the Wagner Act swung the pendulum even farther to labor's side. With the Taft-Hartley Act of 1947, the pendulum began to reverse its swing, and today we are much closer to a true balance of power, although the situation still favors labor somewhat.

FEDERAL LAW AFFECTING LABOR RELATIONS

A large number of labor laws have been enacted over the past forty years. Not all of them were concerned directly with collective bargaining and labor relations. Some, for example, refer chiefly to safety and health, compensation, or training and development. The purpose of this chapter is to describe briefly the principal features of major pieces of legislation aimed primarily at labor relations.

National Labor Relations Act of 1935

This act, also known as the Wagner Act, is the major labor law affecting labor relations. It was brought on by the Great Depression of the 1930s and gave impetus to collective bargaining. The act applies to employers in or affecting commerce, but it excludes employers covered by the Railway Labor Act of 1926 (which today also covers the air transport industry), government employees at all levels, and agricultural laborers.

Stated briefly, Section 7 of the Wagner Act gave employees the right to do the following.

1. Organize, that is, to form or join labor unions.
2. Bargain collectively and select their own bargaining representative.
3. Engage in concerted activities of all types.

Section 8 of the Wagner Act identified and made illegal a number of *unfair labor practices* by employers. Specifically, it forbade employers to do any of the following.

1. Coerce or otherwise interfere with employees in the exercise of their rights, including threats to close or move the plant and spying on union meetings.
2. Dominate or interfere with the formation of a union, or contribute financial support to it.
3. Discrimination in any way so as to encourage or discourage membership in any union.
4. Discharge or discriminate against an employee because the employee has filed charges or given testimony under this act.
5. Refuse to bargain collectively and in good faith.

Additionally, the Wagner Act established the *National Labor Relations Board* (NLRB) to enforce the act. Major functions of the board are determining bargaining units, conducting representation elections by secret ballot, and prosecuting cases of unfair labor practices. As originally enacted, this last function meant prosecuting employers who violated these provisions. As amended in 1947, the function of prosecuting cases of unfair labor practices by unions was added to the board's duties.

Labor-Management Relations Act of 1947

Known also as the Taft-Hartley Act, this was essentially an amendment to the Wagner Act. A serious wave of strikes and labor unrest followed World War II. In fact, the year 1946 set a record for the number of strikes. Public reaction tended to blame the unions. Wages and working conditions had improved greatly since the Depression. The public and the Congress apparently felt that the unions now were going too far and that there were too few restraints on organized labor's actions. The result was passage of the Taft-Hartley Act in 1947 over presidential veto.

The Taft-Hartley Act retained most of the basic provisions of the Wagner Act. A major new feature was that the act identified and forbade several unfair labor practices by unions. The unions are specifically forbidden to do the following.

1. Restrain or coerce employees, for example, mass picketing or violence to prevent nonunion employees from entering a plant.
2. Attempt to cause an employer to encourage or discourage an employee to join a union.
3. Refuse to bargain in good faith.
4. Require an employer or self-employed person to join a union.
5. Force an employer to bargain with one union when another union already is the certified representative.
6. Engage in *secondary boycotts*, that is, attempting to force an employer to stop doing business with, or handling the products of, another employer.
7. Engage in *jurisdictional strikes*, that is, forcing an employer to assign certain work to employees belonging to one union rather than to another union.
8. Charge excessive initiation fees.
9. Engage in *featherbedding* practices, that is, requiring the payment of wages for services not performed.

An effect of these restrictions was to ban the closed shop, although the union shop remains legal under the act. In a *closed shop*, all eligible present workers must be members of the union and all newly hired workers must be members or become members at the time of hiring. In a *union shop*, all eligible present workers are required to join the union and all newly hired workers must join within a specified period, usually 30 days.

The Taft-Hartley Act contains several other significant provisions. It relaxed the earlier Wagner Act's restrictions on management's privilege of free speech in labor matters. It removed supervisors and foremen from protection by the act if they should form or joint a union. In effect, it considers supervisors and forepeople to be part of management rather than just employees. In the event of labor disputes causing national emergencies, the President of the United States may seek an injunction against strikes or lockouts. A cooling-off period of up to 80 days is provided for, along with certain other requirements and actions.

Labor-Management Reporting and Disclosure Act of 1959

This act is commonly referred to as the *Landgrum-Griffin Act*. It was enacted chiefly as the result of congressional investigations in the late 1950s into corrupt practices within a few unions and within certain areas of union-management relations.

The Landrum-Griffin Act is divided into seven titles (parts), the first six of which pertain to internal union affairs whereas the seventh amends and strenghens certain provisions of the Taft-Hartley Act, as follows.

1. Bill of rights. Union members must be given the right to nominate candidates for union office and to participate and vote in union meetings, elections, and referendums; to testify and bring suit when unions infringe on the rights of members; and to receive notice and a fair hearing before any union disciplinary action can be taken other than for nonpayment of dues.
2. Reporting. Unions, union officers, employers, and consultants must file various reports with the Secretary of Labor. These cover certain administrative practices and financial matters designed to show conflict of interest, if any.
3. Trusteeships. Certain rules are established governing the use of trusteeships by national or international unions over their local unions. The rules protect the rights of local members.
4. Union elections. This section specifies time periods within which elections must be held and spells out democratic procedures governing how the elections are to be conducted.
5. Fiduciary. The trust relations in connection with union funds are detailed. Willful misappropriation, embezzlement, or stealing of union funds becomes a federal crime.
6. Miscellaneous financial provisions.
7. Amendments to Taft-Hartley Act. Restrictions on organizational and recognition picketing were strengthened; the right of strikers to vote in new representation elections held up to one year after the strike began was added; and "hot cargo" agreements were made illegal. The latter is similar to, but technically different from, a secondary boycott.

Concessions to the unions included repeal of the anti-Communist affidavit requirements of the Taft-Hartley Act and a provision that, in effect, permits closed shop agreements in the construction industry.

Civil Rights Legislation

The past two decades have been notable for an increasing awareness of discrimination against minority groups within our society. In some instances, discrimination is a conscious, overt act. In other instances, it is more subtle—a subconscious reflection of cultural attitudes. In either case, discrimination may occur in any aspect of life: education, work, recreation, shopping, residential, and so on.

In line with the purposes of this text, our primary concern here is with discrimination, and resulting legislation, as this affects work and labor relations at the supervisory level. Discrimination at work most commonly occurs in connection with the number and kinds of jobs available, pay scales, work assignments, opportunities for promotion, attitudes of supervisors and co-workers, and the like.

One effect of the increasing awareness of discrimination has been the enactment during the 1960s and 1970s of a series of laws collectively described as "civil rights legislation." The purposes of these laws, and regulations promulgated under them, are to affirm and protect the civil rights of minorities, to eliminate (or at least minimize) discrimination, and to redress (to some extent) the effects of past discrimination. The civil rights laws most relevant to the work situation are described briefly.

The Equal Pay Act of 1963 was perhaps the first of such laws. It prohibited differences in pay based on sex. It applies to all employees who are covered by the Wagner Act, plus executive, administrative, and professional employees and outside salespeople. Court rulings under this act in the early 1970s stated that jobs need not be identical, merely substantially equal, for the law to apply.

The Civil Rights Act of 1964 is considered by many to be the single most important piece of legislation of this type. Title VII of the act is directed specifically at terms and conditions of employment. It bans all discrimination in employment because of race, color, religion, sex, or national origin, and holds the employer responsible for any discrimination occurring within the organization. Title VII also created the *Equal Employment Opportunity Commission (EEOC)* to administer and implement these provisions.

The Equal Employment Opportunity Act of 1972 amended the 1964 Act. It changed Title VII to cover all private employers of 15 or more persons. It extended coverage to all public and private educational institutions, state and local governments, public and private employment agencies, labor unions, and joint labor-management committees for apprenticeship and training. It also strengthened appreciably the enforcement powers of the EEOC. For example, the latter is now empowered to file class-action suits against an employer in federal court if it believes that individual complaints indicate a pattern of discrimination. Financial damages can be obtained for each affected employee, past and present, which can be extremely costly.

Executive Order 11246, as amended by Executive Order 11375, applies to most federal contractors and subcontractors. It requires every contract to contain a clause against discrimination because of race, color, religion, sex, or national origin. It also requires written affirmative action programs by most such contractors and subcontractors. This order is enforced by the *Office of Federal Contract Compliance (OFCC)*.

The Age Discrimination in Employment Act of 1967 prohibited employers of 25 or more persons from discriminating against persons in any area of employment because of age. The age bracket initially covered by this law was 40 to 65. In January 1979, regulations under an amendment to this act extended the upper limit to age 70.

Regulations recently issued under an amendment to the Rehabilitation Act of 1963 prohibit discrimination in employment practices on the basis of handicaps. The nature and extent of handicaps covered under this regulation is not completely clear. Future rulings by the appropriate enforcement bodies, and possibly the federal courts, presumably will clarify the bounds of this law.

With respect to all of the laws, regulations, and Executive Orders described above, it must be emphasized that companies acting in good faith can be accused of discrimination. Even practices that are not discriminatory on their face, and that are not intended to be discriminatory, can be in violation of the law. In determining violations, the EEOC and other enforcement bodies consider the effect or result of a practice, not its intent. For these reasons, and because of the variety and complexity of the laws and regulations, the supervisor must be particularly careful with respect to work assignments, evaluations, promotions or transfers, and other work practices when dealing with women and minority members of the work force.

THE UNIONIZATION PROCESS

The supervisor needs to be familiar with the process by which unions are formed. Otherwise, it could be very easy to say or do something during an organization campaign that might be construed as an unfair labor practice and which could subject the employer to severe penalties. Ignorance of the constraints on management is no excuse for failure to comply.

The Organizing Campaign

The initiative for unionization may come from (1) the employees, (2) a union already representing employees in some other part of the company, or (3) an "outside" union having no representation in the plant in question. In any event, a union organizer will start the compaign. The organizer usually begins by contacting a few employees, probably at their homes or at some place frequented by the employees such as a restaurant or bowling alley near the company premises. If there is sufficient interest in unionization, he may set up an in-plant committee of workers to contact others, solicit interest, and otherwise help in the process. Handbills may be distributed and advertisements placed in local newspapers.

The organizer's goal at this stage is to sign up the required percentage of the total number of employees in the *bargaining unit* that he is trying to organize. A bargaining unit is a group of employees who make up a logical unit for collective bargaining because of the place of the proposed unit in the company's organization structure, skills, working conditions, or some other basis of commonality. A frequently used method of obtaining signatures is *authorization cards,* which (1) authorize the union to represent the employee, (2) state that the employee wishes a representation election to be held, or (3) both.

The organizer's next step can vary, depending on circumstances. If sufficient signatures have been obtained (normally over 50 percent of the employees in the unit), the organizer may decide to go directly to the employer and ask for recognition of the union as sole bargaining agent for the unit. The employer may accept. However, another union or some employees could challenge this at a future date. Many employers consider it safer, therefore, to go through the NLRB-supervised election process to be sure that a majoirty of employees truly desire representation by that particular union. Thus the employer may refuse recognition of the union at this stage, but the employer must have a reasonable doubt of the majority claim by the union. If the employer does refuse, the union organizer will petition the NLRB for a representation election.

The organizer does not have to go first to the employer. The organizer may take the petition directly to the NLRB. Before the NLRB will act on the petition under either situation, the organizer must have obtained signatures of at least 30 percent of the employees in the unit and the NLRB must agree that the unit is an appropriate bargaining unit.

If the proper conditions are met, an agent of the NLRB will ask the union and the employer if they will agree to a *consent election.* If they so agree, various details are taken care of and an election date is set.

If the employer does not agree to a consent election, the NLRB holds a formal hearing at which both parties present their arguments. Several reasons exist for which the NLRB may deny an election. If the NLRB rules that an election must be held, details are agreed upon and a date is set for a *representation election.*

The actions of both the union and the employer during the period between petition and election (usually 30 to 50 days) are subject to various constraints under the acts described in the preceding section of this chapter. Both parties will try to influence the employees, and both must be careful about how far they go.

The Representation Election

The NLRB provides ballots to be used in the secret election. If more than one union is to be listed on the ballot, each subsequent union must have obtained signatures from at least 5 percent of the employees in the unit requesting that it represent them. The ballots also contain a space for employees to indicate that they do not wish representation by any union.

The NLRB agent sets up a polling place, usually on company premises. Both parties may have observers present and may challenge individual voters. Both parties may file objections to the election within five days. For example, if the union lost the election but could prove unfair labor practices by the employer during the preelection period, the NLRB might order the employer to accept the union as bargaining agent.

A simple majority of those who vote is needed to win. There are provisions for a runoff election if none of the available choices receives a majority vote. In either event, the winning union is certified by the NLRB as the exclusive bargaining representative for all workers in the bargaining unit.

The Role of the Supervisor

The supervisor must, of course, follow company policy with respect to the unionization process. Depending on the employer's attitude, this can put the supervisor in a difficult position. An organizing campaign often is supercharged emotionally. Feelings run high and tempers may flare. The supervisor must be very careful to follow all of the applicable contraints placed on management by the Wagner Act, Taft-Hartley Act, and Landrum-Griffin Act.

The supervisor must remember that during the preelection campaign, employees ordinarily can solicit for the union on company premises during nonworking hours.

Also, employers may not interfere with, restrain, or coerce employees in connection with the unionization process. This includes no direct or implied threats of reprisal or force and no promises of rewards or benefits for not joining. No wage increases or other benefits may be given to influence an organizing campaign.

Employers may not discriminate against workers for filing unfair labor practice charges or for testifying in an NLRB Hearing. Employers may not dominate or interfere with formation or administration of a union, and may not discriminate against any employee for union activity.

Payments of money or things of value by management or its representatives to an official of a union attempting to organize a company's employees is illegal. It is also illegal to accept or demand such payments.

CHARACTERISTICS OF UNION ORGANIZATIONS

The basic unit of the organized labor structure is the *local union*. There are about 78,000 local unions, most of which are affiliated with a *national or international union*. International unions are so called because they include local unions in Canada. The larger national or international unions will have regional or district offices for administrative purposes at an intermediate level between the national/international headquarters and the locals.

The American Federation of Labor (AFL), composed chiefly of craft unions, was founded in 1886. The Congress of Industrial Organizations (CIO) came into being in 1935, in part as a spin off from the AFL, and consisted of industrial unions. The two merged in 1955 as the AFL-CIO, a loose federation of semiautonomous national/international unions. There are about 175 national/international unions in this country, of which about 115 belong to the AFL-CIO, and the remainder are known as *independent unions*. The two largest unions in existence, the Teamsters and the United Automobile Workers (UAW), are independents. The former was expelled from the AFL-CIO about 1960 and the latter voluntarily disaffiliated from the AFL-CIO about 1969 because of disagreements over policy. Other large independents include the United Mine Workers, International Longshoremen, District 50, United Electrical, Chemical, and National Federation of Federal Employees.

National/international union officers and headquarters staff are involved chiefly with establishing labor policy, lobbying with respect to legislation, conducting organizing drives, industrywide contract negotiations, education and training, and other miscellaneous activities.

At the local union level, the organization structure normally will include elected officers such as president, secretary-treasurer, business agent, and several stewards. Exact titles of these officers may vary. The *business agent* and *stewards* are particularly important to labor relations. The business agent usually is responsible for negotiation of contracts, grievance problems, and protection of the union's job jurisdiction. The stewards' primary responsibility is handling grievances at the worker-supervisor level. Stewards almost always are workers elected by their fellows and given some released time by the employer to perform their union duties. The other local union officers, including the business agent, may work full time at their union jobs (and be paid by the union), or they may be company employees performing union duties in their spare time. This situation will depend on the size of the local union and on whether the union represents employees at one company or several.

The two primary purposes of all unions are contract bargaining and grievance handling. Some unions also may have social programs as a third objective. How individual unions achieve these purposes depends in part on whether they are craft unions or industrial unions. Both types are concerned with wages, of course, but beyond that factor their approaches tend to differ.

A *craft union* represents all workers in a specific skilled trade (such as electricians, or plumbers, or clerical workers) in a given locality, regardless of the company for which they work. Craft unions base their power on controlling the labor supply for a specific skill, and to this end they tend to keep union dues high and to restrict their membership. In negotiating with management, they emphasize job rights, work standards, work pace, and the like. Craft union strikes tend to be peaceful. By controlling the local supply of a specific skill, they often can shut down an entire operation so that it doesn't matter if other workers enter the plant or not.

Industrial unions attempt to sign up and represent all workers, regardless of jobs, in a given company or industry. Industrial unions base their power on large membership and therefore tend to keep dues low. In negotiating with management, they emphsize union and job security, dues checkoff, job change procedures (usually based on seniority), work pace control, and the like. Industrial union strikes may involve violence more frequently than is the case for craft unions. The industrial union cannot control the total labor supply—many of its members on strike can be replaced—and therefore seeks concerted action by all workers.

In recent years, the thrust of union organizing efforts has been directed at those areas least organized: white collar and professional people, public sector employees, and agricultural workers. White collar and professional people in industry have resisted unionization in the past because they often thought of themselves as being part of management or they felt that they would lose status. These attitudes are beginning to change.

Unionization in the public sector (federal, state, and municipal employess) is in a state of flux. President Kennedy's Executive Order 10988 issued January 17, 1962, required federal agencies to recognize as exclusive bargaining agents unions representing a majority of employees in a bargaining unit. On the other hand, the Taft-Hartley Act prohibits strikes by federal employees, which eliminates one of labor's strengths in the bargaining process. Many states and municipalities also have laws prohibiting collective bargaining with, and/or strikes by, public employees. Recent years have seen a marked increase in slowdowns, sickouts, and similar actions by both federal and local public employees which accomplish the same purpose as a strike.

The problem of collective bargaining, and the possibility of resultant strikes, by public employees has raised a number of philosophical and practical questions. Do public employees have the right to withhold such vital services as police and fire protection, or even garbage collection? Does a government have sovereign powers or not? Can collective bargaining contravene public budgets and the tax structure? What are the respective powers of the executive and legislative branches of government in labor relations? Where do civil service commissions fit in? The answers to most of these questions remain to be worked out.

SUMMARY

The industrial revolution of the seventeenth and eighteenth centuries gave rise to the factory system of production. The work patterns required under this system changed the former relationships between master and worker and widened the social and economic gap between workers and the enterprise owners.

The common law and statutes of the nineteenth century were sympathetic to the employer. They were based on the sanctity of private property rights and a belief in the necessity to preserve free competition.

The work pattern of the factory system, and the prevailing views of the legal rights of employer versus employee, resulted in considerable exploitation of the worker. Men, women, and children worked from sunup to sundown six days a week in the factories and mines in the early 1800s.

Efforts of workers to organize in order to improve their economic and working conditions were stifled under the conspiracy doctrine. This doctrine was not overthrown until 1842.

In spite of occasional setbacks, the position of the worker gradually improved through the nineteenth century. Much labor violence marked the second half of the century. Even so, or perhaps partly because of it, a number of individual pieces of favorable legislation were passed. However, the balance of power remained on the side of the employer until 1935.

The Wagner Act, passed in 1935, guaranteed and affirmed by law the worker's right to organize and to bargain collectively. It identified and forbade a number of unfair labor practices by management. The balance of power now was in the hands of the worker.

A wave of strikes and labor unrest following World War II caused a public reaction that resulted in the Taft-Hartley Act of 1947. This act retained the basic provisions of the Wagner Act but added and made illegal a number of unfair labor practices by unions. Investigations of corruption in several unions during the 1950s led to the Landrum-Griffin Act in 1959. Provisions of this act were designed primarily to protect the rights of the worker in his relationship with the union.

Various pieces of civil rights legislation enacted during the 1960s and 1970s have added a new dimension to factors the supervisor must consider in relations with the work force.

KEY CONCEPTS

Collective bargaining. This is the concept of rule by mutual agreement between labor and management developed under established rules. It is the foundation on which labor relations rest. The extent to which trust and respect for this process exist between the two parties generally determines how well the process works.

Balance of power in labor relations. Bargaining implies positions of relative strength. The balance of power between labor and management is largely determined by current labor legislation, but it can swing in either direction according to congressional attitudes as influenced by public opinion. The nature of this balance at any time has a strong bearing on contract negotiations and on labor-management relations in general.

IMPORTANT TERMS

Apprentice	Conspiracy doctrine
Authorization card	Craft union
Bargaining unit	Equal Employment Opportunity
Business agent	Commission (EEOC)
Closed shop	Featherbedding
Collective bargaining	Hot cargo agreement
Collective bargaining agreement	Independent union
Consent election	Industrial Revolution

International union	National union
Journeyman	Representation election
Jurisdictional strike	Secondary boycott
Labor agreement (or contract)	Steward
Local union	Unfair labor practice
National Labor Relations Board (NLRB)	Union shop
	Yellow dog contract

INCIDENTS

Trouble on the Loading Dock

Jim Sullivan, foreperson in the shipping department of Intercity Distributors, came out onto the warehouse loading dock to see what was going on. The men were just sitting around. No one was loading the trucks backed up to the dock.

"What's the trouble, Bill?" Jim asked. "Why aren't you fellows on the job?"

"That truck over there is from the XYZ Company," Bill replied. "Our union is on strike at the XYZ store. The steward just came by and told us not to touch anything going to their place. He's gone now to call the local and get a picket line set up here."

What type of practice is described in this incident? Is it lawful or not? Which labor law covers this particular situation?

A Bad Day at the Office

Glenna Hartke, a clerical supervisor, walked out of the accounting office of Euphoria Mail Orders, Inc., in a highly disturbed state of mind. She had just heard from Mr. Johnson, the chief accountant, that a petition had been filed for union election for all the white-collar workers in Accounting. She had heard rumors, of course, but had dismissed them as just rumors. Pay and working conditions were good. Why should her people bother with such things as unions? As Glenna passed the water fountain, she noticed several women in muted conversation. She knew what they were talking about. Glenna stopped to say a few words.

"Look, ladies, I know what's going on around here. If you go ahead with this ridiculous idea of a union, it will cause nothing but trouble. If you push for this, we will just have to get more machines and let some people go." Satisfied that she had set them straight, Miss Hartke walked away.

Were Glenna Hartke's comments to the women proper or improper? Why?

QUESTIONS FOR DISCUSSION

1. Discuss the background factors contributing to exploitation of workers in the early 1800s.
2. In what sense did World War I and the two decades prior to 1935 represent a transition period between the old and the new in labor relations?
3. In what way was the Sherman Anti-Trust Act used against union activities?
4. How did the Wagner Act swing the balance of power into the hands of the employee?
5. Define collective bargaining. What purpose does it serve?
6. What is a bargaining unit?
7. What was the main purpose of the Landrum-Griffin Act?
8. What is a union unfair labor practice? Which act makes such practices illegal?
9. What must be done to persuade the NLRB to schedule a consent election? A representation election?
10. Enumerate a number of things that a supervisor would have to be careful about doing during an organizing campaign.
11. What are the different kinds of discrimination banned by the several "civil rights laws" described in the chapter?
12. Attempt to describe a work practice that at first glance does not appear to be, and is not intended to be, discriminatory, but which might be ruled so because of its effect.
13. What objectives and practices would craft unions and industrial unions ordinarily have in common?

CHAPTER XXIV

Safety and Health Responsibilities Under OSHA

LEARNING OBJECTIVES

- *To recognize the need for safety and health programs in business and industry.*
- *To understand something of the background of the Occupational Safety and Health Act (OSHA), the organization created to administer the act, and the role of the states in safety and health.*
- *To learn the record keeping and other requirements prescribed by the act, how safety and health standards and regulations are developed and promulgated, how provisions of the act are enforced, and the employer's rights with respect to appeal and variances.*
- *To determine the effects of OSHA on the activities of employers and supervisors and to identify precautions that should be taken.*
- *To recognize that accidents are the result of identifiable causes and to learn the necessary elements of safety programs designed to eliminate or minimize safety and health hazards.*
- *To identify the duties and responsibilities of the supervisor with respect to safety programs, with particular emphasis on developing checklists for self inspections of the work place.*

Introduction

"SAFETY comes from Man's mastery of his environment and himself. It is won by individual effort and group cooperation. It can be achieved only by informed, alert, skillful people who respect themselves and have a regard for others."

anonymous

Prior to the turn of the century, industry as a whole paid little attention to the physical well-being of its workers. Although industry in theory was responsible for the results of accidents and occupational diseases, there were so many loopholes in the body of common law that, in actual fact, the worker had little recourse in the event of injury or job-related illness. In the early 1900s, however, a wave of social awareness and reform was beginning to sweep across the country. One consequence of this was the enactment of industrial compensation laws by some states. Today, all states have laws of this sort with certain basic similarities, although specific provisions and extent of coverage vary from state to state.

The development and spread of compensation laws provided a financial incentive for companies to improve working conditions and to make serious efforts to prevent accidents. The attitudes and expectations of industry and society have progressed over the intervening years. Most organizations today recognize social and moral responsibilities, as well as legal and economic reasons, for providing work environments that protect the health and safety of employees. As a result, the American worker is healthier and safer on the job than workers in any other country. From 1913 to the early 1970s, the frequency of injuries had dropped by 78 percent, the seriousness of those injuries was reduced by 72 percent, and the frequency of fatal accidents was cut by 78 percent.

Even though American industry has a good record, it can be improved. Partly because of an upward trend in work injuries during the 1960s and partly because of the lack of uniformity between various state laws covering job safety and health, Congress enacted the *Occupational Safety and Health Act of 1970 (OSHA)*, effective April 28th, 1971. The act authorizes the federal government to establish and enforce standards relating to occupational safety and health. It is applicable to businesses affecting interstate commerce.

Industry now has had somewhat over nine years of experience under OSHA. The effectiveness of the act is a controversial subject. Many in both industry and government contend that there is little or no solid evidence that OSHA regulations have improved the safety or health of the American worker. A Senate study in 1979 and a bill introduced into the House of Representatives the same year both recommended drastic alternatives to OSHA. Recent court decisions have jeopardized compliance inspections without an employer's consent.

Even though OSHA is in difficulty and may be changed in the foreseeable future, it has had, and will continue to have, numerous side effects in the areas of management practices and industrial relations. These effects are of particular concern to the supervisor, along with the normal responsibilities for the safety and health of the work group.

WHAT IS OSHA?

Public Law 91-596, entitled "Occupational Safety and Health Act of 1970" (OSHA) also is known as the *Williams-Steiger Act* after its sponsors in the Congress. It became effective on April 28, 1971. The purpose of OSHA is as follows.

"To assure safe and healthful working conditions for working men and women; by authorizing enforcement of the standards developed under the Act; by assisting and encouraging the States in their efforts to assure safe and healthful working conditions; by providing research, information, education, and training in the field of occupational safety and health; and for other purposes."[1]

ADMINISTRATION OF THE ACT

The Department of Labor; the Department of Health and Welfare; and several independent agencies and bodies are involved in the administration of OSHA.

The Department of Labor has primary responsibility for administration and enforcement, including promulgation of standards and inspection for compliance. The *Occupational Safety and Health Administration* within the Labor Department has ten regional offices located in Boston, New York City, Philadelphia, Atlanta, Chicago, Dallas, Kansas City, Denver, San Francisco, and Seattle.

The Department of Health and Welfare (HW) is responsible for research, education, and related functions authorized by the act. The *National Institute for Occupational Safety and Health (NIOSH)* has been established to carry out these functions within HW. Both the Labor Department and HW perform certain functions in consultation and cooperation with each other.

OSHA establishes a new and independent federal agency, the *Occupational Safety and Health Review Commission,* a quasi-judicial body whose three members are appointed by the President. The commission's functions are the following.

1. To hear and review cases of alleged violations brought before it by the Secretary of Labor.
2. To issue corrective orders, where warranted.
3. To assess civil penalties.

THE ROLE OF THE STATES

It was the intent of the Congress to have the states assume full responsibility for development, administration, and enforcement of their own occupational safety and health standards and programs. The states are en-

---

[1] Introduction to Occupational Safety and Health Act of 1970.

couraged to submit plans for approval by the Secretary of Labor. There are several conditions for approval, the most important of which is that state standards, and enforcement of these standards (including inspection procedures), must be at least as effective as the federal program. The federal government retains concurrent enforcement jurisdiction with the states for at least three years after initial approval of *state plans*. After that period, the federal government remains in a monitoring role. As of 1979, 24 state plans had been approved.

Employers in states not submitting approved plans are subject to the federal act. However, state agencies and courts may assert jurisdiction under state law over any occupational safety and health issue for which no federal standard is in effect under OSHA.

WHO MUST COMPLY

The terms of OSHA apply to every employer who is engaged in a business affecting commerce. It applies not only to manufacturing operations but also to offices, farms, service organizations, nonprofit organizations, transportation, places of entertainment, and other employers. For all practical purposes, therefore, the great majority of employers are affected. There are, however, some exclusions and some provisions for separate but equally effective coverage.

Self-employed farmers, professional workers, and business people are excluded from provisions of the act if they have no paid employees. Similarly, unpaid family workers are excluded. In other words, a business operated entirely by members of a family and with no paid employees would not be covered. Federal government employees are specifically excluded, but are covered by a separate program. State and local government employees also are excluded, but potentially may be covered under separate programs.

Finally, the act specifically provides that its terms shall not apply to working conditions protected under other federal occupational safety and health laws. Major groups affected by this provision are workers already covered by the Federal Mine Safety and Health Amendments Act of 1977 and the Atomic Energy Act of 1954, as amended, including state agreements under that act.

RECORD-KEEPING REQUIREMENTS

Employers subject to the act are required to keep records of *recordable occupational injuries and illnesses*—defined as those resulting in fatalities, or lost work days, or which involve medical treatment, loss of consciousness, restriction of work or motion, transfer to another job, termination of employment, or any diagnosed occupational illness. *Minor injuries* requiring only first aid treatment not involving any of the above conditions need not be recorded. These records must be kept up to date, be available to government representatives and to employees, and be retained for five years following the end of the current year. The records are to be kept in the *establishments* where the employees usually report to work. There are two kinds of records to be kept.

1. A *log and summary* of all recordable occupational injuries and illnesses. Each case must be recorded on form OSHA No. 200 (see Figure 24-1), or on an equivalent, within six working days of its occurrence.

    The summary section of form OSHA No. 200 showing the year's totals must be completed and certified by February 1 of the following year. Copies must be posted in a conspicuous place by February 1 and remain in place until March 1. No alternate form is acceptable for the posted summary section.

2. A *supplementary record* of each case recorded on form OSHA No. 200 also must be completed within six working days. It is kept on form OSHA No. 101 (see Figure 24-2) or on an equivalent.

To acquaint employees with the job safety and health protection provided under the act, an *informational poster* (available from OSHA) must be posted in a prominent place in the establishment to which employees usually report to work.

An employer must report within 48 hours to the nearest office of the Occupational Safety and Health Administration any accident or health hazard that has resulted in one or more fatalities, or the hospitalization of five or more employees.

An amendment to the act, enacted in 1972, exempts from the preceding occupational injury and illness record-keeping requirements all employers with fewer than eight employees. The amendment does *not* exempt them from compliance with standards or from other provisions of the act.

Certain standards promulgated under the act require the keeping of other records, for example, records of employee exposures to toxic substances or harmful physical agents. Employers should carefully check all standards applicable to their places of business to determine what additional record keeping may be necessary.

ENFORCEMENT OF THE ACT

The enforcement of employer compliance with OSHA standards and regulations is accomplished through inspections of work places and records; through citations, notices, or court orders issued in the event that alleged violations are found; and through assessment of civil or criminal penalties. Provisions exist for hearings and appeals.

Inspection Procedures

Inspection of work places for purposes of standards regulations enforcement is made by *compliance officers* of the Labor Department, or by inspectors of state safety and health agencies. Officials of HW also may

Bureau of Labor Statistics
Log and Summary of Occupational Injuries and Illnesses

NOTE: This form is required by Public Law 91-596 and must be kept in the establishment for *5 years*. Failure to maintain and post can result in the issuance of citations and assessment of penalties. *(See posting requirements on the other side of form.)*

RECORDABLE CASES: You are required to record information about every occupational **death**; every nonfatal occupational **illness**; and those nonfatal occupational injuries which involve one or more of the following: loss of consciousness, restriction of work or motion, transfer to another job, or medical treatment (other than first aid). *(See definitions on the other side of form.)*

Case or File Number	Date of Injury or Onset of Illness	Employee's Name	Occupation	Department	Description of Injury or Illness
Enter a nonduplicating number which will facilitate comparisons with supplementary records.	Enter Mo./day.	Enter first name or initial, middle initial, last name.	Enter regular job title, not activity employee was performing when injured or at onset of illness. In the absence of a formal title, enter a brief description of the employee's duties.	Enter department in which the employee is regularly employed or a description of normal workplace to which employee is assigned, even though temporarily working in another department at the time of injury or illness.	Enter a brief description of the injury or illness and indicate the part or parts of body affected. Typical entries for this column might be: Amputation of 1st joint right forefinger; Strain of lower back; Contact dermatitis on both hands; Electrocution—body.
(A)	(B)	(C)	(D)	(E)	(F)

PREVIOUS PAGE TOTALS ⟶

TOTALS (Instructions on other side of form.) ⟶

OSHA No. 200

Figure 24-1 Form OSHA No. 200 for log and summary of occupational injuries and illnesses.

What is OSHA? 463

U.S. Department of Labor

For Calendar Year 19 _____   Page ____ of ____

Company Name
Establishment Name
Establishment Address

Form Approved
O.M.B. No. 44R 1453

Extent of and Outcome of INJURY | Type, Extent of, and Outcome of ILLNESS

DATE	Nonfatal Injuries				Type of Illness							Fatalities	Nonfatal Illnesses				
	Injuries With Lost Workdays				Injuries Without Lost Workdays	CHECK Only One Column for Each Illness (See other side of form for terminations or permanent transfers.)							Illness Related	Illnesses With Lost Workdays				Illnesses Without Lost Workdays
Enter DATE of injury. Mo./day/yr.	Enter a CHECK if injury involves days away from work, or days of restricted work activity, or both.	Enter a CHECK if injury involves days away from work.	Enter number of DAYS away from work.	Enter number of DAYS of restricted work activity.	Enter a CHECK if no entry was made in columns 1 or 2 but the injury is recordable as defined above.	Occupational skin diseases or disorders	Dust diseases of the lungs	Respiratory conditions due to toxic agents	Poisoning (systemic effects of toxic materials)	Disorders due to physical agents	Disorders associated with repeated trauma	All other occupational illnesses	Enter DATE of death. Mo./day/yr.	Enter a CHECK if illness involves days away from work, or days of restricted work activity, or both.	Enter a CHECK if illness involves days away from work.	Enter number of DAYS away from work.	Enter number of DAYS of restricted work activity.	Enter a CHECK if no entry was made in columns 8 or 9.
	(2)	(3)	(4)	(5)	(6)	(a)	(b)	(c)	(d)	(e)	(f)	(g)	(8)	(9)	(10)	(11)	(12)	(13)

INJURIES   ILLNESSES

Certification of Annual Summary Totals By _____ Title _____ Date _____

OSHA No. 200   **POST ONLY THIS PORTION OF THE LAST PAGE NO LATER THAN FEBRUARY 1.**

OSHA No. 101
Case or File No. _____

Form approved
OMB No. 44R 1453

Supplementary Record of Occupational Injuries and Illnesses

EMPLOYER
1. Name _____
2. Mail address _____
   (No. and street)   (City or town)   (State)
3. Location, if different from mail address _____

INJURED OR ILL EMPLOYEE
4. Name _____ Social Security No. _____
   (First name)   (Middle name)   (Last name)
5. Home address _____
   (No. and street)   (City or town)   (State)
6. Age _____   7. Sex: Male _____ Female _____ (Check one)
8. Occupation _____
   (Enter regular job title, *not* the specific activity he was performing at time of injury.)
9. Department _____
   (Enter name of department or division in which the injured person is regularly employed, even though he may have been temporarily working in another department at the time of injury.)

THE ACCIDENT OR EXPOSURE TO OCCUPATIONAL ILLNESS
10. Place of accident or exposure _____
    (No. and street)   (City or town)   (State)
    If accident or exposure occurred on employer's premises, give address of plant or establishment in which it occurred. Do not indicate department or division within the plant or establishment. If accident occurred outside employer's premises at an identifiable address, give that address. If it occurred on a public highway or at any other place which cannot be identified by number and street, please provide place references locating the place of injury as accurately as possible.
11. Was place of accident or exposure on employer's premises? _____ (Yes or No)
12. What was the employee doing when injured? _____
    (Be specific. If he was using tools or equipment or handling material, name them and tell what he was doing with them.)
13. How did the accident occur? _____
    (Describe fully the events which resulted in the injury or occupational illness. Tell what happened and how it happened. Name any objects or substances involved and tell how they were involved. Give full details on all factors which led or contributed to the accident. Use separate sheet for additional space.)

OCCUPATIONAL INJURY OR OCCUPATIONAL ILLNESS
14. Describe the injury or illness in detail and indicate the part of body affected. _____
    (e.g.: amputation of right index finger at second joint; fracture of ribs; lead poisoning; dermatitis of left hand, etc.)
15. Name the object or substance which directly injured the employee. (For example, the machine or thing he struck against or which struck him; the vapor or poison he inhaled or swallowed; the chemical or radiation which irritated his skin; or in cases of strains, hernias, etc., the thing he was lifting, pulling, etc.)
_____
16. Date of injury or initial diagnosis of occupational illness _____
    (Date)
17. Did employee die? _____ (Yes or No)

OTHER
18. Name and address of physician _____
19. If hospitalized, name and address of hospital _____

Date of report _____ Prepared by _____
Official position _____

Figure 24–2 Form OSHA No. 101 for supplementary record of occupational injuries and illnesses.

make inspections and question employers and employees in carrying out its functions under the act. Inspections may originate in several ways:

1. After reports of serious accidents or where an imminent danger situation is believed to exist.
2. As a result of special emphasis programs targeting on industries with high accident-frequency rates.
3. As a result of a specific complaint by any employee (or representative) to the Department of Labor alleging a violation or imminent danger. The identity of the employee must be kept confidential if he so requests.
4. Through routine or random inspections.

In most instances there will be no advance warning of an inspection. In fact, the act provides criminal penalties for giving any unauthorized advance notice of any inspection.

The act states that compliance officers may enter an establishment at any reasonable time and must not be subjected to undue delay. Compliance officers may review any pertinent records and visit and examine any work place, pertinent condition, equipment, machines, materials, and so on. They have the right to question privately any employer, owner, agent, operator, or employee. Any trade secrets learned in the process must be kept confidential. Inspectors with the proper clearances are available for inspecting areas in which classified government work may be under way.

The employer or representative has the right to accompany the inspector during the *walkaround inspection.* An employee, or a representative authorized by the employees, also has the right to accompany the inspector. The employer must excuse the employee from regular work duties for the walkaround inspection.

An *opening conference* normally precedes the walkaround inspection. The inspector will indicate the investigation's scope, the records she/he wishes to review, and the employees with whom the inspector wishes to talk. After the inspection, the compliance officer holds an informal *closing conference* with the employer advising the employer of any apparent violations. The inspector may hold a separate closing discussion with the employees if they so request.

Many persons have objected to involuntary OSHA inspections on the grounds that they violate the Fourth Amendment. A U.S. Supreme Court decision on May 23, 1978, banned on this basis inspections without warrants by agents of OSHA unless an employer consents to the entry. The court ruling left open a legal opportunity for the Secretary of Labor to seek *ex parte warrants* if an employer refuses entry for an inspection. An *ex parte* warrant is one signed by a court without first providing the employer with a chance to appear in court and oppose the warrant.

In a later case (the Weyerhaeuser case), the courts held that the warrant must be based on evidence of probable cause.

More recently, in *Marshall* v. *Gibson's Products, Inc.*, the Fifth Circuit Court ruled that the Secretary of Labor cannot file suit to enforce an OSHA inspection even when OSHA has secured a warrant. The ruling held that the courts lacked subject jurisdiction because the Congress had not granted that authority to the Secretary of Labor. The Secretary is expected to appeal this decision to the U.S. Supreme Court, or ask the Congress for more authority, or both.

At the time this is written, the right of entry for an OSHA inspection without employer consent is left up in the air. It probably will be settled, one way or the other, in the near future. It should be noted that during the first four months after the May 1978 Supreme Court decision, federal and/or state agents conducted 59,171 safety inspections out of which only 612 employers refused access to the inspectors.

Citations and Abatement In the event that a violation is found, the employer will be issued a written *citation* by the OSHA Area Office describing the specific nature of the violation and fixing a reasonable time period for *abatement* of the violation. A copy of each citation must be posted prominently at or near the location where the violation occurred.

The employer must be notified of the penalty (if any) proposed to be assessed. The Area Office attempts to deliver the notification of penalty concurrently with the situation.

If the employer does not abate the violation within the prescribed time, a penalty may be assessed for exceeding this time. If the abatement time limit has been contested, the abatement period does not start until after a final order has been issued by the Review Commission.

Citations are not issued if violation of a standard has no immediate or direct relationship to safety or health. Instead, a *notice of de minimis violation* shall be issued with no proposed penalty.

If the inspector believes that an *imminent danger* of death or serious harm exists, and that such harm might occur before the hazard could be eliminated through normal enforcement channels, the Secretary of Labor may petition a U.S. District Court for a restraining order to eliminate the conditions or practices in question.

Appeals An employer may contest or appeal (1) a citation for an alleged violation of standards or regulations of the act, (2) the time period allowed for abatement of a violation, (3) the penalty assessed for a violation, and (4) a penalty assessed for exceeding the abatement time limit.

An employer's contest of one of these actions is heard by the Occupational Safety and Health Review Commission whose decision may be appealed in the federal court system.

Employees or their representatives also may contest an abatement period (usually one they consider unreasonably long) by filing a notice within 15 days. This also goes to the Review Commission for a hearing.

Specific Penalties   The act provides both civil and criminal penalties for violations of standards, rules, orders, or regulations. However, no penalty shall be proposed for a *de minimis* violation.

With respect to citations and penalties, one alleged violation consists of all instances of the same violation of a single standard at a single establishment. Thus 10 fork lift trucks without overhead guards at one establishment would comprise 1 violation, not 10.

A *serious violation* is one where there is substantial probability that death or serious physical harm could result from existing conditions or practices. To be a violation, the employer must have been aware of the presence of the hazard, or have been able to be aware of its presence through exercise of reasonable diligence. A *nonserious violation* is one where there is little probability of death or serious harm resulting, but where a direct or immediate relationship to safety or health does exist.

A distinction is made between serious violations and all other violations with respect to civil penalties. A penalty is *mandatory* for a citation issued for a serious violation. The maximum penalty in this instance is $1,000. Civil penalties are *not mandatory* for other nonserious violations, but *may be* proposed. The maximum penalty that may be proposed in these instances is $1,000. In the case of willful or repeated violations, a civil penalty of up to $10,000 *may be* proposed.

In the event of failure of an employer to abate a violation within the period allowed, a civil penalty *may be* assessed up to $1,000 for each day that each violation continues after the expiration of the abatement period.

When there is reason to believe that violations or actions have occurred that are subject to criminal penalties, the matter is referred to the appropriate authorities. Criminal violations or actions under the act include the following.

1. Willful violations causing death.
2. Giving unauthorized advance notice of inspection.
3. Knowingly giving false information (statements, records, reports, and so on).
4. Assaulting or resisting the work of OSHA enforcement personnel.
5. Assaulting such personnel with a deadly weapon.
6. Murder of such personnel.

The act provides specific penalties upon conviction for criminal violations or actions which include fines and/or imprisonment.

OCCUPATIONAL SAFETY AND HEALTH STANDARDS   OSHA defines an *occupational safety and health standard* as a standard that requires conditions—or the adoption or use of one or more practices, means, methods, operations, or processes—reasonably necessary or appropriate to provide safe or healthful employment and places of employment. These standards are a body of rules for avoiding hazards that experience and research have shown to be harmful. Some standards apply to all employees, for example, walking and working surfaces. Many others are applicable only to workers while engaged in specific types of work.

It is beyond the scope of this book to attempt to list or describe the large number of standards in effect. OSHA and many industrial organizations publish booklets describing standards pertinent to specific trades and industries.

Promulgation and Development

The Secretary of Labor has authority to promulgate new occupational safety and health standards. He also may revise, modify, or revoke existing standards. All new standards and any actions relative to existing standards must be published in the *Federal Register* along with the proposed effective date.

An exception is *emergency temporary standards,* which are effective immediately upon publication in the *Federal Register*. These can be established where it is found that employees are exposed to grave danger.

The National Institute for Occupational Safety and Health (NIOSH), which is under HW, has the power to formulate standards in addition to its other duties. It specializes in the area of health standards whereas the American National Standards Institute (ANSI) and other industry groups are playing a major role in safety standards.

Industry has complained extensively about proliferation of regulations that it claims provide few, if any, benefits for employees. A Presidential Task Force has made numerous recommendations to OSHA on ways to minimize the undesirable side effects of government regulation. As a result, OSHA has initiated a program to revoke or simplify regulations that OSHA itself calls "nitpicking" or "irrelevant." In October 1978, it revoked 607 general industry regulations (e.g., toilet partitions) and 321 regulations applicable only to certain trades. In December 1978, it proposed replacing 2400 mandatory regulations with voluntary guidelines which would condense 400 pages of complex and detailed requirements into 10 pages.

Continuation of this program will do much to relieve management and supervisors of some of their headaches.

Appeals and Variances

Any person adversely affected by a standard may challenge its validity by petitioning the U.S. Court of Appeals within 60 days after promulgation. Such a petition does not operate as a stay of the standard unless the court so orders.

An employer may apply to the Secretary of Labor for a *temporary variance* from a standard if he needs more time to come into compliance. The variance normally is granted if the employer can show genuine need and if there exists a protective plan of action. A *permanent variance* (no time limit) may be granted if it can be shown that safety measures are being used that are as safe as those required in a standard.

Affected employees must be notified of all applications for all types of variances and must be given the opportunity for a hearing. An *interim variance* may be granted until a decision is issued on the result of the hearing.

The Secretary of Labor may allow reasonable variations, tolerances, and exemptions from any and all of the act's provisions if he finds these necessary to avoid serious impairment of the national defense. If such are in effect for more than six months, employees must be notified and given an opportunity for a hearing.

THE EFFECT OF OSHA

The preceding description of OSHA makes it obvious that almost all businesses and other organizations have many safety and health obligations and responsibilities, along with their associated costs. This is true even for those firms already having good safety and health programs in operation. Some of the obligations and responsibilities are primarily the concern of top management, but many will fall directly on the shoulders of the supervisor.

EFFECT ON EMPLOYER

It is quite evident that employers have a massive record-keeping job. Care must be taken that the proper records are kept at appropriate locations in multiestablishment firms.

Complete compliance with OSHA standards is difficult; some firms contend that it is next to impossible. This means that evidence of *intent to comply,* or *good faith,* is very important. Business and industrial establishments should conduct their own internal safety and health surveys, record in writing any action taken, and develop and record in writing plans for handling each actual or potential hazard. Doing so may minimize mandatory fines and may eliminate, or at least minimize, discretionary fines.

The possibility of monetary penalties for violations is not the only financial cost. Bringing an establishment into compliance with applicable standards will involve large sums for some companies. American industry spent an estimated $4.8 billion in 1978 complying with OSHA regulations.

The company's labor relations undoubtedly are affected. Two examples are evident today, and others will likely occur.

The act requires employers to excuse an employee from regular work duties to accompany the walkaround inspection, but it does not require the employer to pay for this time. The subject of "walkaround pay" is likely to show up in labor contract negotiations.

Similarly, employers are fully responsible for any violations resulting from employee actions or conduct. The act does not provide for citations or penalties for employees who refuse to abide by safety standards, but does state that employers should take all necessary action to assure employee compliance with standards. Employers are likely to press for union agreement to more stringent disciplinary action in the case of safety violations by workers.

Employers have a problem in keeping up to date with new standards and with new rules, regulations, orders, guidelines, and precedent-setting decisions. The *Federal Register* has been mentioned previously as one source of information. OSHA makes available through the U.S. Government Printing Office a low-cost subscription package of basic OSHA documents plus a monthly update entitled "Job Safety and Health." Subscription commercial news reports that deal solely with activities and developments related to OSHA are available from several reliable sources.

EFFECT ON SUPERVISORS

Supervisors in all types of establishments play a key role in helping their organizations satisfy the requirements of OSHA. The safety and health of the work force always has been a responsibility of the conscientious, effective supervisor. However, OSHA almost certainly will add to supervisory duties and responsibilities in greater or lesser degrees. Safety is now a major part of the job.

The initial tasks of the supervisor will be to familiarize himself thoroughly with those OSHA standards applicable to his work unit and then to take whatever steps are necessary in putting them into practice. The supervisor must, of course, have the cooperation of superiors in providing anything necessary in the way of special equipment, safety devices, protective garments, and so on. At the same time, there is much that only the supervisor can do. For example, alleged violations of the regulation concerning walking and working surfaces are one of the most frequent citations. Only the supervisor is in a position to assure that aisles are kept clear and free of obstruction at all times, and that floors always are swept up and kept free of grease, oil, turnings, and other trash.

With the proper training, education, and example, the average worker will come to recognize a safety and health responsibility to self, fellow workers, and the employer. The fact remains, however, that the worker has very little legal responsibility under the act, because there are no provisions for citations or penalties for employees.

Many supervisors will have to run more of a "taut ship" with respect to enforcing safety rules than they have in the past. Turning a blind eye to the removal of safety guards in order to step up production can be tolerated no longer. Even when uncomfortable or inconvenient, workers must be made to wear hard hats, safety goggles, protective gloves, and so on, when specified by standards. Because an employee's action or conduct can result in a citation and penalty for his employer, the supervisor must develop a stern attitude in disciplinary measures for persistent offenders.

At the same time, one of the major considerations of any supervisor will be to assure that the workers' rights under the act are not obstructed. It is easy to obstruct these rights inadvertently. Specifically, the supervisor should remember that employees have the right to file complaints of alleged violations, and to do so anonymously if they wish. An employee, or the authorized representative of the employees, may accompany the compliance officer on his walkaround inspection. Private discussion between the inspector and a reasonable number of employees is permitted during the inspection, as well as a closing discussion afterwards.

Employees may contest abatement periods and applications for all types of variances. They may contest a national defense variation, tolerance, or exemption after it has been in effect for six months.

The act specifically protects employees against discharge or any other form of discrimination for filing complaints, testifying in any proceedings, or exercising any other right under OSHA.

SAFETY AND ACCIDENTS

The primary purpose of a *safety program* is accident prevention. Business and industry have made considerable progress over the years in making jobs safer, but room for improvement still exists. This is one reason for OSHA.

Safety is an important program. In 1978, accidents that occurred at work accounted for 13,000 deaths and 2.2 million disabling injuries. The costs are estimated at $23 billion, including invisible and indirect costs.[2] The accident frequency and severity rates of a number of the country's principal industries are shown in Figure 24-3.

Every company should have a safety program aimed at accident prevention. It can be a simple program in a comparatively small company, or an elaborate, formal structure within a corporate giant. The kind of company and the nature of its work will determine the size and kind of program needed. A bank or insurance compny with hundreds of clerical and other office workers will require a program quite different in its elements (but not in principle) from that needed by, say, a steel mill.

WHAT CAUSES ACCIDENTS? Before considering the different aspects of a safety program and accident prevention, we must look at the cause of accidents. It is difficult to prevent something for which you do not know the cause.

---

[2]*Accident Facts*, National Safety Council, Chicago, 1979, pp. 23-24.

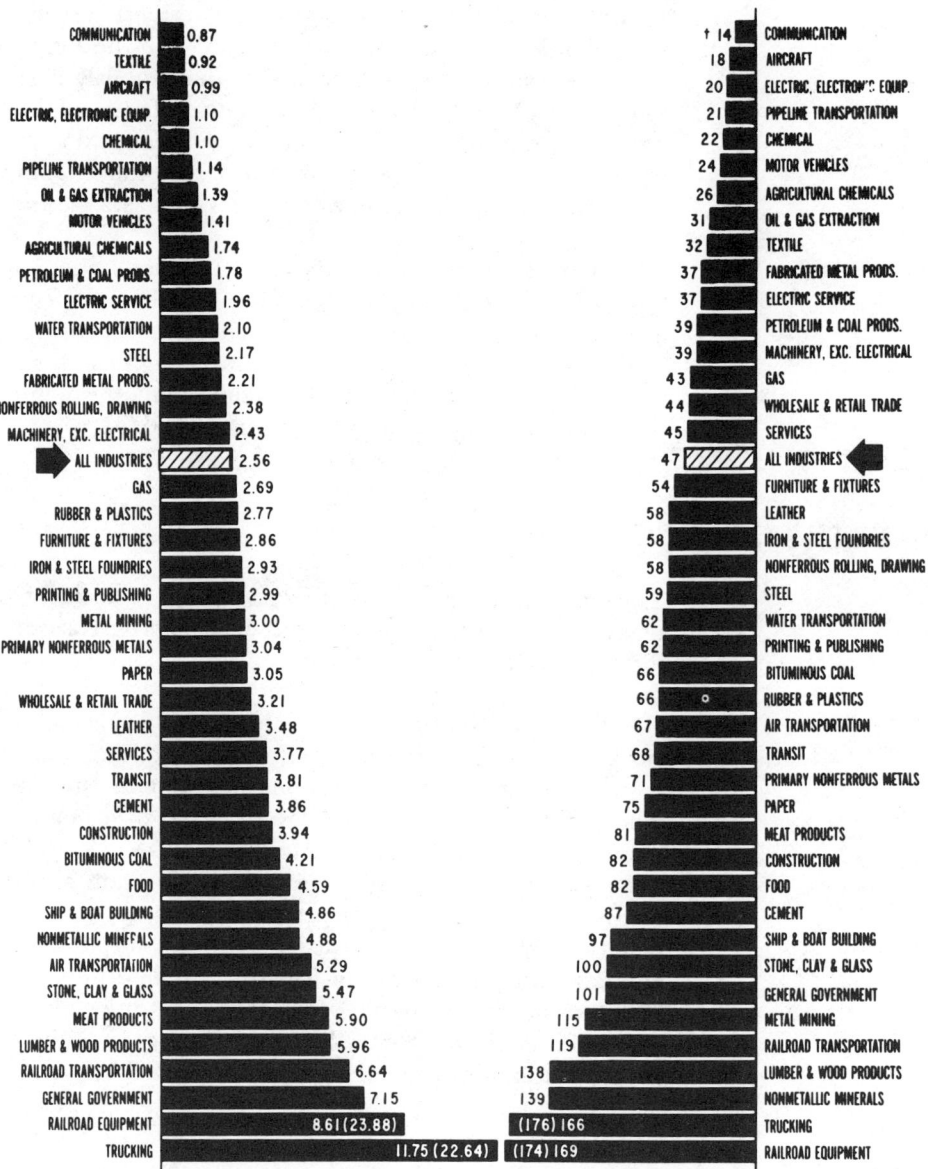

Figure 24–3   *Accident frequency and severity rates of principal industries in 1978. (Source. Adapted from Accident Facts 1979 Edition, © 1979 by the National Safety Council.)*

Some people describe accidents as "acts of God." Others go to the opposite extreme and say, in the words of a popular TV comedian, "The Devil made me do it." These views place the blame where it does not belong. Accidents do not just happen—they are the result of identifiable causes. It may be an unrealistic goal to attempt to eliminate accidents entirely, but a competent supervisor can reduce the frequency rate by a great deal.

Basically, there are two *immediate causes* of accidents: *unsafe personal acts* and *unsafe conditions.* It is estimated that roughly 80 percent of industrial accidents result from unsafe acts and 20 percent from unsafe conditions. However, at least some unsafe conditions are themselves created through unsafe acts. It is likely, therefore, that unsafe acts are responsible directly and indirectly for almost 90 percent of industrial accidents.

Some examples of unsafe acts and unsafe conditions are indicated in Figure 24-4. As illustrated in this figure, an accident is the result of a process, a sequence of happenings subjected to various influences. If we are to prevent accidents, we must look behind the immediate cause to the *contributory causes.* What factors led to the unsafe act or to the unsafe condition? Both the mental and the physical characteristics and traits of the individual are contributory. Another major factor is the broad environment in which he works, with the principal contributory influence here being the attitudes and actions of the supervisor in particular and of higher management in general.

No discussion of accidents is complete without mention of the so-called *accident-prone* individual. This is a somewhat controversial subject. Numerous studies have shown, beyond any question, that a small percentage of people have a high percentage of the accidents. These are "apparent accident prones." It generally is agreed that not all of these people are "true accident prones." The kind of work being done, age, time, and other factors play a part. The important thing for the supervisor to remember is that true accident prones exist, whether their numbers are relatively large or small. The supervisor should not, on the other hand, fall into the trap of blaming everything on accident proneness.

THE SAFETY PROGRAM

Every organization should have a safety program. This is another name for an accident prevention program. As noted before, the program's structure, and whether the program is informal or formal, will depend on the size and nature of the organization as a whole.

Before any effective safety program can be established, three vital criteria must be met: *top management support,* a *safety policy,* and a *safety director.* Top management support is mentioned first because everything else depends on it. If top management does not truly and sincerely support the concept of safety, then the safety program will be lackadaisical

474 Chapter XXIV Safety and Health Responsibilities under OSHA

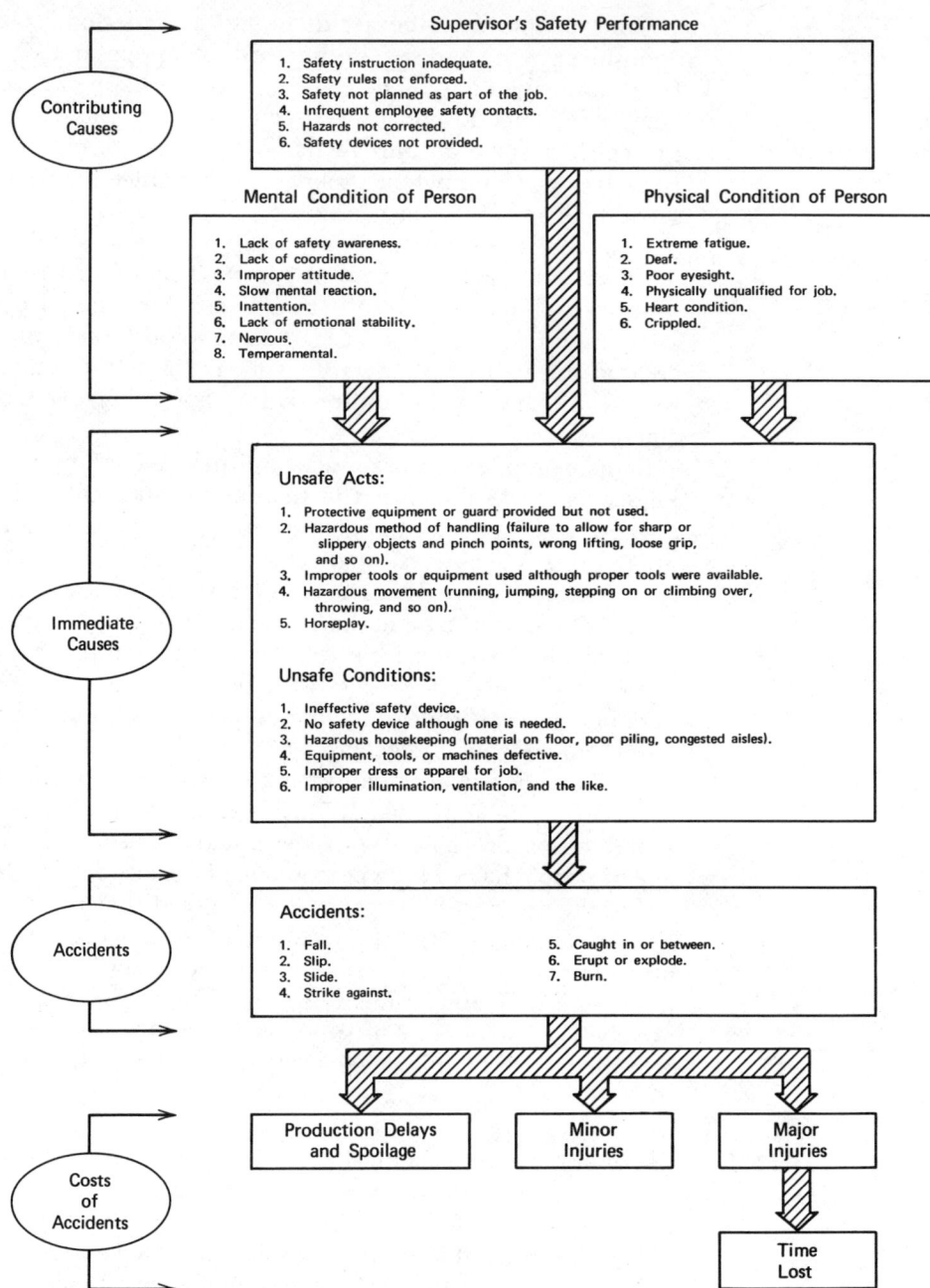

Figure 24-4 The accident process.

at best. We have emphasized many times that leadership styles and attitudes flow downward from the top.

A comprehensive and meaningful safety policy is *prima facie* evidence of support, but it must be followed. A good safety policy will spell out in some detail the safety responsibilities of management in general, of the supervisor in particular, and of the employees. Many labor contracts contain clauses specifying the rights and obligations of management and the worker in matters of safety.

Regardless of whether the program is informal or formal, one individual should be in charge. The title of Safety Director is common, but other titles are used. This may be a part-time job, along with other duties, in a small company or in an informal program. It will be a full-time job in many establishments. Whether part-time or full-time, it is important to success that one person be recognized as having primary authority and responsibility in matters of safety. It has been said, truthfully, that safety is the responsibility of everyone. However, it requires someone to coordinate, guide, and control the efforts of everyone concerned.

Assuming that the preliminary criteria have been met, a comprehensive safety program will include certain specific elements of activity, function, or structure:

1. Safety committee.
2. Education and training.
3. Enforcement.
4. Job safety analysis.
5. Safety engineering.
6. Inspections.
7. Accident investigation and analysis.
8. Record keeping.
9. Treatment of injuries.
10. Periodic review of program.

It is quite possible that some of these elements might be combined — job safety analysis could be assigned to the safety engineer, or record keeping could be part of the investigation and analysis function. They are listed separately to insure that they are not overlooked.

Safety committees normally are made up of a balanced group of hourly employees, supervisors and, possibly, a member of higher management. There are several types of safety committees that may be used; the exact type and its function depend on the organizational structure.[3] The purpose is to aid and advise management on matters of worker safety. The safety committee provides the important factor of employee participation in the safety program. In so doing, it helps advertise and sell safety to the workers. It provides a channel for action on suggestions and ideas submitted by workers. The on-the-job experience of committee

---

[3] *Organizing a Safety Committee*, OSHA 2231, June 1975. Obtainable from any OSHA regional office.

members is valuable in determining hazardous conditions and methods of work, suggesting corrective measures, and obtaining participation of all personnel.

Safety education and training have the objectives of developing an awareness of safety responsibilities in the worker and developing his skills in the use of safe working practices. Much of this is a matter of developing the proper attitudes toward safety. New employees should receive orientation in health and safety matters relevant to their jobs.

People tend to forget and grow careless. Education and training should be a continuous process aimed at all employees. Educational and training tools include posters, films, displays, manuals, safety meetings, safety contests, and short courses. Good materials are available from the National Safety Council, the Department of Labor,[4] the Department of Health and Welfare, and from many other sources. Supervisors should receive even more comprehensive and intensive safety training than the average employee.

Enforcement of safety and health rules and practices is a necessary factor in a successful program. Employees forget, grow careless, take a chance, or fail to learn. Disciplinary action has its place when other approaches fall down. The importance of this may increase under OSHA.

Job safety analysis is a key element in accident prevention. Conducting such analyses is one of the first things to do in a safety program. Job analysis to improve work methods is common practice (see Chapter XI). Job safety analysis goes a step farther. Essentially, it is a study of all work elements of a particular job, the identification of potential hazards, and the determination of work methods or means to avoid or overcome the hazards. Most jobs can be divided into three sections: (1) preparation—make ready or setting up; (2) operation—the actual doing of the job; and (3) disposal—the removal of the product of the operation.[5] A separate analysis should be made of each phase of the job. The cited publication contains examples of convenient forms and charts for conducting job safety analyses.

Safety engineering, as originally conceived, involved the design of machinery and equipment to eliminate potential hazards. If these could not be eliminated completely, then some sort of protective guard or safety device was designed into the machine. This still is one function of safety engineering. However, safety engineering has expanded to cover broader aspects of the work environment—lighting; ventilation; heating and air conditioning; noise; control of fumes, gases, and dust; and so on. New OSHA standards are stringent in these areas. In fact, OSHA has been described as an engineering law by some people. The act will increase the importance of safety engineering dramatically.

---

[4]*Principles and Practices of Occupational Safety and Health,* U.S. Department of Labor, Washington, D.C. This is a six-part, self-study program designed to help the supervisor.
[5]*Ibid.* In particular, Booklet Two (OSHA 2214) and Booklet Three (OSHA 2215) of this series cover job hazard analysis.

Inspections by compliance officers, now faced by almost every type of working establishment, have been described earlier in this chapter. However, safety programs should provide for periodic inspections by appropriate company personnel. These are useful in connection with the overall program as well as assisting in meeting OSHA compliance requirements. Supervisors also should conduct their own inspections at frequent intervals of the work places, equipment, and facilities for which they are responsible. A number of trade associations and other organizations have developed and made available check lists for various types of industry that are convenient in conducting internal company inspections.

Accident investigation and analysis should be conducted for every accident that occurs. It is necessary with respect to prevention of similar occurrences in the future as well as to provide data for records and reports required under OSHA and by insurance companies. The primary purpose should not be to place blame, but rather to determine causes and corrective measures needed. Serious accidents should be investigated by a safety specialist with the involvement of the supervisor. Minor accidents usually can be investigated by the supervisor alone.

Record-keeping requirements under OSHA have been described. However, most companies were keeping accident and health records long before OSHA was enacted. In addition to the OSHA requirement, various kinds of health and accident records are required by state workmen's compensation laws. Records also are useful in analysis of accidents and as a check on the performance of the safety program. They are a necessity in calculating frequency rates and severity rates.

Treatment of injuries, including the rehabilitation of workers disabled on the job, is a recognized responsibility of the employer. Every organization, large or small, should have adequate first aid facilities and personnel trained to use them. Larger establishments may find that it pays them to have a full-time physician and nurses on their staff. This general subject now is covered by OSHA standards. For example, if an establishment has fifteen or more employees on duty at any one time, and if it is not in near proximity to a hospital, clinic, or infirmary, then the employer is required to have (1) a first aid kit approved by a consulting physician, and (2) an employee who is trained to render first aid.

A *periodic review* of the program is the final element in the recommended safety program. This is desirable in order to assure that the program continues to be effective in achieving its objective.

THE ROLE OF THE SUPERVISOR

We have noted at appropriate places throughout this chapter the particular duties or responsibilities of supervisors in safety matters. Because the supervisor is the one person in management who is in daily contact with hourly-wage and nonexempt salaried employees and who is responsible for their work, most of the day-to-day safety job falls on him. This role can be summed up in the following listing of what the supervisor must know and do.

1. What the safety policy is, and what it specifies concerning responsibility and authority.
2. What the total responsibilities are and how the supervisor is expected to accomplish them with safety; which areas, operations, machines, personnel he/she directs; what is to be done about maintenance and repairs, working conditions, provision of guards, and protective devices.
3. What's to be done about determining qualifications of workers in his/her area; what disciplinary action is permitted and advisable and under what circumstances.
4. Who is to instruct and train workers in safety, first aid, and fire prevention, protection, and extinguishment.
5. What the safe work methods are for each job, and where information about them may be obtained.
6. What safety devices and personal protective equipment are to be used on each job, and procedures for making them available and using them correctly.
7. What the supervisor's relationship is to be with the safety committee.
8. What commitments the supervisor may make to correct unsafe conditions, and the cost limit below which the supervisor needs no additional authority.
9. What to do in case of accident: first aid, calling doctor, ambulance, hospital — notifying relatives of injured person.
10. What reports are required: inspection, accident, accident investigation, corrective actions taken or recommended.
11. Basic accident causes and how to apply them as preventive measures in supervisory activity.
12. What to include in continuous and special safety inspections.
13. How to investigate an accident, what to look for, and how to determine recommendations for preventing recurrence.
14. How to conduct the indoctrination and orientation of new employees.

SAFETY SELF-INSPECTIONS

In preceding discussions of safety programs and the role of the supervisor, one of the elements specified was periodic inspections of work places by appropriate company personnel. Because self-inspection of the work place is one aspect of the safety program in which the supervisor is directly and importantly involved, the subject is discussed further.

Self-inspections are a necessity if the supervisor is to know where potential hazards exist and whether they are under proper control. Such inspections must be systematic if they are to be comprehensive and effective. *Checklists* are recommended as a useful aid to this end. The first thing to consider in designing a checklist is its scope. The listing below suggests broad areas of scope and specific items to be looked at, as appropriate, within each subject area.

1. Processing, Receiving, Shipping and Storage. Equipment, job planning, layout, heights, floor loads, projection of materials, materials-handling methods.
2. Building and Grounds Conditions. Floors, walls, ceilings, exits, stairs, walkways, ramps, platforms, driveways, aisles.
3. Housekeeping Program. Waste disposal, tools, objects, materials, leakage and spillage, methods, schedules, work areas, remote areas, windows, ledges, storage areas.
4. Electricity. Equipment, switches, breakers, fuses, switchboards, junctions, special fixtures, circuits, insulation, extensions, tools, motors, grounding, code compliance.
5. Lighting. Type, intensity, controls, conditions, diffusion, location, glare and shadow control, standards applied.
6. Heating and Ventilating. Type effectiveness, temperature, humidity, controls, natural and artificial ventilation and exhaust.
7. Machinery. Points of operation, flywheels, gears, shafts, pulleys, keyways, belts, couplings, sprockets, chains, frames, controls, lighting tools and equipment, brakes, exhaust, feeding, oiling, adjusting, maintenance, grounding, how attached, work space, location, purchasing standards.
8. Personnel. Training, experience, methods of checking machines before use, type clothing, personal protective equipment, use of guards, tool storage, work practices, methods of cleaning, oiling, or adjusting machinery.
9. Hand and Power Tools. Purchasing standards, inspection, storage, repair, types, maintenance, grounding, use and handling.
10. Chemicals. Storage, handling, transportation, amounts used, warning signs, supervision, training, protective clothing and equipment.
11. Fire Prevention. Extinguishers, alarms, sprinklers, smoking rules, exits, personnel assigned, separation of flammable materials and dangerous operations, explosive-proof fixtures, waste disposal.
12. Maintenance. Regularity, effectiveness, training of personnel, materials and equipment used, method of locking out machinery, general methods.
13. Personal Protective Equipment. Type, size, maintenance, repair, storage, assignment of responsibility, purchasing methods, standards observed, rules of use, method of assignment.

Not every subject area in the above listing will be applicable to every work place. The supervisor should select only those broad areas of scope pertinent to a given work place or operation. Checklists for each area of scope then are prepared. A common format is to prepare the checklist in the form of a series of questions for each subject area. A portion of a sample checklist is shown as follows.

		OK	Action Needed
Exits and Access			
1.	Are all exits visible and unobstructed?	☐	☐
2.	Are all exits marked with a readily visible sign that is properly illuminated?	☐	☐
3.	Are there sufficient exits to ensure prompt escape in case of emergency?	☐	☐
4.	Are controls in place for areas requiring limited occupancy?	☐	☐
5.	Do you take special precautions to protect employees during construction and repair operations?	☐	☐
Fire Prevention/Protection			
1.	Are portable fire extinguishers provided in adequate number and type?	☐	☐
2.	Are fire extinguishers inspected monthly for general condition and operability and noted on the inspection tag?	☐	☐
3.	Are fire extinguishers recharged regularly and properly noted on inspection tag?	☐	☐
4.	Are fire extinguishers mounted in readily accessible locations?	☐	☐
5.	If you have interior stand pipes and valves, are these inspected regularly?	☐	☐
6.	If you have a fire alarm system, is it tested at least annually?	☐	☐
7.	Are plant employees periodically instructed in the use of extinguishers and fire protection procedures?	☐	☐
8.	If you have outside private fire hydrants, were they flushed within the last year and placed on a preventive maintenance schedule?	☐	☐
9.	Are fire doors and shutters in good operating condition?	☐	☐
	Are fusible links in place?	☐	☐
	Are they unobstructed and protected against obstruction?	☐	☐
10.	Is your local fire department well acquainted with your plant, location, and specific hazards?	☐	☐
11.	Automatic Sprinklers: Are water control valves, air and water pressures checked weekly?	☐	☐

Are control valves locked open?	☐	☐
Is maintenance of the system assigned to responsible persons or a sprinkler contractor?	☐	☐
Are sprinkler heads protected by metal guards where exposed to mechanical damage?	☐	☐
Is proper minimum clearance maintained below sprinkler heads?	☐	☐

In preparing a checklist, the scope and specific items or questions should be tailored to the nature and characteristics of the work place and the operations and activities being carried out. Some excellent examples of self-inspection checklists covering many areas of scope may be found in *OSHA Handbook for Small Business,* OSHA 2209, revised 1977, available from the U.S. Department of Labor, Washington, D.C., or from any OSHA local or regional office.

In carrying out periodic self-inspections, the supervisor should make sure that each item is seen. Nothing should be left to memory or chance. It is a good idea to write down what you see or don't see, and what you think you should do about it.

Once safety hazards have been identified, control procedures in order of effectiveness and preference are as follows:

1. Eliminating the hazard from the machine, the method, the material, or the plant structure.
2. Abating the hazard by controlling exposures to it or guarding against it at its source.
3. Training personnel to be aware of the hazard and to follow safe work procedures to avoid it.
4. Prescribing personal protective equipment for shielding employees against the hazard.

SUMMARY

Management has a recognized responsibility for the job safety and health of its employees. Business and industry have made considerable progress in meeting this responsibility, but room for improvement still exists.

State job safety and health laws are far from uniform. Partly for this reason, Congress enacted the Occupational Safety and Health Act of 1970 (OSHA). Under this act, job safety and health standards are developed and promulgated that are applicable nationwide to almost all business, industrial, and other organizations having employees and affecting interstate commerce. The states may participate by developing and submitting for approval job safety and health plans that must be at least as effective as the OSHA standards and enforcement procedures.

The act requires comprehensive record keeping by employers. It provides for inspection of establishments; for citations and penalties for violations of standards; and for penalties for failure to abate a violation within the prescribed time limit. Employers may contest or appeal citations, penalties, and abatement periods.

Employees or their representatives have the right to file complaints of alleged violations (anonymously if they desire), to accompany compliance officers on inspections, and to contest abatement periods. They are protected against harassment for filing complaints or exercising any other rights under the act.

The Secretary of Labor may promulgate new standards and revise, modify, or revoke existing standards. Provisions exist for hearings and public comment, challenges of the validity of standards, and variances if more time is needed to comply with standards. The majority of standards are developed by recognized standards-producing organizations with assistance and advice from numerous industry and labor organizations.

OSHA has a major impact on business and industry with respect to costs in meeting requirements, labor relations, and management practices. The supervisor bears a large share of this burden in putting standards into practice in his/her work place, in seeing that employees comply with applicable standards, and in assuring that employee rights are observed.

The primary purpose of a safety and health program is to prevent accidents and occupational illnesses. The immediate causes of accidents are unsafe personal acts (80 percent) and unsafe conditions (20 percent). Behind the immediate causes are contributory factors including physical and mental characteristics or traits of the worker and the working environment as it is influenced by the supervisor and by management in general.

Requisites of a safety and health program are sincere support of top management, a comprehensive safety and health policy, and a safety director with primary authority and responsibility in this area. A good safety and health program will include the following features: safety committee, education and training, enforcement, job safety analysis, safety engineering, inspections, accident investigation and analysis, record keeping, treatment of injuries and illnesses, and periodic reviews. The supervisor is responsible for some of these and is involved in all of them.

KEY CONCEPTS

Employer responsibility. The belief that employers and management have a responsibility to provide safe and healthful working conditions for their employees, and a responsibility for the results of occupational injuries and illnesses that do occur, was slow in taking root. Such a belief was almost nil prior to the late 1800s. This concept has grown gradually over the years and today is widely recognized and accepted. It has pertained largely to physical safety and health. The concept of similar responsibility for the mental health of employees is much more recent and is not yet widely recognized or practiced.

Occupational safety and health standard. It is believed by many people that occupational injuries and illnesses can be greatly reduced in number by compliance with standards specifying conditions—or the adoption or use of one or more practices, means, methods, operations, or processes—that experience and research have shown to be appropriate.

Accident process. An accident, that is, an unplanned and uncontrolled event resulting in personal injury, is the result of a process. In retrospect, every accident resulted from an identifiable flow of interrelated events moving toward an end. Contributory causes (physical and mental characteristics of the worker, the work environment) lead to immediate causes (unsafe acts, unsafe conditions), which result in an accident. This concept holds that accidents do not just happen—it is the opposite of the "act of God" concept.

IMPORTANT TERMS

Abatement
Accident prone
Checklist
Citation
Closing conference
Compliance officer
Contributory cause
De minimis violation
Emergency temporary standard
Ex parte warrant
Good faith
Immediate cause
Imminent danger
Informational poster
Intent to comply
Interim variance
Job safety analysis
Log and summary of occupational injuries and illnesses
Mandatory penalty
Minor injury
National consensus standard

National Institute for Occupational Safety and Health
Nonserious violation
Occupational Safety and Health Act
Occupational Safety and Health Administration
Occupational Safety and Health Review Commission
Occupational safety and health standard
Opening conference
Permanent variance
Recordable occupational injury or illness
Safety committee
Safety director
Safety engineering
Safety policy
Safety program
Self-inspection
Serious violation

State plan
Supplementary record
Temporary variance
Unsafe act

Unsafe condition
Walkaround inspection
Williams-Steiger Act

INCIDENTS

The Untidy Pipe Rack

The supply shed of a major plumbing contractor contained pipe racks for the storage of different sizes of copper water pipe. When the workers were adding pipe to, or removing it from, the racks, they were supposed to be sure that the ends of all lengths of pipe left in the racks were reasonably flush. Most of the men were rather careless about this when they were in a hurry, and it was not uncommon to see random pieces of pipe protruding six or eight inches beyond the end of the rack.

One day a worker tripped over a length of pipe extending two feet into the aisle from the bottom of the rack. The result: a broken leg. Whose fault? No one knew.

For three weeks afterward, not a pipe was out of line. Then, pipe ends began to appear a little uneven, and in two more weeks the pipe rack was its usual untidy self. One day, the superintendent came down the aisle in a hurry and fell over a pipe. As he picked himself up, all that was hurt was his dignity. But you would have thought that he was mortally injured as he bellowed at the foreman, "Who the blankety-blank left these pipes sticking out?"

What basic characteristic of people does this incident illustrate? What are the implications to the foreman? What should he do about the situation?

The Walkaround at Eldorado Electronics

Eldorado Electronics, Inc., employs about 340 people. It has a sizable R & D Department for a firm of this size, because about 30 percent of its work is designing and manufacturing special electronics gear for military aircraft. The balance of its work is assembling purchased components into high-fidelity sound systems for the home entertainment market.

The OSHA compliance officer appeared at Eldorado's office at about 9:30 on Tuesday morning and asked for Mr. Wilson, the General Manager. After some hurried telephoning by the receptionist in an effort to locate Mr. Wilson, she told the officer, "Mr. Wilson is terribly sorry but he is tied up in a very important staff meeting and can't break loose for at least 45 minutes. I'm afraid you'll just have to wait. May I get you some coffee and the morning newspaper?"

In about 50 minutes, Mr. Wilson came hurrying into the lobby full of apologies. In a brief discussion, the compliance officer indicated that he wanted to see the assembly areas. Mr. Wilson and a shop steward accompanied him through the main assembly areas, a series of interconnected bays and clean rooms in which workers were assembling various subcomponents for hi-fi sets.

The inspector had to walk around a number of cartons cluttering the aisle leading into one bay and called this to Mr. Wilson's attention.

"Yes, yes, we'll get those out of the way just as soon as we can clear some space in the store room," answered Mr. Wilson.

As they passed one enclosed bay, the inspector asked, "What's in there?"

"Oh, we're doing some hush-hush government work. No outsiders allowed in that room."

"That doesn't mean me," the inspector replied as he opened the door and took a quick look around. Mr. Wilson shrugged his shoulders, and the shop steward looked sympathetic.

As the trio proceeded on, they came to the testing bay. The inspector noticed that a copper bus-bar ran along two sides of the bay at about table height. It was only partly enclosed by a protective grillework.

"Is that live?" asked the inspector, pointing at the bus bar. "Yes," replied Mr. Wilson, "the test engineers need a heavy-duty power source for some of our high-voltage testing equipment."

"Those guards don't cover its full length. If someone bumped into it just right, he would be a dead duck. Why don't you move it up to the ceiling and bring conduit covered cable down the walls with junction boxes at the ends?"

"Look," said Mr. Wilson impatiently, "the test engineers are experimenting with some new equipment. They have to make different hookups, and this is the most convenient way to handle it. They know what they are doing and are careful."

The three men completed the walkaround without further incident. The shop steward returned to his work while the compliance officer and Mr. Wilson talked over the results of the walkaround briefly. The officer then left.

What did Mr. Wilson do wrong? What should he have done? Did the inspector do anything incorrectly? What should he have done? Eldorado Electronics will receive citations for violation of standards. What is the minimum monetary penalty that might be proposed? The maximum?

QUESTIONS FOR DISCUSSION

1. What are the functions of the Occupational Safety and Health Review Commission?
2. Define a "recordable occupational injury or illness."

3. What different agencies have the right to send inspectors to your establishment in connection with occupational safety and health matters?
4. What safeguards does a company have against what it may consider an unfair citation, penalty, or abatement period? An improper standard?
5. What are the rights of employees with respect to OSHA inspections?
6. Discuss the supervisor's problem with respect to employee observance of safety practices prescribed in an OSHA standard.
7. Why is the subject of "accident-prone" individuals controversial?
8. Why do we consider that an accident is the end result of a process?
9. What is the relationship between work environment and accidents?
10. Describe safety engineering.
11. What are the objectives of safety education and training?
12. Identify at least eight things the supervisor must know and/or do in connection with health and safety responsibilities.
13. Prepare a self-inspection checklist for some specific operation or activity based on some job you have held.

CHAPTER XXV

The Organization and Its Environment

LEARNING OBJECTIVES

- *To gain insight into the three major economic system.*
- *To learn the basic tenets of capitalism.*
- *To learn the role of capital and marketing.*
- *To understand the impact of unionism.*

Introduction

The thrust of business has changed as we have moved through the twentieth century. During the first half, it moved from a production-oriented operation to a market-oriented one. While market is still the controlling factor affecting growth, a new force has arisen to provide a major constraint. This is the price and scarcity of energy, particularly liquid fuels. Today, nearly half of our oil supply comes from overseas, from a very politically unstable part of the world. Its price is up to sixfold what it was a few years ago. Our industrial society has been built on cheap energy and such a price increase is bound to have a major effect.

Nearly as important but not yet as widely recognized is the scarcity and price of certain raw materials. A large segment of the chemical industry is built on pertoleum as a raw material. These increasing prices have had an effect on the market viability of some products. Fifteen or more of our critical (strategic) raw materials come from outside the country and are in short supply. This constrains the development of new product lines, even though the market might demand them.

During this same period, the economic system of capitalism has grown from a system relatively free of restraints to a system hemmed in by government regulations, labor unions, and public attitudes. In more recent years its responsibility to society and the environment has put greater restraints on its freedom. In the early twentieth century if a corporation had a process, a product and the capital, they could embark upon the building of a new facility to meet a market demand. This is no longer true. Environmental regulations may prevent their production or make the product so expensive it is no longer viable. Or society's attitude toward the operation may prevent its development, for example, the nuclear industry in the wake of the Three Mile Island incident.

To further complicate the role of capitalism, profit has become a dirty word among many segments of society. The petroleum industry has most recently been the focal point of the public wrath. The media has publicized percent increases in profit, but disregarded the percent return on investment. The recent "windfall profits tax" was an outgrowth of this mentality. Even at the risk of reducing the amount of drilling for domestic oil, it was passed by Congress since it seemed appropriate, and quite politically desirable in order to recoup most of the extra funds that resulted from decontrol of oil prices.

A few years ago students even failed to enter business because of the stigma associated with profits. And yet profits are the gasoline in the machinery of capitalism. Without profits a capitalistic society can not operate. But business survival in the current age has other factors to contend with that have a major effect on their success. Not very many years ago, the U.S. dollar was pegged to gold at $35 per ounce. It was loosened from that constraint in the early 1970s and in the late 1970s the price of gold soared to over $800 per ounce. Corresponding declines in the value of the dollar against other currencies has taken place. Inflation is raging out of control in the double-digit range. No amount of effort on the part of the government has produced any major positive effect. Interest rates are moving toward 20 percent prime, a far cry from the 4 percent prime of the 1950s.

Government continues to grow larger and larger. The Department of Energy now has 20,000 employees but is providing little positive influence in finding more domestic oil or developing alternate sources of energy. Milton Friedman, the renowned economist, likes to tell his audiences that the government is spending 40 percent of their earnings. He then asks if anyone is satisfied with what they are getting in return.

California residents attempted to take matters in their own hands in the past few years. They passed Proposition 13, designed to make substantive reductions in property taxes, thereby reducing some state income and providing tax relief to residents. This has been followed by another initiative known as Proposition 9, which faced a statewide referendum in early June 1980. These ideas have spread to other states.

This chapter covers some of the major aspects of the environment in which business operates.

BUSINESS DEFINED

EARLY ROLE OF PRODUCTION

During the first half of the twentieth century production was the controlling factor in the sale of goods. The tendency was to produce products and then through salespeople attempt to secure a purchaser. By the early 1940s this procedure was still in vogue. It extended even into research and development. Companies would do research work, develop new products, and then have salesmen take them to the field. Their hopes were that potential customers would be willing to spend their money to determine the usefulness of the product.

World War II aggravated the situation further since the problem was that of being able to produce sufficient materials rather than to find markets. However, as the 1940s drew to a close and the pent-up demands caused by World War II were satisfied, the picture began to change.

GROWING ROLE OF MARKETING

Companies now found that other companies were no longer willing to spend money to investigate the usefulness of, for example unknown chemical compounds. This brought into being a marketing specialist group known as market development. These units would take the new chemical compounds and endeavor to find applications for them in their own laboratory facilities. Armed with the data from such research work, they would visit the most likely companies and use these data to convince the companies that they should try the new product.

The product development system continues today in the chemical industry and is a vital arm of most marketing departments throughout all industries. However, other aspects of *marketing* have developed since the early 1950s. Whereas at one time the job of sales manager was the most desired in the sales field, this position has now been superseded by the marketing manager. The marketing manager has general responsibility for determining the needs of a marketplace in relation to the capabilities of the company. The manager guides the research, development, and production segments of the corporation to provide what the customer needs. In the execution of his duties, the marketing manager employs people in market research, product development, market development, sales, trade relations, and advertising.

Today we can say that the corporation is market oriented. The marketing department, to a large degree, controls the course that the corporation will follow.

While the role of marketing has grown in importance during this century, it's not the sole factor affecting corporate growth today. Because of inflation, the ability to finance projects or to secure sufficient monies to provide adequate working capital may be overriding concerns. Still another concern may reside in availability and price of energy as well as availability of critical raw materials. Despite these factors, however, the planned direction of growth of the corporation must be geared to anticipated market demands. As some sage once said, "Nothing happens until something is sold."

CAPITALISM DEFINED

Capitalism is an economic system in which individuals, with comparative freedom from external restraint, produce goods and services for public consumption in a competitive environment, and with private profit or gain as the principle motivating force,[1] joined today with the will to render public service. These goods and services move from producers to consumers by means of an exchange procedure in which the common medium of payment is usually money or an acceptable substitute for it, such as credit.

Capitalism is an economic, not a political, system. It flourishes best, however, in a country with the democratic form of government. It is important to understand the kind of capitalism that developed in the United States, in view of the attacks now being leveled against it worldwide. To evaluate these criticisms, it behooves us to understand our economic system.

Capitalism thrives best in an atmosphere of freedom, which signifies noninterference by government in the conduct of business by individual businessmen and firms. In its initial phases American business was provided this kind of freedom for the growth of capitalism. However, in the more complex periods of recent years, government restraints have been placed on business, modifying somewhat this free capitalistic movement. For example, local, state, and federal governments exercise control by requiring licenses, charters to incorporate, zoning ordinances, and wage and hours laws. It has been estimated that as many as 1500 governmental regulations are involved with business operations. Since the early 1930s there has been a noticeable increase in government regulation with the advent of commissions and investigation committees.

Capitalism includes three basic freedoms inherent to an understanding of its nature.

1. *Private property*. Capitalism can operate only where the institution of private property prevails. In such cases individual and business firms have the right to purchase, own, and sell property of all kinds. It allows the businessperson/owner to have the right of ownership to the goods produced and to any profits resulting from the sale of these goods.
2. *Private enterprise*. Private enterprise means that most businesses in this

---

[1] Raymond E. Glos and Harold A. Baker, *Introduction to Business*, 6th ed., South-Western Publishing Company, Cincinnati, 1967, p. 3.

country are owned by individuals who have invested their own funds in businesses of their own choosing. These businesses may be as large as General Motors or as small as the neighborhood grocery store. Even though the larger organization may have a corporate format, the method of operation is similar. In this case the ownership may be scattered among many thousands or hundreds of thousands of stockholders.

3. *Freedom of choice.* The democratic form of government provides the environment in which the businessperson is free to choose the field of business in which she/he will engage for the production of profit. The businessperson may also choose her/his customers, workers, and the type and quality of facilities. Workers may work for her/him or not as they choose. Consumers may purchase or not purchase the products involved as they choose. All of the factors seek their own level and their own means for satisfaction within this environment.

COMPARISON OF ECONOMIC SYSTEMS

It might be worthwhile to compare capitalism as the economic system used in the United States with two other major economic systems; market socialism and authoritarian socialism.

Morris Bornstein makes in-depth comparison of these three systems in his book Comparative Economic Systems.[2] Some of the salient features of these three systems are shown in Table 25-1.

Central planning is also used sometimes in a capitalistic society such as ours (e.g., during wartime emergencies).

Table 25-1 Comparison of Three Economic Systems

Capitalism	Market Socialism	Authoritarian Socialism
Private ownership of private enterprise with a means of production	Public ownership	Public ownership
Employer's gain as guiding force in production decisions	Limited inequality in income distribution	Comprehensive and detailed planning and control of almost all phases of economic life
Reliance on markets and prices to allocate resources and distribute income	Uses markets and prices to allocate resources and goods	Resources are allocated primarily by administration commander

[2]Morris Bornstein, "Comparative Economic Systems", Richard D. Irwin, Inc., Homewood, Ill., 1965.

ROLE OF THE INDIVIDUAL IN CAPITALISM

Four groups of individuals interrelate in capitalism as we have described it—*entrepreneurs, management, labor,* and *consumers.* Let us look at each of these individually.

ENTRE-PRENEUR An entrepreneur is one who takes capital and enters some form of business in which he/she believes there is an opportunity for profit. This function may be performed by a single individual in the role of a sole proprietorship, or by several individuals either as a partnership or as a corporation.

The entrepreneur believes that he/she can secure a profit through the business operation and is willing to accept the risk that may be involved. The entrepreneur knows that the more efficiently he/she can operate the business the better the chance of survival will be.

Individuals willing to take these risks for the sake of profit are found in hundreds of thousands of enterprises in the United States. Not all of these entrepreneurs are successful; several thousand fail financially each year.

The successful entrepreneur is encouraged to reinvest his money in new equipment and to expand his operations. At some point the size of the operation exceeds the immediate control of one person, and the need for the next individual is apparent.

MANAGEMENT This term is applied to those individuals charged with responsibility of operating business enterprises in a profitable manner. Today in the large corporation, partnership, and sole proprietorship, they are referred to as professional managers. They may not own very much stock in the company or business, but they are responsible to the shareholders or owners for the stewardship of their money as evidenced by the profits generated.

These individuals are spurred on to outstanding performances by being given opportunities of participating in the profits of the company or by other incentives such as higher salary.

This separation between management and ownership in business has become an important aspect of American capitalism. However, the investors have not abdicated their responsibilities for their funds. The owners continue to hold the management responsible for generating an adequate return on capital invested. This profit generation can be used to measure the efficiency of the managers.

LABOR Capitalism is dependent on individual workers who must perform the physical and mental labor required for the production of goods and services. Workers are normally divided into skilled, semiskilled, and unskilled classes.

As discussed in greater detail in Chapter XXIII "Labor Relations and the Supervisor," the organized labor movement is a formidable aspect of the business environment and American capitalism. Industrywide bargaining and company collective bargaining sessions have become commonplace between management and union representatives.

The upgrading of the worker's standard of living has broadened markets and has helped to enhance existing markets. The shift of income distribution from a triangular shape in the late 1920s to an eggshaped configuration has greatly assisted the rapid economic growth experienced in the nation since the late 1930s.

The effect of unions on the operation of firms in the capitalistic system has become immense. This has been accentuated by industrywide bargaining on the part of management and labor. The supervisor will have to cope with these historical facts in dealing with union representatives. Moreover, the supervisor will have to practice the participative leadership style more often with the strong force of the union organization looking over the supervisor's shoulder. No longer will managers be able to accept workers as a factor of production; they must accept workers as human beings.

CONSUMERS The consumer in the capitalistic ecomony is the reason why firms exist to make products at a profit. By satisfying the consumer's needs at a price the consumer is willing to pay, a firm can exist in the capitalistic economic system. The consumer is the final judge of a given product or service. Regardless of labor and management disputes, if the product does not do its job, the disputes become academic because sooner or later the firm will cease to exist.

Although consumers do not determine what products to make, or what products to research, they do determine whether those products will survive. It is still the prerogative of management to determine what products to make; when, where, and how to make them; and what price to charge. If consumers don't like it, they will not buy if substitutes are available. If no substitutes are available, a quasimonopoly exists, which is illegal, and this is covered by antitrust legislation and the Federal Trade Commission. Protection of the consumer from illegal and fraudulent practices has helped to develop the consumerism movement. Consumers dislike products that don't work, products that don't last, and products that have shoddy workmanship. Both labor and management can be guilty of these practices.

ROLE OF CAPITAL IN CAPITALISM

NEED FOR CAPITAL As we have seen, *capital* in the form of a liquid asset (money) is needed to purchase the tools, equipment, buildings, fixtures, patents, and land required for the manufacture and sale of a product. This money is sometimes referred to as capital funds, and those items that are purchased are referred to as capital goods. This capital may be obtained by the individual entrepreneur borrowing from others, or by financing through the profits that he makes in his business enterprise.

The owners of these capital funds invest their money in the enterprise either as owners purchasing a share of stock or as creditors. As creditors they may have provided loans or have provided extended credit for raw materials. In any event, this owner of capital is going to desire a satisfactory return on his/her investment. If this does not seem possible there will be reluctance to make a loan or to invest money in the enterprise.

WORKING CAPITAL

In addition to capital required to purchase machinery and equipment, capital also is required to furnish funds in sufficient quantities to meet payrolls, pay for raw materials, provide inventories, and furnish credit extension for consumers. This capital, known as *working capital*, is just as important as the capital required for the fixed assets.[3] Many corporations have failed to make ends meet because of the lack of sufficient working capital. One might even say that adequate working capital provides considerable insurance for the stability of the business and the future of the workers. Viability of jobs is directly related to a firm's ability to meet its payroll.

Either the entrepreneur or the professional manager must often seek additional capital for machinery and for working capital. He may seek this from the banker, the life insurance corporation, the individual investor or, at times, a business investment corporation. The financial institutions secure funds from private investors, but certain guarantees are provided by the government. Although the financial institution will make loans, it frequently is interested in securing a certain portion of the equity.

Often the entrepreneur or company is not anxious to give up some of the ownership in exchange for money. All too frequently such moves have ultimately brought the downfall of small corporations. Every new share sold represents dilution of ownership for the current shareholders.

ROLE OF MARKETING

DISTRIBUTION OF GOODS

Distribution is the way in which the output of production is made available to its users, the consumers. The distribution channels are made up of entrepreneurs or corporations interested in making profit by providing the means for reaching this consumer. To achieve this goal the businessperson will use labor, capital, management, and facilities. However,

---

[3]Working capital is the difference between current assets and current liabilities, as covered at greater length in Chapter VII "Financial Control."

as mentioned earlier, distribution is only a small part of the marketing function.

Marketing has as one of its major efforts the discovery of what goods and services the consumer needs and wants. The second stage is the providing of these items to the consumers at the time and place they desire them and at the prices they are willing to pay. In addition to *form utility, time, place, and possession utilities* are extremely important.[4] Of time and place, time utility gets the greatest attention today. Through market surveys, test markets, and similar activities, companies go to great lengths to assure that the product they make will be wanted and purchased at the time they can deliver it. Once that decision is made, then countless millions of dollars go into advertising this product to the consumer. This continual placing of the product before the eyes and ears of the consumer tends to create a demand (want) proportional to the effort applied. Much forecast of consumer demand is based on a firm's ability to influence and communicate its products to the buyer. This is a very difficult task, since it is extremely hard to communicate with the consumer. As mentioned in Chapter IX, people tend to see and hear what they want to see and hear. The consumer is no different.

PRICING THE PRODUCT   The acceptable price of the product represents what the buyer is willing to pay and what the seller is willing to accept in exchange for the goods. This price is determined in part by demand and supply. As the price of the commodity increases, the supply of the commodity tends to increase and its demand tends to decrease. The reverse is also true.

However, the corporation must take many factors into account in setting a price. It is obviously interested in the competitive price situation. For the same quality of product capable of performing the same service, what price should be established? When this price is compared with the probable cost of production at the volume anticipated, the company may decide not to put the product on the market. However, companies that have failed to investigate matters in this manner have frequently entered the market with products that could not be produced for a price that was competitive. Needless to say, they did not last long in this business. Their only alternative was to enter another and more profitable business. In summary, the price must be such that at the likely demand, there will be an adequate profit between the cost of production and the sales price to allow a reasonable and acceptable return to the investor.

A company always faces competition in the capitalistic system.[5] If a company is able to produce and sell a product at a profit, many other en-

---

[4]Utility is defined as the satisfaction of human wants and needs. If no one wants or needs a product, it has no form utility. How many people want or need a mink-covered golf ball?
[5]Competition may be in price, product development, promotion, location, product features, service, and/or timing. Most industries are controlled by a few large firms. This is known as an oligopoly. Other industries, such as power companies, are monopolies as sanctioned by government.

trepreneurs or corporations feel free to enter into this market to secure similar benefits. As a result, these entries have an affect on price. If a company has held a strong position in the marketplace, it may tend to drop the price in an effort to force a new company out of business. Because of its longer period of establishment it is frequently able to survive under a lower production cost than is the new company with a limited market.

Another factor that is involved in the matters of pricing, production costs, and profit is *risk*. The capitalistic society's success is built on accepting risk for rewards. High risks warrant high rewards; low risks warrant low rewards. The production of any product can never bring guaranteed success for an extended period of time. Changing competitive positions, changing economic conditions, new technology, new government regulations, foreign trade, and a host of other items may change the economic posture in the particular field in question. However, it is acceptance of risk that has helped to make America as strong as it is today.

ROLE OF PROFIT

Profit is the fuel in the machinery of capitalism. Without it a capitalistic society cannot operate. It is the incentive that induces investors and lenders to provide money for the operation of business.

Without this incentive, no money will be available for equipment and working capital. With no machinery to use and no workers to be employed and paid, there will be an inadequate number of consumers because the potential consumers will not have the money with which to buy products. As a result, the machine comes to a grinding halt.

Profit may be considered as the excess of income of an enterprise over the costs of its operation. The question is often asked, "What amount of return on investment is required to induce capitalists to invest in an enterprise?" It is impossible to answer this question absolutely. However, if a company goes into the marketplace to secure funds and they are unavailable, it is evident that the return on investment or anticipated profits are less than the lender considers desirable.

Because the capitalist assumes certain risks when he invests in the enterprise, he obviously expects a greater return than he would get if he were to invest his money in the bank. Therefore interest rates represent a floor on the expected return. However, this is not an absolute judgment factor. Many major corporations on the stock market today return earning much less than the interest rates paid on deposits or bonds. Nevertheless, people still continue to invest. Why? Because other factors such as the long-term growth potential, active research and development activities, and rapidly changing needs in American society, may encourage an increase in the return on investment at a later date.

Today industries are in a financial bind. Chrysler and Lockheed have sought government help for survival. The steel industry has passed through such severe circumstances that it has been pointed out they were paying dividends from assets, not profits. Inflation has made it difficult for them to finance replacement of worn-out equipment and to finance new equipment. Profits in real dollars have trended downward at a steady rate as has profits as a percent of national income. Some major industries have been paying dividends to stockholders out of equity. On the other side of the ledger, governmental regulations tie the hands of business and cause even greater expenditures to meet tough standards in areas such as environmental control. So securing an adequate profit to attract more investors for expansion and growth will be difficult in the coming years.

THE ENVIRONMENT OF BUSINESS

PUBLIC OPINION

A firm must operate within an environment made up of many segments of society. One of the most pervading is that of *public opinion*. The large firm is subject to this at an ever-increasing degree. Pressure is brought to bear on the large corporation by editorials, commentators, government, special interest groups, and anyone else who finds it useful for some reason to accuse the large business of some malfeasance. These actions have been aimed against both the business community and the individual corporations. One favorite target, of course, is profit. It continues to be the belief of many that the profits of firms are excessive. Many in Congress would like to reduce the size of corporations, feeling that this might reduce profits, prices, and influence.

In recent years the consumer has directed his voice toward the corporation, and the consumerism movement has grown rapidly. The government now has established a consumer protection agency. Public opinion is a very real thing in the operation of business because it is closely allied with the consumer who is also a voter, worker, manager, or entrepreneur.

GOVERNMENT

When public opinion comes to bear on the business community, it will generally seek support through some element of government. It may be through one of the regulating agencies or it may be through Congress. Over the years many commissions have been established to provide consumer protection, and to act as a government control arm over industry. Among them are the Food and Drug Administration, Federal Communication Commission, Federal Trade Commission, and Interstate Commerce Commission. The power of these agencies is significant. Their influence on the operation of the corporation cannot be discounted. In recent years the Occupational Safety and Health Act and the Environmental Protectional Agency have exerted immense influence upon the operation of business and industry.

The Sherman Anti-Trust Act (1890) has had far-reaching effects on the general format of business in this country. Suits continue to be filed under this act, with the aim to protect the consumer and the public.

Another major federal statute is the Clayton Act of 1914, which forbids trade restraints such as tying contracts and interlocking directorates. A *tying contract* requires a person who wishes to be the exclusive dealer for a manufacturer's product to also carry other of the manufacturer's products. *Interlocking directorates* exist where competitive companies have identical or partially overlapping directors.

The Robinson-Patman Act of 1936 outlaws price discrimination that is not based on quality or quantity differences and that injures competition. It plays a major role in the day-to-day operating activities of corporations.

It is apparent that in every kind of business the manager is surrounded by a complete web of laws, commissions, official regulations, and court decisions. Some are designed to protect workers, consumers, and communities. Others are designed to regulate the behavior of managers and their subordinates in business and industry. All of them together control the manager and influence the success of his enterprise.

UNIONS

We have previously mentioned the growth of unions. From a union membership of 3 million in 1934, we have today almost 20 million union members. Their power has become great in terms of both action and politics. They have acted as a constraint on some firms that might overmaximize their profits at the employees' expense. If union's management believes the return on investment for a firm is extremely high, it will attempt to force higher wages so that labor may share the fruits of victory. This places an obstacle in front of maximizing profit and pricing techniques in addition to the obstacles of competition, government regulation, and what price the consumer will pay.

In the operation of the business enterprise, the role of the union is not to be discounted. It is one of the most active and powerful voices in the business environment.

The supervisor is the man most closely associated with union members. He will have a small booklet—the union contract—that defines in detail his relationship to union members. It circumscribes his authority, and it outlines many things he must do in order to avoid breaking the contract or being accused of an unfair labor practice. It is important then that he understand the background of labor union development and that he clearly understand his legal relationship to the union members as defined in the contract.

With the so-called blue-collar union membership tending to level off, the union leadership has turned its attention to white collar and professional employers. Considerable progress has been made among white-collar workers and professional unions are being formed in increasing numbers. From industry, unions have spilled into the public sector. In the past 20 years, federal, state, and local governments have shown increases in union membership of two and a half fold. Such membership now stands at nearly 2.5 million, not counting an even larger number of employee associations that perform the bargaining function. A prime example of professional unionization is exemplified by the National Education Association with nearly 2 million members.

BIG AND LITTLE BUSINESS The advent of the large business firm with its extensive and efficient research facilities has brought small firms under significant economic pressures. It has become necessary for some of them to adopt the methods of operation of the large companies in order to survive. Even under such circumstances, some have failed to survive. Many laws have been adopted in order to relieve the pressure of competition on small business by the large companies. The Small Business Administration, established by Congress in 1953, was designed to provide some measure of relief.

As long as our capitalistic society exists, the arguments about big and little will persist. Perhaps it can be said that there are certain industries and some product lines that require the extensive resources of big business. There are others in which the more maneuverable and less monolithic small business enterprise can perform a greater service, at greater profit, than can the big business. Smaller firms do not suffer from extensive lines of communication. They can act and react to changes in the marketplace faster than large firms. A small firm can capitalize on an opportunity sooner, but it must stay within its production and financial capabilities.

Regardless of the size of a firm, competition is one of the major constraints faced by a corporation. Competition to gain markets with the right product at the right place at the right time at the right price is, indeed, a most difficult chore. Companies are attempting to do this very thing as they compete with each other for market share and market control. The most severe form of competition is price decreases, which, if carried to extremes, can force all the participants out of business. The most prevalent form of competition is new product competition. New techniques, new technology, and more economical or faster ways of doing a job are the market and product objectives reflected in product competition. Without competitors, there would be no competition and the capitalistic economy would not be serving the needs of the public.

THE LABOR FORCE The labor force in America has now reached 100 million. The big story is the increase in the number or women. They represent 40 percent of the present labor force or 40 million.[6] By 1985 it is projected that the total labor force will be 113 million with 50 million of it women. The market

---

[6]Andrew M. Sum, "Female Labor Force Participation: Why Prospectives Have Been Too Low," *Monthly Labor Review*, Vol. 100, No. 7 (July 1977), pp. 18-24.

of blue-color and white-collar workers has also changed dramatically. In 1946, white-collar workers comprised 33.4 percent of all employed persons; in 1972 this had grown to 47.7 percent.

Women are steadily moving into the professions also. Engineering, once the province of men, is now populated by several percent of women. Women comprise more than 10 percent of all graduating engineers. If the trend continues perhaps 15 to 25 percent of the graduating engineers will be women. They are finding positions in engineering research and development as well as in production and marketing. Their technical education and ability to work with and through people is making them highly sought after by industry.

THE MULTINATIONAL CORPORATION

The multinational corporation is the outstanding social innovation of the 1950s to 1970s. It is also the most dramatic economic develpment during the same period. It is commonly believed to be something radically new and indeed unprecedented, but is really a revival of an old trend. There were many multinationals in the nineteenth century, encouraged in the United States and in Europe by major scientific and technical inventors. In simple terms multinationals are companies making and selling goods in many countries.

The surge of multinationals in the 1950s and 1960s represented in a large measure a resumption of this nineteenth-century trend. While the expansion of these companies during the 1950s was led by American companies, this leadership came to an end in the 1960s. By the 1970s little more than half of the business done by multinationals was done by companies headquartered in the United States.

The explosive upsurge of the multinational corporation is important to the future of business. It shows the emergence of a genuine world market, that is, a market that is not limited or defined by national, cultural, or ideological boundaries. For example, the political and religious changes in Iran have impacted the world business community. This was preceded by a show of Arab solidarity through OPEC controlling the price of oil available on the world market. Such changes in the world economy cause every business, even a purely local one, to be managed as if it operated in a worldwide economy. Such changes affect every aspect of both the small and large business.

FOREIGN COMPETITION

Foreign competition in recent years has become a very important factor in the economic growth of America. The United States has provided resources to help Europe, Japan, and Korea to recover from the ravages of war. In doing so they have bolstered these economies to the point that they are now very strong competitors. As of this date, Japan and Germany are surpassing the United States as export nations. With the ever-increasing cost of wages, it becomes very difficult to compete with countries having more favorable wage situations and more progressive production techniques. During World War II all major industries in Germany and Japan were destroyed. After the war, these countries built, with funds chiefly from the United States, the latest technical production processes. This has forced many American firms to spend billions of dollars in order to modernize their own production facilities. This segment of world environment will perhaps have a greater effect on the economic situation of this country in the future than any other one single factor.

The growth in foreign competition in recent years is revealed by looking at the exports of West Germany, Japan, Taiwan, and Korea. From 1965 to 1978, these four countries increased their exports from $4.2 to 25.3 billion. They have captured major segments of our economy, notably automobiles and electronics. There is no indication of a slackening of their impact on our economy, barring further changes in energy and capital availability.

LEGAL FORMS OF BUSINESS

There are normally three basic legal forms of business: (1) sole proprietorship, (2) partnership, and (3) corporation.

SOLE PROPRIETORSHIP

As the name indicates, this is a business owned by one person and operated for profit. It represents the simplest form of business ownership. It is the easiest to get into, and easiest to get out of.

It has the advantage of single ownership of all the profits. The sole proprietor looks only to himself/herself for business decisions. He/she is free from much government control that is exercised over other forms of business. The sole proprietor has certain tax savings not enjoyed by corporations.

The *sole proprietorship* has certain financial disadvantages. The owner is liable for all of the debts of the business to the extent of his/her worth, including house, car, stockholdings, and other financial instruments in his/her name. The sole proprietor is limited in the extent to which he/she can grow; generally, he/she must maintain a size consistent with one-person management. Moreover, in the event of death, there may be no one to carry forward the business.

PARTNERSHIP

This form of business was developed in order to overcome some of the disadvantages of the sole proprietorship. Two or more individuals may come together to form a *partnership*. The bulk of partnerships consist of two people, although a partnership may include numerous partners.

Some common partnership types of enterprises include wholesale firms, accounting firms, advertising agencies, law firms, and stock brokerage houses.

Because there are now two or more people to provide the capital, this form of ownership has somewhat more financial flexibility. Also there are two or more owners whose credit is available for inspection, and two or more people to pool their efforts in making decisions. Because partnerships have been in existence for such a long period of time, many court decisions exist that provide them with a legal status.

The partnership, however, suffers from some of the same problems as the sole proprietorship, There is unlimited liability on the part of the partners. There is still lack of continuity of ownership and a limitation on growth because of the lack of investment capital. Partners may fail to be compatible and find it difficult to work in harmony. As they fight, their business fails. Partners' spouses have been known to have a "falling out" that precipitated discontinuity between the partners.

CORPORATION

The *corporation* is a legal entity that overcomes many of the disadvantages of the sole proprietorship and partnership. It is a structure made up of shareholders, managers, and workers.

The corporate form of business operation accounts for 80 percent of the total receipts of all business units and three-fifths of all net profits. The corporation is a legal entity—an artificial being endowed with the rights, duties, and powers of a person. The document that creates this being is a state charter. A corporation is a legal entity within a state.

The owners of a corporation are called shareholders. Since in large corporations such as General Motors there are hundreds of thousands of shareholders, the management must be vested in a smaller group. These representatives of the shareholders (or stockholders) are the board of directors. They are normally elected once a year at a stockholders meeting. The number of members on this board ranges from 3 to 25. The board of directors elects the *officers* of the corporation such as president, secretary, and treasurer. These people take care of the day-to-day operations. Periodically the president reports to the board and seeks approval of certain actions beyond her/his authority.

The corporate form of business has a number of advantages. A major one is the limited liability of the stockholders. Each stockholder shares the risk of loss only in proportion to the amount invested in the corporation and is not personally liable for corporate debts. In contrast, if a sole proprietorship or partnership fails, its owners are liable to the extent of all their worldly possessions to pay off any obligations.

The corporation can develop to a much larger size because it can secure its capital from many thousands of stockholders. If a stockholder becomes uninterested in the corporation in which he/she has invested, the stockholder can sell the interest and invest in another corporation. This is done through a stock certificate and with the aid of a stockbroker.

The existence of a corporation is not threatened by the death of a stockholder or officer. It offers the opportunity for the use of professional managers. If it has vast resources, it may expand at will if it has a viable product to offer. As a legal entity it can make contracts or be sued in its name and not the name of individuals.

There are, however, some disadvantages. The corporation is subject to many state and federal taxes. It is expensive to organize, and its operation requires the filing of many reports. Depending on its size, many departments at the state and national level take an interest in its operation and provide their own restrictions. Larger corporations are watched more closely than small ones because large size makes a firm more conspicuous.

The corporation may also suffer from lack of personal interest. With only a few exceptions, large corporations usually are not owned chiefly by an individual or a family. The managers draw a salary and do not necessarily own any stock in the company, although in most corporations executives do have stock options as an incentive. This permits some managers to buy the firm's stock at reduced prices. The more profitable is the firm, the more valuable are its stock holdings. Like a democracy, it has trouble with secrets since it must report its ideas and its plans to its stockholders. Finally, a corporation's character prevents its promiscuous entrance into other businesses.

There are numerous other forms of business ownership, including cooperatives, credit unions, mutual companies, and savings and loan associations. All of these forms are peculiar to their particular areas of business.

SUMMARY

Our industrial society has changed in this century from a system controlled by production to a system controlled by marketing.

Capitalism is built on the basic freedoms of private property, private enterprise, and freedom of choice.

The entrepreneur, management, worker, and consumer all interrelate in the framework of capitalism. Their interrelationship brings about "value added by manufacture" and contributes to the growth of the gross national product. The firm exists to satisfy the needs of the consumer at a profit to itself. The consumer can be the ultimate consumer, or the industrial consumer or user.

Availability of capital is at the base of successful business enterprises. Working capital is necessary to meet payrolls and other current expenses, and investment capital is necessary for new equipment, expansion of production facilities, and research.

The marketing manager is responsible for developing and operating a distribution system, pricing the product, and guiding the corporation toward profitable growth areas.

Profit is the necessary element for a successful capitalistic system. This is a major incentive in accepting the risk of producing a new product for a new market or expanding facilities or changing or being more efficient.

In today's environment of inflationary spiral, securing an adequate profit for replacing and expanding facilities is difficult.

Business exists in a competitive environment made up of public opinion, government regulations, unions, and foreign and domestic competition. These elements may work a hardship on both large and small businesses, but should be looked upon as a challenge.

Business operates in several forms such as sole proprietorships, partnerships, and corporations. Sole proprietorships have flexibility in change and management processes, but may lack skills of a larger organization, capital, and know-how. Partnerships have more owners and managers, but incompatible owners can do damage to the partnership. Corporations have limited liability of individual owners and can acquire many more resources, but may lack flexibility in change and are restricted to their charter stipulations.

The multinational corporation is the outstanding social innovation in the period since World War II.

KEY CONCEPTS

Capitalism. This economic system requires the use of capital or funds to be invested in an organization that can produce a product or service that will satisfy given needs in the marketplace at a profit to the firm. Since numerous firms may be competing for the same market, supervisory efficiency and worker productivity are paramount requirements to economic survival.

Supervisory activities and the environment. Although types of business, economic systems, foreign trade, and the consumer seem remote to the supervisor, conceptually, he/she is in the best position to relate their importance and necessity to the workers. Regardless of motivational factors, a person's survival on the job is still a very important variable. Moreover, the supervisor's understanding of the organization's environment can help to focus attention on why he/she has this position and why the workers are doing what they are doing. The environment provides the sum of rewards of our endeavors and helps to provide direction and purpose.

IMPORTANT TERMS

Capital
Capitalism
Consumers
Corporation
Entrepreneur
Foreign competition
Freedom of choice
Labor
Labor force
Management

Marketing
Multinational corporation
Partnership
Private enterprise
Private property
Profit
Public opinion
Sole proprietorship
Working capital

INCIDENTS

Consumerism and Jerry Walker's Job

George Ullman has just been called into his office to be severely criticized by his boss concerning shoddy workmanship in his department. "We can't have this many turndowns in unit production in this plant," yells George's boss. "Either you shape up your people, George, or division office will have our scalps. We have to make a profit, and the only way we can is by assembling cars that go out the front door. Before they go out the front door, they have to pass inspection."

"I know," said George, "but since Division raised the quality control specs on us it's hard to convince the men why they have to be met. Take Jerry Walker, for instance, I told him he had to check the windshield for leaks more closely now. All I got was a blank stare and then the comment to the effect that management was trying to get his last drop of blood for no increase in pay."

"All that may be true, George," his boss responded. "We must find some way to communicate to the shift workers that the consumerism movement has really convinced management that the consumer is 'sick and tired' of buying cars that will not function properly. Last year we could ship a car that passed 70 percent of its checkpoints and let the dealer worry about the other 30 percent. Today we can't. The darn consumer is forcing us to improve quality with all their complaints to the dealers—that we get in turn. Government regulation and compliance people are visiting us all the time. This forces better quality, whether we like it or not."

If you heard this conversation, how would you explain to the Jerry Walkers (workers) how the consumerism movement affects his job? How would you explain it to all the plant's supervisors? Are there many things that George Ullman's boss should understand and use to help George Ullman in this task?

A Question of Social Responsibility

John Hobbs is plant manager of a large chemical plant outside of Warren, Ohio. One of the products made in the plant is phthalic anhydride, an ingredient in paint. It is an extremely corrosive material and the workers find it necessary to take extreme precautions in manufacturing and packaging the product.

Across the road from the plant is a house occupied by a man, woman, and a six-month old child. Word came to John that the child is ill, and that the parents are blaming the illness on the phthalic anhydride vapors that are coming across the road.

The legal department of the corporation advises John that he must be careful not to admit that this product is having any deleterious effect upon the baby. John, out of courtesy, visits the home. He, of course, is charged by the husband and wife with creating vapors that have been detrimental to their child and some vague threats of a law suit are extended to him. He suggests that while there is no evidence that the vapors from his plant have any bad effect on the child it might be a good idea for them to move to a more attractive environment, and perhaps his company would help in the cost of the move.

Discuss the responsibilities of the corporation in a situation such as this. What is their liability for doctor bills, for reduction in value of housing, or potential long disability of a growing child? How should John pursue this matter to a reasonable conclusion? What do you feel is a reasonable disposition of the case?

QUESTIONS FOR DISCUSSION

1. Has there been any change in the major problems in American industry since the early part of the century? If so, what have they been?
2. What is capitalism? Why can it exist in this country?
3. Discuss the roles that we play in causing the capitalistic system to work.
4. Why is capital important? Discuss its role in the operation of our economic system.
5. We are all exposed to endless streams of advertising. What roles does it play in the success of our economic system? Could it succeed if advertising were outlawed?
6. As consumers we all tend to look at the prices of products. Of the following, what is the most important factor? (a) Having a price below the competitor? (b) Having a better quality product? (c) Having a price so that an adequate profit is available?
7. Is it possible for the capitalistic society to operate without profit? Explain what profit is. How much profit is too much? Too little?
8. What are some of the things affecting the environment of business?

Discuss what effect they have on the successful operation of a corporation.
9. What is your perception of the effect of unionization on the successful operation of a corporation? Discuss the role of the multinational corporation in future worldwide industrial development.
10. Why is the corporate form of business an important one?

PART V
Final Word

This single chapter section wraps up the previous four sections and then concentrates on the supervisor and the future.

CHAPTER XXVI
Closing Remarks

LEARNING OBJECTIVES

- *To realize that constant study and research is needed in the supervisory management area.*
- *To review the major concepts of the previous chapters.*
- *To see supervisory management in persepctive.*
- *To appreciate the future of supervisory management.*

Introduction

Much has been and can be said about supervision and its practice in an organization. Indeed, this subject is far from becoming a run-of-the-mill area of management. Supervision is dynamic, growing, and at times frustrating. The confusion that surrounds management and supervision, specifically, stems from the complex nature of managing people. The obvious system of writing or discussing the supervision of people soon fades into a mass of uncertainty as one attempts to practice the supervision of people. Leading, motivating, and controlling people is still a fine art with scientific overtones.

Getting along with people and liking people is a very necessary part of the supervisor's job, but this cannot be construed as the only tool necessary for any individual to become a supervisor. Constant study and research are necessary before practicing supervisors can consider themselves successful. The ever-changing dynamic environment in which supervisors work forces them to undertake this constant vigil and research. Once they give up and refuse to learn, supervisors, and employees for that matter, have taken a direction that can only lead to oblivion, defeat, or unhappiness.

512   Chapter XXVI   Closing Remarks

CONSTANT STUDY AND RESEARCH NEEDED

What are these things that supervisors must constantly study and research so that they may be successful in their professional lives? The following list of 25 areas may provide some of the answers.

1. They must know and understand the needs of people.
2. They must know how and why leadership of people is necessary and how to practice it effectively.
3. They must know which personal characteristics are required for successful supervisory activity.
4. They must know how to motivate so that employees can achieve the organizational goals.
5. They must know how to plan, organize, and control time, work flow, and the people within their department.
6. They must understand the importance of, and be able to practice the art of, proper human communication.
7. They should be able to cope with the formal and informal organizational structures they encounter on the job.
8. They must be effective disciplinarians and be able to handle grievances and workers' complaints.
9. They must be able to maintain high morale among the workers.
10. They should understand the corporate organization and its economic and political environment.
11. They should understand their position within the total organization and know how their position interrelates to other positions within the organization.
12. They should know how to train and develop the workers and themselves.
13. They should understand how and why control is an important supervisory and production function within their department, and among departments.
14. They must be able to coordinate all the resources at their command so that worker and organizational goals are achieved.
15. They must have an understanding of organizational financial control and the use of financial language.
16. They should understand the use of financial budgets to that they can supervise and manage their work crews effectively.
17. They must be able to make decisions based on a relevant fact or facts within a short time frame.
18. They must understand labor unions and complex labor relations.
19. They must understand and know how to cope with state and federal labor legislation and regulation.
20. They must know how to cope with minority group members and how to practice without legal or ethical discrimination.
21. They must know enough about work methods analysis and job design

analysis so as to work closely with industrial engineers and behavioral scientists.
22. They must know the skills of selecting, interviewing, counseling, appraising, promoting, and compensating workers.
23. They should be an expert at giving orders, introducing change, and conducting meetings.
24. They have to be expert in safety and health responsibilities under OSHA.
25. They should be able to put all these points together or be able to use them individually whenever necessary.

Listing the 25 areas that a supervisor should study constantly sheds light on the complexities of a supervisor's position. This helps to indicate why the practice of effective and efficient supervision is so difficult to attain. It also indicates why a supervisor must act as a researcher. The supervisor must constantly ask how he or she can improve his or her performance and increase the efficiency of the work crew. Working with, communicating, motivating, understanding, directing, and leading people is a monumental challenge. Satisfying workers' needs, satisfying group pressures, and achieving the organizational goals of output and efficiency—helps to increase the size and scope of the supervisor's position and requires a broader comprehension of the supervisory position be taken by its practitioners.

SUPERVISION IN PERSPECTIVE

The need for supervisors to understand the major variables or resources with which they must work cannot be overemphasized. An overview can be extremely difficult to produce. The paramount problem encountered is the leadership of people, or how to motivate and lead the workers. It is also important to the functions of management, to possess management skills, and to understand the local and organizational environment, but people generate the greatest number of problems that face the practicing supervisor. Figure 26-1 illustrates the various approaches or supervisory styles that can be of assistance for analysis of the overviews of supervision.

The three styles—"boss," parental, and motivational—require different inputs and create different outputs. For example, the "boss" style supervisor depends on raw power, whereas the parental style, or "big brother" style, depends on how many economic resources the company has to give to the workers. In the parental style, the supervisor becomes the intermediary because he or she is carrying out the company's policies in fringe benefits and other custodial functions. The motivational style depends on leadership between the supervisor and his workers within the organization.

	"Boss" Style	Parental Style	Motivational Style
Depend on:	Power	Economic resources	Leadership
Supervisory orientation:	Authority	Material rewards	Support
Worker orientation:	Obedience	Security	Performance
Worker psychological result:	Personal dependency	Organizational dependency	Participation
Worker needs met:	Subsistence	Maintenance	Higher Order
Measure of morale:	Compliance	Satisfaction	Motovation

Figure 26–1 Supervisory styles and objectives. (Source. Adapted from Human Relations at Work: The Dynamics of Organizational Behavior by Keith Davis. Copyright 1967, McGraw-Hill Book Co. Used with permission of McGraw-Hill Book Co.)

SUPERVISORY ORIENTATION

Implementing these styles requires a different orientation for each. The "boss" style orients the supervisor to protect jealously his authority over the workers. The parental style's orientation lies in material rewards. Do a good job and you will receive a carrot. However, do a bad job and you will get the stick. The motivational style has the supervisor oriented toward support of the staff. This style is the most difficult to practice because support is not as tangible, in the view of the leader, as material rewards or pure authority. A support orientation on the part of the supervisor requires more self-confidence, recognition of workers' needs, and respect for others. These are difficult attributes to maintain under the pressures of a managerial position. A weak manager tends to use pure authority or material rewards as a basic orientation, whereas a strong manager will tend to support the employees and delegate authority to subordinates.

WORK ORIENTATION

Worker orientation varies by supervisory style as abruptly as supervisory orientation under the "boss" style; the worker succumbs to obedience as a general perspective. The parental style provokes the worker into a security state. The worker looks to the organization as the provider of all the things he must have to maintain security. The supervisor is the agent or intermediary in the process. The motivational style encourages the worker to regard performance as a basic orientation.

WORKER PSYCHOLOGICAL RESULT

The three different supervisory styles psychologically affect the worker in different ways. The "boss" style forces personal dependency of the worker on the supervisor. The boss has personal power to hire, fire, and reprimand the worker. The worker produces only with a minimum of effort. In contrast, the parental style forces organizational dependency. The motivational style differs greatly in that it encourages participation by the worker in the group activities and promotes self-realization of the worker.

WORKER NEEDS MET

Each supervisory style of management meets workers' needs in differing degrees. The "boss" style tends to meet the subsistence needs of the worker and the worker's family. The parental supervisory style meets the maintenance needs of salary, working conditions, job security, and technical supervision. The motivational supervisory style includes a task involvement in that the worker, through greater participation, can satisfy the higher-level needs of appreciating work itself, achievement, growth, advancement, and recognition. These higher-order needs tend to be satisfied as the worker responds with a "we" instead of a "they" attitude toward work, group, and superior.

MEASURE OF MORALE

The measure of morale varies by supervisory style as well. The "boss" style uses compliance to rules and regulations. The compliant worker takes orders and does not talk back. The parental style uses the measure of contentment or satisfaction. If the organization has showered sufficient material gifts on him to provide contentment, then the worker's morale is high. Moreover, a happy worker is considered a good worker. The motivational style measures how much the worker shows motivation in doing tasks. The worker is given recognition, the right to participation, and support from the supervisor. These stimulate the satisfaction of the employees' higher-order needs and tend to motivate the worker into greater industriousness.

SUPERVISORY STYLE IN PRACTICE

The three styles of supervision discussed here are not independent of each other but are inexorably intertwined in actual practice. Rather than jump into the complexities and gray areas of supervisory practice, it is easier to portray the black and white styles and then discuss their interrelationships. The "boss" style of supervision has the longest history and in today's modern organization can be exercised if and when tight control of the employees warrants such a style. The "boss" style can be a very effective way to accomplish work in the short run. Historically, great empires have been built using this style in various shades of gray. It remains the inherent basis for a supervisor's authority. The chief disadvantage of this style, if practiced to the extreme or used too frequently, is its production of side effects. The workers' lack of enthusiasm, motivation, and desire to succeed are strong limiting factors.

The parental style requires a strong economic back-up before working conditions, safety factors, adequate salaries, pensions, and other very pertinent but mundane variables, can be maintained. These aspects can provide workers with some peace of mind. They will not be concerned with the day-to-day struggle of mere survival. However, the parental style encourages the peaceful, contented worker image, which can be an obstacle to production. In undeveloped societies that possess strong cultural values favoring contentment, such a style may be extremely successful. Production, however, can fail miserably. Excessive use of the parental organizational style or "big brother" style can help to retain poverty rather than dispel it. Dependency, security, and handouts tend to restrict growth, and throttle aspirational levels and motivation. A little hunger, in a figurative sense, can assist growth. The motivational style supports growth and rests on the strong leadership of the supervisor.

In actual practice, a mixture of all three styles is most appropriate. However, a constant mix without a change is not desirable. A reasonable amount of parental and "boss" ingredients is necessary for a foundation for growth and implementation of the motivational style of supervision. The exact amount of each ingredient in the mix cannot be answered precisely. The mix of the three styles is dependent upon the supervisor's personality and on the situation that confronts the supervisor. This is where the supervisor's true ability and training in leading, motivating, understanding, communicating and managing the work crew is tested. He or she must understand all the variables that are important and that may affect the situation. Moreover, the supervisor must be able to make a decision or a set of decisions that will satisfy both the needs of the organization and the needs of the workers.

THE SUPERVISOR OF THE FUTURE

The need for more sophsticated supervisors has forced some industrial and manufacturing firms to reassess their supervisory training programs. Instead of relying wholly on promoting hourly workers to salaried supervisory positions, many companies have started to hire college graduates, right off the campus, to fill these jobs. The demand for formally educated supervisors has risen appreciably, and many of the graduates of two-year community colleges, as well as four-year colleges and universities, are expected to become supervisors of tomorrow.

Hiring people fresh from a college campus presents problems for the organization. Although this is one of the easiest ways for a college man to step into a managerial position on his first job, the transition can present difficulties both for the company and for the applicant. Bridging this obstacle has taken the form of on-the-job training programs. Supervisors-in-training programs have been developed. These programs can include learning about the company, the plant, and its departments. The participants cover corporate philosophy, policies, people, and products. In a second phase, the trainees become acquainted with specific departments, such as industrial relations, administrative services, technical, utilities, and general services. Then the trainees are assigned to specific departments to work with a trainer.

Successful on-the-job training programs for supervisors help to fill the need for more well-qualified people. Despite the inclusion of college-trained people in supervision, the need to upgrade hourly people to be placed into shift foreperson positions and the general upgrading of supervisors through training programs still remain. The quest for the educated supervisor for today and the future will remain high. The supervisor is the keystone of the organization. The better the supervisor operates, the more efficient the firm will be.

The supervisor of the future must cope with changing economic, social, technical, political and organizational changes. Since the latter part of the 20th century, the U.S. economy can no longer boast that it is the most viable in the world. Intensive competition from worldwide, multinational firms, an ever-shrinking world due to better communications and transportation and more highly educated and militant countries developing in the Third World have upset our way of life appreciably. The high cost of energy and the need to maintain a high quality of life, as well as our standard of living, forces supervisory management, at all levels, and in all organizations, to become more skillful in human, technical, and social skills. This enables the supervisor to direct, implement, activate, and control to achieve the highest quality production available. No longer can supervisory management exercise power over employees because they hold the position; but leadership, human relations, and participative management are processes that must be used to ensure the continuity of quality output.

In the final analysis, an organization's viability rests solely on supervisory management's ability to practice excellent management. Anything less could provoke the organization's eventual demise.

QUESTIONS FOR DISCUSSION

1. Why isn't getting along with people and liking people the only tool necessary for a practicing supervisor?
2. Is it even possible to know all there is about supervision in an organizational structure? Why or why not?
3. If a supervisor understands the major variables of a supervisor, is it necessary to know all the techniques?
4. Of the three supervisory styles—"boss," parental, motivational—which style do you like the best? Why? Which style would you attempt to practice, if different from the one you liked? Why?

5. Are the three supervisory styles discussed in the chapter independent of each other, or are they styles that can be combined? Why or why not?
6. Why have the propsects of hiring college or junior college graduates for first-line supervisory positions increased in the last ten years?

For continued search and updating, subscribing to or reading current periodicals in the supervisory field could prove to be advantageous.

Supervisory Management, American Management Association, Inc., 135 West 50th St., New York, N.Y. 10020; *Supervision, The Magazine of Industrial Relations and Operating Management*, Employee Relations Bureau, Division of National Research Bureau, Inc., 1970 Main Street, Sarasota, Florida 33577.

Index

Accidents, 471-473
  process of, 483
Accounting records, 150
Accounting systems, balance sheet, 132-133
  income statement, 131-132
Arbitrators, award, 430
  concept of, 432
  hearing, 430
  legal aspects of, 430-431
  sources of, 429
Argyris' theories of motivation, 263
Attitude, formation of, 185
Authority, concept of, 66
  definition of, 54
  delegation process of, 54
  functional, 58-59
  line and staff, 56-58
    defined, 56
  line of direct, 54-56
  responsibility in organizing, 49

Balance sheet, acid test ratio, 133
  analysis of, 133-134
  current ratio, 133
Breakeven analysis, 145
Budgets, concept of, 150
  direct labor costs, 147
  direct materials costs, 147
  overhead costs, 148
  use for control, 146-148
  variance, 148
Business corporation, 502-503
  defined, 489-492
  environment of, 497-501
  partnership, 502
  role of marketing, 489-490
  sole proprietorship, 501
Business environment, 497-501
  big and little business, 499
  foreign competition, 500-501
  government, 497-498
  labor force, 499-500
  public opinion, 497
  supervisory activities, 504
  unions, 498-499

Capitalism, defined, 490-491, 504
  role of capital in, 493
    individual in, 492-493

marketing in, 494-496
  profit in, 496-497
Cash budgets, 135-140
  inventory control with, 138-140
  production, 137-138
  sales, 136-137
Cash outflows and inflows, 136
Chain of command, 54
Change, introducing, 363-367
  resistance to, 364-367
    preparation for, 373
    reducing resistance, 366-367
    types of, 364
    why exists, 364-366
Cliques, 75-76
Collective bargaining, 455
Communication, emotional state of sender, 231
  grapevine groups, 73
  spoken word, 231
  written word, 231-233
Communications, downward, 240-241
  elements of, 231-234
  external, 243
  good, 244-245
    listening, 245
    speaking, 244
    writing, 244-245
  human barriers to, 237-238, 249
  and leadership, 245-246, 249
  multidirectional, 242-243
  nature of, 234-238
  one way vs. two way, 236-237
  on the job, 238-240
  process of, 234-236, 249
  steps in process, 234-235
  types within organization, 240-243
  upward, 241-242
Communicative skills, on the job, 238
Communicators, personality states of, 249
Competition, importance of, 191-192
Complaints, and grievances, 414-431
  nature of, 415-418
  sources of, 418-421
Computers, and information flows, 119-122
Consumers, 493
Control, concept of, 126
  exception principle, 94
  formal group resistance to, 99

519

informal group, resistance to, 99
information flows, 119-122
interdepartmental, 122-125
intradepartmental, 111-122
line-staff conflict, 100-101
managerial function of, 88-89
material and supply flows, 116-119
nature of, 89-97
organizational, process of, 110-111
process of, 90-93
work flows, 111-116
Control function, definition of, 89
Control people, aggressive, attack, 100
compliance with, 102
concept of, 105
correcting deviations, 92-93
effectiveness, 102-105
escape through absenteeism, 101-102
escape through advancement, 99
flexibility, need for, 95
human response to, 98-102
human innovative deviation, 99
neutrality or apathy, 101
overemphasis on goals, 101
performance, measuring, 91-92
problem, why, 97-98
problem of, 97-102
standards, 90-91
Control systems, characteristics of, 94-97
concept of, 105
elements of, 93-94
Cost reductions, 224-225
Counseling, employees need to recognize danger signals, 357-358
role of supervisor, 356-358
Counseling employees, 355-359
advantages of, 356-357
directive vs. non-directive, 358-359, 372
effective situations, 359

Data gathering, 159
Decision making, concept of, 167
evaluating alternative solutions, 159-160
definition of, 156-157
identifying key uncertainties, 159
process of, 156-161
supervisory application of, 162-166
supervisory function and, 154-166
supervisor's need to know, 154-155
Departmentation, basis for, 65
Development employee, 341-344
coaching, 343
delegation of, 343
job rotation, 344
off the job methods, 344

on the job methods, 343-344
principles of, 342-343
special assignments, 343-344
Direct labor costs, 143-144
Direct material costs, 142-143
Disciplinary actions, applying penalty, 404-405
collecting facts, 403
concept of, 410
deciding on penalty, 403-404
follow-up, 405
procedures in, 402-405
stating problem, 403
role of union, 405
Discipline, approaches to, 396-398
concept of, 410
consistency in, 400-401
correction of, 401-402
interdependency, 397-398
keeping records, 402
as last resort, 402
maintaining, 394-405
meaning of, 395-396
negative, 397
positive, 397
progressive, 410
supervisor's role in, 399-402
working environment, 399-402
Dispatching, work flows, 114-115

Economic systems, comparison, 491
Employee productivity, concept of, 199
Entrepreneur, 492
Expediting work flows, 115

Factory rate, determination of, 146
Financial control, 130-149, 150
Fixed costs, 144-145
Flextime, 204-205
Flows, concept of, 126
Four day workweek, 205-206

Gellerman's theories of motivation, 262-263
Gestures, 231
Giving orders, 359-363
characteristics of, 359-360
common errors in, 363
process of, 360-361
supervisory consultative with, 361-362
Grievances, arbitration of, 428-431
concept of, 432
desirable features of, 426
formal procedures of, 424-426
importance of early settlement, 421-422
nature of, 428-429
non-union firm in, 426-428

pertinent factors, 422-423
settling at supervisory level, 421-424
supervisory procedures in, 423-424
Group needs and the individual, 179

Hawthorne studies, 256-257
Herzberg studies, 257-258
Human barriers in attitude, 237
  believability, 237
  communication, 237
  reasoning process, 238
Human behavioral patterns, motivation, 180-181
Human needs vs. wants, concepts of, 186

Individual uniqueness, concept of, 186
Induction, 324-328
  procedures, good, 327, 328
  process of, 329
  supervisory responsibility, 325
  supervisory role in, 325, 327
Industrial engineering department, 124
Informal groups, concept of, 84
  power concept, 84
Informal organizations, activities of, 76-80
  attitudes of, 76-77
  conformity with, 78-79
  morale of, 77-78
  nature of, 72
  rumors, 76
  supervisor's relationship with, 80-83
  threaten by, 78
  true or false information, 78
  types of, 72-76
Interviewer, what makes a good, 322-323
Interviewing, directive and non-directive, 319
  selection, 321-324
  supervisory purpose in, 322
Interview techniques, 323-324
  common errors to avoid, 324
Inventory control, 138-140

Job design, 206-214
  assumption of approaches to, 221-222
  barriers to, 222-223
  concept of, 226
  methods for, 217-221
  motivation and employee satisfaction, 223-224
  traditional views, 216
Job design and job boredom, 216-224
  and the supervisor, 223
Job enlargement, 218
Job enrichment, 218
Job instruction training (JIT), 340

Job responsibility and accountability, concept of, 227
Job rotation, 218
Job training methods, 339-340

Labor market, available skills, 315
  boundaries to, 315
  economics, conditions of, 315
Labor movement, era, early, 440-443
  era modern, 443-453
  federal laws, 444
    Landrum-Griffin, 446-447
    NLRB, 444-445
    Taft-Hartley, 445-446
Labor relations, and civil rights legislation, 447-449
  supervisor and, 439-453
Led, the, 291
Leader, 290-291
  employee oriented, 289
Leadership, 285-297
  concept of, 298
  developing group morale, 297
  leading, 295-296
  maintaining discipline, 296
  nature of, 289-292
  persuasiveness of, 298
  securing cooperation, 293-294
  situation, the, 291-292
  styles, analysis of, 289, 298
  types of, 286-289
    autocratic, 287-288
    democratic, 288
    laissez-faire, 288-289
  use of authority, 294-295
  and you, 297
Leadership development, informal, 79
Leadership pattern, choice of, 292-293
Leadership techniques, 293-297
Leader vs. boss, 12
Line manager, definition of, 57
Line of balancing, 113-114

McGregor's theories of motivation, 261-262
Maintenance department, 123
Management, definition of, 1
  by exception, 148-149, 150
  by objective, 382-384, 389
Management vs. supervision, 1-2
Managers, concept of, 12
  contribution:
    direct, 56-58
    indirect, 56-58
Manpower systems flow, 329
Market competitiveness, concept of, 199

Marketing department, 124-125
Maslow's need priority model, 177
Materials handling, 118-119
Meetings, benefits and limitations to, 368-369
   conducting, 367-371
   sales, 369-371
   supervisor and, 367
   types of, 367
Methods study, objectives of, 208
   techniques for, 208-209
Micromotion study, 210
Morale, 405-410
   concept of, 411
   development of, 406-407
   employee oriented supervisor, 409
   improvement programs of, 408-410
   informal interview in, 407
   meaning of, 405-406
   measuring, 407-408
   motivational programs, 409
   personal observation, 407
   statistical methods, 408
   survey and questionnaire, 408
Motion study, principles of, 209
   use of human body, 211-212
Motivation, competitive economy and, 254-255
   frustration and unsatisfied needs, 265
   importance of, 255
   research, 256-261
Motivational theory, in perspective, 266-267
   supervisory use of, 268
Motivating worker, 253-268
Multinational corporation, 500

Order giving, 359-363
Organization, charts, 47, 49, 50, 51, 55
   concepts of, 65
   corporate, 44-51
   development, 219-220, 349
   environment, 487-503
   informal, 71-83
Organizational control, 126
Organizing, 43-64
   by customer, 51
   definition of, 43
   by function, 46-47
   grouping activities, basis for, 45-51
   by matrix, 48-49
   process, 44-45
   by process or equipment, 49
   by product, 47
   by territory, 49
   by time, 51
   by sample number, 51

supervisor's job, and, 62-63
OSHA, administration of act, 459
   effect on employer, 469-470
   effect on supervisor, 470-471
   record keeping, 460-461
   role of states, 459-460
   standards of, 483
   who must comply, 460

Participative leadership, democratic, 288
   management, concept of, 199
People, as individuals, 182
   motivation, 267
   needs, biological and psychological, 176-178
   needs and wants of, 176-180
   participation, recognition, 183
   societal influences, 179-180
   supervisor's response to wants, 256
   what we know about them, 255-256
   workers, 173-185
Performance appraisals, 376-388
   employees reaction to, 377
   limitation of, 384-386
   process of, 378
   rating scales, 379-382
   by supervisor, 386-388
   supervisor's role in, 377-378
   systems, concept of, 389
   types of, 378-384
Personnel characteristics of supervisor, competence of, 276
   concept of, 282
   decision making, 273-274
   emotional stability, 275
   enjoyment of responsibility, 275
   initiative and drive, 273
   integrity and courage, 274
   intellectual capacity, 274
   motivation, 275-276
   persuasiveness, 276-277
   use of time, 277-278
   vitality and endurance, 276
PERT, 115
Plan - Do - Control, 219
Planning, 19-37
   definition of, 19
   flexibility in, 39
   mathematical techniques for, 34-35
   pervasiveness of, 38
   steps in, 26-30
Planning for change, 35-37
   company policy, 37
   equipment, 36
   personal, 35-36

products, 36
workload, 37
Planning process, 26-30
  alternative plans, 29
  analysis of data, 27-28
  concept of, 38
  developing derivative plans, 29-30
  establishing premises and constraints, 27
  follow-up, 30
  objective definition, 27
  selecting best plan, 29
  supervisor, and, 30-31
Plans, adopting old, 31
  advanced scientific approaches, 34-35
  based on breadth or scope, 24-25
  based on duration, 23-24
  based on function or use, 24
  basis for change, 21-23
  continuous, 38
  Gnatt charts, 31-32
  line balancing, 32-34
  objective, 20-21
  types of, 23-25
  understanding corporate, 20-23
Porter and Lawler model of motivation, 265
Problem existence, determination of, 156-157
Problem recognition, 157-158
Problem solution, action and follow-up, 161
  choice of, 160-161
Product, pricing of, 495-496
Product cost budgets, elements of, 140-146
Production budgets, 137-138
Productivity, 3
  business view, 193
  government's view, 193
  labor's view, 193
  need to improve, 190-198
  slowdown, 193
  supervisor, 195-196
  U.S. compared with other countries, 191
  worker and supervisor relations, 204
Productivity improvement, a human approach, 194-196
  supervisory training, 196-198
  training, 334
    concept of, 350
Productivity problem, a synthesis, 194
Profit planning, definition of, 130
  supervisor and, concept of, 150
Purchasing, 116

Quality control, nature of, 122-123
Quality work life, 203-204
  nature of, 220-221

Recruitment, labor market, 314-315
  methods of, 316-317
  minorities, 317
  selection, 317-319
  sources of manpower, 315-316
Research and development department, 125
Routing work flows, 112

Safety and accidents, 471-481
  inspection, 478-481
  program for, 473-477
  supervisory role in, 477-478
Safety and health under OSHA, 457-481
  employer's responsibility, 482-483
Sales, forecast, 136-137
Scalor chain of command, 54
Scheduling work flows, 112-114
Scientific management, 261
Selection, filtration process, 320
  philosophies of, 318-319
  process of, 319-320, 329
  supervisor's role in, 318
  testing in, 320-321
Self-centered view of individual, 176
Shipping, 116-117
Skinner's operant conditioning, 263-265
Social groups, 75
Span of management, 51-53
  concept of, 66
  lines of communication, 52
Staff managers, 57
  personal staff, 57
Storage of materials, 117-118
Supervision, challenge of, 4
  concept of, 186
  consultative, 372
  human aspects on job activity, 9
  key to improved productivity, 196
  people centered, 182-183
  perspective, 513-516
  productivity, 195-196
  research, 512-513
  study, need for constant, 512-513
Supervisors, another worker, 6
  awareness of selves, 175
  concept of, 12
  definition of, 1
  faces, the many of, 5-9
  future, 516-517
  human relations specialist, 6
  job design, 206
  key person, 5
  keystone of organization, 6-9, 12
  learning by listening, 184
  marginal person, 6

modern, 4
organization, 4-5
people, 174-176
personal characteristics, 272-281
   conceptual, 273-274
   human, 275-276
   technical, 276-278
person in the middle, 5-6
planning, role in, 25-26
selection process, 314-328
technical and human understanding, 13
technical aspects of job, 9
Supervisory behavioral patterns, successful, 278-281
   concept of, 167
Supervisory control, informal groups, 81-83
   control of information, 82
   departmentation at, 59-60
Supervisory management, need for effective, 2-4
   universality of, 2
Supervisory organization, 59-64
Supervisory organizing, typical demand on, 61-62
   work force, 63-64
Supervisory orientation, morale, 575
   style in practice, 515-516
   work orientation, 514
   worker's needs met, 515
   worker's psychological results, 515
Supervisory personal goals vs. company objectives, 10-11
Supervisory planning, practical aids, 31-35
Supervisory responsibility within organization, 1-11
Supervisory self development program, suggested, 348-349, 351
Supervisory training and productivity improvement, 196-198
   training, responsibility for, 334-335

Teamwork, 183-184
Texas Instrument studies, 258-259
Therblig analysis, 210
Time management, 303-309
   guidelines, 308
   productivity, 304, 311
Time management, self discipline, 307
   as system, 309-310
   techniques of, 307-309, 311
Time study, limitations of, 215-216
   observed time study, 214-215
Time wasters, 304-307, 311
Traffic, 116-117

Training, employee, 337-341
   case method, 339
   classroom, 338
   how to instruct, 340-341
   importance of people investment, 334-335
   learning theory in, 335-337
   on the job, 338
   programmed, 338
   types of, 337-339
Training and development, supervisors, 345-349
   conferences, 347
   content of, 345
   job rotation, 347
   lectures, 347
   methods of, 347-349
   objectives of, 345
   people centered programs, 345-347
   simulation and role playing, 347-348
Transactional analysis, 246-248
   adult state, 247
   child state, 247
   parent state, 247
     supervisor and, 246, 248

Unionization, process of, 449-453
   organizing campaign, 449-450
   representative election, 450
   supervisory role in, 451
Union organizations, characteristics of, 451-453

Variable costs, 144
Vroom's preference expectation, 265

Workable solutions, determination of, 158-159
Worker productivity, concept of, 226
Worker's attitudes, positive, 184-185
   behavior, summary of factors that affect, 181-182
   goals and responsibilities as perceived, 11
   job satisfaction, 216-217
   as people, 182-185
Work groups, 73
Working capital, 494
   need for, 493-494
Work methods, 207-214
   process charts, 209
Work modules, 219
Work standards, concept of, 227

Zero-Base Budgeting (ZBB), 149
   concept of, 150

ATIC 85